CN00662661

DELICT: LAW AN.

DELICT: LAW AND POLICY

5TH EDITION

Brian Pillans, LLB, Dip LP

Lecturer in Law, Glasgow Caledonian University

W. GREEN · THOMSON REUTERS

First edition published 1989
Second edition published 1993
Third edition published 1998
Fourth edition published 2004

Published in 2014 by Thomson Reuters, trading as W. Green,
21 Alva Street, Edinburgh, EH2 4PS. Thomson Reuters is registered
in England & Wales, Company No.1679046. Registered Office and
address for service: 5 Canada Square, Canary Wharf, London, E14 5AQ.

For further information on our products and services, visit
http://www.sweetandmaxwell.co.uk/wgreen

Orders by email to: trluki.orders@thomsonreuters.com.
General enquiries should be directed to wgreen.enquiries@thomson.com

Typeset by Wright and Round Ltd, Gloucestershire
Printed and bound in the UK by CPI Group (UK) Ltd, Croydon

No natural forests were destroyed to make this product;
only farmed timber was used and replanted.

A CIP catalogue record for this title is available from the
British Library

ISBN 978-0-414-01890-7

Thomson Reuters, the Thomson Reuters Logo and W. GREEN
are trademarks of Thomson Reuters.

© 2014 Thomson Reuters

Crown copyright material is reproduced with the permission of the Controller of
HMSO and the Queen's Printer for Scotland.

All rights reserved. No part of this publication may be reproduced or
transmitted in any form or by any means, or stored in any retrieval system of
any nature without prior written permission, except for permitted fair dealing
under the Copyright Designs and Patents Act 1988, or in accordance with the
terms of a licence issued by the Copyright Licensing Agency in respect of
photocopying and/or reprographic reproduction. Application for permission for
other use of copyright material including permission to reproduce extracts in
other published works shall be made to the publishers. Full acknowledgement
of author, publisher and source must be given.

PREFACE

This book is dedicated to the memory of Bill Stewart, the author of its first four editions. First published in 1989, Stewart's "Delict" was the first student textbook devoted to the subject and was well received, not only by law students but also by practitioners and academics. Stewart took a wide view of the law of delict, not only in the breadth and effect of the subject but also with regard to its origins and its potential for development. It was, in Stewart's own words, a "good radical look at traditional expositions of delict". It is hoped that this edition retains that tradition.

Readers familiar with previous editions will recognise much of the text and themes here as carrying over from previous editions. Equally, such readers will find that much has changed. The immediately obvious change is to the title—*Delict: Law and Policy*. The new title is intended to emphasise the role that policy always has had, and continues to have, on the development and refinement of the law of delict: it being "no doubt based upon a general public sentiment of moral wrongdoing for which the offender must pay".[1] The fact that the role of policy in shaping this area of the law was traditional rather than radical was acknowledged by probably the most famous and influential English judge of the twentieth century, Lord Denning:

> "In previous times, when faced with a new problem, the judges have not openly asked themselves the question: what is the best policy for the law to adopt? But the question has always been there in the background. It has been concealed behind such questions as: Was the defendant under any duty to the plaintiff? Was the relationship between them sufficiently proximate? Was the injury direct or indirect? Was it foreseeable, or not? Was it too remote? And so forth ... Nowadays we direct ourselves to considerations of policy."[2]

Rather than conceal the role of policy in the background, it is hoped that this exposition of the law of delict is transparent in placing firmly in the foreground the role of policy in shaping the law.

Another theme that Bill Stewart adopted in previous editions was to impress upon the reader their own role in the development of the law of delict, emphasising the need for coherence with regard to the origins and future development of the law. It is hoped that this edition retains and builds on this tradition. Although the law of delict in Scotland has no doubt enjoyed the benefit of developments in the understanding of law and policy in England and Wales,

---

[1] *Donoghue v Stevenson*, 1932 S.C. (HL) 31 at 44 per Lord Atkin.
[2] *Dutton v Bognor Regis UDC* [1972] 1 Q.B. 373 at 397 per Lord Denning M.R.

it is important to remember that the origins and traditions of the law in Scotland are distinct from those south of the border, and it remains open to the law in Scotland to follow its own path. Thus, for example, the roots of Scots law in the *actio injuriarum* are emphasised with regard to opportunities for developing a distinct approach to dealing with delictual wrongs which cause affront to the victim—in areas such as privacy and medical negligence. It is hoped that readers, especially those who intend to enter the legal profession or institutions which have an influence on shaping the law, appreciate their own responsibility in exploring these opportunities and in retaining and enhancing the distinctive tradition of Scots law.

I would like to take this opportunity to thank those who have influenced my own thinking on the law of delict, and those who have assisted me in writing this new edition. The former group includes in particular Professor Joe Thomson and Professor Hector MacQueen. The latter group includes many colleagues and especially Alison Britton, William Henderson, Mark Leiser, Nick McKerrell, Aidan O'Donnell and Eleanor Russell.

The law is intended to be stated as at April 1, 2014, although it has been possible to include some developments that have taken place since. Any errors are my own.

Brian Pillans
July 2014

CONTENTS

Section V: Specific Liability Regimes

TABLE OF CASES

(All references are to paragraph numbers)

TABLE OF STATUTES

(All references are to paragraph numbers)

TABLE OF SCOTTISH STATUTES

(All references are to paragraph numbers)

TABLE OF STATUTORY INSTRUMENTS

(All references are to paragraph numbers)

TABLE OF SCOTTISH STATUTORY INSTRUMENTS

(All references are to paragraph numbers)

SECTION I: INTRODUCTION AND KEY THEMES

CHAPTER 1

INTRODUCTION

TERMINOLOGY: WHAT IS DELICT?

A cow falls through the ceiling of your shop, some unidentified person pours a **1–01** pot of urine over your head, you fall through the floor of a building or you are butted by a bull over a wall on to stinging nettles having tried to ward it off by tapping it on the nose. You are wrongfully arrested by a police officer, potholes in the road burst your car's tyre, your luggage is missing when you return to your hotel or you lose business to a supermarket which sells its "own brand" imitation of your product. You are called a liar on Twitter or photos are taken of you and your partner enjoying a private romantic meal and published in the local newspaper. Your doctor fails to treat your illness in time and your lawyer fails to sue him on time. Your workmates play a prank on you that goes badly wrong. It is with stories like these that the law of delict deals. But first, it is only fair to explain what is meant by the strange name of the subject.[1]

Delict might be defined as the body of law which declares certain conduct to be wrongful in a civil law sense.[2] Many other jurisdictions—including England and Wales—use the word "tort" as an equivalent to delict.[3] A person who commits a delictual wrong may be described as a delinquent, capturing the notion of causing harm by failing in one's duty. Tort jurisdictions tend to use the term "tortfeasor". Delict recognises that wrongful conduct may have a damaging impact on individuals, and so is intended to provide for legal responsibility to individual victims of the wrong. The law does this by creating a mechanism for remedying harm to the individual caused by wrongful conduct. The usual

---

[1] "'*Delinquo*', *supine delictum* means 'to be lacking' or 'fail'. It was already used in classical Latin to mean 'fail in one's duty, offend' ": P. Birks, "The Concept of a Civil Wrong" in D.G. Owen (ed.), *Philosophical Foundations of Tort Law* (Oxford: Oxford University Press, 1995), p.39, fn.28. Sabinus was the creator of the category "Delict": D. Visser and N. Whitty, "The Structure of the Law of Delict" in K. Reid and R. Zimmermann (eds), *A History of Private Law in Scotland* (Oxford: Oxford University Press, 2000), Vol.II: Obligations, p.424, fn.7 citing P.G. Stein, *Romisches Recht und Europa: Die Geschichte einer Rechtskultur* (Frankfurt am Main: Fischer Taschenbuch Verlag, 1996), p.38.

[2] Although all delicts are civil wrongs, not all civil wrongs are delicts, e.g. breach of contract is a civil wrong but the related rules fall within the law of contract.

[3] The English approach to tort is quite distinct from the Scottish approach to delict. The English tradition adopts an *inductive* approach to legal principle, placing grounds of action into distinct categories of wrong and relying heavily on precedent prescribing the development of the law. Scotland, on the other hand, has a history rooted in the civilian tradition which takes an *inductive* approach—deriving decisions from principle rather than precedent and relying less heavily on discreet categories. This accounts for Lord Atkin's distinction in his famous speech in *Donoghue v Stevenson*, 1932 S.C. (HL) 31 at 44: "The liability in negligence, whether you style it such (English approach) or treat it . . . as a species of culpa (Scottish approach) . . . ". See para.1–13 below.

remedies are damages and/or interdict. Liability in delict may therefore be defined as civil liability for the harmful consequences of wrongful conduct. Given the remedial focus on the modern law of delict, an alternative term that is used, especially by practitioners, is "reparation". That term more accurately describes a response to a breach of a legal obligation: one commits a delict; one must make reparation.[4] It will already be obvious that there are some parallels with criminal law. However the modern view of criminal law is that its focus is on conduct that is wrongful due to its impact on society, hence why liability upon conviction is in the form of punishment rather than responsibility for a remedy.[5]

WHERE IN THE LAW DOES DELICT FIT?

The law of obligations

1–02   Delict is treated in Scots law as part of the law of obligations. The law of obligations is generally divided into three areas: contract, delict and unjustified enrichment.[6] Delict may be distinguished from contract in that delictual obligations arise *ex lege* (i.e. out of law) whereas contractual obligations arise *ex voluntante* (i.e. by consent). Accordingly delictual obligations are involuntary, or imposed by law; contractual obligations being, on the other hand, voluntary, or imposed by agreement.[7] Obligations created by the law of unjustified enrichment are also viewed as arising *ex lege*, but differ from delictual obligations only in that in unjust enrichment cases the obligation to pay or to do something arises without the necessity of any wrong being done by the defender.[8] Delict imposes *ex lege* obligations to refrain from wrongful conduct, and to make up the damage caused by any breach of the obligation to refrain from wrongful conduct. On the other hand, the obligations imposed by the law of unjustified enrichment to make repetition of money, restitution of property or recompense are based on concepts of equity or fairness. The following three examples will attempt to clarify the distinctions:

---

[4] Reparation is no longer thought to refer to liability for breach of contract: *Miller v Glasgow DC*, 1989 S.L.T. 44; *Middleton v Douglass*, 1991 S.L.T. 726. The practitioner publications are called *Green's Reparation Law Bulletin* (Edinburgh: W. Green) and *Reparation: Liability for Delict* (Edinburgh: W. Green).

[5] Note the difference in the standard of proof: in delict, the standard is on the balance of probabilities; in criminal cases it is beyond reasonable doubt.

[6] A fourth may be unilateral promise.

[7] A practical riposte to this distinction may point out that most of us enter many contracts without being able to negotiate our preferred contractual position (i.e. we enter contractual obligations involuntarily), examples being most consumer contracts. A more theoretical analysis posits that a voluntary agreement does no more than create a moral obligation—the obligation capable of enforcement by legal process being added by the law's recognition that the agreement amounts to a valid contract, i.e. the moral obligation is transposed to a legal obligation *ex lege*. Thus *policitatio + conventio = pactum*; *policitatio + conventio + vinculum juris = contractus*. The distinction is further undermined by the idea that delictual obligations may be undertaken by a *voluntary* assumption of responsibility. See paras 11–36 to 11–38 below.

[8] J. Blackie, "Enrichment and Wrongs in Scots Law" [1992] Acta Juridica 23; J. Blackie, "Enrichment Wrongs and Invasion of Rights in Scots Law" in D. Visser, *The Limit of the Law of Obligations* (Cape Town: Juta Legal and Academic Publishers, 1997). *Teacher v Calder* (1899) 1 F. (HL) 39; *Exchange Telegraph v Guilianotti*, 1959 S.C. 19.

1. If we have a contract and I fail to perform my contractual obligations to you, if you suffer harm you can sue me for damages for breach of contract. The legal obligation to perform the contract was created by agreement (contract) rather than imposed by law. Breach of the *ex voluntante* obligation is a private law wrong—albeit in the area of contract law rather than delict. Breach of the obligation to perform the contract results in the creation of a secondary obligation—to provide a remedy;

2. If you inadvertently pay a sum of money into my bank account, e.g. because you made a mistake in typing in an account number when online banking, I will be obliged to return the funds to you based on principles of equity—enforceable by an action for repetition in unjustified enrichment. There is no wrongful conduct on my part, but nevertheless the law imposes an obligation on me to return the money to you based on concepts of what is fair in the circumstances;

3. If I drive my car without paying sufficient attention and as a result drive into the wall of your house, causing damage to your wall, you can sue me for damages for negligence. The legal obligation to take reasonable care in my driving was imposed on me by law. Breach of the *ex lege* obligation is a private law wrong—this time delictual. Breach of the obligation to take reasonable care results in the creation of a secondary obligation—to provide a remedy (i.e. to make reparation).

It may be observed that both in contract and in delict there are two distinguishable general obligations. The first is a positive obligation in the law of contract—to perform the contractual obligation as agreed. In delict the primary obligation, or duty, may be described generally as a negative duty—to *avoid* wrongful conduct. In both cases, breach of the first, or primary, obligation gives rise to a secondary obligation to provide a remedy. In delict this is often called the obligation to make reparation. In practice the modern law of delict functions by attempting to provide an efficient enforcement mechanism for the secondary obligation, i.e. the obligation to make reparation. Although delict nevertheless may be intended to have a deterrent effect, this is accepted as considerably weaker than the deterrent function of criminal law. Thus many delictual wrongs are also treated as so offensive and harmful to society that they will also be crimes.

Hierarchy and overlap within the law of obligations

A question to consider is whether there is a hierarchical relationship between **1–03** these aspects of the law of obligations.[9] Taking the view that "the law of (delict) is the general law, out of which the parties can, if they wish, contract,"[10] arguably places contract at a higher level than delict in a hierarchy of obligations. It is submitted that it is consistent with this view to raise concerns that concurrent

[9] There is considerable academic discussion concerning the interrelation of the various categories of the law of obligations: P.S. Atiyah, *Rise and Fall of Freedom of Contract* (Oxford: Clarendon Press, 1979), Ch.20 and P. Birks, *An Introduction to the Law of Restitution* (Oxford: Clarendon Press, 1989). See the discussions in H. MacQueen and J. Thomson, *Contract Law in Scotland*, 3rd edn (London: Bloomsbury Professional, 2012) and M. Hogg, *Obligations* (Edinburgh: Avizandum Publishing Ltd, 2003).

[10] *Henderson v Merrett Syndicates* [1995] 2 A.C. 145 at 193 per Lord Goff of Chieveley.

liability in delict and contract may undermine such a hierarchy of obligations.[11] Nevertheless, concurrent liability appears to have been accepted in some cases. The case of doctors and other professionals has made it look as if there is no problem but these cases can be explained by a principle whose status and origin is not entirely clear, *spondet peritiam artis*[12] that a person who professes a skill must answer for the failure to deliver it.[13] Cases of carriage are easier and do suggest that Scots law was within a general civilian tradition of allowing concurrent liability.[14] Given that English law has accepted concurrent liability even in claims for economic loss for negligence,[15] it can be said that Scots law most certainly accepts concurrent liability and will do so even in a contractual matrix.[16]

An aspect of Scots contract law that may at first sight provide assistance where concurrent liability gives rise to such theoretical problems is the concept of the *jus quaesitum tertio*.[17] However, in *Scott Lithgow Ltd v GEC Electrical Projects Ltd*,[18] it was held that where it was sought to establish the constitution of a *jus quaesitum tertio*, it was not sufficient merely that the *jus* be one in which the *tertius* had an interest. It was instead necessary that the *jus* was intended to be of benefit to the *tertius*. Averments merely that a contract referred to a third party and had been concluded for the advancement of that third party's interests were sufficient to plead a relevant case for a *jus quaesitum tertio*. There was, in general, no reason why a *tertius* should not be entitled to sue for damages, but that had to be a matter of the *intention* of the contracting parties to be ascertained from the terms of their contract.

The distinct functions of delict and unjustified enrichment respectively suggests that there is little scope for overlap. Although a delinquent should not profit from his wrong, the purpose of delictual damages is to compensate, i.e. to put the victim in the position he would have been in but for the wrong. Delictual remedies are not intended to balance the equities of a situation, and certainly are not designed to punish.[19]

Obligation or duty?

1–04 The terms "obligation" and "duty" are frequently treated as synonyms. Although it is submitted that there is nothing wrong with that approach per se, it

---

[11] See, e.g. *Tai Hing Cotton Mill Ltd v Liu Chong Hing Bank Ltd* [1986] A.C. 80 at 106 per Lord Scarman; *Downsview Nominees Ltd v First City Corp Ltd* [1993] A.C. 295 at 316 per Lord Templeman; *Marc Rich & Co A.G. v Bishop Rock Marine Co Ltd* [1996] A.C. 211 at 238–242 per Lord Steyn; *British Telecommunications Plc v James Thomson & Sons (Engineers) Ltd*, 1999 S.C. (HL) 9; *Realstone Ltd v J&E Shepherd* [2008] P.N.L.R. 21.

[12] *Et emperitia culpae enumeratur.*

[13] See paras 12–11 to 12–17 below.

[14] This has been generally ill-articulated. But it is possible to align Scots law more with a German model, where concurrent liability is allowed. In German law liability itself is constrained to certain interests, a line which has not been taken in Scots law in such a dogmatic fashion This is in direct contrast to a French model where concurrent liability is not generally allowed. An explanation for this French position can be found in J. Gordley, "Contract and Delict: Towards a Unified Law of Obligations" (1997) 1 Edin. L.R. 345.

[15] *Henderson v Merrett Syndicates* [1995] 2 A.C. 145. See P. Cane, "Contract, Tort and the Lloyd's Debacle" in F.D. Rose, *Consensus Ad Idem* (London: Sweet & Maxwell, 1996).

[16] See paras 11–34 to 11–35 below.

[17] Right on account of a third party.

[18] *Scott Lithgow Ltd v GEC Electrical Projects Ltd*, 1992 S.L.T. 244.

[19] See paras 5–03 to 5–04 below.

is also suggested that one word may fit better than the other into the context in which the concepts are being discussed. As suggested above[20] and explored in further detail below,[21] two distinct delictual obligations may be distinguished: a *primary* obligation to avoid wrongful conduct, and a *secondary* obligation, which operates upon breach of the primary obligation, to make reparation for resulting harm. It is suggested that the term "duty" may be more apposite in describing the primary obligation to avoid wrongful conduct. This is because the primary obligation operates on a more general basis, i.e. a duty to respect others' rights and interests. In the law of negligence this manifests in a duty to take care. Although that duty is not owed to the world at large,[22] it is generally owed to a range of persons. For example, in driving a motor car, the driver owes an *ex lege* duty of care to persons who are physically within the immediate area of impact, or who own property situated within that area. The duty to respect the rights and interests of others may be breached either intentionally or unintentionally. Examples of the former include fraud, assault, passing off and defamation.[23] The law of delict provides only a weak enforcement mechanism with regard to delictual duties so defined, the main example being interdict.[24]

Breach of a delictual duty then creates an *ex lege* obligation to make reparation for the resulting harm, subject to the rules on remoteness of damage.[25] It is suggested that the word "obligation" be used in this sense so as to capture the personal aspect of a wrong now committed against a person and for which there will now be liability for the resulting harm. This obligation is secondary in the sense that the primary duty to avoid wrongful acts or omissions has to already have been breached. The obligation is personal—in principle it is owed only to the person or persons who have suffered harm as a direct consequence of the breach of duty. The corollary is that only those persons may invoke the mechanism provided by the law of delict for enforcement of the secondary obligation, which generally will be an action for damages as reparation for the harm.[26]

Crime

Stair made a clear division between these two areas of law which had hitherto **1–05** been extremely closely related, although obviously links remain.[27] What has most certainly gone is any penal aspect of damages in Scotland for delict. However, since the Criminal Justice (Scotland) Act 1980 Pt IV, a criminal court can, in certain circumstances, make an order called a compensation order. Such

---

[20] At para.1–02.

[21] At para.1–11.

[22] The law does not permit "liability in an indeterminate amount for an indeterminate time to an indeterminate class": *Ultramares Corp v Touche* (1931) 255 N.Y. 170 at 179 per Cardozo C.J.

[23] These four examples are listed in a sort of hierarchy—it is difficult in practice to prove the intention required in fraud (see para.10–12 below); it is considerably less difficult to prove the intention required in the delict of assault (see para.6–13 below); in passing off there may be a rebuttable presumption of intent (see para.10–14 below), and in defamation there is a generally irrebuttable presumption of intent (see para.7–17 below).

[24] See paras 5–23 to 5–24 below.

[25] See paras 13–19 to 13–25 below.

[26] Although where the victim dies, claims may be brought under the Damages (Scotland) Act 2011 by the executor of the deceased victim's estate and by certain relatives of the deceased (see paras 5–19 to 5–22 below).

[27] Visser and Whitty, "The Structure of the Law of Delict" in Reid and Zimmermann (eds), *A History of Private Law in Scotland* (2000), Vol.II: Obligations, pp.432–434.

an order makes an offender pay a sum compensating the victim of the crime, as well as any fine or sentence of imprisonment that may be imposed. Compensation orders cannot be made in motor collision cases. The offender who does not pay the order—which can be paid by instalments—can be imprisoned for a specified period.

Public law

1–06   Reparation for delict is a branch of private law. The "farming out" of government functions to private or partly private bodies taken with the Crown Proceedings Act[28] are two important developments that have meant that the State, in some shape or form, finds itself in arguments about reparation. The state may also incur a delictual type of liability for failure to implement EU law.[29] Of even more significance is the "bringing home" of the rights set out in the European Convention on Human Rights by the implementation of the Scotland Act 1998 and the Human Rights Act 1998.[30]

The landmark case in negligence, *Dorset Yacht v The Home Office*,[31] brought the State more closely into the scope of liability as some of its functions were now thought justiciable and remain so, albeit there has been a growing reticence to finding public bodies liable in private law.[32]

New procedures for judicial review allowing a claim for damages for results of an unreasonable or wrongful decision has the look of delict. When the Inner House then made it clear that judicial review was not exclusively a matter of reviewing public bodies, it even more so resembles a new area of delict—that of wrongful administration.[33]

The delicts that control intentional harms are essentially bastions of the constitution. In Scotland, as in England, our Claim of Right and Bill of Rights are not documents upon which the citizen regularly has recourse to protect any civil rights that he or she may have. The Constitution depends upon the fact that people are free to do what is not prohibited and delict is one of the major prohibitions. As Fraser put it, in the first half of the 20th century:

> "The British subject has no rights which are guaranteed by the constitution. For the protection of his rights to personal freedom, as of all his other rights, the British subject must look to the ordinary law, particularly parts of it dealing with crimes and delicts, and not to any constitutional guarantees. It is an important feature of these branches of the law that they afford protection whether the citizen's rights are wrongfully invaded by a private person or a public official."[34]

Delict as much as crime regulates what we may or may not do the one to the other. Verbal injury is one of the most obvious examples. If free speech is indeed pivotal to civilisation, then in Scotland it is largely verbal injury that regulates

---

[28] See para.3–29 below.
[29] See paras 17–18 to 17–22 below.
[30] See Ch.2.
[31] *Dorset Yacht v The Home Office* [1970] A.C. 1004.
[32] See discussion below at Ch.17.
[33] See para.17–17 below.
[34] W.L.R. Fraser, *Constitutional Law* (London: W. Hodge, 1938), p.179. See also pp.194 and 200.

it.[35] Rules that seem unfortunate in the context of compensation or insurance or risk may well have significance in maintaining the balance of freedoms in society.[36]

Evidence and procedure

The rules of civil evidence and of court procedure are clearly of vital **1–07** importance in practice,[37] although not necessary to know in order to understand the law of delict itself. In general the onus is upon the pursuer to aver and to prove the necessary elements of the delictual wrong that is alleged of the defender.[38] The onus is also upon the pursuer to aver and to prove, by leading evidence, causation and harm.[39]

It will be noted that many of the great cases did not proceed to a proof.[40] The pursuer's case may be challenged as incompetent or the pleadings may be challenged as irrelevant. Such a challenge will be dealt with in a debate, where the sheriff or Lord Ordinary will decide whether to dismiss the action or to allow it to proceed to a proof or to a proof before answer.[41] Where, following debate, the case is allowed to proceed, it is not infrequent that the parties reach an out of court settlement.

THE EVOLUTION OF DELICTUAL LIABILITY IN SCOTS LAW

The modern law of delict in Scotland is the product of a number of influences **1–08** including indigenous custom, Roman law and English common law,[42] supplemented by statutory provisions in certain areas and now subject to the advancing influence of the European Convention on Human Rights.[43] Although in recent times English law has undoubtedly become the most significant influence on the development of the law of delict in Scotland,[44] it is helpful to glance at the

---

[35] See Ch.7.

[36] P.Q.R. Boberg, *The Law of Delict* (South Africa: Jutta, 1989), pp.26–27: "The law of delict . . . is close to the core problem of balancing individual freedom against collective security—a balance that it seeks to achieve by tempering broad principles of liability with limiting interpretations of wrongfulness, fault and causation. It follows that a proposition should never be propounded without due regard to its social implications, and that the merit of a rule depends on its functional effects rather than the purity of its ancestry."

[37] See generally, R.E. Conway, *Personal Injury Practice in the Sheriff Court*, 3rd edn (Edinburgh: W. Green, 2011).

[38] Subject to the maxim res ipsa loquitur: see paras 12–18 to 12–21 below.

[39] See Ch.13.

[40] The most famous example being *Donoghue v Stevenson*, 1932 S.C. (HL) 31.

[41] A broad equivalent in England and Wales is the application to "strike out". Although deprecated on the basis of a misunderstanding in *Osman v United Kingdom* (2000) 29 E.H.R.R. 245, the European Court of Human Rights has recognised the role of the preliminary hearing in confirming disputed points of law, and in dispensing with unmeritorious claims, at an early stage in procedure: *Z v United Kingdom* (2002) 34 E.H.R.R. 3. See paras 17–05 to 17–06 below.

[42] Itself shaped to a significant extent by developments in other common law jurisdictions—most notably Australia, New Zealand and North America.

[43] By virtue of the Human Rights Act 1998 and, to a lesser extent in relation to the traditional domain of the law of delict, the Scotland Act 1998.

[44] Especially due to the common role of the House of Lords from 1711 as the ultimate appeal court from both jurisdictions.

Roman and indigenous origins of the law[45] as—and in this regard the European Convention on Human Rights should in theory sit more comfortably with Scots law than English —Scots law is still perceived to pursue developments by deduction from general principles rather than by analogy to established precedents.

Roman origins

1–09   The earliest form of Roman law was based on the recognition of the family unit headed by the *paterfamilias*. In the event of a wrong being perpetrated against (a member of) a *familia*, early Roman law recognised a right of seizure enjoyed by that *familia* over the body of the perpetrator. Initially vindication of the right of seizure was the infliction of death upon the wrongdoer. However, with the strengthening of the power of the State, the right of seizure was restricted to a right of *taliation*[46] under the supervision of the State,[47] which was gradually reduced to redemption of the right of seizure by a composition[48]—initially of cattle,[49] and later of a sum of money.[50] The amount of composition for various wrongs became determined by the State.[51]

As Roman society matured, various forms of action emerged—in particular the *actio legis aquiliae* (from the *lex Aquilia*) and the *actio injuriarum*,[52] both based on the *ius civile*. To these *actiones poenales*[53] were added various praetorian edicts[54] each of which identified circumstances in which a (prescribed) remedy could be sought. The *lex Aquilia* dealt with *damnum injuria datum*; *damnum* initially involving damage to property but latterly encompassing personal harm, *injuria* meaning contrary to law and eventually requiring either *dolus* (intent) or *culpa* (lack of care),[55] and *datum* indicating the requirement of a causal link

---

[45] There is now a near complete *History of Scots Law* by Professor Walker. There is a very extensive series of detailed historical, historiographical and theoretical essays in Reid and Zimmermann, *A History of Private Law in Scotland* (2000), Vol.II: Obligations. See also D.M. Walker, "The Development of Reparation" (1952) 64 J.R. 101; R. Black, "An Historical Survey of Delictual Liability in Scotland for Personal Injuries and Death", 1975 C.I.L.J.S.A. 46, 189, 316; 1976 9 C.I.L.J.S.A. 57; R. Evans-Jones, *The Civilian Tradition in Scots Law* (Edinburgh: The Stair Society, 1995); R. Zimmermann, *The Law of Obligations: Roman Foundations of the Civilian Tradition* (Oxford: Oxford University Press, 1996).

[46] Under the *lex talionis*.

[47] Via State controlled legal proceedings (*manus iniecto*).

[48] Although a composition may be considered compensatory, Roman law did not abandon the penal element—so avoiding a clear distinction between criminal and civil liability. Thus, if neither the wrongdoer nor a third party was able or prepared to provide the composition, the wrongdoer was potentially liable to be sold into slavery or in theory to be killed.

[49] *Pecus*.

[50] *Pecunia*—where the wrongdoer was a person in power (son, daughter or slave) the action was available against the *paterfamilias* on the basis of *noxal* liability.

[51] *Poenae*—either the equivalent of the estimated value of the relevant property, or in some cases a multiplier of the value, or in others left to the discretion of the judge.

[52] Action for affront or insult. Readers of earlier case reports will note a different and now disapproved use of the term *actio injuriarum*. See *McKendrick v Sinclair*, 1972 S.L.T. 110 (HL); and also in the Court of Session: 1971 S.L.T. 17; T.B. Smith, "Designation of Delictual Actions: Damn Injuria Damn", 1972 S.L.T. (News) 125; T.B. Smith, "Damn Injuria Again", 1984 S.L.T. (News) 85.

[53] Actions for a sum of money.

[54] On an ad hoc basis to deal with the emerging demands of a developing society—echoed in modern statutory developments.

[55] G. MacCormack, "Aquilian Culpa" in Alan Watson, *Daube Noster: Essays in Legal History for David Daube* (Edinburgh: Scottish Academic Press, 1974).

connecting the harm to the wrongful conduct.[56] The *actio injuriarum* apparently initially provided a remedy for minor physical assaults that probably caused little if anything more than an affront to the honour of the victim. Following praetorian overhaul, the *actio injuriarum* later focussed on *contumelia* (insult), occasioned by harm to *corpus*, *fama* or *dignitas* (body, reputation or dignity), but requiring *animus injuriandi* (intention to insult).[57]

Ironically, although classical Roman law is credited as being at the roots of deductive civilian legal systems, it has been claimed that in the Roman law of delict there was "more affinity between the Roman jurist and the common lawyer than . . . between the Roman jurist and his modern civilian successor."[58] Roman law developed a range of nominate delicts which were modified or expanded by ad hoc praetorian action to provide for exigencies that arose, rather than being developed according to any logical system of general principles. The work of Roman jurists "did not culminate in a streamlined law of *delict* but remained a somewhat haphazard assemblage of individual *delicts*."[59] Thus, developments in the *lex Aquilia* resulted in remedies for direct and consequential damage arising from a lack of due care without an overall consideration of benchmarking limits on potential liability.[60] The practical significance of the *lex Aquilia* is that it was this statute and its interpretation in the *Digest* that was discovered and attracted the attention of the great Roman jurists in post-medieval Europe—the start of the *jus commune* period when European states worked with the raw materials of the ancient law to fashion law for their own time and place.

Scots origins

Early Scots law followed a similar line of development to early Roman law. **1–10** The transition from bloodfeuds and *talio* to pecuniary compensation was completed with the emergence around the 14th century of the remedy of *assythment*.[61] This remedy was typical of the lack of a clear distinction between criminal and civil liability characteristic of developing legal systems[62]—it was an action for pecuniary compensation to be paid by the wrongdoer to the next-of-kin of a victim whose death had been criminally inflicted. From the latter part of the 18th century *assythment* became replaced by solatium.[63] In the 20th century it was suggested that *assythment* had fallen into desuetude[64] but it was only formally abolished by s.8 of the Damages (Scotland) Act 1976.

---

[56] D.9.2.5.1. (Ulpian).

[57] There was possibly a presumption of *animus injuriandi*, reflected in the Scots law of defamation (for which the *actio injuriarum* is an acknowledged primary source). See Ch.7.

[58] W.W. Buckland and A.D. McNair, *Roman Law and Cannon Law, A Comparison in Outline*, 2nd edn (Cambridge: Cambridge University Press, 1952), p.XIV.

[59] R. Zimmermann, *The Law of Obligations: Roman Foundations of the Civilian Tradition* (1996), p.914.

[60] A perennially difficult issue in modern cases involving the law of negligence—see Ch.11.

[61] Assythment was initially competent in respect of all bodily injuries but later became restricted to death.

[62] S. Pollock and T. Maitland, *The History of English Law* (London: Cambridge University Press, 1898), Vol.II, p.449.

[63] *Hamilton v Rutherford* (1771) Mor. Dic. 13924; *Innes v Magistrates of Edinburgh* (1798) Mor. Dic. 13189; *Black v Caddell* (1804) Mor. Dic. 13905; affirmed (1812) 5 Pat.567; *Eisten v North British Railway Co* (1870) 8 M. 980.

[64] *McKendrick v Sinclair*, 1972 S.L.T. 110 at 117 per Lord Simon of Glaisdale.

The remedy of *novel dissasine*[65] was available in early Scots law to restore possession of property. At around the beginning of the 15th century this remedy was superseded by ejection and intrusion[66] in respect of heritage, and *spuilzie*[67] in respect of moveable property. The remedies were concerned with enforcing a right of possession rather than compensating for damage done to the property and the criminal aspect of wrongful dispossession of property was emphasised in the sense that the dispossessed owner was entitled to recover violent profits.[68] Common to the three remedies of *assythment*, ejection and intrusion, and *spuilzie* was the need to prove fault in the sense of intention on the part of the wrongdoer to commit the wrongful act.

Institutional writers

1–11   A gradual reception of the Roman principles, as discovered and developed by civilian jurists, into Scots law is apparent in the work of the Institutional Writers. Stair, having identified that reparation may be claimed in respect of delinquencies injuring a pursuer's person, liberty, fame and honour, object of affection or property,[69] preceded a description of specific obligations[70] with reference to a general obediential obligation of reparation for damage and interest,[71] the measure of damages later being acknowledged as calculated according to the *actio legis Aquiliae*.[72] Bankton continued and refined the theme, hinting at a distinction between the public and private, or criminal and civil, aspects of delinquencies.[73] In particular, injury,[74] damage,[75] extortion[76] and circumvention and fraud[77] were described in Roman law terms, and were complemented by a number of specific delinquencies, including *assythment*, ejection and intrusion, and *spuilzie*.[78]

---

[65] Apparently copied from the English assise of novel disseisin, which itself originated from canon and Roman law—see D.M. Walker, *The Law of Delict in Scotland*, 2nd edn (Edinburgh: W. Green, 1981), pp.23–24.

[66] Whether an action for ejection and intrusion is competent in modern Scots law has been questioned—see *Price v Watson*, 1951 S.C. 359 at 368 per Lord Keith.

[67] *Spuilzie* could originally be pursued either criminally or civilly, with the latter eventually superseding the former. Although the last recognised case of *spuilzie* proper was *Stove v Colvin* (1831) 9 S. 633, whether it has fallen into desuetude appears open to debate—see, e.g. *FC Finance Ltd v Brown & Son*, 1969 S.L.T. (Sh. Ct) 41; *Harris v Abbey National Plc*, 1997 S.C.L.R. 359; A. Rodger, "Spuilzie in the Modern World", 1970 S.L.T. (News) 33; D.L. Carey Miller, *Corporeal Moveables in Scots Law*, 2nd edn (Edinburgh: W. Green, 2005), pp.276–286.

[68] Rent or profit from the estate at double the actual rate for urban land or the highest possible yield for rural land.

[69] Stair, I, 9, 4.

[70] Of which 12 (*assythment*, ejection and intrusion and *spuilzie* being three) intentional wrongs were listed: Stair, I, 9, 7–30.

[71] Which " . . . hath as many branches and specialities as there can be valuable and reparable damages": Stair, I, 9, 6.

[72] Erskine, III, 1, 14.

[73] Bankton, I, 10, 13.

[74] Harm caused either by assault or defamation to the pursuer's fame and reputation—based on the *actio injuriarum*: Bankton, I, 10, 21.

[75] Harm (distinct from dispossession) caused to goods composed of *damnum injuria datum* and reparable under the *actio legis Aquilae*: Bankton, I, 10, 40.

[76] The Roman *vis ac metus*: Bankton, I, 10, 50.

[77] The Roman *dolus*: Bankton, I, 10, 62.

[78] Suggested as evidence that Roman and native delicts existed side by side by the middle of the 18th century: Walker, *The Law of Delict in Scotland* (1981), p.25.

The transition from a system based on nominate delicts dealing with specific actions to one based on a general obediential obligation to make reparation for damage arising from wrongful conduct is most apparent in the work of Erskine who, rather than list any nominate delicts, declared:

> "Everyone who has the exercise of reason, and so can distinguish between right and wrong, is naturally obliged to make up the damage befalling his neighbour from a wrong committed by himself. Wherefore every fraudulent contrivance, or unwarrantable act by which another suffers damage, or runs the hazard of it, subjects the delinquent to reparation."[79]

Erskine then reflected:

> " . . . wrong may arise not only from positive acts of trespass or injury, but from blameable omission or neglect of duty".[80]

Erskine's assertion is worthy of some unpacking. It points out that the obligations to which he referred arise "naturally", i.e. *ex lege* rather than *ex voluntante*. It also suggests that two forms of obligation arise *ex lege*: viz an obligation not to engage in wrongful conduct, referred to as "fraudulent contrivance or unwarrantable act"; and an obligation to make reparation or "make up the damage". Logically, the latter obligation is secondary to the former, in the sense that the obligation to make reparation arises only where the obligation to avoid wrongful acts has been breached. However, Erskine appeared to juxtapose the primary and secondary obligations, referring to the damage before referring to the wrong. This reflects the primary purpose of the modern law of delict, i.e. to provide a remedy for the consequences of wrongful conduct rather than to prevent its occurrence in the first place. However, implicit in the parenthesised part of the latter sentence is the suggestion that reparation can be used to prevent damage occurring, reflecting the availability of interdict as well as damages in the modern law of delict. Also implicit is a distinction between intentional delicts (fraudulent contrivances) and negligence (unwarrantable acts) which explicitly is expanded in the distinction between "positive acts of trespass or injury" and "blameable omission or neglect of duty". It is notable that Erskine also recognised the possibility of liability for omissions in the last part of this extract.

Erskine's explicit distinction between intentional and unintentional wrongful conduct was elaborated by subsequent writers[81] who distinguished between

---

[79] Erskine, III, 1, 13. The influence on Lord Atkin's *locus classicus* in *Donoghue v Stevenson*, 1932 S.C. (HL) 31 at 44 is clear.

[80] Erskine, III, 1, 13. This comes close to the position reached in the French Civil Code—a general principle of reparation not requiring nominate heads—although it should be noted that there are different strands in the civilian tradition: see Zimmermann, *The Law of Obligations: Roman Foundations of the Civilian Tradition* (1996). Stair has a rights-focused general principle that is similar to the German Code and Erskine's is closer to the French. There is much scholarly interest in discovering whether and when any such general principle appeared in Scots law—see D.W. McKenzie and R. Evans-Jones, "The Development of Remedies for Personal Injuries and Death" in Evans-Jones, *The Civilian Tradition in Scots Law* (1995), Vol.2, arguing for a general action in Stair. See however contra, "A general action, and a generalised liability were ideas, the time of which had not yet come": Visser and Whitty, "The Structure of the Law of Delict" in Reid and Zimmermann (eds), *A History of Private Law in Scotland* (2000), Vol.II: Obligations, p.438.

[81] See e.g. P. Stein, "The *Actio de Effusis vel Dejectis* and the concept of Quasi-Delict in Scots Law" (1955) 4 I.C.L.Q. 356.

"delicts" and "quasi-delicts", reflecting the Justinian division of the law of ubligations into four components. It has been suggested that a desire for symmetry was the closest to any practical utility underlying the distinction between "delict" and "quasi-delict" in Roman law,[82] although much deliberation and ink seems to have been devoted to the search for a rational explanation.[83] Thus, some writers compared a distinction between wrongs which are criminally culpable, and those which are not, or at least less so;[84] others distinguished between *dolus* and *culpa* or between intentional and unintentional wrongs or negligence.[85] To add to the confusion, the Roman quasi-delicts included examples of strict and vicarious liability.[86] In practice, the distinction is unimportant[87] as by the beginning of the 19th century[88] a general principle of liability for *damnum injuria datum* was developing in Scots law, based on fault or *culpa*, and encompassing both intentional and unintentional acts. This resulted in the growth of the law of negligence during the 20th century. As a consequence many of the nominate delicts have become irrelevent, or have been superseded by the general action for reparation based upon *culpa*.[89]

The modern era

1–12   Meanwhile, economic and monetary union with England, and the shared supreme jurisdiction of the House of Lords in most civil matters meant that more and more the influence was from England and the Empire and Commonwealth, and less and less from the *jus commune* countries. It is worth noting that since the United Kingdom has been playing a full part in the European Community for nearly half a century, European solutions are now required for economic reasons and those solutions may often find inspiration from the legal systems of France, Germany, Italy or Spain, (to name only four) where the foundations are civilian. The new Scottish Parliament has extensive law-making powers in private law of which delict forms part. Thus interest in *jus commune* solutions is growing both academically and practically. That said, moving on one more step, globalisation, whereby everyone speaks English and eats a Big Mac™ ordered using an app on their iPhone™, while watching a Hollywood movie chosen on their tablet with an Android™ operating system, puts pressure on legislative and other schemes, often of an Anglo-American nature. The Senior Appeal courts in most States will

---

[82] Walker, *The Law of Delict in Scotland* (1981), p.26; although the symbolism of numbers in ancient times was of significant influence see, e.g. Zimmermann, *The Law of Obligations: Roman Foundations of the Civilian Tradition* (1996), p.5.

[83] "(O)ne of the regrettable confusions of Roman law perpetrated in modern Scots law": Walker, *The Law of Delict in Scotland* (1981), p.26.

[84] See e.g. Bankton, I, 4, 26–27; G.C.H. Paton, *Baron David Hume's Lectures* (Edinburgh: Stair Society, 1952), Vol.III, 15, pp.186–198; *Palmer v Wick and Pulteneytown Steam Shipping Co* (1894) 21 R. (HL) 39 at 43 per Lord Watson.

[85] See, e.g. Bell, *Principles*, ss.544–553; J. Guthrie Smith, *A Treatise on the Law of Reparation* (US: Nabu Press, 1864), p.8.

[86] See Ch.4.

[87] See e.g. *Liquidators of Western Bank v Douglas* (1860) 22 D. 447 at 475–476 per Lord Justice-Clerk Inglis, delivering the opinion of the court.

[88] *Black v Caddell* (1804) Mor. Dic.13905; affirmed (1812) 5 Pat. 567, H.L. has been attributed as the first reported case of negligence based upon a general principle of fault based liability, although this case was preceded by the unreported case of *Gardner v Fergusons* (1795), referred to by Lord Kilbrandon in *McKendrick v Sinclair*, 1972 S.C. (HL) 25 at 66.

[89] See e.g. *FC Finance Ltd v Langtry Investment Co*, 1973 S.L.T. (Sh. Ct) 11.

now consider cases from other jurisdictions and systems where there is a new "big issue" under consideration.

Industrialisation brought about more opportunity for loss to be caused in the form of physical injury whether in the factory, the mill, the mine or by the railway or the motor car.[90] Mass production separated the maker from the product and in many cases resulted in no individual being solely responsible for the finished product. In these situations the wrongfulness triggering liability in theft or assault or in insult was not quite so apparent. More harm was caused through neglect than intent. The concept of fault (*culpa*) recognised in Scots law was a fertile theoretical compost in which liability for lack of care could grow. This rapid change of social factors, which has expanded with production, could not always be accommodated by the common law, which requires litigation between real parties to declare the law, and often parliament has been compelled to intervene to provide remedies for appropriate causes, or to remedy perceived deficiencies in the common law as it develops. It shall be seen that many rules of law are no longer found in the common law but in statute or subordinate legislation—for example, the Occupiers' Liability (Scotland) Act 1960,[91] the Health and Safety at Work etc. Act 1974,[92] the Animals (Scotland) Act 1987,[93] and the Consumer Protection Act 1987.[94] Some of the legislation may now come either directly or indirectly from Europe rather than the United Kingdom or Scottish parliaments.

Differences between Scots law and English law

The English law of torts itself grew out of English criminal law. After that its **1–13** development was closely linked to the forms of action. Basically, unless a person could fit his or her claim into one of the forms of action, there was no remedy. Accordingly, English law is most appropriately seen as being a series of separate torts and not as a number of frequently occurring instances of a general principle of delictual or tortious liability. On the other hand, with the passage of time, the expansion of each of the torts resulted in there being fewer gaps between the torts, and indeed the extension of existing torts or the creation of new torts seems to have been based on principles similar to those informing Scots law, such as liability based on fault.[95] A common market, constitution and culture and a common Supreme Court had tendencies to assimilate the two systems. While both Law Commissions are committed to their own respective legal systems, consultation and collaboration suggest that often reform can be at least along the same lines in effect. That said, it is fair to say that there are still differences between the two systems—outwith liability for negligence, considerable differences. The English law is still affected by precedents which say that a man acts at his peril, but they have moved away from that in many details. The English law of defamation makes a technical distinction between libel and slander, which Scots law does not. The English courts can award exemplary or penal damages

---

[90] J. McLaren, "Nuisance Law and the Industrial Revolution—Some Lessons from Social History" [1983] 3 O.J.L.S. 155. Some of the great cases, however, "were not of a type peculiar to urban or industrialising society": H.L. MacQueen and W.D.H. Sellar, "Negligence" in Reid and Zimmermann (eds), *A History of Private Law in Scotland* (2000), Vol.II: Obligations, p.542.

[91] See Ch.18.

[92] See Ch.21.

[93] See Ch.20.

[94] See Ch.19.

[95] See B.S. Markesinis, "The not so dissimilar tort and delict" (1977) L.Q.R. 78.

and the rules on prescription and limitation are different. The rules on remoteness of damage are no longer different. The English law in relation to property interests is quite different both in concept and result.[96] The law of trespass is much more significant in England than in Scotland. However, in the most frequently litigated area, that of negligence, it cannot be said that the law is not now the same in both jurisdictions.[97]

Function: what does delict do?

Deterrence

1–14   Function changes with time.[98] As indicated above, initially, delict had a quasi-criminal function of penalising wrongdoers. To some extent it still has that function: if you strike me or insult me I will get damages from you. This is sometimes described as a hortatory/deterrent function: as well as punishing, the possibility of delictual liability deters people by creating a fear of punishment, encouraging people to organise their behaviour accordingly. But this criminal/hortatory/deterrent function only operates to a certain extent: if you are unemployed and in receipt of state benefit then you pay no damages and so you may not be so concerned to plan your conduct within the law. If you carelessly run me down in your company car, your employer's insurers pay the damages and it is your employer who loses his "no claims" bonus. The criminal law now fulfils much of the deterrent function: you drive carelessly—you are fined—you may lose your driving licence.

A recent expression of the traditional view can be seen in the judgment of Henry L.J. in the Court of Appeal in *Frost v Chief Constable*.[99] Deterrence, he said, was part of the public policy behind tort law. Prevention was better than cure and potential defendants should face up to their safety responsibilities before rather than after an accident.[100] Stapleton has demonstrated that the idea of deterrence is perhaps quite deeply entrenched in the modern law.[101] What she has identified is the theme in modern cases denying liability, even where the harm caused could be described as reasonably foreseeable, a theme founded on the idea of "alternative means of protection". She shows that in cases of denial of liability in the face of what might be expected to be liability, deterrence is an issue. Looked at in this way, doctrines of volenti non fit injuria and contributory negligence also show deterrence at work—deterring careless behaviour on the part of the pursuer.[102] In economic loss cases, the pursuer must often show that it was reasonable to rely upon the information carelessly given which has caused

---

[96] See the Torts (Interference with Goods) Act 1977.

[97] See Chs 11 and 12. See especially A. Rodger, "Lord MacMillan's speech in *Donoghue v Stevenson*" (1992) 108 L.Q.R. 236.

[98] J. Conaghan and W. Mansell, *The Wrongs of Tort* (London: Pluto Press, 1993) is a good radical look at traditional expositions of tort.

[99] *Frost v Chief Constable* [1997] 1 All E.R. 540.

[100] *Frost v Chief Constable* [1997] 1 All E.R. 540 at 567. See also Lord Hoffmann's speech in *Stovin v Wise* [1996] A.C. 923.

[101] J. Stapleton, "Duty of Care: Peripheral Parties and Alternative Opportunities for Deterrence" (1995) 111 L.Q.R. 301–345. For an argument at an even higher level of theory see R. Wright, "Right Justice and Tort Law" in Owen, *Philosophical Foundations of Tort Law* (1995).

[102] Stapleton, "Duty of Care: Peripheral Parties and Alternative Opportunities for Deterrence" (1995) 111 L.Q.R. 301–345, 305.

the loss.[103] Although the corollary of the deterrence argument is that threatening liability may raise standards, imposing too much liability can result in "over-deterrence". This is the argument often used in professional negligence cases: doctors will do too many, perhaps unnecessary tests. The idea of deterrence may also be a factor in letting some potential defenders escape in order to make sure that liability is focused towards another party whose conduct it is sought to deter, perhaps the negligent builder rather than the busy local authority.[104]

Compensation

The next major function (and that which concerns the practitioner) is **1-15** compensation. Instead of concentrating on penalising the wrongdoer we compensate the victim.[105] If compensation is based on fault then not every injured person is compensated and so it might be said that delict is a poor compensation scheme. If a regime of strict liability is applied, more people are compensated.[106] Thus there are often demands for more strict liability and the last 50 years have seen a considerable expansion in such cases.[107] Because a quite significant amount of compensation is achieved through the delict system, those who wish to extend compensation often urge a strict liability regime. Strict liability is also likely to cover the cost of compensating.[108]

Risk allocation

Aside from penalising some wrongdoers quite effectively (for example, **1-16** defamation actions between persons with money), delict redistributes the cost of certain accidents within the community—a function most clearly seen in the rule that an employer is vicariously liable for his or her employees.[109]

The practice of insuring against certain risks, although it has had a considerable influence on the law, is nonetheless legally irrelevant.[110] It therefore does not matter that a pursuer may already have recovered compensation from his insurers. That said, the availability and practice of insurance may provide a background to a legal approach. For example, if a contractor wrongly cuts a power cable which deprives millions of people of power and causes millions of

---

[103] Stapleton, "Duty of Care: Peripheral Parties and Alternative Opportunities for Deterrence" (1995) 111 L.Q.R. 301–345, 306.

[104] Stapleton, "Duty of Care: Peripheral Parties and Alternative Opportunities for Deterrence" (1995) 111 L.Q.R. 301–345, 317; see the cases discussed in Ch.17.

[105] This is now virtually a subject of study in its own right. The issues and the context are examined fully in P. Cane, *Atiyah's Accidents Compensation and the Law*, 8th edn (Cambridge: Cambridge University Press, 2013).

[106] See generally D.M. Walker, "Strict Liability in Scotland" (1954) 66 J.R. 231; D.R. Harris et al., *Compensation and Support for Illness and Injury* (Oxford: Oxford University Press, 1984); Law Reform Committee, *Report of the Royal Commission on Civil Liability and Compensation for Personal Injury* (HMSO, 1978), Cmnd.7054; Cane, *Atiyah's Accidents Compensation and the Law* (2013); P. Cane, "Does No-Fault Have a Future", 1994 J.P.I.L. 302.

[107] Although 2013 saw a reversal in that trend in liability of employers—the presumption of civil liability for breach of the Health and Safety at Work Act 1974 contained in s.47 was reversed by s.69 of the Enterprise and Regulatory Reform Act 2013 (see paras 21–09 to 21–10 below).

[108] See Cane, *Atiyah's Accidents Compensation and the Law* (2013). The consultation paper "Compensation for Road Accidents" from the Lord Chancellor's Department (May, 1991) has never been acted upon.

[109] See paras 4–05 to 4–20 below.

[110] See e.g. *Winnik v Dick*, 1981 S.L.T. (Sh. Ct) 23. But insurance can be a factor in other enquiries such as fairness: see Lord Rodger in the Outer House in *B.T. v James Thomson & Sons Ltd*, 1997 S.L.T. 767 at 774D.

pounds of financial loss, it would be expensive to insure against such a contingency, whereas if individuals are aware that a power cut is a risk they themselves must carry, they will take steps to minimise the loss they might suffer, for example by buying a petrol-powered generator. Alternatively, people who would suffer from a power cut could arrange insurance themselves.[111] In considering the overall function of the law, insurance is taken into account by the legislature. The delict system would not compensate many injured people if there were not compulsory insurance for drivers and employers. Even that requirement needs to be "patched-up" to meet the function. In road traffic cases there is a Motor Insurers' Bureau scheme to cover cases where a driver is uninsured or unidentified. In employment cases, there is generally no equivalent safety net but the courts have in some cases "bent the rules" so as to permit claims against employers where a strict application of the normal rules would leave victims of the employers' wrongful conduct without a remedy.[112] The courts have also allowed those who failed to obey the law and take out the insurance, to be sued for breach of their statutory duty.[113]

An enforcement mechanism for supranational "rights"

1–17   The delict or reparation systems are essentially "used" to achieve other functions—the best, most recent examples being to meet the demands of European law for a nations failure to transpose directives and the demands of European Human Rights law to provide the citizen with just satisfaction. These topics are embraced in this book because these rules form part of the Scots law of delict or reparation, however alien the source of their content.[114]

Welfare

1–18   Even prior to the expansion of the welfare state after the Second World War, the delict system did not act sufficiently broadly to provide welfare for casualties of industrialisation. So while it has and does provide for the welfare of some of the injured[115]—and through establishing liability provides for many more through compelling insurance payments,[116] it is not a cornerstone of the welfare system. There are freestanding systems. People who are the victims of crime may recover compensation under the Criminal Injuries Compensation Scheme[117] and workers injured at work may receive industrial injury benefit. Indeed the welfare system demands recovery from compensation derived from the delict system through compensation recovery.[118]

---

[111] For an excellent examination of this issue, see M. Davies, "The End of the Affair: Duty of Care and Liability Insurance" (1989) 9 L.S. 67–83.

[112] See e.g. *Fairchild v Glenhaven Funeral Services Ltd* [2003] 1 A.C. 32. This case is discussed, along with other related cases, at paras 13–05 to 13–07 below.

[113] See generally Davies, "The End of the Affair: Duty of Care and Liability Insurance" (1989) 9 L.S. 67–83. See *Quinn v McGinty*, 1999 S.L.T. (Sh. Ct) 27.

[114] See paras 17–18 to 17–22 below.

[115] See e.g. *Simmons v British Steel Plc*, 2004 S.C. (HL) 94.

[116] See e.g. *Durham v BAI (Run Off) Ltd* [2012] 1 W.L.R. 867; *AXA General Insurance Ltd, Petitioners* [2011] 3 W.L.R. 871; 2012 S.C. (UKSC) 122.

[117] See W.J. Stewart, *Reparation: Liability for Delict* (London: Sweet & Maxwell), Ch.29.

[118] See para.5–17 below. The impact on the welfare system of the changes to s.47 of the Health and Safety at Work Act 1974 brought in by s.69 of the Enterprise and Regulatory Reform Act 2013 (see paras 21–09 to 21–10 below) have yet to be seen.

GENERAL PRINCIPLES AND CONCEPTS

Justice—or policy

Law is an application of justice. Such big issues are seldom discussed as such **1–19** in the cases, yet when new big issues arise, the law can look towards issues of justice as much as internal juridical policy. Certainly it might be said that the consideration of "legal policy" factors upon the application of a "fair, just and reasonable" test to novel delict cases—not just in negligence—is essentially questioning how justice should be applied.[119] However, the application of policy, or justice, concepts is often controversial,[120] and undermines predictability in the law.

Delict is essentially about *corrective* justice—fixing things between person and person. Outlined by Aristotle, it was developed by Grotius and Pufendorf and later by Kant.[121] Gordley, speaking of the Natural Lawyers in this tradition, including Grotius, a great influence on Stair, says:

> "They used an Aristotelian principle of corrective justice that no one should gain through another's loss to explain liability both for taking another's property and for causing another harm. They gave a unified explanation of causation and fault: one could not say a person was the cause of another's harm unless he chose to harm him by acting intentionally or negligently. They thought that to avoid negligence, a person must weigh the costs and benefits of a course of action, but they did not think the purpose of the law of negligence was to give him the proper incentives to do so."[122]

Distributive justice is the idea that law concerns itself with a just distribution of losses in the community. So far as Scots law is concerned, this is theoretically alien.[123] Scots law corrects the wrong done by compelling the defender to make reparation. In addition, leaving aside any view that civilian *culpa* is the organising concept of the law, the main focus in practice, by virtue of the rules on written pleading, is of bringing fault home to the defender. That said, vicarious liability,[124] non-delegable duties[125] and liberalisations on proof can be seen as distributive. Strict liability, of which there are innumerable examples, many pertaining to the ordinary incidents of everyday life, do in fact place upon one party the burden of the risk of certain activities and to that extent represent distributive justice—the factory owner is obliged to make reparation to his

---

[119] See in particular paras 4–16 to 4–20; 11–61 to 11–63; 13–17 and Ch.17. See also, e.g. *Fairchild v Glenhaven Funeral Services Ltd* [2003] 1 A.C. 32; *Gregg v Scott* [2005] 2 A.C. 176 at 220–221 per Lord Phillips of Worth Matravers; *Chester v Afshar* [2005] 1 A.C. 134 at 162 per Lord Hope of Craighead; *Lamb v Camden London Borough Council* [1981] Q.B. 625 at 636 per Lord Denning.

[120] See e.g. the dissenting speeches of Lord Hope of Craighead and Lord Nicholls of Birkenhead in *Gregg v Scott* [2005] 2 A.C. 176.

[121] D.G. Owen, "Why Philosophy Matters to Tort Law" and J. Gordley, "Tort Law in the Aristotelian Tradition" in Owen, *Philosophical Foundations of Tort Law* (1995), p.131.

[122] J. Gordley, "Tort Law in the Aristotelian Tradition" in Owen, *Philosophical Foundations of Tort Law* (1995), p.131.

[123] The views of Lord Steyn in *Macfarlane v Tayside Health Board*, 2000 S.C. (HL) 1 are not native and are arguably unnecessary for the decision. They do not in any event represent the view of the majority. See J.M. Thomson, "Abandoning the Law of Delict,", 2000 S.L.T. (News) 43.

[124] See paras 4–05 to 4–20 below.

[125] See paras 4–02 to 4–03 below.

workforce in several situations and, if he manufactures products, to many of his customers or even users of his products who are not customers. The bulk of strict liability is conscious and statutory innovation and thus can legitimately reflect political economic or moral trends. The common law, it is submitted, cannot pick and choose between the mosaic tiles of corrective justice and distributive justice to create whatever picture suits the case in hand.[126]

At the highest level of generality there is the precept that one person should not harm another. This was one of Justinian's three precepts of the law.[127] Below that is the principle that one should not cause loss wrongfully. "Wrongfully" refers to fault or conduct in breach of a duty of care, or conduct causing reasonably foreseeable harm of the kind which in fact results. However, there are cases where loss is caused but no action is possible, for example, some of the secondary pure economic loss cases.[128] These may be explained on the basis that "wrongfully" can be dependent upon a duty of care, which can only be said to exist in certain limited circumstances or, more convincingly, that sometimes as a matter of public policy, discernible from precedent, the courts will not allow recovery.

Causation

1–20   Causation, in the sense of attribution of responsibility, is deep within the law no doubt as being entrenched within ideas of justice.[129] It is essential in negligence cases, although the last century has seen an easing of what proof is required of things that are themselves difficult or impossible to prove. In cases where there is an intended wrongful act, causation may still play a part where consequences are attributable to other conduct or circumstances, although these discussions may take place under remoteness. Statutory schemes which seek to transfer responsibility often require to take account of causation lest ideas of fault are "smuggled back in". So it is possible that the simple happening of an event can be a sufficient condition for liability or there may have to be some link which can more neutrally be expressed as "attribution".

Culpa: fault

1–21   In the modern Scots law of delict, liability for harm arising from wrongful conduct is based on the concept of "fault"[130] or "*culpa*". This is an application of the principle incorporated in the maxim *damnum injuria datum*, taken from the *actio legis acquiliae*. *Damnum* refers to the legally recognised harm for which a

---

[126] This is respectfully the opposite of what Lord Steyn says in *Macfarlane v Tayside Health Board*, 2000 S.L.T. 154 although his analogy is adopted with gratitude.

[127] Inst I, i, 3; originally Ulpian's dictum: D.1,1,10,1. It was revived to an extent by the natural lawyers such as Pufendorf, De jure naturale et Gentium Lib III, Cap 1, 1. See Zimmermann, *The Law of Obligations: Roman Foundations of the Civilian Tradition* (1996), p.1032, fn.224. On the face of it such a rule requires strict liability; see Zimmermann, *The Law of Obligations: Roman Foundations of the Civilian Tradition* (1996), p.1033. The natural lawyers began to mitigate that view by reference to imputability, duty and the foreseeability of wrong; Zimmermann, *The Law of Obligations: Roman Foundations of the Civilian Tradition* (1996), p.1032.

[128] See paras 11–40 to 11–43 below.

[129] See Ch.13. See also H.L.A. Hart and T. Honoré, *Causation and the Law*, 2nd edn (Oxford: Oxford University Press, 1985).

[130] Strict liability arises rarely at common law in Scotland—an example may be in defamation (see para.7–17).

remedy may be sought.[131] Injuria denotes a legally recognised wrong and extends to intentional wrongs and to negligence. Wrongful conduct may also take the form of a positive act or, where the law imposes a duty to act, an omission.[132] *Datum* requires a causal link connecting the harm back to the wrongful conduct.[133] Thus *fault* in the context of delictual liability encapsulates a legal responsibility for the harmful consequences of wrongful conduct. In common speech the word "fault" may be used in at least two senses: firstly in describing a problem that does not necessarily give rise to harmful consequences, e.g. the machine developed a fault requiring repair; and secondly in attributing responsibility or blame for an issue, e.g. the problem was X's fault. Likewise, the word "fault" in the context of delict may be used in both senses: fault can be used to define wrongful conduct, i.e. injuria[134]; and fault can be used to attribute legal responsibility for the consequences of an act or omission. In this latter sense, the word fault may encapsulate the three components of *damnum injuria datum*, and it is "fault" in this sense that is required to attract liability in delict. Thus, without fault, or *culpa*, there will be no liability, even where harm is suffered.[135]

Culpa is a term used frequently by the judiciary, apparently as a synonym for fault.[136] However, the various contexts in which *culpa* has been used suggests that it cannot be attributed with any precise meaning[137] but

> "it is perhaps not too fanciful to suggest that '*culpa*' is often used in preference to 'fault' because it is the more forceful word; it carries a stronger implication of wrongdoing and hence is suitable in a context intended to stress this element".[138]

Professor MacCormack has made other very good points, including:

> "Statements which assert that the law of reparation is founded. upon a principle of *culpa* derived from the Roman law are of a fairly late date . . . the judges have simply taken the word *culpa* and used it in the construction of arguments which consider the incidence of fault or negligence, . . . the sporadic reliance on texts from the Digest or the Institutes which use the

---

[131] Not all "harm" will be regarded by the law as *damnum*, e.g. "secondary" pure economic loss (suffered by a secondary victim) has never been recognised as reparable in delict (see paras 11–40 to 11–43 below) and reparable harm is subject to the rules on remoteness of damage (see paras 13–19 to 13–25 below).

[132] See paras 11–64 to 11–66 below.

[133] See Ch.13.

[134] Fault in this narrower sense does not per se give rise to liability in delict without consequential harm—if I drive carelessly but do not collide with anything or anyone there can be no delictual liability. Delict has no concern with *injuria sine damno*—harm without wrong.

[135] Encapsulated in the maxim *injuria sine damno*. Thus, if I open my shop next door to yours and entice all of your customers by undercutting all of your prices, I have not committed any delict. Even although you suffer harm I am not liable.

[136] On occasions the term *dolus* is used in place of *culpa* in the context of intentional wrongful conduct.

[137] See e.g. W.A. Elliott, "Reparation and the English Tort of Negligence" (1952) 64 J.R. 1; J.J. Gow, "Is Culpa Amoral?" (1953) 65 J.R. 17; W.A. Elliott, "What is Culpa?" (1954) 66 J.R. 6; G. MacCormack, "Culpa in the Scots Law of Reparation" (1974) J.R. 13; W.W. McBryde, "The Advantages of Fault", 1975 J.R. 32.

[138] G. MacCormack, "*Culpa* in the Scots Law of Reparation", 1974 J.R. 13 at 20.

term *culpa* does not prove that Scots law extracted from the Roman sources and applied a principle of *culpa*."[139]

Nevertheless, it is important to distinguish culpa from negligence. These terms are not synonyms:

> "*Culpa* is to be translated as fault and not negligence. Where a jurist presents the facts of the case and draws the conclusion that there has, or has not, been culpa, he is not asking, do these facts constitute negligence? His approach is to ask, do these facts constitute a fault? From this one may infer that where *culpa* is used as a criterion of liability in a general context without the addition of facts which explain what is meant, it should be taken as fault. The texts frequently state that a person is liable under the *lex Aquilia* for *dolus* and/or *culpa*. Such statements do not contrast loss brought about through intention and loss brought about through negligence. The mention of *dolus* in no way shows that *culpa* is negligence. As in other contexts it means fault, specifically fault not falling within the ambit of *dolus*. Whether *culpa* is taken as negligence or as fault is important. To say that someone is at fault implies that he has behaved in some way that he should not have behaved but leaves open the nature of the behaviour. To say that someone has been negligent implies that he has acted in a careless fashion and that he ought to have foreseen that what he did would cause damage."[140]

The distinction between *dolus* and *culpa* raises a question: does the law of delict recognise a taxonomy of fault? Older cases sometimes distinguished between *dolus*, *culpa lata*, *culpa levis* and *culpa levissima*. Although distinctive meanings and specific boundaries are difficult to identify, broadly the continuum might be described as:

- *Dolus*: intent;
- *Culpa lata*: gross fault involving malice or recklessness[141];
- *Culpa levis*: a failure to act reasonably in the circumstances;
- *Culpa levissima*: the slightest fault.

1-22   This classification of fault was criticised as outdated even before the House of Lords decision in *Donoghue v Stevenson*.[142] It is probably appropriate to suggest that any significance of the distinction was swept away by the implementing of

---

[139] MacCormack, "*Culpa* in the Scots Law of Reparation", 1974 J.R. 13 at 14, 18, 27.

[140] G. MacCormack, "Aquilian Culpa" in A. Watson, *Daube Noster: Essays in Legal History for David Daube* (Edinburgh: Scottish Academic Press, 1974).

[141] Might *culpa lata* overcome the "core principle" of police immunity from liability in negligence with regard to the carrying out of the police function of investigation and suppression of crime? See *Robinson v Chief Constable of West Yorkshire Police* [2014] P.I.Q.R. P14 and paras 17–04 to 17–09 below.

[142] *Donoghue v Stevenson*, 1932 S.C. (HL) 31. "*Culpa lata, levis, levissima* have been assigned their own boundaries, although to define them in particular cases has proved no easy task. In my humble opinion the more scientific treatment of the problem is not to predicate different degrees of negligence, but to concentrate on the duty, breach of which constitutes negligence. The duty is to take reasonable care in the circumstances, and will vary in each case, but, having been discharged, negatives any negligence, *lata, levis, or levissima*." *Kolbin & Sons v Kinnear & Co Ltd*, 1931 S.C. (HL) 128 at 139 per Lord Atkin.

the Law Reform (Contributory Negligence) Act 1945. Prior to that contributory negligence was a complete defence, and so it would be appropriate to distinguish *culpa levissima* as insufficient to trigger the defence. However, it remains the case that in road traffic matters, the slightest fault on the part of the driver of a motor car is generally sufficient to impose liability. Thus, it may be suggested that *culpa levissima* is sufficient in cases involving motor vehicles.

Nevertheless, a taxonomy of *culpa* was set out by Lord Hope in his judgment in *Kennedy v Glenbelle*:

> "The essential requirement is that fault or *culpa* must be established. That may be done by demonstrating negligence, in which case the ordinary principles of the law of negligence will provide an equivalent remedy. Or it may be done by demonstrating that the defender was at fault in some other respect. This may be because his action was malicious, or because it was deliberate in the knowledge that his action would result in harm to the other party, or because it was reckless as he had no regard to the question whether his action, if it was of a kind likely to cause harm to the other party, would have that result. Or it may be ... because the defender has indulged in conduct which gives rise to a special risk of abnormal damage, from which fault is implied if damage results from that conduct. In each case personal responsibility rests on the defender because he has conducted himself in a respect which is recognised as inferring *culpa* by our law. So what is required is a deliberate act or negligence or some other conduct from which *culpa* or fault may be inferred."[143]

So, Scots law seems not yet to have completely abandoned the categories of fault.[144]

There is, however, a practical problem with the attribution of liability for the consequences of wrongful conduct purely on the basis of fault, even in the word's wider sense. Like the ripples created by a stone hitting a pool of water, the consequences of a wrongful act can be very far reaching. To hold the wrongdoer liable for all damage that may be traced back to the wrongdoer's "fault" creates the potential for liability without any boundaries and would be detrimental to society in the sense that it would discourage persons from engaging in any activity which may possibly have as its consequence damage to any other person's interests. Thus, a recurring feature in the modern Scots law of delict has been the desire to limit potential liability within appropriately defined boundaries.[145]

At first sight this issue appears to present less of a problem when dealing with "intentional" delicts, provided that the intention, or *dolus*, on the part of the wrongdoer has been to cause the harm complained of to be inflicted upon the complaining individual.[146] A logical, although perhaps superficial, conclusion is that unintended consequences, in terms of either harm suffered or individuals affected, are not reparable as intentional delicts. However, if this was the effect

---

[143] *Kennedy v Glenbelle*, 1996 S.C. 95 at 100–101 per Lord Hope. See paras 8–16 and 8–17 below.

[144] cf. *Holdich v Lothian Health Board* [2013] CSOH 197; 2014 S.L.T. 495; 2014 G.W.D. 10–182 at [70] per Lord Stewart: "We have largely abandoned the categories of fault."

[145] See paras 11–02 and 13–19 below.

[146] i.e. an intention to inflict the harm on the victim rather than merely an intention to engage in the conduct deemed wrongful.

of the law, the law could be seen to condone irresponsible behaviour. Thus, *dolus* is viewed objectively rather than subjectively, in the sense that the wrongdoer will be assumed to have intended the natural and direct consequences of his actions.[147] Even where the alleged wrongdoer can show a lack of such intention to cause harm, this will not necessarily render the harm irreparable in delict, if it can nevertheless be shown that the harm was attributable to the wrongdoer's fault or *culpa*. The issue of boundaries of liability thus also arises in the context of intentional delicts, both in determining liability for the unintended consequences to the intended victim of intended acts and in determining liability for the unintended consequences to the unintended victim of intended acts.

Strict liability

1–23 The term "strict liability" tends to be used in the law of delict to denote liability regardless of fault. It features rarely at common law in the Scots law of delict —it features more frequently at common law in England and Wales.[148] It does operate in the law of defamation and, presuming they are part of Scots law, it forms the basis of liability of several Roman "quasi-delicts".[149] Most strict liability regimes that do operate in Scots law are the product of statute.[150] Such statutes tend to permit certain defences—which will be specified in the respective statutes.

Reasonable foreseeability and the reasonable person

1–24 Reasonable foreseeability is a concept used widely across the law of delict. This is especially so in negligence, where the concept is used in determining whether a duty of care is owed, the standard of care the law demands, whether causal chains will be broken, and what will be the boundaries of liability, beyond which losses become too remote to be reparable. The concept often said to be based on the perception of the reasonable man.[151] Originating as the man on the Clapham omnibus,[152] the reasonable man has more recently graduated to be the man on the underground,[153] then becoming the gender non-specific "commuter".[154] Some of the judiciary have become conscious that the analogy is outdated:

---

[147] "If liability were said to be the result of wilful wrongdoing, it might be quite relevant to inquire what an ordinarily prudent man would have contemplated as the probable consequences of his action." *Golder v Caledonian Railway* (1902) 5 F. 123 at 126 per Lord Kinnear.

[148] See e.g. English law imposes strict liability for non-natural use of land: *Rylands v Fletcher* (1868) L.R. 3 H.L. 330. Scots law does not, at least with regards to actions for damages: *R.H.M. Bakeries v Strathclyde Regional Council*, 1985 S.C. (HL) 17; cf. *Caledonian Railway v Greenock Corp*, 1917 S.C. (HL) 56. Nevertheless, liability may arise for *culpa levissima*—see e.g. *Kerr v Earl of Orkney* (1857) 20 D. 298; *Kennedy v Glenbelle*, 1996 S.C. 95. See paras 8–09 and 8–10 below.

[149] See paras 18–18 to 18–25 below.

[150] Examples include the Animals (Scotland) Act 1987 (see Ch.20) and the Consumer Protection Act 1987 (see Ch.19).

[151] For a discussion of the utility of the concept in the modern era see Hoffmann L.J. "Anthropomorphic Justice: The Reasonable Man and his Friends" (1995) 29 *Law Teacher* 127–141.

[152] Although the origin of the term is frequently attributed to *Hall v Brooklands Auto Racing Club* [1933] 1 K.B. 205 at 224 per Greer L.J., in fact the phrase is recited in *McQuire v Western Mornings News Co Ltd* (1903) 2 K.B. 100 at 109 per Collins M.R. and attributed without citation to Bowen L.J.

[153] *Frost v Chief Constable of South Yorkshire* [1999] 2 A.C. 455 at 495 per Lord Steyn.

[154] *McFarlane v Tayside Health Board*, 2000 S.C. (HL) 1 at 16 per Lord Steyn.

"On its own common sense, and without more guidance, is no more reliable as a guide to the right answer in this case than an appeal to the views of the traveller on the London Underground. As I survey my fellow passengers on my twice weekly journeys to and from Heathrow Airport on the Piccadilly Line—such a variety in age, race, nationality and languages—I find it increasingly hard to persuade myself that any one view on anything other than the most basic issues can be said to be typical of all of them."[155]

Nevertheless the concept remains. Previous editions of this book said the following:

"The reasonable man has a place in many areas of the law, but certainly now spends most of his time as a legal device for determining whether or not there is liability for unintentional harm. The reasonable man is not the average man, for quite often he is far more rigorous in the conduct of his affairs than is the average man. Reasonable foreseeability is partly an objective test—we do not ask: did this defender foresee the harm; but neither do we assume a completely objective approach and say the reasonable man does or does not foresee X or Y. Instead we ask whether a reasonable man in the position of the defender would have contemplated the harm—a technique that might conveniently be described as 'defender objectivity'. We put the reasonable man in the defender's position and ask him what he can see. What is required is the application of reason and not prophecy."[156]

Rights in Scots law of delict

The advent of the Human Rights Act 1998 and, to a lesser extent with regard **1–25** to delict, the Scotland Act 1998, raises the question: to what extent can Scots law accommodate a rights[157] based approach to jurisprudence? The Human Rights Act[158] in particular permits litigation to be pursued where the complaint focuses on a breach of a *right* as pronounced in the European Convention of Human Rights. The recent tradition in the Scots law of delict has been to focus on *obligations* (in the context of duty) and *fault*; i.e. on the *wrong* as opposed to the *right*. But to what extent is Scots law equipped to adopt and develop a rights-based approach to situations that would traditionally be determined on application of the law of delict?

Scots law is often described as a "hybrid" system of law, having weaved elements of the civilian legal tradition[159] and the *ius commune*[160] into its

---

[155] *Chester v Afshar* [2005] 1 A.C. 134 at 161–162 per Lord Hope of Craighead. See also *McLelland v Greater Glasgow Health Board*, 2001 S.L.T. 446 at 458 per Lord Morison.
[156] The reasonable man is linguistically embedded in the language of the law. The test is of course that of the reasonable person. L. Bender, "A Lawyer's Primer on Feminist Theory and Tort" (1988) 38 J. Legal Educ. 3. Bill Stewart acknowledged inspiration from Wright, "Standards of Care in Negligence Law" in Owen, *Philosophical Foundations of Tort Law* (1995) for this trail.
[157] Referring to the traditional language of Scots law, this discussion is concerned with personal rights (*jus in personem*) as opposed to real rights (*jus in rem*). The law of property is the proper province of the latter.
[158] Human Rights Act 1998 s.8.
[159] i.e. the Romano-Germanic system as developed in continental Europe.
[160] Loosely—the system of legal principles derived from Roman law and common to jurisdictions adopting the nascent civilian system.

indigenous cultures, institutions and practices, before adopting features of the English common law system following the Act of Union in 1707. A basic distinction between the respective civilian and common law systems is that whereas the method adopted by the civilian tradition may be described as *deductive*, i.e. decisions in specific cases are derived from principles; in comparison the English common law system would then be described as *inductive*, i.e. decisions are determined by the application of precedents: principles eventually emerging over time as the matrix of precedents develops. The civilian tradition therefore attempts coherence by conceptualising hierarchical levels, cascading down from fundamental principles at the top level to specific applications of those principles at the lower levels. The organisation of legal concepts by the English common law system on the other hand could be described as more linear: institutional hierarchy (i.e. the veneration of precedent based on the status of the court revealing the rule) taking priority over any hierarchy of legal principles, and coherence in legal principle being a consequence rather than an objective of the legal method adopted.

The genesis of civilian legal method is generally accepted to be found in Roman law, as explained by Justinian's Digest,[161] which enjoyed a renaissance among jurists in western continental Europe in the 12th and 13th centuries. Although Roman law did not at any period in its development appear to be based on an active assertion of *rights*, the *actio injuriarum* at least did appear to take as its starting point, or highest hierarchical level, the *protection* of *interests* under the heads of *corpus*, *fama* and *dignitas* (body, reputation and dignity). As for the *lex Aquilia*, it may be an overstatement to suggest that the remedy for damage to property enforceable as *damnum injuria datum* went so far as to protect rights, but nevertheless it cannot be inappropriate to say that the *lex Aquilia* acknowledged and respected *interests* in property.[162]

The approach taken by the early Institutional Writers demonstrates the significant influence of Roman law as developed by the civilian tradition and the *ius commune* on contemporary jurisprudence in Scotland. Thus Stair, having identified that reparation may be claimed in respect of delinquencies injuring a pursuer's person, liberty, fame and honour, object of affection or property,[163] made reference to a general obediential obligation of reparation for damage and interest before describing a number of specific obligations. So, although delict was viewed in terms of obligations rather than rights as such, it is suggested that the classification of delictual obligations under first level principles reflecting Roman law—and adopting its language—confirms that the tradition in the law of delict in Scotland is to at least recognise, if not to provide protection for *rights*.

Subsequent developments in focus[164] continued to emphasise obligations rather than rights, but it is again suggested that the search for principled coherence in obligations, being the corollary of rights, is consistent with the purpose of the law incorporating respect for, if not quite express protection for

---

[161] A compendium of Roman law compiled by order of the Emperor Justinian in the 6th century AD.

[162] Some civilian jurisdictions—especially Germany—did assert something of a rights-based approach within their Civil Codes: see B.S. Markesinis, *The German Law of Torts*, 4th edn (Oxford: Hart Publishing, 2002).

[163] Stair, I, 9, 4.

[164] i.e. from nominate delicts towards a general obediential obligation to make reparation for damage caused by wrongful conduct and ultimately focusing on concepts of duty and breach.

rights. In other words, duty, interest and right are different angles from which to view the same thing.

Even before the European Convention on Human Rights itself was drafted the **1–26** concept of rights had been expressly recognised by the courts—at least in terms of defining of wrongs. For example, in the *Crofter Hand Woven Harris Tweed v Veitch* case, Lord Wright acknowledged

> "how far the courts have gone in upholding the rights of persons to freedom to pursue their own interests in their trade even at the cost of seriously impeding the freedom in a practical sense of other persons in their trade."[165]

This was a conspiracy case and the question was whether the main objective of the common activity complained of was to harm the pursuer's interests or to promote the interests of the defenders. So here the analysis of *rights* was perhaps in a passive sense: i.e. that the law would not interfere with activity that an individual had a right to engage in.

However there were also instances of Scottish delict cases where a more active rights-based approach was at least hinted at. For example, in *Micosta S.A. v Shetland Islands Council*, in approving an "interest-based" approach taken by Professor Walker, Lord Ross asserted:

> "The validity of a claim such as that made by the present pursuers[166] does not depend upon there being any precise Scottish authority. There is no such thing as an exhaustive list of named delicts in the law of Scotland. If the conduct complained of appears to be wrongful, the law of Scotland will afford a remedy even if there has not been any previous instance of a remedy being given in similar circumstances. As Professor Walker puts it at p.9[167]: 'The decision to recognise a particular interest, and consequently to grant a remedy for its infringement, is a question of social policy, and the list recognised has grown over the years. In considering whether or not to recognise particular interests the courts have had regard to such factors as the moral obliquity of the defenders' conduct, the capacity of the parties to bear the loss, and the consistency of recognition with what is conceived to be public policy.'"[168]

The advantages of a principled rights-based approach are obvious in the quote above: the law will be flexible and should not become stale. The law can respond quickly to developments in society without the need for statutory intervention—yet remain predictable and coherent as new developments are fashioned from high-level principles.

If these were indeed features of Scotland's law of delict, it would follow that here would be the ideal place to nurture and grow new branches of law, but one

---

[165] *Crofter Hand Woven Harris Tweed v Veitch*, 1942 S.C. (HL) 1 at 34. There are hints here of the balancing exercise elucidated by Lord Steyn in *Re S (A Child) (Identification: Restrictions on Publication)* [2005] 1 A.C. 593 at 603.

[166] The wrong alleged was a deliberate misuse of a statutory power by a public body. English law recognises this as the tort of misfeasance in public office.

[167] Walker, *The Law of Delict in Scotland* (1981).

[168] *Micosta S.A. v Shetland Islands Council*, 1986 S.L.T. 193 at 198.

rights-based area that has notably failed to blossom in Scotland is a law of privacy. The experience in England perhaps proves the point that an emphasis on precedent can strangle rather than liberate development in the common law.[169]

Perhaps it was for lack of opportunity that no delictual remedy for invasion of a right to privacy developed in Scotland. For the courts to be able to develop jurisprudence on a particular matter, someone needs to bring a case. Scotland has a relatively small population and its local media has perhaps behaved more conservatively than its counterpart in England. In comparison, there was ample opportunity for England to develop a privacy law.[170] However, when the opportunity has arisen, it could be said that the Scottish courts have stepped up to the plate. For example, in *Henderson v Chief Constable of Fife*, Lord Jauncey, in awarding damages for "invasion of privacy and liberty", described a request to a female prisoner that she remove her bra before entering a cell as an "interference with her liberty which was not justified in law."[171]

1–27 Thus there are traces of threads, perhaps rather frayed, of a rights-based approach to the Scots law of delict in the 20th century. However, the coming into force of the Human Rights Act has created the opportunity for the law to refocus at the beginning of the 21st century. The Human Rights Act provides that it is unlawful for a public authority to act in a way that is incompatible with the European Convention on Human Rights,[172] unless required to do so by primary legislation.[173] Public authorities include courts, tribunals and other individuals or bodies that perform public functions.[174] Thus, when actions are pursued in the courts, courts as public bodies must act—i.e. allow access and deliver decisions—compatibly with the Convention, unless required to do otherwise by primary legislation enacted by the UK Parliament.[175] In this way rights set out in the convention can be enforced horizontally[176] as well as vertically.[177] The Scotland Act 1998 also provides that neither the Scottish Parliament[178] nor Scottish Ministers[179] have power to act incompatibly with Convention rights. Damages may be payable for a breach of the relevant provisions of the Human Rights Act[180] or the Scotland Act.[181]

This development therefore adds another ground of complaint in the form of a breach of a human right in actions that would traditionally seek remedies in

---

[169] In spite of the fact that *Prince Albert v Strange* (1849) 2 De G. & Sm. 652 was to all intents and purposes a decision enforcing a right of privacy, the House of Lords was still refusing to acknowledge the existence of a common law tort of invasion of privacy in 2003: *Wainwright v Home Office* [2004] 2 A.C. 406 at 424 per Lord Hoffmann.

[170] See in particular *Kaye v Robertson* [1991] F.S.R. 62—an egregious invasion of privacy for which there was no remedy; *R v Brentwood BC Ex p. Peck* [1998] E.M.L.R. 697; *Wainwright v Home Office* [2004] 2 A.C. 406.

[171] *Henderson v Chief Constable of Fife*, 1988 S.L.T. 361 at 367.

[172] Human Rights Act 1998 s.6(1).

[173] i.e. an Act of the United Kingdom Parliament at Westminster: Human Rights Act 1998 s.6(2).

[174] Human Rights Act 1998 s.6(3).

[175] The Scottish Parliament cannot create law that is incompatible with Convention rights—Scotland Act 1998 s.29(2)(d).

[176] i.e. citizen to citizen.

[177] i.e. citizen to State.

[178] Scotland Act 1998 s.29(2)(d).

[179] Scotland Act 1998 s.57(2).

[180] Human Rights Act 1998 s.8.

[181] Scotland Act 1998 s.100(3).

delict. This has been especially the case in actions pursued against public authorities, where it is beginning to prove fertile in enabling remedies to be obtained which would not have been awarded at common law. It has also had a particularly profound impact on the development of remedies for breach, or threatened breach, of "privacy" rights. Conversely, the right to freedom of expression has become an important counterfoil to assertions of rights to privacy.

So the civilian heritage must always be kept in view. However, the law of delict, especially if widely defined as in this book, is neither explained nor predicted by any one theory. The law of delict is a large amount of precedent and a quantity of statutory provision on top of some solid principle, a body of norms, which are not always consistent. Taking that view there are areas where the law is reasonably clear because of precedent, or institutional authority. In other areas the law is less clear but there are themes, if not precepts or principles, that run through much of the authority that can assist a court, practitioner or student in determining the law. It is all a matter of emphasis: there is no danger in saying that the law of delict is based upon certain principles, so long as one is aware of all of the exceptions and anomalies. The law of delict is largely in the cases (and statutes)—the first task for the student is to know them.

> "Hence we shall insist no further, but come to the obligations by delinquence, which are civilly cognoscible by our custom, according to their known names and titles in our law; which though they do rather signify the acts or actions whereby such obligations are incurred or prosecute, than the obligations themselves, yet will they be sufficient to hold out both."[182]

This Chapter has sought to provide an introduction to the law of delict in the context of Scotland's historic and contemporary legal culture. The continuing influence of historic connections through Roman and civilian traditions, supplemented by affiliation with the law of England and Wales, means that the law of delict in Scotland is well poised to engage fully with new opportunities and challenges for development that are provided by human rights jurisprudence. The remaining chapters of the first part of this book continue by examining key themes that operate generically across all aspects of delictual liability, including parties and remedies. The second part of the book considers the relationship between protected interests and specific wrongs. The third part of the book goes on to examine the law of negligence and how it operates in the 21st century, paying particular attention to the classifications adopted by the courts in the area of duty of care and to the influence of policy factors in shaping and developing the law. The fourth part of the book deals with generic limitations on delictual liability, covering causation, defences and prescription and limitation of actions. Finally, the fifth part of the book deals with specific liability regimes, including occupiers' liability, product liability, liability for animals, employers' liability and liability of public bodies. Before going any further however, it is appropriate to consider what delict cases fall within the jurisdiction of the Scottish courts.

---

[182] Stair, I, ix, 5. See this in context, W. Stewart, *A Casebook on Delict*, 2nd edn (Edinburgh: W. Green, 1997), pp.67–70.

1–28 This is a separate university course.[183] Practically, the first question for the practitioner or other analyst ought to be: to what extent does the problem concern the law of Scotland at all, and can the matter be heard a Scottish court? The case may be one to be decided in a different court or according to a different legal system. Delict is treated specially both for jurisdiction and for choice of law. Jurisdiction in civil or commercial legal disputes between individuals or organisations resident within the European Union and the European Free Trade Association are subject to the Brussels I Regulation of 2001 and the Lugano Convention of 2007. Notably there is a ground additional to domicile allowing actions to be raised "in matters relating to tort, delict or quasi-delict, in the courts for the place where the harmful event occurred".[184] *Lis alibi pendens*[185] applies: there are rules in the convention and at common law[186] to prevent two actions running at the same time on related subject-matter. Where proceedings involving the same cause of action between the same parties are brought in the courts of different Contracting States, any court other than the court first seised must, of its own motion, decline jurisdiction in favour of that court.[187] Forum non conveniens remains a part of the law of jurisdiction,[188] although the Civil Jurisdiction and Judgments Act 1982 restricts the applicability of it in international cases between Convention countries.[189] The essence of the plea is that there is a more appropriate court to try the case taking into account the interests of the parties and the ends of justice. The result can be a sist or dismissal. It is generally safer to sist because it is not always known what will happen in the other jurisdiction.[190]

Choice of law is about which rules of law govern the case whatever court it is heard in. The date when the delictual wrong occurred is important:

- Delictual acts committed prior to April 1, 1996 are subject to the common law double actionability rule. This rule also continues to apply to defamation and related actions (including privacy type actions), and likely will continue to do so until the European Union chooses how to deal with cross-border matters;[191]

---

[183] A.E. Anton and P.R. Beaumont, *Civil Jurisdiction in Scotland*, 2nd edn (Edinburgh: W. Green, 1995); A.E. Anton and P.R. Beaumont, *Private International Law*, 2nd edn (Edinburgh: W. Green, 1990); E. Crawford, *International Private Law* (Edinburgh: W. Green, 1998). There is a full treatment in relation to delict in *Reparation: Liability for Delict*, Ch.2.

[184] Council Regulation (EC) No 44/2001 art.5(3).

[185] Dispute elsewhere pending.

[186] On the details of the plea in a reparation action at common law see *Flannigan v British Dyewood Co Ltd*, 1971 S.L.T. 208.

[187] Council Regulation (EC) No 44/2001 art.27.

[188] See e.g. *Vidal-Hall v Google Inc* [2014] E.M.L.R. 14; *Clark v TripAdvisor LLC*, 2014 S.L.T. 418.

[189] But not in extra-Convention cases: *Re Harrods (Buenos Aires) Ltd* [1992] Ch. 72.

[190] See generally *De Mulder v Jadranska Linijska (Jadrolinija)*, 1989 S.L.T. 269.

[191] The European Parliament requested action from the European Commission in May 2012. The European Commission undertook to publish a report by the end of 2013, but has not yet at the time of writing. Meanwhile, in *Martinez v MGN Ltd* [2012] Q.B. 654, the Grand Chamber of the Court of Justice ruled that a claim in defamation or privacy could be brought in the jurisdiction where the claimant had his "centre of interests" as an alternative to bringing the claim in the jurisdiction where the defendant was domiciled or established. The Court of Justice had previously ruled that a limited claim could be brought in the jurisdiction where the material was distributed: *Shevill v Presse Alliance SA* [1995] 2 A.C. 18.

- Delictual acts (other than defamation etc.) committed within the EU between April 1, 1996 and August 19, 2007, or outwith the EU on or after April 1, 1996, are subject to the rules set out in Pt III of the Private International Law (Miscellaneous Provisions) Act 1995;[192]
- Delictual acts (other than defamation etc.) committed within the EU on or after August 20, 2007 are subject to the Rome II Regulations on non-contractual obligations and the Law Applicable to Non-Contractual Obligations (Scotland) Regulations 2008.[193]

The Rome II Regulations[194] prioritise choice of law within the EU as fol- **1–29** lows:

1. The law of the country where the damage occurs[195];
2. The law of the country where both parties were habitually resident when the damage occurred[196];
3. The law of the country with which the case is manifestly more closely connected than the other countries.[197]

The Rome II Regulations permit the parties to agree their own choice of law, either before or after the occurance of the delictual act in question, but effectively restrict this choice to jurisdictions within the EU when all of the elements of the situation are within one or more EU Member States.[198]

The law relating to choice of law previously was overhauled by the Private International Law (Miscellaneous Provisions) Act 1995.[199] The general rule for actions subject to the 1995 Act is that the applicable law is the law of the country in which the events constituting the tort or delict in question occur.[200] Where elements of these events occur in different countries there are three rules:

---

[192] See e.g. A. Briggs, "Choice of Law in Tort and Delict" [1995] L.M.C.L.Q. 519; J. Blaikie "Choice of Law in Delict and Tort: Reform at last" [1997] 1 E.L.R. 361; B. Rodger "The Halley: Holed and now sunk" [1996] 1 S.L.P.Q. 397.

[193] Article 4 of the Law Applicable to Non-Contractual Obligations (Scotland) Regulations 2008 (SSI 2008/404) makes the provisions of Rome II applicable to choice of law between Scotland and the rest of the United Kingdom. Article 6 of the Law Applicable to Non-Contractual Obligations (England and Wales and Northern Ireland) Regulations 2008 operates likewise across the other United Kingdom jurisdictions.

[194] See, e.g. J.M. Carruthers and E.B. Crawford, "Variations on a Theme of Rome II. Reflections on Proposed Choice of Law Rules for Non-contractual Obligations: Part 1" (2005) 9 Edin. L.R. 65; J.M. Carruthers and E.B. Crawford, "Variations on a Theme of Rome II. Reflections on Proposed Choice of Law Rules for Non-contractual Obligations: Part 2" (2005) 9 Edin. L.R. 238.

[195] Rome II Regulations art.4(1).

[196] Rome II Regulations art.4(2).

[197] Rome II Regulations art.4(3).

[198] Rome II Regulations art.14.

[199] There had been criticism in England and Scotland and the matter was dealt with by the Law Commission and the Scottish Law Commission: see, e.g. P. Carter, "Choice of Law in Tort and Delict" (1991) 107 L.Q.R. 405; R. Black, "Delict and the Conflict of Laws", 1968 J.R. 40, Law Com. No.193; Scot. Law Com. No.129.

[200] Private International Law (Miscellaneous Provisions) Act 1995 s.11(1). See generally J.M. Williams and P. Mead, "Abolition of the Double Actionability Rule: Questions still to be answered" [1996] J.P.I.L. 112. Rules on characterisation are important as a preliminary question. Section 9 provides that that characterisation for the purposes of private international law is a matter for the courts of the forum. The applicable law is to be used for determining issues arising such as whether an actionable tort or delict has occurred. Choice of law rules are excluded from the applicable law. It is provided for the avoidance of doubt that the new law applies to events occurring in the forum as it applies to events occurring in any other country.

1. in cases of personal injury[201] or death the applicable law is that of the territory where the individual was when the injuries were sustained[202];
2. for damage to property it is the place where the property was when it was damaged[203];
3. for all other cases the territory where the "most significant element or elements of the events"[204] complained of occurred, or failing that, the law of the territory with which the subject matter has the "most real and substantial connection".

The general rule may be displaced. If it appears, in all the circumstances, from a comparison of:

a. the significance of the factors that connect a tort or delict with the country whose law would be the applicable law under the general rule; and
b. the significance of any factors connecting the tort or delict with another country, that it is substantially more appropriate for the applicable law for determining the issues arising in the case, or any of those issues, to be the law of the other country, the general rule is displaced and the applicable law for determining that issue or issues (as the case may be) is the law of that other country.

The factors that may be taken into account as connecting a tort or delict with a country for the purposes of this section include, in particular, factors relating to the parties, to any of the events which constitute the tort or delict in question or to any of the circumstances or consequences of those events.[205]

The pre-1995 Act law applies only to delicts committed before April 1, 1996 and to defamation actions.[206] Under the old law, the law of the pursuer's domicile was irrelevant.[207] The defender's domicile was equally irrelevant.[208] The claim had to satisfy both the *lex fori* and the *lex loci delicti*. For a long time the rule known as the double actionability or double delict rule applied under which the claim had to be actionable under both systems.[209]

---

[201] This includes disease or any impairment of physical or mental condition: Private International Law (Miscellaneous Provisions) Act 1995 s.11(3).
[202] Private International Law (Miscellaneous Provisions) Act 1995 s.11(2)(a).
[203] Private International Law (Miscellaneous Provisions) Act 1995 s.11(2)(b).
[204] Private International Law (Miscellaneous Provisions) Act 1995 s.11(2)(c).
[205] Private International Law (Miscellaneous Provisions) Act 1995 s.12.
[206] Private International Law (Miscellaneous Provisions) Act 1995 s.13(1). This is defined as any claim under the law of any part of the United Kingdom for libel or slander of title, slander of goods or of malicious falsehood and any claim under the law of Scotland for verbal injury (s.13(2)(a)) and to claims of the same nature under the law of any country (s.13(2)(b)).
[207] *Convery v Lanarkshire Tramway Co* (1905) 8 F. 117.
[208] *Naftalin v L.M.S. Railway*, 1933 S.C. 259.
[209] See, e.g. *Rosses v Sir Bhagrat Sinjie* (1891) 19 R. 31; *Evans v Stein* (1904) 7 F. 65; *Naftalin v L.M.S. Ry*, 1933 S.C. 259; and *McElroy v McAllister*, 1949 S.C. 110; *Mitchell v McCulloch*, 1976 S.C. 1; *James Burrough Distillers Plc v Speymalt Whisky Distributors Ltd*, 1989 S.L.T. 561. Exceptions developed, see *Boys v Chaplin* [1971] A.C. 356 and *Red Sea Insurance Co v Bouygues* [1995] 1 A.C. 190, PC. See B. Rodger, "Bouygues and Scottish Choice of Law Rules in Delict", 1995 S.L.P.Q. 58.

CHAPTER 2

HUMAN RIGHTS

INTRODUCTION

The introduction to this book explained that on one view delict is about **2–01** protecting rights and interests. That must be so regardless of the original source of the rights and interests. Following the Second World War, various European nations formed the Council of Europe to promote co-operation between European countries in areas including human rights. Drawing on the Universal Declaration of Human Rights adopted by the General Assembly of the United Nations in 1948, the Council of Europe drafted the European Convention on Human Rights in 1950, which entered into force in 1953. Although the United Kingdom was instrumental in drafting the Convention, and indeed was the first signatory state to the Convention, there was no attempt made by any government of the United Kingdom to make Convention rights accessible to citizens, in the sense that Convention rights could be asserted and enforced in domestic court proceedings, until the passing into force on October 2, 2000 of the Human Rights Act 1998. Prior to that date, citizens of the United Kingdom who wished to rely upon Convention rights as such would have to take a case to the European Court of Human Rights in Strasbourg after exhausting domestic remedies,[1] although courts in the United Kingdom had already begun to be influenced by Convention jurisprudence where there was scope in the existing law.[2]

Wherever the forum for enforcement may be, the rights adumbrated in the European Convention on Human Rights are as much rights as any domestic rights.[3] They are legal and are thus juridical or juristic and breach of them, to the extent they apply, is wrongful.[4] The Human Rights Act now provides that it is unlawful for a public authority to act incompatibly with a Convention right,[5] even where the citizen is physically outside of the United Kingdom.[6] A person

---

[1] This remains the case for cases involving facts that occurred before the Human Rights Act 1998 came into force: see, e.g. *Jain v Trent Strategic Health Authority* [2009] 1 A.C. 853. There will be a diminishing number of such cases with the passage of time.

[2] See e.g. *Derbyshire CC v Times Newspapers Ltd* [1993] A.C. 534; *T, Petitioner*, 1997 S.L.T. 724.

[3] For a comprehensive discussion on the impact of Human Rights legislation in Scotland see R. Reed and J. Murdoch, *Human Rights Law in Scotland*, 3rd edn (Edinburgh: Bloomsbury, 2011).

[4] art.13 of the Convention provides that everyone whose rights or freedoms are violated has a right to an effective remedy before a national court.

[5] Human Rights Act 1998 s.6(1). Subject to the detailed provisions of subss.(2)–(6), mainly permitting action in respect of judicial acts but exempting parliament.

[6] Although how Convention rights must be respected extra-territorially will depend upon the context: *Smith v Ministry of Defence* [2014] 1 A.C. 52.

who is a victim of an unlawful act[7] can bring proceedings against the public authority under the Act itself,[8] or can rely on Convention rights in any legal proceedings.[9] Thus the Act may provide additional remedies to those already provided by the law of delict. Accordingly, this section deals with the effect of the Human Rights Act 1998 on the availability of reparation[10] as "just satisfaction" for breach of a Convention right.[11]

There are important debates as to whether this law affects the rights of citizens against other citizens as opposed to just the citizen and the State. Given that courts are themselves public authorities, s.6 of the Human Rights Act requires courts to make decisions that are not incompatible with the Convention, no matter the status of the litigants. Domestic courts and tribunals must also take into account the jurisprudence of the European Court of Human Rights, as well as the European Commission of Human Rights, in considering questions to which Convention rights are pertinent.[12] Also, if it is the case that the Scots law of reparation can operate by virtue of the recognition of an interest by the courts,[13] then these rights and freedoms are the very things—now part of the law in a formal sense—that can be used directly or in combination to recognise new reparable interests.[14] This is often called a horizontal effect. More advanced analysis argues that there can be weak or strong horizontality: the weak, where the courts take into account the convention rights in developing the law; the strong, where the courts are compelled to make the common law compatible.[15] The House of Lords' decision in *Campbell v MGN Newspapers Ltd*,[16] supports at least weak horizontality.

---

[7] If proceedings are brought by way of judicial review then a person is only to have title and interest to sue if he is a victim: s.7(4). Victim of an unlawful act is specially defined: s.7(7)—. See also *Axa General Insurance Co Ltd v Lord Advocate*, 2012 S.C. (U.K.S.C.) 122.

[8] Human Rights Act 1998 s.7(1)(a). This envisages a special procedure and rules, including a one year prescription with an equitable override: s.7(5).

[9] Human Rights Act 1998 s.7(1)(b).

[10] The Scottish Parliament and Executive (now the Scottish Government) was set up in such a way that it immediately required to have regard for Human Rights: Scotland Act 1998 ss.29, 53 and 57(2). These provisions remain in force. They may in some circumstances provide a different route to compensation as where a claim for damages is attached to a judicial review of a decision. Such an alternative route was held not to be subject to the 12 months' time-bar under s.7(5) of the Human Rights Act 1998: *Somerville v Scottish Ministers*, 2008 S.C. (HL) 45; although s.100(3A) of the Scotland Act 1998 was subsequently introduced so as to apply a similar one year prescription with an equitable override. The Human Rights Act 1998 came into effect on October 2, 2000 (SI 2000/1851). A "delictual" type of action such as discussed herein does not necessarily involve a devolution issue: *HM Advocate v R.* 2001 S.L.T. 1366. See also D. Fairgrieve, "The Human Rights Act 1998, Damages and Tort Law" [2001] P.L. 695.

[11] Human Rights Act 1998 s.8.

[12] Human Rights Act 1998 s.2.

[13] See the discussion at paras 1–25 to 1–27 above.

[14] See generally, D. Brodie, "Negligence in the Convention" in A. Reed, *A Practical Guide to Human Rights Law in Scotland* (Edinburgh: W. Green, 2001).

[15] H. MacQueen and D. Brodie, "Private Rights, Private Law and the Private Domain", in A. Boyle et al., *Human Rights and Scots Law: Comparative Perspectives on the Incorporation of the ECHR* (Oxford: Hart, 2002). See also A. Young, "Mapping Horizontal Effect" in D. Hoffman (ed.), *The Impact of the UK Human Rights Act on Private Law* (Cambridge: Cambridge University Press, 2011).

[16] *Campbell v MGN Newspapers Ltd* [2004] 2 A.C. 457 (arts 8 and 10). See also on art.10, e.g. *Reynolds v Times Newspapers Ltd* [2001] 2 A.C. 127; *McCartan, Turkington Breen v Times Newspapers* [2001] 2 A.C. 277; *Jameel v Wall Street Journal Europe SPRL* [2007] 1 A.C. 359; *O'Shea v MGN Ltd* [2001] E.M.L.R. 40; and on arts 2, 3, 8 and 10: *Venables v News Group Newspapers Ltd* [2001] Fam. 430.

Accordingly, these outline treatments should be seen not only as sensitising the student to potential instances of reparation against the State, but also as potentially affecting the scope of the existing law. The cases from many countries over many years provide a vast relevant jurisprudence. Selected are those most relevant to delict and generally from the United Kingdom.

Right to life

Everyone's right to life must be protected by law.[17] No one should be deprived **2-02** of his or her life intentionally, save in the execution of a sentence of a court following his or her conviction of a crime for which this penalty is provided by law.[18] Where there is a "real and immediate threat" to the life of an individual, the State owes a "positive obligation" to the individual to take preventative measures to protect life.[19] Thus, the use of lethal force will not be disproportionate if that is a necessary response to a real and immediate threat to life that is reasonably perceived.[20]

In *Edwards v UK*,[21] the European Court of Human Rights held that there had been a breach of art.2 where the prison authorities put a dangerous prisoner with mental problems in a cell with another. Non-pecuniary compensation was set at £20,000. However, in *Thomson v Scottish Ministers*,[22] the Inner House held that the Scottish Prison Service did not owe a duty under art.2 to a member of the public killed by a prisoner on short-term leave where there was no averment of a real or immediate threat to life. Similarly, in *Mitchell v Glasgow City Council*,[23] the House of Lords confirmed that there could be no breach of art.2 by a failure to warn a council tenant of an aggressive neighbour where there was no real or immediate threat to life. On the other hand, in *Finucane v UK*,[24] the UK's failure to promptly and effectively investigate the death of an individual was held by the European Court of Human Rights to be a breach of art.2.

Prohibition of torture, etc.

No one should be subjected to torture or to inhuman or degrading treatment or **2-03** punishment.[25] As with art.2, State liability will require that a "real and

---

[17] The right to life does not protect an unborn foetus: *Paton v United Kingdom* (1981) 3 E.H.R.R. 408. Nor does the right to life incorporate the corollary of a right to die: *Pretty v United Kingdom* [2002] 2 F.L.R. 45.

[18] art.2(1). Deprivation of life shall not be regarded as inflicted in contravention of this article when it results from the use of force which is no more than absolutely necessary: (a) in defence of any person from unlawful violence; (b) in order to effect a lawful arrest or to prevent the escape of a person lawfully detained; (c) in action lawfully taken for the purpose of quelling a riot or insurrection: art.2(2). See *McCann v United Kingdom* (1996) E.H.R.R. 97; *X v United Kingdom* (1980) 19 D.R. 244.

[19] *Osman v United Kingdom* (2000) 29 E.H.R.R. 245; *Van Colle v United Kingdom* (2013) 56 E.H.R.R. 23; *Venables v News Group Newspapers Ltd* [2001] Fam. 430; *Mitchell v Glasgow City Council*, 2009 S.C. (HL) 21. "Combat immunity" provides a limited exception: *Smith v Ministry of Defence* [2014] 1 A.C. 52.

[20] *Bubbins v United Kingdom* (2005) 41 E.H.R.R. 24.

[21] *Edwards v UK* (2002) 35 E.H.R.R. 19.

[22] *Thomson v Scottish Ministers*, 2013 S.C. 628. See also *Rabone v Pennine Care NHS Trust* [2012] 2 A.C. 72.

[23] *Mitchell v Glasgow City Council*, 2009 S.C. (HL) 21.

[24] *Finucane v UK* (2003) 37 E.H.R.R. 29.

[25] art.3. See also *Ireland v United Kingdom* (1979–1980) 2 E.H.R.R. 25; *Ribitsch v Austria* (1995) 21 E.H.R.R. 573 (assault in police custody); *Wainwright v United Kingdom* (2007) 44 E.H.R.R. 40 (intimate strip search); *Keenan v United Kingdom* (2001) 33 E.H.R.R. 38 (segregation and

immediate" risk to the pursuer was, or ought to have been, apparent to the State.²⁶ In *A v United Kingdom*,²⁷ the applicant had been caned by his step-father sufficient to cause bruising. The step-father was acquitted by a jury on the defence of reasonable chastisement. It was held that the chastisement was excessive by European standards. It was further held that the United Kingdom was liable for not having taken steps to protect persons such as the applicant. The United Kingdom was held liable for damages and costs. Further, in *E v United Kingdom*,²⁸ the European Court of Human Rights specifically raised the question of whether the local authority was, or ought to have been, aware of the abuse or risk of abuse.

The mandatory life sentence for murder applicable in the United Kingdom was not in contravention of the European Court of Human Rights, according to the House of Lords.²⁹

In Scotland a case was raised against the Scottish Ministers complaining of the practice of "slopping out" in Barlinnie prison: *Napier v Scottish Ministers*.³⁰ The principal thrust of the case was for judicial review.³¹ The background to the case was set out by the petitioner based on the report to the UK Government on a visit carried out by the European Committee for the Prevention of Torture and Inhumane or Degrading Treatment or Punishment in May 1994. Barlinnie Prison was the subject of unfavourable conduct and reference was made to the fact that slopping-out was to have ended by 1999. So far as interim measures were concerned, the court granted in the petitioner's favour an order on the Scottish Ministers to secure the transfer of the petitioner to conditions of detention that complied with art.3 of the Convention, whether within HM Prison Barlinnie or in any other prison, and that within 72 hours. Eventually the case proceeded to

---

failure to provide treatment for mental health problems while in custody leading to suicide of prisoner); *Venables v News Group Newspapers Ltd* [2001] Fam. 430 (threat of vigilante attack). Article 3 does not impose an obligation upon the State to treat as lawful a homicide carried out so as to avoid or discontinue inhuman or degrading treatment: *Pretty v United Kingdom* [2002] 2 F.L.R. 45.

²⁶ *E v Chief Constable of the Royal Ulster Constabulary* [2009] 1 A.C. 536; *Webster v Ridgeway Foundation School* [2010] E.L.R. 694.

²⁷ *A v United Kingdom* (1999) 27 E.H.R.R. 611. See also *Z v United Kingdom* [2001] 2 F.L.R. 612; *Tyrer v United Kingdom* (1978) 2 E.H.R.R. 1; *Costello-Roberts v United Kingdom* (1993) 19 E.H.R.R. 112; *Campbell and Cosans v United Kingdom* (1982) 13 E.H.R.R. 441; *D. v East Berkshire Community Health NHS Trust* [2004] Q.B. 558.

²⁸ *E v United Kingdom* (2002) 36 E.H.R.R. 519. The applicants had not sought damages through the Scottish courts as they had been advised that a domestic claim would be incompetent in the light of *X (Minors) v Bedfordshire CC* [1995] 2 A.C. 633. On the impact of the ECtHR decisions in *Osman v United Kingdom* (2000) 29 E.H.R.R. 245 and *Z v United Kingdom* (2001) 34 E.H.R.R. 3 on *X v Bedfordshire* see discussion on art.13 at para.2–15 below.

²⁹ *R. v Lichniak* [2002] 1 A.C. 903. For Scotland see the Convention Rights (Compliance) (Scotland) Act 2001 (asp 7) and the decision of the High Court on Appeal in *Flynn v HM Advocate*, 2004 S.C. (P.C.) 1.

³⁰ *Napier v Scottish Ministers*, 2001 G.W.D. 23–876.

³¹ The petitioner sought inter alia: declarator that the conditions of his detention are contrary to art.3 of the Convention, being conditions which cause him to be subjected to inhuman or degrading treatment; declarator that the failures of the Governor of the prison and of the Scottish Ministers to secure that his conditions of detention are not contrary to art.3 are acts or failures to act incompatible with his rights under that article, and are accordingly unlawful by virtue of s.6(1) of the Human Rights Act 1998 and (as regards the Scottish Ministers) s.57(2) of the Scotland Act 1998; an order on the Scottish Ministers to secure his transfer to conditions of detention compliant with art.3, whether within the prison or in any other prison; and for such an order *ad interim*; and damages.

proof. It was held in *Napier*[32] that indeed there had been an infringement of the petitioner's human rights.[33]

Prohibition of slavery and forced labour

No one can be held in slavery or servitude.[34] No one shall be required to **2–04** perform forced or compulsory labour.[35] There may be a duty incumbent on the State to investigate, where it ought to have been aware of forced labour and human trafficking.[36]

Right to liberty and security

Everyone has the right to liberty and security of person. No one can be **2–05** deprived of his liberty save in the following cases and in accordance with a procedure prescribed by law:

a.   the lawful detention of a person after conviction by a competent court;

b.   the lawful arrest or detention of a person for non-compliance with the lawful order of a court or in order to secure the fulfilment of any obligation prescribed by law;

c.   the lawful arrest or detention of a person effected for the purpose of bringing him before the competent legal authority on reasonable suspicion of having committed an offence or when it is reasonably considered necessary to prevent his committing an offence or fleeing after having done so;

d.   the detention of a minor by lawful order for the purpose of educational supervision or his lawful detention for the purpose of bringing him before the competent legal authority;

e.   the lawful detention of persons for the prevention of the spreading of infectious diseases, of persons of unsound mind, alcoholics or drug addicts or vagrants; and

f.   the lawful arrest or detention of a person to prevent his effecting an unauthorised entry into the country or of a person against whom action is being taken with a view to deportation or extradition.[37]

Everyone who is arrested shall be informed promptly, in a language which he understands, of the reasons for his arrest and of any charge against him.[38] Everyone arrested or detained in accordance with the provisions of para.1(c) of

---

[32] *Napier v Scottish Ministers*, 2005 1 S.C. 229 (affirmed by the Inner House: 2005 1 S.C. 307).

[33] See para.2–23 below on "just satisfaction".

[34] art.4(1).

[35] art.4(1). "For the purpose of this Article the term 'enforced or compulsory labour' shall not include: (a) any work required to be done in the ordinary course of detention imposed according to the provisions of Article 5 of this Convention or during conditional release from such detention; (b) any service of a military character or, in case of conscientious objectors in countries where they are recognised, service exacted instead of compulsory military service; (c) any service exacted in case of an emergency or calamity threatening the life or well-being of the community; (d) any work or service which forms part of normal civic obligations": art.4(3). See *Van der Mussele v Belgium* (1984) 6 E.H.R.R. 163.

[36] *CN v United Kingdom* (2013) 56 E.H.R.R. 24.

[37] art.5(1). For art.5(1)(f) see *Chahal v United Kingdom* (1997) 23 E.H.R.R. 413.

[38] art.5(2).

this article must be brought promptly before a judge or other officer authorised by law to exercise judicial power and is entitled to trial within a reasonable time or to release pending trial. Release may be conditioned by guarantees to appear for trial.[39] Everyone who is deprived of his liberty by arrest or detention is entitled to take proceedings by which the lawfulness of his detention must be decided speedily by a court and his release ordered if the detention is not lawful.[40] Then there is a clear reparation provision:

> "Everyone who has been the victim of arrest or detention in contravention of the provisions of this Article shall have an enforceable right to compensation."[41]

That is not to say either that this is the only provision which will result in reparation, merely that this is a clear instance.

In *McDonald v Dickson*,[42] an accused was granted bail on condition, inter alia, that he remained in his house except between 10am and noon. In the context of a devolution minute the High Court held that this did not infringe art.5. It was a severe restriction on his freedom but not complete. He had *not* been placed in detention.

The rights conferred in the article will not be breached where a group is contained by "kettling" (where the group is contained behind a police cordon) where that is necessary to avert a real risk of serious injury or damage and where the practice is rendered unavoidable by circumstances beyond the control of State authorities.[43]

Right to a fair trial

Generally

2–06   In the determination of his civil rights and obligations or of any criminal charge against him, everyone is entitled to a fair and public hearing within a reasonable time by an independent and impartial tribunal established by law. Judgment must be pronounced publicly, but the press and public may be excluded from all or part of the trial in the interest of morals, public order or national security in a democratic society, where the interests of juveniles or the protection of the private life of the parties so require, or to the extent strictly necessary in the opinion of the court in special circumstances where publicity would prejudice the interests of justice.[44] Denial of legal aid for defamation actions has been held to be incompatible with art.6.[45]

---

[39] art.5(3). There are extensive derogations mainly applicable to this article in respect of the civil insurrection in Northern Ireland which is regulated internally by successive Prevention of Terrorism Acts. See Sch.3 to the Human Rights Act 1998 (c.46). See *Lawless v Ireland* (1961) E.H.R.R. 1; *Fox, Campbell and Hartley v United Kingdom* (1991) 13 E.H.R.R. 157; *Brogan v United Kingdom* (1989) 11 E.H.R.R. 117; *Murray v United Kingdom* (1994) 19 E.H.R.R. 193.

[40] art.5(4). See, e.g. *Ashingdane v United Kingdom* (1985) E.H.R.R. 528; *Thynne, Wilson and Gunnell v United Kingdom* (1991) E.H.R.R. 666; *Beggs v United Kingdom* (2013) 56 E.H.R.R. 26.

[41] art.5(5).

[42] *McDonald v Dickson*, 2003 S.L.T. 467. Cf. *Secretary of State for the Home Department v JJ* [2008] 1 A.C. 385.

[43] *Austin v United Kingdom* (2012) 55 E.H.R.R. 14.

[44] art.6(1).

[45] *Steel v United Kingdom* [2005] E.M.L.R. 15.

Civil cases

This article has already caused considerable controversy. In *Osman v United* 2–07 *Kingdom*,[46] the applicants complained that the police had been negligent in their investigation of a teacher, who eventually shot and killed a pupil's father, shot and injured a pupil, shot and injured the headmaster and shot and killed the headmaster's son. They lost their damages action before the English Court of Appeal on the authority of the exclusionary rule in *Hill v Chief Constable of West Yorkshire*.[47] The European Court of Human Rights held that the *automatic* application of *Hill* was contrary to art.6(1) of the Convention. The fact that they could have sued the killer or the psychiatrists was irrelevant; the applicant had not had the chance to have a determination on the conduct of the police. The applicants were awarded damages for the loss of the chance to have sued the police.[48] However, the European Court of Human Rights subsequently reviewed its position in the light of a better understanding of the distinction between substantive law and procedural rules in England and Wales, holding that where there is a clear rule of law established that is itself a European Court of Human Rights compliant, striking out or dismissal at debate is not a breach.[49] Thus, where an action is dismissed following the sustaining of a plea to the relevancy, given that

> "no advantage is to be gained by sending a case to proof when it is clear from the averments that, even if everything that the pursuer avers is proved, the case must fail ... there is no incompatibility between this way of disposing of a case and the pursuer's right under Article 6 of the Convention to a fair trial."[50]

Because the facts in *Jain v Trent Strategic Health Authority*[51] preceded the coming into force of the Human Rights Act, the House of Lords could not consider a claim with regard to Convention rights. However, their Lordships suggested that art.6 had clearly been infringed where the proprietors of a care home had no opportunity to challenge an application for suspension of their licence which was made by the health authority following a statutory procedure.

---

[46] *Osman v United Kingdom* (2000) 29 E.H.R.R. 245. See also *Golder v United Kingdom* (1979–1980) 1 E.H.R.R. 524 (entitlement of prisoner to consult a lawyer to raise civil proceedings).

[47] *Hill v Chief Constable of West Yorkshire* [1989] A.C. 53. See paras 11–61 and 17–04 to 17–07 below.

[48] Following the decision in *Osman*, the House of Lords accepted that the practice of striking-out is not Convention friendly in relation to negligence cases where the court has the task of weighing up interests: see, e.g. *Barrett v Enfield LBC* [2001] 2 A.C. 550; *Phelps v Hillingdon LBC* [2001] 2 A.C. 619.

[49] It was held in *Z v United Kingdom* (2002) 34 E.H.R.R. 3, the ECtHR sequel to *X v Bedfordshire* [1995] 2 A.C. 633, that disposal of the case without proof was not in itself, in this case, a breach of art.6. Following *Z*, the House of Lords reverted to its pre-*Barrett* approach to *Hill*: see *Brooks v Commissioner of Police of the Metropolis* [2005] 1 W.L.R. 1495; *D v East Berkshire Community Health NHS Trust* [2005] 2 A.C. 373; *Smith v Chief Constable of Sussex*, sub nom. *Van Colle v Chief Constable of Hertfordshire* [2009] 1 A.C. 225.

[50] *Mitchell v Glasgow City Council*, 2009 S.C. (HL) 21 at 26–27 per Lord Hope of Craighead.

[51] *Jain v Trent Strategic Health Authority* [2009] 1 A.C. 853.

Criminal cases

2–08   The substantive protection given in Scots criminal law and procedure to comply with the Convention is not the subject of this text. The concern here is for cases where there may be a claim for reparation or just satisfaction arising out of an inadequacy of the already very compliant procedures. Everyone charged with a criminal offence is presumed innocent until proved guilty according to law.[52] Everyone charged with a criminal offence has the following minimum rights:

a.   to be informed promptly, in a language which he understands and in detail, of the nature and cause of the accusation against him;

b.   to have adequate time and facilities for the preparation of his defence;

c.   to defend himself in person or through legal assistance of his own choosing or, if he has not sufficient means to pay for legal assistance, to be given it free when the interests of justice so require;

d.   to examine or have examined witnesses against him and to obtain the attendance and examination of witnesses on his behalf under the same conditions as witnesses against him; and

e.   to have the free assistance of an interpreter if he cannot understand or speak the language used in court.[53]

So far as criminal cases are concerned, it is usually the case that the human rights are respected and protected *in the criminal process*.[54]

No punishment without law

2–09   No one can be held guilty of any criminal offence on account of any act or omission that did not constitute a criminal offence under national or international law at the time when it was committed. Nor shall a heavier penalty be imposed than the one that was applicable at the time the criminal offence was committed.[55]

Right to respect for private and family life

2–10   Everyone has the right to respect for his private and family life, his home and his correspondence.[56] Private life includes physical integrity[57] and may extend to

---

[52] art.6(2).

[53] art.6(3).

[54] *HMA v R.*, 2003 S.C. (P.C.) 21. It may well be the case that where a "criminal" resolution cannot be achieved, just satisfaction may still be sought by way of reparation as suggested by Lord Reed in *HM Advocate v R*, 2001 S.L.T. 1366. See also *Spiers v Ruddy*, 2009 S.C. (P.C.) 1, where, in determining how to deal with a delay in criminal proceedings, the Privy Council preferred the approach taken in *Re Attorney General's Reference (No.2 of 2001)* [2004] 2 A.C. 72 to that taken in *HM Advocate v R* in giving effect to the relevant Strasbourg jurisprudence.

[55] art.7(1). This article does not prejudice the trial and punishment of any person for any act or omission which, at the time when it was committed, was criminal according to the general principles of law recognised by civilised nations: art.7(2). See, e.g. *Welch v United Kingdom* (1995) 20 E.H.R.R. 247; *SW v United Kingdom* (1996) E.H.R.R. 363; *HMA v H*, 2002 S.L.T. 1380.

[56] art.8(1). See, e.g. *Rees v United Kingdom* (1997) 9 E.H.R.R. 56; *Cossey v United Kingdom* (1991) 13 E.H.R.R. 622.

[57] See, e.g. *Glass v United Kingdom* (2004) 39 E.H.R.R. 15; *Wainwright v United Kingdom* (2007) 44 E.H.R.R. 40; *MAK v United Kingdom* [2010] 51 E.H.R.R. 14.

reputation.[58] There must be no interference by a public authority with the exercise of this right except such as is in accordance with the law and in necessary in a democratic society in the interests of national security, public safety or the economic well-being of the country, for the prevention of disorder or crime,[59] for the protection of health or morals, or for the protection of the rights and freedoms of others.[60] The European Court of Human Rights held that an increase in the level of noise by increased flights from Heathrow airport constituted a breach of the applicants' right to family life.[61] Later the Grand Chamber held that the Heathrow night-flying scheme did not in fact interfere with the applicants' human rights under art.8. There was a finding under art.13 because, until the Human Rights Act was in force, there had been no scope for the applicants to take their arguments under domestic law.[62] In *ADT v UK*,[63] the European Court of Human Rights ruled that the UK liberalisation of homosexual activity was inadequate where it still prohibited male group sex. This was a violation of art.8. The pursuer was awarded reparation of £20,929 in that he had been convicted and conditionally discharged for two years. Legislation providing for the monitoring of inmates' telephone calls was not contrary to art.8 of the European Court of Human Rights.[64] In *Campbell*,[65] the House of Lords took account of the European Court of Human Rights to ensure that the existing law of breach of confidence could equally be treated as misuse of private information, which would safeguard the Convention right as between individuals as much as between the individual and the State. However, art.8 does not impose a positive duty on media organisations to inform individuals in advance of an intention to publish material which may interfere with the individual's Convention rights.[66] Surveillance,[67] and stop and search powers,[68] must be prescribed by law, necessary and proportionate to a legitimate aim, and forced entry searches of residential premises must be based on reasonable and probable cause.[69] Public authorities must ensure that disclosures of information about an individual are

---

[58] *Pfeifer v Austria* (2007) 48 E.H.R.R. 175; *Re Guardian News and Media Ltd* [2010] 2 A.C. 697. Cf. *Karakó v Hungary* (2011) 52 E.H.R.R. 36.

[59] Thus, a proportionality test must be applied to determine whether extradition orders which separate parents from children should be made: *H v Lord Advocate*, 2012 S.C. (U.K.S.C.) 308.

[60] art.8(2). See, e.g. *Gaskin v United Kingdom* (1990) 12 E.H.R.R. 547; *Chappell v United Kingdom* (1990) 12 E.H.R.R. 1; *Silver v United Kingdom* (1983) 5 E.H.R.R. 347; *Campbell v United Kingdom* (1993) 15 E.H.R.R. 137; *Halford v United Kingdom* (1997) 24 E.H.R.R. 523.

[61] *Hatton v United Kingdom* (2002) 34 E.H.R.R. 1.

[62] *Hatton v United Kingdom* (2003) 37 E.H.R.R. 28. See also *Dennis v Ministry Of Defence* [2003] Env. L.R. 34 in which it was held that training flights by the RAF were a nuisance and engaged arts 8 and 1 of Protocol 1. The common law damages of £950,000 were sufficient to constitute just satisfaction.

[63] *ADT v UK* (2001) 31 E.H.R.R. 33.

[64] *Dudley v HM Advocate*, 2003 G.W.D. 138; 2003 S.L.T. 597. (Distinguishing *PJ and JH v United Kingdom* Unreported September 25, 2001 E.C.H.R..

[65] *Campbell v Mirror Group Newspapers Ltd* [2004] 2 A.C. 457.

[66] *Mosley v United Kingdom* [2012] E.M.L.R. 1.

[67] *Liberty v United Kingdom* (2009) 48 E.H.R.R. 1; *Wood v United Kingdom* [2004] Po. L.R. 326. Surveillance by an employer is also subject to art.8: *Copland v United Kingdom* (2007) 45 E.H.R.R. 37.

[68] *Gillan v United Kingdom* (2010) 50 E.H.R.R. 45.

[69] *Keegan v United Kingdom* (2007) 44 E.H.R.R. 33 (the fact that the police had not acted maliciously in breaking down the door of the applicant's home—where the father of the suspect the police were looking for had previously lived—was not decisive under art.8, evidence of negligence being sufficient to confirm that the police had acted disproportionately).

both accurate and do not amount to a disproportionate interference with an individual's art.8 rights.[70] Prisoners will inevitably find that their art.8 rights are restricted,[71] but the European Court of Human Rights has denounced blanket disenfranchisement of prisoners,[72] and prohibitions on access to artificial insemination facilities.[73]

Because of the qualified nature of art.8, and especially where it is likely to conflict with other articles, a proportionality test often requires to be applied.[74] In this context, the European Court of Human Rights have recognised the need for a wide margin of appreciation in the application of art.8 within the domestic laws of signatory states. This is because of the range of cultural differences across signatory states in areas such as privacy[75] and family life.[76] Nevertheless, where a proportionality test is not applied, the European Court of Human Rights may continue to criticise domestic decisions as incompatible.[77]

Freedom of thought, conscience and religion

2–11   Everyone has the right to freedom of thought, conscience and religion; this right includes freedom to change his religion or belief and freedom, either alone or in community with others and in public or private, to manifest his religion or belief, in worship, teaching, practice and observance.[78] Freedom to manifest one's religion or beliefs is subject only to such limitations as are prescribed by law and are necessary in a democratic society in the interests of public safety, for the protection of public order, health or morals, or for the protection of the rights and freedoms of others.[79] The UK ban on corporal punishment in schools did not infringe the religious rights of others who did want the right to punish corporeally: there was a distinction between a religious belief or practice and an

---

[70] *Clift v Slough BC* [2011] 1 W.L.R. 1774; *MM v United Kingdom* (24029/07) Unreported November 13, 2012 E.C.H.R.. See also *S v United Kingdom* (2009) 48 E.H.R.R. 50 (retention of DNA samples). Cf. *Desmond v Chief Constable of Nottinghamshire* [2011] P.T.S.R. 1369, where the English Court of Appeal acknowledged a potential claim under art.8 in rejecting a common law claim in negligence. The police had included reference to an arrest and release without charge in an enhanced criminal record certificate sought by the claimant in relation to his application for a job as a teacher. See also *W v Westminster City Council* [2005] 4 All E.R. 96 (Note), where it was held that a defamatory communication that was protected by qualified privilege nevertheless amounted to a breach of art.8.

[71] See, e.g. *Potter v Scottish Prison Service*, 2007 S.L.T. 1019 (pre-recorded message on all outgoing calls informing recipient call was being made from a prison).

[72] *Hirst v United Kingdom* (2006) 42 E.H.R.R. 41. See also *Smith v Scott*, 2007 S.C. 345.

[73] *Dickson v United Kingdom* (2008) 46 E.H.R.R. 41.

[74] See, e.g. *Re S (A Child) (Identification: Restrictions on Publication)* [2005] 1 A.C. 593 at 603 per Lord Steyn.

[75] See, e.g. *Von Hannover v Germany (No.2)* [2012] E.M.L.R. 16; *Axel Springer AG v Germany* [2012] E.M.L.R. 15; *MGN Ltd v United Kingdom* [2011] E.M.L.R. 20.

[76] See, e.g. *Evans v United Kingdom* (2008) 46 E.H.R.R. 34 (compatibility of legislation which required destruction of stored embryos upon the withdrawal of consent of either prospective parent); *X, Y and Z v United Kingdom* (1997) 24 E.H.R.R. 143 (compatibility of refusal to register X, a transsexual, as father of Z, who had been born to Y, with whom X lived, following artificial insemination by donor).

[77] See, e.g. *MAK v United Kingdom* [2010] 51 E.H.R.R. 14—the sequel to *D v East Berkshire Community Health NHS Trust* [2005] 2 A.C. 373.

[78] art.9(1).

[79] art.9(2).

action motivated by religious belief.[80] Where the right to express one's religious beliefs conflicts with other legitimate interests, a fair balance must be struck.[81]

Freedom of expression

Everyone has the right to freedom of expression.[82] This right includes freedom **2–12** to hold opinions and to receive and impart information and ideas without interference by public authority and regardless of frontiers. This article does not prevent States from requiring the licensing of broadcasting, television or cinema enterprises.[83] The exercise of these freedoms, since it carries with it duties and responsibilities, may be subject to such formalities, conditions, restrictions or penalties as are prescribed by law and are necessary in a democratic society, in the interests of national security, territorial integrity or public safety, for the prevention of disorder or crime, for the protection of health or morals, for the protection of the reputation or rights of others, for preventing the disclosure of information received in confidence, or for maintaining the authority and impartiality of the judiciary.[84] Even before the coming into force of the Human Rights Act 1998, art.10 of the European Convention on Human Rights and the jurisprudence of the European Court of Human Rights had been influential in filling in "gaps" in domestic law.[85]

In *Douglas v Hello! Ltd*,[86] it was held that the wedding of two celebrities could be regarded as a commodity and protected as a trade secret. Where the press took unauthorised pictures, this could be a breach of commercial confidence—not privacy. Because the press were involved, art.10 of the European Court of Human Rights was engaged but, as the conduct in this case was in breach of the Editors' Code operated by the Press Complaints Commission, the balance was in favour of the claimants' existing right under the law of confidence not being eroded by art.10. The detailed application of the extent to which the press are allowed to "misuse private information" was considered in *Campbell*.[87] The interplay between arts 8 and 10 has since been considered extensively, with a proportionality test following an intense focus on the facts of each case being the appropriate method of resolution.[88] The European Court of Human Rights was influential in supporting a refusal of interdict against anticipated publication of

---

[80] *R (Williamson) v Secretary of State* [2002] 1 All E.R. 385. A valuable examination of the religious issues which will no doubt continue to emerge. For a consideration of the issue under other rights systems see the note, J. Eekelaar, "Corporal Punishment, Parents' Religion and Children's Rights", 2003 L.Q.R. 370.

[81] See, e.g. *Eweida v United Kingdom* [2013] 57 E.H.R.R. 8 (wearing of religious symbols in the workplace).

[82] See, e.g. *Handyside v United Kingdom* (1976) 1 E.H.R.R. 737; *Goodwin v United Kingdom* (1996) 22 E.H.R.R. 123; *Sunday Times v United Kingdom* (1992) 14 E.H.R.R. 229; *Tolstoy v United Kingdom* (1995) 20 E.H.R.R. 442; *Financial Times Ltd v United Kingdom* [2010] E.M.L.R. 21.

[83] art.10(1).

[84] art.10(2). Nothing in this article may be regarded as preventing the States from imposing restrictions on the political activity of aliens: art.11.

[85] See, e.g. *Derbyshire CC v Times Newspapers Ltd* [1993] A.C. 534.

[86] *Douglas v Hello! Ltd (No.3)*, sub nom. *OBG v Allan* [2008] 1 A.C. 1.

[87] *Campbell v Mirror Group Newspapers Ltd* [2004] 2 A.C. 457.

[88] See, e.g. *Re S (A Child) (Identification: Restrictions on Publication)* [2005] 1 A.C. 593 at 603 per Lord Steyn; *Von Hannover v Germany (No.1)* [2004] E.M.L.R. 21; *Von Hannover v Germany (No.2)* [2012] E.M.L.R. 16; *Axel Springer AG v Germany* [2012] E.M.L.R. 15; *MGN Ltd v United Kingdom* [2011] E.M.L.R. 20.

allegedly defamatory material.[89] The European Court of Human Rights has upheld the "multiple publication" rule insofar as it prescribes every download of online material as a fresh publication as not a disproportionate interference with freedom of expression and so within a signatory state's margin of appreciation.[90] Likewise, in *Animal Defenders International v United Kingdom*,[91] the European Court of Human Rights held that the prohibition on political advertising in s.321(2) of the Communications Act 2003 also falls within the United Kingdom's margin of appreciation and so does not violate art.10.

Freedom of assembly and association

2–13   Everyone has the right to freedom of peaceful assembly and to freedom of association with others, including the right to form and to join trade unions for the protection of his interests.[92] A trade union is equally free to choose its own members and so accept or reject an application for membership.[93] No restrictions shall be placed on the exercise of these rights other than such as are prescribed by law and are necessary in a democratic society in the interests of national security or public safety, for the prevention of disorder or crime, for the protection of health or morals or for the protection of the rights and freedoms of others. This article does not prevent the imposition of lawful restrictions on the exercise of these rights by members of the armed forces, of the police or of the administration of the State.[94] A Scots example is *Aberdeen Bon-Accord Loyal Orange Lodge 701 v Aberdeen City Council*,[95] in which the pursuers were aggrieved that they were prevented from marching. The defenders were able to plead in defence the Civic Government (Scotland) Act 1982, which permits restrictions on parades. It was held that this legislation was indeed compatible with the Human Rights Act where correctly applied, because it provides a proportionate and reasonable response to public order risks. In this particular case, however, the council had not made out its reasons properly and an appeal against a ban was upheld.[96]

Right to marry

2–14   Men and women of marriageable age have the right to marry and to found a family, according to the national laws governing the exercise of this right.[97]

---

[89] *Dickson Minto WS v Bonnier Media Ltd*, 2002 S.L.T. 776 and s.12 of the Human Rights Act. See also *Massie v McCaig*, 2013 S.C. 343. Cf. *Cook v Gibson* [2013] CSOH 64; 2013 G.W.D. 14–298; *Angiolini v Green* [2013] CSOH 196; 2014 G.W.D. 5–104.

[90] *Times Newspapers Ltd v United Kingdom* [2009] E.M.L.R. 14. The multiple publication rule appears to have been adopted in Scotland: *Robertson v Newsquest (Sunday Herald) Ltd*, 2006 Rep. L.R. 124. Ironically, the multiple publication rule has effectively been abolished in England and Wales, but not Scotland, by s.8 of the Defamation Act 2013.

[91] *Animal Defenders International v United Kingdom* [2013] E.M.L.R. 28.

[92] art.11(1). See, e.g. *Young, James and Webster v United Kingdom* (1982) 4 E.H.R.R. 38.

[93] *Associated Society of Locomotive Engineers and Firemen (ASLEF) v United Kingdom* (2007) 45 E.H.R.R. 34.

[94] art.11(2). Nothing in this article may be regarded as preventing the States from imposing restrictions on the political activity of aliens: art.11.

[95] *Aberdeen Bon-Accord Loyal Orange Lodge 701 v Aberdeen City Council*, 2002 S.L.T. (Sh. Ct) 52.

[96] See also *Wishart Arch Defenders Loyal Orange Lodge 404 v Angus Council*, 2002 S.L.T. (Sh. Ct) 43.

[97] art.12. See, e.g. *Rees v United Kingdom* (1987) 9 E.H.R.R. 66, which confirms a wide margin of appreciation.

Right to an effective remedy

Everyone whose Convention rights or freedoms are violated shall have an **2–15** effective remedy before a national authority.[98] The right under art.13 is parasitic, i.e. there must be a failure to provide a remedy for a breach of another article. Thus, a claim for breach of art.13 requires to be combined with a claim for breach of another article. *Reynolds v United Kingdom*[99] provides an example where the European Court of Human Rights held that a failure to remedy a breach of art.2 constituted a breach of art.13. The applicant's adult son, who had previously been diagnosed with schizophrenia, was admitted as a voluntary patient to hospital after complaining that voices in his head were urging him to kill himself. Later in the evening he broke a window in his sixth floor room from which he fell and died. The applicant's claim for damages for a breach of art.2 of the Convention was struck out on an application of the decision in *Savage v South Essex Partnership NHS Foundation Trust*,[100] even although that decision was subject to an outstanding appeal. Although the European Court of Human Rights acknowledged that the misinterpretation of art.2 was subsequently remedied by the decision of the Supreme Court in *Rabone v Pennine Care NHS Foundation Trust*,[101] this was too late for the applicant. The applicant was awarded €7,000 for non-pecuniary damage.

Prohibition of discrimination

The enjoyment of the rights and freedoms set forth in the Convention must be **2–16** secured without discrimination on any ground such as sex, race, colour, language, religion, political or other opinion, national or social origin, association with a national minority, property, birth or other status.[102] Similarly to art.13, the right under art.14 is also parasitic.[103]

Protection of property

Every natural or legal person is entitled to the peaceful enjoyment of his **2–17** possessions. No one may be deprived of his possessions except in the public interest and subject to the conditions provided for by law and by the general principles of international law.[104] The preceding provisions do not, however, in

---

[98] art.13.

[99] *Reynolds v United Kingdom* (2012) 55 E.H.R.R. 35.

[100] *Savage v South Essex Partnership NHS Foundation Trust* [2006] EWHC 3562 (QB); [2007] LS Law Medical 291. The test applied by the judge was gross negligence sufficient to sustain a charge of manslaughter. An appeal was subsequently allowed in *Savage* ([2008] 1 W.L.R. 1667) and, given that Savage was compulsorily detained in hospital, a test akin to that applied to a person detained in prison was applied. The Court of Appeal's decision was upheld in a subsequent appeal to the House of Lords ([2009] 1 A.C. 681).

[101] *Rabone v Pennine Care NHS Foundation Trust* [2012] 2 A.C. 72. The Supreme Court held that a similar operational duty upon public authorities applied where there was a real and immediate risk of a mentally ill patient's suicide, irrespective of whether the patient was compulsorily detained in hospital or was a voluntary patient.

[102] art.14. Nothing in this article may be regarded as preventing the States from imposing restrictions on the political activity of aliens: art.11.

[103] See, e.g. *Abdulaziz, Cabales and Balkandali v United Kingdom* (1985) 7 E.H.R.R. 471.

[104] Because the facts in *Jain v Trent Strategic Health Authority* [2009] 1 A.C. 853 preceded the coming into force of the Human Rights Act, the House of Lords could not consider a claim with regard to Convention rights. However, their Lordships suggested that Protocol 1 art.1 had clearly been infringed where the proprietors of a care home had no opportunity to challenge an application for suspension of their licence which was made by the health authority following a statutory procedure.

any way impair the right of a State to enforce such laws as it deems necessary to control the use of property in accordance with the general interest or to secure the payment of taxes or other contributions or penalties.[105]

Right to education

2–18   No person can be denied the right to education. In the exercise of any functions which it assumes in relation to education and to teaching, the State shall respect the right of parents to ensure such education and teaching in conformity with their own religious and philosophical convictions.[106]

Right to free elections

2–19   The High Contracting Parties undertake to hold free elections at reasonable intervals by secret ballot, under conditions which will ensure the free expression of the opinion of the people in the choice of the legislature.[107]

The death penalty

2–20   The death penalty is abolished. No one may be condemned to such penalty or be executed.[108]

REPARATION FOR INFRINGEMENT

The basic structure

2–21   Section 8(1) to (4) of the Human Rights Act provides:

> **Judicial remedies.**
> **8.**—(1) In relation to any act (or proposed act) of a public authority which the court finds is (or would be) unlawful, it may grant such relief or remedy, or make such order, within its powers as it considers just and appropriate.
>
> (2) But damages may be awarded only by a court which has power to award damages, or to order the payment of compensation, in civil proceedings.
>
> (3) No award of damages is to be made unless, taking account of all the circumstances of the case, including—
>
> > (a) any other relief or remedy granted, or order made, in relation to the act in question (by that or any other court), and

---

[105] First Protocol art.1.
[106] First Protocol art.2. This right does not confer a right to be educated at a specific or particular school. Thus, exclusion of a child from a school will not per se amount to breach where alternative education may be provided: *A v Head Teacher & Governors of Lord Grey School* [2006] 2 A.C. 363. Neither will a delay in providing special educational needs per se amount to a breach: *A v Essex CC* [2011] 1 A.C. 280. See also *Abdel-Rahman v University of Edinburgh* [2013] CSOH 201; 2014 G.W.D. 4–76.
[107] First Protocol art.3.
[108] Sixth Protocol art.1. A State may make provision in its law for the death penalty in respect of acts committed in time of war or of imminent threat of war; such penalty shall be applied only in the instances laid down in the law and in accordance with its provisions. The State shall communicate to the Secretary General of the Council of Europe the relevant provisions of that law: Sixth Protocol art.2.

(b) the consequences of any decision (of that or any other court) in
   respect of that act,

the court is satisfied that the award is necessary to afford just satisfaction to
the person in whose favour it is made.
   (4) In determining—

(a) whether to award damages, or
(b) the amount of an award,

the court must take into account the principles applied by the European
Court of Human Rights in relation to the award of compensation under
Article 41 of the Convention.

The Act does seem to suggest that the Human Rights Act remedy is not
"subsidiary".[109] This provides that proceedings under the Human Rights Act
must be brought within 12 months of the date on which the act complained of
took place.[110] If no declarator is required of infringement, it may well be actions
could be lost. Until there is jurisprudence on the matter, practitioners should
consider raising and sisting cases.

Relationship between action for just satisfaction and judicial review

In *Ruddy v Chief Constable, Strathclyde Police*,[111] the Supreme Court emphat-   **2–22**
ically distinguished an action for just satisfaction from judicial review. The
pursuer claimed to have been assaulted by police officers following his arrest.
Following a complaint about his treatment, the Procurator Fiscal decided no
proceedings were required against any police officer. The pursuer raised
proceedings in the sheriff court for just satisfaction claiming a breach of his
rights under art.3 with regard to the alleged assault and, in a separate crave,
claiming a breach of his right to an effective investigation of his complaint, also
under art.3. The defenders lodged a plea to the competency, which was upheld by
the sheriff. Upon appeal to the Inner House, Lord Clarke, in delivering the
opinion of the court, articulated a view that claims in respect of alleged breaches
of human rights would have to be brought by way of judicial review.[112] Lord
Hope gave this view short shrift:

> "The fallacy which undermines the Extra Division's whole approach to this
> issue, however, lies in its assumption that the appellant is seeking an
> exercise of the court's supervisory jurisdiction. That is not so. He is not
> asking for the review or setting aside of any decision of the chief constable
> or the Lord Advocate. He is not asking the court to control their actions in
> that way at all. His case in regard to both craves is based on averments of
> things done or omitted to be done and actions that were taken or not taken.
> The allegations are of completed acts or failures to act. He is not seeking to
> have them corrected in order to provide a foundation for his claim, nor does
> he need to do so. What he seeks is just satisfaction for the fact that, on his

---

[109] Human Rights Act 1998 s.7(5).
[110] This is now also the case for claims under s.100 of the Scotland Act 1998—s.100(3A).
[111] *Ruddy v Chief Constable, Strathclyde Police*, 2013 S.C. (U.K.S.C.) 126.
[112] *Ruddy v Chief Constable, Strathclyde Police*, 2011 S.C. 527 at 532–533.

averments, his Art 3 Convention rights have been breached. The essence of his claim is simply one of damages."[113]

Just satisfaction

The heads of claim

2–23   The Strasbourg Court awards damages as just satisfaction under three heads: pecuniary loss; non-pecuniary loss; and costs and expenses. In practice, the court does not always separate its awards into these respective heads of damage, and it has often awarded global sums which combine all of the applicant's losses into a single figure. This is reminiscent of the Scots cases where there have been solatium "employability" awards, which have a pecuniary element but insufficient to establish a patrimonial award.

The Law Commissions[114] note that the European Jurisprudence is opaque on this issue. That said, this does have a resonance with solatium in Scots law, which is our domestic non-pecuniary satisfaction. It is submitted that Scots courts will find it as easy as the European Court of Humnan Rights to take a case by case view of the suffering of the victims. The kind of approach that might be expected can be seen in *Smith and Grady v United Kingdom*[115] (concerning homosexuals banned from military service) in which the Strasbourg Court noted that it was not possible to make a precise calculation of the amount necessary to make complete reparation for the applicants' loss of future earnings because of "the inherently uncertain character of the damage flowing from the violations". Again, however, substantial awards (£19,000 to each applicant) were made for non-pecuniary loss. The Commissions' researches show,

> "Non-pecuniary awards have included compensation for pain, suffering and psychological harm, distress, frustration, inconvenience, humiliation, anxiety and loss of reputation. There appears to be no conceptual limit on the categories of loss which may be taken into account, and the Strasbourg Court is often prepared to assume such loss, without direct proof."

Sometimes just satisfaction may require a civil claim for damages as opposed to the protection from criminal prosecution.[116]

Who may claim?

2–24   Any victim may claim. Corporate entities may suffer non-pecuniary loss. Account should be taken of the company's reputation, uncertainty in decision-planning, disruption in the management of the company (for which there is no precise method of calculating the consequences) and the anxiety and inconvenience caused to the members of the management team.[117]

Type of proceedings

2–25   Proceedings may be brought before a court or tribunal and there are no provisions which prohibit jury trial in the civil courts. However, where the

---

[113] *Ruddy v Chief Constable, Strathclyde Police*, 2013 S.C. (U.K.S.C.) 126 at 132–133.
[114] Law Com. No.266.
[115] *Smith and Grady v United Kingdom* (2001) 31 E.H.R.R. 24.
[116] *HM Advocate v R.* 2001 S.L.T. 1366.
[117] *Comingersoll SA v Portugal* (2001) 31 E.H.R.R. 31.

challenge is to a judicial act of a court or an act done on the instructions of, or on behalf of, a judge, proceedings must be by way of appeal, judicial review or in another forum as prescribed by appropriate rules,[118] which, at the time of writing, do not provide for jury trial in such cases.

The character and conduct of the pursuer

Reminiscent of our domestic scheme, operated by the Criminal Injuries **2–26** Compensation Authority, the character and conduct of the applicant may affect the amount of any award. This is most clearly seen in *McCann v United Kingdom*.[119] The applicants had made claims in respect of the killing of three IRA terrorists suspected of planning a bomb attack in Gibraltar. The European Court of Human Rights found a violation of art.2. However, the court rejected the claim for compensation: the victims were intending a terrorist attack. Accordingly, an award of damages was inappropriate. It is more likely that a judgment will itself be held to provide just satisfaction where the applicant is a criminal or a suspected criminal.

Causation

The approach to causation will bring about interesting arguments. The **2–27** Commissions explain that the view is strict. It is, however, tempered by a flexible approach to loss of opportunity. In *Martins Moreira v Portugal*,[120] the applicant complained that the proceedings in which he sought damages for personal injury were not completed within a reasonable time. The defendant became insolvent. The European Court of Human Rights held that it was reasonable to conclude that, as a result of the long delay, the applicant he suffered a loss of opportunities that warranted an award of just satisfaction in respect of pecuniary damage.

The UK experience thus far

In *R. (KB) v Mental Health Review Tribunal*,[121] it was said that the European **2–28** Court of Human Rights approach to awards was to be taken first. There is no reason for lower awards but it is right even where there is no comparable tort to look at ordinary awards in general. *R. (Bernard) v Enfield LBC*[122] is noteworthy as one of the first domestic human rights damages cases. Sullivan J. in the Queen's Bench declined to follow Law Commission guidance, that is by starting from a tort award. The Council had not sufficiently acted to provide accommodation for over 20 months for a disabled person. He considered that damages, in this case against a public authority, should not be minimal or lower than tort damages. There was, in any event, no directly related tort. Instead he looked towards Ombudsman findings of maladministration. In proceedings under the Scotland Act, the remedy of damages for just satisfaction has been described as a "public law remedy".[123] Thus, in *Docherty v Scottish Ministers*[124] it was noted that there

---

[118] Human Rights Act 1998 s.9.

[119] *McCann v United Kingdom* (1995) 21 E.H.R.R. 97.

[120] *Martins Moreira v Portugal* (1988) 13 E.H.R.R. 517.

[121] *R. (KB) v Mental Health Review Tribunal* [2004] Q.B. 936.

[122] *R. (Bernard) v Enfield LBC* [2003] H.R.L.R. 4.

[123] *HM Advocate v R.*, 2003 S.C. (P.C.) 21 at 42 per Lord Hope of Craighead; *Somerville v Scottish Ministers*, 2008 S.C. (HL) 45 at 62 per Lord Hope of Craighead.

[124] *Docherty v Scottish Ministers*, 2012 S.C. 150 at 170 per the opinion of the court (delivered by the Lord President (Hamilton)).

was a difference in emphasis in damages under the Scotland Act—which were
held to appear essentially vindicatory in character—from damages for reparation
in Scots law generally.

One of the first Scottish cases, *Napier*[125] was a case where there were in fact
physical results from the treatment complained of. In view of that and in view of
the fact that a financial award was made, that, together with the declaration of the
infringement, was sufficient for just satisfaction.

RELATIONSHIP WITH DELICTUAL LIABILITY AT COMMON LAW

The interaction between human rights and delictual liability generally

2–29   Section 2(1) of the Human Rights Act requires a court or tribunal when
determining a question in connection with a Convention right to take into account
the jurisprudence of the European Court of Human Rights. This raises a
fundamental question with regard to the future direction of areas of domestic law
which deal with issues that interrelate with Convention rights, viz will such
aspects of domestic law develop so as ultimately to merge with Convention
jurisprudence, or will two distinct and parallel systems continue? If the latter,
what will be the relationship between these distinct systems.

Consistent with the suggestion that the Human Rights Act and the Scotland
Act may still be said to be bedding in to the law of Scotland, it seems that there
is as yet no clear answer to this question. The Human Rights Act has certainly
had a profound impact on the development of the law of confidence in England
and Wales.[126] However, development may have been stultified had the domestic
law of confidence not provided the growing point for misuse of private
information.[127] Nevertheless, human rights jurisprudence may indeed continue to
have a profound impact on the development of personality rights and liability for
associated delictual wrongs generally.[128]

The interaction between human rights and liability for negligence

2–30   Although the question was identified by the Inner House in *Thomson*,[129] the
interaction between human rights jurisprudence and the law of negligence has not
been considered directly in any negligence actions brought under Scots law, at
least not in the higher courts. Nevertheless, if, as recently re-emphasised by
Baroness Hale in *Mitchell*,[130] the laws of negligence of Scotland and England are

---

[125] *Napier v Scottish Ministers*, 2005 1 S.C. 229 (affirmed by the Inner House: 2005 1 S.C. 307).

[126] See, e.g. *Venables v News Group Newspapers Ltd* [2001] Fam. 430; *Campbell v MGN
Newspapers Ltd* [2004] 2 A.C. 457. Similar developments have tentatively been explored in
Scotland: *X v BBC* 2005 S.L.T. 796; *Response Handling Ltd v BBC* 2008 S.L.T. 51.

[127] "(T)he existence of a Convention right cannot call for instant manufacture of a corresponding
common law right where none exists": *Smith v Chief Constable of Sussex* sub nom. *Van Colle v
Chief Constable of Hertfordshire Police* [2009] 1 A.C. 225 at 267 per Lord Bingham of Cornhill.
See also *Wainwright v Home Office* [2004] 2 A.C. 406.

[128] For example human rights considerations have impacted on the jurisprudence dealing with prior
restraint in defamation cases: *Dickson Minto WS v Bonnier Media Ltd*, 2002 S.L.T. 776 (s.12 of
the Human Rights Act). See also *Massie v McCaig*, 2013 S.C. 343. Cf. *Cook v Gibson* [2013]
CSOH 64; 2013 G.W.D. 14–298; *Angiolini v Green* [2013] CSOH 196; 2014 G.W.D. 5–104.

[129] *Thomson v Scottish Ministers*, 2013 S.C. 628 at 639–640 per Lord Justice-Clerk Carloway
delivering the opinion of the court.

[130] *Mitchell v Glasgow City Council*, 2009 S.C. (HL) 21 at 46.

broadly similar, then dicta of senior members of the judiciary in English appeals are likely to be instructive, especially given that the Human Rights Act itself is a law for the whole of the United Kingdom.

The question came to a head in the English Court of Appeal not long after the coming into force of the Human Rights Act. In *D v East Berkshire Community Health NHS Trust*,[131] the court used the Act to hold that a duty of care was owed by a local authority to children whom they ought to have suspected were victims of child abuse. This enabled the Court of Appeal to circumvent the previous decision of the House of Lords in *X (Minors) v Bedfordshire CC*,[132] which otherwise was binding upon the Court of Appeal but had been discredited in an appeal to Strasbourg and in subsequent decisions of the House of Lords on other related matters.[133] Ironically, the Human Rights Act had not been in force at the time of the alleged violations in *D*, enabling the House of Lords to refuse to hold that a duty of care was also owed to the parents.[134]

Since then there has not been a consistent approach—if anything there appears to have developed an increasing judicial resistance to developing the law of negligence in line with human rights jurisprudence. Accordingly, there currently appear to be two parallel, but separate, systems in operation.[135] Indeed, in *Smith v Chief Constable of Sussex*,[136] Lord Hope seemed to suggest that the Human Rights Act might provide some kind of safety valve in permitting claims that would otherwise be excluded at common law, and that this justified refusing to extend the common law[137]:

> "In my opinion the common law,[138] with its own system of limitation periods and remedies, should be allowed to stand on its own feet side by side with the alternative remedy. Indeed the case for preserving it may be thought to be supported by the fact that any perceived shortfall in the way

---

[131] *D v East Berkshire Community Health NHS Trust* [2004] Q.B. 558.

[132] *X (Minors) v Bedfordshire CC* [1995] 2 A.C. 633.

[133] *Barrett v Enfield LBC* [2001] 2 A.C. 550; *Phelps v Hillingdon LBC* [2001] 2 A.C. 619.

[134] *D v East Berkshire Community Health NHS Trust* [2005] 2 A.C. 373: a decision which contradicted the ECtHR's decision in *TP v United Kingdom* (2002) 34 E.H.R.R. 2. In later proceedings before the ECtHR, the decision of the House of Lords in *D* to reject a duty of care owed to the parents was found to be incompatible with the Convention: *MAK v United Kingdom* (2010) 51 E.H.R.R. 14.

[135] See, e.g. *Rabone v Pennine Care NHS Trust* [2012] 2 W.L.R. 381 at 417–418 per Lord Mance J.S.C.

[136] sub nom. *Van Colle v Chief Constable of Hertfordshire Police* [2009] 1 A.C. 225.

[137] Reminiscent of Lord Templeman's dictum in *Downsview Nominees v First City Corp Ltd* [1993] A.C. 295 at 316: "The House of Lords has warned against the danger of extending the ambit of negligence so as to supplant or supplement other torts, contractual obligations, statutory duties or equitable rules in relation to every kind of damage including economic loss." "Human rights" might very well replace the term "economic loss"!

[138] Note that although Lord Hope was referring directly to a discussion of the "common law" by Lord Hamilton in *Gibson v Orr*, 1999 S.C. 420 at 437, Lord Hamilton appeared to be using the term "common law" in a discussion of cases decided (with the exception of *Maloco v Littlewoods Organisation Ltd*, 1987 S.C. (HL) 37) in England and Wales—where the term "common law" has a special meaning. More recently, Lord Mance J.S.C. has said that, "In some areas, the common law may go further than the Convention, and in some contexts it may also be inspired by the Convention rights and jurisprudence (the protection of privacy being a notable example). And in time, of course, a new synthesis may emerge. But the natural starting point in any dispute is to start with the domestic law, and it is certainly not to focus exclusively on the Convention rights, without surveying the wider common law scene": *Kennedy v The Information Commissioner* [2014] W.L.R. 808 at 835.

that it deals with cases that fall within the threshold for the application of the *Osman* can now be dealt with in domestic law under the 1998 Act."[139]

Whether the rights-based tradition, if that is indeed the "tradition" of Scots law, justifies a different approach to the relationship between liability under human rights legislation and delictual liability at common law remains to be seen.

---

[139] *Smith v Chief Constable of Sussex Police* sub nom. *Van Colle v Chief Constable of Hertfordshire Police* [2009] 1 A.C. 225 at 275. See also Lord Brown of Eaton-Under-Heywood at 285–286.

CHAPTER 3

PARTIES

This Chapter will examine who can sue in delict, and against whom an action **3–01** may be raised.

WHO CAN SUE IN DELICT?

To pursue a private law action in Scotland one requires what Scots law calls "title **3–02** and interest". Title and interest appear never to have been clearly defined in the context of delict,[1] and it is suggested that issues tend to be dealt with intuitively by practitioners and the courts. Thus, practice may have entrenched habits that are arguably inconsistent with theory and, although title and interest are separate concepts—"title" being concerned with the legal status required to sue and "interest" with the benefit to the pursuer of the outcome sought—the concepts often appear convoluted in delict cases.[2]

To illustrate: in *Donoghue v Stevenson*[3] for example, Mrs Donoghue's friend would have enjoyed *title* (as a legal person who was a party) to sue the café proprietor in *contract*, but would have no *interest* in recovering damages for Mrs Donoghue's injuries. Whether the friend had title to sue the manufacturer in *delict* would thus be irrelevant to consider, as it would be obvious that the friend would have no interest in the objective of an action: namely the recovery of damages to compensate for Mrs Donoghue's injuries. So if Mrs Donoghue's friend did attempt to sue, the case could be challenged either on "title", or on "interest", or (probably in practice) on "title and interest". On the other hand, as will be seen,[4] an unborn child who suffers injury within the womb has no *title* to sue unless and until the child is born alive,[5] although the child has an *interest* in

---

[1] See, e.g. *D&J Nicol v Dundee Harbour Trustees*, 1915 S.C. (HL) 7 at 12–13 per Lord Dunedin. For a more detailed discussion see G. Cameron, "Capacity and Parties", in J.M. Thomson, *Delict* (Edinburgh: W. Green/SULI), Ch.3.

[2] See, e.g. *Reavis v Clan Line Steamers*, 1925 S.C. 725. Did the Inner House find Mrs Reavis' claim incompetent through lack of title, or irrelevant through lack of interest? It is unclear beyond that the Inner House did not disturb the Lord Ordinary's assertion that Mrs Reavis had "no title to sue".

[3] *Donoghue v Stevenson*, 1932 S.C. (HL) 31. For a full explanation of the facts, see paras 11–02 to 11–03 below.

[4] See para.3–08 below.

[5] Although Scots law deems that a child acquires legal personality, and thus title to sue, only upon birth, it also applies the *nascituri* doctrine which provides that in matters affecting its interests while *in utero* the child is deemed to be born—see *Elliot v Lord Joicey*, 1935 S.C. (HL) 57; *Cohen v Shaw*, 1992 S.L.T. 1022; *Hamilton v Fife Health Board*, 1993 S.C. 369.

pursuing a case once, upon being born, the child acquires title.[6] If the child is not born alive the parents would not succeed in an action with regard to the harm to the child as they would have enjoyed neither *title*—either upon transmission of the rights of a deceased person[7] or as relatives of a deceased[8] (the child never having become a legal person)—or *interest* as they did not suffer themselves the injuries inflicted upon the unborn child.

To try to provide some clarity, the following analysis is mooted as providing a coherent, if not authoritative, taxonomy of the concepts and their application. It is suggested that this analysis is consistent with Erskine's view on the nature of delictual liability:

> "(E)veryone who has the exercise of reason, and so can distinguish between right and wrong, is naturally obliged to make up the damage befalling his neighbour from a wrong committed by himself. Wherefore, every fraudulent contrivance, or unwarrantable act by which another suffers damage, or runs the hazard of it, subjects the delinquent to reparation."[9]

As discussed above,[10] Erskine appears to acknowledge a distinction between a primary obligation (not to engage in fraudulent contrivances or unwarrantable acts) and a secondary obligation (to make up the damage caused by a breach of the primary obligation) imposed *ex lege* by the law of delict. Given that the corollary of an obligation is a right, it follows that there are two levels of "right" recognised in the law of delict: a "primary" right not to be subject to a delictual wrong and a "secondary" right to reparation if the primary right is infringed.

3–03   The "primary" right not to be a victim of a delictual wrong might be expressed in terms of "respect" for one's rights.[11] The reciprocal obligation owed to the holder of the right might then be described as a "duty" to respect those rights. Thus, a person who in law enjoys a right to respect for his physical integrity has title to sue anyone who owes that person a duty to respect—i.e. not to interfere with—his physical integrity. It follows that a legal person who is a victim of an *intentional* delict such as an assault inevitably enjoys title to sue the assailant,[12] but a victim of *negligence* will only enjoy title to sue if the alleged wrongdoer owed the pursuer a duty of care.

It then follows that the "secondary" right to reparation, i.e. the right to a remedy, relates to the "interest" in the outcome sought, and will be completed upon proof of *damnum injuria datum*.

How then would *injuria sine damno*, or *damnum absque injuria* fit into this analysis? An example of the former case may be where an emergency medical procedure has been carried out without the patient's consent, but the patient has

---

[6] Which in practice would be pursued on behalf of the child by the child's parent or a curator ad litem appointed by the court.

[7] Damages (Scotland) Act 2011 s.2. If the child was born alive the parents would be able to claim under s.2, even if the child only lived for a short time: *Hamilton v Fife Health Board*, 1993 S.C. 369.

[8] Damages (Scotland) Act 2011 s.4.

[9] Erskine, III, 1, 13.

[10] See para.1–11 above.

[11] Consistent with the jurisprudential approach of both the Universal Declaration of Human Rights and the European Convention on Human Rights.

[12] It is suggested that intentional delicts cannot be committed without there being a breach of a notional duty to respect the victim's protected interest—in the case of assault, for example, the protected interest is the victim's physical integrity.

suffered no harm.[13] A delictual wrong (*injuria*) has been committed, namely an assault, but the pursuer has sustained no loss (*sine damnum*). It is submitted that the pursuer will have *title* to sue because the case is grounded in a right enjoyed by the pursuer, but will not have *interest* as there is no beneficial objective to the litigation.[14] An example of the latter case may be where a trader loses business to a rival trading at more competitive prices. The pursuer has suffered a loss (*damnum*), but it has not been caused by a legal wrong (*absque injuria*). There, although the pursuer may have an *interest* in the outcome sought, since the pursuer has no legal right at stake (or, to put it another way, the defender owes the pursuer no duty not to undercut his prices), the pursuer has no *title* to sue.[15]

In summary, a pursuer's title to sue depends upon his *status* as the holder of a legal right. Thus, looking at the other side of the coin, if the pursuer is not owed a legal duty, the pursuer has no title to sue.[16] A pursuer's interest is in there being a personal benefit in the outcome sought, i.e. it is in the *substance* of the claim. Thus, if the pursuer has not suffered reparable harm caused by a breach of the duty the pursuer has no interest to sue.

These matters may be dealt with as preliminary issues, effectively weeding out at an early stage cases that ultimately are hopeless. Logically, a challenge to title should take the form of a plea to the competency,[17] whereas a challenge to interest should be taken as a plea to the relevancy.[18] It should be noted though that if a court takes a plea to the competency the case will be thrown out and can proceed no further; whereas if a plea to the relevancy is taken, the pursuer may be permitted to modify the pleadings so allowing the case to continue. Thus, in negligence actions in particular, a challenge to title to sue is often taken as a plea to the relevancy. This may be explained by the fact that the law on whether a duty of care is owed has become very sophisticated, and the pleadings may initially be inadequate and so fail properly to aver a duty of care, but nevertheless capable of modification so as to state a prima facie case.

Primary and secondary victims

The pursuer's status as either a primary or secondary victim of a delictual wrong is significant in terms of title to sue. As a very rough rule of thumb, generally one must qualify as a primary victim to have title to sue—the relationship between the wrongdoer and the secondary victim is usually too **3–04**

---

[13] For there to be "no harm" to the patient in this context, the non-consensual invasion may have to be likely to *improve*, rather than merely *maintain*, the patient's condition: see *Airedale NHS Trust v Bland* [1993] A.C. 789; [1993] 2 W.L.R. 316; *Law Hospital Trust v Lord Advocate*, 1996 S.C. 301.

[14] The patient may argue that he has title *and* interest on the alternative basis that his autonomy and dignity have been affronted by the non-consensual invasion of his bodily integrity. See, e.g. *Goorkani v Tayside Health Board*, 1991 S.L.T. 94; *McFarlane v Tayside Health Board*, 2000 S.C. 1 at 44–45 per Lord Millett; *Rees v Darlington Memorial Hospital NHS Trust* [2004] 1 A.C. 309; *Chester v Afshar* [2005] 1 A.C. 134.

[15] See *D&J Nicol v Dundee Harbour Trustees*, 1915 S.C. (HL) 7 at 12 per Lord Dunedin.

[16] Likewise, it is not sufficient if the pursuer can show the defender owes the duty contended for to someone else: see, e.g. *Orr v Glasgow, Airdrie and Monklands Junction Railway Co* (1860) 3 Macq. 799; *Borland v Bell* (1895) 23 R. 126.

[17] viz: "You cannot bring that action."

[18] viz: "Your pleadings do not set out a case to answer."

remote.[19] As will be seen throughout this work, the reality is more sophisticated—there are other factors which may militate against a primary victim having title to sue and there are cases where secondary victims are permitted to proceed.[20] It is important to understand the difference—although, perhaps surprisingly, the courts have generally avoided tackling this distinction in a definitive way. Nevertheless, it is suggested that the following definitions are appropriate:

- a *primary* victim suffers harm as a direct consequence of the delictual wrong; and
- a *secondary* victim suffers harm as a consequence of the harm suffered by the primary victim —thus the secondary victim suffers secondary harm as an indirect consequence of the delictual wrong.

The analogy of ripples created upon throwing a stone in a pool is instructive. If these ripples strike a rock protruding the surface of the pool, a second set of ricochet ripples will then fan out from the rock. Ripples from that second set may then strike another object in the water. The first rock may be equated with the primary victim—the ripples striking that rock are a direct consequence of throwing the stone in the water. The ripples striking the second object (equated to the secondary victim) are a secondary, or indirect, consequence of throwing the stone in the pool. But for the ripples from the stone striking the first rock, the second object would not have been struck by the second set of ripples. Thus, the impact of the second set of ripples on the second object is parasitic of the impact of the first set of ripples on the first rock.[21]

The distinction is often attributed to the speech of Lord Oliver of Aylmerton in *Alcock v Chief Constable of South Yorkshire Police*.[22] *Alcock* involved claims in negligence from secondary victims who suffered psychiatric injury as a consequence of the tragedy at Hillsborough Stadium on April 15, 1989. In considering previous psychiatric injury cases Lord Oliver suggested that:

> "Broadly they divide into two categories, that is to say, those cases in which the injured plaintiff was involved, either mediately, or immediately, as a participant, and those in which the plaintiff was no more than the passive and unwilling witness of injury caused to others."[23]

---

[19] This may even be the case with regard to "intentional" delicts where secondary victims may be viewed as "collateral damage". However, this will not be the case if the wrongdoer carried out the delictual wrong with the intention of harming the secondary victim. An example would be inducing a breach of contract: see, e.g. *British Motor Trade Association v Gray*, 1951 S.C. 586.

[20] Ch.11 of this work attempts to set out a taxonomy of tests applied in dealing with the duty of care question in negligence, classified according to the respective variables of primary and secondary victim, and physical, economic and psychiatric harm.

[21] Of course, the second object may be struck by *both* sets of ripples. Applying that to the delictual conundrum, whether the pursuer should be classified as a primary or secondary victim will have to be established by investigating which set of "ripples" caused the harm for which the pursuer seeks reparation.

[22] *Alcock v Chief Constable of South Yorkshire Police* [1992] 1 A.C. 310. It has been traced further back: "The factual distinction between primary and secondary victims of an accident is obvious and of long-standing. It was recognised by Lord Russell of Killowen in *Bourhill v. Young* [1943] A.C. 92, when he pointed out that Mrs. Bourhill was not physically involved in the collision." *Page v Smith* [1996] A.C. 155 at 184 per Lord Lloyd of Berwick.

[23] *Alcock v Chief Constable of South Yorkshire Police* [1992] 1 A.C. 310 at 407.

He went on to describe those falling into the former category as "primary **3–05** victims" and those falling into the latter as "secondary victims".[24] This distinction has been widely accepted and applied in cases involving psychiatric injury[25] but it has not to date been applied in cases involving claims for other types of damage. However, Lord Oliver did not confine his discussion to psychiatric injury claims:

> "The failure of the law *in general* to compensate for injuries sustained by persons unconnected with the event precipitated by a defendant's negligence must necessarily import the lack of any legal duty owed by the defendant to such persons."[26]

On the analysis of title and interest as set out above, Lord Oliver's dictum is consistent with a default position that *normally* secondary victims have no title to sue. Indeed, Lord Oliver was trying to pin down what justified an *exception* in psychiatric injury cases:

> "What is more difficult to account for is why, when the law in general declines to extend the area of compensation to those whose injury arises only from the circumstances of their relationship to the primary victim, an exception has arisen in those cases in which the event of injury to the primary victim has been actually witnessed by the plaintiff and the injury claimed is established as stemming from that fact."[27]

Thus, it is submitted that distinguishing primary from secondary victims is as important in other types of case outside of psychiatric injury. Travelling slightly further back in time, one may read the opinion of Lord Oliver in the "pure economic loss" case of *Murphy v Brentwood DC*:

> "It is true that, in an uninterrupted line of cases since 1875, it has consistently been held that a party cannot successfully sue in tort for the interference with his economic expectations or advantage resulting from injury to the person or property of another person with whom he has or is likely to have a contractual relationship: see *Cattle v. Stockton Waterworks Co.* (1875) L.R. 10 Q.B. 453; *Simpson & Co. v. Thompson* (1877) 3 App. Cas. 279; *Société Anonyme de Remorquage à Hélice v. Bennetts* [1911] 1 K.B. 243. That principle was applied more recently by Widgery J. in *Weller & Co. v. Foot & Mouth Disease Research Institute* [1966] 1 Q.B. 569 and received its most recent reiteration in the decision of this House in *Leigh and Sillavan Ltd. v. Aliakmon Shipping Co. Ltd.* [1986] A.C. 785."[28]

---

[24] *Alcock v Chief Constable of South Yorkshire Police* [1992] 1 A.C. 310 at 410–411. The distinction has been applied in Scotland: see, e.g. *Robertson v Forth Road Bridge Joint Board (No.2)*, 1995 S.C. 364; *Campbell v North Lanarkshire Council*, 2000 S.C.L.R. 373; *Fraser v State Hospitals Board for Scotland*, 2001 S.L.T. 1051; *Cross v Highlands & Islands Enterprise*, 2001 S.L.T. 1060; *Keen v Tayside Contracts*, 2003 S.L.T. 500; *Salter v UB Frozen & Chilled Foods Ltd*, 2004 S.C. 233; *Burns v Boots UK Ltd*, 2011 Rep. L.R. 124.

[25] Although there has been some controversy over the definitions adopted in various judgments—see paras 11–47 to 11–53 below.

[26] *Alcock v Chief Constable of South Yorkshire Police* [1992] 1 A.C. 310 at 410.

[27] *Alcock v Chief Constable of South Yorkshire Police* [1992] 1 A.C. 310 at 410.

[28] *Murphy v Brentwood DC* [1991] 1 A.C. 398 at 485.

3–06   It has also been suggested[29] that this distinction between primary and secondary losses (or victims), can be traced back to the famous dictum of Lord Kinloch in *Allan v Barclay*:

> "The grand rule on the subject of damages is, that none can be claimed except such as naturally and directly arise out of the wrong done; and such, therefore, as may reasonably be supposed to have been in the view of the wrongdoer. Tried by this test, the present claim appears to fail. The personal injuries of the individual himself will be properly held to have been in the contemplation of the wrongdoer. But he cannot be held bound to have surmised the *secondary injuries* done to all holding relations with the individual, whether that of a master, or any other."[30]

The terminology used to describe the pure economic loss in these cases has included "indirect,"[31] "relational,"[32] "secondary (pure) economic loss".[33] However, it is submitted that it would be clearer to describe such a claim as one for pure economic loss pursued by a *secondary victim*.

What connects secondary victim psychiatric injury cases such as *Alcock v Chief Constable of South Yorkshire Police*[34] or *Bourhill v Young*[35] with secondary or relational pure economic loss cases such as *Landcatch Ltd v International Oil Pollution Compensation Fund*[36] or *Allan v Barclay*[37] is that the pursuer is claiming for loss which is parasitic on the harm suffered by another person—the primary victim—which was itself a direct consequence of the alleged wrong.[38] Thus the loss suffered by the secondary victim pursuer can be described as an indirect consequence of the defender's delictual wrong.

Clear examples of the primary/secondary victim dichotomy include:

- the owner of a cargo lost upon the sinking of a ship, where the reason the ship sank was due to the negligence of repairers: repairers were negligent (delictual wrong)—shipowner is primary victim (physical

---

29 *Landcatch Ltd v International Oil Pollution Compensation Fund*, 1999 S.L.T. 1208 at 1213 per Lord Justice-Clerk Cullen. Neither of the terms "primary victim" or "secondary victim" were actually used by Lord Cullen in his speech but it is submitted that he was making a similar distinction to that made by Lord Oliver in *Murphy* and *Alcock*.
30 *Allan v Barclay* (1863) 2 M. 873 at 874 (emphasis added). This was a case involving a claim for pure economic loss (the cost of employing a replacement worker) suffered by an employer of the victim of a road accident. Also quoted in *Reavis v Clan Line Steamers (No.1)*, 1925 S.C. 725.
31 *Landcatch Ltd v International Oil Pollution Compensation Fund*, 1999 S.L.T. 1208 at 1224 per Lord McCluskey
32 *Landcatch Ltd v International Oil Pollution Compensation Fund*, 1999 S.L.T. 1208 at 1218 per Lord Justice-Clerk Cullen.
33 *Alegrete Shipping Co Inc v International Oil Pollution Compensation Fund 1971 (The Sea Empress)* [2003] 1 Lloyd's Rep. 327 at 336 per Mance L.J.
34 *Alcock v Chief Constable of South Yorkshire Police* [1992] 1 A.C. 310.
35 *Bourhill v Young*, 1942 S.C. (HL) 78.
36 *Landcatch Ltd v International Oil Pollution Compensation Fund*, 1999 S.L.T. 1208.
37 *Allan v Barclay* (1863) 2 M. 873.
38 This appears to have been misunderstood in some cases where the classification has been based on a notion that the respective victims are classified according to their relationship with a relevant incident—itself the product of the alleged wrong—rather than according to their relationship with the alleged wrongdoer: see, e.g. the critique provided by Mackay J. in *Harrhy v Thames Trains Ltd* [2003] EWHC 2286 of the judgment of Lady Paton in *Keen v Tayside Contracts* 2003 S.L.T. 500.

harm/loss of property), cargo-owner is secondary victim (physical harm/loss of property[39];

- the employer who has to pay for temporary staff where an employee is injured following an assault: assailant commits assault (delictual wrong)—employee is primary victim (physical harm/personal injury), employer is secondary victim (pure economic loss)[40]; and
- the bystander who develops a psychiatric illness following witnessing the driver of a car suffer a horrific death where the accident is caused by a lorry driver's careless driving: lorry driver negligent (delictual wrong)—car driver is primary victim (physical harm/personal injury and death), bystander as witness is secondary victim (psychiatric injury).[41]

It is important to emphasise that although understanding the distinction between primary and secondary victims is important, that understanding remains in development:

" . . . the categorisation of those claiming to be included as primary or secondary victims is not, as I read the cases, finally closed. It is a concept still to be developed in different factual situations."[42]

Title to sue in negligence

Applying the analysis carried out above, a pursuer will only have title to sue **3–07** in negligence if the pursuer is owed a duty of care. Although the circumstances in which the law of delict recognises a duty of care are covered in detail later in this work,[43] it is appropriate to make some basic points at this stage. The duty of care concept operates as a device to "limit the range of (pursuers)".[44] For a duty of care to be owed by an alleged wrongdoer there must be a sufficiently close relationship between the parties. The plethora of precedent in some areas[45]

---

[39] See, e.g. *Marc Rich & Co AG v Bishop Rock Marine Co Ltd (The Nicholas H)* [1996] A.C. 211. Should the cargo owner have been considered a secondary victim and might that classification have made it easier for the majority of their Lordships to justify their conclusion? See also *Perrett v Collins* [1998] 2 Lloyd's Rep. 255. Compare *Palsgraf v Long Island Railroad Co* 162 NE 99 (1928). Is it feasible for physical personal injury to be suffered by a secondary victim? Would an example be a person who was injured or killed when the ship sank? Could the pursuer's sister in *Duffy v Lanarkshire Health Board* 1999 S.L.T. 906 be viewed as a secondary victim suffering physical harm?

[40] See, e.g. *Allan v Barclay* (1863) 2 M. 873; *Reavis v Clan Line Steamers (No.1)*, 1925 S.C. 725.

[41] See, e.g. *McLoughlin v O'Brian* [1983] 1 A.C. 410; *Keen v Tayside Contracts*, 2003 S.L.T. 500. If the bystander was actually a passenger in the car and the psychiatric injury was attributable to the passenger's fear of his own safety, i.e. that he was involved in a near miss, would that make the passenger a primary victim? See, e.g. *Page v Smith* [1996] A.C. 155. If the passenger's psychiatric injury was triggered by a combination of witnessing the death of the driver and fear of his own safety how should he be classified? Can one be both primary and secondary victim? See, e.g. *Currie v Wardrop*, 1927 S.C. 538; *Schneider v Eisovitch* [1960] 2 Q.B. 430; *Malcolm v Broadhurst* [1970] 3 All E.R. 508; *Brice v Brown* [1984] 1 All E.R. 997.

[42] *W v Essex CC* [2001] 2 A.C. 592 at 601 per Lord Slynn of Hadley.

[43] See Ch.11.

[44] *Donoghue v Stevenson*, 1932 S.C. (HL) 31 at 44 per Lord Atkin.

[45] e.g. liability for road traffic accidents.

clearly defines the boundaries; the paucity of precedent in others leaves the boundaries vague. Where precedent does not confirm on which side of the boundary the relationship lies, tests intended to apply underpinning principles require to be applied.[46] The specific questions to be asked vary, depending on the nature of the harm for which reparation is sought,[47] and whether the pursuer is a primary or secondary victim.[48]

As a general rule, secondary victims are not owed a duty of care.[49] The underpinning principle is that the relationship between an alleged wrongdoer and a secondary victim is too remote. On the analysis above, another way of putting the law's general refusal to recognise a duty of care is to say that a secondary victim of negligence will not enjoy title to sue.

This has indeed been the general approach of the courts in reparation actions brought for pure economic loss suffered by a secondary victim and blamed upon a defender's negligence. For example, in *Nacap Ltd v Moffat Plant Hire Ltd*,[50] the Inner House held that a contractor had no title to sue with regard to the costs involved in carrying out their contractual obligation to repair their client's pipework when it was damaged by the negligence of one of the defender's employees. The damaged pipes were owned by the British Gas Corp, the primary victim. The pursuers thus suffered no loss to their own property; their loss was relational, or secondary, and purely economic. In other words the pursuers were secondary victims suffering pure economic loss. As such the pursuers were not owed a duty of care by the defender's employee, the pursuers had no title to sue and the action was thus incompetent.[51]

However, the courts have occasionally recognised exceptions to the rule that secondary victims of negligence are owed no duty of care and have no title to sue in negligence. For example, in actions involving liability for psychiatric injury, claims by secondary victims have been permitted where they have satisfied "control mechanisms" developed by the courts.[52] Here, cases often turn on very fine points of detail, and it arguably makes sense to treat a defender's challenge to the existence of a duty of care, and thus of title to sue, as a plea to the relevancy rather than to the competency.[53]

Likewise, in some negligence actions for pure economic loss brought by prima facie secondary victims, it may be possible for pursuers to argue that they have

---

[46] See, e.g. *Customs and Excise Commissioners v Barclays Bank Plc* [2007] 1 A.C. 181.

[47] Variables include whether the loss is physical, economic or psychiatric.

[48] See, e.g. *Burns v Boots UK Ltd*, 2011 Rep. L.R. 124.

[49] See, e.g. *Alcock v Chief Constable of South Yorkshire Police* [1992] 1 A.C. 310 at 410 per Lord Oliver of Aylmerton.

[50] *Nacap Ltd v Moffat Plant Hire Ltd*, 1987 S.L.T. 221. The Inner House applied the decision of the House of Lords in *Leigh & Sillivan Ltd v Aliakmon Shipping Co Ltd (The Aliakmon)* [1986] A.C. 785. The approach can be traced back through *Simpson & Co v Thomson* (1878) 5 R. (HL) 40 at 46 per Lord Penzanze to *Allan v Barclay* (1863) 2 M. 873 at 874 per Lord Kinloch. See also *Reavis v Clan Line Steamers*, 1925 S.C. 725; *Dynamco Ltd v Holland & Hannen & Cubitts (Scotland) Ltd*, 1971 S.C. 257; *Landcatch Ltd v International Oil Pollution Compensation Fund*, 1999 S.L.T. 1208; *Hand v North of Scotland Water Authority* 2002 S.L.T. 798; *TCS Holdings Ltd v Ashtead Plant Hire Co Ltd*, 2003 S.L.T. 177.

[51] Albeit that in the opinion of the court the pursuers "failed to make out any relevant case": *Nacap v Moffat Plant Ltd* 1987, S.L.T. 221 at 224.

[52] *Page v Smith* [1996] A.C. 155 at 197 per Lord Lloyd of Berwick.

[53] Indeed, a plea to the relevancy may only be suitable for consideration at a proof before answer—see, e.g. *Burns v Boots UK Ltd*, 2011 Rep. L.R. 124.

sufficient interest[54] in the property that is damaged to provide what might be described as a possessory title to sue. Thus, in *North Scottish Helicopters v United Technologies Inc*, where the pursuer leased a helicopter for a 13-year period during which it had exclusive control of the aircraft, and at the end of which it would nominate a buyer and receive 97.5 per cent of the sale price, the Inner House described the pursuer's relationship with the helicopter as being "in the strongest position that could be conceived of short of ownership".[55] The Inner House so confirmed the pursuer's "possessory"[56] title to sue the manufacturer of the helicopter where it was destroyed by a fire blamed on a faulty component.[57]

It is submitted that it is also the case in actions for reparation in respect of property damage outside of negligence that the extent of the pursuer's interest in the property relates directly to title to sue. Thus, although tenancy of heritable property is distinguishable from ownership, tenancy may nevertheless confer title to sue in nuisance.[58] Tenancy confers a right to enjoy the use of the leased property, and it is submitted that this right confers sufficient title to sue, at least for interdict, where a nuisance interferes with the tenant's use of the property; even if tenancy confers no title to sue in the context of damage to, or devaluation of, the property itself.

Title to sue: the human lifecycle

An unborn child has no title to sue in Scots law. However, if the foetus[59] **3–08** suffers antenatal injuries, the *nasciturus* doctrine deems the child to have already been born. The doctrine is expressed in the maxim *nasciturus pro iam nato habetur quotiens de eius commodo agitur*, meaning that provided the child is ultimately born alive, the child *in utero* is deemed to already have been born in matters to the child's advantage.[60] Thus, although the child does not acquire title to sue until birth, the child may then sue in respect of antenatal injuries caused by a delictual wrong. The same principal applies where a child born posthumously claims as a relative of a deceased under s.4 of the Damages (Scotland) Act 2011. An example would be where the unborn child's father dies before the child's birth from injuries sustained in a road accident caused by the defender's negligence.[61] Usually the action will be pursued on behalf of the child by a parent, although where necessary (e.g. if the parent is a defender) the court may appoint a curator ad litem to look after the interests of the child.

---

[54] Note the different use of the word "interest" here from its use in the phrase "title and interest". Here the word denotes the extent of the connection between the pursuer and the *property* in question, rather than the connection between the pursuer and the *outcome* sought in the action for reparation. Having said that, it is clearly the case that the pursuer's interest in the property and the pursuer's interest in the outcome of the action are directly connected.

[55] *North Scottish Helicopters v United Technologies Inc*, 1988 S.L.T. 77 at 79 per Lord Davidson. See also *Blackburn v Sinclair*, 1984 S.L.T. 368 at 369 per Lord Allanbridge; *Mull Shellfish Ltd v Golden Sea Produce Ltd* 1992 S.L.T. 703.

[56] *North Scottish Helicopters v United Technologies Inc*, 1988 S.L.T. 77 at 81 per Lord Davidson.

[57] Nevertheless, the pursuer could not prove fault and the action ultimately failed.

[58] See, e.g. *Hand v North of Scotland Water Authority*, 2002 S.L.T. 798.

[59] Foetus is the term normally used in legal discussions but strictly speaking denotes the three to nine month period after conception, before which the term used by the scientist is embryo.

[60] Bankton, I, i, 7; *Elliot v Lord Joicey*, 1935 S.C. (HL) 57; *Cohen v Shaw*, 1992 S.L.T. 1022; *Hamilton v Fife Health Board* 1993 S.C. 369.

[61] *Cohen v Shaw*, 1992 S.L.T. 1022.

In such cases the law thus deems the concurrence of *injuria* (to the child) and *damnum* to occur at the time of birth.[62] At first sight this may appear to trigger the three-year limitation period, however, the commencement of the triennium is delayed until the child reaches his 16th birthday.[63] If the child is born alive, but dies before an action is brought, the child's right to sue for damages transmits to his executor under s.2 of the Damages (Scotland) Act 2011. However, if the child is not born alive, there will be no concurrence of *injuria* and *damnum*—in other words it will be a case of *injuria sine damno*—and so no action may be pursued against the wrongdoer.[64] Since the stillborn child never acquired a legal right to sue, no right transmits to an executor under s.2 of the Damages (Scotland) Act 2011, and no damages may be claimed by a relative under s.4.[65]

Thus, if a pregnant woman is involved in a road traffic accident and her unborn child is injured, any action with regard to the unborn child's physical injuries will only be competent if the child is born alive, and will remain competent even if the child subsequently succumbs to those injuries or dies from another cause, provided the child was alive when born. The action remains competent even if the accident was the fault of the unborn child's father or mother. If, however, the child is killed within the womb, no action is competent with regard to the child's injuries or death, whether brought on behalf of the stillborn child, or by the parents as relatives. Nevertheless, the mother will be entitled to damages for the loss of her baby if she miscarries as a result of the defender's wrongful conduct.

Given that in Scots law a foetus as such has no title to sue, it follows that no action may be taken to protect a foetus from a lawful abortion. In *Kelly v Kelly*,[66] a husband sought interdict to prevent his wife from terminating her pregnancy. It was accepted that, in general, interdict would be competent upon application by a person's representative in order to prevent harm occurring to that person where, if the harm did occur, it could be compensated in an action for damages. However, because the foetus enjoyed no right to continued incubation within the womb, no action for damages could be competent unless and until the foetus was eventually born alive. Thus the application for interdict was refused. It may be noted that the decision was made in the context of termination being permitted by the law,[67] and there was some discussion of the incompatibility of an interdict with a woman's "right" to terminate or with her autonomy in choosing to engage in other forms of lawful activity, such as smoking. However, there was no discussion of whether an interdict could be granted to prevent the mother from engaging in activity which would amount to an unequivocally delictual, or criminal, wrong which would likely cause harm to the foetus, such as the intentional consumption of illegal drugs carrying a known risk of injury to the foetus. Nevertheless, following the ratio of the decision, since no action for damages is competent unless the child is born alive, an interdict intending to

---

[62] *Hamilton v Fife Health Board*, 1993 S.C. 369.

[63] Prescription and Limitation (Scotland) Act 1973 s.17(3). If the child is incapax the right to sue is subject to neither prescription nor limitation, although where proceedings are delayed the defender may attempt to plead mora and taciturnity: see, e.g. *D's Curator Bonis v Lothian Health Board*, 2010 S.L.T. 725.

[64] If the mother also suffered injury as a consequence of the wrongful act, the competence of her own action with regard to her own injuries will not be affected.

[65] See *Hamilton v Fife Health Board*, 1993 S.C. 369.

[66] *Kelly v Kelly*, 1997 S.C. 285.

[67] Abortion Act 1967.

prevent the pregnant woman from engaging in activity which would amount to a wrong vis-à-vis the child if it was born alive would appear to be incompetent.

Kelly[68] confirms that a foetus as such has no right to a continued existence. A **3–09** related question is whether the very existence of a foetus could involve a wrong to the unborn child—in other words, can a person assert a right never to have existed? At the time of writing the limited jurisprudence that exists, often described collectively as "wrongful life" cases, confirms the answer to be "no".[69] This conclusion is clearly motivated by various public policy factors, including the divergence of views on when life begins and on abortion generally, as well as on priorities if continuing the pregnancy risks the life of the pregnant woman. Thus, a foetus enjoys no protection derived from the European Convention on Human Rights.[70] So, although the essence of art.8 of the European Convention on Human Rights is to protect human dignity,[71] since a foetus as such does not enjoy the rights provided by the European Court of Human Rights, the resulting child will be precluded from claiming that their art.8 rights were breached by allowing the birth. Furthermore, both domestic courts and the European Court of Human Rights have confirmed that art.2 of the European Convention on Human Rights, which explicitly confers a right to life, does not implicitly confer a right to die.[72] It follows that if an existing human being does not enjoy an autonomous right in law to determine their continued existence, a putative human being does not enjoy a right in law to determine whether or not they come into existence in the first place. Thus, if there is no right to assert, there can be no infringement of that right and therefore no delictual wrong.

Although not directly in point, the case of *P's Curator Bonis v Criminal Injuries Compensation Board*[73] is consistent with this reasoning. An application had been made to the CICB on behalf of a child born with incapacitating physical and mental abnormalities attributed to the consanguinity of the parents: the child had been conceived upon the rape of the mother by her own father. The CICB had rejected the claim and this decision was challenged in proceedings for judicial review. Lord Osborne's judgment is valuable for its wide-ranging review of cases from Scotland, England, the Commonwealth and the United States, but the *ratio* focused on *damnum* and concluded that a definition of injury depends upon "a pre-injury state that is capable of assessment and comparison with the post-injury state." Here, there was no comparable "pre-injury state" as the child had not and could not have had any life other than "a defective state".

Complications may be anticipated if the parent of an unborn child injured *in utero* claims damages for psychiatric injury attributed to witnessing the injury or suffering the loss of the baby.[74] If the child is stillborn the mother's claim may be brought as a primary victim on the basis that her psychiatric injury is

---

[68] *Kelly v Kelly*, 1997 S.C. 285.

[69] *McKay v Essex Area Health Authority* [1982] Q.B. 1166; *P's Curator Bonis v Criminal Injuries Compensation Board*, 1997 S.L.T. 1180. Note that *McKay* confirms that the pregnant woman is nevertheless owed a duty of care by her obstetrician: see also *McLelland v Greater Glasgow Health Board*, 2001 S.L.T. 446.

[70] *Paton v United Kingdom* (8416/78) (1981) 3 E.H.R.R. 408.

[71] *Pretty v United Kingdom* (2346/02) [2002] 2 F.L.R. 45; *R. (Purdy) v DPP* [2010] 1 A.C. 345.

[72] *R. (Pretty) v DPP* [2002] 1 A.C. 800; *Pretty v United Kingdom* (2346/02) [2002] 2 F.L.R. 45.

[73] *P's Curator Bonis v Criminal Injuries Compensation Board*, 1997 S.L.T. 1180. See also *McKay v Essex Area Health Authority* [1982] Q.B. 1166.

[74] Liability for psychiatric injury is covered in detail at paras 11–44 to 11–63 below.

derivative to the pain and suffering she has suffered in miscarrying.[75] However, if the pursuer is the father, he will be classified as a secondary victim and may have some difficulty in satisfying the "control mechanisms", at least if the child is stillborn. In particular, he must show that he had a relationship involving close ties of love and affection with the primary victim—but if the foetus was stillborn then, given the limits of the *nasciturus* doctrine,[76] the unborn child may not be viewed as a primary victim.[77] Furthermore, if the action was pursued by one parent against the other, issues of the sort explored by Cazalet J. in *Greatorex v Greatorex*[78] may raise policy reasons for discouraging interfamilial litigation. Another potential hurdle, especially where the child was born alive, would be in questioning whether the psychiatric injury was triggered by shock, i.e. a sudden appreciation by sight and sound of a horrifying event which suddenly and violently agitated the mind.[79]

Children

3–10   Upon birth, a child is entitled to all the protections due to a human being, and may thus be entitled to a remedy in delict. Young children are clearly more vulnerable to accidents and injury than mature adults and their vulnerability must be taken into consideration in determining what precautions are reasonable in negligence cases,[80] and parents and guardians will be expected to take reasonable steps to protect their offspring from obvious dangers.[81] Although the law of delict as such was not altered by the Age of Legal Capacity Scotland Act 1990, s.2 provides that a person aged under 16 will have capacity to instruct a solicitor and to bring or defend legal proceedings, provided that person has a general understanding of what it means to do so; and it is to be presumed that a person has such understanding upon reaching the age of 12. If a victim of an alleged delictual act has not yet achieved capacity to sue, either the child's parent may pursue proceedings on the child's behalf or the court may appoint a curator ad litem to safeguard the interests of the child. There is no legal rule that prevents a child from suing a parent.[82]

Living human tissue[83]

3–11   The fundamental question here is the extent to which the law recognises that one enjoys rights over one's own body or body parts. One might intuitively refer to "my body" or "my leg" but does that intuition actually reflect the legal

---

[75] This is consistent with the House of Lords' confirmation of liability to the mother in *McFarlane v Tayside Health Board*, 2000 S.C. 1.

[76] The child is only deemed born in matters *affecting his own interest*. Here, it is the parent's interest that is engaged.

[77] Although damages have been awarded for a shock reaction to discovering damage to "property": see *Attia v British Gas Plc* [1988] Q.B. 304; *Yearworth v North Bristol NHS Trust* [2010] Q.B. 1. The "property" in the latter case was donated sperm. See also *Holdich v Lothian Health Board*, 2014 S.L.T. 495.

[78] *Greatorex v Greatorex* [2000] 4 All E.R. 769.

[79] See, e.g. *Walters v North Glamorgan NHS Trust* [2003] P.I.Q.R. P2. Cf. *W v Essex CC* [2001] 2 A.C. 592.

[80] See, e.g. *Taylor v Glasgow Corp*, 1922 S.C. (HL) 1.

[81] *Hardie v Sneddon*, 1917 S.C. 1.

[82] *Young v Rankin*, 1934 S.C. 499.

[83] See generally, N.R. Whitty, "Rights of Personality, property rights and the human body in Scots law" (2005) 9 Edin. L.R. 194. See also below at fn.137.

position? Damages may be awarded in Scots law under two heads: solatium and patrimonial loss. Solatium may be awarded for pain and suffering and for affront or insult[84]; patrimonial loss reflects pecuniary losses, i.e. losses that may be quantified in financial terms such as earnings and loss of, or damage to, property. It follows that if Scots law recognises that one enjoys a property type of right to, e.g. one's leg, should one lose that leg due to the delictual wrong of another, a damages award should, in addition to solatium for pain and suffering, incorporate an amount for patrimonial loss to reflect the loss of the limb itself. It may be the case that the sum awarded in respect of patrimonial loss may include the cost of manufacturing and fitting a prosthetic leg, in which case one might argue that this is consistent with Scots law conferring rights to one's own body parts. On the other hand, if damages are intended to achieve as far as possible restitutio in integrum,[85] providing the funds to replace the lost limb is not the same as to say the law recognises that the person had a property type of right over the limb.[86]

Nevertheless, it is clear that the remedy provided in delict with regard to direct impact on the pursuer's physical integrity is confined to solatium. Thus, if the impact produces no pain and suffering, no remedy will be available.[87] This would tend to confirm that the law continues not to recognise that an individual has an ownership type of right to his or her human tissue.

It may be easier to view as property human tissue which has already been removed from the human being on which it grew. The first lock of hair trimmed from the toddler,[88] or the first baby tooth to be discarded by the child, are frequently kept as sentimental souvenirs by parents, and it is submitted that no distinction need be made between such mementoes and photographs or other keepsakes.[89]

Yearworth v North Bristol NHS Trust[90] was a recent case where this question was explored. Sperm samples produced by six men were taken into storage by the hospital as insurance against the possibility that cancer treatment which they were about to undertake could damage their fertility. Due to the negligence of the hospital the sperm samples were destroyed. The Court of Appeal in England confirmed that the damage to the sperm did not constitute personal injury and that the men were the respective owners of the sperm for the purposes both of claims in negligence and in the law of property. The Court of Appeal concluded that

---

[84] See, e.g. *Duffy v Kinneil Cannel and Coking Coal Co*, 1930 S.C. 596 at 597–598 per Lord President (Clyde).

[85] Stair I, 9, 2.

[86] "*dominus membrorum suorum nemo videtur*: no one is to be regarded as the owner of his own limbs, says Ulpian in D 9 2 13 pr": *R v Bentham* [2005] 1 W.L.R. 1057 at 1061 per Lord Rodger of Earlsferry.

[87] *Cartledge v E. Jopling & Sons Ltd* [1963] A.C. 758 at 778 per Lord Reid; *Grieves v FT Everard & Sons Ltd* [2008] 1 A.C. 281; *Wright v Stoddard International Plc*, 2008 Rep. L.R. 37. Although the decisions in *Grieves* and *Wright* regarding liability for pleural plaques has been superseded in Scots law by the Damages (Asbestos-related Conditions) (Scotland) Act 2009, the general principle remains otherwise unaltered.

[88] Hair salons have apparently become susceptible to "theft" of human hair—such is the current market for hair extensions!

[89] That said, the sentimental value of such a photograph will usually far outstrip the commercial value of the image or of any paper on which it may be printed. Thus, although it is impossible to actually achieve restitutio in integrum, solatium for affront is preferable to compensation for patrimonial loss.

[90] *Yearworth v North Bristol NHS Trust* [2010] Q.B. 1.

" ... developments in medical science now require a re-analysis of the common law's treatment of and approach to the issue of ownership of parts or products of a living human body, whether for (an action in negligence) or otherwise."

At the time of writing the matter is due to be considered in a proof before answer.[91] It is submitted that, following *Stevens v Yorkhill NHS Trust*,[92] resort to the *actio injuriarum* to support solatium for affront will provide sufficient justification for a remedy without the need to engage in a property-based analysis.

Relationships

3–12   Humans form a variety of relationships with others. Some of these will be contractual, others personal, some of which will involve a degree of legal formality, including civil partnerships and marriage. At common law married spouses could not sue each other in delict. This anachronism was removed by s.2 of the Law Reform (Husband and Wife) Act 1962. It is now the case that an individual's ability to sue and be sued will be neither restricted nor expanded by personal relationships per se. Thus, spouses may sue each other, as may civil partners; parents may sue their children and vice versa.[93] One spouse is not as such vicariously liable for the delicts of the other, nor in general is a parent as such vicariously liable for delicts committed by a child.[94]

Although in theory the father of an unborn child is so closely affected by the termination of a pregnancy that he may claim to be a victim, in practice the father will be unable to prevent a legal abortion proceeding given the overriding right of the pregnant woman to terminate the pregnancy.[95]

A person who enjoys a relationship with the victim of a delictual wrong may complain that he or she suffers personal harm as a consequence of the harm suffered by the victim him or herself. It is submitted that such a person should be classified as a secondary victim of the wrong, the primary victim being the person who has suffered the harm as a direct consequence of the wrong. The default position at common law appears to be that, in general, secondary victims have no title to sue.[96] However, there are exceptions.

It is difficult to envisage a situation where a secondary victim will suffer involuntary physical injury as a consequence of the harm suffered by a primary victim and no case appears to have been considered on that basis.[97] However, it has been recognised that a secondary victim suffering recognised psychiatric

---

[91] See *Holdich v Lothian Health Board*, 2014 S.L.T. 495. If it is determined that the sperm remains the property of the donor, it is submitted that an action for damages may be competent under s.1(3)(b) of the Occupiers' Liability (Scotland) Act 1960: see Ch.18.

[92] *Stevens v Yorkhill NHS Trust*, 2006 S.L.T. 889. See para.3–19 below.

[93] *Wood v Wood*, 1935 S.L.T. 431.

[94] Although a parent or guardian of a child may owe a duty to supervise the child, both to the child itself and to third parties.

[95] *Kelly v Kelly*, 1997 S.C. 285; *Paton v United Kingdom* (8416/78) (1981) 3 E.H.R.R. 408.

[96] See, e.g. *Alcock v Chief Constable of South Yorkshire Police* [1992] 1 A.C. 310 at 410 per Lord Oliver of Aylmerton.

[97] Arguably a donor of bone marrow or other body matter to the injured person might be classified as a secondary victim: see, e.g. *Duffy v Lanarkshire Health Board*, 1999 S.L.T. 906.

harm does have title to sue, provided that the secondary victim satisfies the requisite "control mechanisms".[98]

Claims by secondary victims for relational economic loss have been consistently denied at common law.[99] However the Administration of Justice Act 1982 allows the recovery of an economic loss suffered by a secondary victim by providing that, unless it is expressly agreed that no sum shall be payable, services rendered to an injured person by a relative will be a head of loss allowing recovery of reasonable remuneration and repayment of reasonable expenses.[100] Note that it is not competent to claim under s.8 if the secondary victim and the wrongdoer are one and the same, e.g. where a spouse can no longer provide personal services to the partner who was responsible for the accident in which the spouse was injured.[101] The Act also allows damages to be paid to compensate for the inability of the injured person to continue in delivering gratuitous personal services to a relative.[102] Nevertheless, the title to sue approach is respected by refusing the relative who suffers the economic loss title to sue. Instead the loss is recovered in a claim made by the injured person, who is placed under an obligation to account to the person suffering the loss.

Section 4 of the Damages (Scotland) Act 2011 provides for liability to pay damages for loss of support, distress, grief and loss of society to certain relatives of a deceased whose death is attributable to personal injuries for which the defender is, or would be but for the death, liable.[103]

Parenthood and wrongful birth

A medical practitioner will owe a duty of care to a pregnant woman (and her **3–13** partner) to carry out tests and provide information related to physical or mental defects in the foetus so as to enable the woman or couple to consider a termination.[104] Breach of this duty will permit a claim for damages for solatium in respect of the shock, stress and psychiatric wear and tear suffered by the parents on discovery of the defect in the child upon birth, as well as the additional costs in providing for the child (into adulthood if relevant) associated with the physical or mental condition. However, applying the *McFarlane*[105] principle, it would not be fair, just and reasonable to recover costs associated with the rearing of a healthy child.[106] On the other hand, the "conventional award" applied in

---

[98] *Alcock v Chief Constable of South Yorkshire Police* [1992] 1 A.C. 310; *White v Chief Constable of South Yorkshire* [1999] 2 A.C. 455.

[99] *Robertson v Turnbull*, 1982 S.L.T. 96. See also *D v East Berkshire Community Health NHS Trust* [2005] 2 A.C. 273 at 412–416 per Lord Rodger of Earlsferry.

[100] Administration of Justice Act 1982 s.8.

[101] *Kozikowska v Kozikowski*, 1996 S.L.T. 386. See also *Hunt v Severs* [1994] 2 A.C. 350.

[102] Administration of Justice Act 1982 s.9. See also *Ingham v John G Russell (Transport) Ltd*, 1991 S.C. 201.

[103] See para.3–18 below.

[104] See, e.g. *Anderson v Forth Valley Health Board*, 1998 S.L.T. 588; *McLelland v Greater Glasgow Health Board*, 2001 S.L.T. 446.

[105] *McFarlane v Tayside Health Board*, 2000 S.C. (HL) 1. See paras 11–67 to 11–70 below.

[106] *McLelland v Greater Glasgow Health Board*, 2001 S.L.T. 446. This case was one of a wanted child. It is submitted that it is important to see this case with its powerful dissent and to read it against the background that Lord Marnoch, on the evidence in this case that the parents agreed that they took pleasure from the child, was compelled to follow *McFarlane*.

Rees v Darlington Memorial Hospital NHS Trust[107] has not replaced damages awards in wrongful birth claims.

Bankruptcy and sequestration

3–14　　Bankruptcy takes the estate into the hands of the trustee subject to the exceptions in the Act.[108] So far as natural persons are concerned, the debtor retains title and interest to sue for personal wrongs such as assault, unintentional personal injury or defamation.[109] However, the litigation becomes an asset belonging to the estate, and so the trustee in bankruptcy has title and interest to sue and if the bankrupt recovers compensation, the damages go to the estate.[110] It may be that a person whose estates are insolvent has no title to sue unless he can show that the trustee and the creditors have abandoned a claim.[111] In *Watson v Thompson*,[112] the Inner House held that once the action was raised it lost its personal character and vested in the trustee. Thus, the trustee in bankruptcy was entitled to be sisted as a party in a claim for solatium raised by the debtor after his sequestration in respect of injuries sustained before his sequestration.

It should always be remembered that although a person whose estates have been made bankrupt may be discharged, his estate might still be subject to the administration of the trustee. Thus, in *Coutts Trustee v Coutts*,[113] a trustee sought a declarator that the debtor's right to solatium in a claim vested in the trustee and that the trustee should receive that sum. The debtor was injured, then sequestrated. He raised his action before he was automatically discharged, and following discharge he settled his action. The Inner House found in favour of the trustee.

Adults with incapacity

3–15　　Although an incapax person is entitled to all of the protections provided for by the law, a person who is insane lacks title to sue in his or her own name. Prior to the implementing of the Adults with Incapacity (Scotland) Act 2000, a curator bonis appointed by the court could raise proceedings on behalf of an insane person. Proceedings may now be brought on behalf of an incapacitated adult by a person with power of attorney or a guardian appointed by a guardianship order.

The terminally ill

3–16　　The terminally ill are as entitled to the protection of the law as all others. Cases arise where out of duty or affection, it is sought to bring to an end the life of a person who is in distress. Much like the foetus cases, these cases raise moral, ethical, religious, political and economic questions. In considering euthanasia there is some symmetry with abortion, which has now legalised what was killing. The delict system is involved because there is likely to be sought either a

---

[107] *Rees v Darlington Memorial Hospital NHS Trust* [2004] 1 A.C. 309.
[108] Bankruptcy (Scotland) Act 1985, as amended.
[109] *Muir's Trustee v Braidwood*, 1958 S.C. 169.
[110] *Jackson v MacKenzie* (1875) 3 R. 130.
[111] *Grindall v John Mitchell (Grangemouth) Ltd*, 1984 S.L.T. 335.
[112] *Watson v Thompson*, 1991 S.C. 447.
[113] *Coutts Trustee v Coutts*, 1998 S.C. 798.

declarator that to take a certain course is not a legal wrong or an interdict to prevent certain steps. The party to the action may therefore be a relative or a doctor seeking declarator, or a relative or other seeking an interdict. The wrong in question, of course, need not be a delict as such. For interdict or declarator, "wrong" is enough. However, if neither procedure were followed, then a claim for compensation for the euthanasia of relative would be a case of reparation, if it has not already attracted the criminal law.

The leading case in Scotland is a decision of a five-bench court in *Law Hospital NHS Trust v Lord Advocate*.[114] A patient had suffered from irreversible damage to the cerebral cortex and had been in a persistent vegetative state in the hospital since 1992. She had no prospect of recovery and was unable to give a valid consent. She remained alive only because feeding and hydration were provided to her artificially and because of the nursing care she received in hospital. Medical experts considered her case hopeless and there were no useful avenues of treatment to explore. The family agreed with the experts that the treatment should stop. The hospital sought declarator that the cessation of treatment was lawful and would not constitute a delict or crime. The Lord Advocate appeared as defender in the public interest along with the curator ad litem to the patient. The main issue in the case was jurisdiction. A full bench of the Court of Session agreed the court did have *parens patriae* jurisdiction[115] in civil matters[116] such as this where there was no one to consent. The Inner House delegated the decision to the Lord Ordinary (Cameron), who followed the leading English case on withdrawal of treatment[117] and granted declarator.[118] For the law of delict, the main point is that made by Lord Clyde. It is no part of a doctor's duty to continue treatment which serves no purpose beyond the artificial prolongation of existence. They would be in no breach of their general duty of care to the patient in discontinuing such treatment in such circumstances and the substance of their continuing duty would be towards securing the comfort and dignity of the patient for the concluding days of the patient's life.[119] The important and difficult ethical issues involved prompted Lord Milligan to echo a call for legislation[120] made previously in the *Bland* case.[121]

---

[114] *Law Hospital NHS Trust v Lord Advocate*, 1996 S.C. 301.

[115] Thus any authority granted by the court would in law be the equivalent of consent given by the patient.

[116] The Inner House confirmed it had no jurisdiction to deal with questions related to criminal law.

[117] *Airedale NHS Trust v Bland* [1993] A.C. 789; *L, Petitioner*, 1996 S.C.L.R. 538 was approved.

[118] *Law Hospital NHS Trust v Lord Advocate (No.2)*, 1996 S.L.T. 869.

[119] *Law Hospital NHS Trust v Lord Advocate*, 1996 S.C. 301 at 321. See also *R. (Burke) v General Medical Council* [2006] Q.B. 273. For further discussion of the issues raised by withdrawal of treatment and euthanasia referring to English authority since *Bland*, see J. Keown, "Beyond Bland: a critique of the BMA guidelines on withholding and withdrawing medical treatment," (2000) 20 L.S. 66; D. Price, "Fairly Bland: an alternative view of a supposed new 'death ethic' and the BMA guidelines," (2001) 4 L.S. 618; S. McLean and D. Morgan, "Choosing death or life: law, medicine and patient's rights". Also see, British Medical Association, *The BMA's Handbook of Ethics and Law*, 3rd edn (Oxford: Blackwell, 2012).

[120] *Law Hospital NHS Trust v Lord Advocate*, 1996 S.C. 301 at 329. Although "best interests" is dealt with in s.4 of the Mental Capacity Act 2005, this applies only within England and Wales. The Adults with Incapacity (Scotland) Act 2000 does not deal directly with the issue.

[121] *Airedale NHS Trust v Bland* [1993] A.C. 789 at 878 per Lord Browne-Wilkinson; at 891 per Lord Mustill.

The deceased

3–17   Where a person is killed by the wrongful act of another, no action can be brought in respect of the death itself by the deceased's executor. Nevertheless, upon death rights to recover damages in respect of injuries suffered before death[122] transmit to the executor.[123] However, an exception applies to actions with regard to injuries to name and reputation, i.e. defamation and related actions.[124]

Ironically, a literal reading of the maxim "one cannot defame the dead" is oxymoronic! In reality the law generally permits one to defame the dead with impunity, a problem where people take insults upon their kin or clan seriously.[125] In *Broom v Ritchie & Co*[126] a widow on her own behalf and for her children sought damages for defamation for the publication in the press of a false statement that her late husband had committed suicide.[127] She claimed solatium only. The defenders pleaded, inter alia, no title to sue. The Lord Ordinary (Kincairney) sustained the plea primarily on the basis of there being no clear principle on which the case was based, and only some very old doubtful authority to support it. The pursuer reclaimed and the court adhered to the Lord Ordinary's judgment. The Lord Justice-Clerk (MacDonald) said that "an aspersion on a person after death cannot, I hold, give right to anyone else to recover damages as for a wrong done to the deceased."[128] However, it was thought that a slander against the character of a deceased person, which by necessary implication injured others (e.g. the deceased's children), would give those persons a right to sue for the effect on their status or patrimonial interests. But this case was for solatium only.[129]

In *Agnew v Laughlan*,[130] the pursuer sought reduction of a sheriff's order under which his now deceased wife had been detained in an asylum, and of certain certificates by medical practitioners. He brought the action both as an individual and as tutor of his son. The sheriff's order was said to be wrongfully obtained and the doctor's certificates were said to be false and inaccurate. The wife had just given birth and died a few days later. After a procedure roll debate it was held by the Lord Ordinary (MacKintosh) that the pursuer had no title to sue as the document sought to be reduced had long since been spent and inoperative. The action was dismissed. Any prejudice to the pursuer or to his son attaching to the family was too vague and remote to found a patrimonial interest. Any stigma

---

[122] This includes injuries arising from any delictual act, whether or not that delictual act has any causal connection with the death. Where the delictual act shortens the expected life of the victim, damages are payable for the suffering anticipated in the victim's loss of expectation of life: Damages (Scotland) Act 2011 s.1. For a discussion on the application of this provision where the victim realises death will be an immediate consequence of the incident experienced see *Beggs v Motherwell Bridge Fabricators Ltd*, 1998 S.L.T. 1215 at 1223–1224 per Lord Eassie.

[123] Damages (Scotland) Act 2011 s.2. See below at para.5–19.

[124] Which generally may only be continued by an executor if the action was already pursued before death: Damages (Scotland) Act 2011 s.2(3). The executor may also pursue an appeal provided that would be competent if the deceased was still alive.

[125] See para.7–04 below.

[126] *Broom v Ritchie & Co* (1904) 6 F. 942.

[127] It being remembered that then, much more so than now, suicide carried a stigma and indeed was a crime in England.

[128] *Broom v Ritchie & Co* (1904) 6 F. 942 at 945.

[129] Note that Lord Young agreed with the result but not with the reasoning of the Lord Ordinary or the other judges of the Division. He thought the claim irrelevant on the facts.

[130] *Agnew v Laughlan*, 1948 S.L.T. 512.

attending to relatives of the deceased because she was put in an asylum was irrelevant. The right to sue for defamation was the deceased's alone and no claim for defamation arises after the death of the defamed.[131]

Relatives of the deceased victim

The Damages (Scotland) Act 2011 permits two distinct claims from relatives **3–18** of a victim whose death was caused by the delictual wrong.[132] A range of relatives may claim for loss of support,[133] and the victim's immediate family will have an additional claim in respect of the emotional consequences of anticipating and experiencing the death of the victim and for loss of society of the victim. The deceased's immediate family is defined as[134]:

- spouse or civil partner, or living with the deceased as if spouse or civil partner;
- parent or child, or accepted as such, of the deceased;
- brother or sister, or brought up as an accepted child of the family in the same household in which the deceased was a child; and
- grandparent or grandchild, or accepted as such, of the deceased.

For the purposes of a claim for emotional harm associated with the victim's death and for loss of society, the definition of relative extends to[135]:

- other ascendants and descendants;
- uncles and aunts and their descendants;
- the descendants of brothers and sisters of the deceased; and
- former spouses or civil partners of the deceased.

There are several caveats. The relative's claim can be no more competent in law than a claim that could have been brought by the victim. Thus, the victim's death must be directly attributable to a delictual wrong, and any defences available against the victim's claim may be deployed by the defender in a claim brought by a relative. Thus, damages may be excluded by, e.g. a successful plea of volenti non fit injuria or reduced by a successful plea of contributory negligence. Subject to an exception in mesothelioma cases,[136] a relative's claim will be excluded if the victim had before death settled the claim or pursued an action to completion.

---

[131] The Scottish Government published a consultation paper, "Death of a Good Name, Defaming the Deceased" in January 2011. Following receipt of responses, no change in the law was proposed.

[132] See also below at paras 5–19 to 5–21.

[133] Damages (Scotland) Act 2011 s.4(3). Section 6 permits a claim under this head to include a reasonable sum with regard to the loss of personal services from the deceased.

[134] Damages (Scotland) Act 2011 ss.4(5) and 14.

[135] Damages (Scotland) Act 2011 s.14.

[136] Damages (Scotland) Act 2011 s.5. This exception permits a relative's claim for emotional harm and for loss of society where the victim has already settled a claim with the defender. A claim for loss of support remains excluded, it being accommodated in a claim brought by the victim prior to death under s.1.

Cadavers and body parts[137]

3–19   Although the position is not certain, there is some authority that there is
sufficient property in a corpse for it to be capable of being stolen.[138] Whether
there is property in the corpse for other purposes is open to question[139]—and a
further question would concern who owned the cadaver, or at least had rights
with regard to it in priority over others.[140] It is worth noting that normally the
social priority will be in disposing of the body, and courts are keen not to allow
litigation to sidetrack that priority.[141] Nevertheless it is legitimately a title to sue
matter in a delict case for say wrongful intromission or spuilzie of the corpse.

Families in particular often have views as to what should or should not happen
to parts after death as to individuals in life. The Human Tissue (Scotland) Act
2006 regulates consent for organ transplants, post-mortem examinations and
organ retention, providing for criminal sanctions in the event of breach. The
delictual situation remains unaffected.

Following the emergence in the late 1990s that unauthorised removal and
retention of organs from deceased children had been routinely carried out at
Bristol Royal Infirmary and at Alder Hey Children's Hospital in Liverpool, a
group action was brought in England.[142] The court affirmed that English law did
not recognise property in a corpse and thus held that there was no tort as such of
wrongful interference with the body of the child. The court did accept that a duty
of care would be owed in negligence if a doctor-patient type of relationship

---

[137] See generally, Skene, "Proprietary Rights in human bodies, body parts and tissue: regulatory
contexts and proposals for new laws" (2002) 22 L.S. 102. Skene reports that the term "body
parts" was defined for the purposes of the interim report of the inquiry into the management and
care of children receiving complex heart surgery, to include tissue, organs and parts of organs and
amputated limbs. Skene thinks it best to keep tissue preserved in glass slides as a separate concept
(102, fn.1). Brownsword reports that the Convention for the Protection of Human Rights and
Dignity of the Human Being with regard to the application of Biology and Medicine: Convention
on Human Rights and Biomedicine (1996) defines body parts as including "organs and tissues
proper, including blood," but excluding "hair and nails, which are discarded tissues, and the sale
of which is not an affront to human dignity." Brownsword, "Freedom of Contract, Human Rights
and Human Dignity," in Friedman and Barak-Erez, *Human Rights in Private Law* (2001),
p.190.

[138] *Dewar v HM Advocate (No.2)*, 1945 J.C. 5. Recently in England an artist who stole old body parts
from the Royal College of Surgeons to draw them was convicted of theft: *R v Kelly* [1998] 3 All
E.R. 741.

[139] See, e.g. the Independent Review Group on the Retention of Organs at Post-Mortem in Scotland
(the "McLean Report"), para.113: "Can human tissue be sold or otherwise transferred to the
ownership of another in Scots law? In principle, there is no reason why it may not - always
provided that it is not an organ. No Scottish court has ruled on the question of whether human
tissue can or cannot be owned, although Roman law (which has considerably influenced Scots
law) suggests that it cannot be. There is no authority to the contrary in any institutional writings
of Scots law. If human tissue is a *res* (a thing), then it can only be excluded from the normal civil
law rules if it is deemed to be *extra commercium*. A court might declare human tissue to be *extra
commercium* on grounds of principle, but that would have the result of effectively excluding the
legal protection of the sale of any medicinal product which was manufactured from human bodily
materials, unless the critical factor was not the origin of the materials, but rather the way in which
they had been processed or treated." See also J.K. Mason and G.T. Laurie, "Consent or property:
Dealing with the body and its parts in the shadow of the Bristol and Alder Hey," (2001) Mod.
L.R. 710.

[140] The question of priority between interested parties in the context of contested place of burial was
considered, without reaching a conclusion, in *C. v Advocate General of Scotland*, 2012 S.L.T.
103.

[141] See, e.g. *Buchanan v Milton* [1999] 53 B.M.L.R. 176 at 186 per Hale J.

[142] *AB v Leeds Teaching Hospital NHS Trust* [2005] Q.B. 506.

existed between the claimant (as opposed to the child) and the doctor and in such cases there could be liability for the claimant's psychiatric injury if that was sufficiently foreseeable.

The furore spread to Scotland, and the court became involved in *Stevens v Yorkhill NHS Trust*.[143] Following the death of her month old daughter, the pursuer had been persuaded to consent to a post-mortem examination upon being informed its purpose would be to help other babies born with a similar abnormality. The pursuer was not informed that organs might be removed or retained, and only found out that her daughter's brain and other tissue had in fact been removed and retained when she made enquiries following the eruption of the Alder Hey scandal. Reflecting the decision in *AB*, the court held that the pursuer was owed a duty of care, though not by analogy with a doctor-patient relationship. The fact that the doctor had sought her permission for a post-mortem was in itself sufficient to create the duty of care.[144] The court also held that the pursuer was a primary victim in the context of a claim for psychiatric injury, there being "force in the argument that the children were not primary victims".[145]

Perhaps of more significance is that the court accepted an alternative ground which permitted the case to proceed. Reviewing some early 20th century authority,[146] and noting that the decisions had not been superseded by statute, the court held that an independent legal wrong of unauthorised removal and retention of organs[147] from a cadaver was part of the law of Scotland. The court recognised that damages would be by solatium and that the true juridical basis of this type of claim was in the *actio injuriarum*. Thus, there is no need to consider such a claim from a property perspective.

There are also emerging issues, again initially of the law of property, in relation to DNA.[148] Bringing this section around full circle, there has *reportedly* been a tort action for conversion by a woman of the plaintiff's sperm where he alleged she became intentionally pregnant.[149]

Title to sue: non-natural persons

As a general principle, provided that a non-natural person is deemed by the **3–20** law to have sufficient legal personality, it will have sufficient legal status to sue in delict. Thus, an incorporated body, whether incorporated by Royal Charter, by statute, by registration under the Companies Acts or otherwise, may sue (and be

---

[143] *Stevens v Yorkhill NHS Trust*, 2006 S.L.T. 889.

[144] The application of the tri-partite test from *Caparo Industries Plc v Dickman* [1990] 2 A.C. 605 led to the conclusion that a free-standing duty of care was owed.

[145] *Stevens v Yorkhill NHS Trust*, 2006 S.L.T. 889 at 904 per Temporary Judge C.J. Macauley QC.

[146] *Pollok v Workman* (1900) 2 F. 354; *Conway v Dalziel* (1901) 3 F. 318; *Hughes v Robertson*, 1913 S.C. 394.

[147] The unauthorised removal (and retention) would be unlawful only if the purpose of the post-mortem was non-diagnostic or if the diagnostic purpose had been fulfilled.

[148] See, e.g. *Moore v Regents of the University of California*, 793 P. 2d 479 Cal. S.C. (1990), discussed in Skene, "Proprietary Rights in human bodies, body parts and tissue: regulatory contexts and proposals for new laws" (2002) 22 L.S. 102.

[149] See S. Sheldon, "'Sperm bandits', birth control fraud and the battle of the sexes" (2001) 21 L.S. 460. The author lists reported cases from the United States on other grounds such as fraud, deceit and misrepresentation in fn.11. See a peripheral discussion in *Bell v McCurdie*, 1981 S.C. 64.

sued) in its own name provided the wrong is done to the organisation itself.[150] The same is true of unincorporated bodies including partnerships, trade unions, clubs and associations. It is probably the case that clubs and associations can, as such, sue their members in delict, even although vice versa is not.[151] The Lord Advocate may sue on behalf of the Crown.[152] In general some patrimonial interest must be averred and proved[153]: since a non-natural person cannot have hurt feelings or suffer affront, solatium cannot be awarded.[154] Nevertheless, a non-natural person can be injured in its reputation.

In a particularly principled decision, it has been held in England that a local authority cannot sue for defamation at all.[155] The reason is to confirm that criticism of the authority is an important civil right. Lord Keith followed with approval some American decisions, one as old as 1923,[156] in coming to the conclusion that English law would not permit such an action: "Every citizen has a right to criticise an inefficient or corrupt government without fear of civil as well as criminal prosecution."[157] It was appreciated that the truth might be known, but no evidence available to substantiate it and thus the immunity was necessary to allow criticism to be made. Lord Keith agreed with Lord Goff in the "Spycatcher" case[158] that so far as the law of England was concerned, it was in concert with art.10 of the European Court of Human Rights.

Administrators, liquidators and receivers

3-21   Administration is now the preferred process for dealing with failing companies and LLPs. The principal objective of administration is to rescue the company as a going concern, and a company in administration will be subject to the control of an administrator. The administrator has general power to do all such things as may be necessary for the management of the affairs, business and property of the company,[159] including the power to bring or defend any action or other legal proceedings in the name and on behalf of the company.[160] Thus, no proceedings for reparation can proceed without the permission of the administrator or the court.[161]

Receivership is an increasingly rare procedure where a receiver is appointed by a creditor of a company who enjoys a floating charge over the whole of the

---

[150] See, e.g. *Duke v University of Salford* [2013] E.L.R. 259; *Scottish Australian Emigration Society v Borland* (1855) 18 D. 239; *Dunnett v Mitchell* (1887) 15 R. 131. Even where the non-natural person had not yet come into existence at the time when the delictual wrong was committed, if the not-yet-formed juristic person was the intended victim or, in the case of a negligent misrepresentation made in anticipation of contracting the not-yet-formed juristic person, was the anticipated party to the contract, the non-natural person which suffers the loss once formed may nevertheless sue: *Cramaso LLP v Earl of Seafield*, 2014 S.L.T. 521.

[151] See, e.g. *Harrison v West of Scotland Kart Club*, 2004 S.C. 615 at 622 per Lord Marnoch. An analogy may be made with partnerships: see, e.g. *Blackwood v Robertson*, 1984 S.L.T. (Sh. Ct) 68; *Ross Harper & Murphy v Banks*, 2000 S.L.T. 699.

[152] See, e.g. *Lord Advocate v Scotsman Publications Ltd*, 1989 S.C. (HL) 122.

[153] See, e.g. *Highland Dancing Board v Alloa Printing Co*, 1971 S.L.T. (Sh. Ct) 50.

[154] See, e.g. *Highland Dancing Board v Alloa Printing Co*, 1971 S.L.T. (Sh. Ct) 50; *Waverley Housing Management Ltd v BBC*, 1993 G.W.D. 17–1117.

[155] *Derbyshire CC v Times Newspapers Ltd* [1993] A.C. 534.

[156] Supreme Court of Illinois: *City of Chicago v Tribune Co* (1923) 139 N.E. 86.

[157] *Derbyshire CC v Times Newspapers Ltd* [1993] A.C. 534 at 548 per Lord Keith of Kinkell.

[158] *Attorney General v Guardian Newspapers Ltd (No.2)* [1990] 1 A.C. 109.

[159] Insolvency Act 1986 Sch.B1 para.59(1).

[160] Insolvency Act 1986 Sch.1 para.5.

[161] Insolvency Act 1986 Sch.B1 paras 64(1) and 68(2).

company's assets and undertaking. Where appointed, a receiver has power to bring and defend any action or other legal proceedings in the name of and on behalf of the company.[162] In *Myles J Callaghan Ltd v Glasgow DC*,[163] it was pointed out that the action should be raised in the name of the company with an indication that the receivers were bringing it. The company is the pursuer. A failure to do so led to an action for count reckoning and payment being dismissed.[164]

Liquidation is the process of winding up a company. Upon appointment a liquidator takes over control of the company. The liquidator has general power to do all such things as may be necessary for the management of the affairs, business and property of the company, including taking proceedings for reparation on behalf of the company.[165] Thus, no proceedings for reparation can proceed without the permission of the liquidator or the court.[166]

Judicial factors

In *Thurso Building Society's Judicial Factor v Robertson*,[167] a judicial factor **3–22** appointed on the estate of an unregistered building society set up as a joint venture by five individuals in 1878 sued a solicitor in respect of alleged professional negligence. The defender pled no title to sue, arguing that there was no continuing legal persona in the joint venture, that only the descendants of the parties to the joint venture had proprietary rights and therefore title to sue, and that there had been no sequestration of the estate of the joint venture, taking the management away from the descendants. Lady Paton held that the circumstances in which a judicial factor might competently be appointed were not rigidly defined or closed. What was essential was the existence of an estate in the sense of a collection of property, rights and obligations, requiring collection, preservation, administration and distribution, for which purposes the management of the estate was entrusted by the court to the factor. In this particular case, while at the time of the alleged acts of negligence, a duty of care was owed to the descendants, who had the interests in the estate, sequestration of the estate in the sense of removing the descendants' right or title was not necessary in the circumstances, especially where the descendants had never taken steps to hold or administer any of the estate. Accordingly, the pursuer did have title to sue.

Title to sue: assignees

Once it has been accepted, as it has been in Scotland, that a right of action **3–23** vests on the wrong, the right to recover can be assigned mortis causa or inter vivos subject to the usual rules on assignation.[168] Thus, a victim can settle a claim by selling an assignation to one of several defenders who can then use the assignation to pursue the other defenders.[169] A party without title to sue may

---

[162] Insolvency Act 1986 Sch.2 para.5.

[163] *Myles J Callaghan Ltd v Glasgow DC*, 1988 S.L.T. 227.

[164] *Ritchie and Redman v EFT Industrial Ltd*, 1997 S.C.L.R. 955.

[165] Insolvency Act 1986 Sch.4 para.6.

[166] Insolvency Act 1986 ss.112–113.

[167] *Thurso Building Society's Judicial Factor v Robertson*, 2001 S.L.T. 797.

[168] *Traill & Sons Ltd v Actieselskabat Dalbeattie Ltd* (1904) 6 F. 798; *Cole-Hamilton v Boyd*, 1963 S.C. (HL) 1.

[169] *National Coal Board v Thomson*, 1959 S.C. 353 at 356; *Esso Petroleum Co Ltd v Hall Russell & Co Ltd*, 1988 S.L.T. 874 at 885.

acquire such by way of assignation.[170] Care must be taken though to consider the authorities, which suggest that a person who has been paid out has nothing to assign—a view that is probably incorrect. A full examination of assignation, reviewing the older authorities, took place in *Cole-Hamilton v Boyd*. Two straightforward rules were also therein stated:

1. if a person other than an alleged joint-wrongdoer pays a sum to obtain an assignation of the injured person's claims for damages, he can sue for the full sum which the injured person could have recovered; the sum which he paid is irrelevant; and
2. if the injured person claims and receives compensation from an alleged wrongdoer and then sues a joint-wrongdoer, his action is competent (in the absence of a full discharge which releases the defender)—but as he cannot be allowed to receive compensation twice, the sum which he has already received must be deducted from the damages which would otherwise be payable.[171]

In case of damage to the property of others[172] the issue of assignation is practically very important. An assignation should come before the action is raised to demonstrate the title to sue.[173]

In *GUS Property Management Ltd v Littlewoods Mail Order Stores Ltd*[174] a building owned by Rest Property Co Ltd (Rest) was damaged by building operations being carried out on a neighbouring property. Rest was a wholly-owned subsidiary of a company, which transferred its properties to a newly-created, wholly-owned subsidiary company, the pursuers. Rest conveyed the building in question to the pursuers for a figure representing its book value. After that, Rest assigned to the pursuers all claims competent to them arising out of the building operations. The pursuers raised an action of damages against the neighbouring proprietors and those involved in the building operations. The Inner House agreed that the action should be dismissed, both because of the title to sue having been with Rest and because, the building having been transferred at book value, there was no loss. The House of Lords reversed this decision. As a general rule, the owner of a property damaged by delict did not, by parting with it to another, lose his title or interest to pursue a claim for damages. In this particular case, the depreciation in value and the cost of reinstatement of the building were alternative approaches to estimating the damages, the appropriate measure requiring evidence.

WHO MAY BE SUED?

3–24 "Who may be sued?" poses a different question to "Who should be sued?" The latter question is the one that is most important in practice, and the answer should be identified by considering who may be *liable* in delict—determined with reference to culpa/dolus, strict liability and vicarious liability.[175] However, before

---

[170] *Nacap v Moffat Plant*, 1987 S.L.T. 221 at 224.
[171] *Cole-Hamilton v Boyd*, 1963 S.C. (HL) 1 at 14 per Lord Reid.
[172] See paras 11–40 to 11–43 above.
[173] *Symington v Campbell* (1894) 21 R. 434.
[174] *GUS Property Management Ltd v Littlewoods Mail Order Stores Ltd*, 1982 S.C. (HL) 157.
[175] See Ch.4.

there can be liability, the identified person must be capable of being sued, hence the former question.

Erskine once again provides the starting point in answering this question:

> "(E)veryone who has the exercise of reason, and so can distinguish between right and wrong, is naturally obliged to make up the damage befalling his neighbour from a wrong committed by himself."[176]

Clearly any sane, living, adult human being may be presumed to have sufficient capacity to be sued in delict. On the other hand, it is clear that non-natural persons as such do not have the exercise of reason. Nevertheless, non-natural persons may be sued where liability is strict or where they incur vicarious liability for the wrongful conduct of a human being. The specialties of different forms of organisations and other non-natural persons, including specific immunities from liability in some cases, are considered in more detail below.

It may be noted that an individual does not completely escape personal liability upon death. An action may be brought against a deceased's executor and compensation may be paid out of the deceased's estate.[177] In the case of non-natural persons, an action may be competent against a liquidator or administrator, but actions cannot in general be brought against other persons, whether natural or non-natural, just because such persons have acquired or inherited the assets of the proper defender.[178]

Children

Delictual liability of children is governed by the common law.[179] Erskine's **3–25** assertion that the natural obligation falls upon "everyone who has the exercise of reason, and so can distinguish between right and wrong"[180] suggests that whether a child has sufficient capacity to commit a delictual act should be determined on a case by case basis, i.e. on whether the specific child is sufficiently mature to enjoy the "exercise of reason" in the context of the alleged wrong.

However, the law is not clear. It has been suggested that a child aged under seven will be deemed by Scots law as too immature to attract delictual liability.[181] This is based on the civilian distinction between *infans* (aged below seven) and

---

[176] Erskine, III, 1, 13.

[177] See, e.g. *Bourhill v Young*, 1942 S.C. (HL) 78. The estate is liable only to the extent of the estate. It is worth mentioning *Thomson v Duggie*, 1949 S.L.T. (Notes) 53 in case anyone else has the same idea. There was a collision between a motor ship called *Resplendent* and another motor ship, *Marinia*. The master of the *Marinia* died suddenly some time after the accident and before action was raised. The owners of *Resplendent* brought an admiralty action in personam against the widow of the master of *Marinia* in which they claimed damages for loss due to the fault of her husband. The pursuers complained that the widow, or her solicitor, had failed to disclose who were the true representatives of the deceased. Lord Birnam dismissed the case.

[178] It may be different if culpa may be averred on the part of the person acquiring or inheriting the asset from the proper defender: see, e.g. *FC Finance v Langtry Investment Co*, 1973 S.L.T. (Sh. Ct) 11.

[179] Age of Legal Capacity (Scotland) Act 1991 s.1(3)(c).

[180] Erskine, III, 1, 13.

[181] W.J. Stewart, "A Note on the Liabiity of Pupils in Delict", 1989 S.L.T. (News) 404.

pupil.[182] However, taking into account the approach adopted by the Age of Legal Capacity (Scotland) Act 1991 to a child's capacity to consent to medical treatment and to appoint a solicitor, it is suggested that it might be appropriate for the law to apply a rebuttable presumption that a child of under seven would not have the "exercise of reason" whereas a child of over seven would. However, the conclusion in each case should take into account the nature and circumstances of the alleged delictual wrong as well as the child's own development and experience.[183] Thus, a six-year-old child may have sufficient "exercise of reason" to appreciate their responsibility to others to take care in riding a bicycle, but an eight-year-old child may not have sufficient "exercise of reason" to distinguish between right and wrong in the context of an intentional delict such as assault or nuisance. Thus, whether a child may be found to have acted out of malice should also be determined by the child's circumstances and experience. The problem is that the delict where malice is most likely to be pertinent is defamation, and in defamation law in Scotland malice is effectively an irrebuttable presumption unless the relevant communication enjoys at least qualified privilege.[184] It is inevitable that the propensity for immature children with access to social networking innocently to communicate defamatory tweets or other messages will pose a challenge for the law as it stands.

Adults with incapacity

3–26   Reverting to Erskine,[185] if an adult does not have the "exercise of reason", that person will not incur liability in delict. However, drawing a parallel with the approach of the criminal law to automatism,[186] and in delict with the defence of volenti non fit injuria,[187] if the person's incapacity is self-induced the person may be deemed as acting voluntarily and so incur liability.

When reparation was about deliberate harm, then those who could not form such an intention through alienation of reason had to be exempted from liability. Thus the law in the Digest would be correct in Scots law in such cases:

> "accordingly the question is asked whether there is an action under the *lex Aquilia* if a lunatic causes damage. Pegasus says there is not, for he asks how there can be any accountable fault in him who is out of his mind; and he is undoubtedly right."[188]

---

[182] In Scots law, a pupil is a girl under 12 or a boy under 14. Upon reaching, respectively, 12 or 14, the child becomes a minor and remains as such until reaching majority—now at age 16 under the Age of Legal Capacity (Scotland) Act 1991.

[183] Compare, e.g. *Blake v Galloway* [2004] 1 W.L.R. 2844 with *Orchard v Lee* [2009] E.L.R. 178. This would enjoy the symmetry of consistency with the approach taken by courts in deciding a child's contributory fault when dealing with a plea of contributory negligence, where the nature of the danger and the capacity of the child to appreciate the risk are considered. Compare, e.g. *Galbraith's Curator ad Litem v Stewart (No.2)*, 1998 S.L.T. 1305 (eight-year-old boy injured on building site—no contributory negligence) with *McCluskey v Wallace*, 1998 S.C. 711 (four-year-old run over in street—20 per cent contributory negligence). See also *McKinnell v White*, 1971 S.L.T. (Notes) 61.

[184] See para.7–17 below.

[185] Erskine, III, 1, 13.

[186] *Ross v HM Advocate*, 1991 J.C. 210.

[187] See, e.g. *Morris v Murray* [1991] 2 Q.B. 6.

[188] Dig. IX 2, 5, 2.

This is supported by the reasoning in *Waugh v James K. Allan Ltd.*[189] In that case, the defenders' driver who was suddenly disabled by an attack of coronary thrombosis run down a pedestrian. Lord Reid said: "One must have great sympathy with the appellant who has suffered so severely through no fault of his own, but I find it impossible to blame the driver."[190] It is voluntary human conduct that is regulated by delict. Practically, it can be seen from *Waugh* that there can be liability if the person knew or ought to have known his condition would develop.[191]

Bodies associate with state functions

In general, liability of bodies associated with the State will technically be **3–27** vicarious, on account that the relevant delictual acts will be carried out or authorised by employees or other human agents of the relevant authority or body. State, or more generally, public bodies may also incur liability under statute including strict liability. It should also be noted that bodies exercising public functions are particularly susceptible to claims, often pursued in parallel to claims in delict per se, based on breach of the European Court of Human Rights under the Human Rights Act 1998,[192] or in the case of the Scottish Parliament or Scottish Ministers, under the Scotland Act 1998.[193] On the other hand, courts will be careful to consider the wider impact on the ability of the relevant body to carry out its functions, and the impact on the community at large, in deciding whether there should be liability in delict. This is especially so in "novel" negligence cases, where courts will consider in detail whether it would be fair, just and reasonable for the law to recognise a duty of care owed through its employees by the relevant body.[194]

The law of the European Union has provided that the Government shall be responsible to its citizens for failure to carry through properly or at all certain community laws.[195]

---

[189] *Waugh v James K. Allan Ltd,* 1964 S.C. (HL) 102. See also *Mansfield v Weetabix Ltd* [1998] 1 W.L.R. 1263.

[190] *Waugh v James K. Allan Ltd,* 1964 S.C. (HL) 102 at 106.

[191] See *Roberts v Ramsbottom* [1980] 1 All E.R. 7, where a man was held liable although he had been in a state of automatism, but on the basis that he should have taken steps to prevent himself causing harm to others. And generally by comparison, see the German Civil Code: BGB 827—a person who does damage to another in a condition of unconsciousness, or in a condition of morbid disturbance of the mental activity, incompatible with a free determination of the will, is not responsible for the damage. If he had brought himself into a temporary condition of this kind by spiritous liquors or similar means, he is responsible for any damage which he unlawfully causes in this condition in the same manner as if negligence were imputable to him; the responsibility does not arise if he has been brought into this condition without fault. See B. Markesinis, *The German Law of Torts* (Oxford: Hart Publishing, 2002), p.11.

[192] s.6(1). See, e.g. *Thomson v The Scottish Ministers,* 2013 S.C. 628; *Rabone v Pennine Care NHS Foundation Trust* [2012] 2 A.C. 72; *Van Colle v Chief Constable of Hertfordshire* [2009] 1 A.C. 225. There is a direct right to reparation under s.8. This is covered in more detail in paras 2–21 to 2–28 above.

[193] ss.29(2)(d) and 57(2).

[194] See, e.g. *Mitchell v Glasgow City Council,* 2009 S.C. (HL) 21; *Smith v Ministry of Defence* [2013] 3 W.L.R. 69; *Hill v Chief Constable of West Yorkshire* [1989] A.C. 53. This is covered in more detail in Ch.17.

[195] *Francovich v Italy* (C-6/90) [1993] 2 C.M.L.R. 66. This is covered in more detail in paras 17–18 to 17–22 below.

Sovereign and state immunity

3–28   The Sovereign is immune from action.[196] Foreign sovereigns probably continue to enjoy immunity at common law, but immunity for states, heads of state, diplomats and others is now governed by statute.[197]

The Crown

3–29   Liability of the Crown is governed by the Crown Proceedings Act 1947, which generally makes the Crown vicariously liable for the actings of its agents or employees.[198] The Crown is liable both as an employer and as an occupier.[199] The Crown is bound by statute if express or by necessary implication.[200]

Normally interdicts cannot be granted against the Crown and instead declarator needs to be sought.[201] Where it is sought to prevent a breach of European Union law interdict may be appropriate.[202]

Scottish Parliament and ministers

3–30   Scotland has its own devolved Parliament.[203] In terms of the devolution legislation, the Lord Advocate and the Solicitor General for Scotland are now Scottish law officers to the Scottish Government. The Advocate General for Scotland became the adviser to the UK Government on Scottish legal matters. Since July 1, 1999 proceedings may be raised against the Parliamentary corporation,[204] although, in practice, actions on matters within the competence of the Scottish Parliament and ministers are raised either against the Scottish Ministers[205] or the Lord Advocate. Actions in UK matters are raised against the Advocate General for Scotland.[206] So far as the Scottish Parliament is concerned, the court cannot make an order for suspension, interdict, reduction or specific performance if the effect of doing so would be to give any relief against the Parliament.[207] It can, however, interdict a wrong by a member of the Scottish Parliament in the conduct of his duties under its statutes.[208]

The armed forces

3–31   Although in general no special rules apply with regard to the armed forces, the doctrine of "combat immunity" does provide that there is no liability at common law for negligence with regard to acts or omissions carried out while actually

---

[196] But this may require review: I. Dickinson, "Crown Immunities Post-1998", 2003 S.L.T. (News) 107.

[197] See, e.g. State Immunity Act 1978; Diplomatic Privileges Act 1964; Visiting Forces Act 1952; International Organisations and Defence Organisations Act 1964; International Organisations Act 2005.

[198] Historically it was necessary to seek declarator of the wrong and seek ex gratia damages.

[199] Crown Proceedings Act 1947 s.2(1) and the Occupiers' Liability (Scotland) Act s.4.

[200] Crown Proceedings Act 1947 s.2(2).

[201] Crown Proceedings Act 1947 ss.43(a) and 21(a); *Lord Advocate v SRC*, 1990 S.L.T. 158; *McDonald v Secretary of State for Scotland* 1994 S.L.T. 692.

[202] *R. v Secretary of State for Transport, Ex p. Factortame Ltd (No.2)* [1991] 1 A.C. 603.

[203] Scotland Act 1998.

[204] Scotland Act 1998 s.40(1), (2).

[205] See, e.g. *Pratt v Scottish Ministers*, 2013 S.L.T. 590.

[206] See, e.g. *King v Advocate General for Scotland* [2009] CSOH 169; 2010 G.W.D. 1–15.

[207] Scotland Act 1998 s.40(3)–(4).

[208] *Whaley v Lord Watson of Invergowrie*, 2000 S.C. 340.

engaged in armed combat.[209] In *Smith v Ministry of Defence*[210] the doctrine was treated by Lord Hope effectively as a title to sue matter; although similar reasons (in particular that the interests of the State must prevail over the interests of the individual) justify finding that it would not be fair, just or reasonable to impose a duty of care with regard to liability in negligence.[211] The doctrine has been narrowly construed, so that it does not apply to activities indirectly connected to battle, including general preparation and training, and the provision of technology and equipment.[212]

There is also the possibility of statutory immunity where the relevant injuries are certified as pensionable,[213] but an order by the Secretary of State would now be required.[214] The power to make an order is available only if it appears necessary or expedient to do so by reason of any imminent national danger, any great emergency or for the purposes of any warlike operations in any part of the world outside the United Kingdom. Thus a specific conflict must be anticipated and, to date, the power has never been used.

The police and other prosecuting authorities

The police may be sued in negligence,[215] but on a matter of policy the courts **3–32** recognise the potential for susceptibility to negligence claims distorting the focus of police activity and undermining the function of the police force in society.[216] Thus, it has been held that it would not be fair, just and reasonable to recognise a duty of care owed by the police to potential victims of crime as it would almost inevitably result in the police adopting a "detrimentally defensive frame of mind" in the carrying out of their functions.[217]

The police may be sued for wrongful detention or arrest,[218] or for malicious prosecution,[219] as may other prosecuting authorities.[220] However, the police enjoy a general immunity from liability which may be displaced only upon proof

---

[209] *Smith v Ministry of Defence* [2014] A.C. 52; *Mulcahy v Ministry of Defence* [1996] Q.B. 732.

[210] *Smith v Ministry of Defence* [2014] A.C. 52 at 125–132 per Lord Hope of Craighead DPSC. See also *Bici v Ministry of Defence* [2004] EWHC 786 (Q.B.) at [84] per Elias J.

[211] Thus, in battle conditions there is no duty of care incumbent on the State to provide a safe system of work, nor is a duty of care owed by one soldier to another: *Mulcahy v Ministry of Defence* [1996] Q.B. 732.

[212] *Smith v Ministry of Defence* [2014] A.C. 52. Cf. *Multiple Claimants v Ministry of Defence* [2003] EWHC 1134 (Q.B.).

[213] Before 1987 this was the position generally under s.10 of the Crown Proceedings Act 1947. For its historic and ongoing impact see *Adams v War Office* [1955] 3 All E.R. 245; *Derry v Ministry of Defence* (1999) 11 Admin. L.R. 758 (where it was confirmed that s.10 continues to apply with regard to acts predating the 1987 Act); *Matthews v Ministry of Defence* [2003] 1 A.C. 1163 (where the House of Lords held that s.10 was not incompatible with art.6 of the European Convention of Human Rights).

[214] Crown Proceedings (Armed Forces) Act 1987 s.2.

[215] See, e.g. *Gibson v Orr*, 1999 S.C. 420.

[216] *Hill v Chief Constable of West Yorkshire* [1989] A.C. 53; *Brooks v Commissioner of Police of the Metropolis* [2005] 1 W.L.R. 1495; *Van Colle v Chief Constable of Hertfordshire* [2009] 1 A.C. 225.

[217] *Hill v Chief Constable of West Yorkshire* [1989] A.C. 53 at 63 per Lord Keith of Kinkell. This is covered in more detail in Ch.17.

[218] See, e.g. *McKie v Orr*, 2003 S.C. 317.

[219] *McKie v Strathclyde Joint Police Board*, 2004 S.L.T. 982.

[220] See, e.g. *Elguzouli-Daf v Commissioner of Police for the Metropolis* [1995] Q.B. 335; *McKie v Scottish Ministers*, 2006 S.C. 528.

of malice.[221] The police may also be sued for breach of a right to privacy or liberty with respect to the unjustified forcible removal of a detained person's underwear.[222] By analogy, an intimate search of an individual may amount to a similar invasion of privacy,[223] although it may be justified, or authorised by statute, in the circumstances.[224]

Local authorities

3–33   Local authorities perform a wide range of functions which impact directly on individual members of the public. Thus, local authorities have been sued in delict for a very long time. Cases now are raised against the appropriate statutory body in its statutory name.[225] Earlier actions were against the magistrates or other officers depending on the status of the organisation.[226] When sued in negligence with regard to its functions as a public body, the fair, just and reasonable test[227] is of particular significance.[228]

Judges

3–34   Judges have had extensive immunities for a very long time. In *Haggart's Trustees v Lord President*, the pursuers were the trustees of an advocate who had raised an action for damages against the Lord President in respect of certain remarks of censure made from the bench about the conduct of his practice. These remarks were alleged to be motivated by malice and to injure John Haggart in his practice. The case was dismissed on appeal to the House of Lords. Lord Gifford said that an action for damages is not maintainable against a judge for words delivered from the bench in the exercise of judicial duty. If it was otherwise, this would subvert due administration of justice. The judges had a public responsibility, but it did not follow how this action could be maintained.[229] On the other hand, in *Allardice v Robertson*,[230] the House of Lords held, affirming the judgment of the Court of Session, that a justice of the peace is not protected against an action of damages for verbal slander made maliciously in delivering judgment against a party to a trial before him.

The immunity was upheld in a rare modern case. In *Russell v Dickson*,[231] after finding an accused person guilty at the conclusion of a summary criminal trial, a sheriff remanded the accused in custody for investigations to be made into certain aspects of the conduct of the defence by the accused's solicitor! The accused was released by the High Court of Justiciary, which commented that the

---

[221] *McKie v Strathclyde Joint Police Board*, 2004 S.L.T. 982.
[222] *Henderson v Chief Constable of Fife*, 1988 S.L.T. 361.
[223] *Wainwright v United Kingdom* (12350/04) (2007) 44 E.H.R.R. 40.
[224] *Tolmie v Dewar*, 2003 S.C. 265.
[225] Currently unitary authorities created by the Local Government etc. (Scotland) Act 1994.
[226] A perusal of the table of cases will show just how many cases involve such parties as pursuers and defenders.
[227] As set out in *Caparo Industries Plc v Dickman* [1990] 2 A.C. 605.
[228] See, e.g. *Mitchell v Glasgow City Council*, 2009 S.C. (HL) 21; *X (Minors) v Bedfordshire CC* [1995] 2 A.C. 633. This is covered in more detail in Ch.17.
[229] *Haggart's Trustees v Lord President* (1824) 2 Sh. App. 125 at 143.
[230] *Allardice v Robertson* (1830) 2 W. & S. 102.
[231] *Russell v Dickson*, 1997 S.C. 269.

sheriff's decision to remand the accused in custody had been in excess of his common law powers, and that his actions had been an excessive and unreason able step. The accused brought an action of damages against the sheriff for wrongful imprisonment, arguing that, in the circumstances, the sheriff's decision to remand could not be described as a judicial act, and that he was not therefore entitled to the absolute immunity from being sued for damages that applied to the judicial actings of a sheriff. It was held that even although the sheriff's decision to remand the accused in custody was wrong and unreasonable, it was still *an act done in his judicial capacity*, and as the averments of malice which had been made were not relevant, the sheriff was protected by absolute immunity.

Solicitors, advocates and witnesses

Solicitors and advocates enjoy immunity from delictual liability with regard to **3–35** their conduct of criminal cases in court.[232] However, the immunity does not extend to the conduct of civil proceedings.[233]

Witnesses are immune from delictual liability with regard both to evidence presented in court[234] and statements made in its preparation.[235] In *Jones v Kaney*,[236] the Supreme Court held by a majority that expert witnesses no longer enjoy immunity either in evidence presented before or during the trial. However, this was an English case, and given Lord Hope's dissenting judgment there are strong grounds to anticipate that a Scottish court would not reach a similar conclusion.[237]

Incorporated bodies

Logically, incorporated bodies,[238] having no physical existence as such and no **3–36** capacity for *culpa*, may only incur strict liability or be vicariously liable. However, there may be personal liability in delict for third party wrongs, either at common law or under statute.[239] No distinction is made between ultra vires and intra vires acts.[240] It must be determined when suing a corporation as personally liable that it is indeed the corporation and not the individuals in their own right who have done the wrong,[241] although if a corporation is legally responsible for a wrong it is likely that the wrongful actions have been carried out through a human being, who may also be sued.[242]

---

[232] *Wright v Paton Farrell*, 2006 S.C. 404. Lord Osborne found that, given the differences in the rules of court procedure in the respective jurisdictions, the rationale for the decision of the House of Lords in *Arthur J.S. Hall & Co v Simons* [2002] 1 A.C. 615 with regard to immunity in the conduct of criminal proceedings did not transpose into Scots law.

[233] *Wright v Paton Farrell*, 2006 S.C. 404 at 451 per Lord Osborne.

[234] *Williamson v Umphray & Robertson* (1890) 17 R. 905; *Trapp v Mackie*, 1979 S.C. (HL) 38.

[235] *Watson v McEwan* (1905) 7 F. (HL) 109.

[236] *Jones v Kaney* [2011] 2 A.C. 398.

[237] See, e.g. *Karling v Purdue*, 2004 S.L.T. 1067 for the position in Scots law.

[238] Including corporations created by statute or charter, companies registered under the Companies Acts and Limited Liability Partnerships.

[239] See, e.g. Occupiers Liability (Scotland) Act 1960.

[240] *Houldsworth v City of Glasgow Bank* (1880) 7 R. (HL) 53.

[241] *Gordon v British & Foreign Metaline Co* (1886) 14 R. 75.

[242] *Dunbar v Presbytery of Auchterarder* (1849) 12 D. 284.

Proceedings against a company subject to an insolvency procedure require special permission. Where a company is in administration under Pt II of the Insolvency Act 1986, and so the subject of a moratorium, legal proceedings against the company require the consent of the administrator or permission from the court.[243] Where a company is in creditors' voluntary liquidation, the liquidator may apply to the court for a direction that no legal proceedings may be commenced against the company without leave of the court.[244] If the company is in compulsory liquidation, actions cannot proceed against the company without the permission of the court.[245] The court that should be approached is the one dealing with the liquidation and not the one where the reparation action is taking or is to take place.[246] The court looks at the matter from the point of view of expediency and the interests of third parties, such as the pursuer, as an important factor.[247] The liquidator can waive any objection.[248] Without leave the action is incompetent. It has been held that where a joint liquidator is being sued in delict, there is no need to convene the other liquidator.[249]

Directors of a company may be held personally liable where in the conduct of the company's affairs they have broken a statutory duty owed to the pursuer.[250] Every case depends upon the duty in question. One recent instance can be found in *Quinn v McGinty*.[251] The pursuer sued a director of his employer company for his failure to comply with the statutory obligation to insure in terms of the Employer's Liability (Compulsory Insurance) Act 1969. The sheriff found against him, but the Sheriff Principal allowed the action. Whether discussed as title to sue or relevancy, a shareholder has generally no right to sue for diminution in the value of his shares due to injury to that shareholder himself, even where he is the largest shareholder[252]; however, a claim for loss of a dividend in such circumstances is competent.[253]

Although the veil of incorporation will generally insulate a holding company from delictual liability for harm suffered by a victim arising out of the conduct of its subsidiary, if the holding company assumes direct responsibility for the welfare of the victim, the holding company may be sued in delict.[254]

---

[243] Insolvency Act 1986 Sch.B1 para.43(6). See also Insolvency Act 1986 Sch.A1 para.12(1)(h) with regard to the effect of a moratorium for a private company qualifying as "small" which is forming a proposal for a Company Voluntary Arrangement under Pt 1 of the Insolvency Act 1986.

[244] Insolvency Act 1986 s.113.

[245] Insolvency Act 1986 s.130(2).

[246] *Martin v Port of Manchester Insurance*, 1934 S.C. 143; *Coclas v Bruce Peebles & Co* (1908) 16 S.L.T. 7; *D.M. Stevenson & Co v Radford & Bright Ltd* (1902) 10 S.L.T. 82.

[247] *Coclas v Bruce Peebles & Co* (1908) 16 S.L.T. 7.

[248] *Hill v Black*, 1914 S.C. 913.

[249] *Highland Engineering Ltd v Anderson*, 1979 S.L.T. 122.

[250] Without a specific "assumption of responsibility" directors do not owe common law duties with regard to pure economic losses: see, e.g. *Williams v Natural Life Health Foods Ltd* [1998] 1 W.L.R. 830; *Nordic Oil Services v Berman* 1993 S.L.T. 1164. Director liability at common law for property damage, or even personal injury, may be less likely given that recent cases have shown an increased scepticism from the Supreme Court as to the legitimacy of the concept of "piercing the veil of incorporation". See *VTB Capital Plc v Nutritek International Corp* [2013] 2 A.C. 337; *Petrodel Resources Ltd v Prest* [2013] 2 A.C. 415.

[251] *Quinn v McGinty*, 1999 S.L.T. (Sh. Ct) 27. See also *Campbell v Peter Gordon Joiners Ltd*, 2014 S.L.T. 178.

[252] *Young v Ormiston*, 1936 S.L.T. 79; *Fox v P Caulfield & Co Ltd*, 1975 S.L.T. (Notes) 71.

[253] *Anthony v Brabbs*, 1998 S.C. 894.

[254] *Chandler v Cape Plc* [2012] 1 W.L.R. 3111. Cf. *Thomson v Renwick Group Plc* [2014] EWCA Civ 635.

Unincorporated bodies

An unincorporated body as defender may be liable to the extent of any **3-37** property held in trust for all the members and to the extent of the members' interest in the body, e.g. a club subscription.[255]

Clubs and similar unincorporated associations

The former rule that a club cannot be sued in its own name—actions required **3-38** to be raised against the club and the office bearers[256]—has been departed from by rules of court. Arguably, all that does is to allow a decree to be enforced against club assets. It has already allowed an action of interdict against nuisance to be raised against a golf club and it was thought that suitable parties could be found to answer for any breach.[257] It has also been said that it is not necessary to sue the association as constituted at the time of the wrong, but it may be designed as it exists at the time of raising the action.[258] However, prudence suggests that the actual wrongdoers personally or in association at the time ought to be sued at least until parties of substance come forward as opponents. It is more likely that a particular office bearer will be personally liable, or all members approving a certain course of conduct will be liable. However, where the personal wrong of individuals can be established they are personally liable. In *Matthew v Perthshire Cricket Club*,[259] the pursuer sued

> "the Perthshire Cricket Club, and the officials and Committee of the Club, for damages in respect of personal injuries sustained by him through the collapse of a grand stand on the North Inch of Perth on August 1, 1903."[260]

Members suing the association

It may be questioned whether a member has a right to sue for injuries or **3-39** wrongs by the association. Analogies with partnership suggest a case might well fail.[261] In *Graham and Simpson v Hawick Common Riding Committee*,[262] the pursuers sued for declarator under the Sex Discrimination Act 1975 and for "nominal" damages of £1. The defenders were a committee, but it was not clear of what. A plea of no title to sue was repelled and that course approved on appeal. The Sheriff Principal did not find it necessary to comment on the English cases

---

[255] *Gibson v Smith* (1849) 21 Sc.J. 331. Nevertheless, if "the claim against the club or association is based on delict or negligence there is, in my opinion, absolutely no basis in principle or in authority for the proposition that the liability of members would be other than personal with a claim for relief against whatever funds are at the time in the name of the club or association": *Harrison v West of Scotland Kart Club*, 2004 S.C. 615 at 622 per Lord Marnoch, i.e. if there are insufficient club assets the members at fault remain personally liable for the difference. Thus it is important to name members at fault in terms of enforcement of a decree.

[256] *Somerville v Rowbotham* (1862) 24 D. 1187.

[257] *Borland v Lochwinnoch Golf Club*, 1986 S.L.T. (Sh. Ct) 13.

[258] *Gorrie v The Marist Bros*, 2001 G.W.D. 39–1484.

[259] *Matthew v Perthshire Cricket Club* (1904) 12 S.L.T. 635.

[260] More marginal (being before the division on exceptions) is *Glass v Leitch* (1902) 5 F. 14, in which a case for damages based on the collapsing of structure was brought against the race committee who acted gratuitously and had a lease of the premises.

[261] See para.3–40 below. For England see *Prole v Allen* [1950] 1 All E.R. 476; *Robertson v Ridley* [1989] 2 All E.R. 474.

[262] *Graham and Simpson v Hawick Common Riding Committee*, 1998 S.L.T. (Sh. Ct) 42.

Prole[263] and *Robertson*, although he could see some force in the view that, if an association consists of its own members and has no independent existence, then on the basis that a person cannot sue himself, those decisions might well be followed in Scotland.[264] In *Milne v Duguid*,[265] Sheriff Kelbie reviewed the authorities, applied *Prole* and held that a member of an unincorporated association could not sue an association. However, he allowed proof before answer on a case against a member who was being sued on the independent ground of his activities as greenkeeper. In *Carmichael v Bearsden & District Rifle and Pistol Club*,[266] the pursuer, a former member of the defender unincorporated club, sued in respect of alleged negligence resulting in lead poisoning over a period of time. The sheriff and the sheriff principal held that the rule in *Mair v Wood*[267] applied.

In *Harrison v West of Scotland Kart Club*,[268] the Inner House upheld the dismissal of the claim against the club and approved the reasoning of Lady Paton following her review of the authorities. It is accordingly an authoritative statement of the present understanding of the law. The pursuer's case was that, while karting, as he slowed down to enter the pits, the kart suddenly accelerated out of control and collided with an unprotected wall. Decisions regarding track safety were made jointly by the office bearers. For various reasons, it was alleged that they knew or ought to have known that, without some crash protection in the area of the building, there was a danger that a driver might similarly lose control and collide with the wall. The first defenders sought dismissal of the case against them on the basis that a member of an unincorporated club could not sue the club. The action against the club and the committee as representing the club was dismissed. The action so far as directed towards the committee members as individuals was allowed to proceed to a proof before answer. Lady Paton established a number of propositions that are transferable to other cases (authorities omitted):

1. the fact that the five were at all relevant times members of the same club as the pursuer did not give them any immunity;
2. nor was it the fact that the five were members or office bearers which fixed them with a duty of care;
3. it was their knowledge coupled with their de facto assumption of the responsibility for taking executive decisions relating to track safety;
4. liability *ex delicto* does not arise from membership of the club per se; and
5. the first defenders were correct in contending that, in the context of delict, by suing the "West of Scotland Kart Club" the pursuer was in effect suing himself. Where a member of the club seeks to recover damages in respect of negligence on the part of another member or members, he cannot seek to recover damages from all the members of the club.[269]

---

[263] *Prole v Allen* [1950] 1 All E.R. 476.
[264] *Robertson v Ridley* [1989] 2 All E.R. 474 at 932.
[265] *Milne v Duguid*, 1999 S.C.L.R. 512.
[266] *Carmichael v Bearsden & District Rifle and Pistol Club*, 2000 S.L.T. (Sh. Ct) 49.
[267] *Mair v Wood*, 1948 S.C. 83.
[268] *Harrison v West of Scotland Kart Club*, 2004 S.C. 615.
[269] *Harrison v West of Scotland Kart Club*, 2001 S.C. 367 at 386–389.

In the Inner House, Lord Marnoch opined that, since a club has no separate legal personality from its membership, a member attempting to sue the club is in an even worse position that a partner attempting to sue the firm. He went on:

> "The result of all this is that there is simply no place within the structure of an unincorporated association for the operation, as between the members themselves, of the principle of vicarious liability. On the contrary, as has now been recognised in a number of cases in both Scotland and England, and as has indeed been conceded in this case on behalf of the five office bearers, the only delictual liabilities which can arise between members of an unincorporated body are such as arise directly from their personal actings as individuals."[270]

Partnerships

Note that no formality is required to create a "traditional" partnership **3–40** (commonly called a "firm") and a partnership will subsist where two or more persons carry on a business in common with a view to a profit.[271] The firm may be sued as a legal person, and may be liable for the delictual acts of partners either as principal in agency law[272] or vicariously.[273]

The scope of the partnership business determines the scope of the liability.[274] In *Kirkintilloch Equitable Co-operative Society Ltd v Livingstone*,[275] there was an allegation of negligence by a member of a firm of accountants who acted as auditor. The fee was paid to the firm and members of the firm assisted in the audit. However, neither the partners nor the firm were entitled to be appointed as auditors under the appropriate legislation. It was argued that, accordingly, the work was not within the ordinary course of business of the partnership. It is clear from the opinion of Lord President Clyde that s.10 of the Partnership Act 1890 provides two alternative modes of liability: "ordinary course" and "authority" cases. In *Kirkintilloch Equitable Co-operative*, the acts were within the scope of the business and in any event the averments as to authority were sufficient.

A firm is not vicariously liable under s.10 for the delictual wrongs of a partner if it is sued by a fellow partner. In *Mair*,[276] one of five share fishermen was seriously injured by the boat's propeller shaft, which had been left uncovered by the skipper. The partnership as such was not vicariously liable, although an action against the skipper for personal liability would have been competent.

The new approach to vicarious liability in intentional wrong cases applies to partnership cases. In *Dubai Aluminium Co Ltd v Salaam*,[277] the House of Lords decided in these contribution proceedings that the firm were vicariously liable for the actings of a partner who was alleged to have dishonestly assisted in a breach of trust—he was acting in the ordinary course of the business even without the knowledge or authority of the partners. The acts complained of were so closely connected with acts that he was authorised to do that this conclusion followed.[278]

---

[270] *Harrison v West of Scotland Kart Club*, 2004 S.C. 615 at 622–623 per Lord Marnoch.
[271] Partnership Act 1890 s.1.
[272] Partnership Act 1890 ss.5, 11.
[273] Partnership Act 1890 s.10.
[274] *Lloyd v Grace Smith* [1912] A.C. 716.
[275] *Kirkintilloch Equitable Co-operative Society Ltd v Livingstone*, 1972 S.C. 111.
[276] *Mair v Wood*, 1948 S.C. 83. See also *Bruce v Clapham*, 1982 S.L.T. 386.
[277] *Dubai Aluminium Co Ltd v Salaam* [2003] 2 A.C. 366.
[278] See the note C. Mitchell, "Partners in Wrongdoing", 2003 L.Q.R. 364.

Where no "corporate" or systematic failure by the firm can be shown, then it remains essential that the professional failing be identified.[279]

Trade unions

3-41   Trade unions are unincorporated bodies. Their ability to sue and be sued is subject to constraints and immunities as befits organisations that essentially came to have constitutional significance in the 20th century from having been primarily illegal combinations in the 19th.[280] Article 23(4) of the Universal Declaration of Human Rights declares: "Everyone has the right to form and to join Trade Unions for the protection of his interests." The European Convention on Human Rights provides in art.11 the right for a person to form and join trade unions for the protection of his interests, but this is subject to restrictions necessary in a democratic society in the interests of national security or public safety, for the prevention of disorder or crime, for the protection of health or morals or for the protection of the rights and freedoms of others. Thus delict, which protects and enforces the interests of persons, must treat trade unions specially.

A trade union is an organisation which consists mainly or wholly of workers whose principal purpose includes the regulation of worker/employer relations.[281] Workers and employers are specially defined.[282] A trade union is not an incorporated body by statute.[283] A union may sue or be sued in its own name and any judgment is enforceable against any property that is held in trust for its benefit. In so far as unions are entitled to protection from certain delictual actions, these have to have been authorised or endorsed under the legislation, which sets out which officials and committees are effective for this purpose.[284] In relation to certain heads of liability, there are fixed limits on the extent of liability.[285] Trade unions are liable for any negligence, nuisance or breach of duty resulting in personal injury to any person or from any breach of duty imposed in connection with the ownership, occupation, possession, control or use of property, without the protection of the statutory limitation.[286] It has been held that trade unions cannot sue for defamation.[287]

There is a general immunity in respect of "an act done by a person" in respect of acts done "in contemplation or furtherance of a trade dispute." There is protection against an action based on inducing a breach of contract or interfering (or inducing another to interfere) with its performance[288]; and where there is a threat that a contract will be broken or its performance interfered with or that there will be action to induce another to break or interfere with a contract.[289]

---

[279] *Duncan v Beattie* 2003 G.W.D. 28–798.
[280] See the review in *Wilkie v King*, 1911 S.C. 1310.
[281] Trade Union and Labour Relations (Consolidation) Act 1992 s.1.
[282] Trade Union and Labour Relations (Consolidation) Act 1992 ss.30, 295, 296.
[283] Trade Union and Labour Relations (Consolidation) Act 1992 s.10(1).
[284] Trade Union and Labour Relations (Consolidation) Act 1992 s.20(2).
[285] Trade Union and Labour Relations (Consolidation) Act 1992 s.22. The Union funds are protected from enforcement by s.23.
[286] Employment Act 1982 s.15.
[287] *E.E.T.P.U. v Times Newspapers Ltd* [1980] Q.B. 585, applying s.2(1) of the Trade Union and Labour Relations Act 1974 (superseded by s.10(1) of the Trade Union and Labour Relations (Consolidation) Act 1992. Whether this decision is correct has been doubted: see Kenneth McK. Norrie, *Defamation and Related Actions in Scots Law* (Edinburgh: Butterworths, 1995), p.68. See also *National Union of General and Municipal Workers v Gillian* [1946] K.B. 81.
[288] Trade Union and Labour Relations (Consolidation) Act 1992 s.219(1)(a).
[289] Trade Union and Labour Relations (Consolidation) Act 1992 s.219(1)(b).

Compliance with strict rules on balloting and notice is required.[290] An agreement between two or more persons to do or procure the doing of any act in contemplation or furtherance of a trade dispute, if the act is one which, if done without any such agreement, would not be actionable, is protected.[291]

For all of these immunities to apply, the acts must be in contemplation or furtherance[292] of a trade dispute.[293] In *Square Grip Reinforcement Co v MacDonald*,[294] officials and members of the union attended building sites where contractors known to be customers of the company were operating and induced workers there to refuse to offload lorries carrying materials supplied by the company, and to threaten that if the lorries were offloaded all the workers on the site who were members of the union would cease work. The customers were forced to refuse to take delivery of the company's materials, and so to break their contracts with the company. It was held that there was a "trade dispute". However, the conduct, which was an inducement to break a commercial contract rather than an employment contract, was not protected by the legislation. There are many English cases.[295] A political protest is not a trade dispute.[296]

Picketing is expressly declared to be lawful,[297] and often it would be anyway. On occasion, the protection is needed where the conduct constitutes perhaps a trespass or a nuisance.[298] The following conditions must be met—the picket must be at or near his place of work (unless a union official) and be there for the purpose only of peacefully obtaining or communicating information, or peacefully persuading any person to work or abstain from working.[299] "Secondary action", i.e. action taken against someone not a party to the dispute will not, generally, attract the immunity.[300]

---

[290] Trade Union and Labour Relations (Consolidation) Act 1992 ss.226–235.

[291] Trade Union and Labour Relations (Consolidation) Act 1992 s.219(2).

[292] *Milligan v Ayr Harbour Trustees*, 1915 S.C. 937.

[293] Defined in Trade Union and Labour Relations (Consolidation) Act 1992 s.244. See, e.g. *P v NASUWT* [2003] 2 A.C. 663.

[294] *Square Grip Reinforcement Co v MacDonald*, 1968 S.L.T. 65. A case under the earlier Trade Disputes Act 1906 and Trade Disputes Act 1965. See also *Merkur Island Shipping Co v Laughton* [1983] A.C. 570.

[295] See V. Craig and K. Miller, *Employment Law in Scotland* (Scotland: Bloomsbury Professional, 2002), Ch.11. See the English Court of Appeal Decision in *UNISON v Westminster City Council* [2001] I.C.R. 1046. This was a dispute over privatisation of council services. The case shows that it is important to show the practical importance of the issue to actual persons employed as opposed to being about high-minded disputes about public policy.

[296] *Mercury Communication Ltd v Scott-Garner* [1984] Ch. 37. See also *Express Newspapers Ltd v McShane* [1980] A.C. 672; *Duport Steels Ltd v Sirs* [1980] 1 W.L.R. 142; *Dimbleby & Sons Ltd v NUJ* [1984] 1 W.L.R. 427.

[297] Trade Union and Labour Relations (Consolidation) Act 1992 s.219(3).

[298] See, e.g. *Thomas v N.U.M. (South Wales Area)* [1986] Ch. 20.

[299] See, e.g. *Timex Electronic Corp v Amalgamated Engineering Union*, 1994 S.L.T. 438.

[300] See, e.g. *Star Offshore Services Plc v National Union of Seamen*, 1988 S.L.T. 836.

CHAPTER 4

LIABILITY FOR DELICTUAL WRONGS

PERSONAL LIABILITY

4–01 The general rule is encapsulated in the maxim *culpa tenet suos auctores*—fault adheres to its author.[1] Thus, whoever commits the wrong—*injuria*—will be personally liable for the reparable consequences.[2] The corollary is that normally one will not be liable for the consequences of a wrong committed by another:

> " . . . as a general equitable principle, no man ought to be made responsible for the fault or crime of another, with which fault or crime he has nothing to do and for which he is not in anywise to blame."[3]

Thus, one spouse is not as such liable for the delicts of the other,[4] likewise parents and children[5]; landlord and tenant[6]; vehicle owner and driver[7]; employee and colleague[8]; hirer and contractor[9] or owner, etc. However, exceptions may arise in the form of either personal liability or vicarious liability, both of which will result in liability arising on a joint and several basis.[10]

PERSONAL LIABILITY FOR THIRD PARTY ACTS

4–02 For personal liability to arise there must have been some form of wrongful conduct on the part of the defender.[11] Thus, if A conspires with B with a view to

---

[1] Or, more colourfully, "the fox must pay his own skin": *Wood v Fullerton* (1710) Mor. 13960. See also G. MacCormack, "*Culpa Tenet Suos Auctores*: The Application of a Principle", 1973 J.R. 159.

[2] Subject to the various immunities and privileges that are recognised in the law of delict, see paras 3–28 to 3–35, 3–41, 6–16, 7–20 to 7–27, 10–10 and 17–04 to 17–09.

[3] *Woodhead v Gartness Mineral Co* (1877) 4 R. 469 at 504 per Lord Gifford. See also *Weld-Blundell v Stephens* [1920] A.C. 956 at 986 per Lord Sumner.

[4] *Barr v Neilsons* (1868) 6 M. 65; *Bruce v Murray*, 1926 S.L.T. 236.

[5] *McKay v McLean*, 1920 S.L.T. 34.

[6] *Mitchell v Glasgow City Council*, 2009 S.C. (HL) 21. See also *Lyons v Anderson* (1886) 13 R. 1020 at 1024 per Lord Rutherford Clark. Cf. *Caledonian Railway Co v Baird & Co* (1876) 3 R. 839.

[7] *Morgans v Launchbury* [1973] A.C. 127.

[8] Nor will an employee be liable for the wrongs of his employer: *Kinloch v Clark* (1865) 4 M. 107.

[9] *Gourock Ropework Co Ltd v Greenock Corp*, 1966 S.L.T. 125; *Esso Petroleum v Hall Russell & Co Ltd (The Esso Bernicia)*, 1988 S.L.T. 874; *D&F Estates Ltd v Church Commissioners for England* [1989] A.C. 177 at 208–209 per Lord Bridge.

[10] Joint and several liability is traditionally described as liability *in solidum*.

[11] Unless the liability is created by statute. See, e.g. *Cora Foundation v East Dunbartonshire Council* [2014] CSIH 46; 2014 G.W.D. 18–356.

B's engaging in an act intended to cause harm to C, A may be liable in delict to make reparation to C.[12] Similarly, if A engages B to carry out a wrongful act, or engages B who is clearly incompetent or unqualified,[13] or condones the clearly wrongful way in which B is carrying out the work A has instructed,[14] where C suffers foreseeable harm A will be personally liable to C.

Thus, in *Stewart v Adams* a boat owner engaged a joiner to carry out repairs on his boats, which were pulled onto a field. The work required the removal of paint scrapings, which were left in the field. The pursuer's cow was poisoned by the scrapings while grazing. The boat owner was held liable, as he had failed in his duty to ensure that the poisonous scrapings were removed, it being recognised that such duty could not be delegated to the contractor.[15]

On some occasions the courts have recognised that a duty may be delegated to an apparently competent person, thus absolving the delegating party from liability.[16] However, on other occasions the courts have held that certain duties cannot be delegated.[17] It is unclear exactly where the boundary line falls, but in general the more dangerous the activity in question, the more likely a court is to hold that the duty cannot be delegated.[18]

In *Muir v Glasgow Corp*,[19] the delegation of responsibility safely to carry an urn full of hot water past a group of children congregated into a narrow corridor was held sufficient to discharge the duty of care owed by the manageress to the children. On the other hand it has been said:

> "Where a person is under a duty to use care, he cannot get rid of his responsibility by delegating the performance of it to someone else, no matter whether the delegation be to (an employee) under a contract for service or to an independent contractor under a contract for services."[20]

Reconciling these cases is difficult, although it may be appropriate to recall that *Muir* was decided during the Second World War—social attitudes to taking responsibility for what is foreseeably dangerous have changed[21] considerably in intervening years.[22] However, it is clear that an employer's common law duty to take reasonable care in providing a safe system of work is a non-delegable duty,[23] as are many statutory duties[24] including those that have been developed under the Health and Safety at Work Act 1974.

---

[12] See paras 10–07 to 10–09 below.

[13] See, e.g. *Wolfson v Forrester*, 1910 S.C. 675.

[14] See, e.g. *McLean v Russell, MacNee & Co*, 1850 12 D. 887. Cf. *D&F Estates Ltd v Church Commissioners for England* [1989] A.C. 177 at 209 per Lord Bridge.

[15] *Stewart v Adams*, 1920 S.C. 120 at 132 per Lord Dundas.

[16] See, e.g. *D&F Estates Ltd v Church Commissioners for England* [1989] A.C. 177 at 208–209 per Lord Bridge.

[17] See, e.g. *Sanderson v Paisley Burgh Commissioners* (1899) 7 S.L.T. 255; *Stewart v Malik*, 2009 S.C. 265.

[18] See, e.g. *Morris Amusements Ltd v Glasgow City Council*, 2009 S.L.T. 697.

[19] *Muir v Glasgow Corp*, 1943 S.C. (HL) 3.

[20] *Cassidy v Minister of Health* [1951] 2 K.B. 343 at 363 per Denning L.J.

[21] Perhaps fluctuated—see, e.g. *Tomlinson v Congleton BC* [2004] 1 A.C. 46 at 84–86 per Lord Hoffmann.

[22] See, e.g. *Hughes v Lord Advocate*,1963 S.C. (HL) 31; *Jolley v Sutton LBC* [2000] 1 W.L.R. 1082.

[23] *English v Wilsons and Clyde Coal*, 1937 S.C. (HL) 46.

[24] See, e.g. *Stephens v Thurso Police Commissioners* (1876) 3 R. 535; *Riverstone Meat Co Pty Ltd v Lancashire Shipping Co Ltd* [1961] A.C. 807; Carriage of Goods by Sea Act 1971.

4–03   The Supreme Court dealt with the question of non-delegable duties in *Woodland v Essex CC*,[25] and used the opportunity to set out what should be an authoritative statement of the law. A 10-year-old girl suffered brain damage when she got into difficulties during a swimming lesson she attended as part of her schooling, as required by the National Curriculum. It was alleged that the accident was attributable to negligence on the part of the swimming teacher and/ or the lifeguard, neither of whom were employees of the school or the local authority. The Supreme Court unanimously overturned the decision of the Court of Appeal and found that the education authority owed a non-delegable duty to schoolchildren with regard to the functions it was entrusted to perform. Lord Sumption set out five criteria that would, outside of statutory duty, highway and hazard cases, give rise to a non-delegable duty of care:

1. "The claimant is a patient or a child, or for some other reason is especially vulnerable or dependent on the protection of the defendant against the risk of injury. Other examples are likely to be prisoners and residents in care homes.

2. There is an antecedent relationship between the claimant and the defendant, independent of the negligent act or omission itself, (i) which places the claimant in the actual custody, charge or care of the defendant, and (ii) from which it is possible to impute to the defendant the assumption of a positive duty to protect the claimant from harm, and not just a duty to refrain from conduct which will foreseeably damage the claimant. It is characteristic of such relationships that they involve an element of control over the claimant, which varies in intensity from one situation to another, but is clearly very substantial in the case of schoolchildren.

3. The claimant has no control over how the defendant chooses to perform those obligations, i.e. whether personally or through employees or through third parties.

4. The defendant has delegated to a third party some function which is an integral part of the positive duty which he has assumed towards the claimant; and the third party is exercising, for the purpose of the function thus delegated to him, the defendant's custody or care of the claimant and the element of control that goes with it.

5. The third party has been negligent not in some collateral respect but in the performance of the very function assumed by the defendant and delegated by the defendant to him."[26]

Although the Court of Appeal had expressed concerns that the imposition of a non-delegable duty of care on education authorities may have a "chilling effect" on the willingness of authorities to provide pupils with a valuable range of experiences,[27] Lord Sumption emphasised that it was fair, just and reasonable to impose such duties.[28] Lady Hale agreed, adding that it would be unsatisfactory if some pupils could sue their education authority (where functions were not

---

[25] *Woodland v Essex CC* [2014] A.C. 537.
[26] *Woodland v Essex CC* [2014] A.C. 537 at 583.
[27] *Woodland v Essex CC* [2014] A.C. 537 at 563 per Tomlinson L.J.
[28] *Woodland v Essex CC* [2014] A.C. 537 at 584–585.

outsourced) but others, whose authorities outsourced those functions, could not.[29]

Dorset Yacht v Home Office[30] provides House of Lords authority that there may be occasions where A owes C a general duty of care with regard to the conduct of B, a third party.[31] There, prison officers were held to owe a duty of care to the owners of property situated beside a campsite where the officers were employed to supervise young offenders on a camping trip. Lord Morris suggested that:

> "If A can reasonably foresee that some act or omission of his may have the result that loss or damage may be suffered by (C) who is someone who would be closely and directly affected by the act or omission, there will be some circumstances in which a legal duty will be owed by A to (C) and some in which it will not. The question arises as to what is the dividing line."[32]

In *Maloco v Littlewoods Organisation Ltd*,[33] Lord Goff attempted to provide an answer to Lord Morris' question and set out three alternative occasions where a defender would owe a duty to take care with regard to the actions of a third party:

1. Special relationships: a "special relationship" may exist between either the defender and pursuer (where usually an assumption of responsibility from the defender to the pursuer is required), or between the defender and the third party.
2. The defender negligently creates a source of danger where it is reasonably foreseeable that third parties are likely to intervene and cause harm.[34]
3. The defender is aware of the third party's actions but fails to take reasonable steps to prevent them from continuing.

JOINT AND SEVERAL LIABILITY

Culpa tenet suos auctores confirms that liability attaches to the person at fault. **4–04** What if two or more persons have engaged in wrongful conduct that has resulted in the harm suffered by the victim? If these are separate wrongs respectively causing distinct hazards,[35] each wrongdoer will be separately, in law severally, liable for only the harm attributable to his wrongful act. However, if the wrongful

---

[29] *Woodland v Essex CC* [2014] A.C. 537 at 587.
[30] *Dorset Yacht v Home Office* [1970] A.C. 1004.
[31] The duty of care with regard to the acts of third parties is covered in more detail at paras 11–20 to 11–24 below.
[32] *Dorset Yacht Co Ltd v Home Office* [1970] A.C. 1004 at 1034.
[33] *Maloco v Littlewoods Organisation Ltd*, 1987 S.C. (HL) 37 at 77–79 per Lord Goff of Chieveley.
[34] For examples, see *Connor v Secretary of State for Scotland*, 2000 Rep. L.R. 18. A factor in the equation may be the extent of the danger arising from the negligence of the defender, see e.g. *Philco Radio and Television Corp of Great Britain v J Spurling Ltd* [1949] 2 All E.R. 882.
[35] See, e.g. *Fleming v McGillivray*, 1946 S.C. 1; *Reid v Sir Robert McAlpine & Son*, 1986 S.L.T. 108.

acts combine, effectively to become a single wrong,[36] causing indivisible harm,[37] the wrongdoers may be liable on a joint and several basis. Joint and several liability may also arise because of a matrix of statutory and/or conventional rules applying to the situation.[38]

An example of the former was *Hook v McCallum*.[39] A servant girl complained that she had been slandered by her mistress and later by her husband when he adopted his wife's statement and so repeated the allegation. It was held that the husband and wife were not jointly and severally liable as the wrongs were separate and distinct. An example of the latter was *Drew v Western S.M.T.*[40] where a van boy was crushed while unloading a van in the early morning before daylight. The driver of the van had failed to ensure the rear lights were visible (they were obscured by the tailgate) and the driver of the bus that collided with the back of the van was driving negligently. Since the separate wrongful acts had combined to result in a single harmful outcome, the respective drivers (and, vicariously, their respective employers) were jointly and severally liable. Since it was impossible to identify the causative effect of each wrong with any degree of precision, contributions were assessed equally.[41]

If liability is joint and several, each wrongdoer is liable for the whole of the harm, regardless of the contribution his delictual act made to the harm.[42] Thus, the pursuer may choose to sue any one (or more) of the wrongdoers and recover in full.[43] However, the court will apportion liability among the wrongdoers,[44] and if a defender has to pay more than his proportion of the liability that defender may take action against the other wrongdoers to recover their contributions as allocated by the court.[45]

VICARIOUS LIABILITY

4–05 Vicarious liability means "liability in place of another". The concept arises most frequently in employment situations, and it may also be encountered in other

---

[36] See, e.g. *Ruddy v Chief Constable of Strathclyde*, 2013 S.C. (U.K.S.C.) 126; *Ellerman Lines Ltd v Clyde Navigation Trustees*, 1909 S.C. 690; *Grunwald v Hughes*, 1965 S.L.T. 209.

[37] See, e.g. *McGillivray v Davidson*, 1993 S.L.T. 693. The definition of "divisible" harm is unclear: compare *Holtby v Brigham and Cowan (Hull) Ltd* [2000] 3 All E.R. 421; *Barker v Corus (UK) Plc* [2006] 2 A.C. 572; *Wright v Stoddard International*, 2008 Rep. L.R. 2.

[38] See, e.g. *Cairns v Northern Lighthouse Board*, 2013 S.L.T. 645.

[39] *Hook v McCallum* (1905) 7 F. 528. See also *Barr v Neilson* (1868) 6 M. 651.

[40] *Drew v Western S.M.T.*, 1947 S.C. 222.

[41] The boy was also held to have been contributorily negligent, and the court stated that the discount (under the Law Reform (Contributory Negligence) Act 1945) should be applied before apportioning liability between the wrongdoers.

[42] The wrong must nevertheless be *causa causans* (i.e. a *sufficient* cause of) the harm—see Ch.13.

[43] If the pursuer recovers all of the damages he claims from one wrongdoer, he cannot thereafter sue any other, even if he realises he could have claimed for more: *Balfour v Archibald Baird & Sons Ltd*, 1959 S.C. 64. On the other hand, if the decree against one joint wrongdoer is not satisfied, he may sue any other: *Steven v Broady, Norman & Co*, 1928 S.C. 351.

[44] Based on the contribution of the wrong to the harm, rather than culpability: *Drew v Western S.M.T.*, 1947 S.C. 222 at 240 per Lord Justice-Clerk Cooper.

[45] Law Reform (Miscellaneous Provisions) (Scotland) Act 1940 s.3. See also *Farstad Supply AS v Enviroco Ltd*, 2010 S.C. (U.K.S.C.) 87.

areas such as agency,[46] partnership[47] and unincorporated bodies.[48] Companies may also be vicariously liable for company directors,[49] the Crown will generally be liable for the delicts of its servants or agents[50] and separate statutory schemes can impose vicarious liability upon, respectively, the Chief Constable of Police[51] and trade unions.[52]

A justification for vicarious liability is encapsulated in the maxim *qui facit per alium facit per se* (he who does something through another does it himself).[53] Thus, in employment situations an employer will be vicariously liable for the consequences of an employee's delictual act, provided that the wrong is committed within the scope of the employment contract. Another maxim associated with vicarious liability is *respondeat superior* (let the master answer). In other words, the employer is liable because the employer has required the employee to carry out the act but has failed to ensure that the act is carried out by the employee both lawfully and carefully. An alternative interpretation of vicarious liability, which may be applied to the latter maxim, although perhaps not the former, and which has been articulated in recent cases which have been significant in extending the doctrine, is that vicarious liability is a policy device intended to ensure that victims are compensated by those who can afford it:

> "The policy objective underlying vicarious liability is to ensure, in so far as it is fair, just and reasonable, that liability for (delictual) wrong is borne by a (defender) with the means to compensate the victim. Such (defenders) can usually be expected to insure against the risk of such liability, so that this risk is more widely spread. It is for the court to identify the policy reasons why it is fair, just and reasonable to impose vicarious liability and to lay down the criteria that must be shown to be satisfied in order to establish vicarious liability."[54]

It is submitted that the former justification is consistent with the traditional "corrective justice" approach of the law of delict in Scotland. However, the latter

---

[46] Provided the agent's delictual act is within his actual or ostensible authority. See, e.g. *Percy v Glasgow Corp*, 1922 S.C. (HL) 144 at 151 per Viscount Haldane.

[47] Partnership Act 1890 s.10. The firm will be vicariously liable to third parties for the delictual acts of a partner carried out while acting in the firm's ordinary business—see, e.g. *Kirkintilloch Equitable Cooperative Society Ltd v Livingstone*, 1972 S.C. 111, even where the partner has committed an intentional wrong—*Dubai Aluminium Co Ltd v Salaam* [2003] 2 A.C. 366. The firm will not be vicariously liable to a partner harmed by the delictual act of a fellow partner—see, e.g. *Mair v Wood*, 1948 S.C. 83.

[48] *Various Claimants v Institute of the Brothers of the Christian Schools* [2013] 2 A.C. 1. Cf. *Harrison v West of Scotland Kart Club*, 2004 S.C. 615.

[49] See, e.g. *Scobie v Steele & Wilson Ltd*, 1963 S.L.T. (Notes) 45.

[50] Crown Proceedings Act 1947; Crown Proceedings (Armed Forces) Act 1987.

[51] Police and Fire Reform (Scotland) Act 2012 s.24, but see *Cropper v Chief Constable of Dumfries and Galloway*, 1998 S.L.T. 548.

[52] Trade Union and Labour Relations (Consolidation) Act 1992 s.20. For the position at common law see, e.g. *Heatons Transport (St Helens) Ltd v Transport & General Workers Union* [1972] I.C.R. 308.

[53] There is an inherent dichotomy in the maxim: it can be seen alternatively as an exception to the *culpa tenet suos auctores* rule, i.e. vicarious liability, or indeed as an application of it—personal liability! Alternatively, the maxim justifies the concept of non-delegable duty—see discussion at paras 4–19 to 4–20 below.

[54] *Various Claimants v Institute of the Brothers of the Christian Schools* [2013] 2 A.C. 1 at 15 per Lord Phillips of Worth Matravers. See also *Viasystems (Tyneside) Ltd v Thermal Transfer (Northern) Ltd* [2006] Q.B. 510 at 528 per May L.J.

may be seen as an application of "distributive justice", i.e. attributing liability in terms of social pragmatics such as affordability rather than culpability. This approach is not consistent with the tradition of the law in Scotland. It is further argued below that recent developments in vicarious liability are conceptually inconsistent, and may be more coherently explained as developments in personal liability for the delictual acts of third parties.[55]

However, returning to the practical application of the concepts, it is imperative to remember that the employee must be personally liable before the employer will incur vicarious liability: so the elements of whatever delictual wrong is contended for by the pursuer must be proved as against the employee before the employer can be held vicariously liable. The liability is then joint and several in nature—so the pursuer may choose to sue either the employee as personally liable, or the employer as vicariously liable. Obviously, a pursuer would normally choose to sue the employer, as the employer would be expected to have deeper pockets and to be insured.

Note that an employee also owes a duty to the employer not to carry out the work in a way that amounts to a delictual wrong. This duty is viewed as an implied term in the contract of employment.[56] Thus, if an employer is exposed to vicarious liability, the employer will have an action against the relevant employee for breach of contract[57] and can recover the damages and expenses incurred in defending (or settling) the claim. The employer's rights against the employee, and against any third parties who have contributed to the incident, will be subrogated to an insurance company which has paid the damages arising from the liability.

As well as the need to prove the elements of personal liability with regards to the employee, there are a further two essential elements which must be admitted or established for a court to hold an employer vicariously liable. First, the wrongdoer must be an employee, and secondly the wrong must be committed within the scope of employment.

Employee or independent contractor?

4–06   The traditional view is that an employer may be vicariously liable for wrongs committed by an employee, but will not be vicariously liable for wrongs committed by an independent contractor.[58] There must be a contract for service (*locatio operarum*) as opposed to a contract for services (*locatio operis, faciendi*).[59] For example, an employer may be vicariously liable for the delicts of his chauffeur, but not for a taxi-driver he has engaged. Distinguishing these

---

[55] See discussion at paras 4–19 to 4–20 below.

[56] It follows that the employer may be viewed as overriding such an implied term if the employer gives the employee specific instructions which require doing the work in an unlawful manner.

[57] *Lister v Romford Ice & Cold Storage Co Ltd* [1957] A.C. 555. Thus vicarious liability does not involve an implied indemnity provided by the employer in favour of the employee. Indeed, *Lister* confirms that the reverse is the case. An employment contract could *expressly* indemnify the employee against liability for negligence, although an indemnity against fraud would be unlawful as contrary to public policy.

[58] The circumstances in which vicarious liability may arise have evolved substantially in recent years, and boundaries are permeable—see, e.g. *Various Claimants v Institute of the Brothers of the Christian Schools* [2013] 2 A.C. 1. Whatever developments occur in the future, it should be remembered that an employer may be *personally* liable for the wrongs of an independent contractor—see paras 4–02 to 4–03 above.

[59] Note that, unlike statutory provisions related to employment protection, vicarious liability requires no qualifying period of continuous employment.

relationships is often difficult and the courts have frequently been called upon to decide whether a worker is an employee or an independent contractor.[60]

It is often the case that the relationship will be expressly set out in the contract. Although this may be persuasive, it is not conclusive, and the courts have developed tests to deal with the matter. The control test is the most primitive, asking whether the employer controls how the worker carries out the work.[61] As skilled employees enjoy substantial autonomy over the way in which they carry out their work, especially where particular technical expertise is required, the control test is inadequate and the integration test may be applied: asking whether the work is integrated into the employer's organisation, or is carried out independently.[62] A more sophisticated multiple test requires the identification and evaluation of a range of factors pertinent to the situation, often paying close attention to the economic reality of the relationship, i.e. who bears the most significant economic risk with regard to the venture.[63]

Factors may include:

- the intention of the parties;
- freedom of selection of employees;
- duration of the contract;
- whether payment is by salary/wages or by the job/unit;
- whether the tools and equipment belong to the employer or employee; and
- the nature of the arrangements for termination.[64]

A key factor in recent employment related cases has been mutuality of obligations: the employer being obliged to make work available and the worker being obliged to do it. Thus, casual workers,[65] and workers supplied by an employment agency,[66] have been held to be employees rather than independent contractors. It must be noted that each case will be decided on its own merits, with consideration of individual factors adding detail to the picture; but the overall decision requires "standing back from the detailed picture ... and making an informed considered qualitative appreciation of the whole."[67]

The significant, if not seismic, change in approach to vicarious liability heralded by the decision of the House of Lords in *Lister v Hesley Hall*[68] appears also to have penetrated the boundary constraining vicarious liability to employer/employee relationships. Focusing on the need for a relationship between the

---

[60] Many of these cases involve issues related to common law and statutory protection for employees, or tax and national insurance. Although such cases may not raise the question of vicarious liability, they are nevertheless relevant in the context of vicarious liability when dealing with a dispute over the status of a worker's contract.

[61] See, e.g. *Yewens v Noakes* [1880] 6 Q.B. 530; *Stagecraft Ltd v Minister of National Insurance*, 1952 S.C. 288.

[62] See, e.g. *Cassidy v Minister of Health* [1951] 2 K.B. 343; *McDonald v Glasgow Western Hospitals Board*, 1954 S.C. 453.

[63] See, e.g. *Park v Wilson's and Clyde Coal Co*, 1928 S.C. 121; *Ready Mixed Concrete (South East) Ltd v Minister for Pensions and National Insurance* [1968] 2 Q.B. 497.

[64] See *United Wholesale Grocers Ltd v Sher*, 1993 S.L.T. 284 for an examination of key factors.

[65] See, e.g. *O'Kelly v Trusthouse Forte Plc* [1984] Q.B. 90.

[66] See, e.g. *Motorola Ltd v Davidson* [2001] I.R.L.R. 4; *Toms v Royal Mail Plc*, 2006 S.L.T. 431.

[67] *Hall v Lorimer* [1994] I.R.L.R. 171 at 174 per Nolan L.J.

[68] *Lister v Hesley Hall* [2002] 1 A.C. 215—see discussion at para.4–16 below.

wrongdoer and the defender creating both the right and the obligation to control the wrongdoer, the courts in England and Wales have extended vicarious liability beyond employment, partnership and agency relationships to include the relationship between a Roman Catholic diocese and its parish priests[69] and the relationship between an unincorporated association of lay brothers of the Catholic Church and brother teachers.[70] In the latter case, the Supreme Court intimated a two stage test for vicarious liability.[71] The first stage required the relationship between wrongdoer and defender to be such as to be capable of giving rise to vicarious liability. If the relationship was "sufficiently akin to an employment relationship,"[72] the test would be satisfied. The second test, discussed further below, required a sufficiently close connection linking the relationship between the wrongdoer and defender to the delictual act or omission in question.

Pro hac vice employment

4–07   It is often the case that a worker will be sent to a place outwith his own place of employment. When he arrives he will be instructed what to do by a third party. If he is negligent and someone is injured, the injured person will need to know who to sue, and will ask the question: which of the two people who ordered around the negligent worker is vicariously liable? It is clear that the starting position is that the original employer remains vicariously liable, although each case turns on its own merits and it may be accepted that responsibility has transferred to the third party. However, it is also clear that there is a heavy onus on the original employer who wishes to prove that the employee has been transferred *pro hac vice*[73] to the third party.

The leading authority is *Mersey Docks and Harbour Board v Coggins and Griffiths Ltd*.[74] The harbour authority let a mobile crane and driver to a firm of stevedores to assist in loading a ship. Although the driver was paid by the Board, which also retained the right to dismiss, the hire contract provided that the driver would be the servant of the hirers. A dock-worker was injured due to the negligence of the driver whilst operating the crane. He sued both of the driver's "employers" in the alternative, leaving it to the court to determine which had responsibility. The House of Lords refused to follow the terms of the hire contract and held that the Board remained the employer and was vicariously liable. Lord MacMillan pointed out:

> "That the crane driver was in general the servant of the appellant board is indisputable. The appellant board engaged him, paid him, prescribed the jobs he should undertake and alone could dismiss him ... Prima facie therefore it was as the servant of the appellant board that (the crane driver)

---

[69] *E v English Province of Our Lady of Charity* [2013] Q.B. 722.

[70] *Various Claimants v Institute of the Brothers of the Christian Schools* [2013] 2 A.C. 1.

[71] *Various Claimants v Institute of the Brothers of the Christian Schools* [2013] 2 A.C. 1 at 12 per Lord Phillips of Worth Matravers.

[72] *Various Claimants v Institute of the Brothers of the Christian Schools* [2013] 2 A.C. 1 at 18 per Lord Phillips of Worth Matravers.

[73] Literally "for this turn".

[74] *Mersey Docks and Harbour Board v Coggins and Griffiths Ltd* [1947] A.C. 1. See also *Park v Tractor Shovels Ltd*, 1980 S.L.T. 94; *Moir v Wide Arc Services*,1987 S.L.T. 495; *Century Insurance v Northern Ireland Road Transport Board* [1942] 1 All E.R. 491 at 517 per Lord Wright.

was driving the crane when it struck the plaintiff. But it is always open to an employer to show, if he can, that he has for a particular purpose or on a particular occasion temporarily transferred the services of one of his general servants to another party so as to constitute him *pro hac vice* the servant of that other party with consequent liability for his negligent acts. The burden is on the general employer to establish that such a transference has been effected . . . I am of opinion that, on the facts of the present case, (the crane driver) was never so transferred . . . as to render the stevedores answerable for the manner in which he carried on his work of driving the crane. The stevedores were entitled to tell him where to go, what parcels to lift and where to take them, that is to say, they could direct him as to what they wanted him to do; but they had no authority to tell him how he was to handle the crane in doing his work."[75]

The language used by Lord MacMillan confirms his emphasis on determining **4–08** which employer was in control of the way in which the worker carried out the work.[76] Historically, it has probably been rare that the general employer has been willing to surrender such control to the person or organisation to whom the employee has been "loaned".[77] Occasionally, however, the courts have concluded that such control has been so transferred from the general employer to the temporary employer so as to conclude that the worker is *pro hac vice* an employee of the temporary employer. In *McGregor v J.S. Duthie & Sons*,[78] two passengers were injured in an accident caused by the negligence of the driver of the lorry in which they were traveling. The driver was in the general employment of a partnership which had been contracted to saw timber for a company. However, he had been "loaned" to the company to drive the company's lorry as instructed by the company. The arrangement provided that the company would reimburse the partnership for the driver's wages. In spite of the fact that one of the partners of the general employer was sitting beside the driver at the time of the accident, and that the passengers were also employed by the firm, the Inner House agreed that the extent to which the company enjoyed the right to control how the driver carried out his work, coupled with the driver's consent so to be controlled by the company rather than the partnership, meant that the driver was *pro hac vice* in the employment of the company. Thus, vicarious liability would attach to the company and not the partnership.

With the growth in the secondment of employees and in the use of agency workers and outside contractors to provide services such as security,[79] catering, cleaning and crèche facilities within the workplace, the significance of *pro hac vice* employment is likely to rise as these trends continue. Another factor which may now enter the equation is the closeness of the connection between the

---

[75] *Mersey Docks and Harbour Board v Coggins and Griffiths Ltd* [1947] A.C. 1 at 12–13 per Lord MacMillan.

[76] See also *Malley v London Midland and Scottish Railway Co*, 1944 S.C. 129 at 137 per Lord Justice-Clerk Cooper.

[77] The employee's input into the decision to transfer has also been held to be significant: see, e.g. *Malley v London Midland and Scottish Railway Co*, 1944 S.C. 129 at 137 per Lord Justice-Clerk Cooper. See also *Boyle v Glasgow Corp*, 1975 S.C. 238.

[78] *McGregor v J.S. Duthie & Sons*, 1966 S.L.T. 133. See also *Wright v Edinburgh Royal Infirmary Joint Venture*, 2008 S.L.T. (Sh. Ct) 90.

[79] See, e.g. *Hawley v Luminar Leisure Ltd* [2006] P.I.Q.R. 17.

delictual act committed by the worker and the employers' respective operations.[80] Thus, in addition to examining issues of control and employee assent to transfer, the close connection test was applied in *Royal Bank of Scotland v Bannerman Johnstone Maclay*.[81] A firm of accountants had seconded an employee, McMahon, to act as financial controller of a company called APC Ltd. The employee had, as part of a fraud, presented false accounts to a bank in order to procure for the company a loan from a bank. The question was which of the employers, the accountancy firm or the bank, should be vicariously liable? Although Lord MacFadyen's conclusion that the fraudulent conduct had virtually no connection with the accountants' business was challenged upon appeal to the Inner House, the Lord Justice-Clerk nevertheless appeared to approve the application of the close connection test from *Lister*.[82]

A question that appears never clearly to have been addressed in case law is whether circumstances could arise where a self-employed worker may be deemed an employee *pro hac vice*. This analysis may provide a rationale for the otherwise difficult decision in *Marshall v Sharp*.[83] Marshall, a quarry manager, sent for the quarry's on-call electrician to investigate why an industrial burner/ dryer was not working. The electrician, Dean, who although self-employed was the only person who did electrical work at the quarry, went into the control-room and pressed both the problematic ignition button and the fuel supply button at the same time. As a result Marshall, who had gone into the burner to check that the ignition device was sparking, was burned to death. The court accepted that the employer was not personally liable for breaching the non-delegable duty to implement a safe system of work. However, the court confirmed that the employer was vicariously liable for Dean's negligence, even although he was an independent contractor, "or at least a contractor with a degree of independence."[84] Nevertheless, in the opinion of the Lord Justice-Clerk, Dean had become part of the quarry company's "workforce" and as such was subject to the quarry company's "supervision and control". The benefit of this formulation is that it does not challenge the general rule that there is no vicarious liability for independent contractors. The language that was used is also consonant with the application of the doctrine of *pro hac vice* employment, by which a worker is transferred from a de jure employer (in this case himself) to a de facto employer (in this case the quarry company). This appears to be the effect of the Inner House decision, which is innovatory and unsupported by any authority. It is also remarkable in that the presumption against transfer in *pro hac vice* vicarious liability cases is very strong, yet in this case, the onus in proving the transfer from the sui juris workman to de facto employee was achieved.

4–09   In the cases considered so far, the courts seem to have been preoccupied with determining which of two "employers" should incur vicarious liability. It has been suggested that there is no principled objection to holding that both employers may be vicariously liable.[85] However, in *The Esso Bernicia* this

---

[80] See *Lister v Hesley Hall* [2002] A.C. 215, discussed at para.4–16 below.

[81] *Royal Bank of Scotland v Bannerman Johnstone Maclay*, 2005 1 S.C. 437.

[82] *Royal Bank of Scotland v Bannerman Johnstone Maclay*, 2005 1 S.C. 437 at 451 per Lord Justice-Clerk Gill.

[83] *Marshall v Sharp*, 1991 S.L.T. 114.

[84] *Marshall v Sharp* 1991 S.L.T. 114 at 121 per Lord Justice-Clerk Ross.

[85] P.S. Atiyah, *Vicarious Liability and the Law of Torts* (London: Butterworths, 1967), p.165.

suggestion was rejected by both the Lord President,[86] and then in the House of Lords.[87] Nevertheless, in *Viasystems (Tyneside) Ltd v Thermal Transfer (North ern) Ltd*, the Court of Appeal in England considered that there was no binding authority preventing dual vicarious liability, and that the focus of an inquiry should be on which of the employers enjoyed such control over the way in which the employee carried out the work so as to incur the duty to ensure that the employee acted with reasonable skill and care. May L.J. explained the approach thus:

> " . . . vicarious liability is a policy device of the law to redistribute the incidence of loss from a supposedly impecunious employee, who is personally at fault, to one or more supposedly solvent and insured employers, who are not personally at fault. The court is not, therefore, concerned to look for personal responsibility in the employer based on what might otherwise have been direct responsibility, for example, whether (the employer) trained (the employee) adequately or not. Vicarious liability derives from the relationship between the employee and the employers, the critical relationship being the employers' right (and theoretical obligation) to control the relevant activity of the employee. If the relationships yield dual control, it is highly likely at least that the measure of control will be equal, for otherwise the court would be unlikely to find dual control."[88]

Thus, although in principle liability in dual vicarious liability cases will be joint and several, May L.J. suggested that the contribution from each employer will inevitably be assessed equally, as it would be illogical to make a finding of dual control if more control is enjoyed by one employer than the other. However, it is worth noting that Rix L.J. alluded to the distributive justice function of vicarious liability in predicting that the concept of dual liability would be refined further in future cases—clearly anticipating a more sophisticated approach to contributions from respective employers than a straight 50:50 split.[89]

Various Claimants v Institute of the Bros of the Christian Schools[90] is a case that may in time be viewed as even more significant than *Lister*.[91] In *Various Claimants*, the Supreme Court endorsed the approach mooted in *Viasystems* by Rix L.J. in preference to that proposed by May L.J., stating:

> "Where two defendants are potentially vicariously liable for the act of a tortfeasor it is necessary to give independent consideration to the relationship of the tortfeasor with each defendant in order to decide whether that defendant is vicariously liable."

---

[86] *Esso Petroleum Co Ltd v Hall Russell & Co Ltd (The Esso Bernicia)*, 1988 S.L.T. 33 at 48 per Lord President (Emslie).

[87] *Esso Petroleum Co Ltd v Hall Russell & Co Ltd (The Esso Bernicia)*, 1988 S.L.T. 874 at 888–889 per Lord Jauncey of Tullichettle. See also *Park v Tractor Shovels Ltd*, 1980 S.L.T. 94 at 101 per Lord Cowie.

[88] *Viasystems (Tyneside) Ltd v Thermal Transfer (Northern) Ltd* [2006] Q.B. 510 at 528 per May L.J.

[89] *Viasystems (Tyneside) Ltd v Thermal Transfer (Northern) Ltd* [2006] Q.B. 510 at 536–537 per May L.J.

[90] *Various Claimants v Institute of the Bros of the Christian Schools* [2013] 2 A.C. 1.

[91] *Lister v Hesley Hall* [2002] 1 A.C. 215.

It is submitted that the Supreme Court has thus confirmed that dual vicarious liability will remain joint and several, but has signposted that contributions will be determined on an aliquot basis.

Scope of employment: traditional view

4–10   If it is established that the person who committed the delict is an employee, it must then be considered whether the delict was committed within the scope of the employee's employment. What is within the scope of employment will not be confined to what is specifically required of the employee by the contract of employment. Indeed, what is expressly prohibited by the contract may never-theless be deemed within the scope of employment.[92] The traditional approach adopted by the authorities was summarised by Lord President Clyde in *Kirby v National Coal Board*:

> " . . . four different types of situation have been envisaged as guides to the solution of this problem. In the first place, if the master actually authorised the particular act, he is clearly liable for it. Secondly, where the workman does some work which he is appointed to do, but does it in a way which his master has not authorised and would not have authorised had he known of it, the master is nevertheless still responsible, for the servant's act is still within the scope of his employment. On the other hand, in the third place, if the servant is employed only to do a particular work or a particular class of work, and he does something outside the scope of that work, the master is not responsible for any mischief the servant may do to a third party. Lastly, if the servant uses his master's time or his master's place or his master's tools for his own purposes, the master is not responsible."[93]

Category 1: authorised activity

4–11   Thus, if it can be proved that the employer has expressly or impliedly authorised the delictual act, there should be little difficulty in concluding that the employer will be vicariously liable. The view taken by the courts has been that the employer's authority extends to activities that are incidental to the carrying out of express instructions. For example, in *Neville v C&A Modes*[94] an employer was held vicariously liable for defamation when two sales assistants accused an innocent woman of shoplifting. The court held that the actions of the employees in taking steps to protect their employer's property were incidental to their main duties.[95]

Categories 2 and 3 contrasted: unauthorised mode or outside the scope?

4–12   However, it has often been said that it is difficult to distinguish between the second and third categories. Lord President Clyde suggested:

---

[92] See, e.g. *Rose v Plenty* [1976] 1 W.L.R. 141.
[93] *Kirby v National Coal Board*, 1958 S.C. 514 at 532–533. See also *Williams v Hemphill Ltd*, 1966 S.C. (HL) 31 at 44 per Lord Pearce. Lord President Clyde acknowledged various earlier iterations of the principles he articulated, including J.W. Salmond, *Salmond's Law of Torts* (London: Stevens and Haynes, 1907), pp.83–84 and *Canadian Pacific Railway Co v Lockhart* [1942] A.C. 591 at 600 per Lord Thankerton.
[94] *Neville v C&A Modes*, 1945 S.C. 175.
[95] See also *Poland v John Parr and Sons* [1927] 1 K.B. 236.

" . . . the criterion is whether the act which is unauthorised is so connected with acts which have been authorised that it may be regarded as a mode—although an improper mode—of doing the authorised act, as distinct from constituting an independent act for which the master would not be liable . . . "[96]

Thus, a bus driver was held to have been acting within the scope of his employment when he caused injury while racing his bus along the route,[97] whereas a bus conductor employed to collect fares was held to have been outwith the scope of his employment when driving a bus to turn it around at the end of the route.[98] Driving a bus, albeit in an unauthorised and reckless manner, was within the scope of employment of a bus driver, but not a bus conductor. Driving a vehicle has also been held to be within the scope of employment of a garage apprentice, even where the apprentice had no authority, or indeed licence, to drive.[99]

The distinction between the scope of employment and the mode of execution of employment is particularly apparent in *Williams v Hemphill*.[100] A lorry driver was instructed by his employers to carry a group of boys, returning from a Boys Brigade camp, from Benderloch to Glasgow. Apparently after some persistence by several of the boys, the driver was persuaded to take a detour via Connel, then Stirling, and finally Dollar, so that the boys could say a final farewell to the members of a Girl Guildry group they had met at camp. On the way to Dollar, the driver caused an accident in which one of the boys (who was not one of the group who had prevailed upon the driver to make the detour) was seriously injured. Even although at the time of the accident the driver was driving in the opposite direction to Glasgow, because the driver was nevertheless still transporting the boys he was still within the scope of his employment and his employer was confirmed by the House of Lords to be vicariously liable. Interestingly, opinions were reserved on the position if the action had been raised by one of the passengers who had requested the detour.

If a driver deviates from the route he has been instructed to take for his own purposes, he may be engaged "on a frolic of his own" and so in Lord President Clyde's fourth category of activity.[101] However, there is authority that requires it

"to be established that the purpose of the journey on which the employee had embarked in the course of his employment had been wholly abandoned and superseded by a purpose entirely unconnected with the employer's business."[102]

In *Smith v Stages*,[103] the House of Lords provided guidance on whether traveling **4–13** to or from work is within or outwith the scope of employment. Two peripatetic

---

[96] *Kirby v National Coal Board*, 1958 S.C. 514 at 533. See also *Canadian Pacific Railway Co v Lockhart* [1942] A.C. 591 at 599 per Lord Thankerton.

[97] *Limpus v London General Omnibus Co* (1862) 1 H. & C. 526.

[98] *Beard v London General Omnibus Co* [1900] 2 Q.B. 530.

[99] *Mulholland v William Reid & Leys Ltd*, 1958 S.C. 290; *London CC v Cattermoles (Garages) Ltd* [1953] 1 W.L.R. 997.

[100] *Williams v A&W Hemphill Ltd*, 1966 S.C. (HL) 31.

[101] *Storey v Ashton* (1868–1869) L.R. 4 Q.B. 476. Cf. *Angus v Glasgow Corp*, 1977 S.L.T. 206.

[102] *R.J. McLeod (Contractors) Ltd v South of Scotland Electricity Board*, 1982 S.L.T. 274.

[103] *Smith v Stages* [1989] A.C. 928.

workers were sent by their employer from their residence in Staffordshire to work for one week in a location in Pembrokeshire. They were paid for their traveling time and, although the employer did not stipulate the mode of travel, they were provided with the cost of a return rail fare. The two decided to travel in one employee's own car. On the return journey, after working a double shift to complete the job early, the passenger was seriously injured in a crash caused by the driver's negligence. The House of Lords held that, in the circumstances, the driver was acting within the scope of his employment and the employer was vicariously liable. Lord Lowry set out the following general propositions on employee travel:

"1. An employee travelling from his ordinary residence to his regular place of work, whatever the means of transport and even if it is provided by the employer, is not on duty and is not acting in the course of his employment, but, if he is obliged by his contract of service to use the employer's transport, he will normally, in the absence of an express condition to the contrary, be regarded as acting in the course of his employment while doing so.

2. Travelling in the employer's time between workplaces (one of which may be the regular workplace) or in the course of a peripatetic occupation ... will be in the course of the employment.

3. Receipt of wages (though not receipt of a travelling allowance) will indicate that the employee is travelling in the employer's time and for his benefit and is acting in the course of his employment, and in such a case the fact that the employee may have discretion as to the mode and time of travelling will not take the journey out of the course of his employment.

4. An employee travelling *in the employer's time* from his ordinary residence to a workplace other than his regular workplace or in the course of a peripatetic occupation or to the scene of an emergency ... will be acting in the course of his employment.

5. A deviation from or interruption of a journey undertaken in the course of employment (unless the deviation or interruption is merely incidental to the journey) will for the time being (which may include an overnight interruption) take the employee out of the course of his employment.

6. Return journeys are to be treated on the same footing as outward journeys.

All the foregoing propositions are subject to any express arrangements between the employer and the employee or those representing his interests."[104]

Another common incident connected to driving is the giving of lifts to passengers. Where a driver is employed specifically to carry passengers, doing so will be within the scope of employment. What is the situation where the employee carries a passenger without express authority, or contrary to his employer's express instructions? The answer appears to depend upon the

---

[104] *Smith v Stages* [1989] A.C. 928 at 955–956 per Lord Lowry. Whether proposition 5 is consistent with earlier Scottish authority is open to question: see *Williams v A&W Hemphill Ltd*, 1966 S.C. (HL) 31; *R.J. McLeod (Contractors) Ltd v South of Scotland Electricity Board*, 1982 S.L.T. 274.

connection between the lift and the employer's business. Giving a lift to a hitch-hiker, family member, or even a colleague, would be outwith the scope of employment,[105] unless authorised by the employer.[106] However, carrying a passenger in order to further the employer's business will be within the scope of employment, even if that is expressly prohibited by the employer. Thus, in *Rose v Plenty*,[107] the employer of a milkman was held vicariously liable for injuries sustained by a 13-year-old boy who had been employed by the milkman to assist in delivering milk to customers on his round. Even although the employer had specifically prohibited this practice, going as far as posting notices to that effect in the depot, because the boy was carried as part of the employer's business the milkman's negligent act (which caused the crash in which the boy was injured) was within the scope of his employment. The milkman was doing what he was employed to do at the time, albeit in an unauthorised manner.

Categories 2 and 4 contrasted: unauthorised mode or frolic of one's own?

It may also be difficult to distinguish between the second and fourth categories **4–14** of employee activity described by Lord President Clyde in *Kirby*.[108] The extent to which the delictual act complained of is connected to the work of the employee is important: if the act is directly connected the employee will be in category two and within the scope of employment; whereas if the employee is engaged on a "frolic of his own"[109] he will be in category four and the employer will not be vicariously liable.

In *Kirby v National Coal Board* itself, a miner went onto waste ground adjacent to the mine in order to take a cigarette break. The miner was not authorised to be there, and smoking was prohibited by statute. When he struck his match, the gas present in the atmosphere exploded, injuring the miner himself and several colleagues. The Inner House confirmed that because at the time the miner was not mining, but smoking, he was outside of the scope of his employment (engaged in activity falling into category four) and the Coal Board was not vicariously liable. The court contrasted these facts with those in *Century Insurance Co v Northern Ireland Transport Board*,[110] where, while waiting for petrol to transfer from his petrol tanker into the underground tank at a petrol filling station, an employee struck a match in order to light a cigarette. He threw the match onto the ground, which ignited spilt petrol and which in turn caused a large explosion. The House of Lords agreed that the employee's job at that moment was to "stand and wait", which was precisely what he was doing when he committed the careless act. Thus, although he was engaged in a "madness",[111] never mind a "frolic", it was not a "madness of his own": he was doing what he was employed to do, albeit in an unauthorised manner.

---

[105] See, e.g. *Twine v Bean's Express Ltd* [1946] 1 All E.R. 202; *Conway v George Wimpey & Co Ltd* [1951] 2 K.B. 266; *Gormanley v Evening Citizen*, 1962 S.L.T. (Sh. Ct) 61. The injured passenger would now be covered by s.149 of the Road Traffic Act 1988.

[106] See, e.g. *Young v Edward Box Ltd* [1951] 1 T.L.R. 789.

[107] *Rose v Plenty* [1976] 1 W.L.R. 141.

[108] *Kirby v National Coal Board*, 1958 S.C. 514.

[109] This quaint phrase has been attributed to Parke B's judgment in *Joel v Morison* (1834) 6 C. & P. 501.

[110] *Century Insurance Co v Northern Ireland Transport Board*, 1942 A.C. 509. See also *Jefferson v Derbyshire Farmers Ltd* [1921] 2 K.B. 21.

[111] *Harrison v Michelin Tyre Co Ltd* [1985] I.C.R. 696 at 701 per Comyn J.

Several cases have involved the playing of practical jokes by one employee on another, and again the outcomes have not been consistent. Kicking a tin of burning paint thinners towards a colleague was held to amount to a frolic of one's own,[112] whereas pushing the trolley one was employed to push under a duckboard upon which a colleague was standing so as to topple him (for a joke) was "part and parcel" of the employment: a frolic on the job![113] In the latter case the employer was vicariously liable, whereas in the former the employer was not.

Considering that courts make such fine distinctions in cases involving negligence, it would follow that intentional delicts committed by employees, such as assault and fraud, would almost inevitably fall outside of the scope of employment. However, historically that was not necessarily the case, although the decisions were not entirely consistent. In 2001 a new and more liberal approach was endorsed by the House of Lords,[114] but it is appropriate first to examine some of the history.

4–15　　In *Lloyd v Grace, Smith & Co*,[115] a managing clerk employed by a firm of solicitors defrauded a client of the firm. The House of Lords, considering that the acts by which the clerk perpetrated the fraud were within his ostensible authority in his capacity as an agent of the firm, held the firm to be vicariously liable. The justification for imposing vicarious liability for fraud where an agent acts within his ostensible authority was explained by Lord Keith of Kinkel, the Scots Lord of Appeal, in an English appeal, *The Ocean Frost*:

> "[T]he question is whether the circumstances under which a servant has made the fraudulent misrepresentation which has caused loss to an innocent party contracting with him are such as to make it just for the employer to bear the loss. Such circumstances exist where the employer by words or conduct has induced the injured party to believe that the servant was acting in the lawful course of the employer's business. They do not exist where such belief, although it is present, has been brought about through misguided reliance on the servant himself, when the servant is not authorised to do what he is purporting to do, when what he is purporting to do is not within the class of acts that an employee in his position is usually authorised to do, and when the employer has done nothing to represent that he is authorised to do it." [116]

That an employer may be vicariously liable for a fraud committed by an employee within the scope of employment has since been endorsed repeatedly,[117] and in *Taylor v Glasgow DC*[118] Lord Sutherland stated that since *Lloyd* it had not been necessary to show that the employer received any benefit from the fraud, and that since *Uxbridge Permanent Building Society v Pickard*[119] it has not been

---

[112] *Coddington v International Harvester Co of Great Britain Ltd* (1969) 6 K.I.R. 146. See also *Smith v Crossley Bros Ltd* (1951) 95 S.J. 655; *McLean v Remploy*, 1994 S.L.T. 687.

[113] *Harrison v Michelin Tyre Co Ltd* [1985] I.C.R. 696.

[114] The "close connection" test: *Lister v Hesley Hall* [2002] 1 A.C. 215.

[115] *Lloyd v Grace, Smith & Co* [1912] A.C. 716.

[116] *Armagas Ltd v Mundogas SA (The Ocean Frost)* [1986] A.C. 717 at 782–783.

[117] See, e.g. *Meridian Global Funds Management Asia Ltd v Securities Commission* [1995] 2 A.C. 500 at 507 per Lord Hoffmann; *Stone & Rolls Ltd (In Liquidation) v Moore Stephens (A Firm)* [2009] 1 A.C. 1391.

[118] *Taylor v Glasgow DC*, 1997 S.C. 183 at 185.

[119] *Uxbridge Permanent Building Society v Pickard* [1939] 2 K.B. 248.

necessary to show that the employers and the defrauded party have been in some contractual relationship.

Decisions over vicarious liability for assault before the *Lister* case tended towards finding that the employee was on a frolic of his own, although an employer was held to be vicariously liable where an employee had slapped a 12-year-old boy whom he reasonably believed was attempting to steal his employer's goods.[120] However, where a dispute over payment for petrol culminated in the attendant assaulting the customer, the court found that the dispute between the customer and the employee had become personal and the assault was thus a retaliation for personal affront.[121] Agency concepts were referred to so as to justify the decision in *Keppel Bus Co v Sa'ad Bin Ahman*, where a bus conductor, for no apparent reason, used his ticket machine to assault a passenger. Lord Kilbrandon concluded

> "that there was no evidence which would justify the ascription of the act of the conductor to any authority, express or implied, vested in him by his employers; there is, accordingly, no legal ground for holding that the facts of this case justify a departure from the ordinary rule of *culpa tenet suos auctores*."[122]

The passenger, who was blinded in one eye, could sue only the employee—in other words the passenger had no effective remedy.

Scope of employment: recent developments

As stated above, a justification for vicarious liability is provided by the maxim **4–16** *qui facit per alium facit per se* (he who does something through another does it himself). One difficulty in limiting vicarious liability to fit in with this concept is that where an employee does the very thing that the employee is actually employed to prevent, the employee cannot be said to be acting within the scope of his employment. Nowhere is this issue more vividly in focus than in cases where children in care have been physically or sexually abused by those employed to look after them.[123]

The House of Lords was confronted with this problem in *Lister v Hesley Hall*. In a watershed judgment, the Law Lords unanimously held that employer of a warden of a residential school who had abused boys at the school was vicariously liable because the "close connection" between the employment and the wrongful conduct made it "fair and just to hold the employers vicariously liable".[124] In reaching this conclusion, which was heavily influenced by a series of Canadian decisions,[125] the Law Lords purported to return to basic concepts. However, it is submitted that it is difficult to decipher a consistent rationale underpinning the

---

[120] *Poland v John Parr and Sons* [1927] 1 K.B. 236.
[121] *Warren v Henlys Ltd* [1948] 2 All E.R. 935. See also *Mohamud v WM Morrison Supermarkets Plc* [2014] EWCA Civ 116; [2014] W.L.R. (D) 68; *Deatons Pty Ltd v Flew* (1949) 79 C.L.R. 370. Cf. *Pettersson v Royal Oak Hotel Ltd* [1948] N.Z.L.R. 136.
[122] *Keppel Bus Co v Sa'ad Bin Ahman* [1974] 1 W.L.R. 1082 at 1086. See also *Power v Central S.M.T. Co*, 1949 S.C. 376.
[123] See, e.g. *Trotman v North Yorkshire CC* [1999] L.G.R. 584 at 591 per Butler-Sloss L.J.
[124] *Lister v Hesley Hall* [2002] 1 A.C. 215 at 230 per Lord Steyn.
[125] *Bazley v Curry* (1999) 174 D.L.R. (4th) 45; *Jacobi v Griffiths* (1999) 174 D.L.R. (4th) 71.

conclusions across their speeches.[126] Nevertheless, what was agreed was suc-
cinctly summed up by Lord Millett:

> "What is critical is that attention should be directed to the closeness of the
> connection between the employee's duties and his wrongdoing and not to
> verbal formulae."[127]

Whatever, *respondeat superior* now takes priority over *qui facit per alium facit
per se* and it is submitted that all previous decisions on vicarious liability require
to be reconsidered in the light of this liberalising judgment. It has been accepted
that *Lister* is now the leading authority on vicarious liability in Scotland as well
as in England.[128]

A factor that was identified in *Lister*, and which has provided a growing point
for the close connection test in subsequent cases, was the "inherent risk" in the
nature of the job that delicts may be committed by the person employed in that
job. Lord Millett explained:

> "Experience shows that in the case of boarding schools, prisons, nursing
> homes, old people's homes, geriatric wards, and other residential homes for
> the young or vulnerable, there is an inherent risk that indecent assaults on
> the residents will be committed by those placed in authority over them,
> particularly if they are in close proximity to them and occupying a position
> of trust."[129]

However, the Law Lords did take care to distinguish cases where the employee
has merely been afforded the opportunity to commit the wrong from cases where
the wrong is closely connected to what the employee is employed to do. It would
follow that there would not be a sufficient connection between an employee's
duties and sexual harassment,[130] or assault,[131] of a colleague so as to engage
vicarious liability, unless there was a significant risk inherent in the nature of the
job; likewise the opportunistic use of an employer's telephone to make malicious
calls.[132] However, if in the latter case the employee was employed specifically to
operate a telephone, there would be a sufficiently close connection, or nexus,
between the purpose of the employment and the delictual wrong; the inherent risk
being higher than where an employee was employed in a job where he merely
had access to a telephone.

Extrapolating this distinction, abuse committed upon children by the gardener,
canteen assistant or baker[133] employed at the residential school would not be

---

126 See discussion at paras 4–19 to 4–20 below.
127 *Lister v Hesley Hall Ltd* [2002] 1 A.C. 215 at 245 per Lord Millett.
128 *Sharp v Highlands and Islands Fire Board*, 2005 S.L.T. 855 at 862 per Lord Macphail.
129 *Lister v Hesley Hall Ltd* [2002] 1 A.C. 215 at 250 per Lord Millett. The Canadian Supreme Court
   had already identified an "enterprise" risk test to establish vicarious liability in *Bazley v Curry*
   (1999) 174 D.L.R. (4th) 45.
130 See, e.g. *Ward v Scotrail Railways Ltd*, 1999 S.C. 255. Cf. *Majrowski v Guy's & St Thomas's NHS
   Trust* [2007] 1 A.C. 224, where the House of Lords recognised that vicarious liability could arise
   for an employee's breach of statutory duty under the provisions of the Protection from
   Harassment Act 1997.
131 *Wilson v Exel UK Ltd* [2010] S.L.T. 671; *N v Chief Constable of Merseyside Police* [2006] Po.
   L.R. 160; *Vaickuviene v J. Sainsbury Plc*, 2014 S.C. 147.
132 See, e.g. *Heasmans v Clarity Cleaning Co* [1987] I.C.R. 949. Cf. *Brink's Global Services Inc v
   Igrox Ltd* [2011] I.R.L.R. 343.
133 *EB v Order of Oblates of Mary Immaculate* [2005] 3 S.C.R. 45.

sufficiently closely connected to their employment to impose vicarious liability. Indeed, it may be difficult to draw a sufficient "nexus" between sexual abuse and a teacher's duties, where he is employed to teach children only during daytime periods and on school premises yet he carries out the abuse in his own home on a child he has befriended.[134] The inevitable question to raise is whether that conclusion is "fair and just"?

As cases with facts such as these have arisen, the answer to the question posed **4-17** at the end of the last paragraph is increasingly "no", and the outcomes of the cases, especially where appeals are taken to the top of the judicial hierarchy, suggest an inexorable expansion of vicarious liability. Thus, a firm has been held vicariously liable for the fraud of one of its partners,[135] an employer for an employee's theft of silver bars from a third party's transport container the employee was instructed to fumigate,[136] the Attorney General of Jamaica for a shooting carried out by an off-duty police officer using a weapon provided by the police but clearly acting exclusively for his own benefit[137] and an employer for the stabbing outside a nightclub of a customer by an unlicensed doorman, apparently in retaliation after the doorman was chased out of the premises by the victim and others when they intervened to prevent him persisting in an assault he had already perpetrated against two other customers.[138]

Whether vicarious liability would extend to a breach of statutory duty was considered in *Majrowski v Guy's and St Thomas's NHS Trust*.[139] The statute in question was the Protection from Harassment Act 1997, which explicitly provides for a civil claim by the victim to be competent against the harasser.[140] However, in the provisions of the Act applicable to England and Wales, the question of vicarious liability is not specifically dealt with.[141] Nevertheless, the House of Lords held that vicarious liability was competent. Lord Nicholls justified this position by reference to policy factors underpinning vicarious liability including its risk-shifting, loss distribution and deterrence functions, concluding that "with these policy considerations in mind, it is difficult to see a coherent basis for confining the common law principle of vicarious liability to

---

[134] *Jacobi v Griffiths* (1999) 174 D.L.R. (4th) 71. Cf. *Kelly v Gilmartin's Executrix*, 2002 S.C. 602 at 614 per Lady Paton. Lady Paton held (obiter) that the daily mental and physical control exerted over a pupil by a form-teacher indicated a sufficiently close connection between sexual abuse and employment. However, the action was time-barred. See also *Maga v Archbishop of Birmingham* [2010] 1 W.L.R. 1441.

[135] *Dubai Aluminium Co Ltd v Salaam* [2003] 2 A.C. 366.

[136] *Brink's Global Services Inc v Igrox Ltd* [2011] I.R.L.R. 343.

[137] *Bernard v Attorney General of Jamaica* [2005] I.R.L.R. 398. The off-duty officer had announced "police" immediately before shooting the victim, and had later turned up at the hospital where the victim was being treated where he purported to arrest the victim and charge him with an offence! Cf. *Attorney General of the British Virgin Islands v Hartwell* [2004] 1 W.L.R. 1273.

[138] *Mattis v Pollock (t/a Flamingos Nightclub)* [2003] 1 W.L.R. 2158. The Court of Appeal indicated that it would have been prepared, if necessary, to hold the employer personally liable since the evidence showed that the employer had chosen to employ the doorman and had encouraged his violence and aggression.

[139] *Majrowski v Guy's and St Thomas's NHS Trust* [2007] 1 A.C. 224.

[140] If no claim by the victim for personal liability is competent against the person in direct breach of statutory duty, it follows that a claim for vicarious liability against an employer will not be competent either.

[141] As pointed out by Lord Hope of Craighead (at 237), s.18A(2)(b) of the Prescription and Limitation (Scotland) Act 1973 (inserted by the Protection from Harassment Act 1997) implicitly recognises vicarious liability under the 1997 Act.

common law wrongs."[142] However, his fellow Law Lords preferred to follow the justification put forward by Lord Hope, that if Parliament had expressed (albeit indirectly) an intention to impose vicarious liability for breach of the Act in the provisions applicable to Scotland and there was no suggestion that Parliament intended to take a different approach in England and Wales, it could be presumed that it was Parliament's intention to legislate for vicarious liability across both jurisdictions.[143]

Recently there have been several significant cases dealing with vicarious liability for abuse of children by those entrusted with their care. A series of historic abuse cases have come before the courts in Scotland in recent years, and although some of the decisions with regard to vicarious liability issues were decided more conservatively than more recent decisions in comparable cases south of the border, most of the Scottish cases were out of the limitation period and so time-barred under the Prescription and Limitation (Scotland) Act 1973.[144]

Various Claimants[145] is the most significant of those cases, and indeed in the longer term it may transpire to be more so than *Lister*.[146] The question in *Various Claimants* was whether an unincorporated Institute of the Catholic Church could be held vicariously liable for abuse perpetrated upon children in their care by brothers who had joined the Institute and who had been assigned teaching duties at various schools owned by the Institute. The brothers were not employees of the Institute, but were bound together by lifelong vows of chastity, poverty and obedience to very strict rules of conduct.

4–18   *Various Claimants* is significant in that it brings together various threads in the scope and operation of vicarious liability following a decade of seismic change. The judgment was unanimous, with Lord Phillips of Worth Matravers delivering effectively the opinion of the Judicial Committee. Lord Phillips set the new tests in their legal context thus:

> "The law of vicarious liability is on the move ... The courts have developed the law of vicarious liability by establishing the following propositions:
>
> (i) It is possible for an unincorporated association to be vicariously liable for the tortious acts of one or more of its members ...
> (ii) D2 may be vicariously liable for the tortious act of D1 even though the act in question constitutes a violation of the duty owed

---

[142] *Majrowski v Guy's and St Thomas's NHS Trust* [2007] 1 A.C. 224 at 229 per Lord Nicholls of Birkenhead.

[143] *Majrowski v Guy's and St Thomas's NHS Trust* [2007] 1 A.C. 224 at 244 per Lord Hope of Craighead. Lord Hope reinforced this conclusion with reference to Hansard.

[144] See, e.g. *M v Hendron* 2007 S.C. 556, where an attempt to argue vicarious liability based on agency concepts was struck out as an attempt to circumvent problems with demonstrating that the foreseeability of damage criterion required for a duty of care to exist as a pre-requisite to personal liability would be satisfied. Whether this decision represents good law in the light of the Supreme Court decision in *Various Claimants v Institute of the Brothers of the Christian Schools* [2013] 2 A.C. 1 (which was described as "almost a carbon copy of (*M v Hendron*)" (at 8 per Lord Phillips of Worth Matravers) is open to question.

[145] *Various Claimants v Institute of the Bros of the Christian Schools* [2013] 2 A.C. 1. The decision was considered to apply in Scotland by the Inner House in *Vaickuviene v J. Sainsbury Plc*, 2014 S.C. 147.

[146] *Lister v Hesley Hall* [2002] 1 A.C. 215.

to D2 by D1 and even if the act in question is a criminal offence
...

   (iii) Vicarious liability can even extend to liability for a criminal act
of sexual assault ...

   (iv) It is possible for two different defendants, D2 and D3, each to be
vicariously liable for the single tortious act of D1 ...

These developments of the law of vicarious liability ... represent sound
and logical incremental developments of the law. They have, however, made
it more difficult to identify the criteria that must be demonstrated to
establish vicarious liability than it was 50 years ago ...

The test requires a synthesis of two stages:

   (i) The first stage is to consider the relationship of D1 and D2 to see
whether it is one that is capable of giving rise to vicarious liability;

   (ii) ... What is critical at the second stage is the connection that
links *the relationship between D1 and D2* and the act or omission
of D1, hence the synthesis of the two stages."[147]

So, with regard to stage 1, vicarious liability is no longer confined to employer/
employee relationships—the features of each relationship will be examined to
determine whether these are consistent with imposing vicarious liability. Important factors may include:

- the extent to which the defender has the right, and related obligation, to
control the wrongdoer;
- whether the relationship is "akin" to that of employer and employee,
significant sub-factors to consider here include:

  - where the defender is an institution or organisation, its structure;
  - how the wrongdoer fits into that structure;
  - what direction is given by the defender to the wrongdoer;
  - whether what the wrongdoer was doing was mutually intended to
further the objectives of the defender;
  - whether the wrongdoer was obliged, whether by contract or
otherwise, to follow rules laid down by the defender;

- whether the defender and the wrongdoer are engaged in a common
purpose;
- the extent to which the activity that the wrongdoer is engaged to do
carries an inherent risk that a delictual wrong may be committed by an
individual in the position of the wrongdoer; and
- whether the defender is insured, or is in a position where it would be
reasonable to expect him to obtain insurance.

This is not likely to be a comprehensive list of factors, and the decision must be
made in the round, taking into account that

---

[147] *Various Claimants v Institute of the Bros of the Christian Schools* [2013] 2 A.C. 1 at 11–12 per
Lord Phillips of Worth Matravers.

"the policy objective underlying vicarious liability is to ensure, in so far as it is fair, just and reasonable, that liability for (delictual) wrong is borne by a (defender) with the means to compensate the victim."[148]

The Supreme Court was careful to highlight the synthesis of stages 1 and 2. It is the closeness of connection between the *relationship* linking the defender with the wrongdoer and the wrong that is crucial, rather than the closeness of connection between the *duties* of the wrongdoer and the wrong. The test as applied to vicarious liability for abuse was defined in terms of economics, risk and causation:

"Vicarious liability is imposed where a defendant, whose relationship with the abuser put it in a position to use the abuser to carry on its business or to further its own interests, has done so in a manner which has created or significantly enhanced the risk that the victim or victims would suffer the relevant abuse. The essential closeness of connection between the relationship between the defendant and the tortfeasor and the acts of abuse thus involves a strong causative link."[149]

4-19 At the beginning of this section, it was suggested that recent developments in vicarious liability have subverted the justification encapsulated in the maxim *qui facit per alium facit per se* and have promoted concepts which are perhaps more consistent with the maxim *respondeat superior*. A related question is to ask whether these developments have changed the underlying nature of the liability in question. Vicarious liability means liability in place of another. Going back to basics the *culpa* element will be attributable to the wrongdoer, rather than the defender. The wrongdoer must be capable of being held *personally* liable before the defender may be *vicariously* liable, so although there is a need to aver fault on the part of the wrongdoer, there should be no need to aver fault on the part of the defender.

As judicial opinions have been delivered in judgments developing and extending vicarious liability, those judges have frequently emphasised that liability remains vicarious, even although the justifications are often explained in language not inconsistent with personal liability. For example, taking into account the "inherent risk" associated with certain activities implies that the employer must bear some personal responsibility in ensuring that they employ individuals who are of sufficient honesty or integrity to be trusted with the task at hand. Similarly, to say that the right to control carries an associated obligation to control, especially in the context of activities carrying such inherent risks, reinforces the idea that there is some personal responsibility to be borne by the employer. Even definitions of the various iterations of the close connection test, especially where a causative link is drawn between the relationship linking defender and wrongdoer and the wrong, may be said to impute some personal responsibility on the employer or equivalent defender.

At the other end of the scale, it has often been mooted that vicarious liability is an example of strict liability. That is not necessarily inconsistent with the

---

[148] *Various Claimants v Institute of the Bros of the Christian Schools* [2013] 2 A.C. 1 at 15 per Lord Phillips of Worth Matravers.

[149] *Various Claimants v Institute of the Bros of the Christian Schools* [2013] 2 A.C. 1 at 26 per Lord Phillips of Worth Matravers.

concept underpinning the maxim *respondeat superior*, although strict liability sits less comfortably with *qui facit per alium facit per se*. Given that strict liability means, in the context of delictual liability, liability regardless of fault, noting that on one view fault on the part of the employer is irrelevant to vicarious liability would tend to justify an assertion that this provides an example of strict liability. However, if indeed factors related to the employer are to enter the discussion in determining whether it is fair, just and reasonable to impose vicarious liability, it becomes more difficult to justify the assertion that vicarious liability involves strict liability. In any event, it remains important to remember that fault on the part of the wrongdoer must be proved or admitted, so even if it is not mistaken to describe vicarious liability as a type of strict liability, fault must nevertheless be averred in the pursuer's pleadings.[150]

One way of understanding and explaining vicarous liability that has largely **4–20** been ignored by the judiciary is to treat it as a species of liability for third party wrongs. This would firmly classify vicarious liability as a form of personal liability, which some might view as heresy![151] In *Maloco*,[152] Lord Goff identified three situations where a defender would owe a duty of care with regard to the delictual acts of a third party. The first situation was described as being where the defender had a "special relationship" with either the pursuer or with the third party. Examples provided by Lord Goff of special relationships included contractual relationships, specifically incorporating employment relationships, and non-contractual relationships where the defender had "assumed responsibility" to the pursuer and controlling or protecting against the activities perpetrated by the third party would fall within the scope of the responsibility assumed. It is submitted that this analysis could provide a coherent understanding of the liability of the defenders in the abuse cases such as *Lister*[153] and *Various Claimants*.[154] Indeed, Lord Hobhouse, albeit almost merging a range of relevant concepts, appeared at least to acknowledge such an analysis in his speech in *Lister*:

> "The classes of persons or institutions that are in this type of special relationship to another human being include schools, prisons, hospitals and even, in relation to their visitors, occupiers of land. They are liable if they themselves fail to perform the duty which they consequently owe. If they entrust the performance of that duty to an employee and that employee fails to perform the duty, they are still liable. The employee, because he has, through his obligations to his employers, adopted the same relationship towards and come under the same duties to the plaintiff, is also liable to the plaintiff for his own breach of duty. The liability of the employers is a *vicarious* liability because the actual breach of duty is that of the employee.

---

[150] Given that in some cases the courts have indicated that they would be prepared to hold the employer as personally liable, as an alternative to or in addition to vicariously liable, there would appear to be no harm in also averring fault on the part of the defender in the pleadings. See, e.g. *Mattis v Pollock (t/a Flamingos Nightclub)* [2003] 1 W.L.R. 2158; *Maga v Archbishop of Birmingham* [2010] 1 W.L.R. 1441. See also *X (Minors) v Bedfordshire CC* [1995] 2 A.C. 633 at 739–740 per Lord Browne-Wilkinson.

[151] Although it is suggested that the decision of the Supreme Court in *Woodland v Essex CC* [2014] A.C. 537 is consistent with this approach.

[152] *Maloco v Littlewoods Organisation Ltd*, 1987 S.C. (HL) 37 at 77–79 per Lord Goff of Chieveley.

[153] *Lister v Hesley Hall* [2002] 1 A.C. 215.

[154] *Various Claimants v Institute of the Bros of the Christian Schools* [2013] 2 A.C. 1.

The employee is a tortfeasor. The employers are liable for the employee's tortious act or omission because it is to him that the employers have entrusted the performance of their duty. The employers' liability to the plaintiff is also that of a tortfeasor. I use the word 'entrusted' in preference to the word 'delegated' which is commonly, but perhaps less accurately, used. Vicarious liability is sometimes described as a 'strict' liability. The use of this term is misleading unless it is used just to explain that there has been no *actual* fault on the part of the employers. The liability of the employers derives from their voluntary assumption of the relationship towards the plaintiff and the duties that arise from that relationship[155] and their choosing to entrust the performance of those duties to their servant. Where these conditions are satisfied, the motive of the employee and the fact that he is doing something expressly forbidden and is serving only his own ends does not negative the vicarious liability for his breach of the 'delegated' duty."[156]

However, with respect, it is suggested that Lord Hobhouse's juxtaposition of the concepts of liability for third party wrongs, assumption of responsibility, delegation of duty, personal liability, vicarious liability and strict liability ultimately actually add to, rather than subtract from, the confusion permeating this area of law! Nevertheless, this does reflect an increasing difficulty in distinguishing vicarious from personal liability.

So, is there a coherent way of understanding the nature of vicarious liability and how it relates to other concepts operating within the law of delict? It is suggested that the answer is probably "no", and that may also have a lot to do with the apparent policy objective of vicarious liability in providing distributive, as opposed to corrective, justice.

---

[155] This passage reflects the "assumption of responsibility" element that was a central feature of the type of "special relationship" described by Lord Goff in his speech in *Maloco v Littlewoods Organisation Ltd*, 1987 S.C. (HL) 37 at 77–79.

[156] *Lister v Hesley Hall* [2002] 1 A.C. 215 at 239 per Lord Hobhouse of Woodborough.

CHAPTER 5

REMEDIES

INTRODUCTION

There is scope for a victim legitimately to resort to self-help in averting a **5–01** threatened or ongoing delictual wrong. Thus, force may be used in defending against an assault, provided the force is reasonable and proportionate.[1] It is less clear whether force may be used in ejecting a trespasser,[2] or in protecting or recovering property.[3] The Animals (Scotland) Act 1987 permits the detention of stray animals[4] and the destruction of animals where that is necessary for self-defence or for the protection of other persons or, where the individual falls into a defined class (e.g. the farmer who owns the land), for the protection of live-stock.[5]

The principle remedies which may be sought in reparation of a suffered or threatened delictual wrong are damages and interdict. Either remedy (or any other remedy which is within the court's competence) may also be awarded as just satisfaction against any act or proposed act of a public authority which is unlawful under the Human Rights Act 1998 as incompatible with European Convention on Human Rights.[6] Damages are intended to compensate the victim for the harm whereas interdict prohibits the wrongful conduct. These are covered below, along with a discussion of miscellaneous related issues at the end of the Chapter.

DAMAGES

There are rules that apply to damages no matter what area of the law triggers the **5–02** remedy.[7] An example is the rules applying in cases of fatal accidents where the same rules apply to cases of delict or breach of contractual duties.[8] *Aquilian* liability depends upon damage and so the existence of an actionable head bears

---

[1] See, e.g. *Ashmore v Rock Steady Security Ltd* [2006] S.L.T. 207.

[2] Compare, e.g. *Wood v North British Railway* (1899) 2 F. 1 with, e.g. *Kennedy v Young* (1854) 1 Irv. 533.

[3] Professor Walker asserted, without authority, that reasonable force may be used to protect or recover property: D.M. Walker, *The Law of Delict in Scotland*, 2nd edn (Edinburgh: W. Green, 1981), p.450.

[4] Animals (Scotland) Act 1987 s.3.

[5] Animals (Scotland) Act 1987 s.4.

[6] Human Rights Act 1998 s.8(1).

[7] The subject of damages in delict is covered in detail by R.M. White and M.J. Fletcher, *Delictual Damages* (Edinburgh: Tottel, 2000).

[8] Thus the Damages (Scotland) Act 2011 does not distinguish between types of wrongful conduct in the context of damages for wrongful death.

upon liability itself.[9] No attempt is made to track current awards even indicatively.[10] Damages for defamation are sufficiently different that they are treated in context in this work.[11] Damages issues are properly separate from liability. Where the rule of liability is for loss wrongfully caused, then it is no surprise and equally proper to ask, "what, in that context, is loss?" If an apparent head of damage is not a loss for this purpose, there is no liability at all.[12]

PRINCIPAL THEMES

Compensatory damages

5–03   Damages awarded for a wrong may seek to compensate the pursuer for the wrong. This is said to be by way of restitutio in integrum—restoring the situation, so far as money can, to where it was before the wrong was committed.[13] There are innumerable dicta on this matter.[14] One often cited is:

> "The dominant rule of law is the principle of *restitutio in integrum* and subsidiary rules can only be justified if they give effect to that rule".[15]

Another oft-cited passage[16] is that containing Lord Dunedin's four propositions in the *Susquehanna*:

> "(1) There is no difference in this matter between the position in Admiralty law and that of the common law, and the common law says that the damages due either for breach of contract or for tort are damages which, so far as money can compensate, will give the injured party reparation for the wrongful act and for all the natural and direct consequences of the wrongful act. (2) If there be any special damage which is attributable to the wrongful act that special damage must be averred and proved ... (3) If the damage be general, then it must be averred that such damage has been suffered, but the quantification of such damage is a jury question. (4) For a jury question no rigid rules, or rules that apply to all cases, can be laid down, but in each set of circumstances certain relevant considerations will arise which, were

---

[9] For an exposition of that important relationship see J. Stapleton, "The Gist of Negligence" (1988) 104 L.Q.R. 213.

[10] See *McEwan & Paton on Damages for Personal Injuries in Scotland* (Edinburgh: W. Green); *Greens Reparation Law Bulletin* and *Greens Reparation Law Reports* (Edinburgh: W. Green).

[11] See para.7–36.

[12] It has been well put by Lord Hoffman in the House of Lords: "Before one can consider the principle on which one should calculate the damages to which a plaintiff is entitled as compensation for a loss, it is necessary to decide for what kind of loss he is entitled to compensation" (*South Australia Asset Management Corp v York Montague Ltd* sub nom. *Banque Bruxelles Lambert v Eagle Star Insurance Co* [1997] A.C. 191 at 211).

[13] Where alternative analyses would produce different figures, evidence is required to confirm the most appropriate approach: see, e.g. *GUS Property Management Ltd v Littlewoods Mail Order Stores Ltd*, 1982 S.L.T. 533.

[14] See the complete theoretical overhaul in J. Stapleton, "The Normal Expectancies Measure in Tort Damages" (1997) 113 L.Q.R. 257.

[15] *Liesbosch Dredger v S.S. Edison* [1933] A.C. 449 at 463 per Lord Wright. However, the result in that case was not always followed and indeed has been comprehensively rejected by the House of Lords in *Lagden v O'Connor* [2004] 1 A.C. 1067.

[16] See, e.g. *Hutchison v Davidson*, 1946 S.L.T. 11.

the matter before a judge, it would be the duty of the judge in the case to bring before the jury."[17]

The Scottish courts generally like to keep the issue open. A good example is the following hypothesis from Lord Normand in *Hutchison v Davidson*:

"The law of damages ought not, it has been said, to be reduced to a mere rule of thumb, and, whatever subordinate rules may be formulated, there must be some cases which cannot fairly be brought within them. If the garage of a country house is destroyed, and it would cost £300 to replace it, it would in my view be less than just to award £100 because a garage could be bought for that sum in a neighbouring town. The defender's counsel conceded that in such a case the reasonable cost of restoration was the proper measure of damages, and I think that this concession was in no way rash, for a garage in the neighbouring town is not comparable as regards the proprietor's convenience with a garage which is an adjunct of his country house."[18]

Penal, punitive and exemplary damages

Scots law does not award punitive or exemplary damages so as to punish, or **5–04** to make an example of, the wrongdoer.[19] Exemplary and punitive (or aggravated) damages are competent in English law,[20] although they are rarely awarded other than in the most egregious of wrongs,[21] and so are virtually unheard of in negligence cases. Violent profits, which is an almost defunct remedy, can on one view be said to be partly penal, but can reflect a primitive attempt to ensure that the pursuer does not suffer in the mensuration process where consequential losses are sought.

Conventional award

In *Rees v Darlington Memorial Hospital NHS Trust*[22] the House of Lords, by **5–05** a bare majority in a seven-judge committee, controversially adopted the concept of a "conventional award" conjured by Lord Millett for loss of "an important aspect of their personal autonomy" in *McFarlane v Tayside Health Board*.[23] Both cases arose following failed sterilisation operations—in each case a pregnancy followed. In *McFarlane*, the House of Lords had refused a claim for the costs involved in healthy parents bringing up a healthy child on "legal policy"

---

[17] *Admiralty Commissioners v Owners of the SS Susquehanna* [1926] A.C. 655 at 661.

[18] *Hutchison v Davidson*, 1946 S.L.T. 11 at 19.

[19] *Gibson v Anderson* (1846) 9 D. 1; *Muckarsie v Dixon* (1848) 11 D. 4; *Black v North British Railway Co*, 1908 S.C. 444.

[20] See generally *Clerk and Lindsell on Torts*, edited by A. Dugdale and M. Jones, 20th edn (London: Sweet & Maxwell, 2013), paras 28–137 to 28–151. For the current English approach see *Kuddus v Chief Constable of Leicestershire* [2002] 2 A.C. 122. Exemplary damages are intended as a "carrot and stick" to persuade print and online news media to sign up to a regulator deriving its authority from a Royal Charter—see Crime and Courts Act 2013 ss.34–42.

[21] For example, where the defendant has engaged in wrong having calculated that the gain will outstrip the compensation award: see, e.g. *Mosley v News Group Newspapers Ltd* [2008] EWHC 2341 (Q.B.).

[22] *Rees v Darlington Memorial Hospital NHS Trust* [2004] 1 A.C. 309.

[23] *McFarlane v Tayside Health Board*, 2000 S.C. (HL) 1 at 44–45. Apparently, this idea was not completely unprecedented: see *Benham v Gambling* [1941] A.C. 157.

grounds. However, in *Rees*, the mother suffered a pre-existing disability—which was why she underwent the sterilisation operation itself—and so the majority decided that she should receive a sum to reflect that she was denied the mother's right to "live her life in the way that she wished and planned."[24] According to Lord Bingham, the figure of £15,000

> "would not be, and would not be intended to be, compensatory ... But it would not be a nominal, let alone a derisory award. It would afford some measure of recognition of the wrong done."[25]

Whether such a conventional award is competent in Scots law is unclear. Lord Hope was in the dissenting minority who distinguished *Rees* from *McFarlane* and no such award has been granted since. In *Chester v Afshar*,[26] Lord Hoffmann (in a dissenting speech) wondered whether "there might be a case for modest solatium" given that if the patient had been fully advised by the surgeon, she would have retained the right to choose not to have the operation or to have it on a different day.

Mitigation

5–06   Mitigation is a principle of the law of damages and thus applies to damages for delict.[27] It is arguable that the concept applies more obviously to a duty to take reasonable steps to reduce patrimonial losses than to reduce solatium. So if something damaged can be more cheaply repaired than replaced, that ought to be attempted.[28] The onus of proof with regard to a breach of the duty to mitigate is upon the defender.[29] In practice, mitigation as a *duty* is found very seldom in personal injuries cases, where the plea is usually that the sum sued for is excessive, and the pursuer is put to proof of his losses.[30] Nevertheless, in personal injury cases, it may be suggested that the pursuer could have gone back to work sooner, could have found other work, has not tried to find other work or is malingering.

Super-mitigation and *res inter alios acta*

5–07   Here the defender says that a gain that the pursuer has acquired should go to reduction of the damages. The pursuer argues to the contrary, saying that this benefit is nothing to do with the case between them—that it is *res inter alios acta*. This can be seen at work in the Scots case *Cantwell v Criminal Injuries Compensation Board*.[31] Loss of pension rights is a recognised head of recovery

---

[24] *Rees v Darlington Memorial Hospital NHS Trust* [2004] 1 A.C. 309 at 317 per Lord Bingham of Cornhill.

[25] *Rees v Darlington Memorial Hospital NHS Trust* [2004] 1 A.C. 309 at 317 per Lord Bingham of Cornhill.

[26] *Chester v Afshar* [2005] 1 A.C. 134 at 147.

[27] A particular problem touching on mitigation is considered below and should be read in conjunction with this section.

[28] See, e.g. *Nolan v Advance Construction (Scotland) Ltd* [2014] CSOH 4; 2014 G.W.D. 5–107, where damages were limited taking into account that the pursuer had unreasonably refused to accept the defender's offer to remedy the problem that defender had caused.

[29] *Medicina Ltd v Midlothian Council*, 2014 Rep. L.R. 36.

[30] For a theoretical discussion which also takes this view of mitigation in tort see J. Stapleton, "The Normal Expectancies Measure in Tort Damages" (1997) 113 L.Q.R. 257.

[31] *Cantwell v Criminal Injuries Compensation Board*, 2002 S.C. (HL) 1.

of damages for personal injury. The question before the court was the effect of s.10 of the Administration of Justice Act 1982 as amended, which provides that in assessing damages pensions are not to be taken into account. (For the purposes of *Cantwell* the police statutory pension was treated as if contractual). The First Division applied the letter of s.10, allowed a claim for lost pension rights, but did not reduce the award by the actual ill-health pension that was received. The House of Lords upheld an appeal, holding that the proper approach is, first of all, to identify the category of loss: loss up to retirement is loss of earnings; loss after that is pension loss. The next task is to assess that loss before considering any deductions. In this case, there was a loss of pension and a gain of a pension from the same source and they had to be aggregated as a first step. This is an exercise prior to any possible exercise of mitigation. The purpose of s.10 was to protect, say, loss of earnings from the deduction of a pension. This decision clarified the law on the particular practical point.[32] Another leading example of these issues being worked out (this time not a personal injury case) is in the important English House of Lords appeal, *Dimond v Lovell*.[33] The issue arose in the following way. The plaintiff's car was damaged by the defender and she obtained a substitute car pending repair from a credit hire company. As it turned out, the House of Lords accepted that because of consumer protection legislation, the credit hire agreement was legally unenforceable and so the pursuer did not need to pay for the hire and so did not require to recover it from the defendant. This was a windfall for the defendant, who would otherwise have had to pay for some loss of use of the vehicle at the very least.

Lost chances and opportunities

The defender argues that the pursuer has actually been unable to show that a **5–08** wrong has actually caused a loss and should thus lose. The pursuer reformulates the case as the loss of a chance. A basic example is *Kyle v P&J Stormonth Darling WS*.[34] The actual blunder in *Kyle* was the failure by the pursuer's solicitor to lodge appeal papers in a case against a third party that the pursuer had lost before the sheriff and the sheriff principal. It was held by an Extra Division that loss of the chance to press a legal right, if it had an ascertainable value, was actionable. It was not necessary to show that the action, which it was alleged had not been raised, would have been successful. The actual appeal had been marked and legal aid granted. This case involved a consideration of two important cases on the general topic of loss of a chance, namely *Kenyon v Bell*[35] (a personal injury/medical negligence case) and *Yeoman's Executrix v Ferries*[36] (a professional negligence/economic loss case). The former was distinguished and the latter followed.[37] So legal right cases appear to be easier than medical negligence

---

[32] See generally, *McEwan & Paton on Damages for Personal Injuries in Scotland*, para.8–09; S.A. Bennet, "Setting Off on the Wrong Foot", 2000 S.L.T. (News) 214.

[33] *Dimond v Lovell* [2002] 1 A.C. 384.

[34] *Kyle v P&J Stormonth Darling WS*, 1993 S.C. 57. See also *Paul v Ogilvy*, 2001 S.L.T. 171; *McCrindle Group Ltd v Willis Corroon Scotland Ltd*, 2002 S.L.T. 209; *McCrindle Group Ltd v Maclay Murray & Spens* [2013] CSOH 72; 2013 G.W.D. 19–389.

[35] *Kenyon v Bell*, 1953 S.C. 125.

[36] *Yeoman's Executrix v Ferries*, 1967 S.C. 255.

[37] See also *Eldin v Campbell Middleton Burness & Dickson*, 1988 S.C. 204 in the Inner House.

cases.[38] It may also be that misrepresentation cases are easily amenable to this approach. Reece cites Lord Lowry in *Spring v Guardian Assurance Plc*,[39] the case where the worker got a "kiss of death" reference:

> "Once the duty of care is held to exist and the defendants negligence is proved, the plaintiff only has to show that by reason of that negligence he has lost a reasonable chance of employment ... he does not have to prove that but-for the negligent reference, Scottish Amicable would have employed him."[40]

Once and for all

5–09   The general rule is that all loss must be recovered in one action. A further extension of this is that all heads of loss are assumed to have been sought in any action raised.[41] There are exceptions and indulgences.

Re-opening the proof

5–10   In personal injury cases, and perhaps in any other case where the damages incorporate an attempt to measure future loss, it is possible to alter what is claimed for even if it has the effect of opening up a proof or requiring further proof. This was decided by a court of seven judges in *Rieley v Kingslaw Riding School*,[42] in which, pending appeal on liability, the pursuer's leg required to be amputated. The Lord Ordinary had indicated that a higher award would have been appropriate had the leg needed to be amputated. The Inner House in these circumstances agreed to hear the additional proof. Such cases are exceptional.

Renewed claims

5–11   A possible exception to the once and for all rule is that a further claim (e.g. after conclusion of a first action or after a time limit) may be regarded as being so different that it constitutes a new claim.[43] Such cases are likely to be found under either (i) prescription and limitation—it being too late to include a new head,[44] or (ii) res judicata.[45]

Interim damages

5–12   By virtue of special rules, a pursuer may get an advance payment.[46] This is not so much an exception in spirit but in the letter, in that the pursuer obtains

---

[38] The position is similar in English law: see, e.g. *Allied Maples Group v Simmons and Simmons* [1995] 1 W. L. R. 1602; *Gregg v Scott* [2005] 2 A.C. 176. For a full discussion of liability for loss of chance see paras 13–08 to 13–09 below.

[39] *Spring v Guardian Assurance Plc* [1995] 2 A.C. 296.

[40] *Spring v Guardian Assurance Plc* [1995] 2 A.C. 296 at 327. Quoted in H. Reece, "Losses of Chance in the Law" (1996) M.L.R. 188, 203.

[41] *Smith v Sabre Insurance Co Ltd*, 2013 S.C. 569.

[42] *Rieley v Kingslaw Riding School*, 1975 S.C. 28.

[43] This possibility was severely curtailed by the decision in *A v Glasgow City Council* sub nom. *F v Quarriers*, 2010 S.C. 411.

[44] See Ch.15.

[45] These issues are discussed below at para.25–18.

[46] There is a full treatment in *McEwan & Paton on Damages for Personal Injuries in Scotland*, Ch.1. For a general discussion, albeit regarding English law, see S. Ashcroft, "Law Commission Paper No. 224: Structured Settlements and Interim and Provisional Damages—A Practitioner's Review" [1995] J.P.I.L. 3.

damages "twice or more and for all".[47] There is a balancing exercise at the end, and the pursuer might have to repay in certain circumstances,[48] The application of the rule has been settled to a considerable degree by *Cowie v Atlantic Drilling*,[49] in which the First Division upheld a finding of interim damages in favour of a workman injured on a North Sea oil rig. There were a number of alleged breaches of duty and a plea and averments of contributory negligence. There were two issues:

(1) Would the pursuer succeed on liability to any extent? The court considered this matter well settled by an existing line of authority[50]: the test is whether the pursuer will succeed, or will certainly succeed, or will almost certainly succeed. In this case, the accident was admitted; an absolute duty was applicable and the court was satisfied that the test was met.

(2) Would the pursuer succeed without any substantial finding of contributory negligence? Here the court settled a divergence of view on the proper interpretation. The court preferred the view that said it meant "considerable" or "big", which was defined as more than a quarter or a third.[51] The First Division found it impossible to come to an estimate; however, that operated in the pursuer's favour as the court was, therefore, unable to say that there would be a considerable finding.[52]

Provisional damages

The public policy arguments that cases should finish or that people should not **5–13** be troubled too often by the same action has less force when the defender is a public authority or an insured body. On that assumption, UK legislation provides for provisional damages.[53] This is still, as will be seen from the text following, not a true exception to the common law,[54] but, practically, it is a huge divergence. Section 12 of the Administration of Justice Act 1982, which applies in Scotland, provides that if there is proved or admitted to be a risk that at some definite or

---

[47] The practice is governed by the Act of Sederunt (Rules of the Court of Session 1994) (SI 1994/1443) r.43.11 and the Act of Sederunt (Sheriff Court Ordinary Cause Rules) (SI 1993/1956) Sch.1 rr.36.8–36.10. The payment may itself be by instalments: Damages Act 1996 s.2.

[48] See observations in *Walker v Infabco Diving Services Ltd*, 1983 S.L.T. 633.

[49] *Cowie v Atlantic Drilling*, 1995 S.C. 288. The decision applied the Act of Sederunt (Rules of Court, Consolidation and Amendment) 1965 (SI 1965/321) r.89A(1)(c).

[50] *Douglas's C.B. v Douglas*, 1974 S.L.T. (Notes) 7; *Walker v Infabco Diving Services Ltd*, 1983 S.L.T. 633; *Nelson v Duraplex Industries Ltd*, 1975 S.L.T. (Notes) 31 and *Reid v Planet Welding Equipment Ltd*, 1980 S.L.T. (Notes) 7.

[51] *McNeill v Roche Products Ltd*, 1988 S.C. 77.

[52] In *Hogg v Carrigan*, 2001 S.C. 542 an interim award was made in face of a possible no-seatbelt contribution of 25%. See also *Cleland v Campbell*, 1998 S.L.T. 642, where in a head-on vehicle collision case an interim payment was ordered when photographs confirmed the need for the defender to lodge averments as to why he had not seen mud which was clearly a hazard on the road.

[53] There is a full treatment in *McEwan & Paton on Damages for Personal Injuries in Scotland*, Ch.2. See generally J. Blaikie, "Provisional damages: A Progress report", 1991 36 J.L.S. 109; J. Blaikie, "Provisional damages: Please may I have some more?", 1995 S.L.P.Q. 65 and albeit regarding English law, S. Ashcroft, "Law Commission Paper No.224: Structured Settlements and Interim and Provisional Damages—A Practitioner's Review" [1995] J.P.I.L. 3; R. Milligan, "Provisional Damages," 2002 Rep. L.B. 2.

[54] See *Potter v McCulloch*, 1987 S.L.T. 308 at 310 per Lord Weir.

indefinite time in the future the injured person will, as a result of the act or omission which gave rise to the cause of the action, develop some serious disease or suffer some serious deterioration in his physical or mental condition the court may, on the application of the injured person order that damages may be paid and the right granted to come back at some specified later time for more. It is a condition of such an indulgence that the person responsible for paying the damages is a public authority or public corporation; or insured or otherwise indemnified in respect of the claim.

In *White v Inveresk Paper Co Ltd (No.2)*,[55] as anticipated in *Potter* the word "serious" in s.12 had to be considered. Lord Murray, accepting there was a 5–10 per cent risk of osteoarthritis, found this to be material and not de minimis, and did not consider this to be serious deterioration. "Serious" qualifies "deterioration" rather than "effects". The persuasive factor seems to have been the argument that was put by counsel that a clear line needed to be drawn in such cases. Lord Murray pointed out that

> "the deterioration in question does not provide a clear cut and severable threshold of the kind which is really needed to enable the reservation to be properly applied in future. The line between permanent minor residual restrictions of the knee and the onset, probably gradually, of osteo-arthritic symptoms would be difficult or impossible to draw."[56]

In *Meek v Burton's Gold Medal Biscuits Ltd*,[57] Lord Prosser rejected the idea that the Act could not be used where the subsequent claim would depend upon a subsequent triggering event. However, in this case an award was not made. Although there was a risk of serious deterioration, even then there might not be serious consequences.

Quantification of damages (property and economic loss)

5–14   There are certain general approaches. The approach to moveable property can be seen in the following opinion of Lord Jamieson in *Pomphrey v James A. Cuthbertson Ltd*:

> "The owner of an article which has been damaged through the fault of another is entitled to reparation for the wrongful act and for all the natural and direct consequences of the wrongful act. He is entitled to *restitutio in integrum*. To give effect to that general principle of law certain rules have been evolved in practice. If the article can be economically repaired the measure of damages is the cost of the repairs, together with any consequential damage naturally and directly flowing from the wrongful act. If on the other hand the article is totally destroyed or cannot be economically repaired, and is an article which has a marketable value, the measure of damages is in the general case its value immediately before it was damaged. The owner of a damaged article must therefore decide whether the article is capable of being economically repaired or is to be treated as a constructive

---

[55] *White v Inveresk Paper Co Ltd (No.2)*, 1987 S.C. 143.
[56] *White v Inveresk Paper Co Ltd (No.2)*, 1987 S.C. 143 at 150. See also *McMenemy v Argyll Stores Ltd*, 1992 S.L.T. 971.
[57] *Meek v Burton's Gold Medal Biscuits Ltd*, 1989 S.L.T. 338.

total loss. If he makes a wrong decision, he may lay himself open to the charge by the wrongdoer that he has failed in his duty to minimise the damage. The test is: What would a prudent owner, who had himself to bear the loss, do in the circumstances?"[58]

In a professional negligence case where, for example, there has been a negligent valuation, the basic rule is the difference between the careless valuation and the valuation that ought to have been made at the time. Repairs are a cross-check.[59]

South Australia Asset Management *principle ("SAAMCO", "Banque Bruxelles")*

Some economic loss cases give rise to real difficulties where there has been a change in market conditions. There is authoritative guidance on these problems as a result of many cases at the end of the last century. The leading case is now *South Australia Asset Management Corp v York Montague Ltd.*[60] Damages issues are properly separate from liability. Where the rule of liability is for loss wrongfully caused, then it is no surprise and equally proper to ask, what in that context is loss. If an apparent head of damage is not a loss for this purpose there is no liability at all. The present position is most easily seen in the decision in the *Nykredit* associated appeal. The lenders, on March 12, 1990, advanced £2.45 million on the security of a property valued by the defendants at £3.5 million. The correct value had been said by the judge to be between £2 and £2.375 million. The price obtained at auction in February 1993 when the market had taken a fall was £345,000. The judge quantified the damages at £3,058,555. On appeal, the House of Lords said the figure should be the difference between £3.5 million and the true value at the date of the valuation. So the negligent surveyors escaped the consequences of the fall of the market. The reasoning of the House of Lords was based on limiting the scope of the duty itself—the surveyors were not advising on a course of conduct, but relaying information upon which the pursuers would act. The test in tort was: how much worse off were the pursuers because the information was wrong? Lord Hoffmann explained the reasoning by way of the doctor and mountaineer analogy. The mountaineer, who is worried about his knee, goes to the doctor who says it is OK when actually it is not. Reassured, he goes mountaineering and is injured, but not through anything wrong with his knee. The doctor cannot be liable to the mountaineer. It has been

---

[58] *Pomphrey v James A. Cuthbertson Ltd*, 1951 S.C. 147 at 161. For an example which makes a practical point, see *McQueen v Hepburn*, 1979 S.L.T. (Sh. Ct) 38 which considers some of the older dicta. See also *Nolan v Advance Construction (Scotland) Ltd* [2014] CSOH 4; 2014 G.W.D. 5–107.

[59] *Stewart v H.A. Brechin & Co*, 1959 S.C. 306, assumed to be the correct measure in *Martin v Bell Ingram*, 1986 S.C. 208.

[60] *South Australia Asset Management Corp v York Montague Ltd* [1997] A.C. 191 and other related cases. The case is sometimes known as the *Banque Bruxelles Lambert* appeal because that decision in the Court of Appeal was the leading decision. It settled before getting to the Lords. See P.J. Wade, "High Valuations versus Bad Lending", 1995 Rep. L.B. 4–2 and *Leeds Permanent Building Society v Fraser & Steele*, 1995 S.L.T. (Sh. Ct.) 72, both pre-dating *South Australia Asset Management*.

followed (but not applied) in Scotland in *Newcastle Building Society v Paterson, Robertson & Graham.*[61]

Quantification of damages (personal injuries)

5–15   There are a number of special rules about the computation of damages, particularly in the area of personal injuries or in respect of the death of a relative. A distinction is made between loss to a person's estate or wealth, known as patrimonial loss and, on the other hand, pain and suffering, which is compensated by an award of solatium. A complex example dealing with claims for solatium, past wage loss, future wage loss and pension loss is found in *McGlone v Greater Glasgow Health Board,*[62] where the court found that medical negligence had a devastating effect on the pursuer's expected family life and career.

Patrimonial loss: items recoverable

5–16   These are as follows:

    i. Wages lost to the date of the proof, together with an award for projected future loss due to the continuing effects of the injury are recoverable. In computing the amount to be paid in respect of wage loss, the following calculation is made:

- calculate a figure for annual wage loss (called the multiplicand)
- multiply by a figure (called the multiplier) which reflects the years over which there will be a wage loss

The multiplier is necessarily less than the actual number of years over which wages are prima facie lost (e.g. until retirement) because of two main factors:

    a. the fact that damages are paid in a lump sum and can, therefore, gain interest; and

    b. the possibility that the injured person would die at some time during the period over which damages are being awarded.

Thus there is usually a bigger multiplier for a young person than an old person, especially (in the latter case) if the pursuer is soon to retire. Until recently lawyers were content to look at previous cases and the facts of a case to come to a suitable multiplier. After some consideration, reflected clearly in *O'Brien's C.B. v British Steel,*[63] the position has been reached as a result of the decision of the House of Lords in *Wells v Wells,*[64] where "official" Ogden tables are used to start finding the multiplier. Further, in using the tables, it has now been accepted that in

---

[61] *Newcastle Building Society v Paterson, Robertson & Graham,* 2001 S.C. 734. See also *Bristol & West Building Society v Rollo Steven & Bond,* 1998 S.L.T. 9; *Royal Bank of Scotland Plc v Bannerman Johnstone Maclay,* 2005 1 S.C. 437; *Preferred Mortgages Ltd v Shanks* [2008] P.N.L.R. 20; *Kirkton Investments Ltd v VMH LLP* [2012] P.N.L.R. 11; *Henderson (t/a Henderson Group Development) v Wotherspoon* [2013] P.N.L.R. 28.

[62] *McGlone v Greater Glasgow Health Board* [2013] S.C.L.R. 459.

[63] *O'Brien's C.B. v British Steel,* 1991 S.C. 355. See generally See S.A. Bennett, "The Future's Bright; the Future's Ogden", 2001 S.L.T. (News) 54; I. Artis, "The Present is Brighter for Ogden", 2001 S.L.T. (News) 153.

[64] *Wells v Wells* [1999] 1 A.C. 345.

working out the rate of return, which a prudent pursuer would seek, the pursuer does not need to be a risk taker. That suggests that the return will be quite low, which in turn provides a bigger damages award. The particular rate of return to be selected is that set by statutory instrument.[65] The Ogden tables provide only for the contingency of mortality and judicial experience is still needed to enhance or discount multipliers from the tables.[66] Alternatively, rather than apply a multiplier to a multiplicand, and especially if it seems that the pursuer will be able to find work or continue working, the court may award a lump sum to reflect general disadvantage in the job market.

ii. Where the pursuer's life expectancy is diminished as a consequence of the wrong, the Damages (Scotland) Act 2011 s.1(5)–(7) provides that the court should take into consideration lost wages that a pursuer would have earned during the "lost period", i.e. the period between the expected date of death of the pursuer and the expected date of death had the pursuer's life expectancy not been reduced by the accident. Thus damages for patrimonial loss are limited to compensate only for the lost period.

iii. Medical expenses generally are recoverable and will cover the cost of necessary transport between hospital and home. The cost of wheelchairs, crutches and prosthetics is recoverable.

iv. Interest on such damages is due (subject to the court's discretion) usually from the date of the accident, by virtue of the Interest on Damages (Scotland) Act 1971. The damages are divided between prior and future loss. Thus, interest is given on the actual loss sustained to the date of the proof. Interest at half the "court rate" is usually awarded, to reflect the fact that the loss occurred, on a week-by-week basis.

Deductions from patrimonial loss

These are as follows: **5–17**

i. Any benefits received, other than from the injured person's own estate which the person would, in the court's opinion, have received or have been acquired.

ii. Income tax from the loss of earnings sum.

iii. In terms of the Social Security (Recovery of Benefits) Act 1997, benefits are effectively taken back from damages awards.[67] The defender compensator is made liable to the Secretary of State.[68] The pursuer will appreciate that the defender has this liability and must know the extent of the clawback to enable decisions as to settlement or continued conduct of the litigation to be made. The compensator is allowed to deduct the payments he is obliged to make from the

---

[65] Presently the Damages (Personal Injuries) (Scotland) Order 2002. See also *Tortolano v Ogilvie Construction Ltd*, 2012 S.L.T. 1233 (affirmed 2013 S.C. 313).

[66] See, e.g. *Robertson v Smith*, 2000 S.C. 591. Cf. *O'Neill v Dowding & Mills Plc*, 2008 Rep. L.R. 40.

[67] And the associated Social Security (Recovery of Benefits) Regulations 1997 (SI 1997/2205). See generally F. Maguire, "Compensation Recovery: all change in October" (1997) 42 J.L.S.S. 352–354.

[68] Social Security (Recovery of Benefits) Act 1997 s.6.

pursuer.[69] The Act provides how this is to be done, the principle being "like for like".[70] Deductions from each category of damages awarded may only extend to those paid over the relevant period, normally five years from the accident.[71] A full and final settlement brings the relevant period to a premature end.[72] Compensation has to be broken into three heads from which associated benefits are recoverable: (1) earnings lost during the relevant period[73]; (2) cost of care incurred during the relevant period[74]; (3) loss of mobility during the relevant period.[75] Courts must now specify in their orders the amount of any compensation payment that is attributable to each of these three heads over the relevant period.[76] Settlements and tenders will have to be arranged to take account of recoupment. The 1992 Scheme allowed for a small settlement figure of £2,500. The 1997 Act permits this, but it has not been reintroduced at the time of writing. The effect of the scheme is that if the defender or insurer is liable for a penny, they are liable for all the benefits. Under the previous scheme, this State clawback could come out of the injured person's solatium or pain and suffering money—but no longer.

   iv. The full amount of any earnings from employment, or unemployment benefit, and any payment made by the wrongdoer (unless through a trust).

   v. Again against income, there is to be deducted any saving made by the injured person by being maintained at the public expense, e.g. in a hospital.

No account is to be taken of any contractual pension, or pension or retirement benefit from public funds, nor of any payment made by an employer subject to any obligation to repay in the event of the recovery of damages, nor of the proceeds of an insurance policy.[77] Deductions will not be reduced to compensate for the defender's impecuniosity.[78]

There is a modern approach to compensation damages in general (this applies to solatium below) which argues for a structured settlement:

> "A structured settlement is an extra-judicial settlement under which the defender's insurers undertake to pay periodic payments to the insured party in lieu of the whole or part of the traditional lump sum. The defender's

---

[69] Social Security (Recovery of Benefits) Act 1997 s.8.

[70] Social Security (Recovery of Benefits) Act 1997 Sch.2.

[71] In the case of disease, it is five years from the first listed benefit claim.

[72] Social Security (Recovery of Benefits) Act 1997 s.3(4).

[73] Benefits recoverable are: disability working allowance; disablement pension payable under s.103 of the Social Security Contributions and Benefits Act 1992; incapacity benefit; income support; invalidity pension and allowance; jobseekers allowance; severe disablement allowance; sickness benefit; statutory sick pay; unemployability supplement; unemployment benefit.

[74] Recoverable benefits are: attendance allowance; care component of disability living allowance; disablement pension increase payable under s.104 or 105 of the Social Security Contributions and Benefits Act 1992.

[75] Recovered from mobility allowance; mobility component of disability living allowance.

[76] Social Security (Recovery of Benefits) Act 1997 s.15.

[77] Administration of Justice Act 1982 s.10. The common law position is the same: *Parry v Cleaver* [1970] A.C. 1; *Forgie v Henderson* (1818) 1 Murray 410; *Davidson v Upper Clyde Shipbuilders Ltd*, 1990 S.L.T. 329.

[78] *Crossett v Upper Clyde Shipbuilders Ltd*, 2009 Rep. L.R. 126.

insurers (the general insurers) then reinsure their obligation using a life office."[79]

There are tax advantages to such schemes and it may be argued by the defender that the benefit should be split.[80] The system, seldom seen in practice, has now been approved and enhanced by the legislature.[81] In December 2013 the Scottish Government announced a proposal to provide Scottish courts with a power to impose a periodical payment order and to vary such orders in the future.[82]

Solatium

The injured person can recover for, among other things, pain and suffering, **5–18** loss of faculties and shortened expectation of life. If the injured person's expectation of life has been reduced by the injuries and the injured person is, was, or at any time would be, likely to become aware of that reduction, the court must have regard to the consequence of that awareness he has suffered or is likely to suffer.[83] There are complicated rules on interest on damages that are beyond the scope of this book.[84] Generally, past solatium, i.e. pain and suffering suffered before the proof, will attract interest at a figure representing approximately the average "court rates" for the period from the date the injuries were healed, or approximately one-half the average rate where pain continues and part of the solatium is apportioned to the past.[85]

The courts will generally take a broad brush approach to questions of quantification. Courts are assisted by awards in clearly similar cases, but obviously every case has its own peculiarities.[86] It should be remembered that inflation affects the value of money and that care should be taken in comparing awards in older cases. Awards in England still tend to be higher than those in Scotland and those in the United States are many times higher.[87] Until recently, jury trials were rare, yet judicial awards were based on what reasonable men

---

[79] S. Eden, "Structured Settlements" (1992) 37 J.L.S.S. 207. See also *D's Parent and Guardian v Greater Glasgow Health Board*, 2011 S.L.T. 1137 at 1139 per Lord Stewart.

[80] The English Law Commission has issued a consultation paper on this and related topics.

[81] Damages Act 1996 ss.4, 5 and 6. Structured settlements require to be agreed between the parties. Although s.2 of the Damages Act 1996 (as amended by the Courts Act 2003 and which now provides a court in England and Wales with the power to make a periodical payment order (PPO) without the consent of the parties—for discussion see *Flora v Wakom (Heathrow) Ltd* [2007] 1 W.L.R. 482) does not apply in Scotland, the scheme has been considered as "new thinking" in approving a settlement by joint minute which included periodic payments: *D's Parent and Guardian v Greater Glasgow Health Board*, 2011 S.L.T. 1137. In the absence of formal guidance, anonymised versions of the joint minute and settlement agreement are appended at the end of Lord Stewart's opinion.

[82] Scottish Government, *Civil Law of Damages: Issues in Personal Injury, Scottish Government Response to the Consultation* (December 2013), found at *http://www.scotland.gov.uk/Publications/2013/12/7197/0* [Accessed July 4, 2014].

[83] Damages (Scotland) Act 2011 s.1(2). This overturns the rule in *Dalgleish v Glasgow Corp*, 1976 S.C. 32 in which an award was made to a comatose child.

[84] The reader is referred to the Interest on Damages (Scotland) Act 1971 and *McEwan & Paton on Damages for Personal Injuries in Scotland*.

[85] The court rates are laid down in various Acts of Sederunt.

[86] See *Barker v Murdoch*, 1979 S.L.T. 145; *Bowers v Strathclyde RC*, 1981 S.L.T. 122.

[87] This leads to what is sometimes called forum shopping—considering in detail whether jurisdiction can be established in a more generous state. Regular reference to the Judicial Studies Board Guidelines may be bringing Scottish and English awards closer in practice.

would award.[88] Jury cases, albeit still relatively rare, have become more common. Until very recently limited guidance on damages awards was given to juries who would have to rely upon instinct and knowledge brought in from outside of the proceedings and a broad approach was to be taken in terms of deviation of jury awards.[89] This led to an increase in awards.[90] Eventually, in *Hamilton v Ferguson (Spean Bridge) Ltd*[91] a five judge bench in the Inner House declared that the time had come for the court, in furtherance of European Court of Human Rights jurisprudence,[92] to set a framework for civil juries to assist juries in reaching awards that were consistent and to narrow the gap between jury and judge awards. A particular problem with awards for loss of society was perceived. Guidance was proposed by the Lord President (Hamilton):

> "(T)he current absence of judicial guidance to juries on levels of damages is an unsatisfactory feature of our practice. It should, in my view, now be changed. There was some discussion as to how procedurally this might be done. There was a broad consensus that, at the conclusion of the evidence, the parties should, in the absence of the jury, briefly address the trial judge on their suggestions as to the level of non-pecuniary damages which would be appropriate. In light of these submissions and having regard to his own experience and judgment, the trial judge would, in addressing the jury, suggest to them a spectrum within which their award might lie. That spectrum, he would inform them, was for their assistance only; it was not binding on them.
>
> These suggestions appear to me to be sensible. What form the guidance took would of course depend on the particular circumstances of the case. Where a spectrum was deployed, this might not be of the whole span of the parties' suggested figures but would be the range within which, in the judge's opinion, a just award might properly lie. In some cases a single, non-prescriptive figure or series of figures might be appropriate. Where there was a conflict in the evidence what was appropriate by way of damages would, of course, also depend on what the jury determined as to the extent of loss of society actually sustained. In such cases it might be appropriate to offer the jury more than one spectrum, figure or series of figures. Counsel in addressing the jury would be free to suggest figures as to what they maintained was appropriate (*John v MGN Ltd*, [1997] QB 586, at 615, 616) but would not cite authority to them. The issue would no longer contain a figure for 'Damages claimed' but the actual sum for which decree could ultimately be granted would be limited by the sum concluded for in the summons. If a party conceived that the guidance given by the trial judge on damages was unsound in law, it might except to his charge. The note of exceptions could then be considered in due course in any motion for a new trial."[93]

---

[88] See *Bellingham v Todd*, 2011 S.L.T. 1124 at 1130 per Lord Woolman.

[89] *Girvan v Inverness Farmers Dairy (No.2)*,1998 S.C. (HL) 1.

[90] A.M. Hajducki, "Changing Values: Bereavement Awards in the post-Shaher World", 2003 S.L.T. (News) 189.

[91] *Hamilton v Ferguson (Spean Bridge) Ltd*, 2012 S.C. 486.

[92] In particular Protocol 1 art.1—the right to peaceful enjoyment of property.

[93] *Hamilton v Ferguson (Spean Bridge) Ltd*, 2012 S.C. 486 at 520–521.

Transmission on death and the relatives' claim on death

The law is regulated by the Damages (Scotland) Act 2011. This law applies **5–19** where a person dies in consequence of personal injuries[94] sustained by him as a result of an act or omission of another person, being an act or omission giving rise to liability to pay damages to the injured person or his executor.

In brief, it allows the deceased's pain and suffering to be inherited by his executor and it allows various relatives to have a claim in their own right for the wrongful death. There are detailed procedural rules to pull all of these individuals together. The right to solatium in consequence of personal injuries (subject to exceptions) now transfers to the executor in the same way as patrimonial loss cases.[95] The executor may only claim in respect of patrimonial losses incurred prior to death.[96] Solatium is likewise calculated up to the date of death.[97] The relatives' claims depend upon the category or categories into which they fall. Everyone who is in the immediate family is a relative, but not all relatives are in the immediate family: "immediate family" is a subset of "relatives". Loss of support is dealt with under "immediate family", below, but is also relevant to the treatment of "relative".

"Immediate family"

Immediate family is defined as including[98]: **5–20**

   (i) a person who was a spouse or civil partner of the deceased immediately before the death or was then living with the deceased as if married to, or in civil partnership with, the deceased;

   (ii) a (grand)parent or (grand)child of the deceased, or a person who was accepted as a (grand)child of the deceased's family or a person who had accepted the deceased as a (grand)child of the person's family[99];

   (iii) a sibling of the deceased, or brought up in the same household as the deceased and accepted as a child of the family in which the deceased was a child.

"Spouse" has been held to cover a woman who married a man after the delict had been committed.[100] It includes in-laws.[101] Section 4 of the 2011 Act provides for sums of damages payable to relatives who are members of a deceased's immediate family for:

---

[94] Defined as any disease or any impairment of a person's physical or mental condition: Damages (Scotland) Act 2011 s.14(1).

[95] Damages (Scotland) Act 2011 s.2(1).

[96] *Mackintosh v Morrice's Executors*, 2006 S.L.T. 580; *Milligan's Executors v Hewats*, 2013 S.L.T. 758.

[97] In relation to verbal injury cases, a claim in respect of injury transmits to the executor, but, with the exception of patrimonial loss cases, only if the claimant brought an action while alive: s.2(3). While s.2(1)(b) of the Damages (Scotland) Act 2011 distinguishes injuries to "name or reputation" from "personal injuries", the term "personal injuries" in the Administration of Justice Act 1982 was amended to include injury from defamation, verbal injury or any other verbal injury or injury to reputation.

[98] Damages (Scotland) Act 2011 s.14(1).

[99] A child in utero is a child for these purposes: *Cohen v Shaw*, 1992 S.L.T. 1022.

[100] See Administration of Justice Act 1982; *Phillips v Grampian Health Board (No.2)*, 1992 S.L.T. 659.

[101] *McAllister v ICI Plc*, 1997 S.L.T. 351; *Monteith v Cape Insulations*, 1998 S.C. 903.

    (i) loss of support and reasonable expenses incurred in connection with the deceased's funeral[102];

    (ii) distress and anxiety suffered in contemplation of the deceased's death[103];

    (iii) grief and sorrow caused by the deceased's death[104]; and

    (iv) the loss of non-patrimonial benefit from the deceased's society and guidance.[105]

5–21 Liability may be excluded or discharged by statute or by the agreement of the deceased prior to death.[106] Awards for loss of support to immediate family do not take into account the relative's income and are based on 75 per cent of the deceased's net annual income being available to support such relatives.[107] For other relatives (excepting any dependent child under 18) the award will be based on the actual amount of support that was usually received.[108] It is appropriate to take account of likely increases in support that would have followed,[109] but not speculative matters.[110] In assessing loss of support, the court will not take into account remarriage prospects.[111] Nor will the court deduct social security benefits paid or money that will accrue from the deceased's estate, such as insurance policies. Any multiplier applied by the court will apply only to future loss of support and will run only from the date of the interlocutor.[112] According to the English Court of Appeal, the rule that a wrongdoer takes his victim as he finds him means that any reduction in a relative's claim for loss of support, due to the shortening of the relative's own life expectancy being itself caused by a delictual wrong, will be borne by a delinquent whose wrong shortens the life expectancy of the relative, whether that delinquent is the same, or an independent, wrongdoer.[113]

The court may take a broad brush to the three other elements of the award and need not ascribe particular sums to any head. Note that the transfer provisions noted above mean that if an immediate family member dies shortly after the person who died as a result of the defender's negligence, the s.4 claim, having vested, will transmit to the immediate family member's executor.[114] However, of the various heads it is more likely that the grief and sorrow element will transfer

---

[102] For discussion of reasonable funeral expenses see, e.g. *Porter v Dickie*, 1983 S.L.T. 234; *Prentice v Chalmers*, 1985 S.L.T. 168.

[103] See, e.g. *Gallagher v SC Cheadle Hume Ltd* [2014] CSOH 103.

[104] In December 2013 the Scottish Government announced a proposal to enact a provision to ensure that a bereaved relative may not secure damages for psychiatric injury under this provision of the Act. However, this would not preclude a claim for damages for psychiatric injury at common law where the relative was owed a common law duty of care by the defender; see Scottish Government, *Civil Law of Damages: Issues in Personal Injury, Scottish Government Response to the Consultation* (December 2013).

[105] See *Dingwall v Walter Alexander & Sons*, 1981 S.L.T. 313; *Donald v Strathclyde Passenger Transport Executive*, 1986 S.L.T. 625.

[106] Damages (Scotland) Act 2011 s.4(1). This is restricted in certain mesothelioma cases by s.5 of the Damages (Scotland) Act 2011.

[107] Damages (Scotland) Act 2011 s.7(1)(a) and (b).

[108] Damages (Scotland) Act 2011 s.7(1)(c). See, e.g. *Hatherley v Smith*, 1989 S.L.T. 316.

[109] *Smith v Comrie's Executrix*, 1944 S.C. 499.

[110] *Daniell v Aviemore Station Hotel Co*, 1951 S.L.T. (Notes) 76.

[111] Law Reform (Miscellaneous Provisions) Act 1971 s.4.

[112] Damages (Scotland) Act 2011 s.7(1)(e).

[113] *Haxton v Philips Electronics UK Ltd* [2014] 2 All E.R. 225.

[114] Damages (Scotland) Act 2011 s.9.

than the non-patrimonial element because of the restriction on the transfer to the position before the death of the relative. An award is also competent for any personal services rendered to the deceased[115] and it is a legitimate head of claim to include a sum in respect of the services that the deceased would have rendered to the relative in terms of the Administration of Justice Act 1982.

"Relatives"

Relatives, according to s.14(1) of the Damages (Scotland) Act 2011, are **5–22** immediate family as defined above, with the addition of the following: ascendants and descendants; uncles and aunts; any person who was, or was the issue of, a brother, sister, uncle or aunt of the deceased, and any person who, having been a spouse or civil partner of the deceased, had ceased to be so by virtue of a divorce or dissolution of the civil partnership. It does not matter that the relationship is through the mother's line rather than the father's, nor that a child or parent is a stepchild or step-parent, nor that a child is illegitimate. These relatives who are not part of the deceased's immediate family can recover loss of support suffered or likely to be suffered. They may recover reasonable funeral expenses.[116] The relatives, who are not also members of the immediate family, have no right to a loss of society award or to an award in respect of distress and anxiety, grief or sorrow. By s.9 of the 1982 Act, the same extended body of relatives are entitled to claim for personal services, which (i) were or might have been expected to be rendered by the deceased, (ii) were of a kind which when rendered by a person other than a relative would ordinarily be obtainable on payment, and (iii) the deceased might have been expected to render gratuitously. This allows, inter alia, a working widow or widower to claim for the services of, for example, a cook or a housekeeper.

REMEDIES OTHER THAN DAMAGES

Interdict

Interdict[117] is defined by the Scottish judiciary as: **5–23**

> "A judicial prohibition or court order preventing someone from doing something. In an emergency, interim interdict can be obtained in the absence of the person against whom the order is sought (i.e. ex parte)."[118]

Interdict, even in the sheriff court, is governed by a specialised body of rules relevant to such actions. The reasons may be that ultimately the defender can be imprisoned for breach of interdict, and that urgent action is often required. Interdict is a preventative remedy, and so is incompetent as a mechanism to enforce positive action.[119] Interdict looks forward to future conduct, and so is not

---

[115] Damages (Scotland) Act 2011 s.6.
[116] Damages (Scotland) Act 2011 s.4(1)(b).
[117] The term used in England and in many other jurisdictions is injunction.
[118] *http://scotland-judiciary.org.uk/29/0/Glossary* [Accessed May 24, 2014].
[119] *Hampden Park v Dow*, 2002 S.L.T. 95. See also *Phestos Shipping Co Ltd v Kurmiawan*, 1983 S.C. 165; *Shell UK v McGillivray*, 1991 S.L.T. 667.

in itself a mechanism for restoring the parties to the position they were in previously.[120] Nevertheless, there is often the need for interim interdict[121]—it might be useless to await the outcome of a contested case if the damage is already done. There is also a set of other rules that apply to the granting of interim interdict. Many of these cases have to be dealt with immediately, when the balance of convenience is an important consideration which often operates in favour of the status quo. The essential requirements for an interim interdict are title and interest to sue, a prima facie case[122] and the balance of convenience being in the applicant's favour.[123] Normally, interdict cannot be granted against the Crown or the Scottish Parliament.[124]

In cases involving wrongs to the person there is little difficulty. Interdict will be granted against, for example, apprehended assault.[125] In the same way, molestation[126] will be interdicted. For some time, in the case of parties who are married, a matrimonial interdict—one that restrains or prohibits any conduct of one spouse towards the other or a child of the family or prohibits a spouse from entering or remaining in a matrimonial home or in a specified area in the vicinity of a matrimonial home—had the special privilege of being able to be fortified by a power of arrest.[127] More recently, this has been extended to parties who are not married, as conduct that amounts to harassment is now restrained by a special statutory remedy.[128]

Economic delicts[129] may be restrained. Many cases involving economic delicts involve trade unions and account must be taken of their immunities in delict.[130] Unless the immunity applies, strikers, sitters-in and illegal picketers will be restrained.[131] An important rule is that interdict cannot be granted in absence if the defender claims or is likely to claim that he acted in contemplation or furtherance of a trade dispute.[132]

Regarding delictual wrongs to property, passing-off is regularly restrained by interdict: by its nature, if it continues, irreparable damage may be done.[133] The balance of convenience in interim interdict applications will normally favour an established trader. In relation to heritage, interdict operates as a possessory remedy as well as preventing wrongs. It is best to see these cases as adjuncts of

---

[120] *Church Commissioners for England v Abbey National Plc*, 1994 S.C. 651.
[121] The terminology adopted in England and Wales is "interlocutory" injunction.
[122] *Osborne v BBC*, 2000 S.C. 29; *Discovery Communications Inc v Discovery FM Ltd*, 2000 S.C. 69.
[123] *Deane v Lothian Regional Council*, 1986 S.L.T. 22.
[124] Crown Proceedings Act 1947 s.21; Scotland Act 1998 s.40. See also *Davidson v Scottish Ministers (No.1)*, 2006 S.C. (HL) 41.
[125] See paras 6–13 to 6–19.
[126] In the contemporary sense of harassment rather than the traditional sense of troubling of possession in lands: see Stair I, 9, 26 which also imported a right to obtain an order ordering the wrongdoer to desist.
[127] Matrimonial Homes (Family Protection) (Scotland) Act 1981 ss.14(1) and 15(1).
[128] See para.6–28 below.
[129] See Ch.10.
[130] See para.3–41 above. See also K. Ewing, "Interdicts in Labour Law", 1980 S.L.T. (News) 121.
[131] See dicta in *Galt v Philp*,1983 J.C. 51; *Phestos Shipping Co Ltd v Kurmiawan*, 1983 S.C. 165; *Timex Electronic Corp v Amalgamated Engineering and Electrical Union*, 1994 S.L.T. 438.
[132] *Scotsman Publications Ltd v Society of Graphical and Allied Trades*, 1986 S.L.T. 646.
[133] See paras 10–14 to 10–17.

the rights conferred by the law of property rather than as wrongs to property.[134] Cases of nuisance have proved to be difficult to analyse. While from the standpoint of interdict, nuisance incurs a strict liability, so far as damages are concerned "nuisance" *culpa* must be averred and proved, albeit this may be by inference.[135] A fear of repeated trespass can be restrained.[136] So far as moveables are concerned, it is clear from *Leitch & Co v Leyden*[137] that where appropriate, wrongs to moveables will be interdicted.[138]

Interdict against a repeat of a defamatory statement is an obvious and **5-24** uncontroversial protection from harm on the basis of an existing finding of wrongdoing.[139] Even before the coming home of human rights, cases of interdict prior to publication have been treated as much more of a problem. An application is competent.[140] At the interim stage, the balance of convenience remains the test, taking into account the reparability of the harm in damages and the public interest.[141] It may be that asking simply whether or not the statement is prima facie defamatory[142] may not give enough protection to the freedom of speech.[143] An anticipated breach of confidence may be restrained,[144] although similar issues with regards to freedom of speech arise.[145]

Professor Munro has re-examined the issue against the background of human rights law in Scotland and readers are respectfully referred to that study,[146] which considers, inter alia, European Court of Human Rights jurisprudence[147] suggesting that, in future, issues of pressing social need and the necessity of interference will be live issues—there being no bright line rule against prior judicial restraint.[148] However, s.12 of the Human Rights Act 1998 is engaged where there

---

[134] See, e.g. *Colquhoun v Paton* (1859) 21 D. 996; *Maxwell v Glasgow and South-Western Railway Co* (1866) 4 M. 447. And for a third party enforcing a real burden see *Lees v North East Fife DC*, 1987 S.L.T. 769. See also *Wills Trustees v Cairngorm Canoeing and Sailing School Ltd*, 1976 S.C. (HL) 30; *Cowie v SRC*, 1985 S.L.T. 333; *Nicol v Blott*,1986 S.L.T. 677; *Burton's Trustees v Scottish Sports Council*, 1983 S.L.T. 418; *Stewart v Malik*, 2009 S.C. 265.

[135] See paras 8–11 to 8–18. See, e.g. *G.B. & A.M. Anderson v White*, 2000 S.L.T. 37.

[136] *Hay's Trustees v Young* (1877) 4 R. 398; *Steuart v Stephen* (1877) 4 R. 873; *Colquhoun and Cameron v Mackenzie* (1894) 22 R. 23; *Wallace-James v Montgomerie & Co* (1899) 2 F. 107.

[137] *Leitch & Co v Leyden*, 1931 S.C. (HL) 1.

[138] See also paras 8–20 to 8–21.

[139] Walker, *The Law of Delict in Scotland* (1981), p.453. See, e.g. *H v H* [2013] CSIH 82; 2013 G.W.D. 34–675; *Angiolini v Green* [2013] CSOH 196; 2014 G.W.D. 5–104.

[140] *Waddell v BBC*, 1973 S.L.T. 246.

[141] In *Waddell* the balance of convenience favoured the publishers.

[142] As in, e.g. *McMurdo v Ferguson*, 1993 S.L.T. 193.

[143] Traditionally the English approach was to be in favour of publication, e.g. *Ferris-Bank (Anguilla) Ltd v Layar* [1991] T.L.R. 68 unless there was a clear exception such as a conspiracy to injure, e.g. *Gulf Oil Ltd v Page* [1987] Ch. 327 (a case described by Tony Weir as egregious and disgraceful: T. Weir, *Economic Torts* (Oxford: Oxford University Press, 1997), pp.19–20). For further discussion see Ch.7.

[144] Indeed that is the best way of implementing the obligation. The topic is dealt with in Ch.9. See *A Family v BBC, The Scotsman*, November 6, 1992; *Osborne v BBC*, 2000 S.L.T. 150; *X v BBC* 2005 S.L.T. 796; *Response Handling v BBC*, 2008 S.L.T. 51.

[145] See, e.g. *LNS (Terry) v Persons Unknown* [2010] E.M.L.R. 16. Cf. *Ferdinand v MGN Ltd* [2011] EWHC 2454 (Q.B.).

[146] C.R. Munro, "Prior Restraint of the Media and Human Rights Law", 2002 J.R. 1.

[147] Such as, e.g. *Handyside v United Kingdom (A/24)* (1979–80) 1 E.H.R.R. 737; *Observer Ltd and Guardian Newspapers Ltd v United Kingdom(13585/88)* (1992) 14 E.H.R.R. 153.

[148] Professor Munro also provides an incisive analysis of the effect of s.12 of the Human Right Act 1998 in this context. In particular he emphasises the need for an applicant for an order to comply with s.12(2) to take all practicable steps to notify the applicant for an order for prior restraint. See also *Dickson Minto WS v Bonnier Media Ltd*, 2002 S.L.T. 776; *Massie v McCaig*, 2013 S.C. 343.

is an application for prior judicial restraint which might affect the Convention right of freedom of expression. An interim interdict should not be granted unless either the person against whom the application is made has been notified in advance or there are compelling reasons to not notify.[149] Thus, ex parte applications generally cannot be brought without the respondent being afforded the opportunity to make representations as to why the application should not be granted. Further, such an interim interdict should not be granted unless the court is satisfied that the applicant is likely to establish that publication should not be allowed.[150] This requirement impacts upon the balance of convenience test and the phrase "likely to establish" has been held by the House of Lords to require that the applicant demonstrate that it is more likely than not that a permanent order be granted following trial.[151] Permanent orders are less controversial.

Declarator

5–25   A litigant may ask the court to declare that a certain course of conduct is a civil wrong. In such a case, the right to the remedy may depend upon the law of delict. A simple declarator might well be sufficient when dealing with a responsible body, which would follow the decision of the court. Indeed, before the enactment of the Crown Proceedings Act 1947, this process was necessary in ordinary reparation cases. A declarator may be sought to declare conduct not delictual if that will have a practical effect in the actual case, although because the Inner House cannot bind the High Court of Justiciary, a declarator of non-criminality is incompetent.[152] In general, a court will decline to grant declarator if it serves no practical purpose. The European Court of Human Rights considers declarations of infringement can be sufficient to constitute just satisfaction and there is no reason at all why Scots courts could not deal with a human rights reparation case in the same way.

Judicial review

5–26   This is a procedure to obtain remedies in matters that concern the Court of Session's supervisory jurisdiction. It is not restricted to matters of public law, but applies also to cases where a jurisdiction is given to a body to take decisions.[153] The private law rules related to title and interest do not apply, and a petitioner may instead confirm "standing" by showing that he will be "directly affected" by the decision under challenge.[154] It might well be the only remedy where there is an alleged liability by omission by a local authority that is causing a continuing loss. While this may well be actionable in damages, a better remedy might be to obtain an order against the authority to prevent further loss.[155] Indeed, it is possible to obtain any remedy in an application for judicial review, including damages and including restitution, unlike the equivalent English jurisdiction.[156]

---

[149] Human Rights Act 1998 s.12(2).
[150] Human Rights Act 1998 s.12(3).
[151] *Cream Holdings Ltd v Banerjee* [2005] 1 A.C. 253. This approach has been applied in Scotland: *X v BBC*, 2005 S.L.T. 796; *Response Handling v BBC*, 2008 S.L.T. 51. See also *Scottish National Party v BBC*, 2010 S.C. 495.
[152] *Law Hospital NHS Trust v Lord Advocate*, 1996 S.L.T. 848.
[153] See, generally, *West v Secretary of State for Scotland*, 1992 S.C. 385.
[154] *Axa General Insurance Ltd, Petitioners* [2012] 1 A.C. 868.
[155] See *Rowling v Takaro Properties Ltd* [1988] A.C. 473 for an illustration.
[156] See *Woolwich v Inland Revenue* [1993] A.C. 70.

If a case raises a several case for reparation that might best be pursued as an ordinary action rather than being tacked on to a judicial review,[157] Damages for abuse of office[158] may be in a different category and might perhaps best be considered in the context of the judicial review action.

Actions of harassment

The Protection from Harassment Act 1997[159] is implemented, inter alia, by a 5–27 separate action of harassment.

State systems

At various times, the reparation system has not been adequate to meet the ends 5–28 of social policy, either domestic, supra-national or international. Thus many wrongs may be compensated, for example through workers compensation systems, the Criminal Injuries Compensation Scheme or the Motor Insurers Schemes.

Court of Session simplified procedure

The Court of Session has introduced special procedures for allowing repara- 5–29 tion cases to be case managed and fast-tracked. Pleadings are reduced in significance and complexity. The law of delict is not affected by any of these rules, but it is likely that more cases will go to proof and more decisions will be reached after proof, which should make the law less abstract but more difficult to state concisely!

---

[157] *Shetland Line (1984) Ltd v Secretary of State for Scotland*, 1996 S.L.T. 653.
[158] See para.17–17 below.
[159] See para.6–28 below.

SECTION II: PROTECTED INTERESTS AND SPECIFIC WRONGS

CHAPTER 6

PERSONALITY RIGHTS AND WRONGS TO THE PERSON

In principle, delictual liability arises in Scots law upon proof of the elements **6–01** encapsulated in the maxim *damnum injuria datum*; meaning loss wrongfully caused. *Damnum*, referring to loss or harm, implies that conduct may be classified as *injuria* where it has a detrimental impact (*datum*) upon an individual's legally protected interests.[1] *Damnum* and *injuria* are thus interrelated. However, it is suggested that *damnum* and *injuria* may also be disaggregated so as to provide two distinct perspectives from which to view liability in delict. One view is from the perspective of what makes conduct wrongful; the other is from the perspective of what legal interests the law should protect. Thus the former perspective may be seen as condemning "wrongs" whereas the latter may be seen as protecting "rights". The law of delict in Scotland arguably may be in the process of relocating from the former to the latter view, accelerated by the new significance given to the rights-based approach of the European Convention on Human Rights by virtue of the Scotland Act 1998 and the Human Rights Act 1998. Thus, a traditional explanation of delictual liability may have taken as its starting point wrongful conduct, whereas a progressive approach may take as its starting point the legally protected interests, or rights, which may be harmed by wrongful conduct. This work attempts to consider delictual liability from both perspectives, and so a discussion of legally protected interests with regard to the "person" will precede a discussion of wrongful conduct, taking a more traditional approach to the classification of wrongs.

"Rights-based" jurisprudence may be traced to Roman law. Ulpian deciphered *corpus*, *fama* and *dignitas* (bodily integrity, reputation and dignity) as interests protected by the *actio injuriarum*.[2] Several institutional writers followed this theme,[3] and recent work has identified a taxonomy of personality rights protected in Scotland by the law of delict.[4] These personality rights include:

- the right to life;
- the right to bodily integrity and personal security;

---

[1] It may be said that there is a sense of circularity in this analysis: the conduct is only wrongful if it causes harm and harm is only reparable if it is caused by wrongful conduct. However, it is suggested that it is inevitable that the elements are interrelated and that each relies upon the others to confirm the concept of *culpa*.

[2] D.47, 10, 1, 2.

[3] Stair, I, 9, 4; Bankton, I, 1, 21; Erskine,.IV, 4, 80.

[4] N. Whitty, "Overview of Rights of Personality" in N. Whitty and R. Zimmermann (eds), *Rights of Personality in Scots Law: A Comparative Perspective* (Dundee: Dundee University Press, 2009), Ch.3.

- the right to identity;
- the right to autonomy;
- the right to dignity;
- the right to liberty;
- the right to physical privacy;
- the right to control private and personal information;
- the right to reputation;
- the right to society in family relationships; and
- the right to bodily integrity of family members after death.

The right to life

6–02   The right to life is recognised in Scots law from birth, although not before.[5] Danger to life by threatened or continuing wrongful conduct, whether intentional or negligent, may be averted by interdict. Section 4 of the Damages (Scotland) Act 2011 permits claims for damages for wrongful death by surviving family members. The right is also recognised by art.2 of the European Convention on Human Rights, although the Convention right is not absolute. Nevertheless, a positive obligation is placed upon the state where there is a real or imminent threat to life.[6] An action may be pursued directly against a public authority under s.7 of the Human Rights Act 1998.

The right to bodily integrity and personal security

6–03   The right to the integrity of one's own body reflects the protected interest in *corpus* as described by Ulpian,[7] whereas the right to personal security, i.e. the right not to be threatened with damage to bodily integrity, reflects the protected interest in *dignitas*. The right to bodily integrity is the corollary of the nominate delicts of assault and seduction, and is also a protected interest with regard to liability for negligence. The right to personal security is traditionally protected by the remedy of lawburrows and is now given statutory recognition in the Protection from Harassment Act 1997. Interdict and damages are competent remedies both at common law and under s.8(5) of the 1997 Act. The right to bodily integrity and personal security is also reflected in art.3 of the European Convention on Human Rights, which prohibits torture, inhuman or degrading treatment.[8]

   The right to bodily integrity is enforceable only from birth but is retrospective upon the application of the *nasciturus* doctrine.[9] The right clearly protects the physical integrity of one's own body and also extends to providing a remedy for the invasion of one's dignity that accompanies a real or threatened interference

---

[5] *Hamilton v Fife Health Board*, 1993 S.C. 369; *Kelly v Kelly*, 1997 S.C. 285. See paras 3–08 to 3–09 above.

[6] *Osman v United Kingdom* (2000) 29 E.H.R.R. 245; *Mitchell v Glasgow City Council*, 2009 S.C. (HL) 21; *Thomson v Scottish Ministers*, 2013 S.C. 628.

[7] See para.6–01 above.

[8] See, e.g. *Venables v News Group Newspapers Ltd* [2001] Fam. 430; *X v Hounslow LBC* [2009] P.T.S.R. 1158.

[9] Bankton I, 1, 7. See, e.g. *Hamilton v Fife Health Board*, 1993 S.C. 369. See paras 3–08 to 3–09 above.

with one's physical integrity. Thus, without statutory or judicial authority, one cannot be compelled to undergo medical treatment[10] or be compelled to provide a blood or urine sample.[11] It is also suggested that the right extends to protection of one's "personal space".[12]

The right may extend to the integrity of living human tissue that was once part of one's body. In *Yearworth v North Bristol NHS Trust*[13] the Court of Appeal in England treated sperm samples as property rather than as remaining a part of the donor's body. However, the classification of sperm samples as falling within personality or property (or some sui generis classification) has yet to be decided in Scotland. At the time of writing the matter is due to be considered in a proof before answer.[14] It is submitted that an analysis recognising an affront to a personality right would provide coherence with the decision in *Stevens v Yorkhill NHS Trust*,[15] where it was recognised that the *actio injuriarum* provided the proper legal basis for solatium for the unauthorised retention of human organs.

The right to identity

Identity may be viewed as an aspect of an individual's personality and also as a personal asset. However, protection of one's right to identity in delict has traditionally been weak in Scots law. Although the appropriation of one's identity has become an issue in the electronic era, so far no specific civil remedy has been recognised by the courts in Scotland for identity theft as such. Fraud is available to deal with the economic consequences of identity theft, but fraud does not deal directly with the impact of identity theft on one's personality.[16] Verbal injury, albeit litigated rarely, is an actionable wrong which provides for solatium for non-patrimonial loss.[17] Whether the developing branch of law described in England and Wales as the tort of misuse of private information can gain sufficient traction so as to be capable of protecting the personality aspect of one's image has yet fully to be tested.[18]

Similarly, the law in Scotland does not appear to incorporate a direct mechanism for the protection or enforcement of an "image right" as such. In England, in treating identity as an asset rather than as an aspect of personality, the law of passing off has been used to obtain an injunction and damages for unauthorised use of a celebrity's name or image.[19] It is considered that a similar action would be competent in Scots law.

6–04

---

[10] See, e.g. *Re T (Adult: Refusal of Treatment)* [1993] Fam. 95. See also *L v L's Curator ad litem*, 1997 S.L.T. 167; *Re B (A Minor) (Wardship: Sterilisation)* [1988] A.C. 199; *Re F (Mental Patient)* [1990] 2 A.C. 1. See discussion of the defence of necessity at para.14–10 below.

[11] See, e.g. *Whitehall v Whitehall*, 1958 S.C. 252.

[12] See, e.g. *McKie v Orr*, 2002 Rep. L.R. 137 (affirmed sub nom. *McKie v Chief Constable of Strathclyde*, 2003 S.C. 317). The action failed for lack of averments of malice.

[13] *Yearworth v North Bristol NHS Trust* [2010] Q.B. 1.

[14] See *Holdich v Lothian Health Board*, 2014 S.L.T. 495.

[15] *Stevens v Yorkhill NHS Trust*, 2006 S.L.T. 889. See para.3–19 above.

[16] See paras 10–12 to 10–13 below.

[17] See Ch.7.

[18] See, e.g. *Murray v Express Newspapers Plc* [2009] Ch. 481; *Weller v Associated Newspapers* [2014] EWHC 1163 (QB). See also Ch.9.

[19] *Clark v Associated Newspapers* [1998] 1 W.L.R. 1558; *Irvine v Talksport Ltd* [2003] 2 All E.R. 881.

The right to autonomy

6–05   "Autonomy" may mean different things in different contexts,[20] but the concept of a right to autonomy simplistically may be described as the right to make one's own decisions. Given that an individual's decisions inevitably impact on others, no person can claim an absolute right of autonomy. The question is then the extent to which the law recognises an individual's right to autonomy as a factor to consider in balancing competing interests.

Autonomy has been described as a "personality" as opposed to a "proprietory" right.[21] In principle an individual enjoys autonomy in determining the size of his or her family.[22] Likewise, in principle a patient enjoys autonomy in deciding whether or not to undergo medical treatment.[23] However, the doctrine of informed consent has not found its way into Scots law,[24] and so it may be said that the law compromises a patient's autonomy by taking a paternalistic approach to the issue of consent for medical treatment.

The right to dignity

6–06   The *actio injuriarum* provided for solatium for *contumelia* (insult). Thus, Roman law appeared to recognise a distinct right to dignity or self-esteem, i.e. how one values oneself. That Scots law echoes this approach may be confirmed in that a defamatory statement need not be communicated to a third party to sound in damages.[25] The *actio injuriarum* may thus provide a basis for the development of a remedy for breach of privacy in Scotland.[26] The now antiquated wrongs of seduction and enticement also provided a remedy for the impact on the dignity of the pursuer. Statutory provisions such as those found in the Protection from Harassment Act 1997 and the Protection from Abuse (Scotland) Act 2001 may be said to recognise a right to dignity.

The right to liberty

6–07   Scots law protects the right to liberty through the delicts of wrongful detention, arrest or imprisonment and through malicious prosecution. Damages may be for affront as well as for patrimonial loss. The right to liberty is also protected by art.5 of the European Convention on Human Rights, although the European Court has accepted that "kettling" of demonstrators did not breach art.5(1), provided that it had been rendered unavoidable by circumstances beyond the control of the authorities and was necessary in order to avert a real risk of serious injury or damage.[27] The right to liberty is also reinforced by the right to respect for private life set out in art.8 of the Convention. Thus, even where police are given statutory powers to detain and stop and search or arrest an individual,

---

[20] See, e.g. G. Dworkin, *The Theory and Practice of Autonomy* (Cambridge: Cambridge University Press, 1988).

[21] *Holdich v Lothian Health Board*, 2014 S.L.T. 495 at 520 per Lord Stewart.

[22] *McFarlane v Tayside Health Board*, 2000 S.C. (HL) 1; *Rees v Darlington Memorial Hospital NHS Trust* [2004] 1 A.C. 309.

[23] *Goorkani v Tayside Health Board*, 1991 S.L.T. 94; *Chester v Afshar* [2005] 1 A.C. 134; *Re C (Adult: Refusal of Medical Treatment)* [1994] 1 W.L.R. 290.

[24] *Moyes v Lothian Health Board*, 1990 S.L.T. 444, following the approach taken by the House of Lords in *Sidaway v Board of Governors of the Bethlem Royal Hospital* [1985] A.C. 871.

[25] See, e.g. *Ramsay v Maclay* (1890) 18 R. 130; *Gall v Slessar*, 1907 S.C. 708.

[26] See para.9–19 below.

[27] *Austin v United Kingdom* (2012) 55 E.H.R.R. 14.

unless there are reasonable grounds to suspect wrongdoing the statutory authority will violate art.8.[28]

The right to physical privacy

Voyeuristic activity may be actionable at common law under general principles **6-08** of *culpa*, given the elements of *damnum* (affront), *injuria* (the intentional but clandestine activity demonstrating an *animus injuriandi*) and *datum* being present. A traditional definition of voyeuristic activity may have operated in parallel with what would amount to criminal conduct punishable as a breach of the peace. Article 8 of the European Convention on Human Rights provides substantial impetus to the protection of the right to be "let alone"[29] and may result in an exponential increase in "privacy" litigation. Although the House of Lords has held it not to be a tort to carry out, without consent, an intimate search of a visitor to a prison, the European Court of Human Rights has confirmed that that decision is incompatible with the Convention.[30]

The right protects against unwarranted surveillance, whether by the police[31] or other state authorities,[32] or by private individuals including employers.[33] The right also protects against intrusion into seclusion, such as by the media. Intrusion may be justified in some circumstances, such as where there is an asserted public interest. In such cases a "balancing exercise" must be carried out to consider the extent to which any interference with privacy rights is proportionate to a legitimate aim.[34]

The right to control private and personal information

This is another aspect of a more general right to privacy, as protected by art.8 **6-09** of the European Convention on Human Rights. The opportunity for this right to be protected by the delict of verbal injury appeared to be lost in the 19th century when truth emerged as a complete defence to virtually all forms of verbal injury.[35] The extent to which Scots law is adopting the "tort of misuse of private information" (arguably rooted in protection of property rights rather than personality rights) as opposed to looking to the *actio injuriarum* for inspiration towards an indigenous approach to the protection of private and personal information is discussed in Ch.9 below.

The right to reputation

The right to the integrity of one's reputation reflects the protected interest in **6-10** *fama* as described by Ulpian.[36] This right is protected in Scots law principally by the law of defamation, which is discussed in detail, along with verbal injury generally, below in Ch.7. The right to reputation also enjoys protection by virtue

---

[28] *Gillan v United Kingdom* (2010) 50 E.H.R.R. 45.
[29] S. Warren and L. Brandeis, "The Right to Privacy" 4 Harvard L.R. 193 (1890).
[30] *Wainwright v United Kingdom* (2007) 44 E.H.R.R. 40.
[31] See, e.g. *Connor v HM Advocate*, 2002 J.C. 255.
[32] See, e.g. *HM Advocate v Higgins*, 2006 S.L.T. 946 (prison authorities).
[33] *Martin v McGuiness*, 2003 S.L.T. 1424; *McGowan v Scottish Water* [2005] I.R.L.R. 167.
[34] *Von Hannover v Germany (40660/08 and 60641/08)* [2012] E.M.L.R. 16; *Re S (A Child) (Identification: Restrictions on Publication)* [2005] 1 A.C. 593.
[35] *MacKellar v Duke of Sutherland* (1859) 21 D. 222 (defamation); *Paterson v Welch* (1893) 20 R. 744 (verbal injury).
[36] See para.6–01 above.

of the delicts of wrongful detention and imprisonment and malicious prosecution, and arguably is reinforced by art.8 of the European Convention on Human Rights.[37]

The right to society in family relationships

6–11   The enforcement of this right may now be confined to damages under s.4 of the Damages (Scotland) Act 2011, which requires the family member to have died as a result of the defender's delictual act or omission. Historically, a parent or spouse may have a claim for enticement,[38] a husband a claim against his wife's "paramour" for adultery, and a jilted fiancé a claim for breach of promise of marriage. Most of these claims have been abolished by statute.[39] Article 8 of the European Convention of Human Rights may provide reinforcement if any actions in delict remain competent.

The right to bodily integrity of family members after death

6–12   This right is enjoyed directly by surviving family members and permits an award of solatium for affront upon discovery that the deceased's body has been the subject of an unauthorised operation.[40] An independent legal wrong of unauthorised removal and retention of organs[41] from a cadaver has also been held to be part of the law of Scotland. The court recognised that damages would be by solatium and that the true juridical basis of this type of claim is in the *actio injuriarum*.[42]

WRONGS TO THE PERSON

Assault

6–13   Assault is an overt act intended to interfere with another's physical or psychiatric integrity done without justification or excuse. The *actio injuriarum* root of Scots law infuses the delict of assault as much as any development of the *lex Aquilia*. Accordingly, assault as a delict includes notional assaults, such as threats of harm, whether by words, silence,[43] actions[44] or gestures, if sufficiently immediate.[45] Assault includes conduct that might also be criminal. However, the issue of mens rea (guilty mind) in the criminal law does not feature to any significant extent in the civil law and motive is irrelevant.[46] Thus, where four farm labourers were building a straw stack and three of them began frolicking,

---

[37] *Pfeifer v Austria* (2009) 48 E.H.R.R. 8. Cf. *Karakó v Hungary* (2011) 52 E.H.R.R. 36.
[38] *McKeen v Chief Constable, Lothian and Borders Police*, 1994 S.L.T. 93 would appear to limit the potency of this delict.
[39] Divorce (Scotland) Act 1976 s.10; Law Reform (Husband and Wife) (Scotland) Act 1984 s.1(1).
[40] *Pollok v Workman* (1900) 2 F. 354; *Conway v Dalziel* (1901) 3 F. 318; *Hughes v Robertson*, 1913 S.C. 394.
[41] The unauthorised removal (and retention) would be unlawful only if the purpose of the post-mortem was non-diagnostic or if the diagnostic purpose had been fulfilled.
[42] *Stevens v Yorkhill NHS Trust*, 2006 S.L.T. 889.
[43] Silent telephone calls: see, e.g. *R v Ireland* [1998] A.C. 147.
[44] "Stalking": see, e.g. *Ward v Scotrail Railways Ltd*, 1999 S.C. 255.
[45] See the charge to the jury of Lord President Boyle in *Ewing v Mar* (1851) 14 D. 314.
[46] Although *animus injuriandi* may be inferred from the conduct: *MacDonald v Robertson* (1910) 27 Sh. Ct Rep. 103.

when one of the frolicking workers hit the labourer who had continued to work, Lord Young treated it as a case of assault:

> "Technically he assaulted him, although he did it playfully and without any bad intention, for if a man playfully attacks another to make him engage in sport, I am of the opinion that that is an assault, and if harm results that is an actionable wrong."[47]

Although assault is an intentional wrong, delictual assault is distinguishable from criminal assault with regard to the operation of intent. For an assault to be criminal, generally there must be an intention to *harm* the victim, i.e. motive is relevant. However, a delictual assault will be committed even where the motive is to benefit the victim, if there is an intention to interfere with the victim's physical or psychiatric integrity. Thus, a medical procedure carried out on a patient without the patient's consent is a delictual assault. Although typically the procedure will be carried out for the benefit of the patient, it may be that the patient is harmed as a result. That may be because the medical practitioner has operated on the wrong part of the patient's body, or it may be because the patient has not consented to the operation. Nevertheless, there being a concurrence of *damnum* and *injuria*, an action in assault is competent. However, an accident is not actionable as assault as there will be no element of intent to interfere with the victim's integrity.[48]

Causation

Causation arises as an issue. A person who allegedly kicked a boy was **6–14** assoilzied, the death being caused by a fall, the boy surviving for over two years.[49] In negligence it is appreciated that causation and remoteness of damage are connected and it is more likely in cases of assault that chains of events would be dealt with on the basis of remoteness. Some authority for that might be found in *Scorgie v Lawrie*,[50] where it was held that although paralysis of a pupil's thumb was caused by a blow with the cane, it was not attributable to the fault of the headmistress. *Ewart v Brown*[51] is even clearer in that the schoolmaster who hit a boy on the head with a pointer was held liable for damages for being at fault in hitting him, but not for his subsequent illness.

Defences

Justification

There are many justifications for assault both at common law and by statute. **6–15** Many of the statutory protections are connected with arrest or detention and are noted below. A recent example was the decision of the Inner House that where the prison rules permitted visual examination of the external parts of the body, it was not an assault to part a prisoner's buttocks to examine his anus.[52] Scots law

---

[47] *Reid v Mitchell* (1885) 12 R. 1129.
[48] *Hall v Watson* (1896) 12 Sh. Ct Rep. 117, although a negligence action might attack some "accidents".
[49] *Milne v Thomson* (1841) 5 D. 759.
[50] *Scorgie v Lawrie* (1883) 10 R. 610.
[51] *Ewart v Brown* (1882) 10 R. 163.
[52] *Tolmie v Dewar*, 2003 S.C. 265. Cf. *Wainwright v United Kingdom* (2007) 44 E.H.R.R. 40.

allows a defence to a claim of assault (both criminal and civil) in the case of certain instances assaulting of children. The defence applies in criminal cases and probably in the same way to civil cases. However, the defence is limited to reasonable chastisement—it is supposed to be a disciplinary matter. The defence is available to parents of children and to others having a position of authority and responsibility over the child, such as teachers[53] and probably cohabitants.[54] What is or is not considered reasonable is a matter for the court and clearly there is likely to be uncertainty as a result.[55] In the case of teachers, the defence was limited by the Education Act 1986 in the public sector and removed completely for all schools by the Education Act 1993. It is not corporal punishment, however, to strike a child out of the way of immediate danger of harm or to prevent immediate danger to property of a person, as by rugby tackling a child about to throw a brick through the windscreen of someone's car. There are often proposals for reform, with some favouring complete abolition and others fearing many spoiled children. The debate continues into the 21st century with human rights arguments from freedom of religious expression. It has been held that the UK ban on corporal punishment in schools did not infringe the religious rights of others who did want the right to punish: there was a distinction between a religious belief or practice and an action motivated by religious belief.[56]

The police

6–16   The police do not have a special immunity in relation to assault, but where they are using force in the exercise of their duty, it is necessary to aver that the conduct is outwith the scope of the duty.[57] *Mason v Orr*[58] purports to lay down some guidance in such cases. Mason was bundled down his own stairs from his own pavement as an officer tried to clear the pavement of Mason and his workforce who were watching a royal visit. The Lord Ordinary allowed an issue, but on reclaiming the case was held to be irrelevant. Lord McLaren, in whose opinion the rest of the division concurred, said:

> "To make a relevant case of assault on the part of a police officer on duty it appears to me to be necessary to aver either (1) that the order which the officer was seeking to enforce was unlawful, that is, not within the scope of his duty; or (2) that the pursuer was willing to comply with the order, in which case the use of force would be unnecessary; or (3) that the force used was manifestly in excess of the requirements of the case."[59]

The test is the balance of probabilities,[60] the view sometimes expressed that the evidence of the officer has to be of "more than ordinary persuasive weight" only

---

[53] *Stewart v Thain*, 1981 S.L.T. (Notes) 2.

[54] *Byrd v Wither*, 1991 S.L.T. 206.

[55] *B v Harris*, 1989 S.C. 278; *Peebles v MacPhail*, 1990 S.L.T. 245.

[56] *R. (Williamson and Others) v Secretary of State* [2002] 1 All E.R. 385 is a valuable examination of the religious issues which will no doubt continue to emerge. For a consideration of the issue under other rights systems, see the note: J. Eekelaar, "Corporal Punishment, Parents' Religion and Children's Rights", 2003 L.Q.R. 370.

[57] *Lennox v Rose* (1824) 2 S. 650; *Wallace v Mooney* (1885) 12 R. 710.

[58] *Mason v Orr* (1901) 4 F. 220.

[59] *Mason v Orr* (1901) 4 F. 220 at 223. See also *Baillie v Edinburgh Magistrates* (1906) 14 S.L.T. 344.

[60] *Ward v Chief Constable*, 1991 S.L.T. 292; *Mullan v Anderson*, 1993 S.L.T. 835; *Gilchrist v Chief Constable* Unreported January 7, 1988 Glasgow Sheriff Court.

means that the officer is assumed, as any other citizen, to be honest and truthful until the evidence is heard, tested and scrutinised. There have been far too many cases in which the police have not been believed in recent years for any general rule of law to be acceptable.[61] Although there is clear authority that it is necessary to aver and prove malice and want of probable cause when suing the police, that applies where the conduct complained of is, on the face of it, within the competence of the officer concerned.[62] However, where it is not there is no need to aver malice and want of probable cause.[63]

Provocation

Provocation is not a defence, but will serve to mitigate (reduce) the dam- **6–17** ages.[64]

Self-defence

Self-defence is a complete defence.[65] Where parties are involved in a brawl, **6–18** there is no defence where one party clearly becomes an assailant, as where one man hit another with a bottle at a time when he had ample opportunity to disengage.[66] The defence of *ex turpi causa non oritur actio* may be relevant in such circumstances, although that defence will be bound to fail if the assault is a distinct retaliation to the perpetrator's wrongful act.[67]

Autonomy and consent

Even a good motive does not justify an assault; thus medical treatment without **6–19** a patient's consent is an assault and actionable.[68] However, in an English case,[69] the court refused to impose a rule that a patient's consent has to be fully informed, a rule that does apply in some of the United States of America.[70] The rationale of the informed consent doctrine is that if to touch is prima facie actionable as assault, then if the patient's consent has been obtained on the basis

---

[61] *Downie v Chief Constable, Strathclyde Police*, 1998 S.L.T. 8; *Airnes v Chief Constable, Strathclyde Police*, 1998 S.L.T. (Sh. Ct) 16; *Rae v Chief Constable, Strathclyde Police*, 1998 Rep. L.R. 63.

[62] *Ward v Chief Constable, Strathclyde Police*, 1991 S.L.T. 292.

[63] *Robertson v Keith*, 1936 S.C. 29 (court of seven judges). It is submitted that this is also established by *Mason v Orr* (1901) 4 F. 220, where the Lord Ordinary had thrown out the argument: "This is an action for damages for assault, and if assault be well averred there is no need for an averment or an issue of malice or want of probable cause." This argument was not taken further although it was suggested that there needed to be "an averment to make him responsible analogous to the averment of malice in a case of wrongful apprehension" at 222.

[64] *Ross v Bryce*, 1972 S.L.T. (Sh. Ct) 76; *Anderson v Marshall* (1835) 13 S. 1130. See contra in England, *Lane v Holloway* [1968] 1 Q.B. 379.

[65] For a discussion on the relationship between self-defence, provocation and *ex turpi non oritur actio*, see *Ashmore v Rock Steady Security Ltd*, 2006 S.L.T. 207.

[66] *Marco v Merrens*, 1964 S.L.T. (Sh. Ct) 74.

[67] See, e.g. *McLaughlin v Morrison*, 2014 S.L.T. 111. Nevertheless, where the tables are turned and the assault is escalated the originator of a minor assault may resort to self-defence: see, e.g. *Burns v HM Advocate*, 1995 J.C. 154.

[68] *Thomson v Devon* (1899) 15 Sh. Ct Rep. 209.

[69] *Sidaway v Board of Governors of the Bethlem Royal Hospital* [1985] A.C. 871 (HL); and see also *Gold v Haringey Health Authority* [1987] 3 W.L.R. 649. For Scotland see *Bonthrone v Secretary of State for Scotland*, 1987 S.L.T. 34; *Craig v Glasgow Victoria and Leverndale HBH* Unreported December 1, 1972 Outer House; *Moyes v Lothian Health Board*, 1990 S.L.T. 444.

[70] For a perspective from another jurisdiction see A.C. Malcolm (The Hon. David K.), "The High Court and Informed Consent: The Bolam Principle Abandoned" (1994) 1 Tort L. Rev. 81.

of misinformation or a withholding of available information, the consent given is vitiated and the treatment given thereafter becomes actionable even if the treatment that follows is carried out without fault or negligence. While this reasoning appears quite sound, it was rejected by a majority in the House of Lords on the basis that the whole matter fell to be dealt with on principles of negligence, asking the question: would a reasonable doctor have given more information than that upon which the consent was based? There is support for this approach in Scotland.[71]

Nevertheless, where a reasonable doctor would have given more information which on the balance of probabilities would have persuaded the patient to delay the operation while she sought a second opinion, even where the operation would merely have been delayed and that the risk of complications would have been no higher or lower, if that risk eventuates the harm does become actionable even if the treatment is carried out without fault or negligence.[72]

Contravention of lawburrows

6–20   The remedy of lawburrows was introduced by the Lawburrows Act 1429 where it was concerned with bodily harm. That named delicts can cover more than one interest is demonstrated in that the remedy was extended by the Lawburrows Act 1581 to protect against intrusion on property as well as injury to the person. Although ancient, clearly the remedy remains competent.[73] A person who has been required to find caution (a sum of money or an insurance bond for a sum of money) not to harm another or his family (called "lawburrows") may, if he contravenes the non-molestation order, be sued in an action of contravention of lawburrows for forfeiture of the caution.[74] Although this procedure is rarely used, it was recently used with success in a dispute between neighbours.

In *Liddle v Morton*,[75] the defender admitted breaking the pursuers' windows. He threatened violence and shook his fist. He left a gate off its hinge so that it would fall. It did, but on the postman. A log was thrown through the pursuers' front window. The sheriff granted lawburrows. On appeal to the High Court of Justiciary, counsel for the appellant accepted, as did the court, that the test for granting lawburrows was that set out by Sheriff Macphail in *Morrow v Neil*[76]:

> "The pursuer must establish that he has reasonable cause to apprehend that the defender will harm the person or property of the pursuer or his family, tenants or servants."

---

[71] The Outer House decision in *Moyes v Lothian Health Board*, 1990 S.L.T. 444 is support for the *Sidaway* case: indeed it is argued that Scots law had already come down against the need in all cases for informed consent. See also *M's Guardian v Lanarkshire Health Board*, 2013 S.C. 245. For further reading see K. Norrie, "Informed consent and duty of care", 1985 S.L.T. (News) 289; L. Sutherland, "A Relationship of Mutual Trust", Rep. L.B. 5–4; for England, P.M.D. Grundy and A.P. Gumbs, "Bolam, Sidaway and the Unrecognised Doctrine of Informed Consent: A Fresh Approach" [1997] J.P.I.L. 211. See paras 12–12 to 12–14 below.

[72] See, e.g. *Chester v Afshar* [2005] 1 A.C. 134.

[73] *Duff v Strang*, 2008 J.C. 251.

[74] Lawburrows Acts 1429 and 1581. See generally D.M. Walker, *A Legal History of Scotland* (Edinburgh: Bloomsbury, 2001), Vol.II, pp.615–616.

[75] *Liddle v Morton*, 1996 J.C. 194.

[76] *Morrow v Neil*, 1975 S.L.T. (Sh. Ct) 65 at 67.

The "reasonableness" aspect of this may require to be reviewed if challenged-
—such subtlety was not a feature of 15th century Scottish jurisprudence.[77]

Relatively recently it was unsuccessfully used in two tenement disputes.[78] In
1986, an unsuccessful attempt was made to have a chief constable find caution
for the alleged behaviour of his officers: it was held that lawburrows would only
be granted in respect of the personal behaviour of the defender and not on the
basis of his vicarious responsibility.[79] An attempt to have a chief constable find
caution on the alternative ground of incitement of his officers to cause harm to
the pursuer failed as irrelevant due to a lack of an averment of any apprehension
of physical violence or harm to the pursuer, his family or his property, the point
on incitement being undecided.[80] Although it was confirmed in that case that an
appeal from a decision of a sheriff on lawburrows to the High Court of Justiciary
is not competent,[81] opinion was reserved on whether appeal could be taken to the
Sheriff Principal or to the Inner House. An appeal has since been taken to, and
lost before, the Inner House following a sheriff's dismissal of the claim on its
relevancy.[82]

There are divergent views as to whether it is an elegant remedy or an absurd
form.[83]

Enticement

A right of action exists where a person, even a relative, entices a member of **6–21**
someone's family away from him or her, without justification. There is now,
however, no delictual liability in the most common instance of enticement-
—where a person has induced someone's spouse to leave, or remain apart from,
the other spouse.[84] This delict might provide a remedy in cases where children
are "attracted" to a religious cult. Contrary to that view is the case of *McKeen
v Chief Constable*,[85] where a man was claiming a sum for the intervention of the
police in taking away his child during a custody dispute with his wife. A
particular statement of Professor Walker's was relied upon:

> "A claim may even lie against a parent not entitled to custody who seeks to
> entice a child out of the custody of the parent lawfully entitled
> thereto."[86]

---

[77] See *Porteous v Rutherford*, 1980 S.L.T. (Sh. Ct) 129 and *Tahir v Gosal* Unreported May 16, 1974 Glasgow Sheriff Court.

[78] *Morrow v Neil*, 1975 S.L.T. (Sh. Ct) 65; *Porteous v Rutherford*, 1980 S.L.T. (Sh. Ct) 129.

[79] *Handy v Bowman* Unreported September 22, 1986 Dundee Sheriff Court.

[80] *Duff v Strang*, 2008 J.C. 251.

[81] Criminal Procedure (Scotland) Act 1995 ss.175 and 176 permit appeal to the High Court of Justiciary by way of stated case only with regard to criminal proceedings.

[82] *Duff v Chief Constable, Dumfries and Galloway Police*, 2012 S.L.T. 975.

[83] See generally, W.J. Stewart, "Lawburrows: Elegant Remedy or Absurd Form", 1988 S.L.T. 181 and related correspondence; *Stair Memorial Encyclopaedia*, "Lawburrows"; Kenneth McK. Norrie, "Intentional Delicts" in Reid and Zimmermann, *A History of Private Law in Scotland* (2000), Vol.II: Obligations, pp.497–500 and G. Jamieson, *Summary Applications and Suspensions* (Edinburgh: W. Green, 2000).

[84] Law Reform (Husband and Wife) (Scotland) Act 1984 s.2(2).

[85] *McKeen v Chief Constable of Lothian and Borders*, 1994 S.L.T. 93.

[86] D.M. Walker, *The Law of Delict in Scotland*, 2nd edn (Edinburgh: SULI/W. Green, 1981), p.713.

Lord Morton thought that if such a right existed it was strange that it had not come before the court.[87] He hazarded the opinion that there might be social reasons why recognition of such a right might be inappropriate. It is submitted that the authorities on enticement generally support Professor Walker's view. Contempt of court and criminal sanctions (plagium) might explain why such cases are rare, although even plagium has difficulty with the "new" contact/ residence.[88]

Wrongful detention and arrest

6–22   Generally, the simple act of preventing a person moving around freely is actionable in damages for the affront caused. In *MacKenzie v Cluny Hill Hydropathic Co Ltd*, in which the pursuer was prevented from leaving a room for 15 minutes, the apparently attractive de minimis argument was rejected until, if at all, after proof. Lord Low said:

> "I have no doubt that a wrong and in my view not a trifling wrong, has been averred. It is averred that the manager detains this lady in his room for fifteen minutes after the assault had been committed, and refused to let her go until she made an apology. If that be true it was an outrage, and a relevant case has been stated."[89]

Perhaps the most practical modern significance of this particular delict relates to store detectives detaining persons suspected of shoplifting. Wrongful detention is enough to constitute the delict. There is no need to establish defamation of character.[90]

Henderson v Chief Constable of Fife[91] is a good illustration of how the law applies. Indeed it might be seen as advancing the law: the reasoning is directed at the individual's interest in personal integrity. Some workers barricaded themselves in their employer's laboratory. Action was taken by the police under the Trespass (Scotland) Act 1865. They arrested the workers, who sued for damages on four counts: (1) the arrest and detention were unjustified; (2) if detention was justified there was no need to detain in cells; (3) if detention in cells was necessary then the removal of one worker's brassiere was unjustified; (4) there was no justification for handcuffing one of the individuals. It was held that, in terms of the 1865 Act, the police had been given a discretion to arrest or detain and that they had exercised it reasonably. Moreover, it was also reasonable in the circumstances to keep the admittedly intelligent and articulate employees in cells. However, the claim in respect of the request to remove the brassiere succeeded. Although there had been no previous case where a request to remove clothing had been held to be actionable, Lord Jauncey, then in the Outer House, said that such a request

---

[87] *McKeen v Chief Constable of Lothian and Borders*, 1994 S.L.T. 93 at 96A.
[88] See e.g. *Hamilton v Wilson*, 1994 S.L.T. 431. In *Orr v K*, 2003 S.L.T. (Sh. Ct) 70 the sheriff refused to treat as plagium a mother's failure to return a child on time after contact.
[89] *MacKenzie v Cluny Hill Hydropathic Co Ltd,* 1907 S.C. 200 at 204. See also *Harris v North British Railway Co* (1891) 18 R. 1009; *Walker v Commissioner of the Metropolis* [2014] EWCA Civ 897. In *Walker* the English Court of Appeal held unlawful the unjustified detention by a police officer of a man for only a few seconds.
[90] See, e.g. *Neville v C&A Modes*, 1945 S.C. 175.
[91] *Henderson v Chief Constable of Fife*, 1988 S.L.T. 361.

"must amount to an infringement of liberty . . . I see no reason why the law should not protect the individual from this infringement, just as it does from other infringements."

It was conceded that it was wrongful in the circumstances to handcuff one of the workers. The case illustrates how this delict, like many others, is based upon the protection of the legitimate interests of the citizen.

Statutory detention

In many cases it may be permissible to detain a person either at common law **6–23** or under a statute, for example, where someone wants to leave in breach of contract; or a child may be detained so far as reasonable and necessary in his interests. The master of a ship may detain people for the preservation of good order or the safety of persons, property or the vessel itself,[92] and a mentally ill person may be detained if a danger to himself.[93] Commanders of aircraft have statutory powers ever more requiring to be exercised as a result of a recent phenomenon of "air-rage".[94] To keep a person in prison longer than necessary is a form of wrongful detention.[95] The opinion has been expressed that detention based on identification of a person's photograph as resembling a perpetrator, together with another accusation, was not unlawful.[96] The courts will scrutinise statutory powers carefully.[97]

Arrest

A special form of detention is arrest. Police officers have powers of arrest and **6–24** if properly exercised no wrong is done.[98] It is important to distinguish between cases of unlawful arrest *simpliciter* and cases where there was a power or warrant to arrest but one which turned out to be ineffective. In the former case there is no need to aver malice and want of probable cause; in the latter case the pursuer must prove malice and want of probable cause.[99] In *Robertson v Keith*,[100] the Lord President (Normand) said:

"It is not doubtful that any unwarranted and unlawful proceedings by a public officer resulting in injury to anyone will subject him to liability, and that in such a case proof of malice or want of probable cause is not required of the pursuer."[101]

---

[92] Merchant Shipping Act 1995 s.105.

[93] Mental Health (Care and Treatment) (Scotland) Act 2003; H. Patrick, "New Act Heralds Major Reform of Scottish Mental Health Law", 2003 S.L.T. (News) 255. For a full discussion of issues of principle see *B v F*, 1987 S.L.T. 681.

[94] Anti-terrorism, Crime and Security Act 2001 s.82.

[95] *Walsh v Secretary of State for Scotland*, 1990 S.L.T. 526.

[96] *McLaren v Procurator Fiscal for Lothian and Borders*, 1992 S.L.T. 844.

[97] *Miborrow Petitioner*, 1996 S.C.L.R. (Notes) 314.

[98] If the pursuer is assaulted in the process, an action for damages is competent: *Ruddy v Chief Constable of Strathclyde*, 2013 S.C. (U.K.S.C.) 126.

[99] This point was made in *McKinney v Chief Constable of Strathclyde*, 1998 S.L.T. (Sh. Ct) 80 and rejected by Lord Kingarth in *Woodward v Chief Constable of Fife*, 1998 S.L.T. 1342. *McKinney* was upheld on appeal by the First Division: 2000 G.W.D. 24–919. See also *McKie v Chief Constable of Strathclyde*, 2003 S.C. 317; *Dahl v Chief Constable of Central Scotland Police*, 1983 S.L.T. 420; *Beck v Chief Constable of Strathclyde*, 2005 1 S.C. 149.

[100] *Robertson v Keith*, 1936 S.C. 29.

[101] *Robertson v Keith*, 1936 S.C. 29 at 41.

In *Leask v Burt*,[102] where a man was arrested without warrant and many months after the alleged offence, the case was relevant without averment of malice. In the recent case of *McKinney v Chief Constable of Strathclyde*,[103] decided by the Inner House, the police got it wrong when they, with some reason, thought they had a power of arrest in a matrimonial interdict case but did not in fact have that power. It was conceded the arrest was unlawful in this sense. Therefore, the defenders could not insist upon the pursuer showing malice and want of probable cause.

Where proof of malice is required, each case will be judged on its facts. In *McKie v Chief Constable of Strathclyde*[104] the Inner House refused a reclaiming motion where the pursuer, a serving police officer, complained that the actions of the arresting officers in keeping a watch while she showered, holding her at the charge bar in front of other officers for 10 minutes, and carrying out an intimate search amounted to a series of assaults upon her. None of these actions individually would amount to a breach of duty, and so there was insufficient evidence to infer malice.

In *Louden v Chief Constable of Police Scotland*,[105] a police officer was awarded damages in the sheriff court for wrongful arrest and detention, and for consequent psychiatric illness. It followed from the lack of corroboration with regard to the proposed charge of attempting to pervert the course of justice that her arrest and detention were based on evidence which, at its highest, could not even begin to secure a conviction. Thus, there was no need to aver or prove malice. However, Sheriff Veal opined that had it been necessary, malice would readily have been inferred given that although the district procurator fiscal had already advised one of the arresting officers that there was insufficient evidence against the pursuer, while off-duty she was called to urgently attend police headquarters where she was interviewed and then arrested, that following arrest and for no apparent purpose the pursuer was taken to the police office where she was normally stationed and there cautioned and charged, photographed and had DNA samples taken, and that the husband of one of the arresting officers appeared previously to have been in a relationship with the pursuer.

Malicious prosecution

6–25   To succeed in an action for malicious prosecution against the police or a prosecuting authority requires proof of malice to a high standard in order to displace the immunity generally afforded to the various authorities involved in the prosecution process. In *McKie v Strathclyde Joint Police Board*,[106] a former police officer sued after being tried and acquitted of committing perjury following an allegation that she had lied about her presence at a murder scene based on mistaken fingerprint evidence. Although Lord Wheatley permitted a proof before answer, his Lordship warned that averments of malice and lack of reasonable and probable cause were essential in order to establish an action of malicious prosecution. Thus, the standard of averment and proof was high, requiring the basis of any claim of malice to be described with particular clarity in the pleadings. Furthermore, there had to be a direct connection between the

---

[102] *Leask v Burt* (1893) 21 R. 32.
[103] *McKinney v Chief Constable of Strathclyde*, 1998 Rep. L.R. 82.
[104] *McKie v Chief Constable of Strathclyde*, 2003 S.C. 317.
[105] *Louden v Chief Constable of Police Scotland*, 2014 G.W.D. 20–381.
[106] *McKie v Strathclyde Joint Police Board*, 2004 S.L.T. 982.

malice complained of and the course of action subsequently undertaken. Nevertheless, Lord Wheatley held that it was not necessary to show that the defenders were the sole procurers or instigators of the prosecution.

Wrongful imprisonment

To be actionable the imprisonment has to be shown to have been legally **6–26** unjustifiable in the first place. Superior court judges are immune. Justices of the Peace may be liable for a grossly ultra vires sentence, without proof of malice or lack of probable cause but not for an honest error in statutory interpretation. In *McPhee v Macfarlane's Executor*,[107] Lord President Clyde thought it clear that there could be no liability for an honest error in statutory interpretation. In that particular case, if there had been an error in interpretation of the Summary Jurisdiction (Scotland) Act 1908, it would have been one that magistrates all over the country would have been applying since 1908 and so would not be actionable as grossly ultra vires. Generally, in terms of s.170 of the Criminal Procedure (Scotland) Act 1995, the wrongfully imprisoned pursuer must aver and prove both malice and lack of probable cause, and the action must be commenced within two months of the act complained of.

Seduction

Seduction is a delict perhaps not litigated nearly as often as it is committed and **6–27** to many it may seem like a paternalistic, sexist anachronism in today's society. Professor Walker defines it as "obtaining sexual relations with a virgin by fraud, circumvention, guile, misrepresentations or other persuasive practices and deflowering her."[108] The difference between seduction and fornication (or adultery in particular) is that in the latter there is genuine and full consent. In rape, which is itself actionable as assault, consent is never given at all. In seduction, there is consent, but it is vitiated by the trickery or wiles involved. An example is *Murray v Fraser*,[109] where the pursuer was a headmaster's daughter and alleged that sexual intercourse took place on two occasions, once in a bicycle shed and another time in a wood. She became pregnant. The defender was a tenant farmer about 30 years of age. He was a friend of the family. He said he regarded the girl as a child and the girl said he treated her as such. She was ignorant of sexual matters and believed his assurance that she would come to no harm. Lord Dundas pointed out that the popular meaning of seduction is different from its legal meaning. In general speech, full consent is implied. What he considered important was the defender's relationship with the family and the girl's amazing ignorance of matters sexual. Other examples of wiles are promises to marry not later implemented, courtship with apparent intention to marry and taking advantage of the woman's dependency, as when she is in the man's employment.[110]

Harassment and abuse

Under the Protection from Harassment Act 1997, every individual in Scotland **6–28** has a right to be free from harassment and, accordingly, a person must not pursue

---

[107] *McPhee v Macfarlane's Executor*, 1933 S.C. 163.
[108] Walker, *The Law of Delict in Scotland* (1981), p.698.
[109] *Murray v Fraser*, 1916 S.C. 623.
[110] *Macleod v MacAskill*, 1920 S.C. 72.

a course of conduct which amounts to harassment of another and: (a) is intended to amount to harassment of that person; or (b) occurs in circumstances where it would appear to a reasonable person that it would amount to harassment of that person.[111] Conduct includes speech.[112] Harassment of a person includes causing the person alarm or distress.[113] A course of conduct must involve conduct on at least two occasions.[114] It is not otherwise defined and the matter is for the courts.[115]

There is a defence as a result of the Secretary of State certifying that the conduct related to national security, the economic well-being of the United Kingdom or the prevention or detection of serious crime.[116] Alternatively, it is a defence to show that the conduct complained of was pursued for the purpose of preventing or detecting crime.[117] The other defences are legal authority[118] and that the conduct was reasonable.[119] The Scottish Parliament moved to meet similar mischief. Scottish courts now have power in terms of the Protection from Abuse (Scotland) Act 2001 to attach a power of arrest to an interdict where there is the threat of abuse defined as including violence, harassment, threatening conduct, and any other conduct giving rise, or likely to give rise, to physical or mental injury, fear, alarm or distress. For these purposes, "conduct" includes speech and presence in a specified place or area.

---

[111] Protection from Harassment Act 1997 s.8(1). Conduct intended to cause fear and alarm, such as "stalking", is actionable at common law: *Ward v Scotrail Railways Ltd*, 1999 S.C. 255.

[112] Protection from Harassment Act 1997 s.8(3). "Speech" includes flying banners behind an aircraft: *Howlett v Holding* [2006] EWHC 41; (2006) 150 S.J.L.B. 161.

[113] Protection from Harassment Act 1997 s.8(3). The Act has been used to obtain an injunction to prevent further uploading of photos to the internet by an unknown person in possession of a stolen phone: *AMP v Persons Unknown* [2011] Info. T.L.R. 25.

[114] Protection from Harassment Act 1997 s.8(3). A course of conduct may be constituted by the publication of a series of newspaper articles: *Thomas v News Group Newspapers Ltd* [2002] E.M.L.R. 4.

[115] It has been said that the courts are well placed to distinguish between "the ordinary banter and badinage of life and genuinely offensive and unacceptable behaviour": *Majrowski v Guy's and St Thomas's NHS Trust* [2007] 1 A.C. 224 at 245 per Baroness Hale of Richmond.

[116] Protection from Harassment Act 1997 s.12 (1). The certificate is conclusive. A certificate which purports to be of such type is presumed to be so unless the contrary is proved: s.12(3).

[117] Protection from Harassment Act 1997 s.8(4)(b). The suspicion that crime has been committed must be reasonable and the conduct must be rational: *Hayes v Willoughby* [2013] 1 W.L.R. 935.

[118] Protection from Harassment Act 1997 s.8(4)(a).

[119] Protection from Harassment Act 1997 s.8(4)(c).

CHAPTER 7

REPUTATION AND DIGNITY: DEFAMATION AND RELATED ACTIONS

INTRODUCTION

This Chapter deals principally with delictual wrongs which cause harm to the **7–01** victim's reputation.[1] The essence of reputation was described by Lord Nicholls in *Reynolds v Times Newspapers Ltd*:

> "Reputation is an integral and important part of the dignity of the individual. It also forms the basis of many decisions in a democratic society which are fundamental to its well-being: whom to employ or work for, whom to promote, whom to do business with or to vote for. Once besmirched by an unfounded allegation in a national newspaper, a reputation can be damaged for ever, especially if there is no opportunity to vindicate one's reputation. When this happens, society as well as the individual is the loser. For it should not be supposed that protection of reputation is a matter of importance only to the affected individual and his family. Protection of reputation is conducive to the public good".[2]

Considerable literature has been devoted to the provenance of the areas of law in question, and although the history of the law has been debated at length, the original purpose of some aspects of law —which remain clouded in mysterious terminology—continue to be contested.[3]

Actions for "verbal injuries" and "slander" have been permitted in the Scottish courts for a very long time. Indeed, there is a record of a case of slander coming before the Court of Session as early as 1542.[4] That, however, was exceptional, for at that time the church courts had jurisdiction in such matters. Stair considered fame, reputation and honour to be among the interests that the

---

[1] Victims may include natural and non-natural persons. "Reputation" cannot impact on a non-natural person's "dignity" since a non-natural person cannot have any sense of self-awareness. Thus, harm to a non-natural person's reputation must be measured with reference to patrimonial loss, rather than solatium. Natural persons who are victims of harmful communications may suffer affront and/or patrimonial loss.

[2] *Reynolds v Times Newspapers Ltd* [2001] 2 A.C. 127 at 200 per Lord Nicholls of Birkenhead.

[3] See, e.g. D.M. Walker, *The Law of Delict in Scotland*, 2nd edn (Edinburgh: W. Green, 1981), p.732; Kenneth McK. Norrie, "Hurts to Character, Honour and Reputation: A Re-appraisal", 1984 J.R. 163; Kenneth McK. Norrie, *Defamation and Related Actions in Scots Law* (Edinburgh: Butterworths, 1995); N.R. Whitty and R. Zimmermann (eds), *Rights of Personality in Scots Law: A Comparative Perspective* (Dundee: Dundee University Press, 2009); Elspeth C. Reid, *Personality, Confidentiality and Privacy in Scots Law* (Edinburgh: W. Green/SULI, 2010).

[4] Stair Society, "Delict", Vol.20, p.268.

law protects and described them, somewhat enigmatically, as being "in some way reparable".[5] The last centuries have seen a considerable English influence. Unfortunately, our law of verbal injuries is not clear. One reason is that this is not simply an application of *culpa* as derived from the *lex Aquilia*, but there was an influence from the Roman *actio injuriarum* for insult, affront or (as it is sometimes known) *contumelia*. The history of the subject, that it was dealt with by church courts, makes it likely that it has become something of a mixture of doctrines. A recent critical history will help anyone trying to discover why the law appears so very "organic".[6]

A serious problem is the identification of different wrongs within the overall rubric. Professors Walker and T.B. Smith alerted the community to these problems. Professor Norrie attempted a more fundamental partial deconstruction.[7] Professor Blackie has succeeded in explaining why so many terms have such fluid meanings. Hardly any terms have been stable throughout history making older cases very difficult to place. Professor Norrie has suggested a way forward.[8]

The "bringing home" of human rights in the Human Rights Act 1998 and Scotland Act 1998 has the potential to provide a new stimulus to this area of Scots law. However, a question that has yet to be definitively answered is whether reputation is protected as such by the European Convention on Human Rights. In describing interests protected by Roman law, Ulpian distinguished between *corpus* (body), *fama* (reputation) and *dignitas* (dignity).[9] These were protected by the *actio injuriarum*, which provided solatium for *contumelia* (insult or affront). Although it is beyond question that dignity is a right protected by art.8 of the European Court of Human Rights, it is less clear whether or not reputation is also so protected.[10] Reputation is only explicitly referred to in para.2 of art.10, which sets out the criteria where restrictions on freedom of expression may be permitted. However, the trend in decisions emanating from the European Court of Human Rights in Strasbourg seems to be towards acknowledging that reputation is a right implicitly protected by art.8.[11]

A taxonomy of verbal injury

7–02   Verbal injury was a term used by institutional writers apparently to describe the genus of wrongs to personality which were distinct from "real" injury.[12] The

---

[5] Stair, I, ix, 4.

[6] J. Blackie, "Defamation" in K. Reid and R. Zimmermann (eds), *A History of Private Law in Scotland* (Oxford: Oxford University Press, 2000), Vol.II: Obligations, p.633.

[7] K. Norrie, "Hurts to Character, Honour and Reputation: a Reappraisal", 1985 J.R. 163.

[8] Kenneth McK. Norrie, "The Scots Law of Defamation: Is There A Need For Reform", in Whitty and Zimmermann (eds), *Rights of Personality in Scots Law, A Comparative Perspective* (2009).

[9] D 47, 10, 1, 2.

[10] Reputation is explicitly protected in art.12 of the Universal Declaration of Human Rights, United Nations, 1948.

[11] *Lindon v France* (2008) 46 E.H.R.R. 35; *Pfeifer v Austria* (2007) 48 E.H.R.R. 175; *Putistin v Ukraine* (16882/03) [2013] ECHR 1154. Cf. *Karakó v Hungary* (2011) 52 E.H.R.R. 36. See also *Polanco Torres and Movilla Polanco v Spain* (34147/06), September 21, 2010 (3rd section); *Re BBC* [2010] 1 A.C. 145 at 166 per Lord Hope of Craighead; *Re Guardian News and Media Ltd* [2010] 2 A.C. 697 at 717–718 per Lord Rodger of Earlsferry; *Clift v Slough BC* [2011] 1 W.L.R. 1774; *M v A Scottish Local Authority* 2012 S.L.T. 6.

[12] See, e.g. Erskine, IV, 4, 80.

personality rights that are accordingly susceptible to verbal injury were recognised by Ulpian as *fama* and *dignitas*,[13] Thus, the term "verbal injury" was used to distinguish an affront to personality rights caused by words (*iniuria verbis*) from an affront to personality rights caused by actions (*iniuria realis*).[14] According to Professor Walker, within this generic category there were three species of verbal injury: *convicium*,[15] defamation and malicious falsehood.[16]

An alternative view is that verbal injury is a distinct alternative species to defamation, the distinction being that to amount to actionable verbal injury a communication need not be defamatory. In that sense, verbal injury might be equiparated with malicious falsehood and may also incorporate slander of title, slander of property and slander of business.[17] Given that slanders to title, property or business involve patrimonial losses, rather than affront, or *contumelia*, logically such a view of verbal injury would have it placed elsewhere in a taxonomy of delictual wrongs. Lord Wheatley, suggesting that the law "now appears to be settled," neatly dispensed with this objection in *Barratt International Resorts Ltd v Barratt Owners Group*[18] by distinguishing verbal injury to the owner of a business from slanders, presumably to title, property, goods and business:

> "The term 'verbal injury' is therefore distinct from defamation, which is the remedy available to someone whose personal reputation has been injured by the expression of written or verbal falsehoods. It is also distinct from *convicium* which is concerned with the hurt to an individual's feelings and public reputation, by being brought into public hatred, contempt and ridicule. Further, there are various types of slanders, recognised principally in the English authorities, but which are of no concern in the present case. Different considerations clearly apply to these various kinds of action."[19]

Lord Wheatley went on to explain that the "ingredients" of this distinct action for verbal injury

> "are that false statements, either written or verbal, must be maliciously communicated to third parties, which are calculated or likely to produce, and which in fact do produce, actual damage to the pursuers' business interests."[20]

Accordingly it is suggested that there may be two distinct forms of verbal injury to business interests: an "injurious falsehood" variant where impugning the character of the *person* harms that person's business interests; and a "slander of title, goods, property or business" variant, which appropriately might be described as "malicious falsehood", where impugning *property* harms the

---

[13] D 47, 10, 1, 2.

[14] D.M. Walker, *The Law of Delict in Scotland*, 2nd edn (Edinburgh: W. Green, 1981), p.732.

[15] Whether *convicium* remains part of Scots law is disputed, although it may have the potential to form a growing point for a distinctively Scots law of privacy: see paras 7–42 to 7–43 below.

[16] Walker, *The Law of Delict in Scotland* (1981), p.732.

[17] See, e.g. *Argyllshire Weavers Ltd v A Macaulay (Tweeds) Ltd*, 1965 S.L.T. 21 at 35 per Lord Hunter; *Westcrowns Contracting Services Ltd v Daylight Insulation Ltd* [2005] CSOH 55.

[18] *Barratt International Resorts Ltd v Barratt Owners Group* [2002] Scot CS 318 at [24].

[19] *Barratt International Resorts Ltd v Barratt Owners Group* [2002] Scot CS 318 at [25].

[20] *Barratt International Resorts Ltd v Barratt Owners Group* [2002] Scot CS 318 at [26].

owner's business interests.[21] Adopting Lord Wheatley's taxonomy, harm to non-business interests falls outside of the two forms of verbal injury, and so requires to be dealt with by defamation or by *convicium*. *Convicium* might alternatively be described as "malicious truth", and it is suggested that it remains helpful to use the term verbal injury, but note that the injury is to *feelings* rather than to *business interests*.

This may provide a workable framework distinguishing four categories of case:

1. defamation;
2. verbal injury to feelings: *convicium* and malicious truth;
3. verbal injury to business interests: injurious falsehood; and
4. verbal injury to business interests: malicious falsehood.

Damages as a remedy for defamation include solatium for *contumelia* (insult or affront) to *dignitas* (dignity)[22] and to *fama* (reputation),[23] as well as compensation for patrimonial losses.[24] Damages as a remedy for verbal injuries to feelings will be confined to solatium, and as a remedy for verbal injuries to business interests will be confined to patrimonial loss. It is submitted that there is nothing illogical in suggesting that a single verbal wrong may cause injuries to both feelings and to business interests, in which case the single verbal wrong would be actionable under two or more heads. Interdict is a competent remedy where there is a threat that any wrong will be repeated.

DEFAMATION

7–03 The term defamation encapsulates the concept of reputational harm. To be actionable, a communication must be capable of causing a reasonable person to associate a defamatory imputation with the character of the pursuer. The principal remedy for the harm caused is damages,[25] and for an action to succeed a court must be satisfied that six elements exist. However, a pursuer need prove only three of those elements: that (1) a *communication* carries (2) a *defamatory statement* which (3) a reasonable reader or viewer would *associate with the pursuer* as an individual. The law then presumes the defamatory imputation to be (4) *false* and to (5) have *caused harm* to the pursuer's reputation (6) *inflicted intentionally* by the defender. Thus, to avoid liability the communicator must

---

[21] Arguably it follows that this category should include harm to the business interests of the pursuer caused by the impugning of a third party (who may be deceased).

[22] Given that Scots law does not require communication of a defamatory imputation to a third party, where the defamatory statement is made privately to the pursuer, any remedy may be confined to solatium for *contumelia* to *dignitas*.

[23] Deriving from the *actio injuriarum*.

[24] Deriving from the *Lex Aquilia*.

[25] Interdict is competent but, unless there is a threat of repetition of the libel, rare, at least on an interim application: see, e.g. *Waddell v BBC*, 1973 S.L.T. 246; *Woodland Trust v MacMillan* [2001] Scot CS 236; *ZAM v CFW* [2013] E.M.L.R. 27. Cf. *McMurdo v Ferguson*, 1993 S.L.T. 193. If an application is made for an interim interdict, at least against the media, s.12 of the Human Rights Act 1998 now effectively requires the media interest to be informed. If the person threatening to communicate insists that the allegation is privileged, provably true and on a matter of concern to the public or honest comment then a court is likely to take the approach of "publish and be damned": *Dickson Minto WS v Bonnier Media Ltd*, 2002 S.L.T. 776.

ensure that statements are either free of calumny, protected by law or provably true. Indeed, it might be said that the tradition of the law in Scotland requires the communicator to publish at his peril.[26]

This position is to some extent being tempered by developing jurisprudence which takes into account the right of freedom of expression.[27] However, in England and Wales, recently it has been thought that statutory intervention is required for the law to strike a balance between protection of reputation and freedom of expression that is fit for the 21st century.[28]

The three elements that a pursuer must prove are communication, identification and defamation, whereas the three legal presumptions that then arise are that the defamatory imputation is false, that it causes reputational harm to the pursuer and that it is communicated with the intention to cause harm, i.e. with a form of malice. Before considering these elements it is appropriate to examine who may sue and who can be sued in defamation.

Who may sue?

The starting point is that any natural or legal person has the capacity to sue for **7-04** harm to reputation. This includes registered companies,[29] partnerships[30] and other associations[31] that enjoy sufficient legal personality. However, non-natural persons cannot recover solatium for hurt feelings and so must lead proof of patrimonial loss in order to recover damages.[32]

If an organisation has no legal personality it cannot sue. It has been held that even although a trade union can sue in tort (or delict), it cannot raise proceedings in defamation.[33] The House of Lords confirmed in *Derbyshire CC v Times Newspapers Ltd* that neither a central nor local government body could sue as such in defamation, citing the "chilling effect" that the threat of proceedings would have on freedom of expression.[34] This restriction has been extended to other government bodies[35] and to political parties,[36] but not to universities.[37] It should be noted that the principle does not prevent identifiable individual

---

[26] See, e.g. *Morrison v Ritchie* (1902) 4 F. 645. This decision would seem to impose strict liability, which may now be incompatible with art.10 of the European Convention on Human Rights: see, e.g. *O'Shea v MGN* [2001] E.M.L.R. 40.

[27] See, e.g. *Lait v Evening Standard Ltd* [2011] 1 W.L.R. 2973 at 2990–2992 per Laws L.J.

[28] Defamation Act 2013. Other than ss.6 (qualified privilege applied to peer-reviewed statements in scientific or academic journals), 7(9) (qualified privilege applied to fair and accurate reports of scientific or academic conferences and related publications) and 15 (related definitions) the Act does not apply in Scotland. The Act came into force on January 1, 2014.

[29] See, e.g. *McDonald's Corp v Steel (No.4)*, *Independent*, May 10, 1999; *Jameel v Wall Street Journal Europe Sprl* [2007] 1 A.C. 359; *Tesco Stores Ltd v Guardian News & Media Ltd* [2009] E.M.L.R. 5.

[30] See, e.g. *Baigent v BBC*, 1999 S.C.L.R. 787.

[31] See, e.g. *British Chiropractic Association v Singh* [2011] 1 W.L.R. 133.

[32] *Woodland Trust v MacMillan* [2001] Scot CS 236 at [17] per Lord Eassie.

[33] *E.E.T.P.U. v Times Newspapers Ltd* [1980] Q.B. 585, applying s.2(1) of the Trade Union and Labour Relations Act 1974 (superseded by s.10(1) of the Trade Union and Labour Relations (Consolidation) Act 1992). Whether this decision is correct has been doubted: see Norrie, *Defamation and Related Actions in Scots Law* (1995), p.68. See also *National Union of General and Municipal Workers v Gillian* [1946] K.B. 81.

[34] *Derbyshire CC v Times Newspapers Ltd* [1993] A.C. 534 at 548 per Lord Keith of Kinkell.

[35] *British Coal Corp v National Union of Mineworkers* Unreported June 28, 1996 QBD.

[36] *Goldsmith v Bhoyrul* [1998] Q.B. 459.

[37] *University of Glasgow v Economist Ltd* [1997] E.M.L.R. 495; *Duke v University of Salford* [2013] E.L.R. 259. In *Duke* Eady J. held that the university's action was an abuse of process as the attack was on the reputation of a member of staff rather than the university itself.

members of the relevant body from raising proceedings in their own name,[38] although courts will be vigilant to ensure that this is not used as an attempt to subvert criticism of the public body "by the back door".[39]

The pursuer must have a sufficient connection with Scotland to bring defamation proceedings in the Scottish courts. In *Ewing v Times Newspapers Ltd*[40] the pursuer, a "determined recreational" litigant, travelled to Scotland from his home in England (where his application had already been refused in the High Court) and used a facility in a public library to download and read an article in the *Sunday Times* in which he was named. The pursuer was ordered to find caution for expenses, which he could not. The practical effect was that the pursuer could not continue the action. This was justified by the Inner House:

> "The present action arises because the pursuer came to Scotland to acquire a cause of action. He has no connection with Scotland and has no apparent reputation here to defend. If he should have suffered hurt feelings when he read the article here, his hurt is self-inflicted. Even if there were to be a vestige of merit in the claim, this action would be disproportionate to its value."[41]

However, in *Kennedy v Aldington*,[42] a proof before answer was permitted in a defamation action that was admittedly brought in Scotland because it was time-barred in England. Although the pursuer had no more than a tenuous connection with Scotland, the matter was determined by the fact that the magazine in question circulated in Scotland and the defender admitted that the court in Scotland had concurrent jurisdiction, the onus being on the defender to persuade the court of forum non conveniens.

The dead cannot sue, although a deceased's executor may continue an action for injuries to name or reputation that had already been raised by the deceased before death.[43] Neither relatives nor others can sue in defamation where a deceased has been defamed, whether the defamatory statement was communicated before or after death. Arguably, however, it may be feasible for a third party to bring an action for verbal injury if the pursuer's business interests are harmed by the slander of a deceased.[44]

Who can be sued?

7–05   "(T)he general rule is that a person circulating a slander is answerable equally with the author of the slander."[45] The "repetition" rule here defined by Lord

---

[38] See, e.g. *Brooks v Lind*, 2000 G.W.D. 8–307; *McLaughlin v Lambeth LBC* [2011] E.M.L.R. 8; *Thompson v James* [2013] EWHC 515 (Q.B.) (affirmed [2014] EWCA Civ 600).

[39] See, e.g. *R. (on the application of Comninos) v Bedford BC* [2003] B.L.G.R. 271.

[40] *Ewing v Times Newspapers Ltd*, 2010 S.L.T. 1093.

[41] *Ewing v Times Newspapers Ltd*, 2010 S.L.T. 1093 at 1096 per Lord Justice Justice-Clerk Gill. See also *Jameel v Dow Jones & Co Inc* [2005] Q.B. 946.

[42] *Kennedy v Aldington* [2005] CSOH 58.

[43] Damages (Scotland) Act 2011 s.2(3). The executor may also pursue an appeal provided that would be competent if the deceased was still alive.

[44] If *convicium* survives as part of Scots law, arguably solatium may be awarded in an action under that head if a slander of the deceased causes harm to the feelings of the pursuer—see para.7–39 below. See also *Putistin v Ukraine* (16882/03) [2013] ECHR 1154, where the European Court of Human Rights recognised the possibility of a claim under art.8 where the defamation of a deceased impacts on the reputation of the deceased's surviving family.

[45] *Wright & Greig v George Outram & Co* (1890) 17 R. 596 at 599 per Lord Kyllachy. See also *Robertson v Newsquest (Sunday Herald) Ltd*, 2006 S.C.L.R. 792.

Kyllachy traditionally provides that anyone who communicates a defamatory statement may be sued, irrespective of whether the individual was the author of the statement, exercised any editorial control or was aware of the content or even the existence of the communication. However, the repetition rule is now restricted by the concept of privilege (which may be absolute or qualified) and by statutory defences found in s.1 of the Defamation Act 1996 and in reg.17 of the Electronic Commerce (EC Directive) Regulations 2002.[46] These restrictions on liability are discussed below as defences to an action in defamation. However, the courts in Scotland may not have jurisdiction where the defender is domiciled or has a place of principal residence or business in another country outside of the European Union.[47]

Communication

"You can shout a slander to the waves or write reams of libelous invective—if   **7–06** nobody hears or reads there will be no defamation."[48] Communication of some sort is essential. Unlike in some other jurisdictions,[49] it is sufficient in Scots law for the communication to be restricted to the pursuer.[50] So a defamatory text message that is communicated directly via Bluetooth and read only by the subject of the imputation is actionable in Scotland, although a slanderous verbal insult may be difficult to prove.

Scots law makes no distinction between slanders and libels.[51] Whether a calumny is communicated by permanent or transient form makes no difference in Scots law to what the pursuer must prove, or to the defences available to the defender. Communication may thus take any form: words, gestures, photographs,[52] films[53] and indeed the displaying of a waxwork effigy are all sufficient.[54] The repetition rule provides that anyone who circulates a defamatory statement is liable equally along with its author.[55] Of particular concern in the modern era of social media is the possibility that the author may be liable for the consequences of secondary communication[56] if that was a foreseeable consequence of the author's own actions.[57]

The process of electronic communications is worthy of close examination in this context. If a defamatory statement is uploaded in electronic form by the author onto a web server and later downloaded by web surfers, does the relevant communication occur when the information is uploaded, downloaded, or both? At the time of writing, the answer in Scotland appears to be "both". Thus, each

---

[46] See also, for England and Wales, s.5 of the Defamation Act 2013 and the Defamation (Operators of Websites) Regulations 2013 (SI 2013/3028).

[47] See, e.g. *Clark v TripAdvisor LLC*, 2014 S.L.T. 418. See also paras 1–29 to 1–30 above.

[48] R. McInnes, *Scots Law for Journalists*, 8th edn (Edinburgh: W. Green, 2010), para.26.16.

[49] Including England and Wales.

[50] See, e.g. *Ramsay v Maclay* (1890) 18 R. 130; *Gall v Slessar*, 1907 S.C. 708.

[51] A distinction is made in England and Wales: for example, there is no presumption of harm in slander and the claimant must lead evidence to prove damage. Broadcast defamatory statements, however, are libels: Broadcasting Act 1990 s.166.

[52] See, e.g. *Garbett v Hazel Watson & Viney* [1943] 2 All E.R. 359.

[53] See, e.g. *Youssoupoff v MGM* (1934) T.L.R. 581.

[54] *Monson v Tussauds* [1894] 1 Q.B. 671.

[55] *Wright & Greig v George Outram & Co* (1890) 17 R. 596; *Hayforth v Forrester-Paton*, 1927 S.C. 74, *Robertson v Newsquest (Sunday Herald) Ltd*, 2006 S.C.L.R. 792.

[56] For example, a message that "goes viral".

[57] *Slipper v BBC* [1991] 1 Q.B. 283; *Cairns v Modi* [2013] E.M.L.R. 8; *McAlpine v Bercow* [2013] EWHC 1342.

visit to the relevant web page constitutes a fresh publication and whoever owns any web server that hosts or transmits the web page will be subject to the repetition rule. This situation prompted the enactment of a defence in s.1 of the Defamation Act 1996. This retains the repetition rule but provides that if a mere distributor of a defamatory statement is not its author, editor or publisher, it will be a defence that the person did not know of the defamatory imputation and acted reasonably in the circumstances. This usually means taking down the statement as soon as it is reasonably practicable following being warned of its defamatory nature.[58] The defence has been held to treat Google's Blogger.com service (a platform for blogs) as the electronic equivalent of the provider of a traditional noticeboard.[59]

Another consequence of the so-called "multiple publication" rule[60] is the asserted growth of a phenomenon known as "forum shopping" or "libel tourism". There is nothing new in the concept itself[61]; but if an offending web page is downloaded in a jurisdiction that is more "pursuer-friendly" than the jurisdiction where the web page was uploaded or (where the pursuer is resident in another jurisdiction) the pursuer's own jurisdiction, the download may facilitate the pursuit of litigation in the jurisdiction where the material was downloaded. It has been suggested that England has been a particular target for libel tourists, although the English courts have been careful to ensure that such downloads amount to a "real and substantial" tort.[62] However, although s.8 of the Defamation Act 2013 replaced the multiple publication rule in England and Wales with a single publication rule when it came into force in January 2014, that provision does not apply in Scotland, potentially exposing Scotland's courts to speculative litigation from forum shoppers.

Identification

7–07   It is essential that the defamatory imputation may be understood by the reasonable reader or viewer to refer to the pursuer as an individual.[63] Clearly this requirement will be met where the pursuer is named or otherwise clearly depicted as the subject of the defamatory imputation: for example by photograph, drawing, cartoon, effigy or nickname. On the other hand, it is insufficient for the pursuer to show that he happens to be a member of a group that is libelled as such, unless the group is so defined that the members of the group are defamed as individuals.[64] The test to be applied has been described as

> "whether the words used ... are such as would reasonably lead persons acquainted with the (pursuer) to believe that he was the person referred to."[65]

---

[58] *Godfrey v Demon Internet Ltd* [2001] Q.B. 201; *Robertson v Newsquest (Sunday Herald) Ltd*, 2006 S.C.L.R. 792.

[59] *Tamiz v Google Inc* [2013] 1 W.L.R. 2151.

[60] See, e.g. *Times Newspapers v United Kingdom* [2009] E.M.L.R. 14.

[61] See, e.g. *The Duke of Brunswick v Harmer* [1849] 14 Q.B. 185; *Youssoupoff v MGM* (1934) T.L.R. 851; *Berezovsky v Forbes Inc* [2000] 1 W.L.R. 1004.

[62] *Jameel v Dow Jones Inc* [2005] Q.B. 946; *Karpov v Browder* [2014] E.M.L.R. 8; *Subotic v Knezevic* [2013] EWHC 3011 (Q.B.).

[63] See, e.g. *Harkness v Daily Record Ltd*, 1924 S.L.T. 759 at 762 per Lord President Clyde: " ... the statement complained of was ... of and concerning the pursuers."

[64] *Browne v D.C. Thomson & Co Ltd*, 1912 1 S.L.T. 123. See also *Riches v News Group Newspapers Ltd* [1986] Q.B. 256; *Baigent v BBC*, 1999 S.C.L.R. 787.

[65] *Knuppfer v London Express Newspaper* [1944] A.C. 116 at 119 per Viscount Simon L.C.

In *KC v MGN Ltd*[66] the claimant recovered damages even although he was not named in the offending communication. A newspaper falsely reported that the natural father of "Baby P", a child posthumously famous as a victim of neglect, had been convicted of raping a 14-year-old girl. The court accepted that although the claimant remained anonymous, he was nevertheless identifiable to a limited range of readers of the newspaper.

History is littered with examples of libel litigation brought by an individual or organisation that by coincidence shared a similar name or other characteristic with a fictitious character in a book, film or television programme. Famous examples include *Hulton v Jones*,[67] where Artemus Jones, a Welsh barrister practising in London, recovered substantial damages from the *Sunday Chronicle* after it published a fictitious story coincidentally featuring an eponymous hypocritical church warden. Another case was *Youssoupoff v MGM*.[68] The plaintiff, formerly Princess Irina of Russia (of the Romanov dynasty) was exiled with her husband to Paris following the 1917 revolution. She sued in London when Metro-Goldwyn-Mayer released a film called *Rasputin and the Empress*, in which a character named Princess Natasha, whom Irina claimed was based on herself, was seduced by Rasputin.[69] A jury accepted that this caused Irina to be shunned and avoided.

Although considerably less glamorous, omitting the address or other distinguishing characteristic of the real person that a communication intended to identify can also lead to catastrophic consequences for the communicator.[70]

Again, the traditionally strict approach of the courts may be tempered by reference to the Human Rights Act 1998 and art.10 of the European Convention on Human Rights. In *O'Shea v Mirror Group Newspapers*[71] the court held that it would place an intolerable burden on the media if there could be liability to a "lookalike" of the subject of a published photograph. The claimant sued when she discovered that an advertisement for a pornographic website featured a model who looked so like her that people who knew her would reasonably think it was she. The court held that strict liability for unintentional defamation arising from the coincidence would amount to an interference with freedom of expression which could not be justified as necessary in a democratic society in the absence of a pressing social need.

Defamation

The classic test for a defamatory statement is "would the words tend to lower **7–08** the (pursuer) in the estimation of right thinking members of society generally."[72]

---

[66] *KC v MGN Ltd*, sub nom. *Cairns v Modi* [2013] E.M.L.R. 8.
[67] *Hulton v Jones* [1910] A.C. 20. Ironically, the real Artemus Jones had at one time been employed as a staff writer on the *Sunday Chronicle*!
[68] *Youssoupoff v MGM* (1934) T.L.R. 851.
[69] As part of the settlement eventually negotiated by an American lawyer named Fanny Holtzmann, the now familiar disclaimer "This film is a work of fiction, any similarity to a person living or dead . . . " was added to the end of the film.
[70] See, e.g. *Outram v Reid* (1852) 14 D. 577; *Wragg v D. C. Thomson & Co Ltd* (1909) 2 S.L.T. 315.
[71] *O'Shea v Mirror Group Newspapers* [2001] E.M.L.R. 40.
[72] *Sim v Stretch* [1936] 2 All E.R. 1237 at 1240 per Lord Atkin.

Alternative definitions have been proposed, including a statement "which is calculated to injure the reputation of another, by exposing him to hatred, contempt or ridicule,"[73] or which causes the pursuer to be "shunned or avoided,"[74] or which "impute(s) lack of qualification, knowledge, skill, capacity, judgment or efficiency in the conduct of his trade or business or professional activity."[75]

There appear to be three steps to determining whether an impugned statement is actionable as defamatory of a pursuer:

- Step 1 considers whether the words complained of are *capable* of bearing the meaning ascribed to them by the pursuer.[76] This requires an examination of the actual words or conduct and of any contended inferences, which may be drawn from the context in which the communication occurs. This is a question of law[77] to be decided by the court and a plea to the relevancy may be taken by the defender on the basis that the range of meanings that the words or actions are capable of bearing does not extend to the meaning attributed by the pursuer.[78]
- Step 2, which in practice may be conflated with step 1, requires an assessment of whether the meaning contended for by the pursuer would convey a defamatory imputation to the reasonable reader. This is also a question to the relevancy of the pleadings and so a question of law,[79] although it requires the judge to adopt the perception of the hypothetical reasonable fair-minded person.[80]
- Step 3 applies a *single meaning* rule[81] and asks what particular meaning or inference would be understood by the hypothetical reasonable reader or viewer of the communication? Determining this is a matter of fact and it remains competent to solve this question by civil jury trial.[82] If the understood meaning is not a relevant defamatory meaning as confirmed by steps 1 and 2 the case will fail.

It follows that it is irrelevant to consider what the author intended the communication to mean.[83] An objective test applies: it is whether the circumstances of the communication "provide grounds for a reasonable inference"[84]

---

[73] *Parmiter v Coupland* (1840) 6 M & W 105 at 108 per Lord Wensleydale.

[74] *Youssoupoff v MGM* (1934) T.L.R. 581 at 587 per Slesser L.J.

[75] *Drummond-Jackson v British Medical Association* [1970] 1 W.L.R. 688 at 698–699 per Lord Pearson.

[76] A court cannot be asked to rule on whether words are *arguably* capable of the meaning asserted by the pursuer: Defamation Act 1996 s.7.

[77] *McCann v Scottish Media Newspapers Ltd*, 2000 S.L.T. 256 at 261 per Lord MacFadyen.

[78] *Russell v Stubbs Ltd*, 1913 S.C. (HL) 14 at 20 per Lord Kinnear.

[79] See, e.g. *McCann v Scottish Media Newspapers Ltd*, 2000 S.L.T. 256 at 261 per Lord MacFadyen.

[80] Reflecting the "reasonable person" test in the law of negligence: see para.1–24 above.

[81] See, e.g. *Thornton v Telegraph Media Group Ltd* [2011] 1 W.L.R. 1985 at 1991 per Tugendhat J.

[82] *McCabe v News Group Newspapers Ltd*, 1992 S.L.T. 707.

[83] *Langlands v John Leng & Co Ltd*, 1916 S.C. (HL) 102 at 105 per Viscount Haldane. See also *McAlpine v Bercow* [2013] EWHC 1342.

[84] *Gollan v Thompson Wyles Co*, 1930 S.C. 599.

that the author intended the meaning asserted by the pursuer. Excluding those who are unduly naïve and those who are unduly suspicious[85] from the range of right thinking members of society *generally*,[86] it is also important to note that a court will not permit a "strained and sinister interpretation . . . to form a ground for reparation"[87] and will dismiss an interpretation that is irrational, fanciful or absurd.[88]

Whether a statement is defamatory will depend on contemporary social values, **7–09** at least within the community in which the pursuer hopes to be held in some esteem. Thus, a statement that was viewed as defamatory half a century ago may no longer be harmful to an individual's reputation if communicated today. There are some imputations that will forever be defamatory, such as being accused of committing a criminal act, but changes in attitudes towards homosexuality provide a good example. It was certainly defamatory to call a person a homosexual in the 1950s.[89] But by the 1990s, when homosexual acts between consenting adults had been decriminalised, attitudes had changed, and without at least an innuendo of related deception, hypocrisy or exploitation, an accusation of homosexuality would not be deemed as lowering the individual's reputation in the estimation of right thinking members of society.[90]

In *Thornton v Telegraph Media Group Ltd*[91] it was accepted by Tugendhat J. that, so as to avoid trivial actions, the defamatory statement must also cross a "threshold of seriousness."[92] A similar qualification was applied by Lord MacPhail in *MacLeod v Newsquest (Sunday Herald) Ltd*,[93] citing as "valuable" the following points of guidance provided by Neill L.J. in *Gillick v BBC*[94]:

"(1) The court should give to the material complained of the natural and ordinary meaning which it would have conveyed to the ordinary reasonable viewer watching the programme once. (2) The hypothetical reasonable reader (or viewer) is not naïve but he is not unduly suspicious. He can read between the lines. He can read in an implication more readily than a lawyer and may indulge in a certain amount of loose thinking. But he must be treated as being a man who is not avid for scandal and someone who does not, and should not, select one bad meaning where other non-defamatory meanings are available. (3) While limiting its attention to what the defendant has actually said or written the court should be cautious of an over-elaborate analysis of the material in issue. (4) A television audience would not give the programme the analytical attention of a lawyer to the

---

[85] *Lewis v Daily Telegraph Ltd* [1964] A.C. 234 at 259 per Lord Reid.

[86] *Sim v Stretch* [1936] 2 All E.R. 1237 at 1240 per Lord Atkin (emphasis added).

[87] *Russell v Stubbs Ltd*, 1913 S.C. (HL) 14 at 23 per Lord Shaw of Dunfermline.

[88] *Jeynes v News Magazines Ltd* [2008] EWCA Civ 130.

[89] *Liberace v Daily Mirror Newspapers Ltd*, *The Times*, June 18, 1959.

[90] *Quilty v Windsor* 1999 S.L.T. 346 at 355 per Lord Kingarth. See also *Cowan v Bennett*, 2012 G.W.D. 37–738.

[91] *Thornton v Telegraph Media Group Ltd* [2011] 1 W.L.R. 1985.

[92] This has been codified in England and Wales by s.1 of the Defamation Act 2013.

[93] *MacLeod v Newsquest (Sunday Herald) Ltd*, 2007 S.C.L.R. 555 at 557. The context of the publication indicated that the content was satire: see also *John v Guardian News & Media Ltd* [2008] EWHC 3066.

[94] *Gillick v BBC* [1996] E.M.L.R. 267 at 272–273.

meaning of a document, an auditor to the interpretation of accounts, or an academic to the content of a learned article. (5) In deciding what impression the material complained of would have been likely to have on the hypothetical reasonable viewer the court are entitled (if not bound) to have regard to the impression it made on them. (6) The court should not be too literal in its approach. (7) A statement should be taken to be defamatory if it would tend to lower the plaintiff in the estimation of right-thinking members of society generally, or be likely to affect a person adversely in the estimation of reasonable people generally."

Furthermore, a communication likely to be read as a whole by the reasonable reader must be read as such for the purposes of liability in defamation. Thus, if a defamatory "bane" is cured by an "antidote" the defender will be entitled to challenge the action as irrelevant. In *Charleston v News Group Newspapers*[95] a Sunday tabloid published an article which the plaintiffs argued contained three distinct elements. These included: a photograph with the heads of the plaintiffs (who were famous as actors in the Australian television soap opera *Neighbours*) superimposed onto the bodies of a couple who appeared to be engaged in an act of intercourse or sodomy; the headline "Strewth! What's Harold up to with our Madge?"—and an article that, adopting an outraged tone, explained that the actors were the unwitting stars of a "sordid" computer game. The House of Lords held that the picture and headline (which may have amounted to a "bane") could not be isolated from the related text (providing the "antidote") since the publication would be read as a whole by the notional reasonable and fair-minded reader.

7–10 Conversely, a prima facie "innocent" statement may be made defamatory by the context in which it is communicated. The context may be as ephemeral as what is currently being discussed by those alert to current trends in social media, or even no more than an emoticon attached to a message. In *McAlpine v Bercow*,[96] a guest on a 2012 broadcast of *Newsnight* (a television news and current affairs programme) had stated that he had been sexually abused in the 1980s by a then "prominent conservative politician," whom he did not name, when he was a child resident of a children's home in Wales. The defendant sent a tweet shortly after the programme had been broadcast which asked: "Why is Lord McAlpine trending? *Innocent Face*." It was held that the defendant's tweet provided a final piece to the jigsaw, i.e. the identity of the anonymous individual referred to in the *Newsnight* programme, to the recipients of the tweet (either from the defendant herself or from those who had re-tweeted it) as twitter users would understand the "*innocent face*" phrase to be the equivalent of an ironic emoticon implying a message that the defendant knew very well the answer to her question.[97]

---

[95] *Charleston v News Group Newspapers* [1995] 2 A.C. 65. See also *Russell v Stubbs Ltd*, 1913 S.C. (HL) 14; *McCann v Scottish Media Newspapers Ltd*, 2000 S.L.T. 256; *Robertson v Newsquest (Sunday Herald) Ltd*, 2006 S.C.L.R. 792; *MacLeod v Newsquest (Sunday Herald) Ltd*, 2007 S.C.L.R. 555.

[96] *Lord McAlpine of West Green v Bercow* [2013] EWHC 1342 (QB).

[97] In effect the tweet was treated as saying: "Why is Lord McAlpine trending? *As if I didn't know . . . *"

It may be that a defender admits that a statement is defamatory, but not in the sense that is argued for by the pursuer. In *Lewis v Daily Telegraph*[98] a newspaper report stated that a company's affairs were being investigated by the Fraud Squad. This was literally true, but the plaintiff argued that the reasonable reader would interpret the statement as meaning that the company's affairs were being carried out fraudulently or dishonestly. This interpretation was rejected by a majority in the House of Lords,[99] it being asserted that:

> "It is a grave thing to say that someone is fraudulent. It is a different thing to say that someone is suspected of being fraudulent. How much less wounding and damaging this would be must be a matter of opinion depending upon the circumstances ... What could ordinary reasonable readers think? Some, I consider, might reasonably take the view that there was just an inquiry to find out whether or not there had been any fraud or dishonesty. Some, I consider, might reasonably take the view that the words meant that there was an inquiry because the police suspected that there had been fraud or dishonesty. Some, I consider, might reasonably take the view that the words meant that there was an inquiry because there had been fraud or dishonesty which occasioned or required inquiry by the police."[100]

That three possible levels of defamatory meaning might be derived from a statement made about a police investigation was further acknowledged in *Chase v News Group Newspapers Ltd*.[101] These have been adopted in subsequent case law in England and Wales as:

- *Chase* level 1: the claimant was guilty;
- *Chase* level 2: there were reasonable grounds to suspect the claimant was guilty[102];
- *Chase* level 3: there were grounds for investigating whether the claimant was guilty.[103]

It is suggested that a similar approach would be applied by the courts in Scotland.[104]

---

[98] *Lewis v Daily Telegraph*, sub nom. *Rubber Improvement Ltd v Daily Telegraph Ltd* [1964] A.C. 234.

[99] "A man who wants to talk at large about smoke may have to pick his words very carefully if he wants to exclude the suggestion that there is also a fire; but it can be done": *Lewis v Daily Telegraph* [1964] A.C. 234 at 285 per Lord Devlin.

[100] *Lewis v Daily Telegraph* [1964] A.C. 234 at 267–268 per Lord Morris of Borth-y-Gest. See also Lord Devlin at 282:
"... there could have been three different categories of justification—proof of the fact of an inquiry, proof of reasonable grounds for it, and proof of guilt."

[101] *Chase v News Group Newspapers Ltd* [2003] E.M.L.R. 11.

[102] See, e.g. *Miller v Associated Newspapers Ltd* [2012] EWHC 3721 (upheld [2014] EWCA Civ 39).

[103] See, e.g. *Flood v Times Newspapers Ltd* [2012] 2 A.C. 273.

[104] Although the hierarchy of meaning set out in *Lewis* and in *Chase* was not expressly adopted as such by Lord Reed in *Robertson v Newsquest (Sunday Herald) Ltd*, 2006 S.C.L.R. 792, it is submitted that his discussion of defamatory meaning is consistent with the approach taken in the English cases. See also *McAvennie v Scottish Daily Record and Sunday Mail Ltd*, 2003 Rep. L.R. 93.

Although the range of defamatory imputations may be infinite, it is convenient to group discussion of case examples around several well-established headings.

Immoral character or behaviour

7–11   This area is possibly the most susceptible to differences and changes in community values. There are historical cases where imputations of immodesty[105] or indelicacy[106] in a woman, or "smutty" behaviour in a man,[107] were held defamatory. Early in the 20th century it would also have been defamatory to accuse a person of engaging in sex outside of marriage,[108] and it was even held that it would cause a woman to be "shunned or avoided" to imply that she succumbed to a sexual assault.[109] By the late 20th century an imputation of extra-marital sex would not of itself be defamatory, although where surrounding circumstances indicated hypocrisy,[110] weakness of character[111] or exploitation of position[112] an action may succeed. It may now be defamatory to suggest that a couple's marriage is a hypocritical sham,[113] but imputations of homosexuality are unlikely to be defamatory unless they carry an inference or innuendo of exploitation or hypocrisy.[114]

More general imputations of anti-social character or behaviour that would attract public opprobrium have been the subject of a number of recent cases. Among them, allegations of racism,[115] extreme hubris,[116] embarrassing drunken behaviour,[117] and exploitation of an expenses system[118] have been held capable of carrying a defamatory meaning. However, it should be noted that to be defamatory the imputation as to character must be more than merely unflattering or insulting.[119] It has been held not to be defamatory to publish a description of a politician as a "scab" when made by another politician in the context of a "political skirmish" fought out in public.[120]

Criminal conduct

7–12   Other than minor or technical criminal offences which attract no social stigma, it is undoubtedly defamatory to accuse an individual of being investigated for,[121]

---

[105] *A.B. v William Blackwood & Sons* (1902) 5 F. 25.
[106] *Cuthbert v Linklater*, 1935 S.L.T. 94.
[107] *Garbett v Hazel Watson & Viney* [1943] 2 All E.R. 359.
[108] See, e.g. *Morrison v Ritchie* (1902) 4 F. 645.
[109] *Youssoupoff v MGM* (1934) T.L.R. 581.
[110] See, e.g. *Clinton v Express Newspapers Ltd* [1998] Scot CS 97.
[111] See, e.g. *Hannah v Scottish Daily Record and Sunday Mail Ltd*, 2000 S.L.T. 673.
[112] See, e.g. *Winter v News Scotland Ltd*, 1991 S.L.T. 828 where a prison officer was accused of engaging in a sexual affair with a prisoner.
[113] See, e.g. *Cruise v Express Newspapers Ltd* [1998] E.M.L.R. 780; *Beckham v News Group Newspapers Ltd* [2005] EWHC 2252.
[114] See, e.g. *Prophit v BBC*, 1997 S.L.T. 745 where the pursuer was a nun.
[115] *Fraser v Mirza*, 1993 S.C. (HL) 27; *Moore v Scottish Daily Record and Sunday Mail Ltd*, 2007 S.L.T. 217.
[116] See, e.g. *Cruise v Express Newspapers Ltd* [1998] E.M.L.R. 780.
[117] *Church v MGN Ltd* [2013] 1 W.L.R. 284.
[118] *Cook v Telegraph Media Group Ltd* [2011] EWHC 763 (QB).
[119] *Dell'Olio v Associated Newspapers Ltd* [2011] EWHC 3472 (QB).
[120] *Curran v Scottish Daily Record and Sunday Mail Ltd*, 2012 S.L.T. 359.
[121] *Lewis v Daily Telegraph Ltd* [1964] A.C. 234—see discussion of difference in levels of meaning above at para.7–10.

committing,[122] facilitating,[123] or being punished for[124] a criminal act. However, it is sufficient for reliance upon the *veritas* defence to show that the pursuer has been convicted.[125] This rule still applies even if that conviction is spent, unless the pursuer can prove the defender acted out of malice.[126]

Fitness for occupation or profession

It is defamatory to "impute lack of qualification,[127] knowledge,[128] skill,[129] **7–13** capacity, judgment or efficiency in the conduct of his trade or business or professional activity."[130] Imputations of misconduct,[131] professional negligence,[132] or disregard for professional integrity[133] may also be actionable. Certain occupations are expected to require fairly thick skins[134] so it is not normally actionable merely to insult.[135] Thus, accusing a councilor of sheer lunacy and gross maladministration was not defamatory.[136] However, it has been held defamatory to accuse an actor of being "hideously ugly".[137] It should be noted that employment references will be protected by qualified privilege, so proof of malice will be required to sustain an action for damages in defamation.[138]

Paradoxically, it has been held defamatory to impute that an amateur sportsperson has been acting as a professional.[139]

---

[122] See, e.g. *Wray v Associated Newspapers Ltd*, 2000 S.L.T. 869 (allegations of wife beating); *Waddell v BBC*, 1973 S.L.T. 246 (television programme suggested W involved in the commission of a murder); *Monson v Tussauds Ltd* [1894] 1 Q.B. 671 (placing of waxwork effigy of accused—who had been acquitted on a not proven verdict on a charge of murder—in a Chamber of Horrors alongside other notorious criminals carried an innuendo that M had in fact committed the crime); *Bento v Chief Constable of Bedfordshire* [2012] EWHC 1525 (police issued press release criticising CPS for failing to instigate retrial for murder of B, who in opinion of police was probably guilty).

[123] See, e.g. *Robertson v Newsquest (Sunday Herald) Ltd*, 2006 S.C.L.R. 792; *Tolstoy Miloslavsky v United Kingdom* [1996] E.M.L.R. 152.

[124] See, e.g. *Harkness v The Daily Record Ltd*, 1924 S.L.T. 759.

[125] Law Reform (Miscellaneous Provisions) (Scotland) Act 1968 s.12.

[126] Rehabilitation of Offenders Act 1974 s.8.

[127] See, e.g. *McKeith v News Group Newspapers Ltd* [2005] E.M.L.R. 32; *McKenna v MGN Ltd* [2006] EWHC 1996.

[128] See, e.g. *McKerchar v Cameron* (1892) 19 R. 383; *Auld v Shairp* (1875) 2 R. 940.

[129] See, e.g. *Dee v Telegraph Media Group Ltd* [2010] E.M.L.R. 20 ("World's worst tennis pro . . . ")

[130] *Drummond-Jackson v British Medical Association* [1970] 1 W.L.R. 688 at 698–699 per Lord Pearson.

[131] See, e.g. *McRostie v Ironside* (1849) 11 D. 74; *Winter v News Scotland Ltd*, 1991 S.L.T. 828; *Fraser v Mirza*, 1993 S.C. (HL) 27; *Shanks v BBC*, 1993 S.L.T. 326; *McCann v Scottish Media Newspapers Ltd*, 2000 S.L.T. 256.

[132] See, e.g. *Simmers v Morton* (1900) 8 S.L.T. 285.

[133] See, e.g. *Hay v Institute of Chartered Accountants of Scotland*, 2003 S.L.T. 612.

[134] *Wray v Associated Newspapers Ltd*, 2000 S.L.T. 869 at 869 per Lord Johnston.

[135] *Moffat v West Highland Publishing Co Ltd*, 2000 S.L.T. 335.

[136] *Brooks v Lind*, 1997 Rep. L.R. 83. It was held in the same case that it was defamatory to allege a malicious misuse of public money.

[137] *Berkoff v Burchill* [1996] 4 All E.R. 1008. See also *Cornwell v Myskow* [1987] 1 W.L.R. 630, where a review stated an actress's "bum is too big and she has the sort of stage presence that jams lavatories."

[138] Although carelessly constructed references may attract liability in negligence: *Spring v Guardian Assurance Plc* [1995] 2 A.C. 296. Cf. *Desmond v Chief Constable of Nottinghamshire* [2011] P.T.S.R. 1369.

[139] *Tolley v JS Fry & Sons Ltd* [1931] A.C. 333.

Financial standing

7–14   It is defamatory to allege that a person is bankrupt,[140] insolvent, in financial difficulty,[141] or is otherwise unable or unwilling to meet his financial commitments.[142] "Person" includes juristic, as well as natural persons and damages awards to trading companies might be enormous. It may be sufficient that a person's credit-worthiness is harmed without his solvency necessarily being questioned.[143]

Health

7–15   Communicating that a person is unwell is more likely to arouse feelings of sympathy than hostility.[144] However, if the imputation is of a loathsome disease, such as leprosy,[145] that has been viewed as defamatory. It has also been said to be defamatory to falsely accuse someone of insanity.[146] However, given that both physical and mental health are examples of private information[147] and, under the Data Protection Act 1998, sensitive personal data, the processing of such information, even where it is false, may be unlawful under the 1998 Act and, assuming that the concept is part of Scots law, may also stimulate a "false privacy" action for misuse of private information.[148]

Innuendo

7–16   A statement may on the face of it appear to be innocent, but nevertheless carry a defamatory inference that may only be obvious to those who are aware of extrinsic facts.[149] The test to be applied asks: "Is the meaning sought to be attributed to the language alleged to be libellous one which is a reasonable, natural, or necessary interpretation of its terms?"[150]

An example was *Morrison v Ritchie*,[151] where a newspaper, apparently in good faith, published a false notice announcing the birth of twins to Mrs Morrison. Although such an announcement may typically be expected to attract warm congratulations, here it was held to be defamatory. Acquaintances who knew the Morrisons had married less than two months previously would reasonably understand the words to mean that they had conceived children out of wedlock

---

[140] *Outram v Reid* (1852) 14 D. 577.
[141] *AB v CD* (1904) 7 F. 22.
[142] See, e.g. *Russell v Stubbs Ltd*, 1913 S.C. (HL) 14.
[143] *AB v CD* (1904) 7 F. 22.
[144] See, e.g. *Grappelli v Derek Block (Holdings) Ltd* [1981] 1 W.L.R. 822.
[145] See, e.g. *Farrell v Boyd* (1907) 15 S.L.T. 327.
[146] *Youssoupoff v MGM* (1934) T.L.R. 581.
[147] See, e.g. *Campbell v Mirror Group Newspapers Ltd* [2004] 2 A.C. 457.
[148] "There is a . . . group of cases where there is an overlap (between privacy and defamation), but where it is unlikely that it could be said that protection of reputation is the nub of the claim. These are cases where the information would in the past have been said to be defamatory even though it related to matters which were involuntary e.g. disease. There was always a difficulty in fitting such cases into defamation, but it was done because of the absence of any alternative cause of action": *LNS v Persons Unknown* [2010] E.M.L.R. 16 at 424–425 per Tugendhat J. For a discussion of "false privacy" see para.9–09 below.
[149] A paradigm example may be *McAlpine v Bercow* [2013] EWHC 1342: see para.7–10 above.
[150] *Russell v Stubbs Ltd*, 1913 S.C. (HL) 14 at 23 per Lord Shaw. See also *Massie v McCaig*, 2013 S.C. 343.
[151] *Morrison v Ritchie* (1902) 4 F. 645.

and theirs was a "shotgun wedding". At that time, such an imputation was highly damaging to one's reputation.

The extrinsic facts may not be very extrinsic. Placing a waxwork effigy in a Chamber of Horrors beside a group of convicted murderers carries the obvious implication that the individual shares a similar history.[152]

There have been many cases where a contention that a reasonable person who knew some detail about the pursuer's character or history would view a fictitious character in a book or film as a caricature of the pursuer has been accepted by a court. For example, the pursuer in *Cuthbert v Linklater*[153] was a famous Scottish Nationalist who had come to public attention when she had removed a Union Jack flag from Stirling Castle and tossed it to a guard. She sued the author of the novel *Magnus Merriman*, claiming that her reputation would be harmed in the eyes of reasonable readers who knew this fact about her. She asserted that they would associate a character, Betty Bracken, who in the novel removed a Union Jack from a castle and tossed it into a public urinal, with her and would read into the novel an imputation that she lacked womanly delicacy.

The other situation where a plea of innuendo is necessary is where the pursuer is alleging that the *ex facie* innocent substance of the communication would nevertheless carry a derogatory meaning to certain persons who would place a particular interpretation on, e.g. the words used. Thus, applying the term "fruit-flavoured" to an individual in the 1950s would convey only to the reader familiar with American slang that the object of the epithet was a homosexual.[154]

To support a plea of innuendo, the pursuer must set out:

- the particular meaning asserted[155];
- the extrinsic facts which would support the meaning[156]; and
- that these facts were known to one or more of the persons to whom the statement was made.

A court will reject a plea of innuendo where a reasonable person would not conclude a defamatory inference upon adding the extrinsic facts to the information contained in the communication.[157] If the plea is accepted, it remains a question of fact whether a reasonable person would interpret the defamatory meaning alleged if another interpretation would also be reasonable.

However, a court will not be impressed with a plea of innuendo where that is unnecessary. In *Carroll v BBC*,[158] the court confirmed that the ordinary meaning of the words "a stranger to the truth" imputed that the subject was a liar—there was no need to plead innuendo.

Presumptions

If a communication is established as defamatory of the pursuer, the law then **7–17** applies three presumptions:

---

[152] *Monson v Tussauds* [1894] 1 Q.B. 671.

[153] *Cuthbert v Linklater*, 1935 S.L.T. 94. See also, e.g. *Youssoupoff v MGM* (1934) T.L.R. 581.

[154] *Liberace v Daily Mirror Newspapers Ltd*, *The Times*, June 18, 1959. See also *Russell v Stubbs Ltd*, 1913 S.C. (HL) 14 at 24 per Lord Shaw. The modern electronic equivalent to the ironic epithet may be the emoticon: see, e.g. *McAlpine v Bercow* [2013] EWHC 1342.

[155] *Stein v Beaverbrook Newspapers Ltd*, 1968 S.C. 272.

[156] *James v Baird*, 1916 S.C. (HL) 158 at 165 per Lord Kinnear. See also *Capital and Counties Bank v Henty* (1881–1882) L.R. 7 App.Cas. 741.

[157] See, e.g. *McCue v Scottish Daily Record and Sunday Mail Ltd*, 2000 Rep. L.R. 133.

[158] *Carroll v BBC*, 1997 S.L.T. (Sh. Ct) 23.

- First, a defamatory statement is presumed to be false. This presumption is rebuttable by proof of *veritas*—the onus of proof being on the defender;
- Secondly, a natural person is presumed to have suffered harm in the form of insult, reflecting the Roman law concept of *contumelia*, and harm to reputation. A similar presumption applies with regard to non-natural persons[159] where the defamatory imputation would have a "tendency to damage"[160] its trading reputation, financial status or ability to attract revenue or donations. Rebuttal of this presumption by showing that defamatory imputations (not proved to be true) do not actually harm the pursuer's reputation (since it has already been justifiably harmed by provable imputation(s)) will reflect in a reduced award of damages[161];
- Thirdly, the law presumes that the defender intended to harm the pursuer's reputation by disseminating the defamatory statement. This has been explained as a presumption of malice where the communication is not protected by privilege[162] and has been described as a form of strict liability.[163] A disclaimer (e.g. "Any reference to any person whether living or dead is unintended and coincidental") is unlikely to be reliable.[164] Although a defence of unintentional defamation as such appears never to have been accepted by a court, a procedure for making a formal offer of amends is provided for in ss.2—4 of the Defamation Act 1996.

Defences

7-18   A defender may escape liability by successfully challenging one or more of the elements of the delict, e.g. that the pursuer could not reasonably be associated with the words complained of or that the words would not convey a defamatory imputation. Scots law also recognises a number of specific defences to an action in defamation.

Privilege

7-19   A modern view of the law of defamation is that it strikes a balance between protection of reputation and freedom of expression.[165] The default position taken by Scots law has traditionally preferred protection of reputation but, where privilege is conferred on a communication, freedom of expression will take priority, potentially at the expense of reputation. Thus, privilege will provide

---

[159] i.e. registered companies, partnerships and various unincorporated bodies including charities, professional and other associations.

[160] *Jameel v Wall Street Journal Europe Sprl* [2007] 1 A.C. 359 at 373 per Lord Bingham of Cornhill.

[161] See, e.g. *Grobbelaar v News Group Newspapers Ltd* [2002] 1 W.L.R. 3024. Note also the defences under ss.5 and 6 of the Defamation Act 1952.

[162] *Shaw v Morgan* (1888) 15 R. 865 at 870 per Lord Young; *Morrison v Ritchie* (1902) 4 F. 645 at 650 per Lord Moncreiff.

[163] *O'Shea v MGN* [2001] E.M.L.R. 40.

[164] See *Mazure v Stubbs*, 1919 S.C. (HL) 112 at 120 per Lord Shaw of Dunfermline; *Cuthbert v Linklater*, 1935 S.L.T. 94.

[165] See para.7–01 above.

immunity from liability in defamation. In that sense it may be said that privilege is not a defence as such.

Privilege may be *absolute* or *qualified*. The difference lies in the relevance of malice. If a communication is protected by absolute privilege, the motive of the communicator in making the statement is irrelevant. However, proof of malice will overcome qualified privilege. Note that the onus of proof is upon the pursuer, who must aver malice in the pleadings and, at proof, adduce sufficient evidence to infer malice.

Absolute privilege

Absolute privilege confers protection against liability for all forms of verbal **7–20** injury, including defamation and malicious falsehood, for the following communications:

- statements made in proceedings of the UK Parliament at Westminster,[166] including reports in *Hansard* and reports published under the authority of either House.[167] The effect of art.9 of the Bill of Rights 1688 is to prevent proceedings in Parliament[168] from being impeached in any court or place other than the relevant House of Parliament itself. The rule has been held not to contravene art.8 of the European Convention on Human Rights.[169] An MP may choose to waive this protection with regard to defamation proceedings[170];
- statements made in proceedings of the Scottish Parliament,[171] including reports published under its authority[172];
- statements made in conducting court and certain tribunal proceedings[173] by persons exercising judicial office, prosecutors, advocates and solicitors representing parties,[174] and witnesses. The parties themselves enjoy only qualified privilege[175];

---

[166] *Makudi v Triesman* [2013] EWHC 142. See also Bill of Rights 1688 art.9.

[167] Parliamentary Papers Act 1840. Repetition of what was said in Parliament is not, as such, protected by absolute privilege: *Buchanan v Jennings* [2005] 1 A.C. 115 (cf. *Makudi v Triesman* [2014] 2 W.L.R. 1228), although publication bona fide and without malice of an extract or abstract of proceedings or *Hansard* is protected by qualified privilege: Parliamentary Papers Act 1840 s.3; Defamation Act 1996 s.15; *Makudi v Triesman* [2014] 2 W.L.R. 1228.

[168] Extending to repetition of a statement made in Parliament where there is "(1) a public interest in repetition of the Parliamentary utterance which the speaker ought reasonably to serve, and (2) so close a nexus between the occasions of his speaking, in and then out of Parliament, that the prospect of his obligation to speak on the second occasion (or the expectation or promise that he would do so) is reasonably foreseeable at the time of the first and his purpose in speaking on both occasions is the same or very closely related": *Makudi v Triesman* [2014] 2 W.L.R. 1228 at 1238–1239 per Laws L.J.

[169] *A v United Kingdom* (2003) 36 E.H.R.R. 51.

[170] Defamation Act 1996 s.13; *Hamilton v Al Fayed* [2001] 1 A.C. 395. At the time of writing the Parliamentary Privilege (Defamation) Bill 2014 purports to repeal s.13 of the Defamation Act 1996.

[171] Scotland Act 1998 s.41(1)(a).

[172] Scotland Act 1998 s.41(1)(b).

[173] Where the Tribunal is exercising the judicial power of the State.

[174] *Williamson v Umphray* (1890) 17 R. 905; *Singh v Truscott* [2011] CSIH 84.

[175] *Campbell v Cochrane* (1905) 8 F. 205; *Williamson v Umphray* (1890) 17 R. 905; *Wilson v Scottish Enterprise* Unreported March 28, 2003 (OH).

- fair, accurate and contemporaneous reports[176] of UK court proceedings held in public, including proceedings in the European Court of Human Rights and the European Court of Justice. Absolute privilege may extend to reporting information contained in documents that form an essential part of the proceedings even where the content is not read aloud to the court[177]; and
- certain statements made by or to the Police Investigations and Review Commissioner in relation to a complaint handling review or to a relevant investigation.[178]

Qualified privilege

7–21   Qualified privilege provides protection from liability for defamation (and other "strict liability" forms of verbal injury) to statements made on certain occasions or in certain circumstances. The range is not fixed but changes over time, and common law has been supplemented by statute.[179] Proof of malice will overcome qualified privilege; so it follows that qualified privilege will not provide a defence to any form of verbal injury that requires proof of malice as an element of the delict itself.

Malice is generally difficult to prove, it being concerned with a state of mind, but will be inferred if a privileged occasion is "misused"[180]:

> "The question is whether the respondent . . . 'misused' the occasion. It was for the appellant to prove that he did so. Such proof involved that it should be established that the respondent was actuated by some improper motive which was dominant in his mind. That is what is meant by express malice. The motive with which a person made a defamatory communication can only be ascertained from an examination of his state of mind at the time he made it . . . can only be inferred from what he did or said or knew."[181]

The fact that words are defamatory will not automatically impute malice where qualified privilege applies.[182] However, malice will be established if it is proved that the defender knew the imputation was false,[183] or was reckless as to whether or not it was true. On the other hand, if the defender holds an honest belief in the truth of the imputation it is not sufficient to establish malice to show that belief

---

[176] For discussion of these criteria see *Pelling v Times Newspapers Ltd* Unreported, June 29, 2000, QBD, Eady J.; *Bennett v Newsquest (London) Ltd* Unreported February 22, 2006 QBD, Eady J. See also *Duncan v Associated Scottish Newspapers Ltd*, 1929 S.C. 14.

[177] *Cunningham v The Scotsman Publications Ltd*, 1987 S.C. 107.

[178] Police, Public Order and Criminal Justice (Scotland) Act 2006 s.46A.

[179] Defamation Act 1996 s.15; Defamation Act 2013 s.6; Police, Public Order and Criminal Justice (Scotland) Act 2006 s.46A(1)(c).

[180] *Horrocks v Lowe* [1975] A.C. 135 at 150 per Lord Diplock. See also *Qadir v Associated Newspapers Ltd* [2013] E.M.L.R. 15 at 370–379 per Tugendhat J.

[181] *Fraser v Mirza*, 1993 S.C. (HL) 27 at 33 per Lord Keith of Kinkell.

[182] *Lyons v Chief Constable of Strathclyde Police* [2013] CSIH 46; 2013 G.W.D. 20–401 at [28] per Lord Eassie, delivering the judgment of the court; *Turner v Metro Goldwyn Mayer Pictures* [1950] 1 All E.R. 449.

[183] *Fraser v Mirza*, 1993 S.C. (HL) 27.

was unreasonable.[184] Where material is published in breach of another statutory provision, it does not necessarily follow that qualified privilege is lost.[185]

Duty and interest

At common law qualified privilege protects a statement made in discharging a **7–22** legal, social or moral duty, provided that the recipient or audience has a corresponding interest in receiving the information.[186] An employment or character reference is an example,[187] as is a statement made about a candidate standing in an election by a person entitled to vote.[188] Statements made as part of formal meetings of public authorities[189] and private organisations[190] may also enjoy protection. Statements made as part of public duties may also be protected, even when made outside of a formal meeting.[191] Reporting a concern to an appropriate authority, such as a crime to the police or evidence of child abuse to social services, will also be protected unless malice can be proved.[192] With regard to "whistleblowing", although the relevant legislation does not specifically provide for immunity from liability in defamation, it is suggested that employees making a "protected disclosure" will enjoy qualified privilege.[193]

A proper complaint to the relevant authority will also attract qualified privilege.[194] For example, it has been held that qualified privilege could protect a complaint made to a chief constable about the conduct of a sergeant.[195] However, a complaint to a journalist will not normally satisfy the duty and interest test,[196] unless either the readership has a direct interest in the issue or the only conduit for the complaint is via the media.[197] Even where there is a strong public interest in the issue, qualified privilege will not protect a statement to the media that makes unnecessary defamatory imputations. Thus, when a police force issued a press release criticising a decision by the prosecuting authority not to pursue a retrial following an appeal where the claimant's murder conviction had been quashed, the police could not rely on qualified privilege as the press release carried the unnecessary imputation that the claimant was probably

---

[184] *Horrocks v Lowe* [1975] A.C. 135.

[185] See, e.g. *Nicol v Caledonian Newspapers Ltd*, 2002 S.C. 493.

[186] *Adam v Ward* [1917] A.C. 309 at 334 per Lord Atkinson.

[187] *Spring v Guardian Assurance* [1995] 2 A.C. 296. The provider of the reference owes a duty of care both to the subject of the reference and to the recipient: *Hedley Byrne & Co Ltd v Heller & Partners Ltd* [1964] A.C. 465.

[188] *Bruce v Leisk* (1892) 19 R. 482. Cf. *Anderson v Hunter* (1891) 18 R. 467. Note s.106 of the Representation of the People Act 1983 which makes it an offence to make a false statement about a candidate's personal character or conduct for the purpose of affecting the candidate's return at an election.

[189] *Shaw v Morgan* (1888) 15 R. 865.

[190] *Chapman v Barber*, 1989 S.L.T. 830.

[191] *Mutch v Robertson*, 1981 S.L.T. 217.

[192] Malice may be inferred if the person alleging a wrong does not report it at the earliest opportunity: see, e.g. *Fraser v Fraser*, 2010 S.L.T. (Sh. Ct) 147.

[193] Employment Rights Act 1996 ss.43A–43L and 103A as inserted by the Public Interest Disclosure Act 1998.

[194] *Quilty v Windsor*, 1999 S.L.T. 346; *Pearson v Educational Institute of Scotland*, 1997 S.C. 245.

[195] *Cassidy v Connachie*, 1907 S.C. 1112. Cf. *Fraser v Mirza*, 1993 S.C. (HL) 27.

[196] See, e.g. *Baigent v McCulloch*, 1998 S.L.T. 780.

[197] Note that anonymised publication may compromise privilege: *Brims v Reid & Sons* (1885) 12 R. 1016; *M'Kerchar v Cameron* (1892) 19 R. 383.

guilty.[198] If the media organisation that publishes the statement is itself sued, it may attempt to rely upon the "responsible journalism" variant of the qualified privilege defence.[199]

Response to an attack

7–23   Qualified privilege may protect a response to criticism amounting to an attack on the defender's character.[200] The response may be robust,[201] provided it is not disproportionate to the attack.[202] If no attack has yet been made, qualified privilege will not apply unless the statement is made in reasonable anticipation of an imminent attack and is limited to a proportionate rebuttal of the anticipated attack.[203]

Where the dispute is played out in a public forum, qualified privilege will extend to reports of the dispute carried in the media. In *Curran v Scottish Daily Record and Sunday Mail Ltd*[204] the *Scottish Daily Record* published an interview with Tommy Sheridan, the former MSP who had recently won a defamation case against the *News of the World*, in which he branded the pursuer a "scab". Mr Sheridan had been publicly criticised by former colleagues, including the pursuer, who had alleged in an article published in another newspaper that Mr Sheridan had committed perjury during the case. Although the Inner House confirmed that the use of the epithet "scab" in the context was not defamatory of the pursuer,[205] even if it had been, the newspaper that reported a fair retort to a public attack on the character of an individual would be protected by qualified privilege. The Inner House also rejected an argument that qualified privilege would be lost by the newspaper if it was proved that Mr Sheridan had acted with malice.

Responsible journalism/Reynolds privilege

7–24   A series of cases beginning with *Reynolds v Times Newspapers Ltd*[206] has developed a new jurisprudential creature, which apparently began its life as an application of the duty and interest formulation of qualified privilege, but which became acknowledged as a distinct "responsible journalism" defence.[207] In

---

[198] *Bento v Chief Constable of Bedfordshire* [2012] EWHC 1525. Cf. *Lyons v Chief Constable of Strathclyde* [2013] CSIH 46; 2013 G.W.D. 20–401.

[199] See paras 7–24 to 7–26 below.

[200] *Shaw v Morgan* (1888) 15 R. 865 at 870 per Lord Young. See also *Chapman v Barber*, 1989 S.L.T. 830; *Carroll v BBC*, 1997 S.L.T. (Sh. Ct) 23. There is significant overlap between this application of qualified privilege and the discreet defence available in Scots law of fair retort —see para.7–30 below.

[201] *Curran v Scottish Daily Record and Sunday Mail Ltd*, 2012 S.L.T. 359.

[202] *Gray v Scottish Society for the Prevention of Cruelty to Animals* (1890) 7 R. 1185 at 1198 per Lord Shand.

[203] *Bento v Chief Constable of Bedfordshire* [2012] EWHC 1525 at [104] per Bean J. See also *Fraser v Fraser*, 2010 S.L.T. (Sh. Ct) 147 on timing.

[204] *Curran v Scottish Daily Record and Sunday Mail Ltd*, 2012 S.L.T. 359.

[205] "In our view, the readers of the article would appreciate that they were witnessing a political skirmish, with warring factions within the SSP and diametrically opposed views about how the party and its members should conduct themselves, including a characteristically forthright public berating by Mr Sheridan of those who, in his view, had failed to give him the unquestioning public and political support he needed in whatever way he demanded and at whatever personal cost to the individual": *Curran v Scottish Daily Record and Sunday Mail Ltd*, 2012 S.L.T. 359 at 368 per Lady Paton.

[206] *Reynolds v Times Newspapers Ltd* [2001] 2 A.C. 127.

[207] In England and Wales the defence has been codified by s.4 of the Defamation Act 2013.

Reynolds itself, a former Irish Taoiseach[208] sought damages for a *Sunday Times* article alleging that the plaintiff had been forced to resign after it was discovered that he had deliberately misled the Dáil.[209] The House of Lords did not accept the defendant's argument that "political information" should as such be protected by qualified privilege, but did recognise that the "new legal landscape" following the passing of the Human Rights Act 1998 required protection to the press where a duty and interest test was satisfied. Lord Nicholls identified 10 factors, described by Lord Hope as a "circumstantial test", which might be relevant when a court was deciding whether to recognise *Reynolds* privilege:

> "Depending on the circumstances, the matters to be taken into account include the following. The comments are illustrative only.
>
> 1. The seriousness of the allegation. The more serious the charge, the more the public is misinformed and the individual harmed, if the allegation is not true.
> 2. The nature of the information, and the extent to which the subject matter is a matter of public concern.
> 3. The source of the information. Some informants have no direct knowledge of the events. Some have their own axes to grind, or are being paid for their stories.
> 4. The steps taken to verify the information.
> 5. The status of the information. The allegation may have already been the subject of an investigation which commands respect.
> 6. The urgency of the matter. News is often a perishable commodity.
> 7. Whether comment was sought from the plaintiff. He may have information others do not possess or have not disclosed. An approach to the plaintiff will not always be necessary.
> 8. Whether the article contained the gist of the plaintiff's side of the story.
> 9. The tone of the article. A newspaper can raise queries or call for an investigation. It need not adopt allegations as statements of fact.
> 10. The circumstances of the publication, including the timing."[210]

It was observed by Lord Hope that the application of a "circumstantial test" over and above the "duty and interest test" required questions of fact to be considered in determining a question of law. This was inconsistent with the traditional approach to qualified privilege which applied where the occasion required (a question of law) but could be lost if the occasion was abused (a question of fact). This analysis later led Lord Phillips to consider that *Reynolds* privilege, if established, operated more akin to absolute rather than qualified privilege, concluding that it was a "different jurisprudential creature from the traditional form of privilege from which it sprang."[211] Although no judge has held that this

---

[208] Equivalent of First/Prime Minister.
[209] Lower house of the Oireachtas (Irish Parliament).
[210] *Reynolds v Times Newspapers Ltd* [2001] 2 A.C. 127 at 205 per Lord Nicholls of Birkenhead.
[211] *Loutchansky v Times Newspapers Ltd* [2002] Q.B. 783 at 806 per Lord Phillips of Worth Matravers.

new jurisprudential creature is part of the law of Scotland, it has been accepted as common ground between parties to litigation that it is.[212]

In *Jameel v Wall Street Journal Europe Sprl*, the House of Lords reconsidered *Reynolds* privilege, recasting the concept as a defence of responsible journalism on matters of public interest. In the context of a reprimand to the lower courts that had tended to treat Lord Nicholls' guidance as a "series of hurdles",[213] the Nicholls' factors in *Reynolds* were endorsed as "pointers which might be more or less indicative, depending on the circumstances of a particular case."[214] Lord Hoffmann explained that these factors centred on three basic issues[215]:

    a. whether the subject matter of the article was a matter of public interest;

    b. whether the inclusion of the defamatory statement was justifiable; and

    c. whether the steps taken to gather and publish the information were responsible and fair—the responsible journalism test.

7-25 Although their Lordships offered no definitive guidance on matters of public interest, Baroness Hale did distinguish "vapid tittle-tattle about ... footballers' wives and girlfriends."[216] The subject of the publication itself was that the central bank of Saudi Arabia had, at the request of US federal agencies, been monitoring certain bank accounts to ensure that they were not used for channelling funds to terrorist organisations. This was described as self-evidently of considerable public interest and it was accepted that reference to specific account holders was necessary to convey the point that the investigations were directed at the heartland of the Saudi business world.

Responsible journalism should no longer be determined by the rigid application of the Nicholls' factors as a series of rigid tests.[217] Thus, in *Jameel*, even although the journalist could not prove that the story had been verified through all of the sources claimed and publication had not been held back so as to provide the claimant the opportunity to respond to the allegations,[218] on balance what was done achieved the standard of the responsible journalist.

The three part test set out by Lord Hoffmann in *Jameel* was applied by the Supreme Court in *Flood v Times Newspapers Ltd*.[219] The *Times* had received information from an anonymous source about a report made to the Metropolitan

---

[212] *Adams v Guardian Newspapers Ltd*, 2003 S.C. 425. See also *Ewing v Times Newspapers Ltd* [2008] CSOH 169 at [27] per Lord Brodie.

[213] *Jameel v Wall Street Journal Europe Sprl* [2007] 1 A.C. 359 at 377 per Lord Bingham of Cornhill.

[214] *Jameel v Wall Street Journal Europe Sprl* [2007] 1 A.C. 359 at 377 per Lord Bingham of Cornhill.

[215] *Jameel v Wall Street Journal Europe Sprl* [2007] 1 A.C. 359 at 381–383 per Lord Hoffmann.

[216] *Jameel v Wall Street Journal Europe Sprl* [2007] 1 A.C. 359 at 408 per Baroness Hale of Richmond.

[217] In *Adams v Guardian Newspapers Ltd*, 2003 S.C. 425 at 447, Lord Reed pointed out that the concept "requires the court to make sensitive judgments about the conduct of journalists which may be influenced by the flavour of the case as it emerges from the evidence, and by a fuller understanding of the factual context than can be derived from pleadings alone."

[218] Cf. *Galloway v Telegraph Group Ltd* [2006] E.M.L.R. 11.

[219] *Flood v Times Newspapers Ltd* [2012] 2 A.C. 273.

Police Service (MPS) that Russian oligarchs had paid a police officer using the codename "Noah" for information regarding extradition requests and that "Noah" could be the claimant. *The Times* contacted MPS to ask for confirmation regarding these allegations. As a result of that enquiry MPS raided the claimant's home and office, but established that the allegations were unfounded. *The Times* at that point published a report of the allegations, naming the claimant. The Supreme Court held that the subject matter was in the public interest, identification of the claimant did not preclude the defence, especially given the connection between "Noah" and "Flood", and the journalism was responsible in that the journalists had reasonably satisfied themselves that the facts were true at the time they were reported.[220]

The responsible journalism defence has not been confined to journalism by the English courts.[221] It has also been applied to material published in a book[222] and to political speech delivered at a public meeting.[223] Section 4 of the Defamation Act 2013, which codifies the defence within England and Wales, does not distinguish between different forms of communication.

Reportage

Initially an application of *Reynolds* privilege, "neutral reportage" of a public **7–26** dispute may enjoy protection from liability in defamation. The concept was recognised in *Al-Fagih v H.H. Saudi Research and Marketing (UK) Ltd*, where a newspaper was allowed the defence in neutrally reporting details of a dispute which was accepted to be a matter of public interest. Reportage was defined as "a convenient word to describe the neutral reporting of attributed allegations rather than their adoption by the newspaper."[224] Thus to rely upon the defence the defender must be careful to avoid adopting, embellishing or drawing inferences from the allegations.[225] The publication will also be viewed in the wider context and so the defence will certainly be rejected where publication is part of a sustained campaign vilifying the pursuer.[226]

It is suggested that "neutral reportage" should now be viewed as distinct from the *Reynolds*/responsible journalism defence, given the requirement of the latter that the steps taken to gather and publish information be responsible and fair. Indeed, this concept is arguably a clearer application of qualified privilege in the sense that the occasion is protected and abuse of the occasion is not.

---

[220] The question whether the *Reynolds* defence would continue to protect an online version of the story was not decided, but it is suggested that a responsible journalist would at least remove a defamatory story from an online archive upon discovering that the included defamatory imputations were actually false. This appears to have been accepted by the defendants and damages were subsequently awarded with regard to continued online publication of the original article beyond the date at which the journalist became aware that the allegations were in fact false: *Flood v Times Newspapers Ltd (No.3)* [2013] EWHC 4075.

[221] *Jameel v Wall Street Journal Europe Sprl* [2007] 1 A.C. 359 at 383 per Lord Hoffmann.

[222] *Charman v Orion Publishing Group Ltd* [2008] 1 All E.R. 750.

[223] *Seaga v Harper* [2009] 1 A.C. 1.

[224] *Al-Fagih v H.H. Saudi Research and Marketing (UK) Ltd* [2002] E.M.L.R. 13 at 219 per Simon Brown L.J. See also *Mark v Associated Newspapers Ltd* [2002] E.M.L.R. 38; *Charman v Orion Publishing Group Ltd* [2007] 4 All E.R. 319; *Roberts v Gable* [2008] Q.B. 502.

[225] *Galloway v Telegraph Group Ltd* [2006] E.M.L.R. 11.

[226] *Grobbelaar v News Group Newspapers Ltd* [2002] 1 W.L.R. 3024.

It is also suggested that, although the term was not used in any of the opinions, *Curran v Scottish Daily Record and Sunday Mail Ltd*[227] provides an application of the concept by Scottish courts.

Reports enjoying qualified privilege

7-27   It is probably the case that at common law qualified privilege will protect any fair and accurate report of an occasion open to the public which itself is protected by absolute privilege, in particular, proceedings in the UK and Scottish Parliaments[228] and in court.[229]

The common law has been supplemented by statutory protection of a variety of reports, now provided for by s.15 of the Defamation Act 1996,[230] which sets out general requirements, and the corresponding Schedule, which lists the range of reports covered. In general a report will not be protected if the subject matter is not of public concern, or if publication is prohibited by law or is not for the public benefit. The list of reports is then divided into two parts, Pt 2 reports being subject to an additional caveat: there is no defence if the defender refused or neglected to publish, in a suitable manner,[231] a reasonable letter or statement by way of explanation or contradiction[232] upon being requested to do so by the pursuer.[233]

Part 1 covers fair and accurate reports of, inter alia, proceedings in public of legislatures, courts, certain public inquiries, international organisations and conferences, as well as fair and accurate copies of or extracts from documents and registers etc associated with these types of organisations and open to public inspection. The relevant organisations may be situated anywhere in the world.

Part 2 covers, inter alia, fair and accurate reports of meetings and inquiries held in public of local authorities[234] and other statutory bodies, and of various other lawfully held public meetings including press conferences,[235] general meetings of public companies, proceedings of scientific or academic conferences and their associated publications, decisions of various bodies formed to super-vise, promote or govern professions, sport, religion, art science etc, as well as fair and accurate copies of or extracts from various communications intended for information of the public from bodies exercising judicial and governmental functions, including the police. With the exception of proceedings at scientific or

---

[227] *Curran v Scottish Daily Record and Sunday Mail Ltd*, 2012 S.L.T. 359.

[228] *Wason v Walter* (1868–1869) L.R. 4 Q.B. 73.

[229] *Richardson v Wilson* (1879) 7 R. 237. See also *Pope v Outram & Co* (1909) S.C. 230; *Harper v Provincial Newspapers Ltd*, 1937 S.L.T. 462; *Cunningham v The Scotsman Publications Ltd*, 1987 S.C. 107.

[230] Supplemented by s.7(9) of the Defamation Act 2013.

[231] The prominence of the published correction will be relevant here.

[232] Note that s.15(2) of the Defamation Act 1996 does not demand publication of an *apology*.

[233] Defamation Act 1996 s.15(2). This requirement has been explained as being "subject to the claimant *having been given the right to ask for opportunity* to contradict or explain . . . ": *Qadir v Associated Newspapers Ltd* [2013] E.M.L.R. 15 at 342–343 per Tugendhat J. With respect, it is submitted that this interpretation is wrong. The language of s.15(2) suggests that the right to contradict or explain is given by the statute and so comes into operation *after* publication by the defender. The language of s.15(3) is not consistent with a requirement that the defender *offer* the right to explain or contradict in advance of publication.

[234] See, e.g. *Brooks v Lind*, 2000 G.W.D. 8–307.

[235] Including information distributed but not necessarily read out at a press conference: *McCartan Turkington Breen v Times Newspapers Ltd* [2001] 2 A.C. 277. See also *Thomson v Ross*, 2001 S.L.T. 807.

academic conferences (which may be anywhere in the world), the geographical range of bodies, etc covered by Pt 2 is also restricted.

Statutory qualified privilege also applies to peer-reviewed publications (unless prohibited by law) in scientific or academic journals, and fair and accurate copies of, extracts from or summaries of such publications.[236]

Veritas

Scots law presumes an unprivileged defamatory statement to be false.[237] It is **7-28** therefore up to the defender, if challenged, to adduce evidence sufficient to prove, on the balance of probabilities, that the imputation, including any defamatory inference drawn from the statement,[238] is true or substantially true.[239] *Veritas* thus provides a complete defence to defamatory statements of fact,[240] or at least in principle.[241]

A bare assertion of truth will not be sufficient—there must be averments in the pleadings as to the detail supporting the assertion,[242] and evidence must be adduced to support the averments. The evidence relied upon does not necessarily need to prove every distinct allegation made provided allegations of fact that are not supported by evidence cause no further material damage than those that are proved.[243] The evidence does need to be relevant to the defamatory imputation; for example, it is no good in defending a statement that a man *is* a thief to lead evidence that he has a historic conviction for theft.[244] The evidence also needs to be relevant to the level or degree of the facts alleged.[245]

However, that a pursuer has been convicted of an offence is conclusive evidence that the pursuer committed that offence for the purposes of an action in defamation.[246] This is subject to the conviction being spent,[247] when proof of malice will defeat the defence of *veritas*.[248]

---

[236] Defamation Act 2013 s.6.

[237] This presumption, which applies similarly in England and Wales, has been upheld by the European Court of Human Rights as compatible with art.10: *McVicar v United Kingdom* (2002) 35 E.H.R.R. 22; *Steel & Morris v United Kingdom* [2005] E.M.L.R. 15. It is not enough to offer to prove that the defender honestly believes the defamatory statement to be true: *Angiolini v Green* [2013] CSOH 196; 2014 G.W.D. 5–104 at [42] per Lord Bannatyne.

[238] See, e.g. *Cruddas v Calvert* [2013] EWHC 2298.

[239] See, e.g. *Sarwar v News Group Newspapers Ltd*, 1999 S.L.T. 327.

[240] The equivalent in England and Wales is now simply called "Truth": Defamation Act 2013 s.2.

[241] Proof of *veritas* may dislodge the presumption of malice in an action for defamation. However, harm caused by the statement may nevertheless remain reparable if Scots law continues to recognise *convicium* as an actionable wrong (or if Scots law recognises a similar wrong of "malicious truth", which may be fortified by an averment of infringement of art.8 of the European Convention on Human Rights). See para.7–38 below.

[242] *Angiolini v Green* [2013] CSOH 196; 2014 G.W.D. 5–104 at [43] per Lord Bannatyne.

[243] Defamation Act 1952 s.5.

[244] *Fletcher v Wilson* (1885) 12 R. 683.

[245] See, e.g. *Lewis v Daily Telegraph Ltd* [1964] A.C. 234; *Berezovsky v Forbes Inc (No.2)* [2001] E.M.L.R. 45.

[246] Law Reform (Miscellaneous Provisions) (Scotland) Act 1968 s.12. Note that as a result of an amendment inserted by the Defamation Act 1996 s.12 this rule only applies where the person convicted is the pursuer. Thus, an allegation that the police fabricated evidence against a person who was wrongly convicted as a result is no longer doomed to fail.

[247] See Rehabilitation of Offenders Act 1974.

[248] Rehabilitation of Offenders Act 1974 s.8.

Where a defender persists in insisting on *veritas*, but the defence is rejected, the court may reflect the aggravation of reputational harm by increasing the award of damages.[249]

Fair comment

7–29   This defence, alternatively known as honest comment,[250] protects the right honestly to express one's opinions in a candid and forthright manner. English courts have recently developed this defence significantly,[251] and these developments have recently been codified into s.3 of the Defamation Act 2013. However, the statutory codification does not apply in Scotland and it is not yet clear whether the judicial developments will be accepted as part of the law of Scotland.[252] There appear to be five requirements for the defence to succeed:

   1. The defamatory imputation must be a comment rather than a fact.[253] It will often be clear into which category a statement falls: to describe a person as "a criminal" is a statement of fact; but to state that what the person did was "criminal" is a comment.[254] However, on occasion distinguishing comment from fact may not be simple. Recent jurisprudence has favoured a liberal approach, holding that if the statement amounts to a "value judgment" it will constitute opinion, even where it could satisfy a "verifiable fact" test.[255] Similarly, comment may include inferences of fact.[256] Thus, an assertion that an association "happily promotes bogus treatments", where it makes claims about treatments even though there is not a jot of supporting evidence, has been described as comment.[257] The comment may be express or by innuendo.[258]
   2. The comment must be based on provably true facts[259] or on privileged information.[260] Provided that sufficient provably true facts underpin the comment, not every fact asserted needs to be proved.[261] The defender can rely upon general facts even if he had forgotten them at the

---

[249] *Baigent v BBC*, 2001 S.C. 281.

[250] See *Joseph v Spiller* [2011] 1 A.C. 852 at 889 per Lord Phillips of Worth Matravers on criticism of the "traditional" nomenclature. The equivalent statutory defence in England and Wales is now called "honest opinion": Defamation Act 2013 s.3.

[251] See, e.g. *Joseph v Spiller* [2011] 1 A.C. 852.

[252] *Massie v McCaig*, 2013 S.C. 343 at 353 per Lord Justice-Clerk Carloway. Cf. *Massie v McCaig* [2013] CSIH 37; 2013 G.W.D. 15–310 at [7] per Lord Justice-Clerk Carloway: "Nothing in (the court's) opinion (in *Massie v McCaig*, 2013 S.C. 343) on the nature of fair comment in Scots law is in conflict with the decision in *Joseph v Spiller* [2011] 1 A.C. 852 . . . "

[253] See, e.g. *Adams v Guardian Newspapers Ltd*, 2003 S.C. 425.

[254] See, e.g. *Waterson v Lloyd* [2013] E.M.L.R. 17; *Myerson v Smith's Weekly Publishing Co Ltd* (1923) 24 S.R. (N.S.W.) 20 at 26 per Ferguson J.

[255] *Sorguç v Turkey* (17089/03) [2009] ECHR 979; *Joseph v Spiller* [2011] 1 A.C. 852.

[256] *Tamiz v Guardian News & Media Ltd* [2013] EWHC 2339.

[257] *British Chiropractic Association v Singh* [2011] 1 W.L.R. 133.

[258] *Moffat v London Express Newspaper*, 1950 S.L.T. (Notes) 46; *Massie v McCaig*, 2013 S.C. 343.

[259] See, e.g. *Fairbairn v Scottish National Party*, 1980 S.L.T. 149 at 152 per Lord Ross. "In order to be fair, the commentator must get his basic facts right": *London Artists Ltd v Littler Ltd* [1969] 2 Q.B. 375 at 391 per Denning M.R.

[260] *Brooks v Lind*, 2000 G.W.D. 8–307.

[261] Defamation Act 1952 s.6. See also *Joseph v Spiller* [2011] 1 A.C. 852.

time—since they may have contributed to the defender's opinion,[262] but cannot rely upon any facts that have come to light since the statement was made.[263]

3. The comment must explicitly or implicitly indicate, at least in general terms, the underpinning facts.[264] The facts do not require to be set out in full. In England and Wales it is now sufficient that underpinning facts be merely alluded to.[265]

4. The comment must be on a matter of public interest.[266] Public interest is liberally interpreted in the context of fair comment:

"Whenever a matter is such as to affect people at large, so that they may be legitimately interested in, or concerned at, what is going on, or what may happen to them or others; then it is a matter of public interest on which everyone is entitled to make fair comment."[267]

Thus, commentary or critical review on a variety of political, entertainment and leisure matters, as well as product or performance reviews, are all covered.[268] Whether "vapid tittle-tattle about the activities of footballers' wives and girlfriends"[269] falls within the parameters of the public interest in the context of fair comment has yet to be tested.

5. The comment must be fair; that is, an honest expression of the defender's opinion.[270] However, that provides considerable latitude:

"The expression of an opinion as to a state of facts truly set forth is not actionable, even when that opinion is couched in vituperative or contumelious language."[271]

The legal presumption that the defender's comment was honest will be difficult to rebut,[272] although possible if the evidence shows that the

---

[262] *Lowe v Associated Newspapers Ltd* [2007] Q.B. 580.

[263] *Wheatley v Anderson*, 1927 S.C. 133.

[264] *Archer v Ritchie & Co* (1891) 18 R. 719 at 727 per Lord McLaren; *Wheatley v Anderson* 1927 S.C. 133 at 147 per Lord Anderson.

[265] *Joseph v Spiller* [2011] 1 A.C. 852; *Kemsley v Foot* [1952] A.C. 345. Presumably this is not altered by s.3 of the Defamation Act 2013.

[266] This is no longer a requirement in England and Wales under the statutory honest opinion defence: s.3 of the Defamation Act 2013.

[267] *London Artists Ltd v Littler Ltd* [1969] 2 Q.B. 375 at 391 per Denning M.R.

[268] See, e.g. *Convery v The Irish News Ltd* [2007] NICA 40.

[269] *Jameel v Wall Street Journal Europe Sprl* [2007] 1 A.C. 359 at 408 per Baroness Hale of Richmond, holding that such discourse was not in the public interest in the context of the responsible journalism/*Reynolds* privilege defence.

[270] Albeit that the court in *Massie v McCaig*, 2013 S.C. 343 (at 353 per Lord Justice-Clerk Carloway) was not persuaded that a subjective "honest belief" in the comment was a requirement of the defence. See also *Massie v McCaig* [2013] CSIH 37 at [7] per Lord Justice-Clerk Carloway.

[271] *Archer v Ritchie & Co* (1891) 18 R. 719 at 727 per Lord McLaren. "The comment must be one which could have been made by an honest person, however prejudiced he might be, and however exaggerated or obstinate his views . . . a critic need not be mealy-mouthed in denouncing what he disagrees with. He is entitled to dip his pen in gall for the purposes of legitimate criticism": *Tse Wai Chun Paul v Cheng* [2001] E.M.L.R. 31 at 783 per Lord Nicholls of Birkenhead. See also *Lowe v Associated Newspapers Ltd* [2007] Q.B. 580; *Associated Newspapers Ltd v Burstein* [2007] 4 All E.R. 319.

[272] *Branson v Bower (No.2)* [2002] Q.B. 737.

defender deliberately suppressed facts that would tend to show the comment to be unfair.[273]

It has been held that a newspaper report of a fair comment would itself attract the protection given to fair comment,[274] although this protection may be lost if the reporter knew that the author of the comment was acting dishonestly. It may be arguable that a person repeating a comment could be liable in negligence upon application of *Spring v Guardian Assurance Plc*.[275]

Fair retort

7–30   Fair retort is a form of verbal self-defence and permits a degree of latitude in responding to charges made in public against the defender's character or conduct.[276] Thus, in *Curran v Scottish Daily Record & Sunday Mail Ltd*[277] the Inner House agreed that in the context of a political skirmish carried out in public, the defence could extend beyond a mere denial, possibly to calling the pursuer a liar, and certainly protecting angry comments regarding the defender's loyalty. There is clearly significant overlap between this defence and the qualified privilege conferred on a proportionate response to an attack.[278] Reporting a fair retort may be protected by qualified privilege or as reportage[279] even if there is evidence of malice in the retort itself.[280]

In rixa

7–31   An angry retort to a jibe made in the heat of an argument will not attract liability for defamation unless malice, in the form of intention to harm the pursuer, is proved.[281]

Vulgar abuse

7–32   This provides a defence where, because of the crude or gross nature of the language used or the context in which the words are delivered, a reasonable person would not take what was said seriously. The defence will apply if it would be obvious to the reasonable person that what is said is clearly intended as a distasteful joke.[282] The defence may also be relevant to heated online debates:

> "From the context of casual conversations, one can often tell that a remark is not to be taken literally or seriously and is rather to be construed merely as abuse. That is less common in the case of more permanent written communication, although it is by no means unknown. But in the case of a bulletin board thread it is often obvious to casual observers that people are

---

[273] *Shanks v BBC*, 1993 S.L.T. 326.

[274] *Brooks v Lind*, 2000 G.W.D. 8–307.

[275] *Spring v Guardian Assurance Plc* [1995] 2 A.C. 296.

[276] See, e.g. *Gray v Scottish Society for the Prevention of Cruelty to Animals* (1890) 7 R. 1185; *Carroll v BBC*, 1997 S.L.T. (Sh. Ct) 23.

[277] *Curran v Scottish Daily Record & Sunday Mail Ltd*, 2012 S.L.T. 359.

[278] See para.7–23 above.

[279] *Roberts v Gable* [2008] Q.B. 502.

[280] *Curran v Scottish Daily Record and Sunday Mail Ltd*, 2012 S.L.T. 359.

[281] See, e.g. *Christie v Robertson* (1899) 1 F. 1155.

[282] See, e.g. *MacLeod v Newsquest (Sunday Herald) Ltd*, 2007 S.C.L.R. 555; *Cowan v Bennett*, 2012 G.W.D. 37–738. Cf. *Prophit v BBC*, 1997 S.L.T. 745.

just saying the first thing that comes into their heads and reacting in the heat of the moment. The remarks are often not intended, or to be taken, as serious."[283]

Innocent dissemination

Scots law presumes an unprivileged defamatory statement to be motivated by **7–33** malice and intended to cause reputational harm to the identifiable pursuer. At common law it appears that this presumption is not rebuttable. However, to mitigate against the impact of the repetition rule on innocent parties who do no more than provide the medium for the defamatory statement to be disseminated, two variants of a similar defence are now provided by statute.[284]

Section 1 of the Defamation Act 1996 provides a defence if the defender:

- was not the author, editor or publisher of the statement complained of;
- took reasonable care in relation to its publication; and
- did not know, and had no reason to believe, that what he did caused or contributed to the publication of a defamatory statement.

This defence was clearly targeted at "internet service providers"[285] but may also be applied to anyone who hosts a web page where others are able to post a comment directly to the page.[286]

Clause 19 of the Electronic Commerce (EC Directive) Regulations 2002 is not confined to defamation and provides that where an information service provider merely stores information without knowledge of unlawful activity or content, it is a defence to show that the defender acted expeditiously to remove or disable access to the information on becoming aware of its unlawfulness.[287]

Apology

An apology disseminated as widely and as prominently as the defamatory **7–34** statement is not likely to provide a defence as such but may mitigate damages.[288] Conversely, it is not impossible that an apology could exacerbate damages if it draws the defamatory imputation to the attention of persons who did not receive the original communication.[289]

Offer of amends

Sections 2–4 of the Defamation Act 1996 provide a procedure for making a **7–35** formal apology and offer of amends. If this is accepted by the pursuer that will prevent the bringing of an action in defamation, although an action to enforce

---

[283] *Smith v ADVFN Plc* [2008] EWHC 1797 at [17] per Eady J. See also *Sheffield Wednesday v Hargreaves* [2007] EWHC 2375.

[284] See also, for England and Wales, s.5 of the Defamation Act 2013 and the Defamation (Operators of Websites) Regulations 2013 (SI 2013/3028).

[285] *Godfrey v Demon Internet Ltd* [2001] Q.B. 201; *Bunt v Tilley* [2007] 1 W.L.R. 1243; *Tamiz v Google Inc* [2013] 1 W.L.R. 2151.

[286] See, e.g. *Robertson v Newsquest (Sunday Herald) Ltd*, 2006 S.C.L.R. 792.

[287] See, e.g. *Karim v Newsquest Media Group Ltd* [2009] EWHC 3205.

[288] There is old authority to the effect that an apology may remove any defamatory sting: *Ewart v Mason* (1806) Hume 633.

[289] Cf. *Robertson v Newsquest (Sunday Herald) Ltd*, 2006 S.C.L.R. 792.

what is agreed is competent. If the offer is neither withdrawn nor accepted,[290] the defender may use this as a defence unless it can be shown that the defender knew or had reason to believe that the original communication was defamatory of the pursuer.[291] Reliance on a failure to accept an offer of amends precludes introduction of any other defence, e.g. *veritas* or fair comment.

Remedies

Damages

7–36   Damages may always be awarded for a defamatory statement. Solatium will be awarded for presumed hurt feelings[292] following the *actio injuriarum*, but damages for patrimonial loss, based on the *lex Aquilia*, reflecting loss of business or damage to reputation, must be averred. If all that the pursuer seeks is to clear his name damages will be modest.[293]

It is inappropriate to attempt to make a direct comparison between an award of solatium for pain and suffering caused by physical injury and an award of solatium for injury to feelings and reputation.[294] While it is proper for a court to take account of levels of award made in Scottish defamation cases, English cases, in which awards are assessed on very different principles, will be of little help.[295] Excessive damages awards must be avoided as they will have a chilling effect on freedom of expression.[296] Nevertheless, juries in Scotland have generally been treated as competent in recognising and applying relevant factors in making an award.[297]

Damages may be increased if the harm has been aggravated by:

- repeating the statement, especially after a warning that it was false.[298] A growing phenomenon is the harassment of pursuers through electronic communications such as blogs. Not only will such conduct also be actionable as an intrusion into privacy, it may also be punishable as criminal under the Protection from Harassment Act 1997[299];
- foreseeable secondary publication by others[300]; and
- persisting in the defence of *veritas*.[301]

Certain factors may mitigate the award of damages:

- circulation of the defamatory statement is minimal[302];

---

[290] See, e.g. *Moore v Scottish Daily Record and Sunday Mail Ltd* [2007] CSOH 24.

[291] See, e.g. *Milne v Express Newspapers* [2003] 1 W.L.R. 927.

[292] Extending to continuing emotional and physical consequences: see, e.g. *H v H* [2013] CSIH 82; 2013 G.W.D. 34–675.

[293] See, e.g. *Gilbert v Yorston*, 1997 S.L.T. 879.

[294] *Winter v News (Scotland) Ltd*, 1991 S.L.T. 828; *Baigent v BBC*, 2001 S.C. 281.

[295] *Winter v News (Scotland) Ltd*, 1991 S.L.T. 828; *Baigent v BBC*, 2001 S.C. 281.

[296] *Tolstoy Milosalvsky v UK* (1995) 20 E.H.R.R. 442.

[297] *Baigent v BBC*, 2001 S.C. 281.

[298] *Morrison v Ritchie* (1902) 4 F. 645.

[299] See, e.g. *Law Society v Kordowski* (2012) 109(1) L.S.G. 13; *Cruddas v Adams* [2013] EWHC 145. See para.6–28 above.

[300] *Slipper v BBC* [1991] 1 Q.B. 283; *Cairns v Modi* [2013] E.M.L.R. 8. The latter case identifies the risk of an electronic communication "going viral".

[301] See, e.g. *Baigent v BBC*, 2001 S.C. 281; *Munro v Brown*, 2011 S.L.T. 947.

[302] *H v H* [2013] CSIH 82; 2013 G.W.D. 34–675.

- a prompt correction and apology has been made[303];
- the pursuer has already been compensated for the harm, e.g. where the pursuer has already sued another publisher of the same defamatory imputation[304]; and
- the pursuer already has a bad reputation.[305] However, if anything, the law presumes a pursuer to be of good character, although "Life not being a morality play or a Victorian Melodrama, men do not enjoy reputations for being bad or good simpliciter."[306] The "legal raspberry" (being the damages award intended to add insult to injury) has been a victim of inflation, rising from the traditional farthing to the grand sum of £1.00.[307]

Interdict

There has been a reluctance in England to allow claimants to restrain **7–37** publication in advance as it stifles free speech. The general rule (often described as the rule in *Bonnard v Perryman*[308]) is that interim (known as interlocutory) injunctions should not be issued where the defendant intimates a defence, whether of justification, honest (fair) comment on a matter of public interest or privilege, i.e. publish and be damned.[309] English law permitted an exception where the publication was part of a conspiracy to injure,[310] but this exception has been narrowly construed.[311] However, the recent phenomenon of internet "trolling"[312] is challenging the courts in England to review their tradition, and interlocutory injunctions have recently been awarded in such cases.[313] Scotland has never operated the rule in *Bonnard v Perryman*. If a court is presented with an application for interim interdict there are two factors to consider. First, s.12(3) of the Human Rights Act 1998 provides that no prior restraint on publication should be ordered before trial unless the court is satisfied that the applicant "is likely to succeed in his conclusion for a permanent interdict."[314] Secondly, the court must then apply a "balance of convenience" test.[315] Where appropriate, this ought to involve a balancing of the pursuer's art.8 right to respect for private life with the defender's art.10 right to freedom of expression.[316]

---

[303] *Morrison v Ritchie* (1902) 4 F. 645.

[304] Defamation Act 1952 s.12.

[305] The bad character must be with regard to the imputation in dispute: *C v M*, 1923 S.C. 1.

[306] *Plato Films v Speidel* [1961] A.C. 1090 at 1130 per Lord Radcliffe.

[307] *Grobbelaar v News Group Newspapers Ltd* [2002] 1 W.L.R. 3024.

[308] *Bonnard v Perryman* [1891] 2 Ch. 269.

[309] *Clerk & Lindsell on Torts*, edited by A. Dugdale and M. Jones, 20th edn (London: Sweet & Maxwell, 2013), Ch.22, s.10 (paras 22–256 to 22–257). See, e.g. *Terry (LNS) v Persons Unknown* [2010] E.M.L.R. 16.

[310] *Gulf Oil Ltd v Page* [1987] Ch. 327. Tony Weir has described this case as egregious and disgraceful: T. Weir, *Economic Torts* (Oxford: Oxford University Press, 1997), pp.19–20.

[311] *Femis-Bank (Anguilla) Ltd v Lazar* [1991] Ch. 391, injunction refused.

[312] The posting of deliberately offensive and inflammatory messages on the internet or via social media.

[313] See, e.g. *ZAM v CFW* [2011] EWHC 476; *London Borough of Lambeth v Pead* [2013] EWHC 212.

[314] *Massie v McCaig*, 2013 S.C. 343 at 354 per Lord Justice-Clerk Carloway. See also *Dickson Minto WS v Bonnier Media Ltd*, 2002 G.W.D. 17–551; *Cream Holdings Ltd v Banerjee* [2005] 1 A.C. 253.

[315] *Waddell v BBC*, 1973 S.L.T. 246; *Kwik-Fit-Euro Ltd v Scottish Daily Record and Sunday Mail Ltd*, 1987 S.L.T. 226.

[316] *Massie v McCaig*, 2013 S.C. 343 at 354 per Lord Justice-Clerk Carloway.

Nevertheless, interdict against repetition of a given statement, already held defamatory, is competent.[317]

CONVICIUM AND MALICIOUS TRUTH

7–38   *Convicium* "is concerned with the hurt to an individual's feelings and public reputation, by being brought into public hatred, contempt and ridicule".[318] The roots of this head of liability are in the *Digest*[319] and the *iniuria* originally consisted of shouting loud insults in public. Hume, writing in the early 19th century, included *convicium* in a series of wrongful communications—alongside the divulging of secret personal information, historic misbehaviour, intimate illness or hidden personal defect—where malicious communication meant that truth provided no defence.[320] Guthrie Smith described *convicium* as a species of verbal injury:

> "A specially aggravated kind—the loud and public denunciation of an individual by different persons, one or more, acting in concert. To be hooted and insulted in this way on the public street is evidently a worse wrong than any form of private scandal. It, may, moreover, often lead to public disturbance; and hence, while the truth of the libel is a good plea in all other cases, in this case the maxim applies *veritas convicii non excusat*."[321]

There is a line of relevant cases, the foundation case being *Sheriff v Wilson*. A series of articles was published vilifying the pursuer. The Lord Justice-Clerk considered that a man could be driven to a state of almost desperation by such conduct.[322] It was thus actionable. The basis was that it would have been punished under the old law and there was authority in Erskine.[323] Glegg goes to considerable trouble to demonstrate the existence of this type of liability.[324] While this is considered by Professor Walker to be part of the law of Scotland, other commentators are very much more doubtful.[325] The state has been reached whereby it is described as a myth in the *Stair Memorial Encyclopaedia*.[326]

---

[317] See, e.g. *H v H* [2013] CSIH 82; 2013 G.W.D. 34–675; *Angiolini v Green* [2013] CSOH 196; [2014] G.W.D. 5–104.

[318] *Barratt Resorts Ltd v Barratt Owners' Group* [2002] Scot CS 318 at [25] per Lord Wheatley. Lord Wheatley's description of the use of the term has been criticised: see Norrie, "Actions for Verbal Injury" (2003) 7 Edin. L.R. 390.

[319] D, 47, 10, 15. The Praetor says: "Nothing shall be done to bring a person into hatred, ridicule or contempt." Or even in the 12 Tables: S.C. Smith, "When the Truth Hurts", 1998 S.L.T. (News) 1.

[320] Hume, *Lectures*, III, 156–160.

[321] J. Guthrie-Smith, *The Law of Damages: A Treatise on the Reparation of Injuries, as Administered in Scotland*, 2nd edn (Edinburgh: T. & T. Clark, 1889), p.241.

[322] *Sheriff v Wilson* (1855) 17 D. 528 at 531.

[323] A.T. Glegg, *A Practical Treatise on the Law of Reparation*, 2nd edn (Edinburgh: W. Green, 1905), pp.145–146; Erskine, *Institute*, IV, 4, 80.

[324] Blackie, "Defamation" in Reid and Zimmermann (eds), *A History of Private Law in Scotland* (2000), Vol.II: Obligations, p.702 demonstrates an innocent misinterpretation or misunderstanding by Glegg of the development of the Roman law in the *ius commune*.

[325] Walker, *The Law of Delict in Scotland* (1981), pp.736–740.; see *contra*, Norrie, *Defamation and Related Actions in Scots Law* (1995), Ch.3. See also E. Reid, "Protection of Personality Rights in the Modern Scots Law of Delict", in Whitty and Zimmermann (eds), *Rights of Personality in Scots Law, A Comparative Perspective* (2009); Reid, *Personality, Confidentiality and Privacy in Scots Law* (2010).

[326] *Stair Memorial Encyclopaedia*, 15, 558: "The non-existence of convicium".

An example of the kind of case that could be described as *convicium* is *Steele v Scottish Daily Record*.[327] Counsel before the Inner House agreed to describe the action as one for verbal injury and so the Second Division did not analyse the matter. This action was based on an article appearing in the "Judge" section of the *Sunday Mail*. The paper reported that the pursuer, a motor dealer, had insisted upon holding a man to his contractual obligations. Part of the report stated:

> "But fair's fair—did your firm have to make him take a car he didn't want, a car he can't afford to run? A car that he's going to find very hard to sell with the coming of winter? You're in the big time, Mr Steele. Probably you didn't know the tough times young Mr McLeod was going through. Come on ... let's show us that the big time has a big heart too."

Note that this could not be a defamation case as the facts stated did not allege dishonourable or immoral conduct. In the event, the court held the case of *convicium* was not made out because the pursuer had not shown that the article intended to have the pursuer ridiculed or treated with contempt. An alternative test equivalent to that in defamation—a lowering in public esteem—was rejected.

More difficult is the question whether the maxim *veritas convicium non excusat* (truth does not excuse *convicium*) applies. There were indications in *Steele* that it might not. *Barratt*[328] appears to leave the matter open. Professor Blackie has offered a cogent explanation for how it could be that it was thought by Glegg (mistakenly) that this could be the case.[329]

7–39

Should Scots law support some sort of "malicious truth" delict? If there is to be a "hooting down" delict, then it is not much use if it only applies to false statements. Nor would recognition of a delict of infringement of privacy as such help if the matter were already public—like the hunchback, or where the statements were simply vilificatory. Nor should it be assumed that the publication of the truth is an absolute right. Criminal law, regulatory provisions and human rights law all restrain the truth that the media may publish; and preventing the media publishing abusive, hurtful, hooting and hounding material merely to vilify the target does not of itself restrain the press in carrying out its social role, only the manner in which it does it. Of course, restrictions on communication must now be compatible with art.10 jurisprudence, which requires these to be prescribed by law, necessary in a democratic society and proportionate with regard to the pursuit of a legitimate aim.[330]

It is true that legislation[331] is gradually appearing to criminalise, inter alia, "offensive speech" and, indeed in the modern world, it may be that what is needed is a statutory restatement on this narrow point without the need for a fundamental review of the entire law of defamation and related obligations.

---

[327] *Steele v Scottish Daily Record*, 1970 S.L.T. 53.

[328] *Barratt Resorts Ltd v Barratt Owners' Group* [2002] Scot CS 318.

[329] Blackie, "Defamation" in Reid and Zimmermann (eds), *A History of Private Law in Scotland* (2000), Vol.II: Obligations, p.702.

[330] See, e.g. *Sunday Times v United Kingdom* (1979–1980) 2 E.H.R.R. 245.

[331] See, e.g. Public Order Act 1986 ss.17–22; Data Protection Act 1998—especially with regard to "processing" of "sensitive personal data"; Communications Act 2003 s.127; Offensive Behaviour at Football and Threatening Communications (Scotland) Act 2012 ss.6–8. Section 13 of the Data Protection Act 1998 also provides a civil remedy for certain breaches. See also Rehabilitation of Offenders Act 1974 s.8(5) (proof of malice overrides *veritas* in defamation actions complaining of communication of spent conviction).

Convicium could either be declared to be non-existent or given a modern role. The latter (with statutory intervention being conscious to avoid the potential for chilling free speech[332]) might be desirable given the potential for harm that comes with the explosion of social media such as *Facebook* and *Twitter*. A modern definition of *convicium* may also clarify whether a defamatory statement about a deceased person that causes substantial harm to the feelings of a living relative could be actionable under this head. That may also clarify the role and boundaries of "verbal injury" to business interests.

VERBAL INJURY: INJURIOUS FALSEHOOD

7–40 As discussed in the introduction to this chapter, verbal injury is a term that has been used in at least three different ways:

1. Generically, to distinguish verbal injury from real injury[333];
2. Semi-generically to incorporate actions related to, but distinct from defamation[334];
3. Specifically, in relation to untrue statements which, although not defamatory, nevertheless are intended to harm the pursuer, and cause the pursuer harm to his business interests.[335]

This section considers the third, most specific, meaning of the term, and it is suggested that the term "injurious falsehood" might also be apposite.

The elements of the specific delictual wrong of verbal injury were identified in *Paterson v Welch*,[336] where the Lord President (Robertson) said:

"But assuming, as I now do, that the words sued on do not found a claim of damages on the head of slander, it by no means follows that they are not actionable ... (W)hen speech is ascribed to A by B, A will have an action if: (1) the statement of B is false; (2) the statement was made with design to injure; and (3) injury has resulted."[337]

The pursuer was a governor of college A. The defender was a governor of college A but also a chairman of the school board of B. The pursuer's complaint was that, at a meeting of the board of school B and at another meeting, the defender had said, falsely, that the pursuer had previously said at a meeting of the governors of college A that the pupils from school B would contaminate the genteel children attending college A. It was held that the statement was not defamatory. Nevertheless, the case involved an actionable wrong consisting of a false statement, an ascription of an unpopular view and public hatred. Professor

---

[332] And thus compliant with art.10 of the European Convention on Human Rights.

[333] See e.g. Erskine, *Institute*, IV, 4, 80.

[334] See, e.g. *Argyllshire Weavers Ltd v A Macaulay (Tweeds) Ltd*, 1965 S.L.T. 21 at 35 per Lord Hunter; *Westcrowns Contracting Services Ltd v Daylight Insulation Ltd* [2005] CSOH 55; *Continental Tyre Group Ltd v Robertson*, 2011 G.W.D. 14–321.

[335] *Barratt Resorts Ltd v Barratt Owners' Group* [2002] Scot CS 318.

[336] *Paterson v Welch* (1893) 20 R. 744. See also *Cunningham v Phillips* (1868) 6 M. 926.

[337] *Paterson v Welch* (1893) 20 R. 744 at 749. The facts of the English case of *Grappelli v Derek Block (Holdings) Ltd* [1981] 1 W.L.R. 822, where a claim for "injurious falsehood" succeeded, would appear to fit into this matrix.

Blackie has adduced convincing reasons for saying that the case actually involved specific business losses and was not simply about solatium.[338] Thus, in the taxonomy proposed in this book, *Paterson* goes into "verbal injury" even though arguably it is in a *convicium* line.

These elements were confirmed in *Barratt International Resorts Ltd v Barratt Owners Group*, where Lord Wheatley explained:

> "The ingredients of (verbal injury) are that false statements, either written or verbal, must be maliciously communicated to third parties, which are calculated or likely to produce, and which in fact do produce, actual damage to the pursuers' business interests."[339]

The onus of proof is upon the pursuer to prove that the statement made by the defender was false. It is not necessary to prove that the defender knew that the statement was false, but the pursuer must prove that the defender made the statement out of malice. "Verbal injury" malice comprises three elements, which again must be averred and proved by the pursuer:

1. the defender deliberately made the statement of and about the pursuer or his business;
2. the defender must have made the statement with the intention or design of harming the pursuer—evidenced by "spite, or malevolence, or other improper motive, or intent to injure the pursuers' business, or at least a lack of honest belief in the truth of the statement made,"[340] or made with such recklessness as is tantamount to knowledge that the statement is untrue;
3. the false statement must be calculated or likely to cause the pursuer actual damage.

However, "verbal injury" malice must be interpreted so as to enable persons

> "to exercise their views with reasonable freedom in any debate which legitimately concerns them, and an action of personal injury should not be used to stifle a debate however vigorous between parties in conflict over their respective rights."[341]

VERBAL INJURY: MALICIOUS FALSEHOOD OR "ENGLISH" SLANDER CASES

This species of verbal injury is probably an offshoot from the English law of **7–41** defamation. It may be distinguishable from the above in that what is impugned is the victim's *property* rather than the victim's *person*. There is not much Scottish authority for it but it seems quite unobjectionable in principle and it could easily be viewed as a form of Scottish verbal injury. Indeed, in *Argyllshire Weavers Ltd v A MacAulay (Tweeds) Ltd*, Lord Hunter opined:

---

[338] Blackie, "Defamation" in Reid and Zimmermann (eds), *A History of Private Law in Scotland* (2000), Vol.II: Obligations, p.705.

[339] *Barratt International Resorts Ltd v Barratt Owners Group* [2002] Scot CS 318 at [26].

[340] Walker, *The Law of Delict in Scotland* (1981), p.902.

[341] *Barratt Resorts Ltd v Barratt Owners' Group* [2002] Scot CS 318 at [25].

"The wrong ... (is) that of a wrongful assertion relating to the goods
produced by the pursuers. The nature of the wrong ... falls in my opinion
into the category which has been referred to in Scotland as verbal injury, and
in England by a variety of terms, including the general description injurious
falsehood, of which slander of goods and slander of title or property are
examples. In Scotland the ingredients of the particular type of wrong ...
are not particularly well illustrated by decision, possibly because the
distinction between actions of slander proper involving injury to character
or reputation and actions of verbal injury has not always been clearly
maintained, though they have been the subject of quite considerable
academic discussion. The subject is dealt with in Burn-Murdoch on
Interdict, pages 388–390, para. 380, from which passage it appears that in
the view of the learned author three requirements must be present to make
false assertion relating to another's property or goods an actionable wrong.
First, the pursuer must establish positively the falsity of the assertion
complained of. There is no presumption in his favour, as there is in actions
of defamation proper, that the statement is false. Second, the pursuer must
prove that the false assertion was made maliciously. Malice is not presumed.
Third, actual damage, or as it is called in England special damage, to the
pursuer must be averred and proved. In an action of interdict, reasonable
apprehension of such actual damage would no doubt be sufficient to qualify
a pursuer for the preventive remedy."[342]

Thus the requisites are an actually spiteful communication, which is false, and
which causes or is calculated to cause damage. It differs from *convicium* in that
the statement must be false, and from defamation in that the statement need not
lead to a lowering of the victim's reputation in the estimation of right-thinking
subjects. It is suggested that the term "malicious falsehood" may be helpful here
in describing a false statement designed to impugn *property*, and might be
distinguished from injurious falsehood in describing a false statement designed to
impugn the *person*. It is known under four heads: slander of title (in the sense of
legal ownership); slander of property (in the sense of physical land or buildings);
slander of goods (moveables); and slander of business.[343] Of course, none of
these are slanders as the term is presently used, which implies defamation. An
example is *Bruce v Smith*.[344] In this case, a builder sued in respect of an article
in the *Glasgow Evening News*, which said:

"People ... in the city have discovered a new distraction in watching the
rents which are appearing in the frontage of a new property still unoccupied.
A year or so ago the building collapsed due to an insecure foundation, but
it has been run up again. Signs of fresh weakness are already evident, and
there is much speculation as to the future on the part of small crowds which
gather in the evening, and gaze blankly at the building. The master of works
may hear that his services are required—when the tenement comes down
with a run for the second time."

---

[342] *Argyllshire Weavers Ltd v A MacAulay (Tweeds) Ltd*, 1965 S.L.T. 21 at 35.
[343] Should this list also include slander to a third party, where the third party may be alive or
deceased?
[344] *Bruce v Smith* (1898) 1 F. 327.

The building was, therefore, becoming difficult to sell or to let. The claim was held to be relevant and indeed the court did not require the pursuer to prove malice, merely that the statement was false and calumnious.

In *Philip v Morton*,[345] it was said the pursuer did not own goods he was selling. In *Westcrowns Contracting Services Ltd v Daylight Insulation Ltd*,[346] a supplier of glass told a potential client that the petitioners, with whom the respondents were competing in tendering for work, were "duplicitous" and guilty of "deceit and misrepresentation" in describing their product as "safety glass". The petitioners had applied no such description to their product and were successful in obtaining a perpetual interdict to prohibit the respondents from continuing with the false and damaging claims. A similar example is *Continental Tyre Group Ltd v Robertson*[347] where the defender commented that a competitor was selling tyres that were unsafe and would explode upon inflation, saying that he "would not put them on his worst enemy's car". *Craig v Inveresk Paper Merchants Ltd*,[348] is the kind of case which is often encountered in practice. It was alleged that the defenders were saying the pursuers would be going out of business.[349]

PRIVACY

If *convicium* is indeed "concerned with the hurt to an individual's feelings and **7-42** public reputation, by being brought into public hatred, contempt and ridicule,"[350] arguably it provides a potential growing point for developing the protection of privacy in Scots law. This argument may be fortified by the recent interpretation of art.8 of the European Convention on Human Rights as providing protection of reputation as well as dignity.[351] However, although there may also be scope for application of the *actio injuriarum* to develop a distinctly Scottish approach to dealing with infringement of privacy as harm to dignity, early indications suggest that Scottish courts are following an English lead on the development of protection of privacy, deriving a wrong of "misuse of private information" from the wrong of breach of confidence.[352] As such, although privacy is concerned with personality rights, the subject is dealt with fully in Ch.9.

CONCLUSION

This Chapter began by highlighting questions relating to the classification of **7-43** delictual wrongs impacting on reputation and dignity. Although defamation as a distinct category of wrong may be relatively settled, differing views have been expressed by generations of commentators on the scope of the term verbal injury,

---

[345] *Philip v Morton* (1816) Hume 865.

[346] *Westcrowns Contracting Services Ltd v Daylight Insulation Ltd* [2005] CSOH 55.

[347] *Continental Tyre Group Ltd v Robertson*, 2011 G.W.D. 14–321.

[348] *Craig v Inveresk Paper Merchants Ltd*, 1970 S.L.T. (Notes) 50.

[349] The case failed only on vicarious liability. It is described in the report as a "verbal injury" case.

[350] *Barratt Resorts Ltd v Barratt Owners' Group* [2002] Scot CS 318 at [25] per Lord Wheatley. If Naomi Campbell had been attending a Narcotics Anonymous meeting in Scotland when she was photographed by a *Daily Mirror* photographer, could she have sought a remedy for *convicium*? (See para.9–06 below).

[351] See para.7–01 above.

[352] See, e.g. *X v BBC*, 2005 S.L.T. 796; *Response Handling Ltd v BBC*, 2008 S.L.T. 51.

the distinction between verbal injury and malicious falsehoods, and whether *convicium* still exists as a distinct delictual wrong in Scots law.

Taking these questions in reverse order, *convicium* arguably could still carry out a role in providing a remedy for "malicious truth", which could include communications which infringe privacy or "maliciously" misuse private information. Malice might be widely defined in such a context. However, various statutes have recently occupied parts of this territory, including the Rehabilitation of Offenders Act 1974, the Data Protection Act 1998, the Communications Act 2003 and the Offensive Behaviour at Football and Threatening Communications (Scotland) Act 2012, to name a few.[353] Furthermore, if Scotland does go its own way in the development of a privacy law, there may be scope for application of the *actio injuriarum* more generally to deal with unwarranted intrusion into privacy and misuse of private information impacts harmfully on a victim's dignity.[354] In any event, *convicium* could never be applied to facts such as those in *Henderson v Chief Constable of Fife*.[355] Presuming that the allegations made by the newspaper were true, *Steele v Scottish Daily Record*[356] may yet be a candidate for promoting *convicium* as actionable malicious truth. However, if on those facts the motor dealer was awarded interdict or damages, would that outcome be compatible with art.10 of the European Convention on Human Rights? Taking on board all of those points, the argument for burying *convicium* once and for all is increasingly persuasive. However, might *convicium* provide a remedy for hurt feelings caused by the defamation of a deceased third party? If so, it would be difficult to sustain an argument that truth is irrelevant, and so describing *convicium* as malicious truth would be inappropriate. Perhaps the strongest argument for restating *convicium*, or a modern equivalent, as part of Scots law would be the need for civil law remedies for malicious non-defamatory communications which harm the pursuer's feelings (*dignitas*), a growing problem in today's world of social media.

Is the distinction between verbal injury and "English" slanders made by Lord Wheatley in *Barratt International Resorts Ltd v Barratt Owners Group*[357] justified? Other cases[358] have conflated these strands into one category, described as verbal injury, or injurious or malicious falsehood. There may be a discernible distinction between the *Barratt* categories in that Lord Wheatley's definition of verbal injury impugnes the *person* (natural or non-natural) in a context which harms the person's business interests, whereas the "English" slanders to title, property, goods or business impugn the *property* directly, rather than the person as such. Whether there is any point in dissecting the matter to such a degree is open to question, and so arguably the distinction made in this chapter between injurious falsehood and malicious falsehood is tenuous, if not illusory.

Finally, the impact of the passing of the Defamation Act 2013 in England and Wales on Scots law is as yet unclear. Whether the replacement of the multiple

---

[353] Although these statutes are intended to prevent certain communications by creating criminal offences, not all of them provide for civil law remedies.

[354] See Ch.9.

[355] *Henderson v Chief Constable of Fife*, 1988 S.L.T. 361. This decision suggests that solatium would provide a remedy should the facts in *Wainwright v Home Office* [2004] 2 A.C. 406 occur in Scotland.

[356] *Steele v Scottish Daily Record*, 1970 S.L.T. 53.

[357] *Barratt International Resorts Ltd v Barratt Owners Group* [2002] Scot CS 318 at [25].

[358] See, e.g. *Argyllshire Weavers Ltd v A Macaulay (Tweeds) Ltd*, 1965 S.L.T. 21 at 35 per Lord Hunter; *Westcrowns Contracting Services Ltd v Daylight Insulation Ltd* [2005] CSOH 55.

publication rule with a single publication rule, along with the general strengthening of bulwarks against so-called libel tourists, will send forum shoppers to Scotland has yet to be discovered, as does the extent to which the Scots law of defamation might be unsettled by the implementation of those changes south of the border. The comments of Lord Carloway on the English influence on the fair comment defence in the various hearings in *Massie v McCaig*[359] might suggest that the Scots law of defamation is in for a testing time.

[359] See para.7–29 above.

CHAPTER 8

WRONGS TO PROPERTY RIGHTS

8–01 This chapter will consider various examples of nominate delictual wrongs which impinge on the victim's rights to property.

TRESPASS

8–02 "The proprietor of land has the exclusive right to the use and occupation, not merely of the surface, but of what is below, and what is above the surface, '*a coelo usque ad centrum*'." [1]

Although it is commonly thought that there is no law against trespass in Scotland, trespass infringes the exclusive right to the use and occupation of land identified above by Bell, and may also infringe the rights set out in art.8 (right to respect for private and family life, home and correspondence) and Protocol 1 art.1 (right to peaceful enjoyment of one's possessions) of the European Convention on Human Rights. Thus, trespass may be actionable as a delictual wrong with the claim reinforced by reference to the Human Rights Act 1998 and the ECHR and may, in Scotland, amount to a criminal offence under at least two Acts.[2] Furthermore, the police are given statutory powers to remove trespassers in certain circumstances.[3]

Trespass may be viewed as one of a group of delictual wrongs which relate to intrusion onto another's property. The group also includes encroachment, ejection and intrusion, which are discussed immediately below.

In Scots law, trespass is a temporary intrusion onto another's property without permission or other justification or authority.[4] The primary remedy for trespass is interdict,[5] although interdict will not be granted unless there is a threat of continuation or recurrence of the intrusion.[6] Damages may also be sought where the trespasser causes harm to the property. Although it is lawful to ask a

---

[1] Bell, *Principles*, s.960. This statement must now be qualified by the rights of access to land set out in Pt 1 of the Land Reform (Scotland) Act 2003. See below at para.8–03.

[2] Trespass (Scotland) Act 1865 s.3 and Criminal Justice and Public Order Act 1994 ss.61, 63 and 68.

[3] Criminal Justice and Public Order Act 1994 s.61(1).

[4] The definition of trespass in Scotland provided in s.61(9) of the Criminal Justice and Public Order Act 1994 is "entering, or as the case may be remaining on, land without lawful authority and without the occupier's consent".

[5] *Allen v Thomson*, 2010 S.L.T. (Sh. Ct) 60.

[6] *Winans v Macrae* (1885) 12 R. 1051

trespasser to leave,[7] it is unlikely that Scots law permits the occupier forcibly to remove the trespasser and the occupier who resorts to force may commit a criminal offence and incur delictual liability either for assault or under the Occupier's Liability (Scotland) Act 1960. However, if two or more people are collectively trespassing with the common purpose of residing there, and cause damage or behave in an aggressive or threatening manner towards the occupier, or have six or more vehicles on the land, the police have the power to intervene.[8]

The traditional view is that with regard to trespass in Scots law, "property" applies to heritable subjects. Since ownership of heritable property is *a coelo usque ad centrum* (from the heavens to the centre of the earth), the law is as concerned with the occupier's airspace and what lies beneath the surface as it is with the land itself. Thus, interdict has been granted against builders to prevent a crane's jib swinging over the petitioner's property.[9] However, there will be no liability in trespass for the flight of an aircraft at a reasonable height and not flown dangerously.[10]

Even where the public, and presumably the respondents, have been permitted by the petitioner to use the property in a certain way, that will not preclude grant of an interdict to prevent continuing use of the property that is outside of that permitted or tolerated. Thus, in *PIK Facilities Ltd v Watson's Ayr Park Ltd*,[11] interdict was granted to prevent the respondents from using buses to drop off their clients on the concourse immediately outside the terminal building at Prestwick International Airport. Although the petitioners allowed the area to be used by the public in accessing the terminal building, that was not enough to confirm that the concourse provided a public right of way.

Although it has been argued that trespass applies only to intrusion onto heritable subjects, case law suggests that property extends to moveables that are capable of occupation. For example, in *Shell UK Ltd v McGillivray*,[12] the petitioners averred that workers continuing a "sit-in" on an oil platform were in effect trespassers and sought interdict to prevent the continued occupation.[13] The respondents argued that trespass in Scots law was only applicable to heritable property. However, Lord Cameron of Lochbroom took a more general view:

> "In my opinion, the use of the word 'trespass' has no particular significance in these petitions other than indicating that the actings of the respondents are averred to be wrongful acts of occupation of parts of property of which the petitioners have the exclusive right of occupation."

---

[7] Provided that the "trespasser" does not enjoy a right of access under Pt 1 of the Land Reform (Scotland) Act 2003: see below at para.8–03.

[8] Criminal Justice and Public Order Act 1994 s.61(1).

[9] *Brown v Lee Constructions Ltd*, 1977 S.L.T. (Notes) 61.

[10] Civil Aviation Act 1982 s.76(1). However, there is strict liability for damage caused by objects, animals or persons falling from aircraft: Civil Aviation Act 1982 s.76(2). See also *Steel-Maitland v British Airways Board*, 1981 S.L.T. 110, where a claim for common law trespass or nuisance was dismissed but a proof before answer was allowed with regard to droplets of fuel falling onto the pursuer's property from overflying aircraft.

[11] *PIK Facilities Ltd v Watson's Ayr Park Ltd*, 2005 S.L.T. 1041.

[12] *Shell UK Ltd v McGillivray*, 1991 S.L.T. 667.

[13] Paradoxically, the immediate effect of the interdict was to require a positive act on the part of the respondents, i.e. to leave as soon as transport became available.

Accepting that

> "Scots law offers remedies for the unlawful occupation of property, be it heritable or moveable, even where that occupation is not affecting the owner's pocket,"[14]

Lord Cameron proceeded on the basis that such occupation was a delictual wrong. This decision provides support, along with cases such as *Henderson v Chief Constable of Fife*[15] and *FC Finance v Langtry Investment Co Ltd*,[16] that Scots law continues to remain flexible and principle based, adopting the view of wrongful conduct being actionable on general principles of *culpa* without the need to identify a nominate delict.

Rights of access

8-03   Accessing a proprietor's land will not amount to trespass if the access is authorised or justified. Thus, the exercise of servitude rights or public rights of way, which may be created by positive prescription,[17] will not constitute trespass.

A significant qualification on the right to exclusive enjoyment of one's land is provided by Pt 1 of the Land Reform (Scotland) Act 2003. This provides everyone with the right of access to land, and to cross land, for recreational activity and for educational purposes, including where these activities are being pursued for profit,[18] subject to the exercising of these rights responsibly.[19] The exercise of access rights is specifically declared not to amount to trespass.[20] The legislation is supported by the Scottish Outdoor Access Code[21] which, although not law as such, provides guidance which a court is likely to note. Land is widely defined,[22] although the right of access does not extend to buildings or their curtilage, land set out as a sports ground or where the public is admitted only upon payment, or land where certain specified commercial or engineering activities are taking place including the growing of crops.[23] The right of access is also restricted where access would interfere with the reasonable degree of privacy to be enjoyed by the occupants of houses.

The 2003 Act imposes reciprocal obligations on landowners to use and manage the land responsibly with regard to access rights.[24] Thus, once again, a recent development in Scots law has been drafted using the language of "rights" along with concepts of proportionality where rights come into conflict.

---

[14] *Phestos Shipping Co Ltd v Kurmiawan*, 1983 S.C. 165 at 180 per Lord Dunpark.
[15] *Henderson v Chief Constable of Fife*, 1988 S.L.T. 361.
[16] *FC Finance v Langtry Investment Co Ltd*, 1973 S.L.T. (Sh. Ct) 11. Although the decision in *F.C. Finance* was not followed in *North West Securities Ltd v Barrhead Coachworks Ltd*, 1976 S.C. 68, the inductive reasoning based on *culpa* was not challenged.
[17] Prescription and Limitation (Scotland) Act 1973 s.3.
[18] Land Reform (Scotland) Act 2003 s.1.
[19] Land Reform (Scotland) Act 2003 s.2.
[20] Land Reform (Scotland) Act 2003 s.5(1).
[21] Land Reform (Scotland) Act 2003 s.10.
[22] Land Reform (Scotland) Act 2003 s.32.
[23] Land Reform (Scotland) Act 2003 s.6.
[24] Land Reform (Scotland) Act 2003 s.3.

Defences

The exercise of access rights, whether in the form of servitude rights, public **8–04** rights of way or access rights under Pt 1 of the Land Reform (Scotland) Act 2003, are not defences as such since they do not amount to a trespass in the first place. Similarly, there are many other circumstances where statutory authority overrides the proprietor's exclusive right of use and occupation of land or other premises.

Bell asserted that: "The exclusive right of a landowner yields wherever public interest or necessity requires that it should yield."[25] Thus trespass may be justified to escape an assault, to pursue a criminal, or to extinguish a fire.

Acquiescence may provide a defence,[26] and the right to object may be lost by negative prescription on account of failure to exercise or enforce the right for a continuous period of 20 years.[27]

Encroachment

Encroachment describes where the defender's property intrudes onto the pur- **8–05** suer's land. Examples would include where the defender builds onto the pursuer's land, including on top of a garden wall previously erected by the pursuer on the boundary of his property,[28] or where tree branches or other flora overhang onto neighbouring property. Remedies include interdict, an order for removal and damages, although culpa must be averred and proved in order to sustain an action for damages.[29]

Defences will include statutory authority and acquiescence. An encroachment which has stood for 20 years without judicial challenge may be transformed into a servitude right by prescription.[30]

In *Compugraphics International Ltd v Nikolic*,[31] a property developer had erected a factory which was sold to the pursuers in 1983. External pipework and ducting had been supported by metal stanchions which had been anchored into a footpath. The land on which the footpath ran was not part of the subject of sale to the pursuers but was subsequently sold as part of a separate neighbouring plot which was then purchased by the defender in 2007. When the defender threatened to remove the pipework from above the path the pursuers sought declarator that they were the owners of, or alternatively enjoyed servitude rights over the pipework. The Inner House recognised that the defenders could have demanded the removal of the overhanging pipework as an encroachment had it not been for the fact that the pipes had remained in place for more than 20 years and that prescription may thus have confirmed a servitude right with regard to the pipework specified under s.77 of the Title Conditions (Scotland) Act 2003.

---

[25] Bell, *Principles*, s.956.

[26] A plea of aquiescence was rejected in *Buccleugh Estates Ltd v Telfer*, 2008 S.L.C.R. 1.

[27] Prescription and Limitation (Scotland) Act 1973 s.8.

[28] *Troup v Aberdeen Heritable Securities Co*, 1916 S.C. 918

[29] *Property Selection and Investment Trust Ltd v United Friendly Insurance Plc*, 1999 S.L.T. 975. In this case it was concluded that rock anchors (supporting the defender's property) concealed in the pursuer's ground actually belonged to the pursuers and so could not be described as an encroachment.

[30] Prescription and Limitation (Scotland) Act 1973 s.3.

[31] *Compugraphics International Ltd v Nikolic*, 2011 S.C. 744.

EJECTION

8–06 Ejection describes where someone enters onto land with the intention of remaining indefinitely and removes the rightful occupier,[32] or where someone who remains on land after their right to do so has expired, so preventing the rightful occupier from taking occupation. Examples include the tenant who, without justification, refuses to leave property upon the expiry of a lease, the squatter who moves into occupied property and excludes the rightful occupier or the jilted lover who moves into his erstwhile partner's home and changes the locks. Remedies include ejection,[33] violent profits[34] and damages.

INTRUSION

8–07 Intrusion is similar to ejection, above, except that the interloper enters onto property that is not currently occupied.[35] The paradigm example is the squatter taking up residence in an empty house. Remedies are similar to those applicable to ejection.

USE OF LAND *IN AEMULATIONEM VICINI*

8–08 Liability may arise for harm caused by lawful activity carried out on land if the predominant motive is spitefully to harm a neighbour's enjoyment or use of their own land. This is clearly associated with nuisance but differs in that one incident is sufficient to attract liability and in that it must be demonstrated that the defender acted with malice.

Thus, in *Campbell v Muir*[36] the defender was shown to have fished from a boat on his own side of a river in a way that was deliberately calculated to prevent anglers from the opposite bank being able to cast. It was held that to do this spitefully was actionable and amenable to interdict.

Note that it is not sufficient to obtain a remedy on this ground merely to show that the defender's activity would result in harm the pursuer's interest in land; it must be proved that harm to the pursuer was the predominant motive for, and not merely a by-product of, the defender's lawful act. Thus, the lawful diversion of a stream that stops water from continuing to flow onto a neighbour's land will not be *aemulationem vicini* if the main purpose is to irrigate the owner's fields, or even to fill an ornamental pond.

It has been suggested that the origins of this area of liability are in the *jus commune* rather than in Roman law itself.[37] In spite of (obiter) dicta to the contrary from the Scottish judge Lord Watson in the House of Lords,[38] it has

---

[32] " ... ejection ... is not only the unwarrantable entering in lands, but the casting out violently of the then possessor": Stair, 1, ix, 25.

[33] Note the distinction between the delictual *wrong* of ejection, i.e. usurping the position of the legitimate possessor of property; and the related *remedy* of ejection, i.e. ousting the ejector.

[34] The greatest profit the pursuer could have made if in possession of the property.

[35] " ... intrusion is the entering in possession, being for the time void, without the consent of the parties interested, or order of law": Stair, 1, ix, 25.

[36] *Campbell v Muir*, 1908 S.C. 387.

[37] D. Johnston, "Owners and Neighbours: from Rome to Scotland" in *The Civil Law Tradition in Scotland*, edited by R. Evans-Jones (Edinburgh: The Stair Society, 1995), Vol.2, p.197.

[38] *Bradford Corp v Pickles* [1895] A.C. 587

subsequently been accepted that this head of liability remains part of Scots law.[39]

LIABILITY FOR NON-NATURAL USE OF LAND

If the owner of land creates an *opus manufactum*[40] on it, such as an artificial lake, **8–09** or digs a tunnel under his own ground, and, as a result, his neighbour's land becomes unstable causing the neighbour's house to collapse, can the neighbour obtain a remedy in delict? If so, what does the neighbour have to prove?

In *Kerr v Earl of Orkney*[41] a dam which had been created to block the flow of a stream collapsed only four months after it was completed, following several days of heavy rain. The pursuer's mill, which was situated about half a mile downstream, was swept away in the resulting deluge. The court held that liability could only be avoided if the defender could show that the collapse was due to a *damnum fatale*.[42] Following the decision of the House of Lords in the English case of *Rylands v Fletcher*,[43] a school of thought considered that *Kerr v Earl of Orkney* provided authority for the proposition that Scots law recognised strict liability for damage caused by a non-natural use of land and that there would be no need to prove fault to confirm liability for reparation.

Such thinking appears to have been applied in *Caledonian Railway v Greenock Corp.*[44] The defenders altered the natural course of a stream in order to fill a children's paddling pool. Rainfall which was exceptional for Greenock, but not for Scotland, caused the pool to overflow, triggering a landslide which damaged the pursuer's railway line. The House of Lords refused to accept that the rainfall amounted to *damnum fatale* and held the corporation liable apparently without requiring the pursuer to establish fault.

The House of Lords took the opportunity to review the understanding of these cases in *R.H.M. Bakeries v Strathclyde Regional Council.*[45] Noting that the rule in *Rylands v Fletcher* "has no place in Scots law",[46] the decision in *Kerr v Earl of Orkney* was explained as adopting an inference of fault due to the short period between completion and collapse of the construction. However, the court ducked the question over whether the alteration of the natural course of a stream incurred

---

[39] *More v Boyle*, 1967 S.L.T. (Sh. Ct) 38.

[40] An artificial working of land.

[41] *Kerr v Earl of Orkney* (1857) 20 D. 298.

[42] See para.14–12 below.

[43] *Rylands v Fletcher* (1868) L.R. 3 H.L. 330. "If a person brings, or accumulates, on his land anything which, if it should escape, may cause damage to his neighbour, he does so at his peril. If it does escape, and cause damage, he is responsible, however careful he may have been, and whatever precautions he may have taken to prevent the damage": at 340 per Lord Cranworth.

[44] *Caledonian Railway v Greenock Corp*, 1917 S.C. (HL) 56.

[45] *R.H.M. Bakeries v Strathclyde Regional Council*, 1985 S.C. (HL) 17.

[46] " . . . and the suggestion that it has is a heresy which ought to be extirpated": *R.H.M. Bakeries v Strathclyde Regional Council*, 1985 S.C. (HL) 17 at 41 per Lord Fraser of Tullybelton. The understanding in English law of the rule in *Rylands v Fletcher* has been qualified in several recent English cases: see, e.g. *Cambridge Water Co Ltd v Eastern Counties Leather Plc* [1994] 2 A.C. 264; *Transco Plc v Stockport M.B.C.* [2004] 2 A.C. 1; *Stannard (t/a Wyvern Tyres) v Gore* [2014] Q.B. 1.

strict liability in Scots law, holding that *Caledonian Railway v Greenock Corp* was not in point.[47]

8–10   So, apart in the meantime from alteration of the natural course of a stream,[48] liability for damage resulting from the creation of an *opus manufactum* is based on *culpa* rather than strict liability, although fault may be readily inferred where the artificial creation is dangerous or upon the application of the brocard *res ipsa loquitur*.[49] This approach will also be adopted with regard to the bringing of inherently dangerous things, such as explosive materials, onto one's property.[50] Thus, the law will demand a high standard of care with regard to the storage and use of such things, including the taking of steps to prevent interference by third parties, and where the thing escapes or explodes fault will be readily inferred. Thus:

> "A landowner will be liable to his neighbour if he carries out operations on his land which will or are likely to cause damage to his neighbour's land however much care is exercised. Similarly will a landowner be liable in respect of carrying out operations, either at his own hand or at the hand of the contractor, if it is necessary to take steps in the carrying out of those operations to prevent damage to a neighbour, and he, the landlord, does not take or instruct those steps. In the former case the landowner's culpa lies in the actual carrying out of his operations in the knowledge actual or implied of their likely consequences. In the latter case culpa lies in not taking steps to avoid consequences which he should have foreseen would be likely to flow from one method of carrying out the operation."[51]

Indeed, it is suggested that an inference of *culpa levissima*[52] should be sufficient to establish liability in reparation where damage may be attributed to the creation of a dangerous *opus manufactum* or to the bringing of inherently dangerous things on to property, unless the defender can provide an explanation why it is not his or her fault.

Defences will be limited to proof that the event was caused either by the actions of a third party for whom the defender was not responsible[53] or *damnum fatale*.[54]

---

[47] To overturn the precedent set in *Caledonian Railway v Greenock Corporation*, 1917 S.C. (HL) 56 would therefore require a case in point to be taken to the Supreme Court, or legislation.

[48] In *Kennedy v Glenbelle*, 1996 S.C. 95 it was accepted that this was an anomalous case. See also G. & A. Estates Ltd v Caviapen Trustees Ltd (No. 1), 1993 S.L.T. 1037. See also Gordon D.L. Cameron, "Strict Liability and the Rule in *Caledonian Railway Co v Greenock Corporation*", 2000 (5) S.L.P.Q. 356.

[49] The facts speak for themselves (and thus infer fault). See, e.g. *Macaulay v Buist & Co* (1846) 9 D. 245 at 248 per Lord Fullerton: " . . . as clear a statement of the doctrine of *res ipsa loquitur* (though of course without using that name) as can be found anywhere." *R.H.M. Bakeries (Scotland) Ltd v Strathclyde RC*, 1985 S.C. (HL) 17 at 39 per Lord Fraser of Tullybelton. See also *David T Morrison & Co Ltd v ICL Plastics Ltd*, 2012 S.L.T. 813 (where the application of the doctrine of *res ipsa loquitur* was acknowledged, albeit in the context of the negligence ground for the claim).

[50] *David T. Morrison & Co Ltd v ICL Plastics Ltd*, 2012 S.L.T. 813.

[51] *Noble's Trustees v Economic Forestry (Scotland) Ltd*, 1988 S.L.T. 662 at 664 per Lord Jauncey. See also *Chalmers v Dixon* (1876) 3 R. 461 at 464 per Lord Justice Clerk Moncreiff.

[52] See paras 1–21 to 1–22 above.

[53] *Gourock Ropework Co Ltd v Greenock Corporation*, 1966 S.L.T. 125.

[54] *R.H.M. Bakeries (Scotland) Ltd v Strathclyde Regional Council*, 1985 S.C. (HL) 17 at 45 per Lord Fraser of Tullybelton.

NUISANCE

Nuisance describes where an occupier of land or premises engages in an activity **8–11** there that disrupts others' enjoyment of their own land or premises to an extent beyond that which the law expects them to tolerate. It may thus be said that the law of nuisance engages in a balancing exercise: one has a right to choose what to do on one's own land but, equally, one has a right to enjoy one's own land and so to object to others' use of their land if it unreasonably prevents one's enjoyment of one's own land and vice versa.

> "The balance in all such cases has to be held between the freedom of a proprietor to use his property as he pleases and the duty on a proprietor not to inflict material loss or inconvenience on adjoining proprietors or adjoining property; and in every case the answer depends on considerations of fact and of degree."[55]

This balancing concept is encapsulated in the latin maxim *sic utere tuo ut alienum non laedas*: use your own property so as not to harm another's. The limiting effect of this concept was explained by Lord President Cooper:

> "If any person so uses his property as to occasion serious disturbance or substantial inconvenience to his neighbour or material damage to his neighbour's property, it is in the general case irrelevant as a defence for the defender to plead merely that he was making a normal and familiar use of his own property."[56]

Remedies include damages for harm caused by the nuisance and interdict to prevent the harmful activity continuing.

It may also be said that the function of the law of nuisance is to control the environment,[57] although the control will be applied on objective criteria, the law taking into account relevant factors external to the parties and expecting a reasonable degree of give and take between respective proprietors of property. *Webster v Lord Advocate*[58] provides an example. The pursuer bought a flat near Edinburgh Castle in 1977. She sought an interdict because of the noise involved in the construction of the grandstand on the Esplanade in preparation for the Military Tattoo, and for the noise made by the rehearsals and performances of the spectacle itself. Although the tattoo had been an annual event since 1950 it was acknowledged that the fact that the activity had been ongoing since before the pursuer moved in was irrelevant. The court did consider the public amenity and commercial benefit in the staging of the Tattoo, but rejected the contention that Miss Webster could pursue "self-help" remedies by closing her windows or installing double glazing. Taking those factors as were relevant into account, the court granted an interdict prohibiting "metallic construction noise so as to cause a nuisance ... " in the construction of the venue, but refused interdict to prevent or restrict the staging of the performances themselves, or the rehearsals.

---

[55] *Watt v Jamieson*, 1954 S.C. 56 at 58 per Lord President Cooper.
[56] *Watt v Jamieson*, 1954 S.C. 56 at 58. Cf. *Davidson v Kerr*, 1997 Hous. L.R. 11.
[57] J. Steele, "Private law and the environment: nuisance in context", 1995 L.S. 236.
[58] *Webster v Lord Advocate*, 1985 S.C. 173.

What amounts to a nuisance?

8–12   To constitute a nuisance, the activity complained of must satisfy certain criteria:

- it must involve the use of land or premises;
- it must be continuing;
- it must be *plus quam tolerabile*;
- it must involve *culpa*, at least insofar as an action is for damages as opposed to interdict.

Use of land or premises

8–13   For an action to be based on nuisance both the wrongful conduct and the harm elements must involve the use of land or premises. The pursuer must allege that his enjoyment of his own premises has been or is being unreasonably disrupted. It is not clear to what extent the pursuer must have an interest in the property concerned but the pursuer must be an owner or occupier. Owners and landlords,[59] as well as tenants in occupation[60] have been permitted to proceed, but it is questionable whether a hotel guest, for example, could pursue a case in nuisance unless their stay was for a considerable period of time.[61] It does not matter whether the defender is in actual possession of the land where the activity complained of is carried out, so long as the defender is in control of the activity.[62]

The activity complained of must relate to the use of the defender's land: land in this context incorporates water and air. So using a suburban back garden to keep geese in a pond or from which to fly a noisy radio controlled aircraft at all times of the day and night may stimulate a justified action in nuisance.[63] A natural event will not constitute a nuisance and so it must involve the defender's act or omission.[64]

Continuing activity

8–14   A one-off event cannot amount to a nuisance. This is consistent with interdict being the primary remedy to prevent the continuation of a nuisance—an interdict would be pointless if there was no risk of repetition of the activity. Thus, a "rave" held at an isolated location could not be interdicted as *plus quam tolerabile*, it being a one-off event.[65]

It is not a defence to show that the pursuer came to the nuisance, i.e. that the activity had already been continuing before the pursuer moved in. However,

---

[59] Not necessarily in possession themselves: see, e.g. *McEwen v Steedman & McAllister*, 1912 S.C. 156.

[60] See, e.g. *Hand v North of Scotland Water Authority*, 2002 S.L.T. 798.

[61] In an English appeal to the House of Lords, Lord Hope agreed that a licensee was not protected by the law of nuisance: *Hunter v Canary Wharf* [1997] A.C. 655.

[62] See, e.g. *G.B. & A.M. Anderson v White*, 2000 S.L.T. 37. Cf. *Gourock Ropework Co v Greenock Corporation*, 1966 S.L.T. 125.

[63] See, e.g. *Dennis v Ministry of Defence* [2003] Env. L.R. 34. Cf. *King v Advocate General for Scotland* [2009] CSOH 169. Note that the Civil Aviation Act 1982 s.76(1) provides that there is no liability in trespass or nuisance for the flight of an aircraft at a reasonable height and not flown dangerously.

[64] *Davey v Harrow Corp* [1958] 1 Q.B. 60.

[65] *Cumnock & Doon Valley DC v Dance Energy Associates Ltd*, 1992 G.W.D. 25–1441.

should the pursuer put up with the nuisance for such a period of time as to lead the defender to believe that the pursuer had no objection to the continuing activity, the defender may rely on acquiescence, or *mora* and *taciturnity*,[66] in pleading that the purser is personally barred from objecting. Similarly, if the pursuer puts up with the nuisance for a period of 20 years, the defender's obligation to abate the nuisance will have prescribed[67] and the pursuer will be prevented from seeking damages or interdict. Nevertheless, if a new neighbour moves in, a new right to object arises and the new neighbour will not be bound by the previous occupier's acquiescence.

Plus quam tolerabile

What will the law consider is more than a reasonable neighbour should be **8–15** expected to tolerate? Lord President Cooper's answer was: "serious disturbance or substantial inconvenience ... or material damage to his ... property."[68] Traditional examples include noise, smells, pollution, vibration and flooding, with modern examples likely to include interference with television and other telecommunications reception. Much will depend upon the locality and the nature of the environment: activity that would not be tolerated in an urban environment may be expected on an industrial estate or accepted in a rural setting.

It should be seen that assessing whether an activity is *plus quam tolerabile* involves a balancing exercise. The onus of proof will be upon the pursuer to set out what is objectionable about the activity, with the onus on the defender to set out why the activity amounts to a reasonable use or enjoyment of his property that his neighbour should be expected to put up with. In all of this the nuisance must be seen from the victim's point of view.[69] Ultimately, the court will have to examine the reasons pro and con the activity and apply a proportionality test to examine the extent to which it would appropriate to allow one party's rights to encroach on the other's. A similar proportionality test applied in privacy cases has been described as "the ultimate balancing test".[70]

Factors will include the nature and extent of the harm: substantial loss of amenity will be enough, at least for interdict, but proof of actual or threatened[71] damage to property,[72] economic loss[73] or hazards to health[74] may strengthen a

---

[66] Delay and silence.

[67] See paras 15–05 to 15–06 below.

[68] *Watt v Jamieson*, 1954 S.C. 56 at 58.

[69] *Watt v Jamieson*, 1954 S.C. 56 at 58.

[70] This longstanding approach to nuisance cases is becoming typical of cases brought under the Human Rights Act where the respective parties' human rights appear to be in conflict. Compare, e.g. the approach to conflicts between art.8 (right to private life) and art.10 (right to freedom of expression) of the ECHR set out by Lord Steyn in *Re S. (A Child) (Identification: Restrictions on Publication)* [2005] 1 A.C. 593 at 603.

[71] The extent of the risk will be taken into account: *Canmore Housing Association Ltd v Bairnsfather*, 2004 S.L.T. 673.

[72] See, e.g. *Lord Advocate v The Reo Stakis Organisation Ltd*, 1981 S.C. 104 (damage caused by ongoing building operations).

[73] See, e.g. *Globe Ltd v North of Scotland Water Authority*, 2000 S.C. 392; *Hand v North Scotland Water Authority*, 2002 S.L.T. 798 (loss of business in pubs caused respectively by road works and a burst sewer); *G. B. & A. M. Anderson v White*, 2000 S.L.T. 37 (economic loss caused by flooding to fields caused by overfilling of the defender's dam raising the surrounding water table).

[74] See, e.g. *Ireland v Smith* (1895) 3 S.L.T. 180 (dust kicked up by chickens kept by neighbours claimed to be hazardous to health).

claim for damages in nuisance, provided that these forms of harm flow from the nuisance. It will not be sufficient, however, for the pursuer to complain about no more than noise arising from normal domestic use of property, such as would not seriously disturb nor substantially inconvenience an average person in the locality.[75] The reasonableness of self-help measures may also be taken into account,[76] although in the *Webster* case discussed above the court did not accept that Miss Webster should be expected to close her windows or install double-glazing. Likewise, the sensitivity of the pursuer, who will be expected to be reasonably robust, may be considered.[77]

The nature of the locality may be another factor:

> "Things which are forbidden in a crowded urban community may be permitted in the country. What is prohibited in enclosed land may be tolerated in the open."[78]

The nature of a locality may change over time. However, other than in the application of specific statutory authority for the purpose of redefining the nature of the locality, a planning or licensing decision will not of itself determine such a change.[79] However, the implementation over a continuous period of the activity permitted may change the character of a locality, so that activity that would previously have been a nuisance would no longer be so.[80]

Public interest, i.e. the social utility of the conduct complained of, may also be taken into account in the sense that the more socially beneficial the use of the land, the more serious the impact that would be required to justify an interdict or even damages.[81] Given the balancing nature of the court's approach, it is likely that the court would seek to restrict the way in which a socially valuable activity is carried out, as opposed to prohibiting it altogether.[82]

The European Convention on Human Rights requires respect for home and family life[83] and for peaceful enjoyment of property.[84] The law of nuisance may be used to obtemper those obligations, especially when the infringing conduct is on the part of a public body. Thus, in *Dennis v Ministry of Defence*,[85] it was held that the noise generated by training flights constituted a nuisance and, although the public interest mitigated against an injunction, damages of £950,000 were

---

[75] *Davidson v Kerr*, 1997 Hous. L.R. 11.

[76] "The person complaining of the nuisance must not be too fastidious ... he must use all reasonable means within his own premises to minimise the inconvenience of which he complains": *Wilson v Gibb* (1902) 10 S.L.T. 293 at 294 per Lord Stormonth Darling.

[77] *Davidson v Kerr*, 1997 Hous. L.R. 11. See also *Armistead v Bowerman* (1888) 15 R. 814. Cf. *Shanlin v Collins*, 1973 S.L.T. (Sh. Ct) 21 (noise nuisance from local commercial kennels *caused* pursuer's nervous disposition).

[78] *Inglis v Shotts Iron Co* (1881) 8 R. 1006 at 1021 per Lord Shand. See also *Maguire v Charles McNeil*, 1922 S.L.T. 193 at 200–201 per Lord President Clyde.

[79] *Barr v Biffa Waste Services Ltd* [2012] 3 All E.R. 380.

[80] *Lawrence v Fen Tigers Ltd* [2012] 1 W.L.R. 2127; *Gillingham BC v Medway (Chatham Docks) Co Ltd* [1993] Q.B. 343.

[81] See, e.g. *Dennis v Ministry of Defence* [2003] Env. L.R. 34.

[82] *Webster v Lord Advocate*, 1985 S.C. 173; *Ben Nevis Distillery Ltd v North British Aluminium Co Ltd*, 1949 S.L.T. (Notes) 14.

[83] art.8.

[84] Protocol 1, art.1.

[85] *Dennis v Ministry of Defence* [2003] Env. L.R. 34.

awarded as just satisfaction[86] for the infringement of their human rights to family life and enjoyment of property.

Culpa

Prior to the decision of the House of Lords in *R.H.M. Bakeries v Strathclyde* **8–16** *RC*,[87] it was widely thought that nuisance was an example of strict liability.[88] Given that to constitute a nuisance the offending activity must be ongoing and a disproportionate interference with the pursuer's rights to enjoy his own property, it follows that fault on the part of the defender is irrelevant. That does appear to continue to be the approach taken by the courts when dealing with an application for interdict to abate the nuisance.[89]

However, the House of Lords confirmed in *R.H.M. Bakeries* that for a claim for *reparation* to be competent (which includes a claim for *damages* for nuisance), *culpa* must be proved. The pursuers had claimed they sustained losses when their bakery was flooded due to the collapse of a sewer which the defenders were responsible for maintaining. The pursuers sought damages averring nuisance but failed to allege fault on the part of the defenders in the pleadings, and this omission was held to be fatal to their claim for damages.

What level of fault must then be proved to sustain a claim for damages in **8–17** nuisance? The question was addressed in *Kennedy v Glenbelle*, where damages were sought for harm caused to the pursuer's property by the carrying out of building work including the removal of a supporting wall to a downstairs flat. In his speech, Lord Hope described negligence and nuisance as different species of delictual liability[90] and went on to distinguish *culpa* in the context of negligence from *culpa* in the context of nuisance:

> "The essential requirement is that fault or *culpa* must be established. That may be done by demonstrating negligence, in which case the ordinary principles of the law of negligence will provide an equivalent remedy. Or it may be done by demonstrating that the defender was at fault in some other respect. This may be because his action was malicious, or because it was deliberate in the knowledge that his action would result in harm to the other party, or because it was reckless as he had no regard to the question whether his action, if it was of a kind likely to cause harm to the other party, would have that result. Or it may be ... because the defender has indulged in conduct which gives rise to a special risk of abnormal damage, from which fault is implied if damage results from that conduct. In each case personal responsibility rests on the defender because he has conducted himself in a respect which is recognised as inferring *culpa* by our law. So what is required is a deliberate act or negligence or some other conduct from which *culpa* or fault may be inferred."[91]

---

[86] Required by Human Rights Act 1998 s.8.

[87] *R.H.M. Bakeries v Strathclyde RC*, 1985 S.C. (HL) 17.

[88] This (mis)understanding has been attributed to the connection of the decisions in *Kerr v Earl of Orkney* (1857) 20 D. 298, *Rylands v Fletcher* (1868) L.R. 3 H.L. 330 and *Chalmers v Wm Dixon Ltd* (1876) 3 R. 461.

[89] *R.H.M. Bakeries v Strathclyde RC*, 1985 S.C. (HL) 17 at 44 per Lord Fraser of Tullybelton.

[90] *Kennedy v Glenbelle*, 1996 S.C. 95 at 99.

[91] *Kennedy v Glenbelle*, 1996 S.C. 95 at 100–101 per Lord Hope.

Lord Hope seems to imply that if fault may be demonstrated by proof of breach of a duty of care where there is a foreseeable risk of injury, an action should be brought in negligence rather than in nuisance. This seems sensible, since in negligence there is no need to prove that the wrong involves a continuing activity.[92] It follows that *nuisance culpa* will not include carelessness, but may be established by proof of malice, intention or recklessness; or be inferred where there is a special risk of abnormal damage. This distinction is of practical importance, as the nature of *culpa* alleged must be averred in the pursuer's pleadings, and this must be consistent with a claim in nuisance.

It may thus be concluded that there are four levels of nuisance *culpa*:

- malice—where the defender deliberately engaged in the activity with the objective of causing harm to the pursuer[93];
- intent—where the defender was aware that the consequences of the activity would include harm to the pursuer[94];
- recklessness—where the pursuer paid no regard to whether the activity would cause harm to the pursuer[95];
- inference of fault—where the activity carries a special risk of abnormal damage.[96]

All of these levels may be distinguished from carelessness (i.e. negligence) in that they each involve proof of actual or constructive knowledge on the part of the defender that the activity complained of will harm the pursuer's interests in his enjoyment of his own property.

Nuisance culpa, effectively in the form of constructive intent, was sufficiently averred in *Anderson v White*.[97] The defenders were accused of creating a nuisance by allowing the water level in their dam to rise to a level where it was inevitable, no matter how much care was exercised, that the pursuer's land would be flooded.

Defences

8–18   There may be any number of arguments that could be deployed to justify the conduct complained of, but care must be taken to distinguish between factors to be taken into account in deciding whether the activity is *plus quam tolerabile*, and defences proper that override a proved nuisance. Acquiescence (meaning consent), and *mora* and *taciturnity* (meaning delay and silence), may be pled effectively as defences, but both are forms of personal bar rather than defences as such. Likewise 20 year long-stop prescription, but again prescription is not a defence as such; the obligation to abate the nuisance ceases to exist.[98] It is settled that it is not a defence to plead that the pursuer came to the nuisance[99] and it

---

[92] In practice, it may be that claims in negligence and nuisance run side by side in the same action: see, e.g. *Viewpoint Housing Association Ltd v City of Edinburgh Council*, 2007 S.L.T. 772.

[93] Perhaps to be equiparated with *dolus*: see paras 1–21 to 1–22 above.

[94] Perhaps to be equiparated with *culpa lata*: see paras 1–21 to 1–22 above.

[95] Perhaps to be equiparated with *culpa levis*: see paras 1–21 to 1–22 above.

[96] Perhaps to be equiparated with *culpa levissima*: see paras 1–21 to 1–22 above.

[97] *Anderson v White*, 2000 S.L.T. 37.

[98] See paras 15–05 to 15–06 below.

[99] *Webster v Lord Advocate*, 1985 S.C. 173.

follows that it is unlikely to be open to the defender to plead *volenti non fit injuria*.[100]

It is also established that it is not a defence that the activity amounts to a normal and familiar use of property,[101] or even that the activity has been approved by the grant of planning permission.[102] It is a defence to show that the nuisance was an inevitable consequence of the implementation of an activity that was authorised by statute. Even in such a case, however, if the statutory authority is found in an Act of the Scottish Parliament or in delegated legislation, the legislative authority may be challenged as incompatible with the European Convention on Human Rights. In that context, art 8[103] and art.1 of Protocol 1[104] are most likely to be important.

WRONGFUL INTERFERENCE WITH MOVEABLES: SPUILZIE

Spuilzie (pronounced, approximately, "spoolly") both describes: **8–19**

1. the act of interfering with possession of property, namely, spoliation; and
2. a remedy known to the law of Scotland in respect of such actings.

It is a delict said by some to be obsolete, but which may yet be found to be useful.[105] Stair described the wrong as "civil theft" and noted that a *vitium reale* attached to the goods in question,[106] meaning the pursuer could recover possession of the goods from a bona fide third party purchaser.[107] It has been described by the Scottish Law Commission as "protean and of uncertain scope".[108] It long ago ceased to be important in relation to heritage. It is committed by a person who takes away moveables without the consent of the possessor or without order of law. It is not even necessary for the pursuer to establish ownership of the property, so long as the goods are within the pursuer's possession by virtue of a right of possession or custody.[109] The taking away must amount to *vitious* (unlawful) dispossession, so unauthorised possession will not suffice.[110] Likewise *spuilzie* will be irrelevant if a person lawfully in possession

---

[100] See paras 14–02 to 14–05 below.

[101] *Lord Advocate v The Reo Stakis Organisation Ltd*, 1981 S.C. 104.

[102] *Wheeler v J. J. Saunders Ltd* [1995] 3 W.L.R. 466.

[103] Right to respect for private and family life, home and correspondence.

[104] Right to peaceful enjoyment of one's possessions.

[105] For a fuller treatment see W.J. Stewart, *Reparation: Liability for Delict* (Edinburgh: W. Green).

[106] Stair, I, ix, 16.

[107] Stair presents this proposition in the context of a description of *spuilzie* as "civil theft", leaving open the suggestion that a *vitium reale* applies only where the victim of *spuilzie* is in fact the owner in possession. In such circumstances, the owner need not resort to the law of delict as the owner may, upon proof of ownership, invoke the law of property so as to vindicate (recover possession of) the property in question.

[108] Scottish Law Commission, *Corporeal Moveables: Remedies* (HMSO, 1976), Memorandum No.31, para.23.

[109] Stair, I, ix, 16. Whether constructive possession (e.g. "civil" possession by the owner of property subject to hire or lease) is sufficient is a matter for debate see, e.g. *Mackinnon v Avonside Homes Ltd*, 1993 S.C.L.R. 976; *Lamont v Mooney* [2011] CSOH 82 at [199] per Temporary Judge Morag Wise QC.

[110] *Calor Gas Ltd v Express Fuels (Scotland) Ltd*, 2008 S.L.T. 123 at 136 per Lord Malcolm.

of the moveables voluntarily hands over the goods to the defender. The primary remedy is the returning of the goods to the pursuer, but there is also a liability to violent profits. These are the maximum profits that could have been made with the goods, valued originally by the pursuer's own oath.

Although there is an urge to interpret this remedy as a combination of restitution and damages for delict, this may be misleading. It is the element of violent profits that is of interest. This is not necessarily a matter of delictual damages.[111] Indeed the exciting thing about such a claim is that it means that the pursuer does not have to show the loss that would be required if the case were based on loss wrongfully caused. The better rationalisation might be that this award is essentially restitutionary and is an example of restitution for wrongs.[112] The recognition of loss of use as a head of claim in ordinary delictual actions makes it unlikely that *spuilzie* arguments will be heard often. There have been some interesting cases[113] and some debate as to the relevance of *spuilzie* in cases of hire purchase and financial leasing arrangements.[114] However, recent attempts to revive *spuilzie* have been in vain.

Nevertheless, it is suggested that *spuilzie* may still have a role in the modern world. Although hire purchase is not as widely used as it was in the twentieth century, it remains a common method of financing the acquisition of motor vehicles by consumers. Financial leasing arrangements for high value moveable assets such as aircraft and motor vehicles are also common in business and have been used in private consumer transactions. If such moveable assets are subject to vitious dispossession, an example being the wrongful clamping or towing away of a motor vehicle which is legally parked, it is suggested that the hirer or lessor may assert a right to immediate return of the property in question and claim for violent profits.

WRONGFUL INTERFERENCE WITH MOVEABLES GENERALLY

8–20 If we look now at the wider notion of wrongful interference with moveables, it can be said that *spuilzie* is a species of this wider delictual concept (which is likely to have both proprietary and restitutionary aspects). There are sufficient markers in the Scots authorities for this wider notion. In *Snare v The Earl of Fife's Trustees*,[115] Snare, a bookseller in Reading, bought a picture that he discovered to be Charles I, by Velasquez. He exhibited it and produced pamphlets showing it to have been in the possession of the Earl of Fife. The result of this information was that the Earl of Fife's trustees petitioned the sheriff that the picture had been stolen or surreptitiously abstracted from their possession and

---

[111] As unlike the apparent position in *spuilzie*, reparation generally requires proof of *culpa*: *R.H.M. Bakeries (Scotland) Ltd v Strathclyde RC*, 1985 S.C. (HL) 17.

[112] See para.1–02 above.

[113] *F.C. Finance Ltd v Brown & Son*, 1969 S.L.T. (Sh. Ct) 41; *Mercantile Credit Co Ltd v Townsley*, 1971 S.L.T. (Sh. Ct) 37; *Calor Gas Ltd v Express Fuels (Scotland) Ltd*, 2008 S.L.T. 123.

[114] A. Rodger, "Spuilzie in the Modern World", 1970 S.L.T. (News) 33; C. Anderson, "Spuilzie today", 2008 S.L.T. (News) 257; W. J. Stewart, "The alleged case of the spuilzied helicopter", 2009 S.L.T. (News) 13; C. Anderson, "The alleged case of the spuilzied helicopter: a reply", 2009 S.L.T. (News) 31. The helicopter case referred to was *North Scottish Helicopters Ltd v United Technologies Corp Inc*, 1988 S.L.T. 77. It is respectfully suggested that a better (but still unsatisfactory) candidate would have been *Nordic Oil Services Ltd v Berman*, 1993 S.L.T. 1164.

[115] *Snare v The Earl of Fife's Trustees* (1850) 13 D. 286.

craved (i) restitution or (ii) warrant to the clerk of court to take possession and retain until caution found. Warrant was granted, the painting seized and retained, and eventually returned. Snare claimed for damages for loss of exhibition. The court allowed the case to go to trial on the basis of the wrongful detention—they "obtained and acted upon an illegal warrant". Neither did they require to aver malice and lack of probable cause.

Even more interesting are the bottle cases. An interdict was granted in *Wilson v Shepherd*,[116] where one trader allowed people to fill another's bottles with paraffin. While there is an element of the law of property about this, the interdict was granted on the basis of a wrong to property and therefore was essentially a delict for which damages could be sought. In a later case, *Leitch v Leydon*,[117] a grocer filled bottles belonging to another with aerated water. It had already been intimated to him that the owners retained ownership. It would have taken a careful glance to check the origin of a bottle. It was held there was no duty to inspect bottles. For Viscount Dunedin there was no *culpa*. Interdict was refused. Although *Wilson* was cited in argument, the respondents were not called upon and the case was not mentioned in the speeches. There was no mention of the provisions of the Sale of Goods Act 1893 that allowed a non-owner to pass title if a buyer was in possession of the goods, although the notice on the bottle might well deprive the "consumer" of the right to rely upon it. So far as it goes, the case is correct, but the real issue is whether, if it were clear *ex facie* that a bottle was one of a specific type that was always sold under a retention if there was no specific intimation that the owners expressly prohibited refilling, interdict or damages should be granted.[118]

In modern life it seems strange that we can do what we like with a bottle that **8–21** says "Property of X—do not refill, return or destroy", but cannot do as we please with a DVD or computer disk. The analysis used by the software "vendors" is that the "buyer" pays for a licence rather than the property.

It does appear that there is scope to apply the fundamental principles embodied in the concept of *culpa* to novel situations where what is done with regard to property may be perceived to be wrongful, but where the circumstances do not fall into an accepted category of wrong and there is no direct precedent to assist. This is consistent with the rooting of Scots law in the civilian tradition, i.e. that an inductive approach may be taken to the identification and application of underpinning legal concepts so as to derive a principled decision in a case presenting a novel set of facts.

The concept of *culpa* was the basis of the decision in *FC Finance v Langtry Investment Co Ltd*.[119] FC Finance became the owner of a motor vehicle when the company provided the finance to enable a Mr Allan to acquire a motor car under a hire purchase contract. The fact that the car was subject to the hire purchase agreement was registered by FC Finance with HP Information Ltd (nowadays

---

[116] *Wilson v Shepherd*, 1913 S.C. 300.

[117] *Leitch v Leydon*, 1931 S.C. (HL) 1. This case ran along with, and was reported with, *A.G. Barr & Co Ltd v MacGheoghegan* and was decided in exactly the same way.

[118] *Calor Gas Ltd v Express Fuels (Scotland) Ltd*, 2008 S.L.T. 123 provides the most recent example of such a "bottle" case. However, although a spuilzie argument was taken—and rejected—Lord Malcolm was not asked to consider an argument based on a more general concept of wrongful interference with moveables, and no reference was made to either *Wilson* or *Leitch*.

[119] *FC Finance v Langtry Investment Co Ltd*, 1973 S.L.T. (Sh. Ct) 11. Although the decision in *F.C. Finance* was not followed in *North West Securities Ltd v Barrhead Coachworks Ltd*, 1976 S.C. 68, the inductive reasoning based on *culpa* was not challenged.

known as HPI), a company which maintains a register of details as to the provenance of motor vehicles. In a fraudulent transaction, Mr Allan purported to sell the car to a garage, Medwin Motors. However, because Mr Allan did not have title to the car (i.e. he was not the owner) Medwin Motors did not acquire title from Allan. Nevertheless, Medwin Motors arranged a hire purchase contract with a private individual (a Mr Kennedy) who wished to acquire the car. The transaction was financed by Langtry Investment, which acquired title to the car because of an exception, peculiar to motor cars subject to sales (or hire purchase transactions) to private individuals, to the *nemo dat quod non habet* rule.[120] Thus, FC Finance could not vindicate against the car (it no longer belonging to them). Although Mr Allan had acted fraudulently, there was no point in FC Finance seeking to sue him as he had emigrated to Canada and was in any event a man of straw. The sheriff principal confirmed that Langtry Investment Co was liable, there being a "special duty" upon them to inquire with HP International Ltd as to the provenance of the car because Langtry had previous experience of Medwin Motors offering them cars which were subject to subsisting hire purchase agreements and so not theirs to sell.[121] So, in failing to discharge this duty, Langtry had been negligent and breached a duty of care owed to FC Finance as the true owner of the vehicle at the relevant time.

Nevertheless, the law does require a revision to create a coherent wrongful interference with moveable property regime and to incorporate the miscellaneous wrongs that already apply. It could also be an opportunity to recognise which interests in moveables are reparable when harmed, something which would have a consequence for negligence for economic loss. Just now a summary is as follows:

1. Property destroyed

8-22   The *lex Aquilia* principle applies—loss wrongfully caused. In this case (for a long time) deliberate destruction has fallen clearly within the idea of wrongfulness. This does not depend in any way upon the law of negligence. Examples include the destruction of a horse[122] and the destruction of stakenets.[123] *Spuilzie* is not appropriate in destruction *simpliciter* for there is no taking.

2. Property of another taken

8-23   It is the kind of activity which would have been struck at by *spuilzie* and in modern times attracts an award of damages, albeit damage need not be proved in the sense of loss but rather by proving that the property was taken and evidence given as to its value. The loss of use is an independent head of damages.

3. Property of another used without permission

8-24   In addition to the bottle cases discussed above there is *Brown's Trustees v Hay*.[124] Hay was an employee of a firm of solicitors who, while involved with an

---

[120] Hire Purchase Act 1964 Pt III
[121] That specific facts may impose a duty of inquiry was not novel: see, e.g. *Faulds v Townsend* (1861) 23 D. 437; *Paterson Bros v Gladstone* (1891) 18 R. 403, the Lord President Kincairney focusing on "fault". Duties of inquiry may arise outside of delict: see, e.g. *Smith v Bank of Scotland*, 1997 S.C. (HL) 111.
[122] *Wilsons v McKnight* (1830) 8 S. 398.
[123] *Grubb v Mackenzie* (1834) 13 S. 717.
[124] *Brown's Trustees v Hay* (1898) 25 R. 1112.

estate, discovered papers which he thought implicated the estate in false returns to the revenue. He made a copy of the papers and sent them to the Inland Revenue. It transpired that the returns were substantially correct. Hay was held liable in damages for the ultroneous use of the property even although there was no actual loss and no taking. In another case an auctioneer, who in selling a bankrupt's estate which he had acquired from the trustee sold a car which was not part of the estate, was held liable in damages to the owner of the car.[125] That case may come within this category because the taking itself was permitted. In *Cairns v Harry Walker Ltd*,[126] the owners of a ship had been fined for an excise offence. The cause was the conduct of the steward (attempting to smuggle goods) carried out with the connivance of the defenders (the merchants who had sold the steward the goods). The merchants were held to be liable to the owners for the wrongful and illegal use of the ship.

4. Property detained

In addition to *Snare,* cited above, a person who stopped a coach taking people to a funeral was held liable in damages.[127] **8–25**

ANOTHER APPROACH

As the issue in these cases is intentional violation of interests in moveables, the general theme that common law crimes are delicts might help in this sphere. The Scots indigenous criminal law has developed carefully over the years, while the civil counterpart has been obscured by negligence and duties of care. Thus it is submitted that in cases where the facts fit *Milne v Tudhope*[128] or *Kidston v Annan*[129] or *Black v Carmichael,*[130] civil liability based on wrongfulness ought to succeed without difficulty. Looking at cases in that way means that they can become rather simple, as in *Gemmell v Bank of Scotland,*[131] where the bank repossessed and the pursuers' goods were missing. The learned sheriff thought it did not matter that the case was one of *spuilzie* or restitution, there would be damages including damages for loss of use.[132] **8–26**

[125] *Mackintosh v Galbraith & Arthur* (1900) 3 F. 66.
[126] *Cairns v Harry Walker Ltd*, 1914 S.C. 51.
[127] *Crawford v Mill* (1830) 5 Mur. 215.
[128] *Milne v Tudhope*, 1981 J.C. 53.
[129] *Kidston v Annan*, 1984 S.L.T. 279.
[130] *Black v Carmichael*, 1992 S.L.T. 897.
[131] *Gemmell v Bank of Scotland* Unreported November 5, 1996 Glasgow sheriff court.
[132] Compare with *Harris v Abbey National*, 1996 G.W.D. 33–1993 in which the pursuer was also successful.

CHAPTER 9

PRIVACY AND THE LAW OF CONFIDENCE

INTRODUCTION

9–01 This chapter is anomalous in that it deals with what may be related aspects of delict which, in causing harm, impinge on different protected interests. The most common use of the law of confidence has been to protect property interests. However, if Scotland follows recent developments in England and Wales, a new branch rooted in the law of confidence, described in English jurisprudence as misuse of private information, is developing so as to provide protection where an individual enjoys a legitimate expectation of privacy. This development provides a remedy where the harm impacts on personality interests—in particular to the pursuer's dignity.

LAW OF CONFIDENCE

9–02 Information can be an extremely valuable commodity, not just economically but also emotionally. The question to be considered here is to what extent does the Scots law of delict provide protection for the economic and/or emotional value attached to information. The answer to this question is unclear in many ways, one of which concerns whether the protection that Scots law does provide is grounded in delict, and if so whether it is rooted directly in the *actio injuriarum*, or in unjustified enrichment,[1] or in the law of property,[2] or by some special sui generis aspect of Scots law.[3] The reason for this is that, although there have been many recent cases, some of which may be familiar, very few have been brought in the Scottish courts.[4]

It has been said that the substance of Scots and English law in this area is the same.[5] The approach taken in this section will thus be to treat the case law from England and Wales as illustrative of the probable position of Scots law, but also to question whether the likely juridical basis for the Scots law of confidence may

---

[1] See, e.g. *Douglas v Hello! Ltd (No 6)* [2006] Q.B. 125 at 160 per Lord Phillips M.R. (delivering the judgment of the court).

[2] See, e.g. *Brown's Trustees v Hay* (1898) 25 R. 1112.

[3] This may be more important that at first it appears: where there is an international element to a claim, the area of law that forms the basis of litigation is important in determining questions over jurisdiction.

[4] Even where events at issue have occurred in Scotland, if publication in England and Wales is threatened, the High Court in London has been the preferred forum for litigation: see, e.g. *Murray v Big Pictures (UK) Ltd* [2009] Ch. 481 (application for injunction over surreptitious photos taken of J.K. Rowling's family on an Edinburgh street).

[5] "While the juridical basis may differ to some extent in the two jurisdictions, the substance of the

ultimately make Scots law more or less flexible than its counterpart in England and Wales. This is an important question given the uno of the law of confidence as the basis for the protection of privacy in English cases—should Scotland merely follow suit or is there capacity in Scots law for a more coherent approach?

Section 6 of the Human Rights Act 1998 has acted as a catalyst in the mutation of the law of confidence towards a law of privacy as such, at least in England and Wales. Courts may now be asked to consider, in particular, art.8 of the European Convention on Human Rights in confidence cases. The House of Lords has confirmed[6] that there remains no self-standing law of privacy in England and Wales, but to compensate the court has fashioned the tort of "misuse of private information"[7] as a new growing point from "old-fashioned"[8] breach of confidence. Although the "new methodology" adopted by the English courts[9] seems to have been accepted and applied in Scotland,[10] the Scottish courts have yet fully to have the opportunity to consider whether Scots law needs to follow English precedent or whether a law of privacy may be recognised as such in the law of Scotland.

It is suggested that the primary remedy for breach of confidence is interdict: although the harm resulting from a breach of confidence may be compensatable in damages, compensation does not provide reparation—once the confidentiality is lost it cannot be recovered. Thus, it is common that if an individual is alerted to the threat of divulgence of confidential information there will be an application for interdict, often sought on an interim basis where, at an emergency hearing, the judge will be asked to decide whether to make an order on the balance of convenience.[11] In England, such orders are known as interlocutory injunctions, and a recent development which has attracted particular controversy is the anonymised injunction—the so-called "super-injunction"—which attempts to prohibit anyone from disclosing even the fact that the court order has been made.[12] This issue has not vexed the courts in Scotland to any significant extent, with there being only one (unsuccessful) attempt to obtain a "super-interdict" at the time of writing.[13]

---

law in both of them is the same": *Lord Advocate v Scotsman Publications*, 1989 S.C. (HL) 122 at 164 per Lord Keith of Kinkell. English case law was referred to without comment on its relevance to Scotland in both *X v BBC*, 2005 S.L.T. 796 and *Response Handling Ltd v BBC*, 2008 S.L.T. 51.

[6] *Wainwright v Home Office* [2004] 2 A.C. 406. See also *Watkins v Home Office* [2006] 2 A.C. 395. The facts in each case occurred before the Human Rights Act 1998 came into force. See also *Peck v United Kingdom* [2003] E.M.L.R. 15; *Wainwright v United Kingdom* (2007) 44 E.H.R.R. 40. The complaints that English law failed to protect the respective applicants' art.8 rights were both upheld by the European Court of Human Rights.

[7] *Campbell v Mirror Group Newspapers Ltd* [2004] 2 A.C. 457 at 464–465 per Lord Nicholls of Birkenhead.

[8] *McKennitt v Ash* [2008] Q.B. 73 at 80 per Buxton L.J.

[9] *Re S (A Child) (Identification: Restrictions on Publication)* [2005] 1 A.C. 593 at 603 per Lord Steyn; *Mosley v News Group Newspapers Ltd* [2008] E.M.L.R. 20 at 687–689 per Eady J.

[10] See, e.g. *X v BBC*, 2005 S.L.T. 796; *Response Handling Ltd v BBC*, 2008 S.L.T. 51.

[11] This frequently means that difficult or complex issues are not fully explored: see, e.g. *X v BBC*, 2005 S.L.T. 796.

[12] See, e.g. *JIH v News Group Newspapers Ltd* [2011] 1 W.L.R. 1645; *Giggs v News Group Newspapers Ltd* [2013] E.M.L.R. 5.

[13] See "Sunday Herald beats off 'super-injunction' bid", *Sunday Herald*, October 3, 2010, p.16.

BREACH OF CONFIDENCE

9–03 In principle an obligation of confidence should arise where the reasonable person in the position of a recipient of information would have realised in all of the circumstances that the information was confidential.[14] The test is objective:

> "Now the law imposes a 'duty of confidence' whenever a person receives information he knows or ought to know is fairly and reasonably to be regarded as confidential."[15]

"All of the circumstances" may involve a range of factors, but it is well-settled that three main elements must be proved in order to establish a prima facie case for a remedy in "old-fashioned" breach of confidence cases. These are:

- the information concerned must be confidential in nature;
- there must have been a relationship between the parties consistent with an obligation of confidence; and
- there must be (at least threatened) unauthorised use of that information which is likely to cause harm to the pursuer.[16]

Confidential information

9–04 The categories of confidential information are not closed. Many examples have been the subject of court proceedings, including trade secrets and other commercially sensitive information and ideas,[17] government information and official secrets,[18] information protected by statute,[19] and personal information[20]—including information on an individual's criminal history,[21] health[22] and sex life.[23] Whether or not documentation has been marked "confidential" is not

---

[14] Scottish Law Commission, *Breach of Confidence* (HMSO, 1984), Scot. Law Com. No.90, Cmnd.9385, draft Bill, cl.1(2)(c).

[15] *Campbell v Mirror Group Newspapers Ltd* [2004] 2 A.C. 457 at 464–465 per Lord Nicholls of Birkenhead.

[16] *Coco v AN Clark (Engineers) Ltd* [1968] F.S.R. 415 at 419 per Megarry J. See also *Attorney General v Guardian Newspapers Ltd (No.2)* [1990] 1 A.C. 109; *Douglas v Hello! Ltd (No.3)*, sub nom. *OBG v Allan* [2008] 1 A.C. 1; *Levin v Caledonian Produce (Holdings) Ltd*, 1975 S.L.T. (Notes) 69 at 70 per Lord Robertson.

[17] See, e.g. *Seager v Copydex Ltd (No.1)* [1967] 1 W.L.R. 923; *Fraser v Thames Television Ltd* [1984] Q.B. 44; *Creation Records Ltd v News Group Newspapers Ltd* [1997] E.M.L.R. 444.

[18] See, e.g. *Attorney General v Guardian Newspapers Ltd (No.2)* [1990] 1 A.C. 109.

[19] Examples of statutes include Protection from Harassment Act 1997 (see, e.g. *Trimingham v Associated Newspapers Ltd* [2012] 4 All E.R. 717), Data Protection Act 1998 (see, e.g. *Campbell v Mirror Group Newspapers Ltd* [2003] Q.B. 633), Regulation of Investigatory Powers Act 2000 (see, e.g. *Phillips v News Group Newspapers Ltd* [2013] 1 A.C. 1. Cf. *Francome v Mirror Group Newspapers Ltd* [1984] 1 W.L.R. 892).

[20] See, e.g. *Duchess of Argyll v Duke of Argyll* [1967] Ch. 302; *Stephens v Avery* [1988] Ch. 449. Personal information is also protected by the Data Protection Act 1998.

[21] See, e.g. *Hellewell v Chief Constable of Derbyshire* [1995] 1 W.L.R. 804.

[22] See, e.g. *AB v CD* (1904) 7 F. 72; *Campbell v Mirror Group Newspapers Ltd* [2004] 2 A.C. 457.

[23] See, e.g. *Mosley v News Group Newspapers Ltd* [2008] E.M.L.R. 20.

conclusive, though it may have a persuasive effect where the status of the information is in dispute.

The publication of the book *Spycatcher*, an account by former MI5 operative Peter Wright of his experiences in working for the British secret service, spawned a series of important cases. Wright could not publish in England because of the terms of his contract of employment and because of the Official Secrets Act 1911, so he emigrated to Australia from where he agreed with an American publisher for the book to be published in the United States.[24] The *Sunday Times* newspaper purchased the right to publish extracts from the book in the United Kingdom, and published the first extract two days before the book itself was published in the United States. The United Kingdom government obtained an injunction to prevent publication by the *Sunday Times* of any further extracts, and sought an account of profits from the newspaper with regard to the publication of the first extract. The House of Lords confirmed that the information in the book had the necessary quality of confidence and that the *Sunday Times* owed a duty of confidence to the Crown, given that it had acquired the information in circumstances which would disclose it had been furnished in breach of confidence. However, once the book had been published in the United States, the information had entered the public domain to the extent that it was no longer confidential, and so future publication could no longer damage the public interest. Thus, the injunction could not be continued, and newspapers who had purchased serialisation rights would no longer be restrained from publishing.[25]

An unusual application of the law of confidence occurred in *Venables v News* **9–05** *Group Newspapers*.[26] Jon Venables and Robert Thomson were both 11 years old when they were convicted of the 1993 murder of two-year-old James Bulger in Liverpool. They were both released from detention upon reaching 18, having been given new identities by the state because of concerns about threats from "vigilantes" to their physical safety. The two sought *contra mundum*[27] perpetual injunctions to prohibit any disclosure of their new identities or other information (including where they lived) likely to reveal their identities. They fortified their confidence claim with reference to arts 2,[28] 3[29] and 8[30] of the European Convention on Human Rights whereas the newspaper defendants relied upon art.10 in challenging the application. The English Court of Appeal found that the elements of breach of confidence were satisfied, the confidential information being information about their new identities and locations, and that the claimants' rights under the Convention outbalanced the media's right to freedom of expression.

That photographs convey more information than merely documenting the fact that the event depicted took place was confirmed by the House of Lords in

---

[24] An injunction prevented the book from being sold in England, but it was sold freely in Scotland, confirming the jurisdictional boundaries of the English court. There have been sequels, most recently the publication of the identity of "CTB" (Ryan Giggs) by the *Sunday Herald* on May 22, 2011. See *Giggs v News Group Newspapers* [2013] E.M.L.R. 5 for the background.

[25] *Attorney General v Guardian Newspapers Ltd (No.2)* [1990] 1 A.C. 109.

[26] *Venables v News Group Newspapers* [2001] Fam. 430.

[27] Against the world at large. It remains questionable whether a *contra mundum* interdict is competent in Scots law given the traditional requirement of service upon the party it is made against.

[28] Right to life.

[29] Right not to be subjected to torture or to inhuman or degrading treatment or punishment.

[30] Right to respect for private and family life, home and correspondence.

Douglas v Hello![31] The publishers of *OK!* magazine sought damages in breach of confidence from the publishers of *Hello!* The film stars Michael Douglas and Catherine Zeta-Jones held their marriage ceremony in a hotel in New York. Guests were explicitly prohibited from taking photographs of the proceedings, the couple having sold the rights to photograph the event to *OK!*, who had outbid *Hello!* However, unauthorised photographs taken surreptitiously at the ceremony appeared in a "spoiler" edition of *Hello!* published a matter of hours after the official commemorative edition of *OK!* was published.[32] The House of Lords held that the photographs amounted to commercial information over which the couple had sufficient control to confirm its confidentiality. The publishers, having bought the rights to photograph the event, had effectively bought the benefit of the obligation of confidence and were thus able to take legal action against the interloping paparazzo who was in breach of the obligation of confidence owed to the couple.

Misuse of private information

9–06   In the context of misuse of private information, and in particular in considering the extent to which a pursuer's rights under art.8 of ECHR are engaged, the nature of the activity and the degree of intrusion will be factors for the court to consider. In *Campbell v Mirror Group Newspapers Ltd*[33] where photographs, taken from a public street, of Naomi Campbell leaving a narcotics anonymous meeting had been had been published, the House of Lords placed emphasis on the health aspect of the case. The court defined misuse of private information by applying a test which asked whether a reasonable person of ordinary sensibilities, if placed in the same situation as the subject of the disclosure, rather than its recipient, would find the disclosure offensive.[34] Since the information about Naomi Campbell's therapy and treatment was akin to private and confidential information contained in medical records, a reasonable person of ordinary sensibilities in her position would find the disclosure highly offensive.

This test was applied again in *Murray v Big Pictures Ltd*[35] where a claim was brought on behalf of the 18-month-old son of J.K. Rowling. Again, photographs had been taken from a public street but without the knowledge of the claimant's family. One factor that was viewed as significant by the English Court of Appeal was that paparazzi photographers were almost constantly following J.K. Rowling and taking photographs of her as she went about her daily business, it being impossible to prevent ordinary members of the public taking snapshots as she

---

[31] *Douglas v Hello! Ltd (No.3)*, sub nom. *OBG v Allan* [2008] 1 A.C. 1. Cf. *Sports & General Press Agency Ltd v Our Dogs Publishing Co Ltd* [1917] 2 K.B. 125. See also *Theakston v Mirror Group Newspapers Ltd* [2002] E.M.L.R. 22 (photos taken of a famous television personality in a brothel enjoined from publication although fact of visit allowed to be published); *Campbell v Mirror Group Newspapers Ltd* [2004] 2 A.C. 457 (fact that Naomi Campbell receiving treatment for drug addiction lawful to publish as in public interest, but public interest did not extend to justifying publication of photographs judged to be especially intrusive).

[32] The Douglases and the publishers of *OK!* had obtained an injunction against *Hello!*, but that was discharged upon appeal, the balance of convenience favouring permitting publication by *Hello!* given that it had invested so much in the edition that to pulp it would likely bankrupt the company. The publishers of *OK!* brought forward the publication date to minimise the damage likely to be inflicted upon them by *Hello!*

[33] *Campbell v Mirror Group Newspapers Ltd* [2004] 2 A.C. 457.

[34] Taken from *Australian Broadcasting Corp v Lenah Game Meats Pty Ltd* (2001) 208 C.L.R. 199 at 226 per Gleeson C.J.

[35] *Murray v Big Pictures Ltd* [2009] Ch. 481.

passed. *Murray* was concerned with an application from the defendant to "strike-out" the claim on the basis that it disclosed no legal ground for the action. The claimants having won on that point, the case was then settled out of court. A similar case arose in *Weller v Associated Newspapers*,[36] where the musician Paul Weller's children were awarded damages after "paparrazi" photographs taken of them on a family outing in California were published, without either consent or pixellation of the children's faces, in a national newspaper. Although publication would have been lawful under the law in California, the law to be applied was English law. Dingemans J. was careful to avoid the suggestion that the decision recognised an "image right" as part of domestic law.

European Court of Human Rights

The European Court of Human Rights has issued two important judgments in **9-07** complaints brought by Princess Caroline of Monaco against Germany. The first was in 2004[37] and concerned several paparazzi photographs taken of Princess Caroline and her family as she carried on her daily life. Princess Caroline had sued unsuccessfully in the German courts. The European Court criticised the German courts for placing too much emphasis on her status and too little on her right to privacy. The court's view was that the decisive factor in balancing the competition between art.8 rights to privacy and art.10 rights to freedom of expression was the extent to which the information in question contributed to a debate of general interest. The court considered that the photographs captured Princess Caroline acting as a private individual, and that the only interest to the general public was that she was a member of a royal family. Thus publication of the photographs did not contribute to such a debate. As a private individual Princess Caroline, albeit well-known, was nevertheless entitled to a zone of privacy even if she appeared in places where she might be seen by the public.

Judgment in the second case was issued in 2012.[38] Again, the complaints were related to the treatment by the German courts of claims made in respect of paparazzi photographs taken of Princess Caroline and her husband whilst engaged in private activities (skiing holidays) but in public places. However, on this occasion the European Court of Human Rights refused to interfere with the decisions of the German courts, pointing out that Member States enjoyed a wide margin of appreciation in balancing the competing rights in arts 8 and 10, and complimenting the German courts on the care they had taken in carrying out that balancing exercise. Given the breadth of the margin of appreciation described by the European Court, it is submitted that in finely balanced cases (which would include *Campbell v Mirror Group Newspapers Ltd* given the 3:2 majority in the House of Lords),[39] provided that a domestic court has taken sufficient care in applying the appropriate methodology, the European Court of Human Rights would be very reluctant to interfere with the decision, even if it may have considered the balance to tilt the other way.

---

[36] *Weller v Associated Newspapers* [2014] EWHC 1163 (QB).
[37] *Von Hannover v Germany* [2004] E.M.L.R. 21.
[38] *Von Hannover v Germany (No.2)* [2012] E.M.L.R. 16.
[39] Although the European Court of Human Rights had previously found that the majority decision of the House of Lords did not contravene art.10: *Mirror Group Newspapers v United Kingdom* [2011] E.M.L.R. 20.

False privacy

9–08   The case of *McKennitt v Ash*[40] resolved the question as to whether an action for breach of confidence or misuse of private information could be pursued where the information in question was not true. The defendant had written a book about her relationship with the Canadian folk singer, Loreena McKennitt. The book contained information about Ms McKennitt's relationships and personal feelings, along with a discussion of a property dispute between Ms McKennitt and the author, most of which the trial judge had found to be untrue. The defendant argued that the claim should be struck out effectively on the basis that confidentiality could not be asserted in false information—to do so would be to attempt to circumvent restrictions in the law of defamation. However, the English Court of Appeal held that the truth or falsity of the information was irrelevant both in breach of confidence and in misuse of private information.

The "limiting principles"

9–09   In the *Spycatcher* case, Lord Goff stated:

> "There are three limiting principles . . . The first . . . is that the principle of confidentiality only applies to information to the extent that it is confidential. In particular, once it has entered what is usually called the public domain (which means no more than that the information in question is so generally accessible that, in all the circumstances, it cannot be regarded as confidential) then, as a general rule, the principle of confidentiality can have no application to it. . . . The second limiting principle is that the duty of confidence applies neither to useless information, nor to trivia. The third . . . is that . . . the law's protection of confidence . . . may be outweighed by some other countervailing public interest which favours disclosure."[41]

Public domain

9–10   As discussed above,[42] the House of Lords took the view that the information contained in Peter Wright's book *Spycatcher* was no longer confidential once it had entered the public domain by being published in the United States. More recent cases arguably have taken a more sophisticated approach.

McKennitt v Ash[43] also dealt with the first of Lord Goff's limiting principles. The Court of Appeal refused to accept the defendant's argument that once the plaintiff had discussed a particular topic in public, other information related to that topic could then be published with impunity. Put another way, where the claimant chose to put some information on an aspect of their personal life into the public domain the claimant did not lose the right to control other related information. A parallel may be seen with the approach of the majority in the House of Lords to the publication by *Hello!* of unauthorised photographs of the

---

[40] *McKennitt v Ash* [2008] Q.B. 73.
[41] *Attorney-General v Guardian Newspapers Ltd (No.2)* [1990] 1 A.C. 109 at 280 per Lord Goff of Chieveley. It is suggested that the first two limiting principles impact on what makes information confidential and so should be treated as challenges to what must be proved by a pursuer. However, it is submitted that the third limiting principle: that a countervailing public interest outweighs protection by the law of confidence, is effectively a defence. The text will treat each limiting factor accordingly.
[42] At para.9–04.
[43] *McKennitt v Ash* [2008] Q.B. 73.

Douglas's wedding ceremony even after *OK!* had published its authorised photographs. However, the claimant may compromise the confidentiality of information or a right to privacy by making substantial public disclosures.[44] The court in *McKennitt* were also unimpressed with the argument that because some copies of the book in question had already been sold, the information was effectively in the public domain.[45]

Likewise, just because activity is carried out where it may be observed by the public does not per se prevent information about the activity acquiring the protection of confidence. The degree to which the public have been able to observe the activity will likely have a significant bearing on the case. Photographs taken of a guest at a private party and subsequently posted on Facebook where they could be viewed by the public were held not to have so entered the public domain that the right to privacy in the information had been lost, there being no evidence to confirm wide viewing by the public at large.[46]

Useless information and trivia

Trivial information, such as "trivial tittle-tattle"[47] is not protected by the law **9-11** of confidence. Baroness Hale alluded to this in distinguishing between Naomi Campbell's treatment for drug addiction and popping out to the shops for a bottle of milk.[48] Thus, in *McKennitt v Ash*[49] the judge was justified in refusing protection for information that was banal, mundane or anodyne, such as details of a shopping trip for furniture.

The first Princess Caroline case against Germany was viewed as questioning the correctness of Baroness Hale's distinction. However, it is submitted that the judgment of the European Court of Human Rights in the second Princess Caroline case confirms that the margin of appreciation enjoyed by the United Kingdom as a member state is wide enough to accommodate the distinction.

Pre-existing relationship

In the old-fashioned law of confidence, the obligation had to arise out of a **9-12** relevant relationship between the parties.[50] The most obvious relationship that may incorporate an obligation of confidence is a contractual relationship, and a common example is the employment contract.[51] Others included professional

---

[44] See, e.g. *Trimingham v Associated Newspapers Ltd* [2012] 4 All E.R. 717.

[45] See also *HRH Prince of Wales v Associated Newspapers Ltd* [2008] Ch. 57; cf. *Attorney-General v Guardian Newspapers Ltd (No.2)* [1990] 1 A.C. 109; *Lord Advocate v Scotsman Publications Ltd*, 1989 S.C. (H.L.) 122.

[46] *Rocknroll v News Group Newspapers Ltd* [2013] EWHC 24 (Ch). Cf. *Mosley v News Group Newspapers Ltd* [2008] EWHC 1777 (QB). In *X v BBC*, 2005 S.L.T. 796 whether the fact that the pursuer's embarrassing behaviour had taken place in public was fatal to a claim for breach of confidence or infringement of privacy was not considered before finding that the balance of convenience favoured an interim interdict.

[47] *Coco v AN Clark (Engineers) Ltd* [1968] F.S.R. 415 at 421 per Megarry J. See also discussion of a "threshold of seriousness" in *Trimingham v Associated Newspapers Ltd* [2012] 4 All E.R. 717 at [87]–[88] per Tugendhat J.

[48] *Campbell v Mirror Group Newspapers Ltd* [2004] 2 A.C. 457 at 501 per Baroness Hale of Richmond.

[49] *McKennitt v Ash* [2008] Q.B. 73.

[50] See, e.g. *Roxburgh v Seven Seas Engineering Ltd*, 1980 S.L.T. (Notes) 49.

[51] The extent of the obligation of confidence arising in employment was explored in *Faccenda Chicken Ltd v Fowler* [1987] Ch. 117.

relationships such as between solicitor and client,[52] or (though strictly a non-contractual relationship outside of private health care) doctor and patient.[53]

Where a contractual obligation of confidence is breached, an action for breach of contract is competent. However, if the contractual obligation is between A and B, and without A's authority B discloses the confidential information to C, A cannot take action in contract against C to prevent further disclosure. A's action against C must be in delict. The question is then in what circumstances will C owe A a delictual obligation of confidence which may be enforced by interdict or, if breached, sound in damages? It has been held that a confidentiality agreement between employer and employee is not automatically binding on third parties,[54] but where the third party knows or ought reasonably to appreciate that the information is confidential, a delictual obligation of confidence will be owed by the third party to the owner or confider of the information.[55]

The formality of the relationship required perhaps works in inverse proportion to the extent to which it is obvious that the information is confidential:

> "I realise that, in the vast majority of cases, . . . the duty of confidence will arise from a transaction or relationship between the parties . . . But it is well settled that a duty of confidence may arise . . . independently of such cases; and I have expressed the circumstances in which the duty arises in broad terms, not merely to embrace those cases where a third party receives information from a person who is under a duty of confidence in respect of it, knowing that it has been disclosed by that person to him in breach of his duty of confidence, but also to include certain situations, beloved of law teachers—where an obviously confidential document is wafted by an electric fan out of a window into a crowded street, or where an obviously confidential document, such as a private diary, is dropped in a public place, and is then picked up by a passer-by."[56]

In this passage, Lord Goff quite clearly set the scene for the expansion of the law of confidence towards its capacity for the enforcement of a general right to privacy, although the real catalyst for that change was the significance afforded to art.8 of the European Convention on Human Rights by the implementation of the Human Rights Act 1998 in October 2000.

9–13   Meanwhile, the range of relationships which courts recognised as giving rise to obligations of confidence expanded considerably from the 1960s onwards. In 1964, the English High Court confirmed that marriage gave rise to obligations of confidence owed by each spouse to the other.[57] This was extended in 1988 to relationships between lovers, whether heterosexual or homosexual.[58] However, whether an obligation of confidence could arise in more fleeting sexual relationships was still open to debate in the first half of the 2000s[59]; but in 2008

---

[52] See, e.g. *Kerr v Duke of Roxburgh* (1822) 3 Murr. 126.

[53] See, e.g. *AB v CD* (1904) 7 F. 72.

[54] *Osborne v BBC*, 2000 S.C. 29.

[55] *Prince Albert v Strange* (1849) 64 E.R. 293; *Attorney-General v Guardian Newspapers Ltd (No.2)* [1990] 1 A.C. 109; *Lord Advocate v Scotsman Publications Ltd*, 1989 S.C. (H.L.) 122.

[56] *Attorney-General v Guardian Newspapers Ltd (No.2)* [1990] 1 A.C. 109 at 281 per Lord Goff of Chieveley.

[57] *Duchess of Argyll v Duke of Argyll* [1967] Ch. 302.

[58] *Stephens v Avery* [1988] Ch. 449. See also *Barrymore v News Group Newspapers Ltd* [1997] F.S.R. 600.

[59] *Theakston v Mirror Group Newspapers Ltd* [2002] E.M.L.R. 22; *A v B Plc* [2003] Q.B. 195.

the matter was put beyond debate when it was confirmed that even a casual relationship between a prostitute and a punter may be sufficient.[60]

In *Campbell v MGN*,[61] the House of Lords confronted the artificiality of the relationship requirement in the use of the law of confidence to protect privacy. Although not mentioned at all in the speeches in *Campbell*, and not strictly a privacy case, the approach taken by the court in *Creation Records Ltd v News Group Newspapers Ltd*[62] illustrates the point. A photographer from *The Sun* newspaper booked into a hotel where the musical group Oasis were due to be photographed for the cover of their "Be Here Now" album. *The Sun*'s photographer, using bushes for cover, surreptitiously took photographs of the band as they posed for their "official" photographs beside a swimming pool in the grounds of the hotel. Several of the unofficial photographs were published in the newspaper, and it invited its readers to purchase a poster of an image captured by the photographer which was virtually identical to the one selected by the band to use on the cover of their album. The band's record company sought an injunction on inter alia breach of confidence grounds. Although the photographer was lawfully on the scene, the court accepted that the nature of the operation and the imposition of security measures made it arguable that the shoot was clearly intended to be confidential. This was enough to satisfy the court that the requirements for breach of confidence were met, and an injunction prohibiting *The Sun* from further publication was granted.

Thus, in *Campbell*, where photographs of the model Naomi Campbell leaving a Narcotics Anonymous meeting were taken from a public street, the House of Lords confirmed a new branch of this area of law: misuse of private information. To succeed in an action for misuse of private information it is no longer necessary to demonstrate that an obligation of confidence arose out of a pre-existing relationship. Even if there was a tenuous connection between the photographer and the band in *Creation Records*, there was effectively no relationship beyond serendipity connecting the *Mirror* photographer to Naomi Campbell.[63] Although none of the Law Lords were prepared to say as much at the time, this decision effectively recognised a remedy for breach of privacy.

Unauthorised use causes harm

To obtain a remedy for breach of confidence the pursuer must normally show **9–14** that he has suffered, or is likely to suffer "detriment".[64] Thus, in the *Spycatcher* litigation, the *Sunday Times* newspaper was held to have been in breach of confidence in publishing extracts from Peter Wright's memoirs before they were published in the United States,[65] but no newspaper was injuncted from publishing afterwards, i.e. when all of any potential "detriment" had already been suffered by the British Government.

---

[60] *Mosley v News Group Newspapers Ltd* [2008] E.M.L.R. 20.

[61] *Campbell v MGN* [2004] 2 A.C. 457.

[62] *Creation Records Ltd v News Group Newspapers Ltd* [1997] E.M.L.R. 444.

[63] Although no doubt Miss Campbell's presence at the Narcotics Anonymous meeting had been leaked to the newspaper: see *Campbell v Mirror Group Newspapers Ltd* [2004] 2 A.C. 457 at 470 per Lord Hoffmann.

[64] *Attorney-General v Guardian Newspapers Ltd (No.2)* [1990] 1 A.C. 109 at 282 per Lord Goff of Chieveley. See also *Attorney General v Jonathan Cape Ltd* [1976] Q.B. 752.

[65] At which point the House of Lords accepted copies of the book were freely available in the United Kingdom. Ironically, the book had previously been on public sale in Scotland.

Lord Advocate v Scotsman Publications Ltd[66] provides a Scottish equivalent. A former MI6 officer, Anthony Cavendish, distributed 279 copies[67] of "Inside Intelligence", an account of his experiences as a secret service operative. An interdict was sought by the British Government. The House of Lords confirmed the decision of the lower courts to refuse interdict on the grounds that the government had not asserted that the book contained any material damaging to national security. Proof of a general obligation of confidentiality owed by the author to the Crown was, without an averment of detriment, insufficient to justify the granting of interdict to prevent publication by a newspaper.[68]

PUBLIC INTEREST DEFENCE

9–15 Although the protection of confidentiality has often been justified with reference to the "public interest", there may be a "countervailing public interest[69] in disclosure of the information. This was recognised long before the Human Rights Act 1998,[70] which requires the court to have "particular regard to the importance of the Convention right to freedom of expression" and, where the proceedings appear to relate to "journalistic, literary or artistic material" or connected conduct, to the extent to which it is, or would be, in the public interest for the material to be published.[71]

For publication to be justified, a legitimate public interest must be engaged: it is not enough that the material will be of interest to a prurient public.[72] Section 12(4)(b) of the Human Rights Act 1998 requires a court in dealing with questions relating to the restriction of freedom of expression to have "particular regard" to "any relevant privacy code." Examples of relevant codes include the Editors' Code of Practice and the OFCOM Broadcasting Code. Although the language differs slightly, both provide similar examples of a public interest that may override a right to privacy:

- revealing or detecting crime or serious impropriety;
- protecting public health and safety;
- exposing misleading claims made by individuals or organisations.

The OFCOM Code also includes "disclosing incompetence that affects the public" and the Editors' Code asserts "there is a public interest in freedom of expression itself."

---

[66] *Lord Advocate v Scotsman Publications Ltd*, 1989 S.C. (H.L.) 122

[67] Cavendish described the privately funded copies as "Christmas Cards". A parallel may be seen in *HRH Prince of Wales v Associated Newspapers Ltd* [2008] Ch. 57.

[68] Lord Keith also referred, without commenting on its authority, to the decision of the Second Division of the Inner House that a purported interdict of "any other person having notice" of the order could not be made by a court in Scotland: 1989 S.C. (H.L.) 122 at 163.

[69] *Attorney-General v Guardian Newspapers Ltd (No.2)* [1990] 1 A.C. 109 at 280 per Lord Goff of Chieveley.

[70] *Gartside v Outram* (1856) 26 L.J. Ch. 113 at 114 per Wood V.C.: " ... there is no confidence as to the disclosure of iniquity". See also, e.g. *Lion Laboratories Ltd v Evans* [1985] Q.B. 526; *Hellewell v Chief Constable of Derbyshire* [1995] 1 W.L.R. 804.

[71] Human Rights Act 1998 s.12(4).

[72] For example, "vapid tittle-tattle about the activities of footballers' wives and girlfriends ... ": *Jameel v Wall Street Journal Europe Sprl* [2007] 1 A.C. 359 at 408 per Baroness Hale of Richmond.

In *Mosley v News Group Newspapers Ltd*,[73] the defendants attempted to justify **9–16** publication of an illustrated account of the participation in a "sex party" with five prostitutes of the former President of the FIA[74] by arguing that exposure was in the public interest. The newspaper alleged that the participants had dressed in Nazi uniforms and had acted out a prison camp scene in mockery of how Jews were treated during the Holocaust. Although the court recognised the potential public interest in revealing any hypocrisy that such conduct exposed, the newspaper was unable to provide any evidence to support its assertions of the motive or context in the "role-play" adopted. The newspaper's defence thus fell apart and damages were assessed at £60,000.

A further limitation should be noted. A genuine countervailing public interest may not justify what the eavesdropper or snooper wishes to do with the confidential information. In *Francome v Mirror Group Newspapers Ltd*,[75] the newspaper purchased transcripts of the jockey, John Francome's telephone conversations which had been unlawfully tapped,[76] but which confirmed that he was involved in a criminal conspiracy. Francome sought an injunction to prevent the newspaper publishing the transcripts; the *Mirror* argued that publishing was in the public interest. The judge's view was:

"In the instant case, pending a trial, it is impossible to see what public interest would be served by publishing the contents of the tapes which would not equally be served by giving them to the police or to the Jockey Club. Any wider publication could only serve the interests of the 'Daily Mirror'."[77]

Likewise in *Campbell v MGN*[78] (decided post-Human Rights Act), the House of Lords recognised the public interest in "setting the record straight" where Naomi Campbell, in courting publicity to further her career, had contrived to create a false image of herself by publicly denying that she took drugs. However, although the House of Lords were unanimous in holding that the public interest justified the newspaper in publishing the *facts* revealed by the photographs of Naomi Campbell leaving the Narcotics Anonymous meeting, i.e. that she had a drug problem, by a majority the Law Lords held that the public interest did not require the facts to be accompanied by the *photographs*. Carrying out the balancing exercise in weighing up the competing rights to privacy and freedom of expression, publication of the verbal information was justified as a proportionate interference with the former right, but publication of the visual information was unduly intrusive, and so amounted to a disproportionate interference with the right of privacy unjustified by the right of freedom of expression.

---

[73] *Mosley v News Group Newspapers Ltd* [2008] E.M.L.R. 20.
[74] The FIA represents the interests of motoring organisations and motor car users and is the regulating body for international motorsport including Formula 1.
[75] *Francome v Mirror Group Newspapers Ltd* [1984] 1 W.L.R. 892.
[76] In breach of s.5 of the Wireless Telegraphy Act 1949. The legislation that now outlaws phone tapping (and hacking) is the Regulation of Investigatory Powers Act 2000.
[77] *Francome v Mirror Group Newspapers Ltd* [1984] 1 W.L.R. 892 at 898 per Sir John Donaldson M.R.
[78] *Campbell v MGN* [2004] 2 A.C. 457.

9–17 Examples of the use of the law of confidence to protect privacy may be seen in the English courts as far back as the mid-nineteenth century. In *Prince Albert v Strange*,[79] Queen Victoria's consort obtained an injunction to prevent the sale of prints that had been made from etchings that he and Queen Victoria had created. Prince Albert had delivered the etchings to a printer in order to have prints made for himself, but an employee of the printer had, without permission, made extra copies which he had put up for sale. It was held that the conduct amounted to a breach of the Prince's legal right of privacy.

Nevertheless, the English courts continued to insist that there was no self-standing action for breach of privacy,[80] at least until the implementation of the Human Rights Act 1998. However, the use of respectively art.8 of the European Convention of Human Rights by claimants and art.10 by defendants has forced the English courts to develop the law of confidence so as to provide proportionate protection to the right of privacy, balancing privacy with the right to freedom of expression.

As already noted above,[81] *Campbell v MGN* was a watershed case. The House of Lords acknowledged that the term "breach of confidence" was outmoded, although there remained a resistance to recognising a right of privacy per se: "In this country, unlike the United States of America, there is no over-arching, all-embracing cause of action for 'invasion of privacy'."[82] So the compromise was to adumbrate a taxonomy of actions under the umbrella of the general law of confidence, and to distinguish between "old-fashioned" breach of confidence and misuse of private information. Recognising misuse of private information as distinct from breach of confidence thus represents a "shift in the centre of gravity"[83] in the sense that the old law relies upon a pre-existing relationship between the parties, whereas the new growing point relies upon the private nature of the information.[84] There is clearly the potential for overlap,[85] which is bolstered by the use by litigants in both types of case of relevant articles of the European Convention on Human Rights.

The reliance upon, respectively, art.8 by claimants and art.10 by (especially media) defendants has also resulted in the adoption of a "new methodology" by the English courts:

> "The interplay between articles 8 and 10 has been illuminated by the opinions in the House of Lords in *Campbell v MGN Ltd*.[86] What does . . . emerge clearly from the opinions are four propositions. First, neither article has *as such* precedence over the other. Secondly, where the values under the two articles are in conflict, an intense focus on the comparative importance of the specific rights being claimed in the individual case is necessary.

---

[79] *Prince Albert v Strange* (1849) 64 E.R. 293.
[80] See, e.g. *Kaye v Robertson* [1991] F.S.R. 62; *Wainwright v Home Office* [2004] 2 A.C. 406; *Vidal-Hall v Google Inc* [2014] E.M.L.R. 14 at 361 per Tugendhat J. Cf. *Henderson v Chief Constable of Fife*, 1988 S.L.T. 361.
[81] At para.9–06.
[82] *Campbell v MGN* [2004] 2 A.C. 457 at 464 per Lord Nicholls of Birkenhead.
[83] *Campbell v MGN* [2004] 2 A.C. 457 at 473 per Lord Hoffmann.
[84] In England, "misuse of private information" has recently been judicially acknowledged as a distinct tort: *Vidal-Hall v Google Inc* [2014] E.M.L.R. 14 at 361 per Tugendhat J.
[85] See, e.g. *Terry v Persons Unknown* [2010] E.M.L.R. 16.
[86] *Campbell v MGN Ltd* [2004] 2 A.C. 457.

Thirdly, the justifications for interfering with or restricting each right must be taken into account. Finally, the proportionality test must be applied to each. For convenience I will call this the ultimate balancing test."[87]

Claimants tend to use art.8 to support an assertion that they enjoy a "reasonable **9–18** expectation of privacy". When will an expectation of privacy be reasonable? The test adopted in *Campbell* was:

"whether a reasonable person of ordinary sensibilities, if placed in the same situation as the subject of the disclosure, rather than its recipient, would find the disclosure offensive."[88]

This has been expanded and refined in subsequent cases:

"The question whether there is a reasonable expectation of privacy is a broad one, which takes account of all the circumstances of the case. They include the attributes of the claimant, the nature of the activity in which the claimant was engaged, the place at which it was happening, the nature and purpose of the intrusion, the absence of consent and whether it was known or could be inferred, the effect on the claimant and the circumstances in which and the purposes for which the information came into the hands of the publisher."[89]

Defendants tend to use art.10 to support an assertion that the claimant's reasonable expectation of privacy should give way to the defendant's right to freedom of expression. Article 10 also specifically confirms a right to receive, as well as impart, information and ideas. Thus, what is usually relied upon to justify giving priority to art.10 is that it is in the public interest to disclose the information, and it would be a disproportionate interference with freedom of expression to prohibit publication. The European Court of Human Rights has emphasised the importance of freedom of expression, especially with regard to the role of the press as "public watchdog":

"(F)reedom of expression constitutes one of the essential foundations of a democratic society. Subject to paragraph 2 of Article 10, it is applicable not only to "information" or "ideas" that are favourably received or regarded as inoffensive or as a matter of indifference, but also to those that offend, shock or disturb. Such are the demands of that pluralism, tolerance and broadmindedness without which there is no "democratic society" . . . In that connection the press plays an essential role in a democratic society. Although it must not overstep certain bounds, in particular in respect of the reputation and rights of others, its duty is nevertheless to impart—in a manner consistent with its obligations and responsibilities—information and ideas on all matters of public interest . . . Journalistic freedom also covers

---

[87] *Re S (A Child) (Identification: Restriction on Publication)* [2005] 1 A.C. 593 at 603 per Lord Steyn. See also *Mosley v News Group Newspapers Ltd* [2008] E.M.L.R. 20 at 687–689 per Eady J.

[88] Taken from *Australian Broadcasting Corp v Lenah Game Meats Pty Ltd* (2001) 208 C.L.R. 199 at 226 per Gleeson C.J.

[89] *Murray v Big Pictures Ltd* [2009] Ch. 481 at 502 per Sir Anthony Clarke M.R. (delivering the judgment of the court).

possible recourse to a degree of exaggeration, or even provocation ...
Although freedom of expression also extends to the publication of photos,
this is an area in which the protection of the rights and reputation of others
takes on particular importance."[90]

The European Court of Human Rights has also set out criteria relevant for
carrying out the "balancing exercise" when the rights set out in arts 8 and 10 are
in conflict.[91] Criteria include:

- contribution to a debate of general interest: a distinction may be made
  between on the one hand issues of political and social importance,
  including crime, sporting issues or performing artists,[92] and on the other
  personal information about private persons, or even public figures
  where that is not connected to their public function or activity[93];
- how well known is the person concerned and what is the subject of the
  report?[94]
- prior conduct of the person concerned: although cooperation with the
  press on one occasion will not deprive the person concerned with future
  protection by art.8[95];
- content, form and consequences of the publication: what is the tone of
  the publication, and what is its circulation with reference to the issue
  under discussion?
- circumstances in which photos were taken: were photos taken with or
  without consent, or in a place where the individual would have a
  reasonable expectation not to be photographed. The court has noted that
  photographs may be particularly intrusive.[96]

A privacy law for Scotland

9–19　　So far there have been few opportunities for the Scottish courts to consider
how to deal with privacy cases. On the two occasions post Human Rights Act
1998 that the issue as such has arisen,[97] the Scottish courts have followed English
jurisprudence in determining whether or not to grant interim interdict. There has
yet to be a full trial of the issues in a privacy type case in Human Rights era
Scotland.

It is worth considering whether the Scottish courts should follow the English
jurisprudence –which appears to still maintain there is no indigenous law of

---

[90] *Von Hannover v Germany* [2004] E.M.L.R. 21 at 403–404 (judgment of the court).
[91] *Von Hannover v Germany (No.2)* [2012] E.M.L.R. 16 at 368–369 (judgment of the court).
[92] The "general interest" may actually be confined to a defined group: see, e.g. *Browne v Associated Newspapers Ltd* [2007] E.M.L.R. 19.
[93] See, e.g. *Mosley v News Group Newspapers Ltd* [2008] E.M.L.R. 20. Cf. e.g. *Ferdinand v Mirror Group Newspapers Ltd* [2011] EWHC 2454; *Trimingham v Associated Newspapers Ltd* [2012] 4 All E.R. 717.
[94] See, e.g. *Goodwin v News Group Newspapers Ltd* [2011] E.M.L.R. 27.
[95] See, e.g. *Price v Powell* [2012] EWHC 3257 (QB). Cf. *Ferdinand v Mirror Group Newspapers Ltd* [2011] EWHC 2454.
[96] See, e.g. *Weller v Associated Newspapers Ltd* [2014] EWHC 1163.
[97] *X v BBC*, 2005 S.L.T. 796; *Response Handling Ltd v BBC*, 2008 S.L.T. 51. In *Martin v McGuiness*, 2003 S.L.T. 1424, Lord Bonomy in the Outer House held that the admission of evidence from private investigators following surveillance activity would not be a disproportionate interference with the pursuer's right to respect for private and family life under art.8 of the European Convention on Human Rights.

privacy at common law –or whether the Scottish courts could adopt a distinctive approach to privacy cases. Ultimately, the answer depends upon the extent to which there is a Scottish tradition to fall back upon. In this context it is appropriate to note that

> "(w)hat human rights law has done is to identify private information as something worth protecting as an aspect of human autonomy and dignity."[98]

According to Ulpian,[99] the *actio injuriarum* provided protection for *corpus, fama* and *dignitas*. It has recently been held that the *actio injuriarum* provided the true juridical basis in Scotland for the legal wrong of unauthorised removal and retention of body parts and would provide for solatium as a remedy for relatives with regard to the affront suffered to their dignity. In *Henderson v Chief Constable of Fife*,[100] although he made no direct reference to the *actio injuriarum* or to dignity as such as a protected interest, Lord Jauncey held that solatium provided a remedy for the infringement of privacy and liberty suffered by a woman who had her brassiere unjustly removed following her arrest.

Thus it may be arguable that there is scope in Scots law to recognise a freestanding law of privacy based on the application of the *actio injuriarum* and its protection of dignity.[101]

---

[98] *Campbell v Mirror Group Newspapers Ltd* [2004] 2 A.C. 457 at 472 per Lord Hoffmann.

[99] D47,10,1,2.

[100] *Henderson v Chief Constable of Fife*, 1988 S.L.T. 361. This decision suggests that solatium would provide a remedy should the facts in *Wainwright v Home Office* [2004] 2 A.C. 406 occur in Scotland.

[101] See E. Reid, "Protection of Personality Rights" and H. McQueen, "A Hitchhiker's Guide to Personality Rights in Scots Law, Mainly with Regard to Privacy", in N. Whitty and R. Zimmermann (eds), *Rights of Personality in Scots Law: A Comparative Perspective* (Dundee: Dundee University Press, 2009).

CHAPTER 10

ECONOMIC WRONGS

INTRODUCTION

10–01 This Chapter deals with a number of delicts, some of which have been described in England as economic torts.[1] This is by no means a closed nor a clearly identified category, and distinctions may be made between the "economic delicts", passing off and fraud. Whether there is a coherence in grouping these examples of delictual wrongs together is open to question. However, what these delicts do have in common is that they all define the limits of legal trading and so are usefully considered together. As will be seen, attempts had been made to harmonise some or all of the wrongs. Recent developments have undermined these attempts.

ECONOMIC DELICTS

10–02 It is open to question whether the term "economic delicts" is appropriate in describing a category of delictual wrongs recognised by the law of Scotland. The Scottish courts have not frequently been troubled by cases in this area,[2] and when they have Scottish judges have tended to apply the jurisprudence developed in England and Wales, where apparently the term "economic torts" has gained acceptance. There has never been a *Donoghue v Stevenson*[3] moment in the economic torts, either in the sense of an attempt to define an underpinning principle that connects the various strands[4] or in the sense of an attempt to unify the law across Scotland and England and Wales. Indeed, it might be said that the most significant recent decisions[5] provide a reverse *Donoghue v Stevenson*

---

[1] See *Clerk & Lindsell on Torts*, edited by A. Dugdale and M. Jones, 20th edn (London: Sweet & Maxwell, 2013), Chs 18, 24 and 26.

[2] Although *Crofter Hand Woven Harris Tweed Co Ltd v Veitch*, 1942 S.C. (HL) 1 is recognised as the leading case on lawful means conspiracy in England and Wales, as well as in Scotland.

[3] *Donoghue v Stevenson*, 1932 S.C. (HL) 31.

[4] Several writers have postulated a general tort of wrongful interference with trade: see, e.g. J. Adams, "Is There a Tort of Unfair Competition?" 1985 J.B.L. 26; H. Carty, "Intentional Violation of Economic Interests: the Limits of Common Law Liability" (1988) 104 L.Q.R. 242; P. Sales and D. Stilitz, "Intentional Infliction of harm by Unlawful Means" (1999) 11 L.Q.R. 411; J. Holyoak and F. Mazzocchetti, "The Legal Protection of Economic Interests" (1993) 1 Tort L.R. 185. The House of Lords conceded the existence of such a general tort in *Lonrho Plc v Fayed* [1991] 3 W.L.R. 188. However, development of such an analysis effectively has been stifled by the decisions of the House of Lords in *OBG Ltd v Allan* [2008] 1 A.C. 1 and *Customs and Excise Commissioners v Total Network SL* [2008] 1 A.C. 1174.

[5] *OBG Ltd v Allan* [2008] 1 A.C. 1; *Customs and Excise Commissioners v Total Network SL* [2008] 1 A.C. 1174.

moment—reinforcing the pigeonholing of wrongs into separate and discreet torts. Cases which fall between the cracks will thus be doomed to fail.[6] A celebrated feature of a principle-based method of jurisprudence is that the law is flexible and that novel situations are justiciable through the identification and application of relevant principles—a delictual example being *culpa*. However, enslavement to labels which are attached to concepts adopting rigid criteria risks stagnation in the law and a failure to see the wood for the trees.[7]

In a free market economy such as exists in Scotland and the United Kingdom, competition is valued as promoting public interests. Thus the law will not condemn the undercutting of another's prices, even where the latter is put out of business as a result.[8] On the other hand, the law will not condone violent methods of seeking to achieve a monopoly over a market, such as shooting (or threatening to) those who choose to deal with a competitor.[9] Development of the common law in this area was accelerated through various examples of industrial conflict in the latter half of the nineteenth century, but the main developments in the twentieth were statutory: legislation dealing with trade unions and industrial relations arriving early in the century[10] and legislation dealing with competition in the market place proliferating in the latter half, with the European Union providing a broader dimension.[11] However, consideration of EU and domestic regulation dealing with industrial relations and distortion of competition in the market place is beyond the scope of this book.

The economic wrongs recognised by the law of delict may be arranged under two headings: namely *individual* economic wrongs which are actionable if carried out by an individual; and *collective* economic wrongs which are actionable only if carried out by a collective of persons in combination, i.e. requiring a conspiracy. Following the analysis provided by the House of Lords in *OBG Ltd v Allan*,[12] it appears settled[13] that two separate torts/delicts provide discreet examples of the former: inducing a breach of contract and causing loss by unlawful means.[14] There are also two examples of the latter: lawful means conspiracy and unlawful means conspiracy.

It should be noted at the outset that all of these are examples of *intentional* delicts—the onus of proof with regards to the mental element falling upon the pursuer. As will be seen, this generally requires identification of the predominant motive behind the conduct and, in general, harm suffered by the pursuer must be intended as an end in itself or as a means to an end; if harm to the pursuer was merely a foreseeable consequence of the acts complained of, resulting harm will not be reparable.

---

[6] See, e.g. *McLeod v Rooney*, 2010 S.L.T. 499.

[7] For example, none of the post *OBG Ltd v Allan* Scottish cases on "causing loss by unlawful means" have considered the extent to which the "delict" is a manifestation of the concepts incorporated in the brocard *damnum injuria datum*.

[8] *Mogul Steamship Co. Ltd v McGregor, Gow & Co* [1892] A.C. 25.

[9] *Tarleton v M'Gawley* (1790) 1 Peake NPC 270; *Garret v Taylor* (1620) Cro Jac 567.

[10] Currently the main statute is the Trade Union and Labour Relations (Consolidation) Act 1992 (as amended).

[11] The main statute is the Competition Act 1998.

[12] *OBG Ltd v Allan* [2008] 1 A.C. 1.

[13] *Global Resources Group v Mackay*, 2009 S.L.T. 104; *McLeod v Rooney*, 2010 S.L.T. 499.

[14] The discreet nature of the torts was emphasised in *OBG Ltd v Allan*, where the House of Lords rejected the analysis that there was a general tort of interference with contractual rights of which the two torts were subcategories.

Economic wrongs actionable if carried out by an individual

10–03   Although there are older cases,[15] the starting point in explaining this category of wrongs is the case of *Allen v Flood.*[16] A boilermakers' trade union official was held not to be liable for telling his employers that if shipwrights who had been employed to repair woodwork were not dismissed, the union workers would not work. The workers were all employed on a daily basis and were under no obligation to sign on for work the next day, so a strike would not have been unlawful. The employers capitulated and (lawfully) discontinued their employment of the shipwrights. The shipwrights could not sue the employers for breach of the employment contract (as they were also employed on a daily basis) so they attempted to sue the union official, relying upon the fact that he had acted out of malice. In holding that there was no liability the House of Lords acknowledged the distinction between inducing a breach of contract and causing loss by unlawful means.[17]

An example of inducing a breach of contract would be where A, motivated by spite towards C, refuses to contract with B unless B breaches his pre-existing contract with C. Note that A's actions do not need to be unlawful per se. The reason for this is that A's conduct is secondary, or using English law terminology *accessory,* to B's breach of contract. C's immediate remedy would be to sue B for breach of contract, but C may also pursue A as an accessory to the breach of contract for a remedy in delict.

An example of causing loss by unlawful means would be where A threatens B with physical violence should B contract with C, and B capitulates in breaking off negotiations with C. C cannot sue B in contract as no contract was entered into, but may sue A in delict. Here, A's wrong is independent rather than accessory, given that B is not guilty of any wrong.

Thus, it is worth observing that a clear distinction between the two wrongs is that the former involves two wrongdoers: A, the delinquent (a third party in terms of the contract in question) inducing the breach and B, the party to the contract itself who is in breach; and one victim: C, the innocent party to the contract. Whereas the latter involves only one wrongdoer: A, and possibly one victim: C, or probably two: B and C.[18] Equally, it is worth noting one feature that is common across the two variants, viz that both involve three parties.

Inducing breach of contract

10–04   It was apparent from some dicta in *Crofter Hand Woven Harris Tweed Co Ltd v Veitch,*[19] that inducing breach of contract was assumed to be a wrong recognised by the law of delict in Scotland. This was confirmed in *British Motor Trade Association v Gray.*[20] After the Second World War there was a shortage of

---

[15] See in particular *Lumley v Gye* (1853) 2 E&B 216.

[16] *Allen v Flood* [1898] A.C. 1.

[17] *Allen v Flood* [1898] A.C. 1 at 96 per Lord Watson. A debate that suggested these were two sub-categories of the single tort of unlawful interference with trade was firmly rejected by the House of Lords in *OBG Ltd v Allan* [2008] 1 A.C. 1.

[18] The inclusion in *D.C. Thomsons v Deakin* [1952] Ch. 646 of "direct intervention" and "indirect persuasion" as examples of committing the wrong of inducing a breach of contract was thus overruled in *OBG Ltd v Allan* [2008] 1 A.C. 1. The actions may nevertheless be wrongful as causing loss by unlawful means.

[19] *Crofter Hand Woven Harris Tweed Co Ltd v Veitch,* 1942 S.C. (HL) 1. See below at para.10–08.

[20] *British Motor Trade Association v Gray,* 1951 S.C. 586.

motor vehicles. The BMTA was formed, consisting of manufacturers and their distributors. They developed a scheme whereby every purchaser of a new car signed an agreement undertaking not to resell the car within a specified period. It was alleged that the respondent had purchased such vehicles within the specified period knowing full well that a covenant had been executed, i.e. he had induced the original purchaser of the car to break his covenant with BMTA. The court allowed the case to proceed:

> " . . . by the law of Scotland an actionable wrong is committed by one who intentionally and without lawful justification induces or procures someone to break a contract made by him with another, if damage has resulted to that other, provided that the contract creates contractual relations recognised by law."[21]

Lord President Cooper said that although such conduct had never been stated as a delict in the law of Scotland, that was just a coincidence. Cases where people were held liable for enticing employees away from their employers[22] were just examples of this broader principle.

In *OBG Ltd v Allan* the House of Lords took the opportunity authoritatively to review the economic torts in English law, including inducing a breach of contract. The court reiterated the distinction between inducing a breach of contract and causing loss by unlawful means, although their Lordships acknowledged the potential for overlap. Lord Hoffmann emphasised the intentional aspect of the wrong, holding that the wrong would not be committed unless the alleged wrongdoer "targeted" the claimant, knowing that his act would induce a breach of contract, and that the breach was intended either as an end in itself or as a means to an end. It would not be enough for the breach of contract merely to be a foreseeable consequence of the defendant's action.[23]

The analysis provided by the House of Lords in *OBG* was applied in Scotland **10–05** in *Global Resources Group v Mackay*. Lord Hodge suggested that the delict is committed by the defender (A) where, knowing the terms of a contract between a third party (B) and the pursuer (C), induces B, without legal justification, to breach that contract. Lord Hodge identified five elements of the delict[24]:

1. B must actually breach the contract with C.[25] Thus, if the contract between B and C was in any event void, there could be no breach of a non-existent contract and A could not be liable in delict. There must also be a causal link between A's act of inducement and B's breach; if B would in any event have breached the contract with C,[26] again A cannot be liable in delict.
2. A must know that his actions will procure B's breach of contract with C. This is a subjective test: it is not enough that A ought reasonably to

---

[21] *British Motor Trade Association v Gray*, 1951 S.C. 586 at 603 per Lord Russell.

[22] See, e.g. *Belmont Laundry Co Ltd v Aberdeen Steam Laundry Co Ltd* (1898) 1 F. 45.

[23] *OBG Ltd v Allan* [2008] 1 A.C. 1 at 29–31. *Millar v Bassey* [1994] E.M.L.R. 44 was expressly overruled.

[24] *Global Resources Group v Mackay*, 2009 S.L.T. 104 at 106–107.

[25] Interdict will be refused if there is no realistic threat of a breach of contract: see, e.g. *Barratt Resorts Ltd v Barratt Owners' Group* [2002] Scot CS 318.

[26] Or if the contract was voidable and capable of reduction, B would have in any event reduced the contract.

have known that B's breach of contract with C would be induced by A's conduct (indeed an unreasonable misunderstanding will not be enough),[27] although A's "willful turning of a blind eye as to the details of the contract would be sufficient knowledge".[28]

3. A must intend to procure B's breach of contract either as an end in itself or as a means to a further end; it is not sufficient if B's breach of contract is merely a foreseeable result of A's acts. It should be noted that the reason, or motive, for procuring the breach of contract is irrelevant. Thus, even if A's motive in procuring B's breach of contract was to release C from what A perceived to be for C a loss-making contractual obligation, A will nevertheless commit the delict and be liable for reparation.[29]

4. A must actively persuade, encourage or assist B in breaching his contract with C. "Failing to stop a breach is not enough."[30] The means of persuasion directed at B need not be unlawful or detrimental to B's interests.[31] It is important here to distinguish between, on the one hand procuring or inducing of a breach of contract, and on the other obstructing or preventing the performance of a contract.[32] Thus, if A's tactics are not directed at B, but are rather targeted directly at C, the *accessory* nature of the wrong will be missing and the delict of inducing a breach of contract will not be committed.[33] Likewise, if A's tactics are directed at parties who have not (yet) contracted with C, such as at potential customers of C, there will be no delictual liability, at least on this ground.[34]

5. A defence will be available if A can demonstrate a lawful justification for inducing B's breach of contract with C. A defence of avarice may well be morally repugnant, and indeed *advancement* of the defender's own economic interests per se has been held not to provide a justification.[35] However, *protection* of A's economic interests may provide a justification.[36] Thus, the English Court of Appeal has held that the protection of security for the repayment of a loan justified the security holder in procuring the dismissal of the developer's architects as a condition of providing further credit to the developer.[37] An administrator appointed under the Insolvency Act 1986 to an ailing company or Limited Liability Partnership may plead justification if, in

---

[27] See, e.g. *British Industrial Plastics v Ferguson* [1940] 1 All E.R. 479.

[28] *Global Resources Group v Mackay*, 2009 S.L.T. 104 at 106. See also *Rossleigh Ltd v Leader Cars Ltd*, 1987 S.L.T. 355 at 360 per Lord Mayfield.

[29] See, e.g. *South Wales Miners' Federation v Glamorgan Coal Co Ltd* [1905] A.C. 239.

[30] *Calor Gas Ltd v Express Fuels (Scotland) Ltd*, 2008 S.L.T. 123 at 135 per Lord Malcolm.

[31] Although an incentive offered to B may be an offence under the Bribery Act 2010.

[32] The "unified theory" adopted in *DC Thomson & Co Ltd v Deakin* [1952] Ch. 646 was rejected by the House of Lords in *OBG Ltd v Allan* [2008] 1 A.C. 1.

[33] Although preventing the performance of a contract may incur liability for causing loss by unlawful means.

[34] See, e.g. *Middlebrook Mushrooms v Transport & General Workers Union* [1993] I.C.R. 612.

[35] *British Motor Trade Association v Gray*, 1951 S.C. 586 at 600 per Lord President Cooper. See also *Global Resources Group v Mackay*, 2009 S.L.T. 104 at 107 per Lord Hodge.

[36] Protection of other interests may also suffice: see, e.g. *Findlay v Blaylock*, 1937 S.C. 21.

[37] *Edwin Hill & Partners v First National Finance Corp* [1989] 1 W.L.R. 225.

performing his statutory duties, he refuses to perform a contract entered into by the company or LLP.[38]

One question which was not considered by the House of Lords in *OBG*, and has yet authoritatively to be determined, is whether the tort/delict in question is confined to inducing a breach of contract, or whether it extends to procuring breaches of other duties, such as fiduciary or statutory duties.[39] The early generation of cases would seem to support a wider interpretation. For example, in *Allen v Flood* Lord Watson expressed the principle widely:

> "He who willingly induces another person to do an unlawful act which but for his persuasion, would ... never have been committed, is rightly held to be responsible for the wrong he has procured."[40]

However, although in one recent Outer House case[41] Lord Reed did not doubt "that Scots law also imposes a liability upon a third party who participates in a breach of trust or fiduciary duty", he left open whether such liability is derived from the line of cases stretching from *Lumley v Gye*[42] to *Allen v Flood*,[43] or indeed whether the nature of such liability was delictual or derived from the law of trust.

Causing loss by unlawful means

The decision of the House of Lords in *OBG*[44] clarified that causing loss by unlawful means is a distinct tort in English law. This analysis, along with the settling of the name to be applied to the wrong, has been accepted in Scotland.[45] **10–06**

> "The gist of (the wrong) ... is striking at the (pursuer) through a third party, and doing so by interfering with (the pursuer's) freedom of economic activity."[46]

Thus, the classic example of causing loss by unlawful means requires three parties: the defender (A), who by unlawful means directed at a third party (B) causes economic harm to the pursuer (C). Although both Lord Hoffmann in *OBG* and Lord Hodge in *Global Resources* found there to be two main elements to the wrong, as was noted by Lord Glennie in *McLeod v Rooney* there are

> "really three matters which the pursuer has to aver and, in due course, prove. These are:

---

[38] See *Joint Administrators of Rangers Football Club Plc, Noters*, 2012 S.L.T. 599 at 608 per Lord Hodge (obiter).

[39] It is submitted that, for the sake of coherence and consistency, an accessory liability for inducing a breach of statutory duty should only be contemplated where a delictual remedy would, at least in principle, be available for a breach of the statutory duty itself: see Ch.16.

[40] *Allen v Flood* [1898] A.C. 1 at 107.

[41] *Commonwealth Oil and Gas Co Ltd v Baxter* [2007] CSOH 198. Affirmed 2010 S.C. 156.

[42] *Lumley v Gye* (1853) 2 E. & B. 216.

[43] *Allen v Flood* [1898] A.C. 1.

[44] *OBG Ltd v Allan* [2008] 1 A.C. 1.

[45] *Global Resources Group v Mackay*, 2009 S.L.T. 104; *McLeod v Rooney*, 2010 S.L.T. 499.

[46] *Customs and Excise Commissioners v Total Network SL* [2008] 1 A.C. 1174 at 1254–1255 per Lord Walker of Gestingthorpe.

    a. that the defender had the intention to cause economic harm to the
        pursuer;

    b. that the defender acted unlawfully in relation to a third party; and

    c. that such unlawful action affected that third party's freedom to deal
        with the pursuer."[47]

The first element is consistent with the wrong of inducing a breach of contract: economic harm to the pursuer must be *intended* by the defender as either an end in itself or as a means to some further end. It is not sufficient that harm to the pursuer is merely a foreseeable consequence of the defender's actions.[48] Thus, the subcontractor who breaches his contract with the main contractor does not automatically become liable to the employer for the main contractor's consequential breach of contract with the employer—although the subcontractor may become liable if the employer can prove that the subcontractor's motive was to cause economic harm to the employer. Nevertheless, if the defender's purpose in carrying out the unlawful act is to gain an advantage for himself, the pursuer's loss is likely to be the other side of the same coin.[49] Thus, publication of illicitly taken photographs of a private occasion in a "spoiler" edition of a magazine will result in liability if economic harm to the officially appointed photographer/ publisher is the means used to achieve the end, whether the end is promotion of the defender's publication or satisfaction of the readers' appetite for information.[50]

    The second element requires that the defender's action towards the third party be unlawful. The majority in *OBG* agreed with Lord Hoffmann's analysis[51] that unlawfulness requires that the means would have been actionable as a civil wrong[52] by the third party had the third party suffered a loss.[53] It follows that even where the actions directed at the third party amount to a criminal offence, unless the criminal acts are also civil wrongs against the third party, the pursuer will be unable to sue in delict.[54] Thus, the liability to the pursuer may be described as *secondary*: if a threat of delictually wrongful conduct is directed by the defender at the third party this will be in itself a delictual wrong (albeit incomplete)—had the defender actually carried out the threat the wrong would be

---

[47] *McLeod v Rooney*, 2010 S.L.T. 499 at 505

[48] *Global Resources Group v Mackay*, 2009 S.L.T. 104 at 107 per Lord Hodge.

[49] "When the whole object of the defendants' action is to capture the plaintiff's business, their gain must be his loss": *Sorrell v Smith* [1925] A.C. 700 at 742 per Lord Sumner.

[50] *OBG Ltd v Allan* [2008] 1 A.C. 1 at 50–52 per Lord Hoffmann. Nevertheless, *OK!* did not succeed in their action against *Hello!* on this ground as (similarly to *RCA v Pollard*, see fn.56 below) *Hello!*'s wrongful conduct did not impact on the Douglas's ability to deal with *OK!*.

[51] *OBG Ltd v Allan* [2008] 1 A.C. 1 at 32–33 per Lord Hoffmann.

[52] Lord Hoffmann did not set out the range of civil wrongs contemplated. Presumably, a threatened breach of contract will be within the range, but breaches of statutory duty where the relevant statute does not clearly confer a private law remedy must be outside of the range: see Ch.16.

[53] *OBG Ltd v Allan* [2008] 1 A.C. 1 at 32. Lord Nicholls (at 53–57) took a different view: that acts directed at the third party which were wrongful either under the civil or the criminal law would suffice provided they were "instrumental" in achieving the economic loss suffered by the pursuer. Lord Nicholls' view gained some traction in the later House of Lords decision in an unlawful means conspiracy case: *Customs and Excise Commissioners v Total Network SL* [2008] 1 A.C. 1174. However, Lord Hoffmann's analysis survives with regard to causing loss by unlawful means.

[54] It is clear from the speeches in *Customs and Excise Commissioners v Total Network SL* [2008] 1 A.C. 1174 that their Lordships were somewhat uneasy that the definition of unlawful means differs between the respective wrongs of causing loss by unlawful means and unlawful means conspiracy.

completed, and the defender would incur *primary* liability to the third party, since the third party would have suffered harm. Thus, it follows that intimidation of the third party by threatening a delictual wrong is itself a form of unlawful conduct which is sufficient to establish this element of causing loss by unlawful means.[55]

The third element concerns causation and requires that the third party's ability to deal with the pursuer be curtailed as a consequence of the defender's unlawful act. If the unlawful action does not actually impact upon the third party's freedom to deal with the pursuer, the defender will not incur liability. Thus, the record company that owned the rights to exploit recordings made by Elvis Presley was unable to obtain a remedy against a bootlegger who sold unauthorised recordings of Elvis Presley concerts. Although the defendant's acts may have reduced the profits made by the record company, they did not restrict the record company in its dealings with the Presley estate.[56]

Another question left open in *OBG* is whether the law recognises a two-party variant of the wrong, i.e. the pursuer suffers economic harm as a direct result of conduct targeted directly at the pursuer by the defender. If the defender actually commits a delictual wrong, such as an assault, then the harm will be reparable by pursuing a case recognising the wrong for what it is (i.e. in this example for assault). The situation is less clear if the intimidated pursuer suffered harm upon succumbing to threats of wrongful conduct uttered by the defender but never actually carried out, or if the pursuer was the victim of criminal conduct which did not, of itself, sound in damages. There are dicta which acknowledge the possibility of a two-party variant,[57] but as yet there is no authoritative statement from the courts.

Collective economic wrongs: conspiracy

A conspiracy may be defined as an arrangement between two or more persons **10–07** who collude so as to cause some harm to another.[58] A natural question to raise is why would the law of delict distinguish between harm inflicted by an individual acting alone and the same harm inflicted by persons in concert? After all, the object of delictual liability is to provide reparation for the harm, not punishment for the conduct. The question was recently considered in *Customs and Excise Commissioners v Total Network SL*,[59] where Lord Walker, referring to a range of authorities,[60] identified three reasons.[61] First, a group acting in concert may create a more dangerous situation than one individual could on one's own.[62] Secondly, the very fact that the group "gangs-up" to seize collective

---

[55] Previous cases such as *Rookes v Barnard* [1964] A.C. 1129 and *Micosta S.A. v Shetland Islands Council*, 1986 S.L.T. 193 must now be considered overruled insofar as they distinguished intimidation as a discreet delictual wrong.

[56] *RCA Corporation v Pollard* [1983] Ch. 135.

[57] See, e.g. *OBG Ltd v Allan* [2008] 1 A.C. 1 at 35 per Lord Hoffmann; at 57 per Lord Nicholls of Birkenhead.

[58] "The gist of conspiracy is damage intentionally inflicted by persons who combine for that purpose": *Customs and Excise Commissioners v Total Network SL* [2008] 1 A.C. 1174 at 1255 per Lord Walker of Gestingthorpe.

[59] *Customs and Excise Commissioners v Total Network SL* [2008] 1 A.C. 1174.

[60] Including *Mogul Steamship Co Ltd v McGregor Gow & Co* (1889) 23 QBD 598 at 616 per Bowen L.J.; *Lonrho v Shell Petroleum Co Ltd (No. 2)* [1892] A.C. 173 at 189 per Lord Diplock; *Crofter Hand Woven Harris Tweed Co Ltd v Veitch*, 1942 S.C. (HL) 1 at 8 per Viscount Simon L.C.

[61] *Customs and Excise Commissioners v Total Network SL* [2008] 1 A.C. 1174 at 1247.

[62] Lord Walker treated this justification with a degree of scepticism.

power may confirm that the object of the activity is to carry out an unlawful plan.[63] The third reason is quite startling, and may provide evidence to condemn the distinction between unilateral and collective wrongs as out of touch with modern society:

"I suspect that the judges at the end of the 19th century also had a third reason, largely unarticulated but appearing in Lord Macnaghten's dictum about boycotts in *Allen v Flood*, [1898] A.C. 1. That was the deep suspicion which the governing class had, in Georgian and Victorian England, of collective action in the political and economic spheres, as potential threats to the constitution and the framework of society. It is a theme from the Gordon Riots in 1780 to the Land League in Ireland a century later (see *R v Parnell*, (1881) 14 Cox C.C. 508), with the conventions called by the corresponding societies in the 1790s, the Peterloo Massacre in 1819, the Tolpuddle Martyrs in 1834 and the Chartist Movement (1838–1848) and the rise of the trade unions in between."[64]

In today's world of global enterprise, mergers and acquisitions, it is more likely that the large organisation (in law an individual) wields far more power than a collective of small businesses or even a collective of workers from an employer, or even a range of employers, in the form of a trade union.[65] However, that conspiracy survives as a distinct set of delictual or tortuous wrongs was confirmed unanimously by their Lordships in *Total*.

Total also confirmed the existence of two distinct wrongs requiring a conspiracy to injure: lawful means conspiracy (alternatively described as unlawful *object* conspiracy) and unlawful means conspiracy.

An example of lawful means conspiracy may be where a group of business owners agree to boycott a particular supplier of raw materials with the primary motivation of putting that supplier out of business. Problems regarding proof of motive should immediately be obvious. An example of unlawful means conspiracy may be where a group of business owners agree to fix prices in breach of competition law so as to put a competitor out of business.

Lawful means conspiracy

10–08   This variant may also be referred to as "unlawful object conspiracy" or as "conspiracy to injure by lawful means". Where two or more persons conspire collectively to engage in lawful conduct with the predominant purpose of causing harm to another, the harm is reparable in delict. Provided the predominant motive

---

[63] "Now the moment that that is recognised, i.e. that the essence of conspiracy on which civil action is founded is a criminal conspiracy, though of course unless actual damage has followed no civil action will lie, . . . you at once bring in the spirit of the criminal law, where motive or intention—the *mens rea*—is everything": *Sorrell v Smith* [1925] A.C. 700 at 725 per Lord Sumner.

[64] *Customs and Excise Commissioners v Total Network SL* [2008] 1 A.C. 1174 at 1247 per Lord Walker of Gestingthorpe.

[65] See, e.g. *Lonrho Ltd v Shell Petroleum Co Ltd* [1981] 2 All E.R. 456 at 464 per Lord Diplock. Whether a court is prepared to pierce a company's veil of incorporation may depend upon whether the court accepts that the company has been created as a façade: see, e.g. *Adams v Cape Industries Plc* [1990] Ch. 433; *Trustor AB v Smallbone (No. 2)* [2001] 1 W.L.R. 1177. For an international dimension see also *VTB Capital Plc v Nutritek International Corp* [2013] 2 W.L.R. 398.

is to harm the victim, the lawful acts may be aimed at the victim directly ("two-party" variant) or at a third party ("three-party" variant). Here, although the acts are lawful, it is the object that is unlawful. Thus, it is the coalescence of collusion and harmful objective that renders the whole scheme unlawful.

The most significant Scottish case is *Crofter Hand Woven Harris Tweed Co Ltd v Veitch,*[66] a decision of the House of Lords that is now considered to be the leading authority in this area in both Scotland and England. The facts are quite complicated. The Crofter Company marketed cloth woven by the Isle of Lewis crofters using yarn imported from the mainland. Yarn was also spun on the island itself. The island spinners were members of the Transport and General Workers' Union (TGWU). The union tried to get a higher rate of pay for its members who spun yarn on the island. The island employers said they could not afford to pay their members more money; the TGWU ordered its members not to handle the yarn of the mainland producers. The House of Lords held that this conduct was not actionable, but a number of propositions can be taken from it:

1. Lawful means conspiracy consists in a "conspiracy to injure" with a predominant purpose to injure where injury is actually caused even where there are no unlawful means or unlawful acts. This differs from a "set of acts dictated by business interests" which is not actionable.
2. There is nothing unlawful in giving a warning or intimation that if the party addressed pursues a certain course of conduct, others may act in a manner he will not like, so long as nothing unlawful is threatened or done.
3. It is possible for something that would not be actionable if done by one person to be actionable if he conspires to do it with another. This may be anomalous, but it is said to be firmly entrenched in the law.
4. It is not actionable (absent unlawful means) if the predominant motive is not unlawful. It was this last proposition which proved decisive in the *Crofter* case: the union's predominant motive was to advance the members' interests.

Thus, in lawful means conspiracy, it is the object, rather than the method used to achieve the object, that is unlawful. Thus, if the motivation for the defender's conduct has been the acquiring an advantage (economic or otherwise) for himself, rather than the infliction of harm upon the pursuer, the pursuer's case will fail. In other words, if the harm suffered by the pursuer is a consequence (no matter how foreseeable) of the conduct, rather than the prime motivation for the conduct, a case for reparation will fail. While avarice may be condoned, yet malice is condemned.

Unlawful means conspiracy

Unlawful means conspiracy consists in the agreement of two or more persons **10–09** to do an unlawful act, or to do a lawful act by unlawful means, so long as the acts are actually carried out in pursuance of the conspiracy to the damage of the pursuer.

---

[66] *Crofter Hand Woven Harris Tweed Co Ltd v Veitch,* 1942 S.C. (HL) 1. For a review of the case and conspiracy generally see J.M. Thomson, "An Island Legacy—the Delict of Conspiracy" in D.L. Carey-Miller and D.W. Meyers (eds), *Comparative and Historical Essays in Scots Law: A Tribute to Professor Sir Thomas Smith QC* (Edinburgh: Butterworths, 1992), p.137.

A key difference between this variant and lawful means conspiracy is what is required in terms of motive. Although there remains a need for the pursuer to prove *an* intention on the part of the colluding parties that their scheme should harm the pursuer, there is no need to establish that such harm is the *predominant* motive behind the conspiracy. Nevertheless, consistent with the other economic delicts, the conspirators' scheme must at least intend harm to the pursuer as a means to an end, albeit that the intended end may itself be legitimate. However, it will not be sufficient to prove merely that the harm to the pursuer is a foreseeable consequence of the scheme.

What kinds of act will satisfy the unlawful means requirement of this variant? For the sake of coherence it would seem appropriate to apply a definition consistent with that applied in the wrong of causing loss by unlawful means.[67] However, in *Customs and Excise Commissioners v Total Network SL*,[68] the House of Lords unanimously rejected that view, and held that unlawful means in the context of conspiracy incorporates criminal, as well as delictual wrongs. Again, the anomaly may be observed that it is possible for an act (in this case criminal) which would not be actionable in the civil courts if done by one person to be actionable if he conspires to do it with another.

Ultimately, the justification that was put for the distinction was that the classic three-party variant of causing loss by unlawful means, as was considered in *OBG*,[69] involved a notional secondary liability, in the sense that the third party was the immediate target of the (threatened) wrongful conduct, whereas the liability to the pursuer arising out of unlawful means conspiracy is primary since the wrongful conduct is targeted directly at the pursuer.[70]

Their Lordships left open whether other wrongful conduct, such as breach of contract or breach of statutory duty that does not of itself sound in damages, would fall within the definition of unlawful means for the purposes of liability for unlawful means conspiracy.[71]

Trade union immunity

10–10   The Trade Union and Labour Relations (Consolidation) Act 1992, as amended by the Trade Union Reform and Employment Rights Act 1993, confers immunity from liability for conspiracy and for interfering with the performance of, or inducing a breach of, contract. Threats of inducing a breach or interfering with performance of a contract are also covered. The immunity is limited, and does not cover liability for breach of statutory duty (or liability or inducing a breach of statutory duty, if such a delict/tort exists). The immunity only applies if the relevant provisions of the Act are fully complied with. Thus, the otherwise delictual acts must be carried out in contemplation or furtherance of a trade dispute and various statutory requirements related to balloting of members and

---

[67] See above at para.10–06. Unlawful means must involve a civil wrong for the purposes of causing loss by unlawful means—criminal acts (or breaches of statutory duty) directed at a third party do not qualify unless a private law civil remedy for resulting harm is competent: see *OBG Ltd v Allan* [2008] 1 A.C. 1 at 32–33 per Lord Hoffmann.

[68] *Customs and Excise Commissioners v Total Network SL* [2008] 1 A.C. 1174. The case involved a "carousel VAT fraud".

[69] *OBG Ltd v Allan* [2008] 1 A.C. 1.

[70] *Customs and Excise Commissioners v Total Network SL* [2008] 1 A.C. 1174 at 1256 per Lord Walker of Gestingthorpe.

[71] *Customs and Excise Commissioners v Total Network SL* [2008] 1 A.C. 1174 at 1252 per Lord Walker of Gestingthorpe.

formal sanctioning of industrial action must be satisfied. An interdict or injunction to prevent industrial action will be competent if the statutory requirements are not met.[72] A full treatment of the law must be left to textbooks on employment law.

Conclusion on economic wrongs

It is submitted that it is quite appropriate to describe the law on economic **10–11** wrongs as being in a confused state. There is no clear underpinning principle connecting the various examples of economic wrongs and so an attempt to formulate a coherent taxonomy would be to seek an elusive objective. As was stated at the outset, this ad hoc arrangement of distinct wrongs is more consistent with the characteristics of the common law system of England than those of the civilian systems of continental Europe. Drawing on its historic connections with the latter as demonstrated in the works of the institutional writers, the view of many remains that Scots law should continue to aspire to coherence.

However, on this area of the law there is a paucity of guidance to be found in the works of the institutional writers. Stair did consider extortion to be a delict, but may not have had in mind the threat to commit a breach of contract:

> "Extortion signifies the act of force, or other means of fear, whereby a person is compelled to do that which of their proper inclination they would not have done. It doth also imply the obligation of the injurer to the injured, to repair his loss and damage by such acts."[73]

It has been suggested that the concept of malice that is recognised in liability for harm to a pursuer's enjoyment of his property from actions carried out in *aemulationem vicini* might be applied so as to explain liability for unjustified economic harm.[74] This would require acceptance that the doctrine, which derives from the *jus commune* and was described by institutional writers in the context of neighbour/land issues,[75] could be extended to create liability for malicious abuse of a dominant position, i.e. that the malicious infliction of harm would be actionable, even if the conduct complained of is, on the face of it, lawful. A similar line has been taken in the United States.[76] The European Court of Justice has held that not all price competition can be regarded as legitimate and has penalised predatory pricing.[77] A wider view may also be observed in Scottish cases dealing with wrongful occupation of property.[78]

However, it is difficult to anticipate that there remains potential for this area of the law of delict to be rebuilt from first principles, or even for a peculiarly

---

[72] See, e.g. *British Airways Plc v Unite the Union* [2010] I.C.R. 1316.

[73] Stair, I, ix, 8.

[74] T.B. Smith, "Strange Gods: the crisis of Scots law as a Civilian system" in T.B. Smith, *Studies Critical and Comparative* (Edinburgh: W. Green, 1962), p.83.

[75] See D.E.L. Johnston, "Owners and Neighbours: From Rome to Scotland" in *The Civil Law Tradition in Scotland*, edited by R. Evans-Jones (Edinburgh: Stair Society, 1995), Vol.2.

[76] *TuttleBuck* (1909) 119 N.W. 946. But see the comments on the case in T. Weir, *Economic Torts* (Oxford: Clarendon Press, 1997), pp.72–74.

[77] *AKZO Chemie BV v Commission of the European Communities* (C 62/86) [1991] T.L.R. 432.

[78] *Phestos Shipping Co Ltd v Kurmiawen*, 1983 S.C. 165; *Shell UK Ltd v McGillivray*, 1991 S.L.T. 667. These cases dealt with applications for interim interdict and ultimately were decided on the balance of convenience.

Scottish jurisprudence to develop. The post *OBG*[79] and *Total*[80] Scottish cases[81] seem, so far, to have adopted the respective approaches taken by the House of Lords in these decisions.

FRAUD

10–12 Fraud[82] has been defined as a "machination or contrivance to deceive".[83] There is no substantial body of purely delictual cases.[84] Although the most likely consequence of fraud is economic harm, this delict protects the infringement of many different interests. It may, for example, cause someone mental harm[85] or result in their becoming involved in some dangerous escapade.[86] Often it is encountered in commerce. Fraud involves the making of a false representation of fact without belief in its truth, intending that the person to whom it is made should act in reliance thereon, which causes a consequent loss.[87] The onus of proof with regard to the defender's state of mind (mens rea) is upon the pursuer.[88]

The necessary mens rea for fraud was considered by the House of Lords in *Derry v Peek*.[89] The Plymouth Tramways Company issued a prospectus (inviting investment in the company) stating that the company had statutory authority to use steam power instead of horses. The prospectus omitted the fact that the statute required a licence to be granted by the Board of Trade, for which the company had already applied. However, the Board of Trade rejected the application and the company was wound up, but not before the plaintiff had invested in reliance on the statement in the prospectus. However, an action in deceit was ultimately dismissed, Lord Herschell setting out the law:

> "First, in order to sustain an action of deceit, there must be proof of fraud, and nothing short of that will suffice. Secondly, fraud is proved when it is shewn that a false representation has been made (1) knowingly, or (2) without belief in its truth, or (3) recklessly, careless whether it be true or false. Although I have treated the second and third as distinct cases, I think the third is but an instance of the second, for one who makes a statement under such circumstances can have no real belief in the truth of what he states. To prevent a false statement being fraudulent, there must, I think,

---

[79] *OBG Ltd v Allan* [2008] 1 A.C. 1.

[80] *Customs and Excise Commissioners v Total Network SL*, [2008] 1 A.C. 1174.

[81] In particular: *Global Resources Group v Mackay*, 2009 S.L.T. 104; *McLeod v Rooney*, 2010 S.L.T. 499.

[82] English law recognises the similar tort of deceit.

[83] Erskine, III, i, 16.

[84] Although there is a longer history in connection with bankruptcy: K. McK. Norrie, "The Intentional Delicts" in K. Reid and R. Zimmermann (eds), *A History of Private Law in Scotland* (Oxford: Oxford University Press, 2000), Vol.II: Obligations, p.495.

[85] *Wilkinson v Downton* [1897] 2 Q.B. 57.

[86] See *Burrows v Rhodes* [1899] 1 Q.B. 816, which arose from the Jameson raid. Sir Leander Starr Jameson led a raid against the Transvaal to support rebels (mainly British) to advance Cecil Rhodes' colonial ambitions. Jameson was captured and handed over to the British. The reasoning might be a little coloured by the circumstances.

[87] See generally: *Boyd & Forrest Glasgow & South-Western Ry*, 1912 S.C. (HL) 93.

[88] See, e.g. *Milne v Gray*, 2008 S.C.L.R. 558; *Zurich GSG Ltd v Gray & Kellas (A Firm)*, 2007 S.L.T. 917.

[89] *Derry v Peek* (1889) 14 App. Cas. 337.

always be an honest belief in its truth. And this probably covers the whole ground, for one who knowingly alleges that which is false, has obviously no such honest belief. Thirdly, if fraud be proved, the motive of the person guilty of it is immaterial. It matters not that there was no intention to cheat or injure the person to whom the statement was made."[90]

Where fraud is encountered it is most likely to be in connection with contracts—the fraud inducing a contract either with the person perpetrating the fraud or with another party. Damages are recoverable whether or not the contract can be rescinded, emphasising the independent nature of the delict.[91] Fraud can be carried out in an infinite number of ways, and in particular it is possible to commit the delict without words, but to do so by actions or deeds. An example is *Hillcrest Homecare Services v Tartan Home Care Ltd.*[92] The pursuers alleged that the defenders had induced them to purchase a nursing home by arranging a tour of the premises in such a way that they and their surveyor were fooled into thinking there were more occupants than actually there were![93]

An illustration of the technical nature of the wrong can be seen in *H & J.M. Bennett (Potatoes) v Secretary of State for Scotland.*[94] The government department provided a certificate saying that certain potatoes were found or believed by the inspector to be free from potato cyst eelworm. The potatoes were sold by the pursuers to buyers not parties to the action, who rejected the goods because they were infected. The tests carried out could not have determined whether the problem existed or not. At the very least, this was an example of negligence, but the law on reparation for negligence makes it difficult to recover pure economic loss. In this case, by making the statement there had been an intentional act. Taking into account the wide definition of fraud, and in particular the third element of Lord Herschell's definition (that motive is irrelevant), the official was "guilty" of fraud because he knew the certificate was not stating the true position, albeit another technical person might have read the certificate in a less stringent fashion. There was no need to establish an intention to cheat.

It is not uncommon for a fraudster to use a separate legal entity (usually a **10–13** company) as a vehicle to perpetrate the fraud. Whether the fraudster's mens rea is imputed to the company (or partnership) as a legal person (so as to make the company/firm liable) will depend upon several factors: including the size and structure of the legal entity; the predominant purpose in establishing the legal entity; and the knowledge of other persons associated with the management of the legal entity. Thus, where the sole owner of a "one-man" company deliberately set up the company as a vehicle for a fraud, the court imputed the

---

[90] *Derry v Peek* (1889) 14 App. Cas. 337 at 374 per Lord Herschell. See also *Cramaso LLP v Viscount Reidhaven's Trustees* [2010] CSOH 62; 2010 G.W.D. 20–403.

[91] *Thin & Sinclair v Arrol* (1896) 24 R. 198; and see *Post Office v Morton*, 1992 G.W.D. 26–1492.

[92] *Hillcrest Homecare Services v Tartan Home Care Ltd*, 1996 G.W.D. 4–215.

[93] Perhaps influenced by the "Great Salad Oil Swindle". Businessman Tino De Angelis negotiated millions of dollars in loans from American Express based on his company's inventory of salad oil. American Express inspectors were fooled into thinking tanks were full of oil, when in fact the tanks were filled mostly with water: a thin layer of oil floating on top. To add insult to injury, employees would pump the contents of one tank in to another as inspectors toured the site! Norman C. Miller, *The Great Salad Oil Swindle* (New York: Coward McCann, 1965).

[94] *H & J.M. Bennett (Potatoes) v Secretary of State for Scotland*, 1986 S.L.T. 665. Reversed on appeal on different grounds: 1990 S.C. (HL) 27.

mens rea of the sole owner to the company.[95] However, the court may distinguish between imputation of *knowledge* as such from imputation of *intention* where, for example, one partner in a firm attempts to use the firm in the perpetration of a fraud.[96]

Furthermore, discovering that one's client is engaged in a fraud may impose a positive obligation on a professional person to disassociate oneself from the client's fraud and to warn the victim of the fraud. Failure to do so may result in the professional being deemed an accessory to the fraud and incurring liability to the victim.[97] Failure to appreciate that one's client is engaged in perpetrating a fraud may amount to professional negligence.[98]

Since the policy of the law is to discourage dishonesty, the rules on causation and remoteness of damage are, for the pursuer, more liberal than they are in the law on negligence. Thus, the "but for" test in causation is less stringently applied, and it is enough that the fraud was a factor in persuading the pursuer to act as he did, even where the pursuer may well have acted that way anyway,[99] or indeed where his decision was influenced by his own mistake.[100]

Losses which are attributable to what the pursuer did under the influence of the fraud are recoverable even if they are not reasonably foreseeable, provided that they flow directly from the tainted transaction. Thus, if the pursuer's losses are exacerbated by an unforeseeable fall in the market value of the commodity that the pursuer has been persuaded to purchase, the pursuer will be entitled to recover to the full extent of his loss, subject to a rule that the pursuer must take reasonable steps to mitigate his losses.[101]

It follows from the law's policy of outlawing fraud that consent cannot provide a defence. Nor should volenti non fit injuria, and indeed it has been held that since the common law does not recognise the defence of contributory negligence to fraud, apportionment of damages under the Law Reform (Contributory Negligence) Act 1945 is incompetent.[102] Any exemption clause attempting to exclude liability for fraud will also be contrary to public policy and void. Consistently with this principle, ex turpi causa non oritur actio may be used as a defence when sued in negligence by a fraudster.[103]

PASSING OFF

10–14 The delict of passing off is difficult to classify. It has been viewed as a sub-species of fraud, although such a view does not take into account that passing off is not a delict that requires proof of an intention. The function of the delict of

---

[95] *Stone & Rolls Ltd (In Liquidation) v Moore Stephens (A Firm)* [2009] 1 A.C. 1391.

[96] *Zurich GSG Ltd v Gray & Kellas (A Firm)*, 2007 S.L.T. 917.

[97] *Frank Houlgate Investment Co Ltd v Biggart Baillie LLP*, 2013 S.L.T. 993.

[98] *Stone & Rolls Ltd (In Liquidation) v Moore Stephens (A Firm)* [2009] 1 A.C. 1391.

[99] *Smith New Court Securities Ltd v Scrimgeour Vickers (Asset Management) Ltd* [1997] A.C. 254. Cf. the position in *negligent* misrepresentation: *South Australia Asset Management Corp v York Montague Ltd* sub nom. *Banque Bruxelles Lambert SA v Eagle Star Insurance Co Ltd* [1997] A.C. 191.

[100] *Edgington v Fitzmaurice* (1885) 29 Ch. D. 459.

[101] *Barry v Sutherland*, 2002 S.L.T. 413 at 417 per Lord Eassie. See also *Smith New Court Securities Ltd v Scrimgeour Vickers (Asset Management) Ltd* [1997] A.C. 254 at 265–266 per Lord Browne-Wilkinson; *Doyle v Olby (Ironmongers) Ltd* [1969] 2 Q.B. 158.

[102] *Standard Chartered Bank v Pakistan National Shipping Corp (No.2)* [2003] 1 A.C. 959.

[103] *Stone & Rolls Ltd (In Liquidation) v Moore Stephens (A Firm)* [2009] 1 A.C. 1391.

passing off is to protect "goodwill", but is goodwill a property right, i.e. an asset, or must it be expressed as an economic value? Thus, whether passing off should be classified as a delict pertaining to property or as an economic delict is an open question. Another angle is to consider goodwill as an aspect of reputation, and in that context it arguably might be considered alongside verbal injury generally or slander to goods in particular.[104]

Nevertheless, this well-recognised and often-utilised delict can be used to obtain an interdict or damages or both where one party has represented his goods or services as being those of another in a way calculated to deceive the public, divert custom and cause loss of business to the other. Sometimes, as we shall see, this element of calculating to deceive will easily be inferred from the circumstances. It can result in damages or a restitutionary remedy for the wrong of an account of profits.[105] Passing off may provide a parallel or alternative to statutory remedies under the Trade Marks Act 1994, although it should be noted that passing off cannot be used per se to create or enforce a monopoly in a market.[106] Although most of the authorities deal with direct examples of passing off, it has recently been accepted that what might be described as "indirect" passing off is actionable.[107]

Although the authorities are not completely clear on the matter, it is submitted that there are three essential elements to the delict:

- misrepresentation (by the defender);
- confusion (in persons intending to deal with the pursuer); and
- harm (to goodwill enjoyed by the pursuer).

The *misrepresentation* need not be intentional but it must be shown that the defender acted in a way that would be likely to lead to confusion in persons who intended to deal with the pursuer. Put another way, the defender's actions must, on an objective view, at least have the potential to be causative of confusion in the market place with regard to the provenance of goods or services provided by the defender and/or the pursuer.

The defender's acts must be likely to lead to *confusion* in the market place. The classic example is where the defender places a product in the marketplace in such a way that customers believe it is a product associated with the pursuer's business. Thus, if a manufacturer develops a unique product—such as lemon juice contained within a plastic bottle shaped and coloured to mimic a lemon[108]—which, due to the distinctiveness of its "get-up" becomes wholly

---

[104] "While it is injurious falsehood for a defendant to claim your goods are his, it is passing off for him to claim that his goods are yours": John G. Fleming, *The Law of Torts*, 8th edn (Sydney: The Law Book Company, 1992), p.714. "Injurious falsehood" may broadly be equiparated with verbal injury in Scotland: see paras 7–40 to 7–41 below.

[105] It has been held that a pursuer must claim either an account of profits or damages: *Treadwell's Drifters Inc v RCL Ltd*, 1996 S.L.T. 1048 (decided in 1993).

[106] Although threats of litigation from wealthy businesses may be used to force less wealthy traders to capitulate.

[107] See, e.g. *Clark v Associated Newspapers Ltd* [1998] 1 W.L.R. 1558; *Irvine v Talksport Ltd* [2003] 2 All E.R. 881.

[108] *Reckitt & Colman Products Ltd v Borden Inc* [1990] 1 W.L.R. 491 (the "Jif Lemon" case).

associated by customers with that manufacturer, if another manufacturer adopts a similar "get-up" in marketing a similar product, customers are likely to be confused as to the provenance of the new product, believing it is manufactured by the pursuer when it is in fact manufactured by the defender. Factors which may mitigate the likelihood of confusion include the use of different trading names,[109] differing geographical areas of distribution or operation[110] and the distinctiveness of the products or services.[111]

10–15   *Harm* to the defender's goodwill must be demonstrated as a likely consequence of the defender's acts to justify an interdict, and must be proved to have been caused by the defender's acts to justify an award of damages. The natural objective of an action in passing off is an interdict to prohibit the defender carrying out or continuing the acts complained of. Application for interim interdict is common, and in such cases the court will determine whether or not to grant interim interdict on the balance of convenience.

In *Haig v Forth Blending Co*[112] the court reviewed the existing authorities and provided a useful set of propositions applicable to these cases.

1. It is not permissible to sell goods in such a way that the public may be confused into thinking that the goods are those of the complainer.
2. A trader must show that his goods are recognised by the public or a particular section of it and that any name, mark or get-up is associated in their minds with his goods alone.
3. The trader must show a likelihood of confusion although he need not actually show that any particular member of the public has been confused—certainly where the remedy sought is interdict.
4. There is no right of property in any name, mark or get-up: the essence of the delict is the defender's attempt to appropriate the pursuer's goodwill.
5. "Get-up" includes design, labels and generally the way the thing is packaged for the public—a special design of a useful part of an article may form part of the get-up.
6. In considering whether the public has been deceived, a member of the public is "a person of reasonable apprehension and proper eyesight."
7. A bottle may be part of the get-up and it may be associated with a single trader.
8. If the goods of a trader have, from a peculiar mark or get-up, become known by a particular name, the adoption by another of any mark or get-up which will cause his goods to attain the same name is actionable.

---

[109] *Salon Services (Hairdressing Supplies) Ltd v Direct Salon Services Ltd*, 1988 S.L.T. 414. Cf. *International House of Heraldry v Grant*, 1992 S.L.T. 1021.

[110] *Dunlop Pneumatic Tyre Co Ltd v Dunlop Motor Co Ltd*, 1907 S.C. (HL) 15. Cf. *William Grant & Sons Ltd v Glen Catrine Bonded Warehouse Ltd*, 1999 G.W.D. 15–714.

[111] See, e.g. *The Scottish Union and National Insurance Co v The Scottish National Insurance Co Ltd*, 1909 S.C. 318; *Stringfellow v McCain Foods (GB) Ltd* (1984) R.P.C. 501. Cf. *Lego Systems A/S v Lego M Lemelstrich Ltd* [1983] F.S.R. 155; *Gleneagles Hotels Ltd v Quillco 100 Ltd*, 2003 S.L.T. 812.

[112] *Haig v Forth Blending Co*, 1954 S.C. 35.

9. An innocent manufacturer may have to answer for a dishonest retailer if the manufacturer provides a weapon for the dishonest retailer.
10. Even if there is no intention to deceive on the part of a retailer, he may be interdicted if the public are being misled.

The *Haig* case was an action by a whisky company against blenders and retailers. The complainers were trying to prohibit the use of a bottle of triangular shape similar to one they had used for a long time. There was material before the court that indicated that barmen and customers were confused, thinking that the defenders' product was the complainer's "Dimple". Interdict was granted.

A more recent statement of the nature of the delict in the House of Lords casts some doubt on the possibility of an innocent trader being held liable and tries to focus less on the appropriation of goodwill and more on the elements of loss and misrepresentation. It constitutes an attempt to find a broader principle behind the rules of passing off. In doing so, it admits of the possibility of an expansion of the rules. Lord Diplock, in *Erven Warnink v Townend*,[113] indicated that the following five elements would have to be present to support an action:

1. a misrepresentation[114];
2. made by a trader in the course of a trade;
3. to prospective customers of his or ultimate consumers of goods and services supplied by him;
4. which is calculated to injure the business or goodwill of another trader (in the sense that this is a reasonably foreseeable consequence); and
5. which causes actual damage to the business or goodwill of the trader by whom the action is brought, or which will probably do so.

Thus it is not even permissible to use one's own name in trade if used **10–16** fraudulently or to create avoidable confusion.[115] Interdict might be available if it can be shown that one's own name has attached to some particular product.[116] It is usually permissible to use a word or name that is part of the English language for a product and so it is essential for the complainer to show that any word has become associated with his product alone.[117] For this reason, a trader is well advised to register any new word he or she has invented under the Trade Marks Act 1994 (as amended). If this is not done there is a danger that a concocted word may lose its distinctiveness, becoming by enthusiastic marketing a generic term for products of that kind.[118] Browsing through the *Concise Oxford Dictionary of*

---

[113] *Erven Warnink v Townend* [1979] A.C. 731.

[114] It has been held in Scotland following this authority that a mere misrepresentation is not sufficient: *Treadwell's Drifters Inc v RCL Ltd*, 1996 S.L.T. 1048 (decided in 1993).

[115] *Baume & Co Ltd v Moore* [1958] Ch. 907; *O'Briens v Watts*, 1987 S.L.T. 101. Cf. *HFC Bank Plc v HSBC Bank Plc* [2000] F.S.R. 176.

[116] *Parker-Knoll Ltd v Knoll International Ltd* [1962] R.P.C. 265. See E. Clive, "Goods by Any Other Name", 1963 S.L.T. (News) 106.

[117] See, e.g. *Cellular Clothing Co Ltd v Maxton & Murray* (1899) 1 F. (HL) 29; *Aerators Ltd v Tollitt* [1902] 2 Ch. 319; *British Vacuum Cleaner Co Ltd v New Vacuum Cleaner Co Ltd* [1907] 2 Ch. 312. Cf. *Reddaway v Banham* [1896] A.C. 199.

[118] A process known as "genericide".

Current English (9th edn) one can find "Sellotape: transparent cellulose or plastic tape" and "Hoover: a vacuum cleaner", showing this process in action.[119]

Cases tend to turn on different issues and to an extent the principles set out in the *Haig* case are not exhaustive. In deciding whether there is a likelihood of confusion, the market in which the parties operate is usually important.[120] The geography of the market may be an important factor. Thus, in the case of the *Dunlop Pneumatic Tyre Co Ltd v Dunlop Motor Co Ltd*,[121] although both companies had similar names, it was held that the citizens of Kilmarnock were unlikely to be confused between the pursuers, the Dunlop tyre company from England, and the defenders, a family business in Kilmarnock. In any event, the sort of work carried out by the two companies was, in the main, different. That the market sector is quite often crucial can be seen from the case of *Scottish Milk Marketing Board v Drybrough & Co Ltd*,[122] where the pursuers, who had sold butter under the name "Scottish Pride" for some considerable time, tried to prevent the defenders from selling a lager by the same name. They were unsuccessful on the basis that confusion was unlikely to result. They were also unsuccessful in a slightly more subtle argument. The dairy company had been sponsoring sporting events to associate, in the public mind, their product with health. They complained that the defenders' actions would damage that advertising. This did not seem to carry much weight at the interim hearing.

Where the market area is narrow, confusion is much more likely, as where the International House of Heraldry were able to restrain the use of "International Art of Heraldry".[123] In *Dash Ltd v Philip King Tailoring*,[124] it was argued that the confusion that was said to exist in the case was only such as to amount to the possibility of confusion, whereas the *Haig* case required a likelihood of confusion. Lord McDonald, giving the opinion of the court, stated that the *Haig* case dealt with the similarity of goods rather than names. The court did, however, consider that in the case before it, if the test were likelihood, it had been met. There seems to be no reason why the principles expounded in *Haig* should not apply to names as much as get-up—the test should be the same whether a trader

---

[119] Although it is equally interesting to note that among much erudite philological information in the introduction to the dictionary the following also appears: "This dictionary includes some words which have, or are asserted to have, proprietary status as trade marks or otherwise. Their inclusion does not imply that they have acquired for legal purposes a non-proprietary or general significance, nor any other judgement concerning their legal status. In cases where the editorial staff have some evidence that a word has proprietary status this is indicated in the entry for that word by the abbreviation propr., but no judgement concerning the legal status of such words is made or implied thereby." Both "Sellotape" and "Hoover" are so marked. See *Re Gramophone Co's Application* [1910] Ch. 423. Further researches reveal the position to be even more interesting. It transpires that "Proprietary terms are of more than usual concern to lexicographers since such terms are often the subjects of protracted correspondence or even threatened litigation": R.W. Burchfield, "Controversial Vocabulary in the Oxford English Dictionary" in R.W. Burchfield, *Unlocking the English Language* (London: Faber, 1989), p.96. His further exposition indicates that passing-off would be unlikely to be successful against a dictionary as the publisher is not trying to sell the product. It is the use of dictionaries by Trade Marks registrars and the like that gives the proprietor of a mark an interest in the publication of the word with a lower case first letter indicating generic use.

[120] J. Phillips and A. Coleman, "Passing Off and the Common Field of Activity" (1985) 101 L.Q.R. 242.

[121] *Dunlop Pneumatic Tyre Co Ltd v Dunlop Motor Co Ltd*, 1907 S.C. (HL) 15.

[122] *Scottish Milk Marketing Board v Drybrough & Co Ltd*, 1985 S.L.T. 253. Cf. *Ewing v Buttercup Margarine Co Ltd* [1917] 2 Ch. 1.

[123] *International House of Heraldry v Grant*, 1992 S.L.T. 1021.

[124] *Dash Ltd v Philip King Tailoring*, 1988 S.C. 87.

obtains another's sale by using a name or a get-up. "Likelihood", it is submitted, is still the better verbal formulation [125]

The delict has widened in that the pursuer is permitted to claim in circum- **10–17** stances where the defender, rather than actually pretending to sell someone's goods, pretends that his goods are in some way the same as the pursuer's or by his actions tries to appropriate exclusiveness and style. The Scottish case of *John Walker & Sons Ltd v Henry Ost & Co Ltd*[126] supports this broader view in that the court accepted that a producer was entitled to protect his product from sales of non-Scotch whisky on the basis that there would be damage to his sales where someone tasted the inferior product and decided not to try the real thing. This case need not be restricted to mere geographic appropriation, but applies to the whole image of a product.[127]

So far as whisky itself is concerned, there is a definition of the drink in European Law.[128] It has been held in *Scottish Whisky Association v Glen Kella Distillers*[129] that this regulation was intended not only to protect the public, but also producers who would have title to sue for injunction for breach of the regulation. An injunction was granted where the defendants sold "white whisky". It was produced by re-distilling ordinary whisky. It had not been re-matured after distillation. It would thus constitute passing off, commencing an insidious process of erosion of the integrity and aura of true whisky. The regulation was founded upon, again in protection of Scotch Whisky in *Matthew Gloag and Son Ltd v Welsh Distillers Ltd*.[130] The defendants sold a Welsh whisky called "Swyn y mor" with a big red dragon on the bottle. It said:

> "Welsh whisky … is a spirit unique in taste and origin—a superb blend of malt and grain whiskies blended and bottled by the Welsh Whisky Co. Brecon, Wales, UK, Product of Wales, UK, Blended in the Principality for the world to enjoy."

It was not in dispute that the contents were Scotch whisky. It was held that this was extended passing off on the basis of *Erven Warnick*[131] and *Bristol Conservatories Ltd v Conservatories Custom Built Ltd*.[132] It was accepted that there had been a breach of the European regulation but it was argued that only consumers had a right of action under the regulation. On the basis of *Glen Kella*[133] and *Scotch Whisky Association v J.D. Vintners*,[134] Laddie J. found for the Scottish Whisky companies.

---

[125] And see *John Walker & Sons v Douglas Laing & Co Ltd*, 1993 S.L.T. 156 in which likelihood as opposed to probability was considered sufficient in breach of interdict proceedings. This case, although reported in 1993, was decided in 1976.

[126] *John Walker & Sons Ltd v Henry Ost & Co Ltd* [1970] 1 W.L.R. 917; and see also *J Bollinger SA v Costa Brava Wine Co Ltd* [1960] Ch. 262; *Lang Brothers v Goldwell*, 1980 S.C. 237.

[127] See H.L. MacQueen, "Wee McGlen and the Action of Passing Off", 1982 S.L.T. (News) 225; H.L. MacQueen, "The Wee McGlen case: Representations of Scottishness—Passing off and Unfair Trading" (1983) 5 E.I.P. R. 18. See the cover of W.J. Stewart, *A Casebook on Delict*, 2nd edn (Edinburgh: W. Green, 1997) for the Wee McGlen bottle and generally, W. Stewart, "The Law of Passing-Off—A Scottish Perspective" (1983) 5 E.I.P.R. 64.

[128] Regulation 1576/89 [1989] O.J. L160/1.

[129] *Scottish Whisky Association v Glen Kella Distillers* [1997] Eu. L.R. 455.

[130] *Matthew Gloag and Son Ltd v Welsh Distillers Ltd* [1998] 2 C.M.L.R. 203.

[131] *Erven Warnick B.V. v J Townend & Sons (Hull) Ltd* [1979] A.C. 731.

[132] *Bristol Conservatories Ltd v Conservatories Custom Built Ltd* [1989] R.P.C. 455.

[133] *Scotch Whisky Association v Glen Kella Distillers Ltd* [1997] Eu. L.R. 455.

[134] *Scotch Whisky Association v J.D. Vintners* [1997] Eu. L.R. 446.

Attempts can be made to use passing off as a way of protecting intangible "rights".[135] In *Clark v Associated Newspapers*,[136] the late politician and author, Alan Clark, who enjoyed a somewhat scandalous reputation, used passing off to obtain an injunction to prevent the *London Evening Standard* from continuing to publish the "spoof" Alan Clark's Secret Diaries, which were authored by an employee of the newspaper and intended to parody Mr Clark's own writings. A clearer example of indirect passing off may be found in *Irvine v Talksport Ltd*,[137] where the former racing driver, Eddie Irvine, was successful in using passing off effectively to enforce a form of image right. The defendants, without Mr Irvine's permission, had used a photograph of the sportsman holding a radio in advertising their radio station. The defendant's logo had been superimposed onto the photograph. The Court of Appeal in England agreed that an action for passing off could be based on a false product endorsement and awarded damages to reflect the fee that Mr Irvine would have charged had he been contracted to endorse the defendant's product.

HARBOURING EMPLOYEES

10–18 It is a wrong for an employer to employ a worker when he knows that the worker is already under contract to another. In *Rose Street Foundry and Engineering Company Ltd v John Lewis & Sons Ltd*, the Inner House reviewed the authorities in relation to this wrong. The pursuers sued their former employee Clark and his subsequent employers, the defenders. Interestingly, the defenders complained that Clark had previously worked for them but had been induced by the pursuers to leave. When the matter came before the court, the inducement issue was not live. The Lord Justice-Clerk (Scott-Dickson) reviewed and stated the law which is accurate today albeit there do not appear to be any reported Scottish cases:

> "I hold that the facts that A., knowing that B. is under a contract of service with C., takes B. into his service or continues to employ him during part of the period embraced in said contract and while C. desires implement thereof constitute 'harbouring', and a legal wrong against the original employer."[138]

WRONGFUL REFUSAL TO CONTRACT

10–19 Usually it is not a delict to refuse to contract. But for a long time it has been recognised that persons in certain occupations were compelled to contract, namely the carrier of goods and the innkeeper. An innkeeper, for example, must provide accommodation, food and drink unless: (a) no security for the bill is proffered if requested; (b) the "guest" is accompanied by an animal causing alarm to other guests; (c) the complainer is not actually on a journey; (d) the

---

135 See, e.g. P. Russell, "The Commercial Exploitation of Fictitious Names" (1980) 130 N.L.J. 256; C. Waelde, "Wet? Wet?—a little mystery unresolved", 1996 S.L.T. (News) 1.

136 *Clark v Associated Newspapers* [1998] 1 W.L.R. 1558.

137 *Irvine v Talksport Ltd* [2003] 2 All E.R. 881.

138 *Rose Street Foundry and Engineering Company Ltd v John Lewis and Sons Ltd*, 1917 S.C. 341 at 348, relying, inter alia, on *Lumley v Gye* (1853) 2 E. & B. 216 and *Dickson v Taylor* (1816) 1 Mur 141.

traveller refuses to pay or is of undesirable character; or (e) there is no available accommodation.[139] The rules relating to carriers are now usually considered as part of the law relating to carriage of goods.[140] It has been suggested that this delict "should be kept apart from the economic torts as they develop."[141]

ABUSE OF PROCESS

The incorporation of abuse of process into this chapter may seem incongruous. **10–20** It might well be placed in a chapter dealing with wrongs to personality rights, given the indignity likely to be suffered by the victim dragged into the courts without any good reason, or in a chapter on wrongs to property rights, given that the right to pursue litigation is often described as an asset. However, the most obvious harm risked or encountered in defending malicious or vexatious litigation will be to the victim's economic resources—it will cost the victim money to defend or to lose.

Abuse of process may occur in many ways. Examples include:

- pursuing a claim or presenting a defence in bad faith and with no genuine belief in its merits[142];
- by fraudulent means[143];
- for an improper ulterior motive such as that of publicly denouncing the other party.

Most cases that arise are of wrongful diligence where it is said someone has tried to enforce a decree against the wrong person or against the "right" person for the wrong debt.

Abuse of process is a rarely encountered wrong for obvious reasons—solicitors, advocates, sheriff officers, messengers at arms and prosecutors are educated, trained and ethical. The court has an inherent jurisdiction in civil proceedings to strike out a claim or counterclaim which is challenged as an abuse of process.[144] A petition may be brought by the Lord Advocate to prohibit any person who has habitually and persistently instituted vexatious legal proceedings without any reasonable ground for instituting such proceedings from instituting further proceedings without leave of the court.[145]

---

[139] See *Rothfield v North British Ry*, 1920 S.C. 805.

[140] See *Gloag and Henderson: The Law of Scotland*, edited by Lord Eassie and H.L. MacQueen, 13th edn (Edinburgh: W. Green, 2012), Chs 21, 22 and 23.

[141] H. Carty, "Intentional Violation of Economic Interests: the Limits of Common Law Liability" (1988) 104 L.Q.R. 242 at 284. H. Carty, *An analysis of the Economic Torts* (Oxford: Oxford University Press, 2001).

[142] See, e.g. *Lonrho Plc v Al-Fayed (No.2)* [1992] 1 W.L.R. 1.

[143] See, e.g. *Levison v Jewish Chronicle*, 1924 S.L.T. 755.

[144] See, e.g. *Shetland Sea Farms Ltd v Assuranceforeningen Skuld*, 2004 S.L.T. 30 at [143] per Lord Gill; *McKie v MacRae*, 2006 S.L.T. 43; *Tonner v Reiach & Hall (A Firm)*, 2008 S.C. 1. See also *Moore v Scottish Daily Record*, 2009 S.C. 179; *Hepburn v Royal Alexandra Hospital NHS Trust*, 2011 S.C. 20. Dismissal of a claim due to delay is now dealt with by r.21A of the Rules of the Court of Session (Act of Sederunt (Rules of the Court of Session 1994) 1994 (SI 1994/1443)). See, e.g. *Abrahm v British International Helicopters Ltd* [2014] CSIH 53.

[145] See, e.g. *Lord Advocate v Duff* [2013] CSIH 50; 2013 G.W.D. 22–428; *Lord Advocate v McNamara*, 2009 S.C. 598.

Civil litigation

10–21   In civil litigation, the only penalty for failure in an action is generally an award of expenses as taxed.[146] Generally, a party having title and interest to oppose can oppose any proceedings he wishes subject only to an award of expenses being made against him.[147] In civil cases, two early cases suggest that clear evidence of malice and want of probable cause is required.[148] Using process moderately and in good faith results in no liability and so there must be an averment of malice and want of probable cause.[149] The basic rule applies:

> "Where a person acts in the exercise of a legal right and in the ordinary use of legal forms of procedure, and where it is said that he has abused that right, the law holds that malice or an intention to injure must be proved, and also that it must be shewn that he had no probable cause for what he did."[150]

In relation to the use of diligence (enforcement), the creditor is always liable even although he has employed independent contractors.[151] No one is liable for enforcing an *ex facie* regular decree.[152] An incompetent warrant does not protect the creditor.[153] It is wrongful to do diligence when it has been agreed to delay such.[154] If the creditor has exaggerated the sum, he and neither the agent nor the messenger is liable.[155]

It is accepted that there is a distinction to be made between diligence done as of right, in which malice and want of probable cause must be shown and other cases, such as interdict where the creditor requires to make a representation to the court to obtain the order.

Crime

10–22   In criminal matters it has long been settled that a public prosecutor can only be liable on proof of malice and want of probable cause. It is a prerequisite that the pursuer has been acquitted of the charge or the charge has been abandoned against him.[156] It is not possible by seeking reparation to review a decision of the High Court of Justiciary.[157]

---

[146] *Kennedy v Police Commissioners of Fort William* (1877) 5 R. 302 per Lord Gifford at 307: "The costs of suit are the damages for bringing a groundless claim."

[147] *Gordon v Royal Bank* (1826) 5 S. 164; *Walker v Gemmill* (1846) 8 D. 838.

[148] *Somerville v Thomson*, May 19, 1815, F.C.; 6 Pat. App. 393; *Cleland v Lawrie* (1848) 10 D. 1372.

[149] *Kinnes v Adam* (1882) 9 R. 698 at 702 per Lord President Inglis. This claim was founded on a sequestration which had been recalled on purely technical grounds.

[150] *Henning v Hewetson* (1852) 14 D. 487 at 488 per Lord Justice-Clerk Hope.

[151] *Anderson v Ormiston and Lorain* (1750) Mor. 13949.

[152] *Aitken v Finlay* (1837) 15 S. 683.

[153] *Bell v Gunn* (1859) 21 D. 1008; *Ormiston v Redpath Brown & Co* (1866) 4 M. 488. A case of wrongful diligence was dismissed as recently as 2002 where the diligence was done on the basis of a valid decree from a competent court: *Brougham v Royal Bank of Scotland*, 2002 G.W.D. 13–449.

[154] *Cameron v Mortimer* (1872) 10 M. 817.

[155] *Henderson v Rollo* (1871) 10 M. 104.

[156] The pursuer in *Downie v Chief Constable of Strathclyde Police*, 1998 S.L.T. 8 had been acquitted of charges of charges of breach of the peace and a contravention of s.41(1) of the Police (Scotland) Act 1967. It was admitted this was a malicious prosecution and damages awarded at £1,500 under this head.

[157] *Moore v Secretary of State for Scotland*, 1985 S.L.T. 38. See also *Wright v Paton Farrell*, 2006 S.C. 404.

SECTION III: NEGLIGENCE

A BASIC LIABILITY FOR NEGLIGENCE FLOWCHART

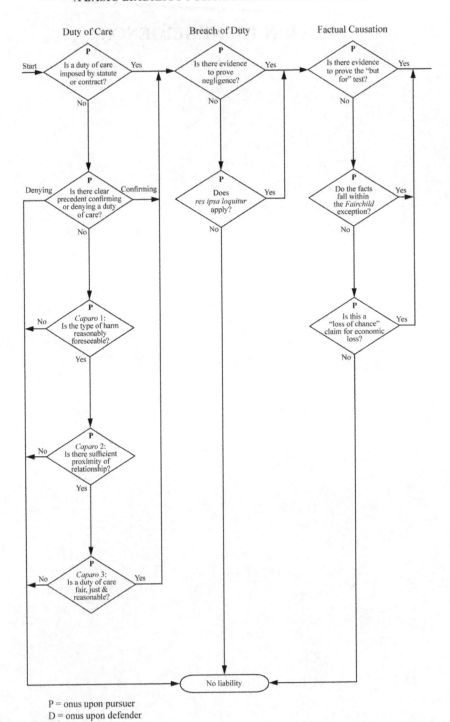

P = onus upon pursuer
D = onus upon defender

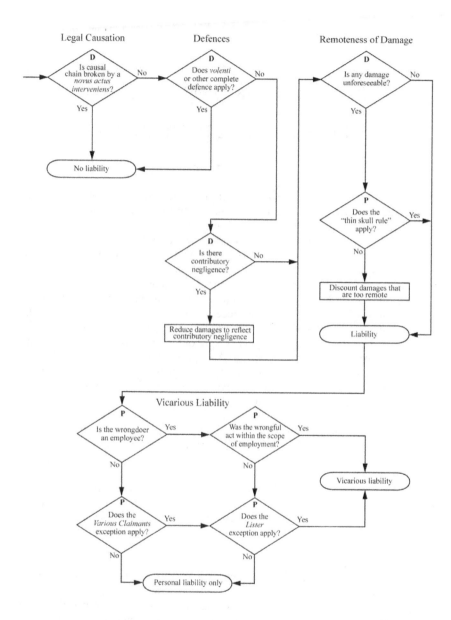

CHAPTER 11

NEGLIGENCE: THE DUTY OF CARE

INTRODUCTION

11–01 "The liability for negligence, whether you style it such or treat it as in other systems as a species of '*culpa*,' is no doubt based upon a general public sentiment of moral wrongdoing for which the offender must pay. But acts or omissions which any moral code would censure cannot, in a practical world, be treated so as to give a right to every person injured by them to demand relief. In this way rules of law arise which limit the range of complainants and the extent of their remedy. The rule that you are to love your neighbour becomes in law, you must not injure your neighbour; and the lawyer's question, Who is my neighbour? receives a restricted reply. You must take reasonable care to avoid acts or omissions which you can reasonably foresee would be likely to injure your neighbour. Who, then, in law, is my neighbour? The answer seems to be—persons who are so closely and directly affected by my act that I ought reasonably to have them in contemplation as being so affected when I am directing my mind to the acts or omissions which are called in question."[1]

Negligence is certainly the most familiar, and has probably become the most commonly litigated aspect of the modern law of delict. The famous 1932 majority decision of the House of Lords in *Donoghue v Stevenson*[2] ultimately provided the foundations of the modern law of negligence, enabling its controversial expansion throughout the later decades of the twentieth century, of which more below. One significant feature of that decision was its treatment of the concepts underpinning the law of negligence as common to Scotland and England, effectively fusing the respective jurisdictions' approach to and development of the law. Thus,

"The liability for negligence, whether you style it such *(the English approach—negligence as a distinct tort)* or treat it as in other systems *(Scotland in particular)* as a species of '*culpa*,' is no doubt based upon a general public sentiment of moral wrongdoing for which the offender must pay."[3]

In order to appreciate how and why the law of negligence continues to develop today in Scotland and in England, it is important to have a basic understanding

---

[1] *Donoghue v Stevenson*, 1932 S.C. (HL) 31 at 44 per Lord Atkin.
[2] *Donoghue v Stevenson*, 1932 S.C. (HL) 31.
[3] *Donoghue v Stevenson*, 1932 S.C. (HL) 31 at 44 per Lord Atkin.

of the respective approaches taken prior to the *Donoghue* decision, and to recognise the social context in which the decision was made. A historical feature of the "common law" in England remains its relatively rigid approach to judicial precedent: case decisions must be consistent with the decisions of superior courts. This approach has tended to inhibit rapid expansion of the law, which can become a problem if the law needs to react quickly to significant developments in society or technology.[4] On the other hand, the development of Scots law has been influenced by the principle-based approach of civilian legal systems, which never recognised judicial precedent as a formal source of law. As has already been seen, the law of delict in Scotland may be said to be based on concepts of *culpa*, so that the law can develop by demonstration of the existence of the elements *damnum injuria datum* in novel situations rather than by analogy to existing precedents.

A common concern in relation to liability for negligence has been what may be called "indeterminate liability".[5] The law should not permit "liability in an indeterminate amount for an indeterminate time to an indeterminate class".[6] Like the ripples created when a stone is thrown into water, a negligent act can trigger a wide range of consequences that may affect a wide range of people over a long period of time. Thus, to avoid indeterminate liability the law must impose limits on liability: in terms of the range of consequences which may be the subject of a claim[7]; the period of time within which a claim may be raised in the courts;[8] and the range of affected persons who may pursue a remedy. Accordingly,

> "acts or omissions which any moral code would censure (*injuria*) cannot, in a practical world, be treated so as to give a right to every person injured (*damnum*) by them (*datum*) to demand relief. In this way rules of law arise which limit the range of (pursuers) and the extent of their remedy."[9]

Judges therefore tend to be reticent in exploring new ground in negligence claims in case one decision opens the floodgates and the courts risk being overwhelmed with claims.[10] Equally, judges may be concerned lest their decisions are seen to endorse a "compensation culture", encouraging frivolous claims to be pursued.[11] Accordingly proof of *damnum injuria datum*, or *culpa*, is insufficient on its own to result in liability in negligence. Thus there is a need to apply legal concepts which impose boundaries on the "range of complaints and the extent of their remedy."[12]

Prior to *Donoghue v Stevenson*, the main mechanism adopted by Scottish judges in setting and patrolling boundaries of liability appears to have been the **11–02**

---

[4] Such criticisms continue to be leveled at the law on liability for psychiatric injury: see, e.g. para.11–53 below.

[5] Prima facie this would not appear a concern as far as *intentional* delicts are concerned—where the delinquent has intended to impact the harm on the victim. However, similar issues may arise where the delinquent's conduct causes unintended harm—either to the intended victim or to others.

[6] *Ultramares Corporation v Touche* (1931) 255 N.Y. 170 at 179 per Cardozo C.J.

[7] Controlled by remoteness of damage concepts: see paras 13–19 to 13–25 below.

[8] Controlled by prescription and limitation concepts: see Ch.15.

[9] *Donoghue v Stevenson*, 1932 S.C. (HL) 31 at 44 per Lord Atkin.

[10] See, e.g. *Hill v Chief Constable of Yorkshire* [1989] A.C. 53; *Alcock v Chief Constable of South Yorkshire* [1992] 1 A.C. 310.

[11] See, e.g. *Tomlinson v Congleton BC* [2004] 1 A.C. 46; *Gorringe v Calderdale MBC* [2004] 1 W.L.R. 1057.

[12] *Donoghue v Stevenson*, 1932 S.C. (HL) 31 at 44 per Lord Atkin.

principle of "remoteness of damage".[13] However, throughout the 18th century, judges in England and Wales developed the concept of the "duty of care" as a device restricting the range of complaints. For a duty of care to be imposed by the law in a given situation, the facts would have to fit into a pre-existing precedent. English judges also tended to prefer a contractual analysis of facts, where a rigid application of the doctrine of privity of contract constricted developments in the law.[14] Thus, a consumer injured by a defective product would generally be unable to obtain a remedy unless the consumer was also a customer and able to claim in the latter capacity for breach of contract under the Sale of Goods Act 1893.[15]

Scots law began to adopt the duty of care concept in negligence cases around the turn of the 20th century,[16] using it as a device to limit claims; and at the same time preferring privity of contract over liability in negligence. Thus, two boys who sued the manufacturer for harm suffered after drinking from a contaminated bottle of lemonade they found, still sealed from the factory, in a field were held not to be entitled to a remedy as they had no claim against a seller in contract.[17]

Meanwhile, the industrial revolution had spawned a new era of (at the time) sophisticated technological products, which were becoming common—and dangerous. The paradigm example was the motor car. The imperative that the law had to accommodate such technological and social changes was recognised in the United States in 1916. Donald MacPherson from New York State was injured when a wooden wheel on his Buick motor vehicle collapsed due to a manufacturing defect. MacPherson had bought the car from a dealer, rather than directly from Buick. Buick had purchased the defective wheel from a supplier before fitting it to the car during the assembly process. Buick admitted the defect could have been discovered upon inspection of the wheel but denied liability, arguing that liability could only arise in contract. In the New York Court of Appeals Cardozo J. had this to say:

> "If the nature of a thing is such that it is reasonably certain to place life and limb in peril when negligently made, it is then a thing of danger. It's nature gives warning of the consequence to be expected. If to the element of danger there is added knowledge that the thing will be used by persons other than the purchaser, and used without new tests, then, irrespective of contract, the manufacturer of this thing of danger is under a duty to make it carefully. That is as far as we need to go for the decision of this case ... If he is negligent, where danger is to be foreseen, a liability will follow."[18]

The facts alleged in *Donoghue v Stevenson* were as follows. At about 9pm on a Sunday evening in August 1928, Mrs May Donoghue, a resident of Cowcaddens

---

[13] *Allan v Barclay* (1864) 2 M. 873 at 874 per Lord Kinloch. For discussion of the concept of remoteness of damage in relation to liability for negligence see paras 13–19 to 13–25 below.

[14] *Winterbottom v Wright* (1842) 10 M. & W. 109. Exceptions were recognised where the product was "inherently dangerous" or had been "fraudulently misdescribed": *Langridge v Levy* (1837) 2 M. & W. 519.

[15] *Priest v Last* [1903] 2 K.B. 148; *Cavalier v Pope* [1906] A.C. 424.

[16] *"Owners of Islay" v Patience* (1892) 20 R. 224; *Kemp & Dougall v Darngavil Coal Co*, 1909 S.C. 1314; *Clelland v Robb*, 1911 S.C. 253.

[17] *Mullen v AG Barr & Co. Ltd*, 1929 S.C. 461.

[18] *MacPherson v Buick Motor Co*, 217 N.Y. 382 at 389–390.

in Glasgow, accompanied by an un-named friend, stopped for refreshment at the Wellmeadow Café on Love Street in Paisley. Mrs Donoghue's friend paid for the refreshments, effectively providing Mrs Donoghue with her "ice cream float"[19] as a gift. The proprietor of the café apparently selected a bottle of "ginger"[20] manufactured by the defenders (a local supplier of soft drinks), opened it, and poured half of the contents over the scoop of ice cream he had already placed in a tumbler. Mrs Donoghue then began to consume the concoction, refilling her tumbler with what remained in the bottle of ginger. It was then that the remains of a decomposed snail emerged from the bottle. Mrs Donoghue claimed that she suffered shock and gastro-enteritis as a consequence of her ingestion of the contaminated confection.

Mrs Donoghue had no claim under the Sale of Goods Act 1893: she had not **11–03** entered into a contract with the proprietor of the café. She therefore sued in delict, claiming that her illness was caused by the negligence of the manufacturer. It is significant to note that the bottle was opaque and that its crimped cap confirmed it could not have been opened following its leaving the factory, thus it would appear to be the manufacturer's fault that the snail was in the bottle. Stevenson, the manufacturer, challenged the relevancy of the claim, arguing that it did not owe Mrs Donoghue any obligations in delict as a consumer's remedies were confined within the law of contract.

This legal point[21] was eventually appealed to the House of Lords; the Inner House having followed its own decision in *Mullen v Barr*.[22] The House of Lords held by a majority of 3:2 that a manufacturer did owe a duty of care in delict to the ultimate consumer of a product as the relationship between the parties was such that the manufacturer could be expected reasonably to foresee that a consumer of a product, whether or not the consumer was the purchaser, would be likely to suffer harm if the product was defectively manufactured. The majority appeared to have been persuaded by Lord Atkin,[23] who was himself clearly influenced by the speech of Cardozo J. in *MacPherson v Buick*.[24] The decision may therefore be seen as a defining moment when the laws of negligence in the respective United Kingdom jurisdictions entered a modern age.

In the course of his leading speech, Lord Atkin observed:

> "The law of both (Scotland and England) appears to be that, in order to support an action for damages for negligence, the (pursuer) has to show that he has been injured by the breach of a duty owed to him in the circumstances by the (defender) to take reasonable care to avoid such injury."[25]

---

[19] A local delicacy created by pouring a soft drink over a scoop of ice cream.

[20] Part of the vernacular of the West of Scotland providing a generic word for a soft drink.

[21] "In the present case we are ... solely concerned with the question whether, as a matter of law in the circumstances alleged, the defender owed any duty to the pursuer to take care": *Donoghue v Stevenson*, 1932 S.C. (HL) 31 at 43–44 per Lord Atkin.

[22] *Mullen v Barr*, 1929 S.C. 461. See para.11–02 above.

[23] A. Rodger, "Lord MacMillan's Speech in *Donoghue v Stevenson*" (1992) 108 L.Q.R. 236.

[24] *MacPherson v Buick Motor Co*, 217 N.Y. 382. See J.D. Gordon, "The American Authorities in *Donoghue v Stevenson*: A Resolution" (1999) 115 L.Q.R. 183.

[25] *Donoghue v Stevenson*, 1932 S.C. (HL) 31 at 43 per Lord Atkin. "Negligence means more than heedless or careless conduct; it properly connotes the complex concept of duty, breach and damage thereby suffered by the person to whom the duty was owing; on all this the liability depends": *Lochgelly Iron & Coal Co Ltd v McMullan*, 1933 S.C. (HL) 64 at 78 per Lord Wright.

Thus, it is possible to recognise three essential elements,[26] which the pursuer must prove to exist, before there may be liability in negligence:

1. the pursuer must be owed a *duty of care* by the alleged wrongdoer;
2. the alleged wrongdoer must be shown to have been in *breach of the duty* of care;
3. the breach of duty must have *caused harm* recognised as reparable by the law.

Within each of these essential elements there are other issues that have to be addressed. In so doing it must be appreciated that there is no such thing as "negligence in the abstract"[27] and that every case turns upon its own facts. It is also said that "the categories of negligence are never closed"[28]: except in cases where the courts have absolutely excluded recovery as a matter of policy or precedent,[29] it is always possible to argue that there is a ground of action.

It should be noted that judgments and speeches in reported negligence cases might not obviously distinguish these three elements. Indeed, speeches delivered in some of the most famous Scottish negligence cases might appear to conflate the components. For example, in *Muir v Glasgow Corp*, where the case concerned precautions taken by a tearoom manageress, Lord MacMillan concluded that "there was *no duty* incumbent upon her".[30] Conversely, his fellow judges[31] agreed that the manageress *did* owe a duty of care to the customers in the tearoom; deciding the case on the basis that the manageress was not in *breach* of her duty of care.

DUTY OF CARE

11-04 Logically, the existence of a duty of care must be confirmed before it is appropriate to examine the elements of *damnum injuria datum* so as to determine liability in a given set of circumstances. Thus, the duty of care question may be viewed as a preliminary issue and so may be challenged as a plea to the relevancy of a claim (as in *Donoghue v Stevenson*[32] itself). Whether or not a duty of care is owed is a question of law, although the answer in any given case will be substantially determined by its distinctive facts. Ultimately what the law demands is that, with regard to the averred facts of the claim, the *relationship* between the alleged victim and alleged wrongdoer is close enough for the law to impose the duty of care.[33] The question is therefore how close (or "proximate")

---

[26] However, "[i]n all these cases you will find that the three questions, duty, causation, and remoteness, run continually into one another. It seems to me that they are simply three different ways of looking at one and the same problem": *Roe v Minister of Health* [1954] 2 Q.B. 66 at 85 per Denning L.J.

[27] *Donoghue v Stevenson*, 1932 S.C. (HL) 31 at 71 per Lord MacMillan.

[28] *Donoghue v Stevenson*, 1932 S.C. (HL) 31 at 71 per Lord MacMillan.

[29] Judges are usually at pains to avoid "absolutely" excluding recovery.

[30] *Muir v Glasgow Corp*, 1943 S.C. (HL) 3 at 11 per Lord MacMillan (emphasis added).

[31] Specifically Lords Romer, Thankerton and Wright.

[32] *Donoghue v Stevenson*, 1932 S.C. (HL) 31. Although the House of Lords allowed Mrs Donoghue's claim to proceed to a proof before answer (i.e. a civil trial), the case was settled out of court. Thus the facts alleged by Mrs Donoghue were never proved to have been true.

[33] Where a plea to the relevancy of a claim is considered, the court will make a decision on the basis that the facts averred are true.

must the relationship be for the alleged wrongdoer to owe the pursuer an *ex lege* duty of care?

Lord Atkin answered that question in his speech in *Donoghue v Stevenson* by asserting that the relationship would be close enough if it was reasonably foreseeable from the perspective of the defender that someone in the pursuer's position may suffer harm if the defender was careless. His Lordship borrowed terminology from the Christian parable of the Good Samaritan and created the "neighbour" test:

> "The rule that you are to love your neighbour becomes in law, you must not injure your neighbour; and the lawyer's question, Who is my neighbour? receives a restricted reply. You must take reasonable care to avoid acts or omissions which you can reasonably foresee would be likely to injure your neighbour. Who, then, in law, is my neighbour? The answer seems to be - persons who are so closely and directly affected by my act that I ought reasonably to have them in contemplation as being so affected when I am directing my mind to the acts or omissions[34] which are called in question."[35]

It is clear that a "reasonable" manufacturer of a product put onto the market for human consumption would "reasonably foresee" that the ultimate consumer of that product might be harmed if the product is unsafe. Thus, a manufacturer has a "neighbour" relationship with the ultimate consumer and the law imposes a duty, owed to the ultimate consumer, upon the manufacturer to take reasonable care in the manufacturing process. So the decision of the House of Lords in *Donoghue v Stevenson* created a precedent that a manufacturer of a product put onto the market owes a duty of care to the ultimate consumer of the manufactured product.[36]

However, Lord Atkin's intention was to identify "a general conception of relations giving rise to a duty of care"[37]—in other words the neighbour test was intended to be ubiquitous: it could be applied to any set of facts to determine whether the law imposed a duty of care. Although it suffered a slow start, certainly by the end of the 1970s Lord Atkin's neighbour test appeared to have achieved that ambition, defining the existence of a duty of care not just in product liability and other relatively straightforward physical harm cases, but extending into economic and psychiatric harm cases. This was relatively uncontroversial when the neighbour test was applied so as to confirm a relationship was too remote for a duty of care to be owed. However, the limitations of the neighbour test as a general principle providing a universal touchstone of liability became apparent when it was applied in unprecedented scenarios so as to create novel categories of liability in negligence, especially in cases involving "pure economic" loss.

An example of the former was *Bourhill v Young* in 1942. Mrs Bourhill, who was eight months pregnant, had taken a tram journey in Edinburgh, alighting at a stop on Colinton Road. As she was collecting her luggage the tram was

---

[34] Note that in spite of Lord Atkin's choice of words here, there is generally no liability for "pure omissions": see paras 11–64 to 11–66 below.

[35] *Donoghue v Stevenson*, 1932 S.C. (HL) 31 at 44 per Lord Atkin.

[36] This precedent has been overtaken by statute: Pt I of the Consumer Protection Act 1987 now imposes strict liability on the producer of a product.

[37] *Donoghue v Stevenson*, 1932 S.C. (HL) 31 at 44 per Lord Atkin.

overtaken by a motorcycle ridden by Mr Young. Young was going too fast and collided with a car about 15 metres further up the road. Young suffered fatal injuries. The tram happened to be between Mrs Bourhill and the collision so that she did not see the accident happen. She did hear the noise, but by the time she walked to the scene, Mr Young's body had already been removed. Nevertheless, she claimed to have suffered such shock from the experience that she miscarried.

11–05   The House of Lords unanimously confirmed that Mr Young did not owe Mrs Bourhill a duty of care. According to Lord MacMillan

> "The duty to take care is the duty to avoid doing or omitting to do anything the doing or omitting to do which may have as its reasonable and probable consequence injury to others, and the duty is owed to those to whom injury may reasonably and probably be anticipated if the duty is not observed."[38]

Although Mr Young undoubtedly owed a duty of care to the occupants of the vehicle with which he collided, the relationship between Mr Young and Mrs Bourhill was too remote. She was not within the range of persons whom a reasonable person in Mr Young's position could reasonably foresee as being affected by the way in which he was riding his motorcycle.

Bourhill v Young may be classified as a "nervous shock" or "psychiatric/ mental harm" case. More recently, additional criteria supplementing the neighbour test have been applied to psychiatric injury cases.[39] In many such cases there has been a fear that a pure application of the neighbour test would impose indeterminate liability, or at least have the potential to trigger a flood of claims.

Similar fears have been expressed in cases involving liability for pure economic loss and liability for third party acts. Thus, when effectively an unqualified application of the neighbour test to pure economic loss cases was approved in 1977 by the House of Lords in *Anns v Merton London BC*,[40] the backlash of academic and judicial criticism[41] resulted in the replacement of the neighbour test with a more sophisticated three part—or "tripartite"—test by the beginning of the 1990s in *Caparo Industries Plc v Dickman*.[42]

Caparo v Dickman was a case involving pure economic loss allegedly caused by auditor negligence.[43] It provided the House of Lords with the opportunity to consolidate various duty of care concepts which had been developed across a range of then recent cases:

> "But since the *Anns* case a series of decisions ... have emphasised the inability of any single general principle to provide a practical test which can

---

[38] *Bourhill v Young*, 1942 S.C. (HL) 78 at 88 per Lord MacMillan.
[39] *Alcock v Chief Constable of South Yorkshire* [1992] 1 A.C. 310: see paras 11–54 to 11–60.
[40] *Anns v Merton LBC* [1978] A.C. 728.
[41] See, e.g. *Governors of the Peabody Donation Fund v Sir Lindsay Parkinson & Co Ltd* [1985] A.C. 210 at 240 per Lord Keith of Kinkel; *Leigh & Sillavan Ltd v Aliakmon Shipping Co Ltd (The Aliakmon)* [1986] A.C. 785 at 815 per Lord Brandon of Oakbrook; *Yuen Kun Yeu v Attorney General of Hong Kong* [1988] A.C. 175 at 194 per Lord Keith of Kinkel; *Sutherland Shire Council v Heyman* (1985) 157 C.L.R. 424 at 480 (HC (Aus)) per Brennan J.
[42] *Caparo Industries Plc v Dickman* [1990] 2 A.C. 605.
[43] See para.11–33 below for the facts.

be applied to every situation to determine whether a duty of care is owed and, if so, what is its scope. What emerges is that, in addition to foreseeability of damage, necessary ingredients in any situation giving rise to a duty of care are that there should exist between the party owing the duty and the party to whom it is owed a relationship characterised by the law as one of 'proximity' or 'neighbourhood' and that the situation should be one in which the court considers it fair, just and reasonable that the law should impose a duty of a given scope upon the one party for the benefit of the other."[44]

In the passage above Lord Bridge enunciates three elements to the duty of care question[45]:

1. foreseeability of damage, i.e. would a reasonable person in the position of the alleged wrongdoer reasonably foresee that someone in the pursuer's position may suffer the type of harm alleged;
2. proximity of relationship, i.e. is the relationship between the parties close enough;
3. fair, just and reasonable considerations, i.e. are there "policy factors" to consider in recognising an *ex lege* duty of care in the circumstances of the case?

However, Lord Bridge also acknowledged that this framework provides sign- **11–06** posts rather than hard and fast rules:

"But the concepts of proximity and fairness embodied in these additional ingredients are not susceptible of any such precise definition as would be necessary to give them utility as practical tests, but amount in effect to little more than convenient labels[46] to attach to the features of different specific situations which, on a detailed examination of all the circumstances, the law recognises pragmatically as giving rise to a duty of care of a given scope."[47]

In *Caparo*, the House of Lords also advocated adopting the wisdom of the Australian judge, Brennan J., who preferred that "that the law should develop novel categories of negligence incrementally and by analogy with established categories".[48] In other words, judges should be very careful in ensuring that a duty of care would only be recognised in new scenarios if those could be connected to precedents where a duty of care had already been held to exist.

---

[44] *Caparo Industries Plc v Dickman* [1990] 2 A.C. 605 at 617–618 per Lord Bridge of Harwich. See also Lord Oliver of Aylmerton at 632–633.

[45] The identification of these three elements was not revolutionary, or even novel. The same three elements may be detected as informing the decision of the House of Lords in *Hedley Byrne & Co Ltd v Heller & Partners Ltd* [1964] A.C. 465 (see para.11–31 below), and may also be detected in the debate in the New York Court of Appeals in *Palsgraf v Long Island Railroad Co*, 162 NE 99 (1928) (see para.11–16 below).

[46] Described as "blunt tools" by Lord Walker of Gestingthorpe in *Customs and Excise Commissioners v Barclays Bank Plc* [2007] 1 A.C. 181 at 209.

[47] *Caparo Industries Plc v Dickman* [1990] 2 A.C. 605 at 617–618 per Lord Bridge of Harwich. See also Lord Oliver of Aylmerton at 632–633.

[48] *Sutherland Shire Council v Heyman* (1985) 60 A.L.R. 1 at 43–44 per Brennan J.

The conservative attitude to development of the duty of care concept, coupled with the apparent preference of precedent over principle, raise questions as to whether the *Caparo* three-stage test is good law in Scotland.[49] However, by the end of the 1990s the three-stage test was clearly accepted as representing the approach to deciding whether the law recognised a duty of care in novel situations (i.e. where there was not already a clear precedent) for physical damage[50] and pure economic loss[51] cases, and by 2006 for psychiatric injury[52] cases. The matter was put beyond doubt by the House of Lords in *Mitchell v Glasgow City Council*.[53]

Meanwhile, an alternative approach was developed across a trilogy of "pure economic loss" negligence cases decided in the House of Lords in the mid-1990s.[54] Drawing on the 1960s case of *Hedley Byrne & Co Ltd v Heller & Partners Ltd*,[55] Lord Goff of Chieveley suggested that an assumption of responsibility may in itself be enough to establish an *ex lege* duty of care:

> " . . . if a person assumes responsibility to another in respect of certain services, there is no reason why he should not be liable in damages for that other in respect of . . . loss which flows from the negligent performance of those services. It follows that, once the case is identified as falling within (this) principle, there should be no need to embark upon any further enquiry whether it is "fair, just and reasonable" to impose liability . . . "[56]

The assumption of responsibility concept has not been confined to pure economic loss cases[57] and has been accepted as good law in Scotland.[58]

11-07   How does all of this fit together? In *Customs and Excise Commissioners v Barclays Bank Plc*[59] the House of Lords accepted that there are potentially three separate tests: incrementalism; the three-stage test; and the assumption of responsibility concept, but also concluded that these all operate at "high levels of abstraction" and in most scenarios application of each of the respective tests is likely to result in the same answer. In practice, most negligence claims arise in circumstances where it has been well established by statute, precedent or even contract that a duty of care is owed, and any dispute will tend to be on whether the alleged wrongdoer breached the duty of care. However, it is novel cases, i.e.

---

[49] See, e.g. G.C. Borland, "The Test for a Duty of Care: Journey's End", S.L.P.Q. 2000, 5(4), 423–429. Scepticism of *Caparo's* utility in Scotland may have involved an element of defensiveness given that much of the criticism of the *Anns* approach had specifically targeted the decision of the House of Lords in the Scottish case *Junior Books Ltd v Veitchi Co Ltd*, 1982 S.C. (HL) 244.

[50] *British Telecommunications Plc v James Thomson & Sons Ltd*, 1999 S.C. (HL) 9; *Gibson v Orr*, 1999 S.C. 420.

[51] *Coleridge v Miller Construction Ltd*, 1997 S.L.T. 485.

[52] *Stevens v Yorkhill NHS Trust*, 2006 S.L.T. 889.

[53] *Mitchell v Glasgow City Council*, 2009 S.C. (HL) 21 at 31 per Lord Hope of Craighead.

[54] *Spring v Guardian Assurance* [1995] 2 A.C. 296; *Henderson v Merrett Syndicates* [1995] 2 A.C. 145; *White v Jones* [1995] 2 A.C. 207.

[55] *Hedley Byrne & Co Ltd v Heller & Partners Ltd* [1964] A.C. 465.

[56] *Henderson v Merrett Syndicates* [1995] 2 A.C. 145 at 180–181.

[57] *Barrett v Enfield LBC* [2001] 2 A.C. 550; *Swinney v Chief Constable of Northumbria* [1997] Q.B. 464. Cf. *Mitchell v Glasgow City Council*, 2009 S.C. (HL) 21; *Desmond v Chief Constable of Nottinghamshire* [2011] P.T.S.R. 1369.

[58] *Royal Bank of Scotland Plc v Bannerman Johnstone Maclay*, 2005 1 S.C. 437; *Realstone Ltd v J & E Shepherd* [2008] P.N.L.R. 21.

[59] *Customs and Excise Commissioners v Barclays Bank Plc* [2006] 3 W.L.R. 1.

cases which introduce new issues which have not already been determined by statute or precedent, that require the application of these complex concepts.[60]

In dealing with those novel cases it is important to remember the purpose of the duty of care concept. It is intended to avoid liability to an indeterminate class, or range, of persons; that is to ensure that the law remains predictable and practical. It may be important to consider the implications of recognising the existence of a duty of care: would that provide a precedent to enable a very wide range of persons affected by a negligent act to sue, and who would pay for the costs and damages involved? If the costs might be borne by an insurance company or a public body, how will such an organisation afford to pay for the potential range of claims? Will the inevitable increase in the premiums charged by insurance companies have a substantially detrimental impact on society, e.g. by actively discouraging entrepreneurship? These are questions of policy, i.e. they are ultimately asking whether it would be fair, just and reasonable to impose a duty of care, considering the implications; but these are also questions about the relationship between the parties. Thus, as well as it being arguable that the three separate tests identified above overlap to the extent that they are synonymous,[61] it might equally be said that the three stage test in *Caparo* itself merely represents three ways of asking the same question.

It is suggested that the nearest it is possible to achieve rationalisation of the tests and concepts would be to adopt the *Caparo* three stage test as a general framework which will require to be populated with specific questions relevant to the particular case under the general headings. Thus, foreseeability of damage is an initial filter—as may be seen in crude operation in comparing *Donoghue v Stevenson*[62] with *Bourhill v Young*.[63] If the case in question survives this test, then the proximity of relationship between the parties may be examined. Fundamentally the object here is to avoid liability to an indeterminate class. As will be seen below the questions to ask here are to a large extent determined by the category of case, usually determined by the type of victim and the type of harm one is dealing with. If there is a contract between the parties, or non-contractual assumption of responsibility by the alleged wrongdoer to the victim, then the relationship will be close, and may even be described as "special".[64] On occasions policy factors may justify holding a relationship to be artificially close.[65] However, even where a relationship is sufficiently "proximate", there may be other policy factors which weigh against a finding that it would be fair, just and reasonable to impose a duty of care.[66] The impact of policy factors may therefore justify the existence of a duty in some cases and undermine such justification in others. Incrementalism, as a useful cross-check, should then mean no more than caution in the face of radical innovation.

Does Scots law need the duty of care concept?

As was stated at the beginning of this chapter, historically Scots law dealt with **11–08** the issue of indeterminate liability by excluding from liability those consequences of a wrongful act that were too remote from the wrong. Thus,

---

[60] See, e.g. *Cramaso LLP v Earl of Seafield*, 2014 S.L.T. 521 at 528 per Lord Reed.
[61] See above at fn.26.
[62] *Donoghue v Stevenson*, 1932 S.C. (HL) 31.
[63] *Bourhill v Young*, 1942 S.C. (HL) 78.
[64] *Hedley Byrne & Co Ltd v Heller & Partners Ltd* [1964] A.C. 465.
[65] See, e.g. the discussion of rescuers in psychiatric injury cases at para.11–49 below.
[66] See, e.g. the discussion of liability for pure omissions at paras 11–64 to 11–66 below.

remoteness was considered in the context of *consequences* or *damage* rather than in the context of relationships.

> "The grand rule on the subject of damages is, that none can be claimed except such as naturally and directly arise out of the wrong done; and such, therefore, as may reasonably be supposed to have been in the view of the wrongdoer."[67]

Given that the predominant concept underpinning the "grand rule" is also reasonable foreseeability, it might be argued that there is no fundamental difference between the Lord Kinloch's grand rule and Lord Atkin's neighbour test.

The duty of care concept has been the subject of sustained criticism dating back to the time of *Donoghue v Stevenson*.[68] Continental jurisdictions adopting civilian systems seem to manage without it. The UK judiciary has acknowledged the debate:

> "A wider approach has also been canvassed. The suggestion has been made that, in effect, the common law should jettison the concept of duty of care as a universal prerequisite to liability in negligence. Instead the standard of care should be "modulated" to accommodate the complexities arising in fields such as social workers dealing with children at risk of abuse: Tort Liability of Public Authorities in Comparative Perspective, ed Fairgrieve, Andenas and Bell (2002), p 485. The contours of liability should be traced in other ways."[69]

Nevertheless, the duty of care concept remains firmly established within negligence jurisprudence in the respective jurisdictions of Scotland and England and Wales. Its principle function remains as a conceptual device intended to control or limit the range of complaints.

DUTY OF CARE: FORESEEABILITY OF DAMAGE

11–09 The first stage of the *Caparo* tri-partite test is foreseeability of damage. This concept, as has already been seen,[70] was confirmed as a basic principle of negligence liability at least as far back as *Donoghue v Stevenson*. As well as underpinning Lord Atkin's neighbourhood test, the concept pops up across the law of delict generally and in negligence in particular: being applied to

---

[67] *Allan v Barclay* (1864) 2 M. 873 at 874 per Lord Kinloch.

[68] "an unnecessary fifth wheel on the coach incapable of sound analysis and possibly productive of injustice": W.W. Buckland, "The Duty to Take Care" (1935) 57 L.Q.R. 637 at 639. The "doctrine is redundant because the same result can be attained by reliance on the broad Roman concept of *culpa* limited by the principle of remoteness, that liability extends only to persons who might foreseeably be harmed by the defender's conduct": D.M. Walker, *The Law of Delict in Scotland*, 2nd edn (Edinburgh: W. Green, 1981), p.46. For a radical proposal on restructuring the law of negligence see B. Hepple, "Negligence: the Search for Coherence", C.L.P. 1997, 50(1), 69–94.

[69] *D v East Berkshire Community Health NHS Trust* [2005] 2 A.C. 373 at 408 per Lord Nicholls of Birkenhead.

[70] See paras 1–24 and 11–04 above.

determining the standard of care demanded by the law,[71] as well as issues arising in the context of causation[72] and remoteness of damage.[73]

In the context of a duty of care, reasonable foreseeability may be seen as a first level control device, limiting the range of complaints. If the pursuer belongs to a class of persons beyond the range of those

> "who are so closely and directly affected by my act that I ought reasonably to have them in contemplation as being so affected when I am directing my mind to the acts or omissions which are called in question,"[74]

then the case falls at the first hurdle. So, in *Bourhill v Young*,[75] a motorcyclist who had already overtaken a tramcar and was travelling away from the vehicle could not be expected reasonably to foresee that a person on the pavement on the other side of the tram could be affected by the way in he was driving his motorcycle.

Types of harm

One caveat that must be considered concerns the distinction between types of **11–10** harm recognised by the law of negligence as reparable. Thus, physical harm, including personal injury and damage to property, may be distinguished from psychiatric harm. A third distinct type of harm is economic loss. Further, a distinction may be made between "pure" and "derivative" harm: the word "pure"[76] being used to distinguish the immediate impact upon the victim of the wrong from the harmful consequences to the victim that derive from the immediate damage.[77] Thus, a victim injured in an accident caused by a defender's negligent driving may sue for damages for the physical injuries inflicted in the accident, as well as any mental trauma involved in dealing with the accident and the resulting injuries, as well as any economic consequences such as loss of earnings or earning capacity. In this example the physical harm is "pure" in the sense of being an *immediate* result of the wrong whereas the economic harm is "derivative" in the sense of being a *consequence* of the immediate (pure) harm. The psychiatric harm may be pure, i.e. the mental anguish experienced in being involved in the accident itself, or derivative, i.e. the mental anguish in coming to terms with the physical injuries suffered and/or the economic consequences of those injuries, or a combination of both. There are thus several permutations:

- pure physical harm—including death, personal injury and damage to property caused immediately by the wrong;

---

[71] See Ch.12.

[72] Especially with regard to novus actus interveniens: see paras 13–14 to 13–17 below.

[73] See paras 13–19 to 13–25 below.

[74] *Donoghue v Stevenson*, 1932 S.C. (HL) 31 at 44 per Lord Atkin.

[75] *Bourhill v Young*, 1942 S.C. (HL) 78.

[76] The term "pure" has been used by the judiciary in the context of a duty of care mainly in claims for economic loss. In the view of the present writer the term is confusing as it suggests no other type of loss may be incorporated in such a claim for reparation. It is suggested that "immediate" would provide a more apposite adjective than "pure".

[77] It is also suggested that a suitable alternative term for "derivative" is "consequential". The latter word imputes causation/remoteness of damage as the applicable legal concepts more than the former.

- derivative physical harm, e.g. if a person was prevented from taking precautions to prevent flooding on his property because he was injured in a road accident as he was travelling home;
- pure economic loss, e.g. where negligent financial advice has been relied upon in making an investment which results in financial loss[78] or where an employer has to pay for a temporary replacement for an employee injured as a consequence of the defender's negligence[79];
- derivative economic loss, e.g. where a person injured due to the defender's negligence is unable to work while recuperating and loses income;
- pure psychiatric harm, e.g. where a person[80] suffers mental trauma in fearing for their own safety where the defender's negligence causes a "near-miss" or where a person[81] suffers mental trauma in witnessing the impact of the defender's negligence on another "primary" victim;
- derivative psychiatric harm, e.g. where a person develops a psychiatric illness in coming to terms with physical injury suffered as an immediate consequence of an incident cased by the defender's negligence.[82]

11–11 It is important to note that the device used to control liability with regard to "pure" harm is the duty of care concept, where the focus of foreseeability is on the relationship between the wrongdoer and the victim; whereas the device used to control liability with regard to "derivative" harm is the remoteness of damage concept, where the focus of foreseeability is on the consequences of the wrong.[83] Take the case of a victim of a defender's negligence who suffers a head injury in the accident itself, but as a result of the incapacity caused by the head injury the victim goes on to develop a psychiatric illness which in turn prolongs the victim's absence from work and exacerbates the financial consequences due to lack of earnings. The head injury, as the immediate damage, is "pure" physical harm and the psychiatric and economic consequences of the physical injury are forms of "derivative" or "consequential" harm. It will be the physical harm that is key to the relationship required between the wrongdoer and the victim for the law to impose a duty of care owed by the wrongdoer to the victim. Thus, if with regard to pure physical harm the relationship is close enough for a duty of care to be owed, the *duty* of care will extend to the derivative consequences, i.e. in this case the psychiatric and economic harm, although the defender's *liability* for the derivative harm may be limited by remoteness of damage rules.[84]

So, in a negligence action where the claim is for damages for pure economic loss, foreseeability of physical harm will be insufficient—pure economic loss must be a reasonably foreseeable consequence of the alleged negligence.

---

[78] See, e.g. *Hedley Byrne & Co Ltd v Heller & Partners Ltd* [1964] A.C. 465. The investor is a "primary victim" of the defender's negligence: see para.11–31 below.

[79] See, e.g. *Allan v Barclay* (1863) 2 M. 873. The employer is a secondary victim of the defender's negligence: see para.11–40 below.

[80] See, e.g. *Page v Smith* [1996] A.C. 155. This person is a primary victim of the defender's negligence: see para.11–11.

[81] See, e.g. *Alcock v Chief Constable of South Yorkshire* [1992] 1 A.C. 310. This person is a secondary victim of the defender's negligence: see para.11–49 below.

[82] See, e.g. *Simmons v British Steel Plc*, 2004 S.C. (HL) 94.

[83] See paras 13–19 to 13–25 below.

[84] See, e.g. *Simmons v British Steel Plc*, 2004 S.C. (HL) 94.

There is, however, at least one exception to the general rule outlined above. In *Page v Smith*,[85] which was a case where the plaintiff was claiming damages for pure psychiatric harm as a primary victim,[86] the House of Lords by a majority held that reasonable foreseeability of "personal injury" was sufficient—personal injury incorporating both pure physical harm and pure psychiatric harm. While driving his Volvo motor car, Mr Page was involved in a minor road accident caused by the negligent driving of Mr Smith. Although neither driver was injured (there were no passengers in either car) and both cars were only lightly damaged, the incident triggered a recrudescence of a psychiatric illness in Mr Page. It was held that Mr Smith owed Mr Page a duty of care because, although psychiatric injury itself might not be reasonably foreseeable in the context of a minor bump, "personal injury" to drivers or passengers was a reasonably foreseeable consequence of a crash involving motor cars.[87]

Page v Smith was distinguished, albeit not overturned, by the House of Lords in *Rothwell v Chemical and Insulating Co Ltd*.[88] The claimant discovered that he had inhaled asbestos fibres due to the negligence of his employer when a medical examination confirmed scarring to the pleural membrane surrounding his lungs (pleural plaques). Pleural plaques are usually symptomless and, although they confirm that asbestos fibres have entered the individual's lungs, they do not increase susceptibility to other asbestos related diseases and have no impact on the individual's life expectancy. The House of Lords held that accordingly, pleural plaques do not amount to *damnum* and so there can be no liability for pleural plaques as such.[89] The House of Lords also rejected a claim for psychiatric harm with regard to the claimant's increased anxiety at the risk of developing a fatal asbestos-related disease, holding that if pleural plaques did not amount to actionable harm, it was unforeseeable that a person developing pleural plaques would suffer psychiatric injury. Putting it another way, if the creation of a risk of disease did not amount to actionable harm,[90] psychiatric injury associated only with that risk equally could not amount to actionable harm.[91] The distinction is at best subtle, and may be viewed as exposing the analysis in *Page v Smith* to the threat of being overturned.

Provided that the *type* of harm is reasonably foreseeable, the duty of care will **11–12** be owed even if the *extent* of harm was greater than might be anticipated. Here, it may be that there is overlap between the duty of care element and the remoteness of damage element of the enquiry into liability for negligence.[92] In

---

[85] *Page v Smith* [1996] A.C. 155.

[86] For the distinction between primary and secondary victims see para.11–14 below.

[87] It was acknowledged (at 186–189 per Lord Lloyd of Berwick) that this was, in effect, an application of the eggshell/thin skull rule to the facts: for discussion of the eggshell/thin skull rule see paras 13–24 to 13–25 below.

[88] Sub nom. *Grieves v FT Everard & Sons Ltd* [2008] 1 A.C. 281.

[89] This decision was effectively reversed by the Scottish Parliament in passing the Damages (Asbestos-related Conditions) (Scotland) Act 2009. There is no equivalent in England and Wales so the House of Lords decision in *Grieves* stands south of the border.

[90] *Gregg v Scott* [2005] A.C. 176.

[91] Damages (Asbestos-related Conditions) (Scotland) Act 2009 s.1(4) provides that "nothing in this section otherwise affects any enactment or rule of law which determines whether and in what circumstances a person may be liable in damages in respect of personal injuries." Thus, it is submitted that psychiatric injury that is derivative of asbestos-related pleural plaques (or pleural thickening/asbestosis: see s.2) is now actionable in Scotland subject to the rules on remoteness of damage.

[92] See discussion at paras 13–19 to 13–25 below.

Hughes v Lord Advocate,[93] workers employed by the Post Office were carrying out work on a cable beneath a residential street in Edinburgh. They accessed the cable by lifting a manhole cover in the road and erecting a canvas shelter over the site. Late in the day the workers went for a tea break, closing the shelter with a tarpaulin but leaving off the manhole cover. They also placed several paraffin fueled warning lamps around the site. Two boys (aged eight and ten) came upon the site and climbed into the shelter, taking with them one of the paraffin lamps. One boy was severely burned when he tripped over the paraffin lamp, knocking it into the manhole. The paraffin vapourised and the mixture ignited in a violent explosion, the effects of which were exacerbated by the confined space in which the accident occurred. Although it was accepted that it was reasonably foreseeable that paraffin would leak out of the lamp if it was dropped or fell over, and that the resulting pool of paraffin would catch fire creating the risk of burning, it was not reasonably foreseeable that the paraffin would vapourise and explode. So the type of harm (personal injury) was reasonably foreseeable, as was the means (by burning), although the extent of the harm was not. The House of Lords held that there was liability. Lord Pearce explained:

> "When an accident is of a different type and kind from anything that a defender could have foreseen he is not liable for it ... But to demand too great precision in the test of foreseeability would be unfair to the pursuer since the facets of misadventure are innumerable ... "[94]

The victim in *Hughes* was a child, and the decision took into account that the unattended site with its assorted paraphernalia would constitute an allurement to children. In the comparable case of *Jolley v Sutton London BC*, the House of Lords focused on the perspectives to be considered when the reasonable foreseeability question is asked. A wooden boat in poor condition had been abandoned on open ground outside a block of flats owned by the local authority. The local authority knew about the boat but failed to remove it. Two years after it had been abandoned, by which time it had fallen into a dilapidated state, two young boys (aged 13 and 14) decided to make repairs to the boat. They raised the boat using a car jack, but when one of the boys climbed under the boat it collapsed onto him, causing him serious injuries which left him paraplegic. In finding the local authority liable, Lord Hoffmann noted that

> "it has been repeatedly said in cases about children that their ingenuity in finding unexpected ways of doing mischief to themselves and others should never be underestimated."[95]

Thus, for all that it may appear to be an objective test, there is a subjective element to the concept of reasonable foreseeability. Ultimately the question, "Was the type of harm a reasonably foreseeable consequence of the allegedly negligent activity?" must be asked from the perspective of the reasonable person (the objective part of the test) in the position of the alleged wrongdoer (which introduces a subjective element to the test), but such a reasonable person must

---

[93] *Hughes v Lord Advocate*, 1963 S.C. (HL) 31.
[94] *Hughes v Lord Advocate*, 1963 S.C. (HL) 31 at 48. See also *Corr v IBC Vehicles Ltd* [2008] 1 A.C. 884.
[95] *Jolley v Sutton LBC* [2000] 1 W.L.R. 1082 at 1093 per Lord Hoffmann.

take into account the subjective features of the range of persons who might be affected by the impugned activity. Thus, on a risk assessment analysis, the law expects those in control of an environment that children may access to take into account what features of the environment may constitute an allurement to children[96] and to take appropriate precautions in order to minimise the risks to inquisitive juveniles.[97] There is obvious overlap with the standard of care element of the law of negligence.

Duty of care: proximity of relationship

The second element of the *Caparo* three-part test concerns proximity of **11–13** relationship.[98] The relationship between the alleged wrongdoer and the victim must be close enough to satisfy a test of "proximity". The word proximity generally means "nearness" or "closeness" and does not provide any empirical form of measurement. It is suggested that its use in the context of the duty of care is equally vague and imprecise. Although such a suggestion implies that the word appears to be more formal than the concept it is intended to represent, it is also submitted that the separation of this concept from reasonable foreseeability and from policy issues is significant. Indeed, it may be said that the concept represented by the term "proximity" is central to the whole point of the duty of care as a conceptual device intended to control or limit the range of claims in negligence.

It has long been acknowledged that the law of negligence cannot permit liability to an indeterminate class[99] of persons. The other side of that coin is that there must be a pre-existing relationship between the parties so as to give rise to the imposition of the duty of care.[100] It is therefore submitted that the purpose of the proximity of relationship element of the tri-partite test is to ensure that liability is confined to those within a determinate class. Put another way, the onus is upon the pursuer to demonstrate a pre-existing relationship with the alleged wrongdoer that is sufficiently proximate to confirm that the pursuer falls within a determinate class of persons who may reasonably be foreseen to be likely to

---

[96] Which, if Lord Hoffmann is correct, can never be predicted!

[97] See, e.g. *Taylor v Glasgow Corp*, 1922 S.C. (HL) 1. Cf. *McGlone v British Railways Board*, 1966 S.C. 1; *Titchener v British Railways Board*, 1984 S.C. (HL) 34; *Devlin v Strathclyde RC*, 1993 S.L.T. 699; *Muir v Glasgow Corp*, 1943 S.C. (HL) 3; *Tomlinson v Congleton BC* [2004] 1 A.C. 46; *West Sussex CC v Pierce* [2014] P.I.Q.R. P5. Similar considerations apply to other vulnerable persons: see, e.g. *Haley v London Electricity Board* [1965] A.C. 778—blind man tripped over hammer left on the pavement intended to alert pedestrians to a trench being dug at that spot.

[98] *Caparo Industries Plc v Dickman* [1990] 2 A.C. 605 at 617–618 per Lord Bridge of Harwich. See also Lord Oliver of Aylmerton at 632–633.

[99] *Ultramares Corporation v Touche* (1931) 255 N.Y. 170 per Cardozo C.J.

[100] An analysis of the facts of *Anns v Merton LBC* [1978] A.C. 728 will reveal that there was no pre-existing relationship between the local authority planners and the plaintiff at the time of the alleged negligence. Looking at the facts of *Donoghue v Stevenson* 1932 S.C. (HL) 31 in the same way, at the time of the alleged negligence was there a pre-existing relationship between the manufacturer of the contaminated bottle of ginger and Mrs Donoghue as the ultimate consumer? If not, was *Donoghue v Stevenson* correctly decided? Today, the question would be irrelevant as the facts would result in liability under Pt 1 of the Consumer Protection Act 1987. In the context of physical damage it has been explained that "[i]t is enough that the plaintiff chances to be (out of the whole world) the person with whom the defendant collided or who purchased the offending ginger beer": *Caparo Industries Plc v Dickman* [1989] Q.B. 653 at 686 per Bingham L.J. Cf. *Sutradhar v Natural Environment Research Council* [2006] 4 All E.R. 490.

suffer harm as a consequence of the alleged wrongdoer's negligent acts or omissions. It is clear that the world at large is an indeterminate class and too wide. That is easy to state, but what is not so easy is to define the boundaries of a determinate class.

Nevertheless, it may be possible to define the boundaries in respect of specific activities. In the context of the driver of a vehicle, a reasonable person might apply Lord MacMillan's assertion that "the duty is owed to those to whom injury may reasonably and probably be anticipated if the duty is not observed"[101] by confining the duty to fellow road users and owners of property within the immediate area of impact.[102] That range will further be refined with reference to the type of vehicle being driven and the manner in which it is driven.

This is indeed the way in which the jurisprudence related to this element of the tri-partite test has developed. As cases carrying different facts have been decided they have added to a developing tapestry and, although the arras may never be complete, a matrix sufficient in detail to identify some broad classifications has emerged. Thus, as well as cases being classified by types of harm (as suggested above), victims may be classified as either primary or secondary, adding a further dimension to the categorisation of cases. This has permitted the courts to become more specific in defining the tests to be applied to determine sufficient proximity of relationship. Different tests may thus be applied to different permutations of type of harm and type of victim.

Primary and secondary victims

11–14   The distinction between primary and secondary victims tends to be associated with liability for psychiatric injury.[103] In *Alcock v Chief Constable of South Yorkshire Police*, Lord Oliver suggested that previous cases involving liability for mental harm

> "divide into two categories, that is to say, those cases in which the injured plaintiff was involved, either mediately, or immediately, as a participant, and those in which the plaintiff was no more than the passive and unwilling witness of injury caused to others."[104]

He later described those plaintiffs falling into the first category as "primary victims" and those falling into the second as "secondary victims".[105]

However, a closer look at Lord Oliver's analysis reveals he may not have intended to confine his analysis to psychiatric injury cases:

---

[101] *Bourhill v Young*, 1942 S.C. (HL) 78 at 88 per Lord MacMillan.

[102] See, e.g. *Gibson v Orr*, 1999 S.C. 420.

[103] See also paras 3–04 to 3–06 above.

[104] *Alcock v Chief Constable of South Yorkshire Police* [1992] 1 A.C. 310 at 407.

[105] *Alcock v Chief Constable of South Yorkshire Police* [1992] 1 A.C. 310 at 410–411. The distinction has been applied in Scotland: see, e.g. *Robertson v Forth Road Bridge Joint Board (No.2)*, 1995 S.C. 364; *Campbell v North Lanarkshire Council*, 2000 S.C.L.R. 373; *Fraser v State Hospitals Board for Scotland*, 2001 S.L.T. 1051; *Cross v Highlands & Islands Enterprise*, 2001 S.L.T. 1060; *Keen v Tayside Contracts*, 2003 S.L.T. 500; *Salter v UB Frozen & Chilled Foods Ltd*, 2004 S.C. 233; *Anderson v Christian Salveson Plc*, 2006 S.L.T. 815; *Burns v Boots UK Ltd*, 2011 Rep. L.R. 124.

"The failure of the law *in general* to compensate for injuries sustained by persons unconnected with the event precipitated by a defendant's negligence must necessarily import the lack of any legal duty owed by the defendant to such persons."[106]

Thus it is submitted that the distinction between primary and secondary victims is not confined to psychiatric injury cases and indeed operates across the whole of the law of negligence, if not the whole of the law of delict.[107]

What ultimately distinguishes between primary and secondary victims is that primary victims suffer harm as a direct consequence of the wrongful conduct whereas secondary victims suffer harm as a consequence of the harm suffered by the primary victim. Thus, the harm suffered by the secondary victim is indirect, in the sense of being secondary to, or parasitic of, the harm suffered by the primary victim. An analogy may be drawn with the consequences of a stone being thrown into a pool of water. A series of concentric ripples will spread out from the point of impact. If these ripples hit an object protruding through the surface of the water (equivalent to a primary victim), a second series of ripples will be formed, spreading out from the object struck by the first series of ripples. If the secondary ripples strike another object, that second object may be equiparated with a secondary victim.[108]

This analysis is borne out by a wide range of case law, albeit that the language used by the respective judges rarely features the terms "primary victim" or "secondary victim". *Allan v Barclay*[109] provides the starting point for a line of cases distinguishing between direct and indirect (or primary and secondary/ relational) economic loss, and *Marc Rich v Bishop Rock Marine Co Ltd*[110] provides a distinction between direct and indirect physical harm which may be analysed as differentiating between physical loss suffered by a primary victim and that suffered by a secondary victim.

---

[106] *Alcock v Chief Constable of South Yorkshire Police* [1992] 1 A.C. 310 at 410 (emphasis added). Lord Oliver was seeking in this part of his speech to identify what was so special about the psychiatric injury cases to which he was referring that distinguished them from the normal approach of the law to secondary victims: "What is more difficult to account for is why, when the law in general declines to extend the area of compensation to those whose injury arises only from the circumstances of their relationship to the primary victim, an exception has arisen in those cases in which the event of injury to the primary victim has been actually witnessed by the plaintiff and the injury claimed is established as stemming from that fact."

[107] See para.3–04 above.

[108] The second object may in fact be struck by both sets of ripples. This aspect of the analogy may be applied to cases such as *Currie v Wardrop*, 1927 S.C. 538; *Schneider v Eisovitch* [1960] 2 Q.B. 430; *Malcolm v Broadhurst* [1970] 3 All E.R. 508; *Brice v Brown* [1984] 1 All E.R. 997. Might the grandmother in *Burns v Boots UK Ltd*, 2011 Rep. L.R. 124 concurrently be a primary and a secondary victim?

[109] "The personal injuries of the individual himself will be properly held to have been in the contemplation of the wrongdoer. But he cannot be held bound to have surmised the *secondary injuries* done to all holding relations with the individual, whether that of a master, or any other": *Allan v Barclay* (1863) 2 M. 873 at 874 per Lord Kinloch (emphasis added). See also *Reavis v Clan Line Steamers (No.1)*, 1925 S.C. 725; *Landcatch Ltd v International Oil Pollution Compensation Fund*, 1999 S.L.T. 1208; *Cattle v Stockton Waterworks Co* (1875) L.R. 10 Q.B. 453; *Leigh and Sillavan Ltd v Aliakmon Shipping Co Ltd* [1986] A.C. 785; *Alegrete Shipping Co Inc v International Oil Pollution Compensation Fund 1971 (The Sea Empress)* [2003] 1 Lloyd's Rep. 327 at 336 per Mance L.J.; *D Pride & Partners (A Firm) v Institute for Animal Health* [2009] N.P.C. 56.

[110] *Marc Rich v Bishop Rock Marine Co Ltd* [1996] 1 A.C. 211 at 237 per Lord Steyn. See also *Perrett v Collins* [1998] 2 Lloyds Rep. 255 at 273 per Buxton L.J.

The relationships between the wrongdoer and the primary and secondary victims is illustrated in the following diagram:

Defender	**Primary Victim**	**Secondary Victim**
Negligence ➝	Personal injury/ damage to property/ loss of money ➝	Personal injury/ damage to property/ loss of money

In general, liability for negligence is confined to providing reparation to primary victims and, even then, only when either there is suitable precedent or the relevant tests are applied to confirm the relationship gives rise to a duty of care. Thus, as a general rule, there will be no liability to secondary victims, although there may be exceptions. The approach of the law will be to require justification for such exceptions when they arise.[111]

Proximity of relationship: physical damage

Primary victim physical damage

11–15   This is the most straightforward category, and in the vast majority of cases there will be a clear series of precedents confirming whether or not a duty of care is owed. Thus, it is well established that a driver owes a duty of care to other occupants of the vehicle, and to the occupants of other vehicles, pedestrians and owners of property situated within the range of possible collision impact. On the rare occasion that an unprecedented set of facts arises, it is submitted that a "neighbourhood" relationship as defined by Lord Atkin[112] and based on the concept of reasonable foreseeability would satisfy the proximity of relationship requirement. Alternatively, the defender may be held to owe the pursuer a duty of care if the defender has assumed responsibility to the pursuer for the issue in question.[113]

Secondary victim physical damage

11–16   This permutation has not clearly been identified as such by the judiciary, at least in so far as it may be a distinct category. In *Palsgraf v Long Island Railroad Co* a bizarre chain of events was set in motion when a railway station porter attempted to help a passenger on to a train by giving the passenger a push. The porter's push dislodged a package carried by the passenger which fell onto the railway tracks. Only when the package exploded did it become apparent that it had contained fireworks! The force of the blast caused a set of scales to fall on to the plaintiff, who had been standing at the other end of the railway platform. In the New York Court of Appeals Cardozo J. hinted at the distinction between primary and secondary victims in a physical harm case when he opined that

---

[111] *Alcock v Chief Constable of South Yorkshire Police* [1992] 1 A.C. 310 at 410 per Lord Oliver of Aylmerton (see fn.106 above).

[112] *Donoghue v Stevenson*, 1932 S.C. (HL) 31 at 44.

[113] See, e.g. *Murphy v East Ayrshire Council*, 2012 S.L.T. 1125.

"(t)he diversity of interests emphasises the futility of the effort to build the plaintiff's right upon the basis of a wrong to someone else."[114]

However, in the present writer's view, Cardozo J. did not hit the nail quite on the head. What makes a person a *secondary* victim is not defined by the fact that they are a victim of a *wrong* to someone else, but that they are a victim of the *harm* suffered by a primary victim. On that definition Mrs Palsgraf might indeed qualify as a secondary victim, the wrong committed by the porter (an assault) caused physical damage to the primary victim's property (the package) which in turn triggered the physical harm suffered by the secondary victim (Mrs Palsgraf). Cardozo J.'s dictum makes sense in the context of Mrs Palsgraf suing in assault, but that would not necessarily preclude a right to a remedy in negligence. However, to succeed in a negligence claim, the secondary victim would have to show that the alleged wrongdoer owed her a duty of care. That brings us to the crux of the issue—what rules are applied to determine sufficient proximity of relationship in secondary victim physical harm cases?

The House of Lords had the opportunity to consider this question in *Marc Rich v Bishop Rock Marine Co Ltd*.[115] However, the court did not recognise the case as concerning liability for physical harm suffered by a secondary victim and so did not lay down any statements of rule or principle with regard to the proximity of relationship question.[116] Rather, the House of Lords focused on the policy question incorporated in the third element of the *Caparo* three part test—viz whether it was fair, just and reasonable for the law of negligence to impose a duty of care. The case concerned a contract, incorporating the Hague Rules, for the carriage of a cargo by sea. The ship (The Nicholas H) developed a crack in its hull during the voyage and was put in to harbour for assessment of the damage and repairs. The surveyor sent out by the defendants (a marine classification society) to inspect the ship at first decided that it would require immediately to be placed in a dry dock and that permanent repairs were necessary to make it seaworthy. However, after discussion with the shipowners the surveyor changed his mind and approved the ship as fit to sail following temporary repairs. Upon recommencing its voyage, the ship broke up and sank, and the cargo was lost. The Hague Rules stipulated that the shipowner would be liable for the lost cargo but limited that liability to a fraction of its value. The owners of the cargo sued the classification society in negligence for the difference between the damages paid by the shipowners under the Hague Rules and the actual value of the cargo. By a 4:1 majority the House of Lords rejected the cargo owners' claim, holding that to recognise a duty of care would upset the delicate balance of interests and liabilities that were incorporated into the Hague Rules, which were in universal use. That point, in combination with the quasi-public role of classification societies and that the additional insurance costs that would arise would ultimately fall upon shipowners (who may then take short-cuts to cut costs and so compromise safety), meant that it would not be fair, just and reasonable for the

---

[114] *Palsgraf v Long Island Railroad Co*, 162 NE 99 (1928) at 100. Students have recreated the story of the case in Lego for a video featured on YouTube—google "Palsgraf Lego Law"! It is also interesting to note that the concepts of foreseeability, proximity and policy were all at large in the delivered judgments— 60 years before *Caparo Industries Plc v Dickman* [1990] 2 A.C. 605.

[115] *Marc Rich & Co AG v Bishop Rock Marine Co Ltd (The Nicholas H)* [1996] A.C. 211.

[116] Indeed, the majority in the House of Lords proceeded on the assumption that the proximity of relationship requirement was satisfied.

law to impose a duty of care owed by the classification society to the owners of cargo.

11–17 Although Lord Steyn did acknowledge a difference between direct and indirect loss, he did not elaborate on the distinction beyond asserting that "(t)he law more readily attaches the consequences of actionable negligence to directly inflicted physical loss than to indirectly inflicted physical loss." This statement may be seen as at odds with the decision in *Clay v A.J. Crump & Sons Ltd*,[117] but Lord Steyn distinguished *Clay* as involving directly inflicted physical loss.

It is submitted that the better analysis of *Marc Rich* would classify it as a secondary victim physical harm case as illustrated in the diagram below. The primary victim of the surveyor's negligence was the shipowner, who suffered physical harm with the loss of the ship. The loss of the ship resulted in the loss of the cargo—so the owner of the cargo may be seen as a secondary victim of the surveyor's negligence. The question as to proximity of relationship may then be met head-on, and if Lord Oliver's analysis in *Alcock* was correct,[118] the presumption should be that secondary victims have too remote a relationship with the wrongdoer, subject to the operation of any control mechanisms that might permit exceptional claims.

Wrongdoer	Primary Victim	Secondary Victim
Surveyor ⟶	Shipowner (Damage to property) ⟶	Cargo owner (Damage to property)

11–18 It is submitted that a similar analysis justifies the decision of Lord MacLean in *Coleridge v Miller Construction Ltd*.[119] The supply of electricity to the pursuer's glass factory was disrupted for twenty minutes when the defenders cut through an electricity cable (belonging to a third party—the electricity board), causing the temperature in a glass furnace to drop suddenly. This caused a heater element from the furnace to break up and fall into the molten glass. The pursuers were advised that they could either drain the contaminated molten glass from the furnace—a process which would take several weeks—or continue operating the furnace as normal so that the flawed glass would gradually be diluted. The pursuers chose the latter and sued for the cost of repairs to the furnace and for the loss of the contaminated glass.

In applying the three part *Caparo* test, Lord MacLean dismissed the action. The harm suffered by the pursuers was held unforeseeable: even if the defenders had consulted the plans that would have confirmed the route of the cables, they could not have been aware of the pursuers' reliance on a constant supply of electricity through the cable. Respectfully, it is submitted that such an analysis is

---

[117] *Clay v A.J. Crump & Sons Ltd* [1964] 1 Q.B. 533. In that case an architect assured a demolition contractor that he could safely leave a wall standing. The demolition contractor acted on this advice but the wall later collapsed on a workman. The workman sued the architect in tort. It was held that the architect owed a duty of care to the workman as the architect was primarily responsible for leaving the wall in a dangerous condition. Was the workman a secondary victim suffering physical harm attributable to the harm suffered (the wall collapsing) by the primary victim (the owner of the wall)? In his speech in *Marc Rich*, Lord Steyn did not view that case that way.

[118] *Alcock v Chief Constable of South Yorkshire Police* [1992] 1 A.C. 310 at 410 per Lord Oliver of Aylmerton (see fn.106 above).

[119] *Coleridge v Miller Construction Ltd*, 1997 S.L.T. 485.

inconsistent with the reasoning in *Hughes v Lord Advocate*.[120] Lord MacLean also held that the lack of awareness of reliance meant that there was insufficient proximity of relationship, and that it would not be fair, just and reasonable to impose a duty of care because the damage was so remote and that it would be reasonable to expect the pursuers to insure against such risks.

The pursuers had argued that a distinction should be made between pure economic losses and damage to property (i.e. asking the court to treat the damage to the furnace as the latter). This approach had been taken in several similar English cases.[121] Lord MacLean said:

> "It seems to me artificial and without justification to make recovery of loss by those supplied in these circumstances turn upon whether the damage sustained was physical or purely economic. After all, in all these cases, loss is computed in money terms so far as the action for recovery of damages is concerned, although loss, no doubt, is more readily identifiable in the one case rather than the other."

Although Lord MacLean had stated that he viewed the *damage* as too remote, it is suggested that what Lord MacLean appears to have had in mind was that, as a secondary victim of the defender's negligence, the *relationship* between the defenders and the pursuers was too remote. It is also submitted that taking such an approach is consistent with what appears to have underpinned the thinking of Lord Steyn in *Marc Rich v Bishop Rock Marine Co Ltd*.[122] Thus, the presumption that secondary victims have too remote a relationship with the wrongdoer may be justified as based on principle, subject to any control mechanisms that might permit exceptional claims.

Such a control mechanism may distinguish between physical harm to the **11–19** secondary victim's property and personal injury inflicted upon the secondary victim. This would perhaps also rationalise the decision of the House of Lords in *Marc Rich* with the decision of the Court of Appeal in *Perrett v Collins*,[123] where the plaintiff claimed damages for injuries sustained when the plane in which he was a passenger crashed. He sued the inspector who had granted a certificate of airworthiness following an inspection of the plane. The inspector had not noticed an incompatibility between two components which was what later caused the plane to crash. The Court of Appeal confirmed that the inspector owed a duty of care to future passengers. In excluding the application of the fair, just and reasonable test, Hobhouse L.J. distinguished *Marc Rich* on the basis that it was an economic loss case and not a personal injury case. Nevertheless, his Lordship found that reasonable foreseeability was not on its own sufficient to determine the matter but concluded that the necessary proximity of relationship was present because of the degree of control exercised by the inspector (if the inspector refused a certificate the aircraft would not be permitted to fly).

---

[120] *Hughes v Lord Advocate*, 1963 S.C. (HL) 31.
[121] *SCM (United Kingdom) Ltd v WJ Whittall & Son Ltd* [1971] 1 Q.B. 337; *Spartan Steel & Alloys Ltd v Martin & Co Ltd* [1973] Q.B. 27; *Londonwaste Ltd v Amec Civil Engineering Ltd*, 53 Con. L.R. 66.
[122] *Marc Rich v Bishop Rock Marine Co Ltd* [1996] 1 AC 211.
[123] *Perrett v Collins* [1998] 2 Lloyd's Rep. 255.

So again, a secondary victim who suffers damage to property (e.g. *Marc Rich*) may be subject to the usual rule,[124] i.e. that there is insufficient proximity of relationship. Whereas a secondary victim who suffers personal injury may pass the proximity test if relevant control mechanisms are satisfied, e.g. that the alleged wrongdoer has complete control over a dangerous situation. There are hints that this may be the law,[125] but the matter has not yet been dealt with head-on by the judiciary. However, if it is the case, is the distinction between personal injury and damage to property justified? Is the broken finger necessarily more serious harm than the wrecked core business asset, bankruptcy and ruin?

In *Perrett v Collins*, Buxton L.J. had this to say:

> "In the straightforward case of the direct infliction of physical injury by the act of the plaintiff there is, indeed, no need to look beyond the foreseeability by the defendant of the result in order to establish that he is in a "proximate" relationship with the plaintiff ... The infliction of physical injury to the person or property of another universally requires to be justified ... The causing of economic loss does not. The root of this distinction therefore lies in the difference ... between physical damage and economic loss ... The distinction is not, however, a simple one between physical damage and economic loss, because the cases of (foreseeable) physical damage that are likely to attract liability without more consideration ... are cases of 'direct' physical damage. That notion is difficult to define, and is not defined in the cases that employ it ... It will of course be noted that this is a different issue from that of causation, since it is perfectly possible for a person to cause damage otherwise than by his own direct act. The existence of this sub-category of physical damage does however mean that where the physical damage is deemed to be indirect, the questions of proximity, justice, fairness and reasonableness remain wholly in issue, and to be established by the plaintiff."[126]

In concluding that these cases demonstrate the inevitable overlap between relationship questions of proximity and policy questions of fairness, justice and reasonableness, one may be reminded of the comment above that the *Caparo* tripartite test may really be three different ways of asking the same question!

Proximity of relationship: liability for the wrongful acts of third parties[127]

11–20 In *Dorset Yacht v Home Office*, prison officers accompanied a group of young offenders on a camping trip to Jackson Island, an island just off the southern coast of England. While the prison officers slept on the job, a group of the boys escaped from the campsite and stole a yacht which they intended to sail to the mainland. However, their lack of sailing skills were revealed when the stolen yacht collided with another. Both vessels were badly damaged. The owners of the

---

[124] *Alcock v Chief Constable of South Yorkshire Police* [1992] 1 A.C. 310 at 410 per Lord Oliver of Aylmerton (see above at fn.106).

[125] See also *Sutradhar v Natural Environment Research Council* [2006] 4 All E.R. 490 at 502 per Lord Hoffmann, referring to *Clay v AJ Crump & Sons Ltd* [1964] 1 Q.B. 533 and *Watson v British Boxing Board of Control Ltd* [2001] Q.B. 1134 as examples of the latter type of case. See also *ICL Tech Ltd v Johnston Oils Ltd*, 2013 S.L.T. 1090 at 1099 per Lord Hodge.

[126] *Perrett v Collins* [1998] 2 Lloyd's Rep. 255 at 273 per Buxton L.J.

[127] See also paras 4–02 to 4–03 above.

second yacht sued the employers of the prison officers, claiming they were vicariously liable for the negligence of the prison officers. The plaintiffs argued that the prison officers owed them a duty of care with regard to the activities of the boys. Lord Diplock pointed out that

> "This appeal, therefore, also raises the lawyer's question: 'Am I my brother's keeper?' A question which may also receive a restricted reply."[128]

Lord Morris of Borth-y-Gest considered that because of the level of control that the officers were empowered by statute to exercise over the boys, a "special relationship" existed between them which was sufficient to impose a duty of care on the officers which was owed to the yacht owners. Both Lord Morris and Lord Reid considered that the harm was the "very kind of thing which would be likely to happen"[129] if the prison officers failed in their duty to supervise the boys. Thus, foreseeability of harm was sufficient to give rise to a duty of care owed by A to B with regard to the wrongful—even criminal—acts of C.[130]

Dorset Yacht was decided principally upon the application of the reasonable foreseeability concept embodied in the neighbourhood test,[131] albeit with a reference to the "special relationship" concept explored by the House of Lords in the earlier *Hedley Byrne* case.[132] Although pre-*Caparo*, *Maloco v Littlewoods Organisation Ltd*[133] provided the House of Lords with the opportunity to revisit the issue of liability for third party acts during the period when the retreat from *Anns*[134] was resulting in a recalibration of the duty of care tests.

The facts of *Maloco* were that unknown third parties, probably young children, set a fire that burnt down a derelict cinema, which Littlewoods had purchased. The fire spread to damage Mr Maloco's café and the church in the charge of Mr Smith, who also sued Littlewoods. When *Maloco* came to the House of Lords, Lord Mackay settled that point by indicating that it is essentially a question of fact and that the intervention should be high on a scale of probability before there can be liability. However, there was quite a difference between the speeches of Lord Mackay and Lord Goff in *Maloco*.[135] Lord Goff was concerned that foreseeability should not impose duties on individuals in their ordinary lives—elderly gardeners leaving french doors open, stone-deaf asthmatics leaving windows open or old ladies leaving their windows open for their cats while they (the old ladies) visit their married daughters. Thus, Lord Goff set out three alternative occasions where a defender would owe a duty to take care with regard to the actions of a third party. These alternatives may be seen as pertinent to the matter of proximity of relationship.

1. Special relationships: a "special relationship" may exist between either the defender and pursuer, or between the defender and the third party. **11–21**

The former may involve an "assumption of responsibility" to the pursuer by the defender. Examples might include contractual relationships, e.g. between

---

[128] *Dorset Yacht v Home Office* [1970] A.C. 1004 at 1061 per Lord Diplock.
[129] *Dorset Yacht v Home Office* [1970] A.C. 1004 at 1034 per Lord Morris of Borth-y-Gest.
[130] Scots law had recognised such a liability as far back as *Scott's Trs v Moss* (1889) 17 R. 32.
[131] *Donoghue v Stevenson*, 1932 S.C. (HL) 31 at 44 per Lord Atkin.
[132] *Hedley Byrne & Co Ltd v Heller & Partners Ltd* [1964] A.C. 465.
[133] *Maloco v Littlewoods Organisation Ltd*, 1987 S.C. (HL) 37.
[134] *Anns v Merton LBC* [1978] A.C. 728.
[135] Lord Keith agreed with both!

employer and employee[136] or contractor[137]; or statutory relationships, e.g. between an occupier and visitor to premises.[138] Although normally the "veil of incorporation" means that a parent company is not liable for the wrongs of its subsidiary, liability may arise where the facts disclose that the parent has assumed responsibility to the victim for the relevant conduct of the subsidiary.[139] Other examples include: the duty incumbent upon schools to take care to protect pupils[140]; the assumption by the police of responsibility to an informant[141] or by prison authorities to a prisoner[142]; and a potential duty owed by a local authority to parents of children abused by a child fostered within the family.[143] However, it should be noted that without clear evidence of an assumption of responsibility, the courts tend to be unwilling to recognise a duty owed to the victim, even in the context of statutory requirements to carry out paternalistic or protective type of activity, and especially where the third party's acts are criminal.[144]

Alternatively, a special relationship may exist between the defender and the third party. An example may be the relationship between a parent and a dependent child. Although parents are not as such liable for the delicts of their children,[145] a parent may owe a duty to supervise a child where it is foreseeable that the child, if left to his own devices, could cause harm to others. An example would be if a toddler was left to wander onto a busy road, resulting in a collision between road users attempting to avoid running over the child.

11–22   **2.** The defender negligently creates a source of danger where it is reasonably foreseeable that third parties are likely to intervene and cause harm.[146] The classic example is found in *Haynes v Harwood*,[147] where a carter left a horse-drawn van unattended in a crowded street. The horses bolted when a boy threw a stone at them and a police officer, who was injured himself when he intervened to stop the horses causing injury to bystanders, was held entitled to recover damages from the carter's employer. It has also been held that a duty was owed by prison officers to a psychologically vulnerable prisoner who, after witnessing

---

[136] See, e.g. *W v Commissioner of Police of the Metropolis* [2000] 1 W.L.R. 1607; *Collins v First Quench Retailing Ltd*, 2003 S.L.T. 1220; *Strathclyde Joint Police Board v McKinlay*, 2005 S.L.T. 764.

[137] See, e.g. *Stansbie v Troman* [1948] 2 K.B. 48. Cf. *P. Perl (Exporters) Ltd v Camden LBC* [1984] Q.B. 342.

[138] Occupiers Liability (Scotland) Act 1960.

[139] *Chandler v Cape Plc* [2012] 1 W.L.R. 3111.

[140] *Woodland v Essex CC* [2014] A.C. 537. See also, e.g. *Brown v North Lanarkshire Council*, 2011 S.L.T. 150. Cf. *Webster v Ridgeway Foundation School* [2010] E.L.R. 694.

[141] *Swinney v Chief Constable of Northumbria* [1997] Q.B. 464. Cf. *Costello v Chief Constable of Northumbria* [1999] 1 All E.R. 550; *An Informer v Chief Constable* [2013] Q.B. 579.

[142] *R (Amin) v Secretary of State for the Home Dept* [2004] 1 A.C. 653.

[143] *W v Essex CC* [2001] 2 A.C. 592. See also *R (Amin) v Secretary of State for the Home Dept* [2004] 1 A.C. 653.

[144] See, e.g. *Hill v Chief Constable of West Yorkshire* [1989] A.C. 53; *Mitchell v Glasgow City Council*, 2009 S.C. (HL) 21; *Gorringe v Calderdale MBC* [2004] 1 W.L.R. 1057; *Jain v Trent SHA* [2009] 1 A.C. 853; *X v Hounslow LBC* [2009] P.T.S.R. 1158; *Thomson v Scottish Ministers*, 2013 S.C. 628; *Desmond v Chief Constable of Nottinghamshire* [2011] P.T.S.R. 1369; *Santander UK Plc v Keeper of the Registers of Scotland*, 2013 S.L.T. 362.

[145] *McKay v McLean*, 1920 S.L.T. 34.

[146] *Maloco v Littlewoods Organisation Ltd*, 1987 S.C. (HL) 37 at 77–79 per Lord Goff of Chieveley. For examples see *Connor v Secretary of State for Scotland*, 2000 Rep. L.R. 18. A factor in the equation may be the extent of the danger arising from the negligence of the defender: see, e.g. *Philco Radio and Television Corp of Great Britain v J Spurling Ltd* [1949] 2 All E.R. 882.

[147] *Haynes v Harwood* [1935] 1 K.B. 146. See also *Flemington Trust Ltd v Brown & Lynn*, 1953 S.L.T. (Sh. Ct) 13. Cf. *Topp v London Country Bus (South West) Ltd* [1993] 1 W.L.R. 976.

(and apparently being blamed for) the suicide of his first cellmate (who was known to be suicide risk), was made to share a cell with another suicidal prisoner.[148] However, in *Maloco v Littlewoods Organisation Ltd*[149] itself, the owner of an empty building was held not to be liable to the proprietors of adjoining properties which were destroyed when an unidentified third party (presumed to be a child) set fire to Littlewoods' premises.[150] Apart from the difficulty in holding that leaving a building empty is, in itself, negligent, the House of Lords confirmed that the circumstances in the case were not such as to conclude it was reasonably foreseeable that third parties may interfere and cause damage.

3. The defender is aware of the third party's actions but fails to take reasonable **11–23** steps to prevent it from continuing. Lord Goff spoke of this in the context of the proprietor of a building who knows that trespassers have been starting fires on his property. The evidence in the *Maloco* case did not point to such knowledge on the part of Littlewoods or its employees. However, a similar approach has resulted in proprietors of football grounds being held liable with regard to the consequences of abuse of the premises by football supporters,[151] and in auditors being held liable for failing to report their suspicions of fraud.[152] Again, however, the courts tend to be reticent in recognising the existence of a duty of care where there is no clear assumption of responsibility by the defender to the pursuer.[153]

Looking in detail at some post-*Maloco* cases raises the interesting question of whether there has been a divergence along national lines.

In England, in *Topp v London Country Bus Ltd*,[154] the owners of a minibus stolen by unknown persons were held not to be liable to the husband of a person run down by the bus. The case was argued on the basis of allurement: the ignition key was left in the lock and the vehicle left unattended. The court held that foreseeability was not enough. The fact that the allurement and danger argument was taken shows the influence of Lord Goff's speech—the attempt was to bring the case within the second of his catalogue of situations in which there could be liability. Lord MacKay's test could, however, bring about the same decision because the need for the intervention to be high on a scale of probability might rule this case out—it is not like untrained borstal boys trying to sail boats. Even if it was foreseeable that the vehicle would be stolen, the next stage—driving such as to injure another—is not perhaps probable: most people, most of the time, do not run people down. On the other hand, there are car thieves and there are car thieves—some are excellent and careful drivers who safeguard their booty; others may be young "neds" who may never actually have learned to drive. The harm of the kind which resulted was not the harm reasonably to be foreseen, namely injury after car theft. However, in another English case a decision was

---

[148] *Butchart v Home Office* [2006] 1 W.L.R. 1155.
[149] *Maloco v Littlewoods Organisation Ltd*, 1987 S.C. (HL) 37.
[150] The speeches in the House of Lords placed substantial emphasis on English precedents, disparaging Scottish precedent as "too wide" (*Evans v Glasgow DC (Negligence)*, 1978 S.L.T. 17) and "wrongly decided" (*Squires v Perth and Kinross DC*, 1985 S.C. 297).
[151] See, e.g. *Hosie v Arbroath Football Club Ltd*, 1978 S.L.T. 122; *Cunningham v Reading Football Club Ltd* [1992] P.I.Q.R. P141.
[152] *Sasea Finance Ltd (In Liquidation) v KPMG (formerly KPMG Peat Marwick McLintock) (No.2)* [2000] 1 All E.R. 676; *Frank Houlgate Investment Co Ltd v Biggart Baillie LLP*, 2013 S.L.T. 993. Cf. *Stone & Rolls Ltd (In Liquidation) v Moore Stephens (A Firm)* [2009] 1 A.C. 1391.
[153] See, e.g. *Hill v Chief Constable of West Yorkshire* [1989] A.C. 53; *Mitchell v Glasgow City Council*, 2009 S.C. (HL) 21; *Smith v Chief Constable of Sussex* [2009] 1 A.C. 225.
[154] *Topp v London Country Bus Ltd* [1993] 1 W.L.R. 976.

reached, albeit against the background of the English equivalent of the Occupiers' Liability (Scotland) Act 1960, which fits more into the "foreseeability with high probability" model. In *Cunningham v Reading Football Club Ltd*,[155] the plaintiffs were injured at a football match by bits of terracing thrown at the police. Four months earlier, concrete had been thrown. The club knew it was a local derby and knew that trouble might arise. The club was held liable.

11-24   In Scotland, in *Fry's Metals Ltd v Durastic Ltd*,[156] a company entered into a lease with another company of factory and office premises for the six-month period to March 23, 1984. Two separate alarm systems protected the premises: a conventional bell system mounted on an exterior wall manually set by a key, and a private system installed by a security company at the request of the tenants, connected to the offices of the security company by landline. The tenants notified the security company that cover would not be required after March 30. On April 2, the tenants sought to hand over the keys to the landlords. The keys were refused because electricity and gas meters were required to be read before the handover was complete. This took place on April 9. On April 7, the premises were broken into and vandalised. Both alarm systems failed to operate. The landlords sued the tenants for loss caused by the failure of the private alarm system. It was argued, on the basis of Lord MacKay's speech, that there is a duty in delict to take care in respect of the occupation of premises to prevent damage by the action of a third party, which arises if, but only if, the injury or damage by third parties arising from the act or omission of the person against whom the duty of care is alleged is highly probable. Lord Dervaird held that test met. In *Gillon v Chief Constable*,[157] a police officer on the track who was told to stand with her back to the playing surface was "run-down" by an enthusiastic footballer. She sued her employer and lost on the basis of *Bolton v Stone*[158] unlikeliness. But it is an example of the fact that, although there was another human being (in this case a footballer) in the chain of events, a case could be made out. In *Hendrie v Scottish Ministers*,[159] half a million pounds was awarded to a prison officer who injured his back intervening in a fight between two inmates. There had been a fight before between them. There had been enough time to separate them. However, the scope of the duty can reach only so far. In *McLean v University of St Andrews*,[160] the pursuer, a student at the defender's institution, claimed she had been raped by three Russian soldiers while an exchange student in Odessa. She had been outside the accommodation provided for her at the time (although allegedly because of a fight there). It was known to be a dangerous area and the University could only be held responsible to provide safe accommodation.

The cases in this area often appear to be inconsistent and difficult to reconcile with each other. Although unlawful acts by third parties should not be expected, sometimes the circumstances are such that they are predictable. One would instinctively suggest that intentional wrongs would be even less predictable than unintentional wrongs, but the duty to guard against theft may exist where the

---

[155] *Cunningham v Reading Football Club Ltd* [1992] P.I.Q.R. P141. See *Hosie v Arbroath Football Club Ltd*, 1978 S.L.T. 122 for a Scottish equivalent.

[156] *Fry's Metals Ltd v Durastic Ltd*, 1991 S.L.T. 689.

[157] *Gillon v Chief Constable*, 1997 S.L.T. 1218.

[158] *Bolton v Stone* [1951] A.C. 850. See para.12–05 below.

[159] *Hendrie v Scottish Ministers*, 2003 S.C.L.R. 642. Cf. *Donaldson v Scottish Ministers*, 2009 S.L.T. 240; *Pratt v Scottish Ministers*, 2013 S.L.T. 590.

[160] *McLean v University of St Andrews*, 2004 Rep. L.R. 54.

duty to anticipate third party negligence may not. Advice given by Lord Nicholls is very pertinent:

> "The better approach is to recognise that, as with the likelihood that loss will occur, so with the likelihood of wrongful third party intervention causing loss, the degree of likelihood needed to give rise to a duty of care depends on the circumstances. In some circumstances the need for the high degree of likelihood of harm mentioned by Lord Reid may be an appropriate limiting factor in cases involving deliberate wrongful human actions. In other cases foresight of a lesser risk of harm flowing from a third party's intervention will suffice to give rise to a duty of care. The law of negligence is not an area where fixed absolutes of universal application are appropriate. In each case the governing consideration is the underlying principle. The underlying principle is that reasonable foreseeability, as an ingredient of a duty of care, is a broad and flexible objective standard which is responsive to the infinitely variable circumstances of different cases. The nature and gravity of the damage foreseeable, the likelihood of its occurrence, and the ease or difficulty of eliminating the risk are all matters to be taken into account in the round when deciding whether as a matter of legal policy a duty of care was owed by the defendant to the plaintiff in respect of the damage suffered by him."[161]

Proximity of relationship: economic loss

11–25 Although economic (i.e. money) losses suffered by a victim as a consequence of personal injury or damage to property have always been recoverable (subject to the rules on remoteness of damage), historically claims for pure economic loss were deemed too remote to be reparable.[162] Judicial reticence was based on the concern that, because of the potential range of persons who might suffer economic harm on account of a wrongdoer's negligence, to permit liability for pure economic loss would be to expose the law of negligence to the possibility of liability to an indeterminate class. However, following a dissenting judgment of Lord Denning M.R.,[163] the House of Lords decision in *Hedley Byrne v Heller & Partners Ltd*[164] opened up the possibility of claims in negligence for pure economic loss, albeit restricted to claims from a primary victim.

Although the principles in *Hedley Byrne* were couched carefully, there followed a period of expansion of liability, culminating in the now notorious decision of the House of Lords in *Anns v Merton LBC*,[165] where simple reasonable foreseeability was held sufficient to trigger a duty of care for pure economic loss. The reaction to *Anns*, fuelled by the critical academic and judicial reception of the House of Lords decision in the Scottish case of *Junior Books Ltd v Veitchi Ltd*[166] resulted in judicial retraction, and a series of court decisions in the later 1980s culminated in the decision of the House of Lords in *Caparo*

---

[161] *Attorney General of the British Virgin Islands v Hartwell* [2004] 1 W.L.R. 1273 at 1280 per Lord Nicholls of Birkenhead delivering the judgment of the court.
[162] See, e.g. *Allan v Barclay* (1864) 2 M. 873.
[163] *Candler v Crane Christmas & Co* [1951] 2 K.B. 164.
[164] *Hedley Byrne v Heller & Partners Ltd* [1964] A.C. 465.
[165] *Anns v Merton LBC* [1978] A.C. 728.
[166] *Junior Books Ltd v Veitchi Ltd*, 1982 S.C. (HL) 244.

Industries Ltd v Dickman,[167] where it was confirmed that foreseeability was necessary but not sufficient to confirm a duty of care in pure economic loss cases. There was a suggestion of further expansion of liability for pure economic loss post-*Caparo* from a series of cases in the mid-1990s, most notably *Henderson v Merrett Syndicates*,[168] but a conservative approach was restated by the House of Lords in *Customs & Excise Commissioners v Barclays Bank Plc*[169] in 2006.

Meanwhile, an exclusionary rule has been consistently applied to claims for pure economic loss suffered by secondary victims of negligence,[170] albeit that occasional recent cases have hinted at the possibility of developing exceptions to the rule.[171] The current position on where a duty of care is owed with regard to economic loss in all of its variants is set out below.

Economic loss—derivative or pure?

11–26   Economic loss may be classified as derivative or pure. *Derivative* (or *consequential*) economic loss describes loss measured in financial terms that flows from the immediate harm caused by the impact of the defender's wrong upon the pursuer. Obvious examples of derivative economic loss include loss of wages while recuperating from personal injury or loss of income from property damaged by the defender's negligence. Derivative economic loss is irrelevant to establishing the existence of a duty of care—the degree of proximity of relationship required is determined by the immediate harm.[172] Presuming that the immediate harm is reparable, limitations on recovery of derivative losses, including derivative economic loss, will be determined by the application of the rules on remoteness of damage.[173] In addition, depending upon the circumstances, courts may apply multipliers or discounts to the assessment of damages for loss of future earnings.[174]

Pure economic loss in principle may be seen as self-standing loss that is the direct consequence of the negligence[175] and that may be measured only in financial terms. Thus, if an investor relying on an expert's negligent advice loses money on an investment, it should be clear that the loss is purely economic. The investor may suffer mental anguish, or even resort to self-harm, as a result of losing money, but there the psychiatric and/or physical harm is derivative of the economic loss; the economic loss itself being "pure". In principle, whether or not the pure economic loss is reparable depends upon whether the expert advisor owes the investor a duty of care with regard to pure economic loss. If no duty of care is owed, the investor will not be entitled to any remedy. However, if a duty of care is owed in respect of the pure economic loss, and that duty is breached,

---

[167] *Caparo Industries Ltd v Dickman* [1990] 2 A.C. 605.
[168] *Henderson v Merrett Syndicates* [1995] 2 A.C. 145. See also *Spring v Guardian Assurance* [1995] 2 A.C. 296; *White v Jones* [1995] 2 A.C. 207.
[169] *Customs & Excise Commissioners v Barclays Bank Plc* [2006] 3 W.L.R. 1.
[170] *Nacap Ltd v Moffat Plant Hire Ltd*, 1987 S.L.T. 221.
[171] See, e.g. *North Scottish Helicopters Ltd v United Technologies Corp Inc (No.1)*, 1988 S.L.T. 77; *Hand v North of Scotland Water Authority*, 2002 S.L.T. 798; *Mull Shellfish Ltd v Golden Sea Produce Ltd*, 1992 S.L.T. 703.
[172] *Conarken Group Ltd v Network Rail Infrastructure Ltd* [2012] 1 All E.R. (Comm.) 692.
[173] See paras 13–19 to 13–25 below.
[174] See para.5–16 above.
[175] The economic delicts cause pure economic loss. There, as liability to an indeterminate class is unlikely to be an issue, the law does not get bogged down in the way it does with pure economic loss in negligence.

the derivative personal injury or damage to property will then be subject to remoteness of damage rules.

The allocation of limiting rules respectively to pure and derivative economic loss is illustrated in the diagram below:

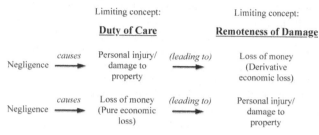

Pure economic loss: definitions

Some examples of pure economic loss are relatively straightforward to **11–27** recognise as such. Such examples include:

- the employer who loses income,[176] or has to pay for a replacement,[177] while his injured employee recuperates;
- the investor who relies upon negligent advice in making a loss-making investment;
- the creditor who relies upon a positive credit reference in making a loan to an insolvent debtor[178];
- the purchaser of an overvalued business or other asset[179];
- the employee who does not get the job application because of an unjust employment reference[180];
- the creditor whose court order to preserve the assets of his debtor is ignored[181];
- the factory owner who has to shut down a production line because his source of power is cut off[182];
- the debtor in a debtor-creditor-supplier agreement who is faced with the supplier's repudiatory breach of contract and who, following justified refusal to continue with the payments to the creditor, suffers harm to his credit rating as a consequence of an unfavourable report to a credit reference agency from the negligent creditor.[183]

Some examples are more difficult to classify. Thus, if a house develops cracks due to a defect in its design should that be classified as damage to property or as pure economic loss? The owner who discovers the cracks has two choices: pay for repairs or sell the house for less than it should have been worth. Either way the owner's loss may be measured purely in money (any mental harm due to the

---

[176] *Reavis v Clan Line Steamers (No.1)*, 1925 S.C. 725.
[177] *Allan v Barclay* (1863) 2 M. 873.
[178] *Hedley Byrne & Co Ltd v Heller & Partners Ltd* [1964] A.C. 465.
[179] *Caparo Industries Plc v Dickman* [1990] 2 A.C. 605; *Smith v Eric S. Bush* [1990] 1 A.C. 831.
[180] *Spring v Guardian Assurance* [1995] 2 A.C. 296.
[181] *Customs and Excise Commissioners v Barclays Bank Plc* [2007] 1 A.C. 181.
[182] *Dynamco Ltd v Holland & Hannen & Cubitts (Scotland) Ltd*, 1971 S.C. 257.
[183] *Durkin v DSG Retail Ltd*, 2014 S.L.T. 468.

expense of repairs or being forced to sell will be *derivative* of the initial harm—the defective property). Would it make any difference if the first sign of the defective design is when the house falls down?

Comparison of two cases illustrates the dichotomy. In *Anns v Merton LBC*,[184] the House of Lords classified such a case as being a claim for physical damage to property. The plaintiff had bought a house from its previous owner. The house had been built a number of years before. Some time after the plaintiff purchased the house, cracks appeared. Investigation revealed inadequate foundations were to blame. There was a risk that the house would become unstable unless expensive repairs were carried out. The purchaser could not sue the seller for breach of contract as the contract contained no express or implied warranties concerning the condition of the house. The builder had gone out of business so the purchaser sued the local authority that had approved the plans and the construction of the house. The House of Lords held that reasonable foreseeability did not need to be qualified by any special rules on proximity of relationship.

11-28   Commentators quickly criticised the decision as opening the gate to a potential flood of claims, analysing the case as an example of pure economic loss. This analysis was formally accepted as correct by the House of Lords in *Murphy v Brentwood DC*,[185] where the facts were virtually identical to those in *Anns*. By this time the courts had recognised that applying reasonable foreseeability as an unqualified test to pure economic loss claims opened the door to liability to an indeterminate class.[186] Thus, in classifying the claim as one for pure economic loss, the House of Lords required a more exacting test of proximity of relationship to be applied. The plaintiff failed that test as, at the time of the local authority's alleged negligence, he was a prospective purchaser of a house yet to be built (which could be "anybody") and clearly had no "special relationship" with the local authority.[187]

Logically, even if the house had collapsed, the physical damage to the house itself would be classified as pure economic loss.[188] This analysis is susceptible to the obvious criticism that it is anomalous to describe what manifests as harm to property as pure economic loss. This criticism is reinforced when one considers that if a motor car is damaged in a collision caused by another driver's negligence, the damage to the vehicle will be classified as harm to property even although in practice what it costs the owner is the money it takes to repair or replace it. Nevertheless, this critique may be answered by pointing out that in the former case the property is the *subject* of the (local authority's) negligence

---

[184] *Anns v Merton LBC* [1978] A.C. 728.
[185] *Murphy v Brentwood DC* [1991] 1 A.C. 398.
[186] See, e.g. *Governors of the Peabody Donation Fund v Sir Lindsay Parkinson & Co Ltd* [1985] A.C. 210 at 240 per Lord Keith of Kinkel; *Leigh & Sillavan Ltd v Aliakmon Shipping Co Ltd (The Aliakmon)* [1986] A.C. 785 at 815 per Lord Brandon of Oakbrook; *Yuen Kun Yeu v Attorney General of Hong Kong* [1988] A.C. 175 at 194 per Lord Keith of Kinkel; *Sutherland Shire Council v Heyman* (1985) 157 C.L.R. 424 at 480 (HC (Aus)) per Brennan J.
[187] For the significance and meaning of the term "special relationship" see paras 11–31 to 11–39 below. Is this analysis reminiscent of the dissenting speech of Lord Buckmaster in *Donoghue v Stevenson*, 1932 S.C. (HL) 31 at 42.
[188] This analysis is consistent with the distinction made in the Consumer Protection Act 1987 s.5(1) between damage to the defective product itself and damage caused to other property by the defect in the product. Indeed, in *Donoghue v Stevenson*, 1932 S.C. (HL) 31, Mrs Donoghue was declared by the majority in the House of Lords to be owed a duty of care by the manufacturer with regard only to the harm to Mrs Donoghue herself (resulting from the defective product), a claim for the defect in the product being restricted to a claim for breach of contract under the Sale of Goods Act 1893 (s.14 of the Sale of Goods Act 1979 would apply today).

whereas in the latter the property is the *object* of the (other driver's) negligence. In the former case the owner acquired an already defective house so the impact upon the owner is the *discovery* of the harm rather than the harm itself. In the latter example the owner began with an undamaged motor vehicle, but ended up with a damaged motor vehicle so the impact upon the owner is the *damage* to the owner's property. Nevertheless, as a means to an end, these distinctions may be described as artificial and accused of being asserted cynically to justify an arbitrary policy distinction made by the courts.

Further anomalies become apparent upon comparison of case law. In a case where the owner of an aircraft had to pay various charges to release an aircraft from impound, it was suggested that had the aircraft been seized by the authorities the loss to the owners would nevertheless have remained classified as purely economic.[189] On the other hand, it has been held that the contamination of property by dust or other chemicals, where no more than cleaning is required to nullify the harmful effect, is nevertheless to be classified as damage to property.[190]

At this point it is worth reminding ourselves that the significance of the distinction is in the proximity of relationship required for a duty of care to be owed. For harm classified as damage to property (or personal injury), reasonable foreseeability is sufficient. However, for pure economic loss a closer relationship is required.

A way to rationalise some of the case law was suggested in *D & F Estates Ltd* **11–29** *v Church Commissioners for England*,[191] where Lord Bridge of Harwich tentatively put forward a "complex structure theory". The theory was that a complex structure such as a dwelling house should not be treated as an indivisible unit, but should be treated as a series of separate divisible units. Thus, if a defect in one part of a complex structure caused damage to another part, that damage should be treated as physical rather than purely economic. The theory has not been adopted as such, and is unlikely to be so in the foreseeable future.[192] However, it does point to a distinction that is supported by case law.[193] If, for example, an extension is built onto an existing building, if a defect in the design of the extension (e.g. inadequate foundations) causes it to collapse, the damage to the extension itself will be classified as pure economic loss. If the collapse of the extension damages the structure of the original building (or other property such as moveables, e.g. furniture, placed inside the extension or original building), that damage will be classified as damage to property.

---

[189] *Nordic Oil Services Ltd v Berman*, 1993 S.L.T. 1164.

[190] *Hunter v Canary Wharf Ltd* [1996] 2 W.L.R. 348 (reversed without disturbing this conclusion by the House of Lords: [1997] A.C. 655); *Losinjska Plovidba v Transco Overseas Ltd (The Orjula)* [1995] 2 Lloyd's Rep. 395.

[191] *D & F Estates Ltd v Church Commissioners for England* [1989] A.C. 177.

[192] Lord Bridge denounced his own theory in his speech in the later case of *Murphy v Brentwood DC* [1991] 1 A.C. 398 at 478. However, Lord Bridge did distinguish "between some part of a complex structure which is said to be a 'danger' only because it does not perform its proper function in sustaining the other parts and some distinct item incorporated in the structure which positively malfunctions so as to inflict positive damage on the structure in which it is incorporated." How does one tell which is which? For example, would a central heating boiler be defined as an integral or as a distinct part of a brand new house?

[193] See, e.g. *Bellefield Computer Services Ltd v E. Turner & Sons Ltd* [2000] 2 T.C.L.R. 759; *Tesco v Costain Construction Ltd* [2003] EWHC 1487.

Nevertheless, anomalies remain.[194] If a complex structure is treated as a single unit when it first enters the market (such as a dwelling house, factory or motor car), it inevitably becomes a complex structure when parts of it are replaced. For example, if the tyre fitted to a wheel on a brand new car is defective and, because of the defect, it causes damage to other parts of the motor vehicle, that damage will be classified as pure economic loss.[195] However, if the original tyre is replaced with a defective tyre which then, because of the defect, causes damage to other parts of the motor vehicle, that damage will be classified as physical, although the damage to the defective tyre itself remains distinctly classified as pure economic loss.[196]

Pure economic loss: primary and secondary victims

11–30   Prior to the decision of the House of Lords in the *Hedley Byrne*[197] case in 1964, courts had consistently refused to recognise liability in negligence for pure economic loss.[198] A different policy was applied to claims for pure economic loss than for physical harm, whereas

> "the infliction of physical injury to the person or property of another universally requires to be justified . . . the causing of economic loss does not."[199]

Several justifications for this distinction have been put forward, including the promotion of competition as being in the interest of the public in a market based economy, and the fear that the unpredictability of the economic consequences of an act could open the floodgates to an unmanageable range of claims.[200]

Hedley Byrne was at first described as a "liability for negligent mis-statement" case,[201] and it is often still referred to as such. However, *Hedley Byrne* may also be analysed as a case brought by a primary victim of alleged negligence for pure economic loss. In that sense *Hedley Byrne* may be distinguished from the line of cases which suggested that the law imposed a rule excluding claims in pure economic loss. Indeed, as will be seen below, the "exclusionary rule" is still applied to claims from secondary victims for pure economic loss. The analysis

---

[194] See, e.g. *M/S Aswan Engineering Establishment Co v Lupdine Ltd* [1987] 1 W.L.R. 1, where a waterproofing compound was lost after the plastic pails in which it had been supplied melted. Lloyd L.J. intimated that he would view the loss of the product as property damage whereas Nicholls L.J. would have viewed the loss as purely economic.

[195] Unless the tyre is a "distinct item incorporated in the (motor vehicle)": *Murphy v Brentwood DC* [1991] 1 A.C. 398 at 478 per Lord Bridge of Harwich.

[196] Consumer Protection Act 1987 s.5 (1). See also *D & F Estates Ltd v Church Commissioners for England* [1989] A.C. 177 at 211–212 per Lord Oliver of Aylmerton.

[197] *Hedley Byrne & Co Ltd v Heller & Partners Ltd* [1964] A.C. 465.

[198] See, e.g. *Allan v Barclay* (1864) 2 M. 873; *Reavis v Clan Line Steamers (No.1)*, 1925 S.C. 725; *Candler v Crane Christmas & Co* [1951] 2 K.B. 164. There were at least two exceptions: *Cann v Willson* (1888) 39 Ch. D. 39; *Morrison Steamship Co Ltd v Greystoke Castle (Cargo Owners)* [1947] A.C. 265.

[199] *Murphy v Brentwood DC* [1991] 1 A.C. 398 at 487 per Lord Oliver of Aylmerton.

[200] See, e.g. *Hedley Byrne & Co Ltd v Heller & Partners Ltd* [1964] A.C. 465 at 534 per Lord Pearce. Cf. at 496 per Lord Morris of Borth-y-Gest; at 517 per Lord Devlin.

[201] See, e.g. *Home Office v Dorset Yacht Co Ltd* [1970] A.C. 1004 at 1061 per Lord Diplock.

applied in this section will therefore distinguish between primary victim pure economic loss and secondary victim pure economic loss.

Proximity of relationship: primary victim pure economic loss

Hedley Byrne v Heller and Partners[202] generally is seen as the first case where   **11-31** the House of Lords acknowledged that the law of negligence might permit a claim for pure economic loss. The plaintiffs were an advertising agency. They were approached by a company, Easipower Ltd, who wanted Hedley Byrne to carry out a lot of work for them on credit. Before committing themselves, Hedley Byrne naturally wanted to make sure that Easipower would pay the bill so Hedley Byrne sent a letter to Easipower's bank (Heller and Partners) asking for a credit reference. Heller responded to the request by supplying a letter stating that Easipower was "considered good for its ordinary business engagements". However, the letter also stated: "without responsibility on the part of this bank"—a disclaimer of liability. Relying on the positive credit reference, Hedley Byrne entered a contract with Easipower and carried out the work, but were not paid before Easipower went into liquidation. Because Easipower was insolvent, there was no point in the advertising agency suing the client for breach of contract, so Hedley Byrne sued the bank in negligence.

The House of Lords decided that where information or advice was provided in circumstances where reliance on that advice would run the risk of financial loss, a duty of care would be imposed if there was a "special relationship" between the parties.[203] A special relationship would be "equivalent to contract"[204] and the indicators of such a relationship would be an assumption of responsibility[205] by the advisor to the advisee, and reliance that was reasonable in the circumstances by the advisee upon the advice.[206] However, the House of Lords held that because of the disclaimer incorporated by the bank into their letter, the bank had denied rather than assumed responsibility, and so the bank avoided the duty of care. Thus, Hedley Byrne lost the case on its facts.[207]

Thus, in a primary victim pure economic loss case where there is no clear precedent to confirm that, on the facts, a duty of care is owed by the defender to the pursuer, there requires to be a special relationship between the parties to satisfy the proximity of relationship requirement from the *Caparo* three-part

---

[202] *Hedley Byrne v Heller and Partners* [1964] A.C. 465.

[203] In reaching this decision, the House of Lords approved the dissenting judgment of Lord Denning M.R. in *Candler v Crane Christmas* [1951] 2 K.B. 164. The term "special relationship" was sourced to *Nocton v Lord Ashburton* [1914] A.C. 932 at 956 per Lord Haldane.

[204] This term was also sourced to *Nocton v Lord Ashburton* [1914] A.C. 932 at 972 per Lord Shaw.

[205] *Hedley Byrne & Co Ltd v Heller & Partners Ltd* [1964] A.C. 465 at 528–529 per Lord Devlin.

[206] *Hedley Byrne & Co Ltd v Heller & Partners Ltd* [1964] A.C. 465 at 502–503 per Lord Morris of Borth-y-Gest. It is interesting to compare the last requirement—reasonable reliance—to the policy element of the *Caparo* three part test where it must be "fair, just and reasonable" in the circumstances for the law to impose a duty of care.

[207] The disclaimer of liability would now be subject to the "fair and reasonable" test under s.16 of the Unfair Contract Terms Act 1977 (non-contractual disclaimers becoming subject to the Act under s.10 of the Law Reform (Miscellaneous Provisions) (Scotland) Act 1990). It is suggested that because the two parties occupied similar bargaining positions the disclaimer would likely pass such a test: see, e.g. *Bank of Scotland v Fuller Peiser*, 2002 S.L.T. 574; cf. *Melrose v Davidson & Robertson*, 1993 S.C. 288.

test.[208] As will be seen below there have been some cases where a voluntary assumption of responsibility has been accepted as sufficient,[209] but generally there are three elements to consider in deciding whether the relationship between the parties is so proximate to qualify as special:

1. relationship equivalent to contract;
2. assumption of responsibility;
3. reasonable reliance.

Special relationship: equivalent to contract

11–32   The first indicator of a special relationship is that it is "equivalent to contract". Lord Devlin defined such a relationship as one "where there is an assumption of responsibility in circumstances in which, but for the absence of consideration, there would be a contract."[210] He went on to explain:

> "Such a relationship may be either general or particular. Examples of a general relationship are those of solicitor and client and of banker and customer. There may well be others yet to be established. Where there is a general relationship of this sort, it is unnecessary to do more than prove its existence and the duty follows. Where, as in the present case, what is relied on is a particular relationship created *ad hoc*, it will be necessary to examine the particular facts to see whether there is an express or implied undertaking of responsibility."[211]

In *Hedley Byrne* the advertising agency had communicated a request for advice to the potential client's bank and the bank had responded by communicating the credit reference to the advertising agency. Although not amounting to an offer and acceptance as such, these communications may be compared with typical negotiations leading to the formation of a contract, i.e. that the communications were direct and reciprocal as between the parties.

Whether it is necessary that communications are communicated directly from each party to the other is open to question. In the *Hedley Byrne* case itself, it was the advertising agency's own bank who in fact sent the letter to Heller and Partners. In doing so, Hedley Byrne's bank may be seen to have been acting in the capacity of agent of the advertising agency, so the communications may still be deemed to have been directly between the parties. However, if the bank had been contacted by an independent credit reference agency engaged by Hedley

---

[208] Generally, proof of a special relationship based on an application of the *Caparo/Hedley Byrne* tests is not required where a negligent misrepresentation is alleged to have been made as part of pre-contractual negotiations, even where the resulting contract is eventually entered between the misrepresenting party and a corporate body created subsequent to the misrepresentation by the misled party: *Cramaso LLP v Viscount Reidhaven's Trustees*, 2014 S.L.T. 521. See also *Hamilton v Allied Domecq Plc*, 2001 S.C. 829 at 836 per Lord Carloway; *BSA International SA v Irvine* [2010] CSOH 78 at [15] per Lord Glennie.

[209] Notably *Spring v Guardian Assurance* [1995] 2 A.C. 296; *Henderson v Merrett Syndicates* [1995] 2 A.C. 145; and *White v Jones* [1995] 2 A.C. 207. See also *Williams v Natural Life Health Food Ltd* [1998] 1 W.L.R. 830.

[210] *Hedley Byrne & Co Ltd v Heller & Partners Ltd* [1964] A.C. 465 at 529 per Lord Devlin. It might be observed that such relationships would create obligations enforceable be the law of contract or of promise in Scotland, given the lack of insistence on consideration as a prerequisite of an enforceable voluntary obligation.

[211] *Hedley Byrne & Co Ltd v Heller & Partners Ltd* [1964] A.C. 465 at 530 per Lord Devlin.

Byrne for that purpose, would that suffice—especially where the bank might not be apprised of either the identity of the credit reference agency's client or the specific transaction the information was to be put to? An indication of the answer may be gleaned from litigation brought against surveyors by purchasers of properties, such as the related cases (the appeals were heard together by the House of Lords) of *Smith v Eric S. Bush* and *Harris v Wyre Forest DC*.[212]

The facts in each were typical of such cases: an individual wishes to buy a house, but has not the means to pay for it in cash, and so applies for a mortgage. The proposed mortgage provider wishes to ensure that the property in question provides good security for the loan, and so insists upon a valuation survey of the property. The proposed mortgage provider instructs the survey (so entering into a contractual relationship with the surveyor). The surveyor provides a report which confirms the value of the property - and so the mortgage provider lends the money required to complete the purchase. Thus, but for the surveyor certifying that the property provides adequate security, the mortgage provider would not advance the funds and the purchaser would not be able to complete the purchase. Accordingly, the purchaser is relying upon such a survey report for two purposes: first, to enable the completion of the purchase transaction; and secondly, to confirm the condition of the property. In both of the cases the question was whether the surveyor owed a duty of care to the purchaser where each of the survey reports had overvalued the respective properties, it being alleged the surveyors had not reported defects in the respective properties which would have been obvious to an ordinarily competent surveyor taking reasonable care. The House of Lords confirmed that a duty of care was owed by the surveyors to the prospective purchasers:

> "The salient feature of all these cases is that the defendant giving advice or information was fully aware of the nature of the transaction which the plaintiff had in contemplation, knew that the advice or information would be communicated to him directly or indirectly and knew that it was very likely that the plaintiff would rely on that advice or information in deciding whether or not to engage in the transaction in contemplation."[213]

Thus, the communication between the parties need not necessarily be direct.[214] **11–33** However, it remains that to be "equivalent to contract" the communications must be reciprocal in the sense of supplied in response to the requirement of a specific individual (or possibly limited class) in respect of a specific transaction.

This requirement of what we might call "reciprocity" was reinforced by the House of Lords in *Customs and Excise Commissioners v Barclays Bank Plc*.[215] The Commissioners had obtained court orders freezing the accounts held with the bank by two companies. Shortly after notice of the orders had been served upon the bank, the accounts were emptied, effectively frustrating the freezing orders

---

[212] *Smith v Eric S. Bush* and *Harris v Wyre Forest DC* [1990] 1 A.C. 831. See also *Martin v Bell Ingram*, 1986 S.C. 208; *Melrose v Davidson & Robertson*, 1993 S.C. 288. Cf. *Scullion v Bank of Scotland Plc (t/a Colleys)* [2011] 1 W.L.R. 3212 (distinguished from *Smith v Eric S Bush* as the purchaser was buying to let rather than as purchaser's residential home, i.e. the transaction was commercial rather than consumer in nature).

[213] *Caparo Industries Plc v Dickman* [1990] 2 A.C. 605 at 620–621 per Lord Bridge of Harwich.

[214] See also *White v Jones* [1995] 2 A.C. 207 at 271 per Lord Browne-Wilkinson; *Hines v King Sturge LLP*, 2011 S.L.T. 2 at 14 per Lord Osborne.

[215] *Customs and Excise Commissioners v Barclays Bank Plc* [2007] 1 A.C. 181.

and putting the funds in question (due for unpaid VAT) beyond the reach of the Commissioners. Having confirmed that there was no question of a voluntary assumption of responsibility by the bank to the Commissioners, the House of Lords reverted to applying the *Caparo* three-stage test. In doing so, the court noted the absence of any reciprocal communication between the parties, leading to the conclusion that the "bank and the applicant are about as far from being in a relationship 'equivalent to contract' as they could be."[216]

The need for reciprocal communication may be seen as a major factor in distinguishing auditor liability cases such as, on the one hand, *Caparo v Dickman*,[217] and on the other *Morgan Crucible v Hill Samuel Bank*.[218] Again the facts in each were typical of such cases. Parties making a takeover bid (i.e. an offer to acquire all of a target company's shares from its existing shareholders) acquired financial information about the target companies which had been prepared by the targets' respective auditors under statutory audit rules. The financial information was inaccurate, overvaluing the respective targets. Relying upon the inaccurate information resulted in financial loss, as the successful bidders paid more for the shares than they would have had they known the true financial state of the respective targets. In *Caparo*, the bidders received the financial information about the target (Fidelity Plc) from the target company itself because they already owned shares in Fidelity Plc. Thus there was no reciprocal communication between the bidders and the auditors. However, in *Morgan Crucible* the bidders received the financial information directly from the target's auditors after already making a takeover offer which had not been accepted by the target's shareholders. The supply of the financial information was likely intended to persuade the bidders to increase the offer, which they did. In *Caparo*, the House of Lords unanimously held that there was insufficient proximity of relationship for a duty of care to be owed (no reciprocal communication) whereas in *Morgan Crucible* the Court of Appeal allowed the case to proceed to a trial to determine on the evidence whether there was sufficient proximity of relationship between the parties.

11-34   So it appears that reciprocity is a prerequisite to a relationship "equivalent to contract". A question that follows is what if there actually *is* a contractual relationship between the parties? Is a contractual relationship the paradigm or the antithesis of a relationship "equivalent to contract"? If "the law of (delict) is the general law, out of which the parties can, if they wish, contract,"[219] whether or not the law of delict will continue to regulate the relationship between

---

[216] *Customs and Excise Commissioners v Barclays Bank Plc* [2007] 1 A.C. 181 at 208 per Lord Rodger of Earlsferry. Cf. *Ministry of Housing and Local Government v Sharp* [1970] 2 Q.B. 223 (described in *Customs and Excise Commissioners v Barclays Bank* as "rightly decided" at 222 per Lord Mance). See also *Braes v Keeper of the Registers of Scotland*, 2010 S.L.T. 689.

[217] *Caparo v Dickman* [1990] 2 A.C. 605.

[218] *Morgan Crucible v Hill Samuel Bank* [1991] Ch. 295. See also, e.g. *Esso Petroleum Co Ltd v Mardon* [1976] Q.B. 801; *Al Saudi Banque v Clark Pixley* [1990] 1 Ch. 313; *James McNaughton Paper Group Ltd v Hicks Anderson & Co* [1991] 2 Q.B. 113; *Galoo Ltd v Bright Grahame Murray* [1994] 1 WLR 1360; *ADT Ltd v BDO Binder Hamlyn* [1996] B.C.C. 808 (where a 45 minute meeting resulted in a £65m liability); *Welton v North Cornwall DC* [1997] 1 W.L.R. 570; *BCCI (Overseas) Ltd v Price Waterhouse Coopers (No 2)* [1998] B.C.C. 617; *Electra Private Equity Partners v KPMG Peat Marwick* [2000] B.C.C. 368; *Esanda Finance Corp Ltd v Peat Marwick Hungerfords* [2000] Lloyd's Rep. P.N. 684; *Partco Group Ltd v Wragg* [2002] 2 Lloyd's Rep. 343; *Royal Bank of Scotland v Bannerman Johnstone Maclay*, 2005 1 S.C. 437; *Man Nutzfahrzeuge AG v Ernst & Young* [2007] B.C.C. 986.

[219] *Henderson v Merrett Syndicates* [1995] 2 A.C. 145 at 193 per Lord Goff of Chieveley.

contracting parties should depend upon the will of the parties themselves. The difficulty though will be in determining the will of the parties where the point has not been addressed within the terms of the contract. Where the intention of contracting parties is unclear, the question then becomes what is the default position? It follows from the dictum of Lord Goff just quoted that, unless clearly the parties have chosen to supersede the general law, there will be a rebuttable presumption that a delictual duty of care will be owed in parallel to the contractual relationship. However, if doctrinally contract takes priority over delict because of the value attached to choice, it is equally (if not more strongly) arguable that the parties in expressing what they have chosen to incorporate have by implication excluded anything else—summed up in the maxim *inclusio unius est exlusio alterius* (inclusion of one excludes the other). It is submitted that the latter approach is also more consistent with the doctrine that contractual obligations arise *ex voluntante* rather than *ex lege*. Thus, it should follow that there should be a presumption (probably rebuttable) that contracting parties' remedies are confined to those set out in the terms of the contract.[220]

If by entering into a contract with each other the parties *ex voluntante* have structured their relationship so as to create a presumption against the super-imposing of *ex lege* delictual duties of care, what is the legal position where the parties are indirectly contractually related through a chain of contracts? A typical example might be where an owner of land wishes to erect a building on that land. The owner may contract with a builder to deliver a fully completed building. The builder may then sub-contract the various specialist works required for completion of the project, e.g. appointing an architect who in turn might appoint a surveyor, and appointing specialists to supply and install foundations, plumbing, electrics, windows, ceilings, firewalls, floors etc. A complex matrix of contracts may be created and it becomes necessary to ask whether, in terms of liability, the relationships are structured to connect[221] or to separate[222] the various parties. The question arose in *Junior Books v Veitchi*,[223] where the House of Lords delivered a decision which has been condemned, probably unfairly, as the "high water mark" of *Anns*[224] liability. The pursuers, who had contracted for the construction of a factory, alleged that due to the negligence of nominated[225] sub-contractors a

---

[220] See, e.g. *Hamilton v Allied Domecq Plc*, 2007 S.C. (HL) 142 at 148 per Lord Rodger of Earlsferry; *Robinson v P E Jones (Contractors) Ltd* [2012] Q.B. 44. Policy reasons (based on a legal hierarchy) for keeping delict out of contract have also been expressed in, e.g. *Downsview Nominees Ltd v First City Corporation Ltd* [1993] A.C. 295 at 316 per Lord Templeman; *Marc Rich & Co. AG v Bishop Rock Marine Co Ltd* [1996] A.C. 211 at 238–242 per Lord Steyn. See also *British Telecommunications Plc v James Thomson & Sons (Engineers) Ltd*, 1999 S.C. (HL) 9; *Realstone Ltd v J & E Shepherd* [2008] P.N.L.R. 21.

[221] Examples of cases where the decisions were consistent with this view include: *Junior Books Ltd v Veitchi Co Ltd*, 1982 S.C. (HL) 244; *Smith v Eric S. Bush* [1990] 1 A.C. 831; *Martin v Bell Ingram*, 1986 S.C. 208; *Melrose v Davidson & Robertson*, 1993 S.C. 288; *Henderson v Merrett Syndicates* [1995] 2 A.C. 145; *Fuji Seal Europe Ltd v Catalytic Combustion Corporation* (2005) 102 Con. L.R. 47; *Riyad Bank v Ahli United Bank (UK) Plc* [2006] 2 Lloyd's Rep. 292; *Realstone Ltd v J&E Shepherd* [2008] P.N.L.R. 21. A proof before answer on inter alia this point was allowed in *Hines v King Sturge LLP*, 2011 S.L.T. 2.

[222] Examples of cases where the decisions were consistent with this view include: *D. & F. Estates Ltd v Church Commissioners for England* [1989] A.C. 177; *Simaan Contracting v Pilkington Glass* [1988] 1 Q.B. 758; *Nordic Oil Services Ltd v Berman*, 1993 S.L.T. 1164; *Williams v Natural Life Health Foods Ltd* [1998] 1 W.L.R. 830; *West Bromwich Albion Football Club Ltd v El-Safty* [2007] P.I.Q.R. P7.

[223] *Junior Books v Veitchi*, 1982 S.C. (HL) 244.

[224] *Anns v Merton LBC* [1978] A.C. 728.

[225] Meaning chosen by the owners rather than the main contractors.

defective (but not dangerous) floor had been installed in their factory, costing substantial sums of money to put right and causing lost profits to the owners in the process. Rather than sue the main contractor for breach of contract the owners chose to sue the specialist flooring contractors in negligence. By a majority, the House of Lords found that the sub-contractors owed the owner a duty of care as their relationship was of very close proximity, only just falling short of a direct contractual relationship. Factors crucial to the decision in *Junior Books* were:

"1. The appellants were nominated sub-contractors;
2. The appellants were specialists in flooring;
3. The appellants knew what products were required by the respondents and their main contractors and specialised in the production of those products;
4. The appellants alone were responsible for the composition and construction of the flooring;
5. The respondents relied upon the appellants' skill and experience;
6. The appellants as nominated sub-contractors must have known that the respondents relied upon their skill and experience;
7. The relationship between the parties was as close as it could be short of actual privity of contract;
8. The appellants must be taken to have known that if they did the work negligently (as it must be assumed that they did) the resulting defects would at some time require remedying by the respondents expending money upon the remedial measures as a consequence of which the respondents would suffer financial or economic loss."[226]

11–35 It follows that each case must be decided on its own merits, requiring an intense focus on its specific facts. This was the approach taken by Lord Clyde in *Scott Lithgow Ltd v GEC Electrical Projects Ltd*,[227] and by Lord Hodge in *Realstone Ltd v J & E Shepherd*.[228] The object is to determine whether, in choosing to structure their relationship through a chain of contracts, the parties have consented to include, or contrived to exclude, a delictual duty of care.

One other question remains to be considered under this heading. It is whether the "assumption of responsibility" concept that was developed by Lord Goff in *Spring v Guardian Assurance*,[229] *White v Jones*[230] and *Henderson v Merrett Syndicates*[231] operates in combination with, or in parallel to, the "equivalent to contract" concept. The answer to that question may be found in determining whether reciprocity was a pre-requisite for "assumption of responsibility" liability. In *Spring*, the provider of an employment reference was held to owe a duty of care to the subject of the reference, having assumed responsibility to the subject of the reference for the information and opinions provided to the potential employer. Although there was no direct communication between the job applicant and the referee (the request for the reference being made by the potential employer) it tentatively could be argued that there was reciprocity in the sense that the applicant was an ex-employee of the referee and an employment

---

[226] *Junior Books Ltd v Veitchi Co Ltd*, 1982 S.C. (HL) 244 at 277 per Lord Roskill.
[227] *Scott Lithgow Ltd v GEC Electrical Projects Ltd*, 1989 S.C. 412 at 426.
[228] *Realstone Ltd v J & E Shepherd* [2008] P.N.L.R. 21 at 578–580.
[229] *Spring v Guardian Assurance* [1995] 2 A.C. 296.
[230] *White v Jones* [1995] 2 A.C. 207.
[231] *Henderson v Merrett Syndicates* [1995] 2 A.C. 145.

reference is part and parcel of the residual relationship between an employer and an ex-employee. However, in *White* there had never been any direct relationship between the relevant parties. In *White*, a solicitor failed to carry out a client's testamentary instructions prior to the client's death. By a majority, the solicitor was held by the House of Lords to owe a duty of care to the disappointed intended beneficiaries. Given that the intended beneficiaries played an entirely passive role in the circumstances, it is surely beyond argument that there never was reciprocity between the parties. Thus, it is suggested that the "assumption of responsibility" concept does not require reciprocity and so operates as an alternative to the "equivalent to contract" concept. It follows that the separate tests may ultimately yield different results.[232]

Special relationship: assumption of responsibility

The second indicator of a special relationship is that the defender must have **11–36** assumed responsibility to the pursuer. The concept was explained by Lord Morris of Borth-y-Gest in his speech in *Hedley Byrne*:

> "(I)f someone possessed of a special skill undertakes, quite irrespective of contract, to apply that skill for the assistance of another person who relies upon such skill, a duty of care will arise. The fact that the service is to be given by means of or by the instrumentality of words can make no difference. Furthermore, if in a sphere in which a person is so placed that others could reasonably rely upon his judgment or his skill or upon his ability to make careful inquiry, a person takes it upon himself to give information or advice to, or allows his information or advice to be passed on to, another person who, as he knows or should know, will place reliance upon it, then a duty of care will arise."[233]

The word "voluntary" frequently precedes "assumption of responsibility" when the phrase is used in this context. That raises the question as to whether the duty of care is imposed *ex lege* or is undertaken *ex voluntante*. If the answer is the latter then it might be said that the law of delict is straying into territory that is the true preserve of the law of contract. The issue has been addressed. In his speech in *Caparo*, Lord Oliver stated:

> " '(V)oluntary assumption of responsibility' ... is a convenient phrase but it is clear that it was not intended to be a test for the existence of the duty for, on analysis, it means no more than that the act of the defendant in making the statement or tendering the advice was voluntary and that the law attributes to it an assumption of responsibility if the statement or advice is inaccurate and is acted upon."[234]

---

[232] Cf. *Bank of Credit and Commerce International (Overseas) Ltd (In Liquidation) v Price Waterhouse (No.2)* [1998] P.N.L.R. 564 at 586–588 per Sir Brian Neill QC. See also *Customs and Excise Commissioners v Barclays Bank Plc* [2007] 1 A.C. 181.

[233] *Hedley Byrne & Co Ltd v Heller & Partners Ltd* [1964] A.C. 465 at 502–503 per Lord Morris of Borth-y-Gest. See also *Caparo Industries Plc v Dickman* [1990] 2 A.C. 605 at 620–621 per Lord Bridge of Harwich. Cf. *Wilson v D M Hall & Sons* [2005] P.N.L.R. 22.

[234] *Caparo Industries Plc v Dickman* [1990] 2 A.C. 605 at 637 per Lord Oliver of Aylmerton.

In *Henderson v Merrett Syndicates*, Lord Goff considered that an objective, rather than a subjective test should be applied.[235] So the state of mind of the defender is irrelevant[236] and the law does not require voluntary, conscious or any other active acceptance of responsibility by the defender.[237] However, the state of mind of the defender must be distinguished from the activity of the defender that is called into question.[238] Engagement in the relevant activity must be voluntary on the part of the defender.[239] Accordingly, although the *act* will be *ex voluntante*, the *duty* arises *ex lege*. Furthermore, there must be evidence to support an averment that the defender assumed responsibility for carrying out the activity. Thus, in *Hamilton v Allied Domecq Plc*,[240] the House of Lords refused an appeal from the Inner House where the appellants argued that the law of delict imposed a duty on the respondents to make clear what was their *understanding* of pre-contractual negotiations. Lord Rodger stated that

> "the simple truth is that counsel for the appellants was unable to point to anything in the facts or evidence to show that, in this particular commercial negotiation, there had been any voluntary assumption of responsibility on the part of (Allied Domecq)."[241]

Although the provision of professional or other specialist services has been the most fertile ground for case law, the concept has not been confined to such cases. "Ancillary" business activity, such as the provision of information to employees[242] or the provision of character references of former employees may be included,[243] as might even the provision of advice provided a person holding himself out as a skilled amateur.[244]

---

[235] *Henderson v Merrett Syndicates* [1995] 2 A.C. 145 at 181 per Lord Goff of Chieveley.

[236] *Williams v Natural Life Health Foods Ltd* [1998] 1 W.L.R. 830 at 835 per Lord Steyn.

[237] *Smith v Eric S Bush* [1990] 1 A.C. 831 at 862 per Lord Griffiths. "Whether a party has assumed responsibility is a question of law. The court does not have to find that the relevant party has voluntarily assumed responsibility ... The word 'assumption' is therefore something of a misnomer. The phrase 'attachment' of responsibility might be more accurate": *Chandler v Cape Plc* [2012] 1 W.L.R. 3111 at 3127 per Arden L.J.

[238] "(T)he assumption of responsibility referred to is the defendant's assumption of responsibility for the task not the assumption of legal responsibility": *White v Jones* [1995] 2 A.C. 207 at 273 per Lord Browne-Wilkinson.

[239] *Customs and Excise Commissioners v Barclays Bank Plc* [2007] 1 A.C. 181 at 200 per Lord Hoffmann: the law of negligence does not impose liability for "pure omissions". However, a duty to take care may still arise in providing information or advice in compliance with a statutory or regulatory duty: see, e.g. *Spring v Guardian Assurance* [1995] 2 A.C. 296. Cf. *Mitchell v Glasgow City Council*, 2009 S.C. (HL) 21; *X & Y v London Borough of Hounslow* [2009] P.T.S.R. 1158; *Desmond v Chief Constable of Nottinghamshire* [2011] P.T.S.R. 1369.

[240] *Hamilton v Allied Domecq Plc*, 2007 S.C. (HL) 142. See also *Banque Keyser Ullmann SA v Skandia (UK) Insurance Co Ltd* [1990] 1 Q.B. 665; *Howard Marine & Dredging Co Ltd v A Ogden & Sons (Excavations) Ltd* [1978] Q.B. 574.

[241] *Hamilton v Allied Domecq Plc*, 2007 S.C. (HL) 142 at 147 per Lord Rodger. See also *Robinson v P E Jones (Contractors) Ltd* [2012] Q.B. 44.

[242] *Lennon v Commissioner of Police of the Metropolis* [2004] 1 W.L.R. 2594. Cf. *Crossley v Faithful & Gould Holdings Ltd* [2004] 4 All E.R. 447.

[243] *Spring v Guardian Assurance Plc* [1995] 2 A.C. 296.

[244] *Chaudhry v Prabhakar* [1988] 3 All E.R. 718. In this case a defendant was held liable after his counsel conceded that he owed a duty of care for the provision of advice in assisting a family fried in the purchase of her first car. It is considered that the case was decided on its own facts. It has never been followed since.

Spring v Guardian Assurance[245] was the first of three cases heard by the House 11–37
of Lords in quick succession in the mid 1990s in which Lord Goff of Chieveley
developed a suggestion that an assumption of responsibility may in itself be
enough to establish an *ex lege* duty of care:

> " . . . if a person assumes responsibility to another in respect of certain
> services, there is no reason why he should not be liable in damages for that
> other in respect of . . . loss which flows from the negligent performance of
> those services. It follows that, once the case is identified as falling within
> (this) principle, there should be no need to embark upon any further enquiry
> whether it is "fair, just and reasonable" to impose liability . . . "[246]

In *Spring*, a former employee sued over an employment reference which was
described by the trial judge as the "kiss of death" on the plaintiff's career in the
insurance market. The reference was based on an inadequate investigation and so
contained information about the plaintiff which was untrue. The plaintiff sued in
negligence so as to circumvent the defence of qualified privilege which would
have protected the reference from liability in defamation. The House of Lords
held by a majority of four to one that the plaintiff was owed a duty of care by his
former employer.[247] Three of the judges justified this decision upon the
application of the *Caparo* three part test, but Lord Goff arrived at the same
conclusion by a different route:

> "(W)here the plaintiff entrusts the defendant with the conduct of his affairs,
> in general or in particular, the defendant may be held to have assumed
> responsibility to the plaintiff, and the plaintiff to have relied on the
> defendant to exercise due skill and care, in respect of such conduct."[248]

Lord Goff went on to consider whether policy considerations should militate
against the existence of a duty of care, referring specifically to the suggestion that
liability in negligence would undermine the function of the qualified privilege
defence in defamation. However, he concluded that because of the *Hedley Byrne*
requirement of a relationship between the parties "equivalent to contract" there
was no good reason to negative the duty of care.[249]

Thus, in *Spring*, Lord Goff's approach was to treat proximity of relationship
as creating a presumption in favour of the existence of a duty of care which

---

[245] *Spring v Guardian Assurance* [1995] 2 A.C. 296. The other two were *Henderson v Merrett Syndicates* [1995] 2 A.C. 145 and *White v Jones* [1995] 2 A.C. 207. Lord Goff had already introduced the concept as almost self-standing in *Maloco v Littlewoods Organisation Ltd*, 1987 S.C. (HL) 37 at 77–79, and revisited the concept in *Williams v Natural Life Health Foods Ltd* [1998] 1 W.L.R. 830.

[246] *Henderson v Merrett Syndicates* [1995] 2 A.C. 145 at 180–181. Cf. *Caparo Industries Plc v Dickman* [1990] 2 A.C. 605 at 637 per Lord Oliver of Aylmerton.

[247] The decision has been applied in Scotland: *Donlon v Colonial Mutual Group (UK Holdings) Ltd*, 1998 S.C. 244.

[248] *Spring v Guardian Assurance* [1995] 2 A.C. 296 at 318 per Lord Goff of Chieveley. Lord Goff distinguished *Mutual Life and Citizens' Assurance Co Ltd v Evatt* [1971] A.C. 793 by pointing out (at 320) that "the skill of preparing a reference in respect of an employee falls as much within the expertise of an employer as the skill of preparing a bank reference fell within the expertise of the defendant bank in *Hedley Byrne* itself."

[249] *Spring v Guardian Assurance* [1995] 2 A.C. 296 at 324.

would only be displaced if policy considerations negatived a duty of care,[250] the onus of proof with regard to the latter being upon the defender. Three weeks later Lord Goff went further in delivering his speech in *Henderson v Merrett Syndicates.*[251]

The facts in *Henderson* were complicated.[252] The case was between Lloyds names and those whose negligence they said had caused them to lose on their Lloyds investment. Superficially, the scheme operates by the "name" joining a syndicate and in so doing agreeing to be responsible to an unlimited amount, being worth a certain sum and depositing a fraction of it. Normally this was easy money and becoming a Lloyds name carried a cachet. Bad weather in the United States and large damages claims—ironically probably based on tort—brought about enormous losses. The names' case, at its most honourable, was that they did not mind losing but the way their involvement was handled by their agents and sub-agents was negligent, lacking all care for their interests. Holding that the existence of a contractual relationship did not per se prevent a duty of care in tort/delict being owed by contracting parties, Lord Goff, with whom all of the other Law Lords agreed, held that a duty of care was owed upon an application of the *Hedley Byrne* principle of voluntary assumption of responsibility. Lord Goff's view was that a duty of care will be owed within a relationship, whether contractual or otherwise, where one party undertakes or assumes responsibility to the other for the supply of information, advice or services in circumstances where the other party relies on the expertise or special knowledge of the supplier. Further:

> "It follows that, once the case is identified as falling within the *Hedley Byrne* principle, there should be no need to embark upon any further enquiry whether it is 'fair, just and reasonable' to impose liability for economic loss."

11–38 Thus, if the case falls within the "*Hedley Byrne* principle" the first *Caparo* criterion is unnecessary and the third *Caparo* criterion is irrelevant.

The third case in the trilogy was *White v Jones.*[253] Sisters sued a negligent solicitor who had failed to carry out their father's instructions on the alteration of his will to the plaintiffs' benefit prior to his death. Lord Goff dispensed with old authority to the effect that a solicitor would incur no liability by declaring Lord Campbell's dictum in *Robertson v Fleming*[254] to be obiter and in any event superseded by a century of jurisprudence. Lord Mustill described the issue:

> "If A promises B to perform a service for B which B intends, and A knows, will confer a benefit on C if it is performed, does A owe to C in (delict) a duty to perform that service? . . . So expressed, this is a new question, and the right way to approach it is . . . to 'see how far the authorities have gone, for new categories in the law do not spring into existence overnight.'"[255]

---

[250] Reminiscent of the discredited approach of Lord Wilberforce in *Anns v Merton LBC* [1978] A.C. 728.

[251] *Henderson v Merrett Syndicates* [1995] 2 A.C. 145.

[252] See P. Cave, "Contract, Tort and the Lloyd's Debacle" in F.D. Rose (ed.), *Consensus Ad Idem: Essays on Contract in Honour of Guenter Treitel* (London: Sweet & Maxwell, 1996), p.5.

[253] *White v Jones* [1995] 2 A.C. 207.

[254] *Robertson v Fleming* (1861) 4 Macq. 167.

[255] *White v Jones* [1995] 2 A.C. 207 at 283 (quoting Lord Devlin in *Hedley Byrne & Co Ltd v Heller & Partners Ltd* [1964] A.C. 465 at 525).

Nevertheless, expressing an "impulse to do practical justice" Lord Goff said:

> "It seems to me that it is open to your Lordships' House ... to fashion a remedy to fill a lacuna in the law and so prevent the injustice which would otherwise occur on the facts of cases such as the present ... In my opinion your Lordships' House should in cases such as these extend to the intended beneficiary a remedy under the *Hedley Byrne* principle by holding that the assumption of responsibility by the solicitor towards his client should be held in law to extend to the intended beneficiary who (as the solicitor can reasonably foresee) may, as a result of the solicitor's negligence, be deprived of his intended legacy in circumstances in which neither the testator nor his estate will have a remedy against the solicitor."[256]

By a three to two majority, the House of Lords held that the solicitor owed a duty of care to the disappointed beneficiaries. The decision has been followed in Scotland,[257] but only on its own facts.[258] There is a risk that to apply the "assumption of responsibility" concept too widely, without insisting on a reciprocal relationship between the parties or concomitant reliance, will be to invite liability to an indeterminate class.[259] Nevertheless, Lord Goff's approach has been cautiously re-validated by the House of Lords, albeit viewed as one of three approaches which should be complementary in effect.[260]

In *Hedley Byrne*, the disclaimer of responsibility inserted into the credit reference by Heller & Partners denied directly any assumption of responsibility. Such a disclaimer would now be subject to the fair and reasonable test under s.16 of the Unfair Contract Terms Act 1977.[261] Note that it has since been held that a disclaimer cannot be inserted so as to avoid a duty of care arising at all—the disclaimer may only avoid liability for *breach* of duty.[262] The test has been applied on several occasions to disclaimers inserted by into survey reports carried out by professional surveyors on properties as instructed by potential mortgage lenders. What is key to the application of the test are the respective bargaining positions of the client of the potential lender (i.e. the person(s) intending purchasing the property in question) and the surveyor. Such disclaimers have been held not to be fair and reasonable where the client is a consumer[263] but have been upheld as fair and reasonable where the client is in business.[264]

---

[256] *White v Jones* [1995] 2 A.C. 207 at 268.
[257] *Robertson v Watt & Co* Unreported July 4, 1995 IH (2 Div); *Holmes v Bank of Scotland*, 2002 S.L.T. 544. See also *Hines v King Sturge LLP*, 2011 S.L.T. 2; *Steven v Hewats*, 2013 S.L.T. 763 at 766 per Lord Tyre. For discussion on the *function* of the *White v Jones* principle see *Milligan's Executors v Hewats*, 2013 S.L.T. 758. Cf. *McLeod v Crawford*, 2010 S.L.T. 1035.
[258] *White v Jones* has been distinguished in, e.g. *Matthews v Hunter & Robertson Ltd*, 2008 S.L.T. 634; *Fraser v McArthur Stewart (A Firm)*, 2009 S.L.T. 31; *McLeod v Crawford*, 2010 S.L.T. 1035.
[259] See, e.g. *Saeed v Waheed*, 1996 S.L.T. (Sh. Ct) 39 at 44 per Sheriff Principal C.G.B. Nicholson QC.
[260] *Customs and Excise Commissioners v Barclays Bank Plc* [2006] 3 W.L.R. 1.
[261] The factors relevant to determining whether a disclaimer is fair and reasonable under UCTA are not necessarily the same as the factors relevant to considering whether a duty of care is owed: *Scullion v Bank of Scotland Plc (t/a Colleys)* [2011] 1 W.L.R. 3212.
[262] *Smith v Eric S Bush (A Firm)* and *Harris v Wyre Forest DC* [1990] 1 A.C. 831; *Royal Bank of Scotland Plc v Bannerman Johnstone Maclay*, 2005 1 S.C. 437.
[263] *Smith v Eric S. Bush* and *Harris v Wyre Forest DC* [1990] 1 A.C. 831; *Melrose v Davidson & Robertson*, 1993 S.C. 288.
[264] *Bank of Scotland v Fuller Peiser*, 2002 S.L.T. 574; *Robinson v P E Jones (Contractors) Ltd* [2012] Q.B. 44.

Special relationship: reasonable reliance

11–39   The third indicator of a special relationship is reliance, which must be reasonable in the circumstances, by the victim upon the alleged wrongdoer. The concept was explained by Lord Morris of Borth-y-Gest:

> "(I)f in a sphere in which a person is so placed that others could reasonably rely upon his judgment or his skill or upon his ability to make careful inquiry, a person takes it upon himself to give information or advice to, or allows his information or advice to be passed on to, another person who, as he knows or should know, will place reliance upon it, then a duty of care will arise."[265]

It has been suggested that a close reading of this dictum suggests that the reliance may be actual or constructive,[266] which may assist in reconciling the decision of the House of Lords in *White v Jones*[267] with the full Hedley Byrne analysis of a "special relationship". However, "reliance in the law is usually taken to mean that if A had not relied on B he would have acted differently."[268] Thus, for a claim to proceed to a proof, facts must be alleged in the pleadings upon which it would be possible to conclude, or at least infer, that the pursuer would have acted differently but for the actions of, or information tendered by, the defenders.[269]

Although it is not necessary that the defender actively intended the pursuer to rely upon the actions taken or advice given,[270] the defender must have at least been aware of the pursuer's reliance with regard to the type of transaction in question.[271] In *Royal Bank of Scotland Plc v Bannerman Johnstone Maclay*[272] the defenders were a firm of accountants that provided audit and other services to an insolvent company, APC Ltd. The defenders had prepared a business plan to assist with a management buyout which led to the formation of the company, and had seconded one of their employees to the company as financial controller. The pursuers had relied on the business plan, monthly management accounts and audited annual accounts in providing overdrafts and loans to the company and in

---

[265] *Hedley Byrne & Co Ltd v Heller & Partners Ltd* [1964] A.C. 465 at 502–503 per Lord Morris of Borth-y-Gest.

[266] *White v Jones* [1993] 3 W.L.R. 730 at 738 per Sir Donald Nicholls V.C.

[267] *White v Jones* [1995] 2 A.C. 207 at 271–272 and 275 per Lord Goff of Chieveley; *Henderson v Merrett Syndicates Ltd* [1995] 2 A.C. 145.

[268] *Customs and Excise Commissioners v Barclays Bank Plc* [2007] 1 A.C. 181 at 194 per Lord Bingham of Cornhill.

[269] *Hines v King Sturge LLP*, 2009 S.L.T. 763. A proof before answer was refused in a claim brought by tenants for business losses resulting from fire damage to the building, part of which they leased for commercial purposes. The defenders were contracted by the pursuer's landlords to maintain a fire alarm system which the pursuers alleged was defective. The pleadings were held not to contain averments that the pursuers were relying on the defenders, and had informed the defenders of their reliance, to maintain a working fire alarm system.

[270] *Electra Private Equity Partners v KPMG Peat Marwick* [2000] B.C.C. 368; *Royal Bank of Scotland Plc v Bannerman Johnstone Maclay*, 2005 1 S.C. 437.

[271] *Caparo Industries Plc v Dickman* [1990] 2 A.C. 605 at 638–639 per Lord Oliver of Aylmerton; *BCCI (Overseas) Ltd v PriceWaterhouseCoopers (No.2)* [1998] B.C.C. 617 at 635 per Sir Brian Neill; *Peach Publishing Ltd v Slater & Co* [1998] B.C.C. 139; *Electra Private Equity Partners v KPMG Peat Marwick* [2000] B.C.C. 368; *Royal Bank of Scotland Plc v Bannerman Johnstone Maclay*, 2005 1 S.C. 437.

[272] *Royal Bank of Scotland Plc v Bannerman Johnstone Maclay*, 2005 1 S.C. 437. Cf. *Man Nutzfahrzeuge AG v Freightliner Ltd* [2007] B.C.C. 986.

buying a shareholding in the company. The pursuers claimed that the close relationship between the defenders and the failed company indicated that the defenders would have an intimate understanding of the relationship between the company and the pursuers, including an awareness of the reliance they had placed on the defenders. The Inner House, in allowing a proof before answer in a claim for damages for the bank's losses, confirmed that it was not necessary to show that the defender provided information or advice with a positive intention that the defender rely upon it, and that the extent of the involvement of the defenders in the company may reveal that objectively, the defenders would be expected to be aware of the reliance placed by the pursuers upon the professional services it rendered to the company.

The reliance must also be reasonable in the circumstances. There is overlap here with the fair, just and reasonable element of the *Caparo* three part test, and ultimately it may be more coherent to consider questions as to the reasonableness of the pursuer's reliance as relevant to the third limb of *Caparo*. Thus, in the auditor liability case of *James McNaughton Paper Group Ltd v Hicks Anderson & Co*,[273] where the bidders who made a takeover offer had communicated directly with the auditors of the target (whose comments suggested that the target was in a poor financial state), the Court of Appeal in England held that because the bidders had access to the accounting information from which the target's auditors had prepared draft accounts, it was not reasonable for the bidders to rely upon the auditors without seeking independent advice from their own accountants. It was not fair, just and reasonable to recognise a duty of care owed by the auditors to the bidders.

Proximity of relationship: secondary victim pure economic loss

Although the terminology adopted here has not so far been adopted by the **11–40** judiciary, courts have distinguished between direct or primary pure economic loss, and "indirect",[274] "secondary"[275] or "relational"[276] pure economic loss that is parasitic of the harm suffered by the person directly affected by negligent act. A close examination of the distinction reveals that it is consistent with the distinction between primary and secondary victims adopted here.

An exclusionary rule consistently has been applied[277] to secondary victim pure economic loss cases by the courts in Scotland and by the courts in England and Wales.[278] In Scotland, the source may be traced to the decision of the Inner House in *Allan v Barclay*,[279] where an employer was held not entitled to reparation for the loss of an employee's services while he recovered from injuries

---

[273] *James McNaughton Paper Group Ltd v Hicks Anderson & Co* [1991] 2 Q.B. 113. Cf. *Royal Bank of Scotland Plc v Bannerman Johnstone Maclay*, 2003 S.C. 125; *ADT Ltd v BDO Binder Hamlyn* [1996] B.C.C. 808; *HSBC Bank Plc v 5th Avenue Partners Ltd* [2009] 1 C.L.C. 503.

[274] *Landcatch Ltd v International Oil Pollution Compensation Fund*, 1999 S.L.T. 1208 at 1224 per Lord McCluskey.

[275] *Alegrete Shipping Co Inc v International Oil Pollution Compensation Fund 1971 (The Sea Empress)* [2003] 1 Lloyd's Rep. 327 at 336 per Mance L.J.

[276] *Landcatch Ltd v International Oil Pollution Compensation Fund*, 1999 S.L.T. 1208 at 1218 per Lord Justice-Clerk Cullen.

[277] An exception is to be found in *Morrison Steamship Co v Greystoke Castle* [1947] A.C. 265.

[278] Traceable to the decision in *Cattle v Stockton Waterworks Co* (1874–75) L.R. 10 Q.B. 453. Not all jurisdictions apply such a rigid rule: see, e.g. *Caltex Oil (Australia) Pty Ltd v The Dredge "Willemstad"* (1976) 136 C.L.R. 529; *Perre v Apand Pty Ltd* (1999) 198 C.L.R. 180 (Australia); *Canadian National Railway Co v Norsk Pacific Steamship Co* [1992] 1 S.C.R. 1021 (Canada).

[279] *Allan v Barclay* (1863) 2 M. 873.

sustained in an accident caused by the fault of the defender. Lord Kinloch declared:

> "The grand rule on the subject of damages is, that none can be claimed except such as naturally and directly arise out of the wrong done; and such, therefore, as may reasonably be supposed to have been in the view of the wrongdoer. Tried by this test, the present claim appears to fail. The personal injuries of the individual himself will be properly held to have been in the contemplation of the wrongdoer. But he cannot be held bound to have surmised the *secondary injuries* done to all holding relations with the individual, whether that of a master, or any other."[280]

The relationships in *Allan v Barclay* are illustrated in the following diagram:

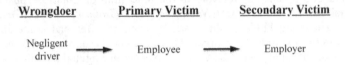

Wrongdoer	**Primary Victim**	**Secondary Victim**
Negligent driver	Employee	Employer

11–41   The exclusionary rule was confirmed by the House of Lords in *Simpson & Co v Thomson*.[281] In *Reavis v Clan Line Steamers*,[282] the exclusionary rule prevented liability in negligence to the leader of an orchestra for loss of profit due to the disbanding of the orchestra after several of its members were killed or injured in a shipping collision. Similarly, in *Robertson v Turnbull*[283] the House of Lords applied the rule to refuse a claim for economic loss sustained by relatives as a consequence of non-fatal injuries inflicted on a primary victim by a defender's negligence.[284]

---

[280] *Allan v Barclay* (1863) 2 M. 873 at 874 (emphasis added). Also quoted in *Reavis v Clan Line Steamers (No.1)*, 1925 S.C. 725.

[281] *Simpson & Co v Thomson* (1878) 5 R. (HL) 40, see especially 46 per Lord Penzance. Exceptions to the "exclusionary rule" may be created by statute. Examples include: the Indemnity Act 1920—see *Elliott Steam Tug Co Ltd v The Shipping Controller* [1922] 1 K.B. 127; s.8(3) of the Damages (Scotland) Act 2011; the Carriage of Goods by Sea Act 1992—see, e.g. *East West Corp v DKBS 1912* [2003] Q.B. 1509; and the Merchant Shipping Act 1995—see, e.g. *Alegrete Shipping Co Inc v International Oil Pollution Compensation Fund 1971 (The Sea Empress)* [2003] 1 Lloyd's Rep. 327. However, it must be clear that the intention of Parliament was to create an exception to the exclusionary rule: see, e.g. *Landcatch Ltd v International Oil Pollution Compensation Fund*, 1999 S.L.T. 1208 where it was held that neither the Merchant Shipping Act 1974 nor the Merchant Shipping (Oil Pollution) Act 1971 provided such exceptions. See also *Alegrete Shipping Co Inc v International Oil Pollution Compensation Fund 1971 (The Sea Empress)* [2003] 1 Lloyd's Rep. 327.

[282] *Reavis v Clan Line Steamers*, 1925 S.C. 725. "In the law of Scotland there is no such thing as a right or interest, in the nature of property, in the services of another; and the person claiming reparation for injury by another's fault cannot go beyond the effects of such injury on his own person, his own health, his own business or other capabilities, and his own property": *Reavis v Clan Line Steamers (No.1)*, 1925 S.C. 725 at 740 per Lord President Clyde.

[283] *Robertson v Turnbull*, 1982 S.C. (HL) 1. See also *Edgar v Postmaster General*, 1965 S.C. 67; *Bonthrone v Secretary of State for Scotland*, 1987 S.L.T. 34

[284] If the primary victim dies a claim may be brought by certain secondary victims under s.4 of the Damages (Scotland) Act 2011 (codifying the decision in *Eisten v North British Railway Co* (1870) 8 M. 980): see para.5–20 above.

In *Dynamco Ltd v Holland & Hannen & Cubitts (Scotland) Ltd*,[285] the Inner House rejected a claim for loss of profit and other economic losses where it was averred that the defenders, who were contractors digging up a road, had been negligent in failing to identify the location of an underground cable belonging to the electricity board which they dug through, disrupting the electricity supply to the pursuer's factory and so preventing the pursuer from operating the factory until the electricity supply was restored. The primary victim was the electricity board, whose cable was physically damaged, with the pursuers suffering pure economic loss as a consequence of the disruption to the electricity supply caused by the damage to the cable.

In *Nacap Ltd v Moffat Plant Ltd*,[286] the pursuers were contracted to lay a pipeline owned by British Gas. The pipeline was damaged by the defenders and, as a result, the pursuers suffered economic loss because they could not complete the work to the deadline set in the contract. Although not using the terms primary and secondary victim as such, the Inner House nevertheless distinguished between on the one hand, ownership or right of possession in property,[287] and on the other, contractual responsibility for the integrity of property belonging to another. The exclusionary rule would apply to the latter and so the pursuers' claim was dismissed.

The exclusionary rule was applied against the owner of property damaged by **11-42** negligence in the English case of *Candlewood Navigation Corp v Mitsui Osk Lines*.[288] The plaintiffs, as owners of the ship in question, had created a "bareboat" charter in favour of a third party, but had then hired the vessel back on a "time-charter". The bareboat charter provided that the third party was responsible for any repairs required to the vessel. The plaintiffs sued for damages in respect of hire payments and lost profits for the period the ship was out of service as it was being repaired following a collision which was due to the defendants' negligence. The plaintiff's losses were purely economic and, although again the plaintiffs were not described as secondary victims in the speeches, the losses were treated as relational. It may seem anomalous to describe the owners of a damaged vessel as secondary victims, but it is suggested that it would be more anomalous to treat one hirer of property (at least in that capacity) any differently to others merely because the specific hirer happened to be the owner of the property in question.

A question that was not considered in the *Candlewood* case was whether the third party with responsibility to repair the boat under the charter could recover

---

[285] *Dynamco Ltd v Holland & Hannen & Cubitts (Scotland) Ltd*, 1971 S.C. 257. See also *Coleridge v Miller Construction Ltd*, 1997 S.L.T. 485, where, in another severing of an electricity supply cable case, a distinction drawn between loss of profit and damage to the equipment in the factory was held to be "artificial". See also *East Lothian Angling Association v Haddington Town Council*, 1980 S.L.T. 213; *Wimpey Construction (UK) Ltd v Martin Black & Co (Wire Ropes) Ltd*, 1982 S.L.T. 239; *Scott Lithgow Ltd v GEC Electrical Projects Ltd*, 1989 S.C. 412; *Strathford East Kilbride Ltd v HLM Design Ltd*, 1999 S.L.T. 121.

[286] *Nacap Ltd v Moffat Plant Ltd*, 1987 S.L.T. 221. See also *Leigh & Sillivan Ltd v Aliakmon Shipping Co Ltd (The Aliakmon)* [1986] A.C. 785; *TCS Holdings Ltd v Ashtead Plant Hire Co Ltd*, 2003 S.L.T. 177; *Colour Quest Ltd v Total Downstream UK Plc* [2009] 2 Lloyd's Rep. 1.

[287] Examples of such a right of possession might include tenancy under a lease: see *Hand v North of Scotland Water Authority*, 2002 S.L.T. 798; *Mull Shellfish Ltd v Golden Sea Produce Ltd*, 1992 S.L.T. 703. See also *North Scottish Helicopters Ltd v United Technologies Corp Inc (No.1)*, 1988 S.L.T. 77.

[288] *Candlewood Navigation Corp v Mitsui Osk Lines (The Mineral Transporter and The Ibaraki Maru)* [1986] A.C. 1. See also *Elliott Steam Tug Co Ltd v Shipping Controller* [1922] 1 K.B. 127.

damages from the negligent defendants. Following the analysis of the Inner House in *Nacap*, the third party incurring the cost of repair would also suffer pure economic loss as the boat did not actually belong to them, and for the same reason they would fall into the category of secondary victim. It follows that the exclusionary rule applied to relational pure economic loss should be applied to the third party too.[289] However, recent cases suggest that where a non-owner possessor's interest in the property in question is such that it might be described as tantamount to ownership, the exclusionary rule may be avoided.

An example is *North Scottish Helicopters Ltd v United Technologies Corp Inc*[290] where the pursuers had leased a helicopter from its owners - a finance company. The lease required the pursuers to indemnify the finance company against any damage to the helicopter. The aircraft was destroyed when a component failed. It was alleged that the component was defective due to negligence in the manufacturing process. In applying "tests" derived from *Leigh and Sillivan*[291] and *Nacap*,[292] Lord Davidson held that the pursuers had more than mere contractual rights in the helicopter, giving them sufficient title to sue for damages. Thus, the pursuers' status was elevated from secondary victim to primary victim. This would avoid the exclusionary rule, but the pursuers' claim would nevertheless be for pure economic loss. Thus the proximity of relationship required for a duty of care to be owed to the pursuers would require to be tested against the *Caparo/Hedley Byrne* criteria as discussed above.

A similar approach was taken by Lord Wheatley in *Hand v North of Scotland Water Authority*.[293] A proof before answer was allowed in an action in negligence against a water authority alleged to be at fault when a public house was flooded because of a damaged sewer. The tenant of the pub sued for solatium and for loss of profit. Although in principle the tenants' rights in the damaged property were contractual (so making the tenant a secondary victim), Lord Wheatley held that the tenant's possessory right in the property was in many respects identical to the interests of ownership.

11–43   The exclusionary rule has been applied to employers and to business partners[294] who parasitically have suffered pure economic loss as a consequence of injuries suffered by a primary victim.[295] It follows that where an employee or director of a company is injured, and as a consequence the company loses profits, shareholders in the company (as well as the company itself) will be treated as

---

[289] In England, the law of bailment may have provided a remedy: see, e.g. *The Winkfield* [1902] P. 42. There is no direct equivalent to the law of bailment in Scots law.

[290] *North Scottish Helicopters Ltd v United Technologies Corp Inc*, 1988 S.L.T. 77.

[291] *Leigh & Sillivan Ltd v Aliakmon Shipping Co Ltd (The Aliakmon)* [1986] A.C. 785 at 809 per Lord Brandon.

[292] *Nacap Ltd v Moffat Plant Ltd*, 1987 S.L.T. 221.

[293] *Hand v North of Scotland Water Authority*, 2002 S.L.T. 798. See also *Mull Shellfish Ltd v Golden Sea Produce Ltd*, 1992 S.L.T. 703, where a tenant was again treated as enjoying equivalent interests in the property in question as a landlord; *Saeed v Waheed*, 1996 S.L.T. (Sh. Ct) 39 where a claim in negligence for pure economic loss brought by a tenant of shop premises against persons alleged to be in wrongful occupation was permitted to proceed.

[294] Although where a partner is injured due to another's negligence, if that partner's incapacity causes a downturn in the firm's profits, the injured partner (as a primary victim) may be entitled to recover his share of the lost profit (as derivative economic loss) from the wrongdoer: *Vaughan v Greater Glasgow Passenger Transport Executive*, 1984 S.C. 32.

[295] See, e.g. *Allan v Barclay* (1863) 2 M. 873; *Quin v The Greenock and Port Glasgow Tramways Company*, 1926 S.C. 544; *Gibson v Glasgow Corporation*, 1963 S.L.T. (Notes) 16; *Sturgeon v Gallagher*, 2003 S.L.T. 67.

secondary victims of any alleged negligence and subject to the exclusionary rule.[296] However, in *Anthony v Brabbs*, the Inner House held that in the context of a typical "one-man" company, where one shareholder owned all or virtually all of the shares, it would be artificial to distinguish between income in the form of a salary as an employee or director of the company, and income received as a dividend out of the company's profits:

> "Although the source of the lost income is different, this does not detract from the fact that the pursuer is seeking to recover a loss of income from his usual work, a loss which is alleged to be due to the defenders' wrongful act. In our view such a loss is foreseeable and not too remote."[297]

The Inner House was careful to confine their decision to the facts, so where the pursuer is one of a number of shareholders, the decision may be distinguished. It is therefore imperative in such cases that the pursuer's pleadings make it clear that the claim for the loss of dividend income is "derivative" of the injury and incurred in the capacity of primary victim rather than as a consequence of the relational economic losses suffered by the company.

Thus, at least two exceptions to the exclusionary rule appear to becoming accepted by the Scottish courts. First, where the pursuer has a possessory interest in the damaged property which, although not actually ownership, is very close to ownership; and secondly, where the pursuer suffers economic loss technically as a secondary victim, but derivative of personal injury[298] suffered as a primary victim. The question that follows is: is there scope for the development of further exceptions? Perhaps in the future a pursuer who suffers pure economic loss as a secondary victim may nevertheless avoid the exclusionary rule if he can show that he has a *Hedley Byrne* type "special relationship" with the alleged wrongdoer.

Proximity of relationship: psychiatric injury

Liability in negligence for psychiatric or mental harm historically was treated **11–44** differently than liability for physical injury, damage to property or economic loss. Judges have tended to be sceptical with regard to claims for mental harm[299]—it is not a visible injury, it may be difficult to confirm and easy to fake or exaggerate. There may be a risk in opening the floodgates to claims. However, as medical science has gradually improved its understanding of mental health, sceptical judicial attitudes have increasingly become viewed as pejorative and

---

[296] See, e.g. *Fox v P. Caulfield & Son*, 1975 S.L.T. (Notes) 71; *Fullemann v McInnes's Executors*, 1993 S.L.T. 259. "The lack of profits reaching (the shareholder's) pocket are in a double sense remote": *Young v. Ormiston*, 1936 S.L.T. 79 at 81 per Lord MacKay.

[297] *Anthony v Brabbs*, 1998 S.C. 894 at 898 per Lord President Rodger delivering the opinion of the court. The court confirmed that any claims made by the company itself or the pursuer's wife in her capacity as shareholder (his wife held the small percentage of the company's shares not owned by the pursuer) would be irrelevant as too remote.

[298] But not damage to property: *Candlewood Navigation Corp v Mitsui Osk Lines (The Mineral Transporter and The Ibaraki Maru)* [1986] A.C. 1.

[299] For a discussion of the concerns see, e.g. *Frost v Chief Constable of South Yorkshire Police* [1999] 2 A.C. 455 at 493–494 per Lord Steyn.

out of touch with modern society.[300] Thus, for example, liability for psychiatric harm in the form of work-related-stress has, since the mid-1990s, become accepted[301] and successful claims have proliferated. Nevertheless, there remains a judicial resistance to recognising liability for mental harm, especially where that has been triggered by the pursuer's experience in witnessing an incident in which another suffers physical harm. Judicial resistance to the development of the law has been further entrenched by conservative precedents.[302] The Law Commissions of England and Wales[303] and of Scotland[304] have separately considered liability for psychiatric injury and each has made recommendations for law reform, neither of which have been taken forward by either Parliament.

Psychiatric injury—derivative or pure?

11–45   Psychiatric harm may be classified as derivative or pure. Where a pursuer suffers personal injury,[305] damage to property[306] or economic loss[307] as the immediate consequence of the wrong, and goes on to suffer psychiatric injury as a reaction to the immediate harm, the psychiatric harm may be described as "derivative" of the immediate harm. Provided a duty of care is owed with regard to the immediate harm, the duty will encompass the derivative psychiatric harm. However, subject to the exception created by the "thin skull rule", liability for derivative psychiatric injury will be controlled by the rules on remoteness of damage.[308]

It is submitted that it is appropriate to describe mental harm that is the immediate consequence of the wrong as "pure" psychiatric harm. This may be suffered as a primary or as a secondary victim. An example of the former would be where the pursuer is put in mortal fear because of the negligence of the wrongdoer, but where the anticipated death or injury does not actually occur. An example of the latter would be where the pursuer suffers psychiatric harm as a consequence of witnessing the death or injury of another person which was a

---

[300] "My Lords, this story of the ebb and flow of tort liability for psychiatric injury has often been told and I have recounted it again at some length only because I think it must be borne in mind when we come to deal with the authorities. In order to give due weight to the earlier decisions, particularly at first instance, it is necessary to have regard to their historical context. They cannot simply be laid out flat and pieced together to form a timeless mosaic of legal rules. Some contained the embryonic forms of later developments; others are based on theories of liability which had respectable support at the time but have since been left stranded by the shifting tides": *White v Chief Constable of South Yorkshire Police* [1999] 2 A.C. 455 at 503 per Lord Hoffmann.
[301] *Walker v Northumberland CC* [1995] 1 All E.R. 737.
[302] Such as *Alcock v Chief Constable of South Yorkshire Police* [1992] 1 A.C. 310. For judicial comment see, e.g. *White v Chief Constable of South Yorkshire Police* [1999] 2 A.C. 455 at 500 per Lord Steyn; at 511 per Lord Hoffmann.
[303] Law Commission, *Liability for Psychiatric Illness* (HMSO, 1998) (Law Com. No.249).
[304] Scottish Law Commission, *Report on Damages for Psychiatric Injury* (The Stationery Office, 2004) (Scot. Law Com. No.196).
[305] See, e.g. *Simmons v British Steel Plc*, 2004 S.C. (HL) 94.
[306] See, e.g. *Attia v British Gas Plc* [1988] Q.B. 304. Cf. *Yearworth v North Bristol NHS Trust* [2010] Q.B. 1 at 24–25 per Judge C.J. (delivering the opinion of the court). It is submitted that the facts in *Holdich v Lothian Health Board*, 2014 S.L.T. 495 disclose an example of derivative psychiatric injury, the "pure" or "immediate" harm being the damage to the stored gametes and/or the loss of autonomy with regard to the opportunity to become a father.
[307] See, e.g. *Martin v Bell Ingram*, 1986 S.C. 208.
[308] *Simmons v British Steel Plc*, 2004 S.C. (HL) 94.

consequence of an accident caused by the defender's negligence. Thus, a passenger in a motor car who escapes physically unscathed may suffer psychiatric injury as a primary victim if that was triggered by fear of their own impending death or injury; or as a secondary victim if their mental harm was triggered by witnessing the death or injury of the driver of the car. It should immediately be clear that there may be evidential difficulties in confirming whether such a pursuer's claim for damages is as a primary or as a secondary victim.

Liability for pure psychiatric injury is controlled by the duty of care device, which operates differently depending on whether the pursuer is a primary or a secondary victim. The allocation of limiting rules respectively to pure and derivative psychiatric harm is illustrated in the diagram below:

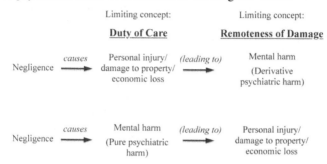

Pure psychiatric injury: definitions

Claims for psychiatric injury have tended to be treated sceptically, if not **11–46** suspiciously, by the judiciary. Reticence to recognise psychiatric harm as reparable can be traced to nineteenth century cases, where the term "nervous shock" was first used.[309] Although the term still appears in pleadings and judgments, it frequently has been denounced as being loaded with a cynical suspicion of bogus claims or a pejorative attitude towards "feeble" minds.[310] As medical science has developed so has the understanding of psychiatric harm, but the law has been criticised as "marching with medicine, but in the rear and limping a little."[311]

However, "as medical science advances, it is important that the law should not be seen to limp too far behind."[312] Various alternative terms have been introduced into litigation, including "post-traumatic stress disorder", "psychiatric illness" and "pathological grief disorder". The Scottish Law Commission adopted the term "mental harm" in its proposal for legislation.[313] The terms psychiatric injury or mental harm are used in this work.

---

[309] *Victorian Railway Commissioners v Coultas* (1888) L.R. 13 App. Cas. 222. See also *Dulieu v White & Sons* [1901] 2 K.B. 669; *Hambrook v Stokes Bros* [1925] 1 K.B. 141; *Wallace v Kennedy* (1908) 16 S.L.T. 485; *Brown v Glasgow Corp*, 1922 S.C. 527; *Currie v Wardrop*, 1927 S.C. 538; *Bourhill v Young*, 1942 S.C. (HL) 78.

[310] See, e.g. *McLoughlin v O'Brian* [1983] 1 A.C. 410 at 418 per Lord Wilberforce; *Alcock v Chief Constable of South Yorkshire Police* [1992] 1 A.C. 310 at 395 per Lord Keith of Kinkel; *Page v Smith* [1996] A.C. 155 at 180–183 per Lord Browne-Wilkinson; *White v Chief Constable of South Yorkshire* [1999] 2 A.C. 455 at 488–489 per Lord Goff of Chieveley.

[311] *Mount Isa Mines Ltd v Pusey* (1970) 125 C.L.R. 383 at 395 per Windeyer J.

[312] *Page v Smith* [1996] A.C. 155 at 187 per Lord Lloyd of Berwick.

[313] Reparation for Mental Harm (Scotland) Bill; Scottish Law Commission, *Report on Damages for Psychiatric Injury*. See, in particular, paras 1.7–1.8.

Nevertheless, although it has been accepted judicially that because medical science no longer distinguishes between bodily and mental harm—the suffering associated with each being attributable to an impact on the central nervous system—neither should the courts; that is a different matter from distinguishing between physical injury and psychiatric harm in terms of the principles governing the recovery of damages in delict.[314] Judges remain concerned at the spectre of creating liability to an indeterminate class and there remains a fear that the range of persons psychologically affected by an incident could be enormous, especially where those persons suffer psychiatric harm as secondary victims.

A "mere fright" will not be reparable as psychiatric injury.[315] Neither will a shock unless it triggers a psychiatric illness.[316] Likewise a typical grief reaction to an event deemed part of the ordinary vicissitudes of life[317] with which is it reasonable to expect a person of normal fortitude or "customary phlegm" emotionally to cope. Thus, to be reparable, the harm must amount to a recognisable psychiatric injury and must be long lasting.

In *Hatton v Sutherland*,[318] the Court of Appeal confirmed that an employer's duty of care to provide a safe system of work extended to the risk of mental harm as well as physical harm. It is now well established that where such a risk of mental harm eventuates following a gradual build up of work-related stress, damages may be awarded. In delivering the opinion of the court Hale L.J. identified four categories in a claim for psychiatric injury[319]:

1. delictual/tortuous claims by primary victims[320];
2. delictual/tortuous claims by secondary victims[321];
3. contractual claims by primary victims[322];
4. contractual claims by secondary victims.[323]

However, although mental harm caused gradually by work-related stress to a primary victim is now recognised as reparable in a "contractual" case (i.e. the third of Hale L.J.'s categories), it remains unclear whether a delictual claim from a primary victim, or a delictual or contractual claim from a secondary victim can succeed where psychiatric harm is caused other by shock, defined as "the sudden

---

[314] *White v Chief Constable of South Yorkshire* [1999] 2 A.C. 455 at 492 per Lord Steyn.
[315] *Wallace v Kennedy* (1908) 16 S.L.T. 485 at 486–487 per Lord Johnston; *Simpson v ICI Ltd*, 1983 S.L.T. 601 at 605 per Lord Robertson.
[316] *Page v Smith* [1996] A.C. 155 at 189–190 per Lord Lloyd of Berwick.
[317] *Alcock v Chief Constable of South Yorkshire Police* [1992] 1 A.C. 310 at 416 per Lord Oliver; *Page v Smith* [1996] A.C. 155 at 171 per Lord Jauncey of Tullichettle. Cf. *Vernon v Bosley* [1997] 1 All E.R. 577 at 610 per Thorpe L.J. who accepted that "pathological grief disorder" could be compensated.
[318] *Hatton v Sutherland* [2002] 2 All E.R. 1. The decision of the Court of Appeal was reversed on appeal to the House of Lords: sub nom. *Barber v Somerset CC* [2004] 1 W.L.R. 1089.
[319] *Barber v Somerset CC* [2002] I.C.R. 613 at 624, [21]. Hale L.J.'s analysis was affirmed by the House of Lords (sub nom. *Barber v Somerset CC* [2004] 1 W.L.R. 1089), although the decision of the Court of Appeal in Barber's appeal (heard by the Court of Appeal along with Hatton's appeal) was overturned.
[320] Such as the car driver in *Page v Smith* [1996] A.C. 155. Hale L.J. suggested that at least in some cases (analogous to contractual claims by primary victims) foreseeability of physical harm would be unnecessary, with foreseeability of psychiatric injury being sufficient.
[321] Such as family and friends of the primary victims in *Alcock v Chief Constable of South Yorkshire Police* [1992] 1 A.C. 310.
[322] Such as the employee in *Walker v Northumberland CC* [1995] I.C.R. 702, or the solicitor's client in *McLoughlin v Jones* [2002] 2 W.L.R. 1279.
[323] Such as the police officers in *White v Chief Constable of South Yorkshire* [1999] 2 A.C. 455.

appreciation by sight or sound of a horrifying event, which violently agitates the mind."[324] In *Sion v Hampstead Health Authority*,[325] a father maintained a vigil while his son slowly died after alleged mistreatment of physical injuries. The father was denied compensation on the basis that his psychiatric injury was not triggered by a shock. However, in *Walters v North Glamorgan NHS Trust*[326] it was held that a mother's severe stress over a 36 hour period during which her baby son's acute hepatitis was misdiagnosed constituted a single horrifying experience and that when she was informed of her son's actual condition (which resulted in a decision to terminate his life support) this had an immediate and devastating impact upon her, constituting a sudden shock. The question was considered, but left undecided, by the House of Lords in *W v Essex CC*.[327]

Proximity of relationship—primary victim pure psychiatric injury

The distinction between primary and secondary victims as such was first made **11–47** by Lord Oliver in his speech in *Alcock v Chief Constable of South Yorkshire Police*, where he described a primary victim as one who "was involved, either mediately, or immediately, as a participant"[328] in the relevant event. Based on an analysis of previous case law Lord Oliver set out three categories of primary victim cases:

1. those who fear physical harm to themselves;
2. those who come to the rescue of the injured; and
3. those who believe they have involuntarily caused the death or injury of another.[329]

Lord Oliver's analysis has been challenged[330] and in *W v Essex CC* Lord Slynn suggested that the categorisation of victims "is a concept still to be developed in different factual situations."[331] It is submitted that the lack of clarity here has been exacerbated by a misunderstanding of what respectively primary and secondary victims are victims of. In his discussion in *Alcock*, Lord Oliver might be seen to connect victims to the incident allegedly triggered by the defender's negligence. However, it is submitted that a correct analysis is to define the status of victims according to their connection to the wrongful conduct rather than their connection to the consequence of the wrongful conduct. Indeed, Lord Oliver ultimately focused on

> "the twin questions of (a) whether injury of this sort to each particular plaintiff was a reasonably foreseeable consequence of the acts or omissions constituting the breach of duty to the primary victim and (b) whether there

---

[324] *Alcock v Chief Constable of South Yorkshire Police* [1992] 1 A.C. 310 at 401 per Lord Ackner.

[325] *Sion v Hampstead Health Authority* [1994] 5 Med. L.R. 170. See also *Wood v Miller*, 1958 S.L.T. (Notes) 49; *Ward v Leeds Teaching Hospitals NHS Trust* [2004] Lloyd's Rep. Med. 530.

[326] *Walters v North Glamorgan NHS Trust* [2003] P.I.Q.R. P16.

[327] *W v Essex CC* [2001] 2 A.C. 592.

[328] *Alcock v Chief Constable of South Yorkshire Police* [1992] 1 A.C. 310 at 407 per Lord Oliver of Aylmerton.

[329] *Alcock v Chief Constable of South Yorkshire Police* [1992] 1 A.C. 310 at 408 per Lord Oliver of Aylmerton.

[330] See, e.g. *White v Chief Constable of South Yorkshire Police* [1999] 2 A.C. 455 at 472 per Lord Goff of Chieveley.

[331] *W v Essex CC* [2001] 2 A.C. 592 at 601 per Lord Slynn of Hadley.

existed between the defendant and each plaintiff that degree of directness or proximity necessary to establish liability."[332]

So a pursuer should be classified as a primary victim only if the pursuer's mental harm was a direct consequence of the defender's wrong; if the pursuer's psychiatric injury was triggered by witnessing or discovering harm to another (i.e. the primary victim) then the pursuer must be classified as a secondary victim.

Thus, in *Burns v Boots UK Ltd*,[333] the victim status of a grandmother should be determined by whether she suffered psychiatric injury as a consequence either of fear for her own safety (in which case she should be classified as a primary victim) or of witnessing her granddaughter being struck on the head by a rolling pin (in which case she should be classified as a secondary victim). The infant's mother and grandfather had gone into a shop while the grandmother waited outside with the infant who was in a child buggy. The rolling pin fell out of a third floor window and struck the child on the head. The mother and grandfather, not having any reason to fear for their own safety, could only be secondary victims. However, the grandmother could be either, or both,[334] and evidence of the trigger for her psychiatric injury (presuming that it could be proved that she suffered reparable mental harm) would be required to confirm in what capacity she would be entitled to sue.[335]

The significance of the distinction was confirmed in *Page v Smith*,[336] where it was held in the House of Lords that the "control mechanisms" which apply to secondary victims claiming for psychiatric injury do not apply to primary victims. Thus, a "neighbourhood"[337] relationship based on the reasonable foreseeability concept will be sufficient to satisfy the proximity requirement in primary victim mental harm cases. A neighbourhood relationship will also be sufficient to confirm the existence of a duty of care in actions brought by a primary victim for mental harm allegedly caused by work-related stress.[338]

Primary victims: fear of own safety

11-48   If the pursuer's mental harm is triggered by their involvement in an incident created by the negligence of the defender and in which it is reasonably

---

[332] *Alcock v Chief Constable of South Yorkshire Police* [1992] 1 A.C. 310 at 406 per Lord Oliver of Aylmerton.

[333] *Burns v Boots UK Ltd*, 2011 Rep. L.R. 124.

[334] A concurrent status has been recognised: *Page v Smith* [1996] A.C. 155 at 190 per Lord Lloyd of Berwick, commenting on *Schneider v Eisovitch* [1960] 2 Q.B. 430. See also *Currie v Wardrop*, 1927 S.C. 538; *Brice v Brown* [1984] 1 All E.R. 997; *Malcolm v Broadhurst* [1970] 3 All E.R. 508. This analysis is consistent with the analogy of the twin sets of ripples striking the protruding object in the pool: see para.11–14 above.

[335] The fact that as a secondary victim a pursuer will be subject to control mechanisms that do not apply to primary victims means that it would be easier to establish liability for fear of one's own safety than for witnessing a horrific accident in which others are injured or killed (even when the pursuer attempts to assist the primary victim given the decision of the House of Lords in *White v Chief Constable for South Yorkshire* [1999] 2 A.C. 455). Is it right that the law should adopt a policy of self-interest over empathy or altruism?

[336] *Page v Smith* [1996] A.C. 155.

[337] *Donoghue v Stevenson*, 1932 S.C. (HL) 31 at 44 per Lord Atkin.

[338] See, e.g. *Flood v University Court of the University of* Glasgow, 2010 S.L.T. 167. See also *Walker v Northumberland CC* [1995] 1 All E.R. 737; *Cross v Highlands & Islands Enterprise*, 2001 S.L.T. 1060; *Barber v Somerset CC* [2004] 1 W.L.R. 1089; *White v Chief Constable of South Yorkshire* [1999] 2 A.C. 455 at 506 per Lord Hoffmann.

foreseeable that a person in the pursuer's position may suffer personal injury, the pursuer will be a primary victim and not subject to the secondary victim control mechanisms. In *Alcock*, Lord Oliver considered that *Dulieu v White & Sons*,[339] was such a case. In *Dulieu*, the plaintiff luckily escaped physical injury when a vehicle crashed through the wall of a public house where she was working, but was held entitled to damages to compensate for the miscarriage inducing shock caused by being "personally threatened"[340] with death or serious injury. It follows that *Brown v Glasgow Corp*[341] should be classified in the same way. In *Brown*, the pursuer suffered a miscarriage following a "near-miss" with an out-of-control tram.

In *Page v Smith*,[342] the House of Lords confirmed that such a primary victim would avoid the control mechanisms applied to secondary victims. The defendant in driving negligently caused a minor road traffic accident in which the plaintiff's car was damaged. Neither driver was physically injured in the accident and there were no passengers in either car. Both vehicles were capable of being driven away. However, the plaintiff suffered a recrudescence of myalgic encephalomyelitis.[343] The House of Lords held that, where the plaintiff was a primary victim of negligence, psychiatric injury should be treated alongside physical harm as a sub-category of "personal injury" and so it was sufficient to establish a duty of care if personal injury was a reasonably foreseeable consequence of the defendant's negligence.[344]

Primary victims: rescuers

For policy reasons the law tends to give special treatment to rescuers. This was **11–49** justified by Cardozo J.:

> "Danger invites rescue. The cry of distress is the summons to relief ... the act, whether impulsive or deliberate, is the child of the occasion. The emergency begets the man."[345]

Thus, the law could be described as antisocial if its operation appeared to discourage altruistic humanitarianism.[346] This policy may be seen to have justified the decision in *Chadwick v British Railways Board*.[347] Mr Chadwick lived close to the scene of the Lewisham train crash, which happened during rush

---

[339] *Dulieu v White & Sons* [1901] 2 K.B. 669.

[340] *Alcock v Chief Constable of South Yorkshire Police* [1992] 1 A.C. 310 at 408 per Lord Oliver of Aylmerton.

[341] *Brown v Glasgow Corp*, 1922 S.C. 527. See also *Wallace v Kennedy* (1908) 16 S.L.T. 485.

[342] *Page v Smith* [1996] A.C. 155

[343] Commonly known as ME, chronic fatigue syndrome or post viral fatigue syndrome. The plaintiff had previously suffered symptoms, which had been in remission immediately prior to the accident.

[344] See, e.g. *Donachie v Chief Constable of Greater Manchester* [2004] Po. L.R. 204 for an extreme example. See also *Ormsby v Chief Constable of Strathclyde*, 2008 S.C.L.R. 783; *Smith v Ministry of Defence* [2014] A.C. 52.

[345] *Wagner v International Railway Co* (1921) 232 N.Y. 176 at 180–181 per Cardozo J. See also *Bourhill v Young*, 1942 S.C. (HL) 78 at 92 per Lord Wright; *Haynes v Harwood* [1934] 2 K. B. 240 at 247 per Findlay J.

[346] Hence the rule that volenti non fit injuria cannot be pled against the volunteer rescuer who has acted on human impulse: *Baker v. T. E. Hopkins & Son Ltd* [1959] 1 W.L.R. 966.

[347] *Chadwick v British Railways Board* [1967] 1 W.L.R. 912. See also *Mount Isa Mines Ltd v Pusey* (1970) 125 C.L.R. 383.

hour in dense fog on a Wednesday evening in December 1957. Two passenger
trains collided under a railway bridge, with the bridge collapsing onto some of
the coaches. Ninety passengers died and hundreds more were injured, with many
trapped in crushed carriages. Mr Chadwick went to help, and spent the whole
night climbing into damaged railway carriages to assist in the rescue operation
where he witnessed many gruesome scenes. Waller J. held that, the railway
accident itself being reasonably foreseeable, it was equally foreseeable that
someone in Mr Chadwick's position would act as a rescuer and suffer shock as
a result of the horrific experience.[348]

In *White v Chief Constable of South Yorkshire*,[349] the House of Lords qualified
the special treatment afforded to rescuers. *White* was the second of two
psychiatric injury cases to reach the House of Lords which stemmed from the
Hillsborough tragedy in April 1989. An FA cup semi-final between Liverpool
and Nottingham Forest to be played at Sheffield Wednesday's Hillsborough
ground resulted in 96 deaths and hundreds of injuries which were caused by a
crush attributed to the negligence of the police force responsible for controlling
the event. In *Alcock v Chief Constable of South Yorkshire Police*,[350] the House of
Lords had applied the secondary victim control mechanisms to reject several
claims brought in a test case to determine the potential liability of the police to
family and friends of some of those who had died. *White* was a series of cases
brought by individual police officers who had been required to attend at the
football ground to assist in dealing with the immediate aftermath of the tragedy.
The plaintiffs in *White* argued inter alia that their role was as rescuers and so,
following the interpretation of *Chadwick* by the House of Lords in *Alcock*, their
claims should not be subject to the secondary victim control mechanisms. The
Court of Appeal had found in favour of the police officer plaintiffs.[351]

In the House of Lords Lord Browne-Wilkinson agreed with Lord Steyn and
Lord Hoffmann that a rescuer might be classified as a primary victim only where
the individual satisfied the "threshold requirement"[352] of actual or perceived
personal exposure to physical danger.[353] As the police officers had not so been
exposed they could not claim as primary victims and so, as secondary victims,
they were subject to the control mechanisms.

Thus, following *White*, where a person who, out of public-spiritedness, assists
in rescuing those in mortal peril but succumbs to the horrors of the experience
and develops a psychiatric illness, that person will only enjoy protection by the
law (unless in the extremely unlikely situation where that person satisfies the
secondary victim control mechanisms) if that person is himself exposed to

---

[348] Although some jurisdictions, including the United States, adopt a "fireman's rule" which
distinguishes professional rescuers, such a rule has never been applied by a court in the United
Kingdom: *White v Chief Constable of South Yorkshire* [1999] 2 A.C. 455 at 471 per Lord Goff
of Chieveley; at 511 per Lord Hoffmann. See also *Ogwo v Taylor* [1988] A.C. 431; *Hale v London
Underground Ltd* [1993] P.I.Q.R. Q30; *King v Sussex Ambulance NHS Trust* [2002] I.C.R.
1413.

[349] *White v Chief Constable of South Yorkshire* [1999] 2 A.C. 455.

[350] *Alcock v Chief Constable of South Yorkshire Police* [1992] 1 A.C. 310.

[351] Sub nom. *Frost v Chief Constable of South Yorkshire Police* [1998] Q.B. 254, Judge L.J. dissenting.

[352] *White v Chief Constable of South Yorkshire* [1999] 2 A.C. 455 at 499 per Lord Steyn.

[353] Lord Goff of Chieveley, in a dissenting speech, was particularly critical of this "new control
mechanism", describing it as "contrary to authority", erecting an "artificial barrier against
recovery" and "misconceived": *White v Chief Constable of South Yorkshire* [1999] 2 A.C. 455
at 486–488.

physical danger. If that approach is consistent with the general approach of liability in negligence, it follows that it must not be reasonably foreseeable that such a rescuer will develop a psychiatric illness unless that person is exposed to a risk of physical injury. Does that make sense, and is it compatible with the principle floridly explained by Cardozo J. in *Wagner*? It is difficult to avoid suspicion that this qualification was a cynical way to avoid the criticism that would have been anticipated if in *White* the House of Lords had confirmed the earlier decision of the Court of Appeal.[354]

Primary victims: involuntary participants

The third group of historic cases analysed by Lord Oliver as brought by primary victims were from those who believed they had involuntarily caused, or were about to cause, the death or injury of another. An example was *Dooley v Cammell Laird & Co Ltd*.[355] The plaintiff was employed as a crane operator at a shipyard. On the occasion in question Mr Dooley was lowering a quantity of materials into a ship's hold when the sling, which was defective, gave way and the load fell, along with scaffolding dislodged in the accident, into the ship's hold. Mr Dooley could not see into the hold from the operating platform on his crane, but he knew that his colleagues were working in the hold and immediately feared that there would have been serious injuries, if not fatalities. Fortuitously there were none, but Mr Dooley nevertheless developed a psychiatric illness. Donovan J. held that **11–50**

> "if the driver of the crane concerned fears that the load may have fallen upon some of his fellow workmen, and that fear is not baseless or extravagant, then it is, I think, a consequence reasonably to have been foreseen that he may himself suffer a nervous shock."[356]

In *Robertson v Forth Bridge Joint Board*,[357] the Inner House accepted the analysis provided by Lord Oliver, but held that to qualify as a primary victim the unwilling or unwitting pursuer must nevertheless have participated actively in another's death and merely to be engaged on the same task was not sufficient. Three colleagues, who were also close friends, were sent to clear an obstruction from the roadway on the Forth Road Bridge during high winds. They found lying on the carriageway a large sheet of steel which was too big to fit in their van. They resolved to load the sheet onto the back of a pickup, and the deceased volunteered to sit on the sheet to hold it down. However, a violent gust of wind caught the sheet and it, along with the deceased, were blown over the parapet. The deceased was killed by the impact when he landed on a steel girder below the roadway. The two surviving colleagues were held to have no greater status than bystanders, and so were classified as secondary victims who did not satisfy the control mechanisms that thus applied.

---

[354] Sub nom. *Frost v Chief Constable of South Yorkshire Police* [1998] Q.B. 254.

[355] *Dooley v Cammell Laird & Co Ltd* [1951] 1 Lloyd's Rep. 271. See also *Galt v British Railways Board* (1983) 133 N.L.J. 870; *Wigg v British Railways Board*, *The Times*, February 4, 1986; *Dillon v British Railways Board* Unreported January 18, 1995 OH.

[356] *Dooley v Cammell Laird & Co Ltd and Mersey Insulation Co Ltd* [1951] 1 Lloyd's Rep. 271 at 277 per Donovan J.

[357] *Robertson v Forth Bridge Joint Board*, 1995 S.C. 364.

The decision of the Inner House in *Robertson* is not inconsistent with the analysis of Lord Lloyd in *Page v Smith*: that to be classified as a primary victim the pursuer must be within the zone of foreseeable physical injury.[358] However, in *Salter v UB Frozen & Chilled Foods Ltd*[359] a proof before answer was allowed where a forklift driver, who was described by the judge as a primary victim, was at no time exposed to physical danger. A colleague of the pursuer who was riding on the forks was killed as the pursuer had manoeuvred the vehicle. The judge considered it to be arguable that the driver was an "active participant" in the incident in which the victim was killed, and specifically referred to the point made by Lord Slynn in his speech in *W v Essex CC*:

> "But the categorisation of those claiming to be included as primary or secondary victims is not as I read the cases finally closed. It is a concept still to be developed in different factual situations."[360]

Primary victims: assumption of responsibility

11–51   Although the assumption of responsibility concept is mainly associated with *Hedley Byrne* liability for pure economic loss, it has also been applied in considering whether the resulting relationship places the victim suffering psychiatric injury in the position of a primary victim. For example, in *Swinney v Chief Constable of Northumbria Police Force*,[361] the plaintiff had supplied the police with information on an armed robbery. Papers containing details of the informant had been stolen from an unattended police car and had found their way to the individual who was the subject of the information, who threatened the informant with violence. The Court of Appeal held that the police owed the plaintiff a duty of care as a primary victim with regard to psychiatric harm as a special relationship was created by the assumption of responsibility by the police to the informant.

In *McLoughlin v Jones*,[362] the claimant sued a firm of solicitors, alleging that their negligence in defending him in a prosecution had resulted in his psychiatric harm as he had been committed to prison upon conviction. Brooke L.J. acknowledged the conservative approach taken by the House of Lords in *White*[363] but nevertheless resorted to principle:

> "Against this background, how could a legally enforceable duty of care arise in the present case where, as in the *Frost* case, the parties' legal relations are ultimately founded on contract? To answer this question one must go once more to the battery of tests which the House of Lords has

---

[358] *Page v Smith* [1996] A.C. 155 at 184 per Lord Lloyd of Berwick. Lord Lloyd's analysis was approved in *White v Chief Constable of South Yorkshire Police* [1999] 2 A.C. 455 at 496–497 per Lord Steyn. Cf. *White v Chief Constable of South Yorkshire Police* [1999] 2 A.C. 455 at 479–480 per Lord Goff of Chieveley. See also *Hunter v British Coal Corporation* [1999] Q.B. 140; *Campbell v North Lanarkshire Council*, 2000 S.C.L.R. 373; *Gilfillan v Barbour*, 2003 S.L.T. 1127.

[359] *Salter v UB Frozen & Chilled Foods Ltd*, 2004 S.C. 233. See also *Anderson v Christian Salvesen Plc*, 2006 S.L.T. 815.

[360] *W v Essex CC* [2001] 2 A.C. 592 at 601 per Lord Slynn of Hadley.

[361] *Swinney v Chief Constable of Northumbria Police Force* [1997] Q.B. 464.

[362] *McLoughlin v Jones* [2002] Q.B. 1312. The claimant's conviction had been overturned on appeal.

[363] *White v Chief Constable of South Yorkshire* [1999] 2 A.C. 455.

taught us to use: see my judgment in *Parkinson v St James and Seacroft University Hospital NHS Trust* [364] I will refer briefly to four of them: the "purpose" test (*Banque Bruxelles Lambert SA v Eagle Star Insurance Co Ltd*[365]); the "assumption of responsibility " test (*Henderson v Merrett Syndicates Ltd*[366]); the "principles of distributive justice" test (*White v Chief Constable of South Yorkshire Police*[367]); and the "three-pronged" test (*Caparo Industries plc v Dickman*[368]). The fact that these tests are usually deployed in cases involving pure financial loss does not mean that they are inappropriate for use when the only damage in question is psychiatric illness."[369]

Thus a variety of other claims have been classified as brought by primary victims on the basis of a relationship created by an assumption of responsibility. These include claims brought by prisoners in respect of alleged ill-treatment from prison officers,[370] claims brought against schools by pupils subject to bullying and against employers by employees subject to harassment,[371] claims by patients in respect of alleged negligent treatment by a psychiatrist,[372] claims brought by children against local authorities for failure to act in suspected child abuse cases[373] and for failure to properly manage children in care,[374] claims brought by parents wrongly suspected of child abuse,[375] claims brought by clients against their legal representatives in respect of the negligent defence of a criminal prosecution,[376] claims brought against the police for negligent delay in the execution of an arrest warrant[377] and for negligence in respect of establishing the status of a witness following a murder[378] and for negligence in appointing the plaintiff as an "appropriate adult" to be present during the protracted questioning of a suspect without giving any indication of the nature or extent of the horrific crimes about which he was questioned,[379] claims by parents whose deceased infant children had their organs retained without permission,[380] claims by patients or their relatives who were provided with distressing information in an

---

[364] *Parkinson v St James and Seacroft University Hospital NHS Trust* [2002] Q.B. 266 at 282–283, [50] per Brooke L.J.

[365] *Banque Bruxelles Lambert SA v Eagle Star Insurance Co Ltd* [1997] A.C. 191 at 211–212 per Lord Hoffmann.

[366] *Henderson v Merrett Syndicates Ltd* [1995] 2 A.C. 145 at 180–181 per Lord Goff of Chieveley.

[367] *White v Chief Constable of South Yorkshire Police* [1999] 2 A.C. 455 at 503–504 per Lord Hoffmann.

[368] *Caparo Industries Plc v Dickman* [1990] 2 A.C. 605 at 617–618 per Lord Bridge of Harwich.

[369] *McLoughlin v Jones* [2002] Q.B. 1312 at 1323, [28] per Brooke L.J.

[370] *Butchart v Home Office* [2006] 1 W.L.R. 1155.

[371] *Bradford-Smart v West Sussex CC* [2002] 1 F.C.R. 425.

[372] *X (Minors) v Bedfordshire CC* [1995] 2 A.C. 633.

[373] *X (Minors) v Bedfordshire CC* [1995] 2 A.C. 633.

[374] *Barrett v Enfield LBC* [2001] 2 A.C. 550.

[375] *D v East Berkshire Community Health NHS Trust* [2005] 2 A.C. 373.

[376] *McLoughlin v Jones* [2002] Q.B. 1312.

[377] *McNern v Commissioner of Police for the Metropolis* [2000] Po. L.R. 117.

[378] *Brooks v Commissioner of Police of the Metropolis* [2005] 1 W.L.R. 149.

[379] *Leach v Chief Constable of Gloucestershire Constabulary* [1999] 1 W.L.R. 1421 at 1435. The plaintiff complained that she was not given proper warning, training or counselling. Prior to acting she was only told that the police wished to interview a 52-year-old male. The suspect transpired to be Fred West.

[380] *Stevens v Yorkhill NHS Trust*, 2006 S.L.T. 889; *A v Leeds Teaching Hospital NHS Trust* [2005] Q.B. 506. Cf. *Powell v Boldaz* [1998] Lloyd's Rep. Med. 116.

insensitive manner,[381] claims by patients who feared for the future after discovering that growth hormone treatment they had received as children was known to be capable of infecting them with Creutzfeldt-Jacob Disease (CJD),[382] and a claim by a prison officer for a lack of counseling provision from an employer where the prison officer had ingested a prisoner's blood when intervening to break up a fight.[383]

Primary victims: employees

11–52   An employer's common law duty to provide a safe system of work extends to psychiatric harm, as well as to physical harm. On its own, the previous sentence would suggest that whenever an employee complains that psychiatric harm is the employer's fault, the existence of the duty of care will be taken for granted and any dispute will focus on proof of damage and/or proof of negligence and/or proof of causation.[384] However, case law confirms that the law is not as straightforward.

In the employer liability case of *Hatton v Sutherland*,[385] Hale L.J. distinguished between contractual claims by primary victims and contractual claims by secondary victims. It is suggested that this distinction should be unnecessary as irrelevant. A contractual relationship is necessarily a direct relationship between the parties, and it follows that it is illogical to suggest that a claim for breach of contract by negligent failure to perform that contract may be made by a secondary victim who, by definition, is claiming on the basis of an indirect relationship, i.e. as parasitic of the harm suffered by a primary victim with a direct relationship with the defender.

The contradiction may be illustrated by the following diagram:

The employment contract itself creates the duty of care owed by the employer to the employee to provide a safe system of work. Thus, whether the employee's

---

[381] *A.B. v Tameside & Glossop Health Authority* [1997] 8 Med. L.R. 91; *Allin v City & Hackney Health Authority* [1996] 7 Med. L.R. 167. See also *Farrell v Avon Health Authority* [2001] Lloyd's Rep. Med. 458.

[382] *Group B Plaintiffs v Medical Research Council* [2000] Lloyd's Rep. Med. 161. Cf. *Rothwell v Chemical And Insulating Co Ltd* sub nom. *Grieves v FT Everard & Sons Ltd* [2008] 1 A.C. 281.

[383] *Pratt v Scottish Ministers*, 2011 S.C.L.R. 446. Lord Brodie's finding that the employer was not in breach of duty was upheld on appeal: 2013 S.L.T. 590. However, the Inner House questioned (without deciding the matter) whether a duty of care was owed at all.

[384] As was settled some time ago to be the case in Australia: *Mount Isa Mines Ltd v Pusey* (1970) 125 C.L.R. 383.

[385] *Hatton v Sutherland* [2002] I.C.R. 613. See also *South Essex Mental Health NHS Trust v Hartman* [2005] P.I.Q.R. P255.

mental harm is a direct result of the employer's fault, or whether it is parasitic of the harm suffered by a primary victim of the employer's fault should be irrelevant in determining whether a duty of care is owed by the employer to the employee. If the duty arises under the contract of employment, the employee inevitably should be a primary victim of the employer's wrong if the employee has been exposed to the traumatic event in performance of his duties under the contract of employment. However, the matter is made complicated by the decisions of the House of Lords in *Alcock v Chief Constable of South Yorkshire*[386] and in particular *White v Chief Constable of South Yorkshire*.[387]

In *White*, the House of Lords held that even as employees exposed to the **11-53** consequences of their employer's negligence because they were performing their contracts of employment, the plaintiffs were subject to the ordinary rules of tort, as to hold otherwise would be unfair on the bereaved relatives of the primary victims who were classified as secondary victims in *Alcock* and thus subject to the control tests. It is thus submitted that the distinction made by Hale L.J. in *Hatton* attempts artificially to rationalise a difficult decision of a superior court rather than being based on a statement of principle capable of withstanding logical analysis.[388]

Nevertheless that is the law that we are faced with at the moment.[389] So, although chronic stress brought on by excessive workload[390] or threats of violence[391] may be treated as impacting on an employee as a primary victim, where a test of reasonable foreseeability is sufficient,[392] post traumatic stress disorder triggered by nervous shock is treated as impacting on the employee as a secondary victim.

This was confirmed by Lady Paton in *Keen v Tayside Contracts*.[393] The pursuer was employed by the defenders as a road worker. He was instructed to attend at the scene of a serious road accident. When he arrived he became aware that there remained four charred bodies in a burnt-out vehicle at the scene. He telephoned his supervisor to complain that he could not cope with the situation, pointing out that he had received no relevant training. His supervisor insisted that he remain at the scene. Lady Paton held the pursuer to be a secondary victim, and as he could not satisfy the secondary victim control mechanisms his employers were held not to owe him a duty of care.

Lady Paton's analysis of the case appears to be based on the pursuer's relationship with the accident rather than on his relationship with the person averred to have acted wrongfully (his employer). With respect it is again

---

[386] *Alcock v Chief Constable of South Yorkshire* [1992] 1 A.C. 310.

[387] *White v Chief Constable of South Yorkshire* [1999] 2 A.C. 455. See also *Robertson v Forth Road Bridge Joint Board (No.2)*, 1995 S.C. 364.

[388] "In this area of the law, the search for principle was called off in *Alcock v. Chief Constable of South Yorkshire Police* [1992] 1 A.C. 310. No one can pretend that the existing law, which your Lordships have to accept, is founded upon principle ... Consequently your Lordships are now engaged, not in the bold development of principle, but in a practical attempt, under adverse conditions, to preserve the general perception of the law as system of rules which is fair between one citizen and another": *White v Chief Constable of South Yorkshire Police* [1999] 2 A.C. 455 at 503 per Lord Hoffmann.

[389] Which has led to the bizarre conclusion that a claimant in one case was neither a primary nor a secondary victim: *French v Chief Constable of Sussex* [2006] Po. L.R. 19.

[390] See, e.g. *Flood v University Court of the University of Glasgow*, 2010 S.L.T. 167.

[391] See, e.g. *McCarthy v Highland Council*, 2012 S.L.T. 95.

[392] See, e.g. *Fletcher v Argyll and Bute Council*, 2007 S.L.T. 1047.

[393] *Keen v Tayside Contracts*, 2003 S.L.T. 500.

submitted that this analysis is based on a misunderstanding of what determines the status of a victim. The pursuer will be claiming to be a victim of a defender's wrong; not a victim of the consequences of the defender's alleged wrong. In *Keen*, the averred wrong was the employer's insistence that the pursuer remain at a scene that the employer had been warned the pursuer was not equipped to cope with. On that analysis, it is submitted that the pursuer should be treated as a primary victim. In *Harrhy v Thames Trains Ltd*,[394] MacKay J. noted that in her judgment in *Keen*, Lady Paton made no reference to the dictum of Lord Slynn in *W v Essex CC*:

> "But the categorisation of those claiming to be included as primary or secondary victims is not, as I read the cases, finally closed. It is a concept still to be developed in different factual situations."[395]

Proximity of relationship—secondary victim pure psychiatric injury

11–54   *Alcock v Chief Constable of South Yorkshire Police* was a test case taken before the House of Lords to determine potential liability arising from the Hillsborough disaster on April 15, 1989. Ninety six people died, and a further 766 were injured, in a crush in the Leppings Lane stand at Hillsborough Stadium in Sheffield during an FA cup semi-final match between Liverpool and Nottingham Forest. Various friends and relatives of the dead brought the proceedings. Some of the plaintiffs had witnessed the events unfold from within the stadium, some had watched the events unfold on live television, and others had been informed of the disaster and had attended at the mortuary to identify their relatives who had died. All claimed for psychiatric injury triggered by the witnessing or discovery of what had happened to their deceased friends or relatives. Since none were directly at risk of physical harm all were classified as secondary victims, and none of the claims succeeded.

In his speech, Lord Oliver described a "secondary victim" as one who "was no more than the passive and unwilling witness of injury caused to others."[396] A secondary victim's psychiatric injury will thus be parasitic of the injury suffered by a primary victim. It is also the case that while the primary victim's legal relationship with the wrongdoer is direct, the secondary victim's relationship with the wrongdoer is indirect.

Wrongdoer	**Primary Victim**	**Secondary Victim**
Police ⟶	Deceased ⟶	Family & friends

11–55   Although not described as such at the time, *Bourhill v Young*[397] was pursued by a secondary victim and was the first psychiatric injury case to reach the House of Lords. The facts are explained above[398] and the relationships are illustrated in

---

[394] *Harrhy v Thames Trains Ltd* [2003] EWHC 2286. MacKay J. commented that the facts in *Harrhy* were very similar to those in *Keen*.

[395] *W v Essex CC* [2001] 2 A.C. 592 at 601 per Lord Slynn of Hadley.

[396] *Alcock v Chief Constable of South Yorkshire Police* [1992] 1 A.C. 310 at 407 per Lord Oliver of Aylmerton.

[397] *Bourhill v Young*, 1942 S.C. (HL) 78.

[398] At para.11–04.

the diagram below. Ironically the primary victim of Mr Young's negligence was Mr Young himself. Mrs Bourhill's shock was stimulated by her witnessing the aftermath of the accident. The House of Lords held that as a reasonable person in Mr Young's situation would not reasonably be expected to foresee that someone in Mrs Bourhill's position would be affected by his acts or omissions, he did not owe Mrs Bourhill a duty of care. Thus, her relationship with the negligent party was too remote.

Wrongdoer	**Primary Victim**	**Secondary Victim**
Motorcyclist ⟶ (Young)	Deceased ⟶ (Young)	Mrs Bourhill

Historically, claims for psychiatric injury brought by secondary victims were **11–56** treated with great suspicion by the judiciary.[399] However, in *Hambrook v Stokes Bros*[400] a claim was allowed when a mother miscarried and later died after witnessing an out of control lorry cause an accident in which one of her children was injured. *Hambrook v Stokes* was followed in *McLoughlin v O'Brian*, where the House of Lords allowed a claim from a plaintiff who today would be described as a secondary victim.

Mrs McLoughlin was informed by a neighbour that her husband and three children had been taken to hospital following a serious accident in the family car. She attended the hospital immediately, where she saw her husband and two of her children, still covered in mud, oil and blood, and awaiting treatment. She was told her youngest daughter had died. Mrs McLoughlin developed a psychiatric illness as a result, and sued the driver of the lorry whose negligence had caused the accident. The House of Lords unanimously upheld Mrs McLoughlin's claim. Lord Wilberforce described three limiting factors which he considered should be applied to such cases:

> "the class of persons whose claims should be recognised; the proximity of such persons to the accident; and the means by which the shock is caused."[401]

Lord Wilberforce's "limiting factors" were adopted unanimously by the House of Lords in *Alcock*,[402] and were subsequently described as "control mechanisms" by Lord Lloyd in *Page v Smith*.[403] It is suggested that the subtle change in language indicates a transition from a liberal approach to liability in *McLoughlin* to a more conservative approach in *Alcock* and subsequent cases. These control mechanisms may be seen as policy mechanisms intended to control the range of

---

[399] See, e.g. *Brown v Glasgow Corp*, 1922 S.C. 527 at 532 per Lord Hunter; *Currie v Wardrop*, 1927 S.C. 538 at 544 per Lord Justice-Clerk Alness; *Smith v Johnson & Co* Unreported January 1897 (Div. Ct), referred to in the judgment of Wright J. in *Wilkinson v Downton* [1897] 2 Q.B. 57 at 61.

[400] *Hambrook v Stokes Bros* [1925] 1 K.B. 141. Bankes L.J. at 152 drew attention to the uncomfortable proposition that if only those in fear of their own safety could claim damages for nervous shock, a mother who witnessed her children caught up in an incident would have to show she was more concerned for herself than for her offspring.

[401] *McLoughlin v O'Brian* [1983] 1 A.C. 410 at 422 per Lord Wilberforce.

[402] *Alcock v Chief Constable of South Yorkshire Police* [1992] 1 A.C. 310.

[403] *Page v Smith* [1996] A.C. 155.

claims from secondary victims, and were summarised in that context by Lord Oliver in *Alcock v Chief Constable of South Yorkshire Police*:

> "The common factors of all the reported cases of this type ... are, first, that in each case there was a marital or parental relationship between the plaintiff and the primary victim; secondly, that the injury for which damages were claimed arose from sudden and unexpected shock to the nervous system; thirdly that the plaintiff in each case was either personally present at the scene of the accident or was more or less in the immediate vicinity and witnessed the aftermath shortly afterwards; and fourthly that the injury arose from witnessing the death of, extreme danger to or injury and discomfort suffered by the primary victim. Lastly in each case there was not only an element of physical proximity to the event but a close temporal connection between the event and the plaintiff's perception of it combined with a close relationship of affection between the plaintiff and the primary victim. It must, I think, be from these elements that the essential requirement of proximity is to be deduced ... In my opinion the necessary proximity cannot be said to exist where the elements of immediacy, closeness of time and space and direct visual or aural perception are absent."[404]

Thus, as well as the need for the mental harm to be triggered by shock and for such shock to be reasonably foreseeable in a person of reasonable fortitude,[405] there are three further control mechanisms that limit the range of secondary victims to whom a duty of care will be held to be owed:

1. the relationship between the primary and secondary victim must involve close ties of love and affection;
2. the proximity of the secondary victim to the incident in which the primary victim suffers injury must be close in terms of time and space;
3. the method of communication to the secondary victim of the harm inflicted upon the primary victim must involve direct visual or aural perception.

Control mechanisms: relationship to primary victim

11–57   The relationship between the primary and secondary victims must involve close ties of love and affection. There is a presumption that the relationship between spouses,[406] and between parent and child,[407] will involve such ties, although that presumption may be displaced by evidence. At the other end of the scale, a bystander will be presumed to have too distant a relationship from the primary victim.[408] However, the courts have been careful not to say that the

---

[404] *Alcock v Chief Constable of South Yorkshire Police* [1992] 1 A.C. 310 at 416-417 *per* Lord Oliver of Aylmerton.

[405] Thus the "thin skull rule" does *not* apply with regard to secondary victims suffering psychiatric injury: *Page v Smith* [1996] A.C. 155.

[406] *McLoughlin v O'Brian* [1983] 1 A.C. 410. "Spouses" will at least include civil partners, if not similar long term, albeit less formal, relationships: see, e.g. *Alcock v Chief Constable of South Yorkshire Police* [1992] 1 A.C. 310 at 416 per Lord Oliver of Aylmerton.

[407] Including foster children: *McLoughlin v O'Brian* [1983] 1 A.C. 410 at 418 per Lord Wilberforce.

[408] *Keen v Tayside Contracts*, 2003 S.L.T. 500; *Bourhill v Young*, 1942 S.C. (HL) 78.

presumption against bystanders can never be displaced if the horror of the experience was sufficiently extreme.[409] Nevertheless, even where a bystander witnessed dozens of colleagues perish when an oil rig exploded and was consumed by fire, the courts have refused to accept that the scene was so shocking as to displace the presumption.[410]

It is legitimate to ask where is the cut-off point? No definitive answer has to date been proposed. Indeed, so far no secondary victim outside of a spouse or parent/child relationship with a primary victim has succeeded in a claim for psychiatric injury. In *Alcock v Chief Constable of South Yorkshire*,[411] for example, of the plaintiffs who satisfied the other two control mechanisms, the closest relative to a primary victim was brother-in-law. That relationship was held to be too remote. Similarly, in *Robertson v Forth Bridge Joint Board*,[412] where evidence confirmed a long history of close friendship between colleagues stretching over many years, the Inner House nevertheless held the relationship to be outside of the boundary.

Control mechanisms: proximity to incident

The secondary victim's experience of the shocking incident must be close in **11–58** time and space. It is sufficient if the secondary victim experiences the incident itself, or its immediate aftermath. In *McLoughlin v O'Brian*,[413] the plaintiff was held to have witnessed the immediate aftermath of a serious road accident in that when she saw the surviving members of her family in hospital two hours after the collision, they were still covered in mud, blood and oil from the accident. If they had already been treated so that the immediate signs of trauma had been removed it may have been a different matter: in *Alcock v Chief Constable of South Yorkshire*,[414] for example, the plaintiffs who satisfied the other two control mechanisms were held not to have witnessed the immediate aftermath as it was several hours after the incident itself before they attended at the morgue to identify the dead, by which time the signs of trauma had been removed from the bodies of the primary victims.

There is no definitive guidance on the cut-off point, and each case is determined on its own facts. Thus, witnessing unsuccessful attempts by rescue services to free children trapped in a car has been held to be within the immediate aftermath,[415] as has the cradling of a daughter's disfigured body in a mortuary shortly after attending the scene of the accident.[416] However, attending a mortuary only to confirm the death of the primary victim has not,[417] nor has being present at the death of a mother a few weeks following an accident at work.[418]

---

[409] Such as a burning petrol tanker crashing into a school playground: *Alcock v Chief Constable of South Yorkshire Police* [1992] 1 A.C. 310 at 403 per Lord Ackner.

[410] See, e.g. *McFarlane v Wilkinson* and *Hegarty v EE Caledonia Ltd* [1997] 2 Lloyd's Rep. 259; *McFarlane v EE Caledonia Ltd* [1994] 2 All E.R. 1; *Keen v Tayside Contracts*, 2003 S.L.T. 500.

[411] *Alcock v Chief Constable of South Yorkshire* [1992] 1 A.C. 310.

[412] *Robertson v Forth Bridge Joint Board*, 1995 S.C. 364.

[413] *McLoughlin v O'Brian* [1983] 1 A.C. 410.

[414] *Alcock v Chief Constable of South Yorkshire* [1992] 1 A.C. 310.

[415] *Vernon v Bosley (No.1)* [1997] 1 All E.R. 577.

[416] *Galli-Atkinson v Seghal* [2003] Lloyd's Rep. Med. 285.

[417] *Taylor v Somerset HA* [1993] P.I.Q.R. P262.

[418] *Taylor v A Novo (UK) Ltd* [2013] 3 W.L.R. 989. See also *Ravenscroft v. Rederiaktiebølaget Transatlantic* [1991] 3 All E.R. 73.

Control mechanisms: direct perception

11–59   To satisfy this control mechanism, the psychiatric injury suffered by a secondary victim must result from witnessing the impact on the primary victim by "her own unaided senses, and not from something that someone told her."[419] Whereas Mrs McLoughlin satisfied this control mechanism in that saw first hand her family in the shocking state in which they had been removed from the stricken car, the secondary victims who watched the events at Hillsborough unfold on live television were held not to have satisfied this requirement.

The justification for this part of the decision in *Alcock* was that, given broadcasting guidelines which required that no pictures be transmitted that would show identifiable people suffering, it was unforeseeable that anyone watching would appreciate by virtue of the television pictures alone that a person with whom the viewer had close ties of love and affection was a primary victim of the tragedy.[420] Nevertheless, it was recognised that in different circumstances, such as where an event featuring a small and distinct group of people was being broadcast live, perception via television of the detail of an incident by a secondary victim who had close ties of love and affection with the primary victim would be sufficient.[421] Thus, if a mother and daughter were involved in a serious road accident in which the daughter was fatally injured, if the mother contacted the father by mobile telephone so that the father heard his daughter's screams of agony as she died, if the underlying test is one of reasonable foreseeability this control mechanism should be satisfied, since such communication by mobile telephone would be very much at the highly likely end of the foreseeability scale.

Primary victim suffers self-inflicted harm

11–60   Although *Bourhill v Young* was decided by the House of Lords simply on the basis that Mrs Bourhill was beyond the range of persons that Mr Young could be expected reasonably to foresee as being affected by his negligent acts, the Lord Ordinary had suggested that no duty of care could be owed to a secondary victim by a wrongdoer who was himself a primary victim.[422]

In *Greatorex v Greatorex*,[423] a fireman arrived at the scene of a fatal road accident whereupon he discovered that his son, whose negligence had caused the collision, had suffered a head injury and was lying unconscious in the car. Cazalet J. held that as the victim of self-inflicted injuries, policy considerations outweighed the imposition of a duty of care. To recognise the potential for liability carried with it the potential to cause acute family strife. This decision has

---

[419] *Hambrook v Stokes Bros* [1925] 1 K.B. 141 at 152 per Bankes L.J. Cf. *A v Leeds Teaching Hospital NHS Trust* [2005] Q.B. 506 where parents of children whose organs were removed without consent were described as primary victims. See also *Stevens v Yorkhill NHS Trust*, 2006 S.L.T. 889. Cf. *Yearworth v North Bristol NHS Trust* [2010] Q.B. 1.

[420] *Alcock v Chief Constable of South Yorkshire Police* [1992] 1 A.C. 310 at 398 per Lord Browne-Wilkinson; at 405 per Lord Ackner; and at 423 per Lord Jauncey.

[421] *Alcock v Chief Constable of South Yorkshire Police* [1992] 1 A.C. 310 at 405 per Lord Ackner; at 417 per Lord Oliver of Aylmerton.

[422] *Bourhill v Young*, 1941 S.C. 395 at 399 per Lord Robertson. To illustrate his point, Lord Robertson suggested the example of the pregnant woman suffering a miscarriage after observing from her window a window cleaner fall from a height to his death, being impaled on railings below. Cf. *Alcock v Chief Constable of South Yorkshire Police* [1992] 1 A.C. 310 at 418 per Lord Oliver of Aylmerton.

[423] *Greatorex v Greatorex* [2000] 1 W.L.R. 1970.

been neither approved nor overruled by higher authority,[424] and it may best be viewed as determined by its own facts. Nevertheless, the decision points to policy factors playing an explicit role as such in determining whether exceptions should be found to the rules that have evolved to date.

DUTY OF CARE: POLICY

The third element of the *Caparo* three part test considers whether it is "fair, just **11–61** and reasonable" to impose a duty of care in the circumstances.[425] This overtly is a policy question, although it tends to overlap with the foreseeability and proximity parts to the test. It is likely to be of crucial importance in dealing with novel negligence cases which are on the boundary of liability, and the question will be pertinent no matter what type of harm the case is dealing with. In such cases, the pursuer may be advised to propose policy reasons in support of a duty of care, whereas the defender may adduce policy reasons which challenge the imposition of a duty of care.[426] The court will then have to consider the weight to attach to each of these factors in assessing the impact each should have on determining the existence of a duty of care.

Policy considerations have played a part in shaping the law of negligence from the beginning of its modern development. Lord Atkin's assertion that liability for negligence "is no doubt based upon a general public sentiment of moral wrongdoing for which the offender must pay" identifies a policy question, which is then countered by another:

> "But acts or omissions which any moral code would censure cannot, in a practical world, be treated so as to give a right to every person injured by them to demand relief."

Thus, "rules of law arise which limit the range of complainants and the extent of their remedy."[427] Policy questions were explicitly raised as such in ground-

---

[424] It has found favour with the Law Commission of England and Wales (*Liability for Psychiatric Illness* , paras 5.34–5.44), but has been criticised by the Scottish Law Commission (*Report on Damages for Psychiatric Injury*, para.3.65).

[425] *Caparo Industries Plc v Dickman* [1990] 2 A.C. 605 at 617–618 per Lord Bridge of Harwich. See also Lord Oliver of Aylmerton at 632–633.

[426] Some jurisdictions, notably Canada (*Cooper v Hobart* [2001] 3 S.C.R. 537), continue to view policy considerations only as limiting factors "negativing" the existence or scope of the duty of care.

[427] *Donoghue v Stevenson*, 1932 S.C. (HL) 31 at 44 per Lord Atkin. The duty of care concept was duly criticised as nothing but a policy device: "an unnecessary fifth wheel on the coach incapable of sound analysis and possibly productive of injustice": Buckland, *The Duty to Take Care* (1935) 57 L.Q.R. 637 at 639. Indeed, all of the legal mechanisms applied to the inquiry into liability in negligence have been acknowledged as policy devices: "In previous times, when faced with a new problem, the judges have not openly asked themselves the question: what is the best policy for the law to adopt? But the question has always been there in the background. It has been concealed behind such questions as: Was the defendant under any duty to the plaintiff? Was the relationship between them sufficiently proximate? Was the injury direct or indirect? Was it foreseeable, or not? Was it too remote? And so forth ... Nowadays we direct ourselves to considerations of policy": *Dutton v Bognor Regis Urban DC* [1972] 1 Q.B. 373 at 397 per Lord Denning M.R.

breaking negligence cases by the late 1960s,[428] so in *Caparo* the judges were merely expressing ideas that had long been part of the law of negligence.

Whether the *Caparo* fair just and reasonable test was part of the law of Scotland was at first unclear. However, the question was put beyond doubt by Lord Hope of Craighead in his speech in *Mitchell v Glasgow City Council*:

> " . . . in the Inner House in *British Telecommunications plc v James Thomson & Sons (Engineers) Ltd*[429] Lord Morison, in his dissenting opinion, had described the 'fair, just and reasonable' test as uncertain and wide-ranging . . . The test is indeed broadly expressed. But I see no good reason why, as a general guide to what is required, it should not be regarded as part of Scots law. It is really no more than an expression of the idea that lies at the heart of every judgment about legal policy. If liability is to attach, it should be in situations where this is readily understandable because, looking at both sides of the argument, it is fair and reasonable that there should be liability. *Smith v Chief Constable, Sussex Police*,[430] . . . provides a recent example of its application in a case of personal injury. It was adopted without criticism by Lord Mackay of Clashfern when he spoke for the House in *British Telecommunications plc v James Thomson & Sons (Engineers) Ltd*.[431] It was applied by Lord Brodie in *West v Castlehill LLP*[432] in a situation where he would not have regarded an analysis based simply on foreseeability to be adequate. There is no principle of Scots law that contradicts it, and the fact that the law of liability for negligence has developed on common lines both north and south of the border provides powerful support for the defenders' argument that it should be applied in this case."[433]

In *Hill v Chief Constable of West Yorkshire*,[434] the House of Lords considered that it would not be fair, just or reasonable for the law to impose a duty of care upon the police owed to potential victims of crime. The plaintiff was the mother of the final victim of Peter Sutcliffe, who, notorious as the "Yorkshire Ripper", committed 13 murders and at least eight attempted murders of young women in the West Yorkshire area between 1975 and 1980. Mrs Hill contended that the police had been negligent in their investigation of these crimes and that, had the police carried out their functions with due care, Mr Sutcliffe would already have been arrested and prosecuted by the time he abducted her daughter. Although the House of Lords were unanimous in holding that there was a lack of proximity, so

---

[428] See, e.g. *Rondel v Worsley* [1969] 1 A.C. 191; *Home Office v Dorset Yacht Co Ltd* [1970] A.C. 1004.

[429] *British Telecommunications Plc v James Thomson & Sons (Engineers) Ltd*, 1997 S.C. 59.

[430] *Smith v Chief Constable of Sussex* [2009] 1 A.C. 225.

[431] *British Telecommunications Plc v James Thomson & Sons (Engineers) Ltd*, 1999 S.C. (HL) 9 at 12.

[432] *West v Castlehill LLP* [2008] CSOH 182; 2009 G.W.D. 1–4 at [23].

[433] *Mitchell v Glasgow City Council*, 2009 S.C. (HL) 21 at 31 per Lord Hope of Craighead.

[434] *Hill v Chief Constable of West Yorkshire* [1989] A.C. 53. Although the decision was disapproved by the European Court of Human Rights in *Osman v United Kingdom* (2000) 29 E.H.R.R. 245, its status was to some extent restored by *Z v United Kingdom* (2002) 34 E.H.R.R. 3. The decision in *Hill* has since been reinforced: *Brooks v Commissioner of Police of the Metropolis* [2005] 1 W.L.R. 1495; *Smith v Chief Constable of Sussex*, sub nom. *Van Colle v Chief Constable of Hertfordshire* [2009] 1 A.C. 225. Cf. *Swinney v Chief Constable of Northumbria (No.2)* (1999) 11 Admin. L.R. 811.

disposing of the case, their Lordships went on to say that public policy required that the police be immune from liability for negligence in respect of their investigative function. To allow for the potential of liability "may lead to the exercise of a function being carried on in a detrimentally defensive frame of mind"[435] and would "do more harm than good."[436] Policing would be conducted so as to avoid liability and scarce resources would be diverted from crime suppression and investigation so as to be invested in defending litigation.[437]

A distinction has been made between *public* policy and *legal* policy con- **11–62** siderations:

> "Limitations on the scope of legal liability arise from legal policy, which is to say 'our more or less inadequately expressed ideas of what justice demands' (see Prosser & Keeton, Law of Torts (5th ed) (1984), p 264). This is the case whether the question concerns the admission of a new head of damages or the admission of a duty of care in a new situation. Legal policy in this sense is not the same as public policy, even though moral considerations may play a part in both. The court is engaged in a search for justice, and this demands that the dispute be resolved in a way which is fair and reasonable and accords with ordinary notions of what is fit and proper. It is also concerned to maintain the coherence of the law and the avoidance of inappropriate distinctions if injustice is to be avoided in other cases."[438]

The difference between public policy and legal policy is not immediately clear in Lord Millett's dictum quoted above. However, it is suggested that the term "public policy" may be concerned with the impact of imposing a duty of care on community interests, whereas the term "legal policy" may be more concerned with perceptions of justice and legal coherence. Although judges are undoubtedly well placed to make decisions on the coherence of the law, whether judges are qualified to appreciate the impact of decisions on community interests, or even to adjudicate on perceptions of justice, is open to question. Without intervention by parties who are likely to be affected by decisions, judges will only have submissions from counsel to guide them, and those submissions necessarily will be biased towards the specific interests of the respective clients.[439] Thus

---

[435] *Hill v Chief Constable of West Yorkshire* [1989] A.C. 53 at 63 per Lord Keith of Kinkell.

[436] *Hill v Chief Constable of West Yorkshire* [1989] A.C. 53 at 65 per Lord Templeman.

[437] Immunity from liability following *Hill* has not been extended to the other "emergency" services: see, e.g. *Kent v Griffiths* [2001] Q.B. 36; *Aitken v Scottish Ambulance Service*, 2011 S.L.T. 822 (ambulance service); *Capital & Counties Plc v Hampshire CC* [1997] Q.B. 1004; *Duff v Highland and Islands Fire Board*, 1995 S.L.T. 1362; *Burnett v Grampian Fire and Rescue Services*, 2007 S.L.T. 61 (fire brigade). Cf. *OLL Ltd v Secretary of State for Transport* [1997] 3 All E.R. 897 (coastguard). Other bodies performing public or regulatory functions may be susceptible to immunity from liability: see, e.g. *Elguzouli-Daf v Commissioner of Police of the Metropolis* [1995] Q.B. 335 (*Hill* immunity applied to Crown Prosecution Service); *Marc Rich & Co AG v Bishop Rock Marine Co Ltd* [1996] A.C. 211 (classification society).

[438] *McFarlane v Tayside Health Board*, 2000 S.C. (HL) 1 at 39 per Lord Millett. See also *Rees v Darlington Memorial Hospital NHS Trust* [2004] 1 A.C. 309 at 345–346 per Lord Millett.

[439] For example, nothing in the speeches in *Hill v Chief Constable of West Yorkshire* [1989] A.C. 53 alludes to any research or evidence to underpin the assertions made concerning the impact of a duty of care on policing practice.

"it is quite impossible for a court to know, within the confines of a particular case and with the benefit of only a sparse amount of evidence and its own common sense, what are the wider implications of the move that it is being asked to make."[440]

Judges may claim to speak for the "man on the Clapham omnibus"[441] or for the "traveller on the London Underground",[442] but these assertions may, with some justification,[443] be criticised as arrogant.[444] Judges may develop the experience to make an "educated reflex to facts",[445] but without evidence decisions are likely to be based on "mere guess work."[446]

Public policy arguments have warned of a variety of invidious consequences if the existence of a duty of care creates the potential for liability including: "detrimentally defensive action" that would harm public interests[447]; the burden on the taxpayer[448]; an "overkill" attitude towards risk aversion creating a "nanny state"[449]; diversion of purpose[450]; a breakdown in the structure of social services[451]; a breakdown in social cohesion[452]; a diversion from duties to the

---

[440] *Islington LBC v University College London Hospital NHS Trust* [2006] P.I.Q.R. P3 at 43 per Buxton L.J.

[441] This phrase was attributed to Lord Bowen by Collins M.R. in *McQuire v Western Morning News Co Ltd* [1903] 2 K.B. 100 at 109.

[442] *McFarlane v Tayside Health Board*, 2000 S.C. (HL) 1 at 16 per Lord Steyn.

[443] "I have no very clear insight into what the ordinary person on the London Underground, or in a Glasgow public house, or in any other place where he or she may be found, would regard as fair in this case": *McLoughlin v Grovers* [2002] Q.B. 1312 at 1324 per Brooke L.J. "On its own common sense, and without more guidance, is no more reliable as a guide to the right answer in this case than an appeal to the views of the traveller on the London Underground. As I survey my fellow passengers on my twice weekly journeys to and from Heathrow Airport on the Piccadilly Line—such a variety in age, race, nationality and languages—I find it increasingly hard to persuade myself that any one view on anything other than the most basic issues can be said to be typical of all of them": *Chester v Afshar* [2005] 1 A.C. 134 at 161–162 per Lord Hope of Craighead.

[444] See, e.g. J. Thomson, "Abandoning the law of delict", 2000 S.L.T. (News) 43.

[445] *Maloco v Littlewoods Organisation Ltd*, 1987 S.C. (HL) 37 at 84 per Lord Goff of Chieveley.

[446] *Marc Rich & Co AG v Bishop Rock Marine Co Ltd* [1996] A.C. 211 at 222 per Lord Lloyd.

[447] See, e.g. *Yuen Kun Yeu v Attorney-General of Hong Kong* [1988] A.C. 175 at 198 per Lord Keith of Kinkell (delivering the judgment of the court); *Hill v Chief Constable of West Yorkshire* [1989] A.C. 53 at 63 per Lord Keith of Kinkell; *Caparo Industries Plc v Dickman* [1990] 2 A.C. 605 at 610–611 (arguments from counsel for the auditors); *X (Minors) v Bedfordshire CC* [1995] 2 A.C. 633 at 750 and at 755 per Lord Browne-Wilkinson; *Jain v Trent SHA* [2009] 1 A.C. 853 at 865–866 per Lord Scott of Foscote; *Mitchell v Glasgow City Council*, 2009 S.C. (HL) 21 at 32 per Lord Hope of Craighead. Cf. *Barrett v Enfield LBC* [2001] 2 AC 550 at 568 per Lord Slynn of Hadley; *Phelps v Hillingdon LBC* [2001] 2 AC 619 at 672 per Lord Clyde; *Spring v Guardian Assurance Plc* [1995] 2 AC 296 at 326 per Lord Lowry and at 336 per Lord Slynn of Hadley; *Three Rivers DC v Bank of England (No.3)* [2003] 2 A.C. 1.

[448] See, e.g. *Home Office v Dorset Yacht Co Ltd* [1970] A.C. 1004 at 1045 per Viscount Dilhorne; *Stovin v Wise* [1996] A.C. 923 at 952 per Lord Hoffmann.

[449] See, e.g. *Stovin v Wise* [1996] A.C. 923 at 954–955 per Lord Hoffmann. Cf. *Home Office v Dorset Yacht Co Ltd* [1970] A.C. 1004 at 1033 per Lord Reid. See also *Wands v Fife Council*, 2009 G.W.D. 30–477.

[450] See, e.g. *Harris v Evans* [1998] 1 W.L.R. 1285 at 1297–1298 per Sir Richard Scott V.C.; *Mulcahy v Ministry of Defence* [1996] Q.B. 732 at 747–748 per Neill L.J.; *Smith v Ministry of Defence* [2014] A.C. 52 at 130–132 per Lord Hope of Craighead; *Marc Rich & Co AG v Bishop Rock Marine Co Ltd* [1996] A.C. 211 at 241–242 per Lord Steyn.

[451] See, e.g. *X (Minors) v Bedfordshire CC* [1995] 2 A.C. 633 at 749–751 per Lord Browne-Wilkinson.

[452] See, e.g. *Greatorex v Greatorex* [2000] 1 W.L.R. 1970 at 1985–1986 per Cazalet J.

community at large to focus on obligations to individuals[453]; a conflict of interest with respect to the range of persons to whom a duty would be owed[454]; a disproportionate failure of businesses[455]; a stimulus for a "compensation culture" opening the floodgates to rampant litigation[456]; a disproportionate relationship between risk and reward[457]; and tacit approval of criminal or socially undesirable conduct.[458]

Legal policy arguments have included: the relationship between statutory **11–63** purposes and common law duties[459]; the hierarchy of the law of obligations[460]; the extent to which any development is incremental[461]; the extent to which a private law remedy would cut across a pre-existing responsibility mechanism[462]; whether the remedy sought should be the subject of a statutory scheme rather than by imposition of an inappropriate duty of care[463]; the impact on the prior allocation of risks[464]; where liability would be grossly disproportionate to

---

[453] See, e.g. *Elguzouli-Daf v Commissioner of Police of the Metropolis* [1995] Q.B. 335 at 349–350 per Steyn L.J.; *X (Minors) v Bedfordshire CC* [1995] 2 A.C. 633 at 749–751 per Lord Browne-Wilkinson; *A v Essex CC* [2004] 1 W.L.R. 1881 at 1899–1901 per Hale L.J. (delivering judgment of the court); *Brooks v Commissioner of Police of the Metropolis* [2005] 1 W.L.R. 1495 at 1509-1510 per Lord Steyn; *Mitchell v Glasgow City Council*, 2009 S.C. (HL) 21 at 32 per Lord Hope of Craighead. Cf. *Swinney v Chief Constable of Northumbria Police Force (No.1)* [1997] Q.B. 464.

[454] See, e.g. *Elguzouli-Daf v Commissioner of Police of the Metropolis* [1995] Q.B. 335 at 352 per Morritt L.J.; *D v East Berkshire Community Health NHS Trust* [2005] 2 A.C. 373 at 405–408 per Lord Nicholls of Birkenhead, at 415–416 per Lord Rodger of Earlsferry and at 418–420 per Lord Brown of Eaton-Under-Heywood; *Jain v Trent SHA* [2009] 1 A.C. 853 at 864–868 per Lord Scott of Foscote. Cf. *Arthur JS Hall & Co v Simons* [2002] 1 A.C. 615 at 671–672 per Lord Steyn and at 738–740 per Lord Hobhouse of Woodborough; *Frank Houlgate Investment Co Ltd v Biggart Baillie LLP* [2010] P.N.L.R. 13.

[455] See, e.g. *Caparo Industries Plc v Dickman* [1990] 2 A.C. 605 at 610–611 (arguments from by counsel for the auditors).

[456] See, e.g. *C.B.S. Songs Ltd v Amstrad Consumer Electronics Plc* [1988] A.C. 1013 at 1059 per Lord Templeman; *Alcock v Chief Constable of South Yorkshire Police* [1991] 3 All E.R. 88; *Frost v Chief Constable of South Yorkshire* [1999] 2 A.C. 455 at 493–494 per Lord Steyn; *Gorringe v Calderdale MBC* [2004] 1 W.L.R. 1057 at 1059 per Lord Steyn; *Tomlinson v Congleton BC* [2004] 1 A.C. 46 at 96–97 per Lord Hobhouse of Woodborough; *Phelps v Hillingdon LBC* [1999] 1 W.L.R. 500 at 516 per Stuart-Smith L.J. Cf. *Phelps v Hillingdon LBC* [2001] 2 A.C. 619 at 672 per Lord Clyde.

[457] See, e.g. *Tartan American Machinery Corp v Swan & Co*, 2004 S.C. 276 at 285 per Lord Abernethy.

[458] See, e.g. *Stone & Rolls Ltd (In Liquidation) v Moore Stephens (A Firm)* [2009] 1 A.C. 1391.

[459] See, e.g. *X (Minors) v Bedfordshire CC* [1995] 2 A.C. 633 at 749–751, 755 and 761–763 per Lord Browne-Wilkinson; *Stovin v Wise* [1996] A.C. 923 at 935 per Lord Nicholls of Birkenhead; *Gorringe v Calderdale MBC* [2004] 1 W.L.R. 1057 at 1087–1088 per Lord Brown or Eaton-Under-Heywood; *Desmond v Chief Constable of Nottinghamshire Police* [2011] P.T.S.R. 1369.

[460] See, e.g. *Tai Hing Cotton Mill Ltd v Liu Chong Hing Bank Ltd* [1986] A.C. 80 at 106 per Lord Scarman; *Downsview Nominees Ltd v First City Corporation Ltd* [1993] A.C. 295 at 316 per Lord Templeman; *Marc Rich & Co AG v Bishop Rock Marine Co Ltd* [1996] A.C. 211 at 238–242 per Lord Steyn; *British Telecommunications Plc v James Thomson & Sons (Engineers) Ltd*, 1999 S.C. (HL) 9; *Realstone Ltd v J & E Shepherd* [2008] P.N.L.R. 21.

[461] See, e.g. *X (Minors) v Bedfordshire CC* [1995] 2 A.C. 633 at 749–751 per Lord Browne-Wilkinson; *Barrett v London Borough of Enfield* [2001] 2 A.C. 550 at 569 per Lord Slynn of Hadley; *Sutradhar v Natural Environment Research Council* [2007] Env. L.R. 10 at 182–183 per Lord Hoffmann.

[462] See, e.g. *Barrett v London Borough of Enfield* [2001] 2 A.C. 550 at 589 per Lord Hutton.

[463] See, e.g. *Jain v Trent SHA* [2009] 1 A.C. 853 at 869 per Lord Scott of Foscote.

[464] See, e.g. *Marc Rich & Co. AG v Bishop Rock Marine Co Ltd* [1996] A.C. 211 at 239–240 per Lord Steyn; *British Telecommunications Plc v James Thomson & Sons (Engineers) Ltd*, 1999 S.C. (HL) 9.

fault[465]; whether gaps in the law require filling[466]; and, more controversially, whether the population at large would consider liability consistent with their sense of right and wrong.[467] In particular,

> "The House of Lords has warned against the danger of extending the ambit of negligence so as to supplant or supplement other torts, contractual obligations, statutory duties or equitable rules in relation to every kind of damage."[468]

Duty of care: pure omissions

11–64   Although Lord Atkin asserted that "[y]ou must take reasonable care to avoid acts or *omissions* which you can reasonably foresee would be likely to injure your neighbour,"[469] it has also been stated that "[t]he common law does not impose liability for what are called pure omissions."[470] This raises the question: what is the difference between an omission and a "pure" omission? The answer would seem to be that a duty to avoid omissions is owed to one's neighbour, but not to others. A further question is then raised:

> "Who, then, in law, is my neighbour? The answer seems to be—persons who are so closely and directly affected by my act that I ought reasonably to have them in contemplation as being so affected when I am directing my mind to the acts or omissions which are called in question."[471]

However:

> "The very parable of the good Samaritan (Luke 10, v. 30) which was evoked by Lord Atkin in *Donoghue v. Stevenson* illustrates, in the conduct of the priest and of the Levite who passed by on the other side, an omission which was likely to have as its reasonable and probable consequence damage to the health of the victim of the thieves, but for which the priest and Levite would have incurred no civil liability in English law."[472]

This discussion appears to be circular. However, a more detailed examination of the parable of the good Samaritan may provide a resolution. Jesus recited the parable in response to the lawyer's question, "Who is my neighbour?" In the

---

[465] See, e.g. *McFarlane v Tayside Health Board*, 2000 S.C. (HL) 1 at 24 per Lord Hope of Craighead and at 36–37 per Lord Clyde.

[466] e.g. " . . . it is open to your Lordships' House . . . to fashion a remedy to fill a lacuna in the law and so prevent the injustice which would otherwise occur on the facts of cases such as the present": *White v Jones* [1995] 2 A.C. 207 at 268 per Lord Goff of Chieveley.

[467] See, e.g. *McFarlane v Tayside Health Board*, 2000 S.C. (HL) 1 at 16 per Lord Steyn.

[468] *Downsview Nominees Ltd v First City Corporation Ltd* [1993] A.C. 295 at 316 per Lord Templeman.

[469] *Donoghue v Stevenson*, 1932 S.C. (HL) 31 at 44 (emphasis added).

[470] *Maloco v Littlewoods Organisation Ltd*, 1987 S.C. (HL) 37 at 76 per Lord Goff. See also *Mitchell v Glasgow City Council*, 2009 S.C. (HL) 21 at 27–29 per Lord Hope of Craighead.

[471] *Donoghue v Stevenson*, 1932 S.C. (HL) 31 at 44 per Lord Atkin.

[472] *Home Office v Dorset Yacht Co Ltd* [1970] A.C. 1004 at 1060 per Lord Diplock. "The (priest), both in England and Wales and in Scotland would have been in breach of no more than a moral obligation": *Mitchell v Glasgow City Council*, 2009 S.C. (HL) 21 at 35 per Lord Scott of Foscote.

parable, a priest and a Levite[473] ignored the predicament of a man lying injured in the road after having been set upon by thieves. The Samaritan,[474] though, took compassion on the man, dressed his wounds and took him to an inn, promising to repay the innkeeper any expenses incurred in looking after the man. Jesus then asked the lawyer which of the three was a neighbour to the man, the lawyer replying, "He who shewed mercy on him." Using modern legal language, the Samaritan assumed a responsibility for the man which the others had not.

Thus, a "pure" omission[475] is a failure to act where there is no responsibility to act. Responsibility giving rise to a duty to avoid omissions[476] may be imposed by statute or may arise where an individual creates a "public danger".[477] Responsibility may also arise due to a pre-existing relationship between the parties. A relationship may exist naturally where an *ex lege* duty of care will be imposed, such as the relationship between a parent and child or between a school and a child in its care,[478] or between a host and a guest.[479] Alternatively the relationship may be created *ex voluntante* by contract, or alternatively, where the defender voluntarily assumes responsibility for the pursuer.[480]

Without an assumption of responsibility there is no duty to warn, even **11–65** although harm may be foreseeable. Thus, there is no liability in negligence

> "on the part of one who sees another about to walk over a cliff with his head in the air, and forbears to shout a warning."[481]

This was confirmed quite emphatically in *Mitchell v Glasgow City Council*,[482] where the House of Lords held that a local authority as social landlord did not owe a duty of care to a tenant to warn him of the risk of injury from an assault by an angry neighbour. The tenant, Mr Mitchell, had complained to the local authority over a number of years about a prolonged campaign of harassment and intimidation, including threats of violence, from his next-door neighbour, Mr Drummond, who had been moved to that address by the local authority following complaints of anti-social behaviour at his previous address. The local authority eventually held a meeting with Mr Drummond where he was informed that he was to be evicted. Mr Drummond lost his temper at the meeting, although he did calm down before the meeting concluded. However, Mr Drummond encountered Mr Mitchell on his return home and carried out a serious assault on Mr Mitchell, who subsequently died as a result of his injuries. Although there was proximity

---

[473] A member of the Hebrew Tribe of Levi.

[474] Samaritans and Jews were reputed to despise each other at the time.

[475] Some other jurisdictions describe a pure omission as "non-feasance".

[476] Described as "misfeasance" in some other jurisdictions. However: "In my opinion the law of Scotland does not draw a distinction between acts and omissions comparable to that which appears to exist in the English law of tort between misfeasance and non-feasance": *Burnett v Grampian Fire and Rescue Services*, 2007 S.L.T. 61 at 67 per Lord Macphail.

[477] See, e.g. *Haynes v Harwood* [1935] 1 K.B. 146.

[478] *Woodland v Essex CC* [2014] A.C. 537. Cf. *Webster v Ridgeway Foundation School* [2010] E.L.R. 694.

[479] See, e.g. *Horsley v MacLaren (The Ogopogo)* [1971] 2 Lloyd's Rep. 410.

[480] *Mitchell v Glasgow City Council*, 2009 S.C. (HL) 21 at 33 per Lord Hope of Craighead. This analysis again suggests an overlap between *ex lege* and *ex voluntante* obligations: see para.11–36 above.

[481] *Yuen Kun Yeu v Attorney-General of Hong Kong* [1988] A.C. 175 at 192 per Lord Keith of Kinkell

[482] *Mitchell v Glasgow City Council*, 2009 S.C. (HL) 21.

here, the House of Lords held that it would not be fair, just and reasonable to impose a duty of care owed by the local authority to Mr Mitchell. Lord Hope of Craighead explored the implications of recognising a duty to warn:

> "(T)he implications of saying that there was a duty to warn in this case are complex and far reaching . . . if there was a duty to warn in this case, must it not follow that there is a duty to warn in every case where a social landlord has reason to suspect that his tenant may react to steps to address his anti-social behaviour by attacking the person or property of anyone he suspects of informing against him? And if social landlords are under such a duty, must social workers and private landlords not be under the same duty too? In this case it is said that the duty was owed to the deceased. But others in the neighbourhood had complained to the defenders about Drummond's behaviour. Was the duty to warn not owed to them also? It is said that there was a duty to keep the deceased informed of the steps that they proposed to take against Drummond, and in particular to warn him that a meeting had been arranged for 31 July. This suggests that the defenders would have had to determine, step by step at each stage, whether or not the actions that they proposed to take in fulfilment of their responsibilities as landlords required a warning to be given, and to whom. And they would have had to defer taking that step until the warning had been received by everyone and an opportunity given for it to be acted on. The more attentive they were to their ordinary duties as landlords the more onerous the duty to warn would become.
>
> These problems suggest that to impose a duty to warn, together with the risk that action would be taken against them by anybody who suffered loss, injury or damage if they had received no warning, would deter social landlords from intervening to reduce the incidence of anti-social behaviour . . . As in the case of the police, it is desirable too that social landlords, social workers and others who seek to address the many behavioural problems that arise in local authority housing estates and elsewhere, often in very difficult circumstances, should be safeguarded from legal proceedings arising from an alleged failure to warn those who might be at risk of a criminal attack in response to their activities. Such proceedings, whether meritorious or otherwise, would involve them in a great deal of time, trouble and expense which would be more usefully devoted to their primary functions in their respective capacities."[483]

11–66 Thus, without an active assumption of responsibility, policy considerations confirm that failure to intervene will normally be classified as a pure omission and attract no liability. This will also be the case where the failure is to perform a statutory function such as the provision of social services or educational facilities to members of the community with special needs.[484] Neither will the

---

[483] *Mitchell v Glasgow City Council*, 2009 S.C. (HL) 21 at 31–32 per Lord Hope of Craighead.

[484] See, e.g. *X v Bedfordshire CC* [1995] 2 A.C. 633. A similar approach is taken to performance of statutory functions of highway authorities: see, e.g. *Stovin v Wise* [1996] A.C. 923; *Gorringe v Calderdale MBC* [2004] 1 W.L.R. 1057; *MacDonald v Aberdeenshire Council*, 2014 S.L.T. 2.

emergency services be liable for pure omissions, even where they fail to respond to an emergency call.[485]

However, a duty to act will arise where the defender has assumed responsibility towards the pursuer. Responding to an emergency call may demonstrate an assumption of responsibility. Thus, a proof before answer was allowed where it was reasonably foreseeable that a delay in dispatching an ambulance would carry a risk to the health of the patient.[486] Likewise, where the fire brigade do attend at an emergency they will owe a duty of care to the victim with regard efficiently to putting out the fire,[487] and where the police actively "take control" of a hazard on a public road, they may owe a duty to other road users likely to be immediately and directly affected by that hazard.[488] Similarly to the responsibility assumed by hospitals to patients,[489] the police and prison authorities may be held to have assumed responsibility towards those whom they have taken into custody,[490] and local authorities may be deemed to have assumed responsibility to children once taken into care.[491] Persons entrusted with property may be held to have assumed responsibility to the owner for its safety.[492] Intervening to assist a person who is too drunk to look after himself may amount to a "good Samaritan" assumption of responsibility, and so the law may then impose a duty to ensure that the person concerned receives medical treatment.[493]

Note that mere engagement with a statutory function will not of itself amount to an assumption of responsibility and so will not, of itself, create a duty of care. This point was made clear in the decision of the House of Lords in *Mitchell*[494] and was made with some force by the English Court of Appeal in *X v Hounslow LBC*.[495] A married couple lived along with their two children in a flat provided by the local authority. The adults and older child had learning difficulties and a social worker was concerned that they were being exploited by local youths who were using the flat to engage in a range of anti-social activities. The social worker had attempted to have the local authority expedite re-housing the family but, before the formalities had been completed, the family were imprisoned in the flat by a gang of youths during which time they were subject to serious physical and sexual assaults. It was held that the local authority, in doing no more than

---

[485] See, e.g. *Hill v Chief Constable of West Yorkshire* [1989] A.C. 53; *Brooks v Commissioner of Police of the Metropolis* [2005] 1 W.L.R. 1495; *Smith v Chief Constable of Sussex,* sub nom. *Van Colle v Chief Constable of Hertfordshire* [2009] 1 A.C. 225 (police); *Aitken v Scottish Ambulance Service,* 2011 S.L.T. 822 (ambulance service); *Capital & Counties Plc v Hampshire CC* [1997] QB 1004 (fire brigade); *OLL Ltd v Secretary of State for Transport* [1997] 3 All E.R. 897 (coastguard).

[486] *Aitken v Scottish Ambulance Service,* 2011 S.L.T. 822.

[487] *Duff v Highland and Islands Fire Board,* 1995 S.L.T. 1362; *Burnett v Grampian Fire and Rescue Services,* 2007 S.L.T. 61.

[488] *Gibson v Orr,* 1999 S.C. 420 at 435 per Lord Hamilton.

[489] See, e.g. *Rabone v Pennine Care NHS Trust* [2012] 2 A.C. 72. The assumption of responsibility may also invoke positive duties with regard to human rights as set out in the European Convention on Human Rights.

[490] *Kirkham v Chief Constable of Greater Manchester* [1990] 2 Q.B. 283; *Reeves v Commissioner of Police of the Metropolis* [2000] 1 A.C. 360. See also *Swinney v Chief Constable of Northumbria* [1997] Q.B. 464 (assumption of responsibility to a police informant). Cf. *Gibson v Orr,* 1999 S.C. 420 at 434 per Lord Hamilton.

[491] *Barrett v Enfield London Borough Council* [2001] 2 A.C. 550.

[492] See, e.g. *Stansbie v Troman* [1948] 2 K.B. 48.

[493] *Barrett v Ministry of Defence* [1995] 1 W.L.R. 1217.

[494] *Mitchell v Glasgow City Council,* 2009 S.C. (HL) 21.

[495] *X v Hounslow LBC* [2009] P.T.S.R. 1158.

attempting to carry out its statutory duties, had not actively assumed responsibility to the family so as to have taken upon themselves a good Samaritan duty of care.

Duty of care: wrongful conception

11-67 A series of cases for "wrongful conception" following failed sterilisation procedures have highlighted a number of difficult issues which deserve individual treatment. The negligence may be in the procedure itself, or in the provision of advice with regard to the efficiency of the procedure. It goes without saying that an unwanted conception is a reasonably foreseeable consequence if a sterilisation procedure fails due to negligence. However, the proximity and policy questions raised are much less straightforward.

The discovery of an unwanted conception may in itself result in shock and distress for the woman or the couple. The woman will also endure pain and suffering associated either with a termination of the pregnancy, or with childbirth. There are also financial costs associated with the birth and the rearing of the child. If the child is given up by the mother or family then there may be further mental trauma.

Proximity questions relate to the classification of the status of the victim, i.e. primary or secondary, and to the classification of the harm. If the failed sterilisation procedure had been carried out on the mother, clearly she should be classified as a primary victim of the surgeon's negligence. The distress upon discovery of pregnancy and the pain and suffering of termination or childbirth are the immediate consequences of the negligence, and establishing proximity of relationship will be straightforward. The financial costs of upbringing may be seen as derivative of the harm and suffering associated with childbirth and so would not be subject to the limitations imposed in the context of proximity, but would only be subject to the rules on remoteness of damage.[496]

Where the failed sterilisation has been carried out on the mother, the status of the father as primary or secondary victim is less clear. If the man began the relationship with the woman only after she had undergone the attempted sterilisation procedure, it is submitted that he should be classified as a secondary victim, at least with regard to the financial costs of raising the child if not also with regard to the emotional distress that follows discovery of the unwanted pregnancy. This analysis would exclude liability to the father under the general exclusionary rule for recovery to secondary victims.[497] However, if the couple were already within a relationship at the time of the operation, if they had been advised as a couple by the surgeon it may be argued that there is a direct

---

[496] See para.11–26 above. Should damages then reflect the standard of upbringing enjoyed by the child's siblings? See, e.g. *Benarr v Kettering Health Authority* (1988) 138 N.L.J. 179. Cf. *McFarlane v Tayside Health Board*, 2000 S.C. (HL) 1 at 24 per Lord Hope of Craighead.

[497] See para.11–14 above. At the time of the negligence and from the perspective of the surgeon, the man, as a future partner of the patient, would belong to an indeterminate class. What would be the position if the woman patient met the man immediately following the operation, and he accompanied her on a visit to the surgeon where the surgeon advised the patient that she was no longer at risk of pregnancy is she engaged in unprotected sex? See also *Goodwill v British Pregnancy Advisory Service* [1996] 1 W.L.R. 1397, where the plaintiff met the man three years after he had undergone a vasectomy operation which spontaneously reversed.

relationship between the surgeon and the man, creating sufficient proximity of relationship.[498]

Where the failed sterilisation operation has been carried out on the man, does that make the woman a secondary victim? If so, where does that leave the woman in terms of a duty of care owed to her by the surgeon with regard to the emotional distress at discovery of the pregnancy, the pain and suffering associated with termination or childbirth, or the financial costs of bringing up the child? As a secondary victim she would find herself subject to the exclusionary rule, at least with regard to financial losses. The exceptions to the exclusionary rule developed with regard to psychiatric injury in the line of cases around *Alcock*[499] clearly are unsuitable for application in such a case,[500] and there is a dearth of guidance on liability to secondary victims for physical harm. Again, if the couple engaged together in a pre-operation consultation with the surgeon, would that affect the mother's status and then should she be classified as a primary victim?[501] Furthermore, should the financial costs in relation to the child's birth and upbringing that were borne by the father be classified as derivative or pure economic loss—after all the father will not have had to endure the physical pain and suffering associated with the birth.[502]

These proximity questions effectively were rendered redundant by the decision **11–68** of the House of Lords in *McFarlane v Tayside Health Board*.[503] The McFarlane couple decided that they did not wish to have any more children so Mr McFarlane underwent a vasectomy procedure in 1989, later receiving a letter received from the health board which stated wrongly that his sperm counts were negative. Mrs McFarlane fell pregnant, giving birth to a healthy child in 1992. Mrs McFarlane claimed for the pain and suffering associated with the birth and the couple claimed for the costs involved in bringing up the child. At first instance Lord Gill took the view that the birth of a healthy child simply was not actionable: labour and childbirth was not "personal injury" and a child was a "gift", the value of which would transcend any patrimonial loss incurred in the child's upbringing.[504] Lord Gill's decision was reversed by a unanimous decision of the Inner House.[505]

On appeal by the Health Board to the House of Lords, four possible outcomes were identified as having been considered in other jurisdictions. One would be to follow the decision of the Lord Ordinary and to reject the claim in its entirety. A second would be to follow the decision of the Inner House, and to allow the claim

---

[498] This conundrum was explored in the context of negligent failure to advise of the risk of Downs Syndrome by Lord Prosser in *McLelland v Greater Glasgow Health Board*, 2001 S.L.T. 446 at 449–450. See also *Anderson v Forth Valley Health Board*, 1998 S.L.T. 588, where, in a wrongful birth case, Lord Nimmo Smith considered whether the cost of upbringing should be classified as pure, or as derivative, financial loss.

[499] *Alcock v Chief Constable of South Yorkshire* [1992] 1 A.C. 310 at 416–417 per Lord Oliver of Aylmerton; *White v Chief Constable of South Yorkshire Police* [1999] 2 A.C. 455.

[500] By analogy see *McLelland v Greater Glasgow Health Board*, 2001 S.L.T. 446 at 450 per Lord Prosser.

[501] This was the situation in *McFarlane v Tayside Health Board*, 2000 S.C. (HL) 1, but Mrs McFarlane's status as primary or secondary victim was not part of the pleadings and thus not considered at any stage in the proceedings.

[502] "The distinction (between pure or consequential economic loss) is technical and artificial if not actually suspect in (such) circumstances": *McFarlane v Tayside Health Board*, 2000 S.C. (HL) 1 at 40 per Lord Millett.

[503] *McFarlane v Tayside Health Board*, 2000 S.C. (HL) 1.

[504] *McFarlane v Tayside Health Board*, 1997 S.L.T. 211.

[505] *McFarlane v Tayside Health Board*, 1998 S.C. 389.

in its entirety with no set-off to account for the benefits accruing from the addition to the family of a healthy child. A third approach would be to allow the claim for pain and suffering, but deny the claim for economic loss. A fourth option would be to allow the claim for the costs involved in bringing up the child, but to discount from the claim the benefits of having a healthy child. Their Lordships noted that all of the first three approaches had found favour in some jurisdictions, but noted that the fourth had generally been rejected as morally repugnant—it being required effectively to put a "purchase price" on the value of a child.[506] By a majority, their Lordships opted for the third outcome, with Lord Millett preferring the first, subject to a "conventional sum" to be paid for compensation for loss of autonomy.

Other than a reliance on "legal policy", it is difficult to detect consensus in their Lordships' reasoning.[507] Indeed, it is submitted that the speeches reveal evidence of decision making by instinct followed up with attempts to justify the conclusions.[508] Such judicial creativity thus exposes their Lordships to accusations of abandoning their judicial function and adopting the role of legislator.[509] Lord Slynn took the view that there would have to be an assumption of responsibility by the surgeon for the pure economic loss and, without there being a contract in place, it would not be fair, just and reasonable to impose a duty of care with regard to that head of claim.[510] Lord Hope suggested that liability for the costs of bringing up the child would be disproportionate to the extent of the negligence,[511] and agreed that it would not be fair, just and reasonable to admit the claim for economic loss, holding that this part of the claim fell "outside the *ambit of the duty of care* which was owed to the pursuers by the persons who carried out the procedures."[512] Lord Clyde expressed his opinion as being based on remoteness of damage rather than duty or no duty:

> "But that the pursuers end up with an addition to their family, originally unintended but now, although unexpected, welcome, and are enabled to have the child maintained while in their custody free of any cost does not seem to accord with the idea of restitution or with an award of damages which does justice between both parties."[513]

---

[506] "If the monetary value of the child is assessed at a sum in excess of the costs of maintaining him, the exercise merely serves to confirm what most courts have been willing to assume without it. On the other hand, if the court assesses the monetary value of the child at a sum less than the costs of maintaining him, it will have accepted the unedifying proposition that the child is not worth the cost of looking after him": *McFarlane v Tayside Health Board*, 2000 S.C. (HL) 1 at 42 per Lord Millett. See also at 34–35 per Lord Clyde.

[507] Indeed it is suggested that it is difficult to observe consensus in their Lordships' understanding of what is meant by "legal policy".

[508] It is submitted that other examples include *Frost v Chief Constable of South Yorkshire* [1999] 2 A.C. 455; *Fairchild v Glenhaven Funeral Services Ltd* [2003] 1 A.C. 32; and *Chester v Afshar* [2005] 1 A.C. 134.

[509] See, e.g. Thomson, "Abandoning the Law of Delict?", 2000 S.L.T. (Notes) 43.

[510] Lord Slynn did not consider the discriminatory impact of this approach, i.e. those who could afford to pay for a procedure may be owed a duty of care, whereas those who sought the procedure on the NHS would not.

[511] *McFarlane v Tayside Health Board*, 2000 S.C. (HL) 1 at 24 per Lord Hope of Craighead. Lord Clyde also considered that the expense of child rearing would be wholly disproportionate to the doctor's culpability at 37.

[512] *McFarlane v Tayside Health Board*, 2000 S.C. (HL) 1 at 29 per Lord Hope of Craighead (emphasis added).

[513] *McFarlane v Tayside Health Board*, 2000 S.C. (HL) 1 at 36 per Lord Clyde.

Lord Steyn delivered one of the most radical speeches in respect of delict theory **11–69** in a century. Acknowledging that corrective justice would demand a remedy for the costs of the child's upbringing, he preferred to resort to "distributive" justice, being "the just distribution of burdens and losses among members of a society."[514] Thus, his Lordship was firmly of the opinion that a survey of commuters on the Underground[515] would provide an overwhelming "No" to the question of liability for the child's upbringing. It is submitted that this amounts to a shameless usurping of the function of legislator, carried out without a shred of evidence to support the presumed conclusions.[516] Indeed, this device has been criticised as judicial subjectivity masquerading as an objective view.[517] Lord Millett's proposed solution was no less radical: in view of the difficulties in a cost/benefit analysis, which Lord Millett perceived as infecting all aspects of the claim, no damages should be awarded but rather the couple should receive a "conventional award" for the loss of their autonomy in determining the size of their family.

The decision in *McFarlane* was applied in *Parkinson v St James and Seacroft University Hospital NHS Trust*[518] where a child was born with congenital disabilities following a failed sterilisation operation. The difficulties associated with the *McFarlane* decision were highlighted by the fact that the Court of Appeal, again relying on the opaque concepts of "legal policy" and "distributive justice", held that the additional costs arising from the special needs of the child were recoverable even although the ordinary costs in bringing up the child were not. What is rather bizarre is that the costs directly traceable to the negligent act are not recoverable whereas costs which are at best indirectly attributable to the negligent act are![519]

McFarlane was not followed in the Commonwealth.[520] That, along with the trenchant criticism of the decision, meant that it was virtually inevitable that

---

[514] *McFarlane v Tayside Health Board*, 2000 S.C. (HL) 1 at 16 per Lord Steyn.

[515] Assuming Lord Steyn was referring to the London Underground one might point out that not every passenger is a "commuter"!

[516] Perhaps even more astonishing is the criticism leveled at the Court of Appeal by Lord Steyn in his speech in *Rees v Darlington Memorial Hospital NHS Trust* [2004] 1 A.C. 309 at 321: "Unfortunately, there was no information before the Court of Appeal as how, if at all, it is more costly for the claimant to look after (the child) than it would be for a mother who does not have her disability." In spite of this criticism, Lord Steyn continued to assume the thoughts of others later in his speech where he asserted (at 327) that Lords Slynn and Clyde had "without doubt" unspokenly rejected Lord Millett's suggestion in *McFarlane* that a conventional sum should have been awarded to the pursuers!

[517] "As is pointed out by Lord Steyn, such a test proceeds in essence on the 'judges' sense of the moral answer to a question' and by 'what a judge reasonably believes that the ordinary citizen would regard as right'. I must confess that my perception of what 'the traveller on the Underground' would think fair does not differ from that which I myself think and that therefore the test appears to me to be no less subjective if expressed in this way": *McLelland v Greater Glasgow Health Board*, 2001 S.L.T. 446 at 458 per Lord Morison (dissenting).

[518] *Parkinson v St James and Seacroft University Hospital NHS Trust* [2002] Q.B. 266.

[519] Although it was not tampered with by the House of Lords in *Rees v Darlington Memorial Hospital NHS Trust* [2004] 1 A.C. 309, there was dissensus across the members of the judicial committee in respect of their view of the decision in *Parkinson*.

[520] See, e.g. *Cattanach v Melchior* (2003) 215 C.L.R. 1. See also L. Sutherland, "Update—Medical Negligence (post-*McFarlane* decisions)", 2001 39 Rep. B. 3; M. Bickford-Smith, "Damages for Failed Sterilisation" [2001] J.P.I.L. 404; J.K. Mason, "Wrongful Pregnancy, Wrongful Birth and Wrongful Terminology" (2002) 6 Edin. L.R. 46. The decision in *Cattanach* was overturned by legislation in Queensland, New South Wales and South Australia, all of which substituted an approach consistent with the decision of the House of Lords in *McFarlane*.

sooner or later a seven-member House of Lords would be required to reconsider the position. That moment arrived sooner rather than later in the case of *Rees v Darlington Memorial Hospital NHS Trust*[521]; a factual variant of *McFarlane*. A disabled mother sought a sterilisation as it would be harder for her to care for a child. It failed, and she gave birth to a healthy child. The case failed on a 4:3 majority decision. To an extent, the House of Lords did not want to be seen to be changing the law according to the personnel deciding the case, especially where no new arguments had been presented. Thus, the decision in *McFarlane* was confirmed; explained as based on legal policy and invoking the theory of distributive justice, considering that it was fair, just and reasonable to construct an exception to the normal principles of damages based on a "recognition of the uniqueness of every human being."[522] Nevertheless, the claimant was not sent away empty-handed. Lord Millett's suggestion in *McFarlane* that a conventional award should be made for loss of autonomy was adopted by the majority, albeit subject to criticism that such an outcome would be unprincipled and unprecedented.[523] Although not compensatory, such an award should not be "nominal or derisory", and so a figure of £15,000 was suggested as affording "a more ample measure of justice than the pure *McFarlane* rule."[524]

11–70   It is submitted that it is highly unsatisfactory that such an anomalous approach should be permitted to become orthodoxy in one isolated branch of the law, at least unless that is the product of a legislature. Indeed, it is suggested that a traditional approach which would apply corrective rather than distributive justice, and so retain coherence in the law of negligence as it stands, could have been adopted so as to reach a similar outcome. Clearly, given that a duty of care with regard to pain and suffering was recognised in both, there was sufficient proximity in *McFarlane* and in *Rees* to put the pursuer/claimants into a determinate class of potential victims from the perspective of the surgeon (the alleged wrongdoer). Thus, rather than distinguish between the various strands of harm at the duty stage, it is submitted that a more coherent approach would be to accept that a duty of care was breached but to apply the principle of causation asserted by the Court of Appeal in *Galoo v Bright Grahame and Murray*.[525] Thus a wrongdoer will not be liable where the wrong merely creates the opportunity for the pursuer to suffer a loss. Losses, or *damnum*, in the sense of "some material prejudice to an interest which the law recognises as a legal interest,"[526] in such cases may include: first, loss of autonomy in determining the size of one's family; secondly, the pain and suffering associated with pregnancy and childbirth; thirdly, the costs of the upbringing of a healthy child; and fourthly, the additional costs in providing for a disabled child. The first of these flows directly from the wrong but, since other factors also have a role to play in creating the

---

[521] *Rees v Darlington Memorial Hospital NHS Trust* [2004] 1 A.C. 309.

[522] *Rees v Darlington Memorial Hospital NHS Trust* [2004] 1 A.C. 309 at 354 per Lord Scott of Foscote.

[523] Ironically, the criticism came from Lord Steyn at 328: "I regard the idea of a conventional award in the present case as contrary to principle. It is a novel procedure for judges to create such a remedy. There are limits to permissible creativity for judges. In my view the majority have strayed into forbidden territory. It is also a backdoor evasion of the legal policy enunciated in *McFarlane*. If such a rule is to be created it must be done by Parliament."

[524] *Rees v Darlington Memorial Hospital NHS Trust* [2004] 1 A.C. 309 at 317 per Lord Bingham of Cornhill. No attempt was made to set out a calculation so as to demonstrate how the award was neither nominal nor derisory—was the figure merely plucked out of the air?

[525] *Galoo v Bright Grahame and Murray* [1994] 1 W.L.R. 1360. See para.13–18 below.

[526] *McFarlane v Tayside Health Board*, 1998 S.C. 389 at 400 per Lord McCluskey

condition, the wrong may be seen as merely providing the opportunity rather than the catalyst for the second and third.[527] As for the fourth category, it would depend on whether any disability arose independently of the wrong, or as its direct consequence, whether the wrong could be said to merely create the opportunity for the loss or should be treated as the catalyst.

---

[527] See also *Sasea Finance Ltd (In Liquidation) v KPMG (formerly KPMG Peat Marwick McLintock) (No. 2)* [2000] 1 All E.R. 676.

CHAPTER 12

NEGLIGENCE: BREACH OF THE DUTY OF CARE

INTRODUCTION

12–01 To establish liability in delict it is not sufficient merely to confirm that the law imposes a duty owed by the defender to the pursuer; it must also be shown that the relevant duty has been breached by the defender. There must be proof of some "culpable act or omission."[1] It may be noted that it is rare that terms such as "breach of duty" are used in the context of intentional or other "nominate" delicts. However, the term is frequently encountered in the context of proof of negligence. Thus, "breach of duty" may be seen as the second stage of an inquiry into liability for negligence[2]:

> "The liability for negligence, whether you style it such or treat it as in other systems as a species of '*culpa*,' is no doubt based upon a general public sentiment of moral wrongdoing for which the offender must pay."[3]

The onus of proof is upon the pursuer and that in general requires the pursuer to lead evidence so as to prove on the balance of probabilities that the defender failed to achieve the standard of care demanded by the law. It follows that two questions must be answered: first, what standard of care was demanded; and secondly, was that standard achieved? The former is a question of law[4] and the latter a question of fact, to be determined by the evidence.[5] In practice, everyday cases tend to involve factual disputes rather than questions of law where the second question requires most attention, with regard to the rules of evidence. Thus, without averments of fact to support an assertion of breach of duty, fault or *culpa* on the part of a defender, any claim for reparation will be dismissed as irrelevant.[6]

STANDARD OF CARE

12–02 The standard of care demanded by the law of negligence is always reasonable care in the circumstances:

---

[1] Erskine, III, 1, 13.
[2] The first stage being the confirmation that a duty of care is owed *ex lege* by the defender to the pursuer: see Ch.11.
[3] *Donoghue v Stevenson*, 1932 S.C. (HL) 31 at 44 per Lord Atkin.
[4] *Bolton v Stone* [1951] A.C. 850 at 859 per Lord Porter.
[5] *Muir v Glasgow Corp*, 1943 S.C. (HL) 3 at 8 per Lord Thankerton.
[6] *Gibson v Strathclyde RC*, 1992 S.L.T. 1243.

"You must take *reasonable* care to avoid acts or omissions which you can reasonably foresee would be likely to injure your neighbour."[7]

In the classic case of *Muir v Glasgow Corp* a Sunday School trip to Kings Park in Glasgow was disrupted by heavy rain. The supervising church elders obtained permission from the manageress of a tearoom in the park for the party of children to shelter inside the tearoom. She also allowed two men from the party to carry a tea urn into the tearoom. As they carried it through the narrow entrance, one of the men apparently lost his grip and some of the hot tea spilled out, scalding several of the children who were queuing for sweets.

The Corporation accepted that the manageress (their employee) owed the children a duty of care, but denied that she had been negligent. The House of Lords made it clear that the standard to be used was that of the *reasonable* man:

" . . . it has long been held in Scotland that all that a person can be held bound to foresee are the reasonable and probable consequences of the failure to take care, judged by the standard of the ordinary reasonable man."[8]

This provided an *objective* test:

"It eliminates the personal equation and is independent of the idiosyncrasies of the particular person whose conduct is in question . . . The reasonable person is presumed to be free both from over-apprehension and from over-confidence."[9]

However, Lord MacMillan went on to add an important *subjective* qualification:

" . . . but there is a sense in which the standard of care of the reasonable man involves in its application a subjective element. It is still left to the judge to decide what, in the circumstances of the particular case, the reasonable man would have had in contemplation, and what, accordingly, the party sought to be made liable ought to have foreseen."[10]

Lord Thankerton put the point this way:

12–03

"The court must be careful to place itself in the position of the person charged with the duty, and to consider what he or she should have reasonably anticipated as a natural and probable consequence of neglect."[11]

In the circumstances of *Muir*, the House of Lords held that the manageress had taken reasonable care in entrusting the carrying of the tea urn to the men and in

---

[7] *Donoghue v Stevenson*, 1932 S.C. (HL) 31 at 44 per Lord Atkin (emphasis added).
[8] *Muir v Glasgow Corp*, 1943 S.C. (HL) 3 at 8 per Lord Thankerton.
[9] *Muir v Glasgow Corp*, 1943 S.C. (HL) 3 at 10 per Lord MacMillan.
[10] *Muir v Glasgow Corp*, 1943 S.C. (HL) 3 at 10 per Lord MacMillan.
[11] *Muir v Glasgow Corp*, 1943 S.C. (HL) 3 at 8 per Lord Thankerton.

allowing the children to remain on site at the time: her duty was only to take reasonable care, not to prevent all accidents occurring on the premises.[12]

There are thus two elements to the test of reasonable care in the circumstances. The *objective* element requires the circumstances to be considered from the perspective of the hypothetical person who is competent in the activity in question.[13] Personal prejudices or inabilities will be ignored, and indeed policy factors may even enter the equation.[14]

Meanwhile, the *subjective* element avoids distortion by the inadvertent application of hindsight,[15] but requires any professional skills or special experience claimed by the defender to be considered.[16] Thus, involuntary acts,[17] emergencies,[18] errors of judgment[19] and actions in the heat of the moment[20] may where appropriate be taken into account.

Negligence may therefore be described as a failure to achieve the standard of care demanded by the law, and has been defined as:

> " . . . the omission to do something which a reasonable man, guided upon those considerations which ordinarily regulate the conduct of human affairs, would do, or doing something which a prudent and reasonable man would not do."[21]

Reasonable care: risk assessment and economics

12–04 "The degree of care of the safety of others which the law requires human beings to observe in the conduct of their affairs varies according to the circumstances. There is no absolute standard, but it may be said generally that the degree of care required varies directly with the risk involved. Those who engage in operations inherently dangerous must take precautions which

---

[12] It is suggested that if similar facts were to arise today, such an omission may now be regarded as unreasonable in the circumstances for two reasons: first, the fact that the accident occurred in *Muir* points to the possibility of its recurrence in similar circumstances; and secondly, current attitudes towards health and safety issues suggest an expectation of a greater awareness of risk and therefore a greater expectation in respect of precautionary measures.

[13] *Wilsher v Essex AHA* [1987] Q.B. 730 (trainee judged by the standard expected of a qualified doctor); *Nettleship v Weston* [1971] 2 Q.B. 691 (learner judged by the standard of the driver who has passed a driving test). Cf. *Mullin v Richards* [1998] 1 W.L.R. 1304 (age taken into account in assessing foreseeability of injury arising from fifteen year olds "fencing" with plastic rulers).

[14] See, e.g. *Tomlinson v Congleton BC* [2004] 1 A.C. 46 at 85 per Lord Hoffmann. See also *Pierce v West Sussex CC* [2014] E.L.R. 62.

[15] "The court must . . . not give undue weight to the fact that a distressing accident has happened or that witnesses in the witness-box are prone to express regret, *ex post facto*, that they did not take some step, which it is now realised would definitely have prevented the accident": *Muir v Glasgow Corp*, 1943 S.C. (HL) 3 at 8 per Lord Thankerton. "The judge must not look at the 1947 accident with 1954 spectacles": *Roe v Minister of Health* [1954] 2 Q.B. 66 at 84 per Denning L.J. See also *Finningham v Peters* (1861) 23 D. 260 at 264 per Lord Justice-Clerk Inglis.

[16] See, e.g. *Dorchester Finance Co Ltd v Stebbing* [1989] B.C.L.C. 498; *Norman v Theodore Goddard* [1992] B.C.C. 14; *Re D'Jan of London Ltd* [1993] B.C.C. 646.

[17] See, e.g. *Waugh v James K Allan Ltd*, 1964 S.C. (HL) 102 (driver taken ill at the wheel); *Baker v TE Hopkins & Son Ltd* [1959] 1 W.L.R. 966 (doctor who died while attempting to rescue trapped miners); *Reeves v Commissioner of Police of the Metropolis* [2000] 1 A.C. 360 (mentally ill prisoner who hanged himself in his cell).

[18] See, e.g. *Gilfillan v Barbour*, 2003 S.L.T. 1127.

[19] See, e.g. *Marshall v Osmond* [1983] Q.B. 1034.

[20] See, e.g. *Wallace v Bergius*, 1915 S.C. 205.

[21] *Blyth v Birmingham Waterworks Co* (1856) 11 Ex. 781 at 784 per Alderson B.

are not required to persons engaged in the ordinary routine of daily life. It is, no doubt, true that in every act which an individual performs there is present a potentiality of injury to others . . . In Scotland, at any rate, it has never been a maxim of the law that a man acts at his peril.[22] Legal liability is limited to those consequences of our acts which a reasonable man of ordinary intelligence and experience so acting would have in contemplation."[23]

Determining reasonable care in a given set of circumstances will therefore involve what economists might call a risk assessment exercise—assessing the probability of injury against the difficulty, expense and other factors involved in preventing or avoiding the injury—albeit carried out on an ex post facto basis. It follows that one must ask what factors may be relevant, and what weight should be attached to each of those factors. Although judges have tended not to use the language of the economist or the scientist, this discussion may be said reasonably to represent an intuitive mechanism applied often in an unarticulated way by lawyers and judges. It might also be said that the new era of rights based jurisprudence has introduced appropriate language to the legal vocabulary in articulating the process applied. Thus, four stages to the analysis may be extrapolated[24]:

1. first, factors to be entered into the equation must be identified;
2. secondly, where conflicts arise between factors an intense focus on the comparative importance of the conflicting factors in the light of the facts of the case is necessary;
3. thirdly, the justifications for discounting factors must be taken into account; and
4. fourthly, a "proportionality test", or "ultimate balancing test" must be applied to each.

So, for example, when a seaman on a grain ship was sent below to fetch some timber and fell from a stair, he alleged breach of duty to provide a handrail. His employer stated that no other employers in that business erected such rails. However, the reasonable person is not necessarily the average person and it was said:

"If a real risk is one which would occur to the mind of a reasonable man and which he would not brush aside as far fetched . . . then surely he would not

---

[22] It is submitted, however, that Scots law imposes a very high standard of care in respect of some types of activity, e.g. employing staff: see, e.g. *Paris v Stepney BC* [1951] A.C. 367; *General Cleaning Contractors v Christmas* [1953] A.C. 180 at 189–190 per Lord Oaksey; driving vehicles, and making "non-natural" uses of land: see, e.g. *Kerr v The Earl of Orkney* (1857) 20 D. 298; *Greenock Corp v Caledonian Railway Co*, 1917 S.C. (HL) 56; *RHM Bakeries (Scotland) Ltd v Strathclyde RC*, 1985 S.C. (HL) 17. On the other hand, the law appears to be less demanding on those who participate in or organise sport, even at a professional level: see, e.g. *Wooldridge v Sumner* [1963] 2 Q.B. 43; *Caldwell v Maguire* [2002] P.I.Q.R. P6; *Gillon v Chief Constable of Strathclyde*, 1997 S.L.T. 1218. Cf. *Cunningham v Reading Football Club Ltd* [1992] P.I.Q.R. P141.

[23] *Muir v Glasgow Corp*, 1943 S.C. (HL) 3 at 10 per Lord MacMillan. See also *McGlone v British Railways Board*, 1966 S.C. 1 at 13 per Lord Reid: "no substantial difficulty or expense".

[24] The methodology is borrowed from *Re S (A Child) (Identification: Restrictions on Publication)* [2005] 1 A.C. 593 at 603 per Lord Steyn.

neglect such a risk if action to eliminate it presented no difficulty, involved no disadvantage and required no expense."[25]

One judge from the United States who did explicitly apply a quasi-scientific formula to the question was Judge Learned Hand:

"If the probability (of risk) be called 'P'; the (extent of) injury 'L'; and the burden (of appropriate precautions) 'B'; liability depends upon whether B is less than L multiplied by P: i.e. whether B<PL."[26]

Frequently, cases have focused on specific factors.

Probability of risk

12–05   A consequence of an activity may be foreseeable, but unlikely. The less likely the harm, the less effort a reasonable person would consider necessary to guard against the harm. In *Bolton v Stone*,[27] the plaintiff, who was walking along a road outside a cricket ground, was injured upon being struck by a cricket ball which had cleared a 17 feet high perimeter fence—itself some 80 yards from the where the batsman had hit the ball. The evidence led pointed to only six previous occasions in 30 years where a ball had been hit over the fence and this was the first occasion where it hit a passer-by. The House of Lords held that, the risk being extremely small, the height of the fence was sufficient to achieve the standard of care required.

A similar decision was reached by the Outer House in *Gillon v Chief Constable of Strathclyde*,[28] where, on account of the negligible (albeit not unforeseeable, if not actually obvious) risk of such an incident, it was held that a football club was not required to erect a barrier to prevent police officers who were monitoring the crowd (and in doing so ordered to face away from the pitch) from being injured in a collision with a footballer who had ran beyond the edge of the pitch.

Conversely, in *Lamond v Glasgow Corp*[29] a pedestrian walking on a footpath adjoining a golf course was struck by one of the six thousand or so golf balls struck out of bounds onto the footpath annually. Although no evidence could be adduced to show that a pedestrian had previously been hit by a stray ball, given the level of traffic on the path and the incidence of stray balls, the likelihood of

---

[25] *Overseas Tankship (UK) v Miller* [1967] 1 A.C. 617 at 642 per Lord Reid. See also *Morris v West Hartlepool Steam Navigation Co Ltd* [1956] A.C. 552 at 574 per Lord Reid; *McErlean v J & B Scotland Ltd*, 1997 S.L.T. 1326 at 1330 per Lord Prosser; *Tomlinson v Congleton BC* [2004] 1 A.C. 46 at 82 per Lord Hoffmann.

[26] *United States v Carroll Towing Co*, 159F. 2d 169, 173 (1947) per Learned Hand J.

[27] *Bolton v Stone* [1951] A.C. 850; see also *Hall v Brooklands Auto Racing Club* [1933] 1 K.B. 205 where an out of control car struck spectators within the sports ground.

[28] *Gillon v Chief Constable of Strathclyde*, 1997 S.L.T. 1218. The facts of this case are reminiscent of the famous case in the *Digest* (D.9.2.11.Pr.) of the barber who was engaged to shave a client next to a place where people were playing ball. When the barber's hand was struck by the ball, his patron's throat was cut rather than shaved!

[29] *Lamond v Glasgow Corp*, 1968 S.L.T. 291.

the occurrence of such an accident was high enough, on a cost/benefit analysis, to require either the erecting of a fence or the redesigning of the golf course.[30]

Foreseeability of risk and/or harm cuts both ways. If the risk is obvious the law may allow the defender to rely on the pursuer's own responsibility in recognising and guarding against the risk. If a pond is clearly unsafe for swimming, or there is clear danger of electrocution or collision with a train while trespassing on a railway line, failure to erect barriers may not be held to amount to negligence.[31] However, the vulnerability of those who may foreseeably come into contact with the offending thing will be taken into account,[32] and policy factors may result in the courts taking the view that the law should be applied so as to provide particular protection to those affected by the activity.[33]

Thus, where the offending thing would constitute an "allurement" to young children, the defender will be expected to go to greater lengths to prevent children from coming into contact with the thing. In *Taylor v Glasgow Corp*[34] for example, a seven-year-old child died after eating poisonous red berries from a bush in Glasgow's Botanical Gardens. The House of Lords held that a reasonable person would have appreciated that the vivid colour of the berries would have been attractive to children too young to appreciate the potential for harm to their health, and so the reasonable occupier of the premises would be required to take steps, by fencing or pruning, to ensure that the berries would be beyond the reach of such children.

Extent of harm

How serious might the harm be if the risk eventuates? The greater the degree **12–06** of harm, the more the reasonable person would do to avoid the risk. This factor will also involve the vulnerability of the potential victim.

In *Paris v Stepney BC*[35] the House of Lords held that an employer was liable for failing to supply goggles to an employee, who was already blind in one eye, where a slight risk of injury did not justify a policy of ensuring that goggles were routinely worn by employees with two healthy eyes. Mr Paris, who was employed as a mechanic, lost his sight when his good eye was penetrated by a fragment of metal that flew off a seized bolt he was trying to free off by striking it with a hammer.

---

[30] See also, e.g. *Whitefield v Barton*, 1987 S.C.L.R. 259; *Lewis v Buckpool Golf Club*, 1993 S.L.T. (Sh. Ct) 43; *Hilder v Associated Portland Cement Manufacturers Ltd* [1961] 1 W.L.R. 1434.

[31] See, e.g. *Tomlinson v Congleton BC* [2004] 1 A.C. 46; *McGlone v British Railways Board*, 1966 S.C. 1; *Titchener v British Railways Board*, 1984 S.C. (HL) 34.

[32] See, e.g. *Reeves v Commissioner of Police of the Metropolis* [2000] 1 A.C. 360 (prisoner known to be a "suicide risk"); *Haley v London Electricity Board* [1965] A.C. 778 (blind person fell into a hole dug up in the pavement); *Kemp v Secretary of State for Scotland*, 2000 S.L.T. 471 (drunk person tripped over a raised kerbstone).

[33] e.g. in employing staff: see, e.g. *Paris v Stepney BC* [1951] A.C. 367; *General Cleaning Contractors v Christmas* [1953] A.C. 180 at 189–190 per Lord Oaksey; driving vehicles, and making "non-natural" uses of land: see, e.g. *Kerr v The Earl of Orkney* (1857) 20 D. 298 (IH); *Greenock Corp v Caledonian Railway Co*, 1917 S.C. (HL) 56; *RHM Bakeries (Scotland) Ltd v Strathclyde RC*, 1985 S.C. (HL) 17.

[34] *Taylor v Glasgow Corp*, 1922 S.C. (HL) 1. See also *Hughes v Lord Advocate*, 1963 S.C. (HL) 31; *Jolley v Sutton LBC* [2000] 1 W.L.R. 1082; *Galbraith's Curator ad Litem v Stewart (No.2)*, 1998 S.L.T. 1305. Cf. *Devlin v Strathclyde RC*, 1993 S.L.T. 699; *McGlone v British Railways Board*, 1966 S.C. 1; *Titchener v British Railways Board*, 1984 S.C. (HL) 34; *Pierce v West Sussex CC* [2014] E.L.R. 62.

[35] *Paris v Stepney BC* [1951] A.C. 367. See also *McKinlay v British Steel Corp*, 1987 S.L.T. 522; 1988 S.L.T. 810.

Burden of precautions

12–07   Issues such as the financial and social cost, as well as the technical development, awareness of, and availability or practicality of precautions will weigh in the scales. The assessment will be based on what was known and what was available at the time of the incident so where a risk and an associated precaution has only become known or obvious since the date in question, it will be discounted. Thus, in *Roe v Minister of Health*[36] a hospital was not liable for the presence of phenol in anaesthetic solution when medical science at the time of the incident could not have discovered the tiny cracks in glass containers that had enabled the contamination to occur.

Financial cost was the predominant factor in the decision of the House of Lords in *Latimer v AEC Ltd*.[37] A factory floor was flooded with oily rainwater following an overnight rainstorm. The owners instructed the spreading of sawdust across the floor before allowing workers to enter; but there was insufficient sawdust to cover the whole floor. An employee slipped on the untreated part of the floor, suffering a leg injury. It was held that taking into account the loss of production, and therefore the loss of profit that would result from closing the factory, coupled with the lack of evidence to show that any other member of the substantial workforce had slipped as a result of the flood, the employers had done as much as would be expected of a reasonable employer and so had not breached the duty owed to the employee.

The social value of the activity and, conversely, the social cost of precautions, may also be factors to consider. In *Tomlinson v Congleton BC* Lord Hoffmann said:

" . . . the question of what amounts to 'such care as in all the circumstances of the case is reasonable' depends upon assessing . . . not only the likelihood that someone may be injured and the seriousness of the injury which may occur, but also the social value of the activity which gives rise to the risk and the cost of preventative measures. These factors have to be balanced against each other."[38]

Thus, a local authority was held to have acted reasonably in not actively preventing persons diving into a flooded disused quarry that the authority had already recognised as being dangerous for swimming. The only effective preventative measure would have been to destroy the facility, which had been used for many years by the local community for leisure purposes such as sunbathing and paddling: activities which involved minimal risk.

The social utility of optimising the use of emergency vehicles in wartime was held to justify the increased risk to other road users in *Daborn v Bath Tramways*

---

[36] *Roe v Minister of Health* [1954] 2 Q.B. 66. See also *McTear v Imperial Tobacco Ltd*, 2005 2 S.C. 1 (medical risks associated with smoking tobacco products); *Smith v P&O Bulk Shipping Ltd* [1998] 2 Lloyd's Rep. 81 (medical risks associated with inhalation of asbestos fibres).

[37] *Latimer v AEC Ltd* [1953] A.C. 643. See also *Smith v Littlewoods Organisation Ltd* and *Maloco v Littlewoods Organisation Ltd*, 1987 S.C. (HL) 37 (financial cost of preventing unlikely risk of fire to unoccupied property). Cf. *Henderson v Carron Co* (1889) 16 R. 633 (substantial financial cost did not justify failure to close down a dangerous furnace where operator fatally incinerated).

[38] *Tomlinson v Congleton BC* [2004] 1 A.C. 46 at 82 per Lord Hoffmann.

Motor Co Ltd,[39] where the plaintiff was injured in a collision with an ambulance with defective signaling equipment which was being used during the hours of darkness.

It may also be the case that precautions which would have avoided the incident were available, obvious and not disproportionately expensive, yet would be inappropriate since implementing the precaution would create a greater risk of a different harmful incident. Not taking such precautions may then be justified as the lesser of two evils.[40]

Reasonable care: other factors

Common practice

Compliance with common practice may be a significant factor pointing to **12–08** reasonable care having been taken. In times past, evidence of adoption of a practice which has been carried on consistently without incident likely would have been conclusive in considering the standard of care to be exercised.[41] However, the courts have reduced the significance of compliance with common practice so that it may be strongly presumptive of reasonable care; but the presumption may be rebutted by evidence.[42] Thus, "[n]eglect of duty does not cease by repetition to be neglect of duty."[43]

For instance, in *Cavanagh v Ulster Weaving Co Ltd*,[44] the House of Lords held that a system of work operated by the defendants fell below the standard demanded by the law, in spite of the fact that such a system was commonly adopted by other employers. The plaintiff had, while carrying a bag of cement and wearing rubber boots which were too big for him and which had become wet, slipped from a ladder which had no handrail onto a glass roof.[45]

Where developments in knowledge and understanding of risks reveal that common practice is inadequate, continuing with that common practice will be at least negligent. A defender will be expected to keep abreast of such developments,[46] and where the defender may reasonably be expected to be ahead of the field in developing understanding of risk, that defender will be judged according to his own knowledge.[47] Nevertheless, although "an absence of initiative in seeking out knowledge of facts which are not in themselves obvious" may amount to negligence, "the court must be slow to blame him for not ploughing a lone furrow."[48]

---

[39] *Daborn v Bath Tramways Motor Co Ltd* [1946] 2 All E.R. 333. Cf. *Gilfillan v Barbour*, 2003 S.L.T. 1127. See also, e.g. *Ward v London CC* [1938] 2 All E.R. 341; *Gaynor v Allen* [1959] 2 Q.B. 403.

[40] See, e.g. *Wyngrove's Executrix v Scottish Omnibuses Ltd*, 1966 S.C. (HL) 47 at 81 per Lord Reid.

[41] See, e.g. *Morton v Wm Dixon*, 1909 S.C. 807 at 809 per Lord Dunedin.

[42] *Wyngrove's Executrix v Scottish Omnibuses Ltd*, 1966 S.C. (HL) 47 at 81 per Lord Reid.

[43] *Brown v Rolls Royce Ltd*, 1960 S.C. (HL) 22 at 27–28 per Lord Denning; *Bank of Montreal v Dominion Gresham Guarantee and Casualty Co Ltd* [1930] A.C. 659 at 666 (P.C. (Can.)) per Lord Tomlin. See also *JD Williams & Co Ltd v Michael Hyde & Associates Ltd* [2001] B.L.R. 99.

[44] *Cavanagh v Ulster Weaving Co Ltd* [1960] A.C. 145.

[45] See also, e.g. *Morris v West Hartlepool Steam Navigation Co Ltd* [1956] A.C. 552.

[46] *Stokes v GKN* [1968] 1 W.L.R. 1776 at 1783 per Swanwick J.; *Thompson v Smith Shiprepairers Ltd* [1984] Q.B. 405 at 416 per Mustill J.

[47] *Baker v Quantum Clothing Group Ltd* [2011] 1 W.L.R. 1003.

[48] *Thompson v Smith Shiprepairers Ltd* [1984] Q.B. 405 at 416 per Mustill J.

On the other side of the coin, while failure to follow common practice may indicate negligence, it is not conclusive. This is especially so in medical negligence cases: if deviation from common practice per se confirmed negligence that would destroy any incentive to engage in medical research and development.[49] Similarly, in *Brown v Rolls Royce Ltd*[50] an employee claimed that his employer's failure in providing barrier cream to guard against dermatitis amounted to negligence, asserting that supply of such cream was common practice among other employers. However, the House of Lords rejected his claim. There were questions regarding the efficacy of the cream, so the employers had not acted negligently in dealing with the potential problem of dermatitis in a different way.

It should be noted that common practice will never cure conduct that amounts to an intentional delict.[51]

Errors of judgment

12-09   In some cases a mere "error of judgment" has been held not to amount to negligence.[52] This seems to have been particularly so in sport where, without evidence of recklessness, even a "foul" tackle resulting in harm will be regarded as no more than an error of judgment.[53] In *Blake v Galloway*,[54] such an approach was taken where an injury resulted from spontaneous participation in an informal game where the "rules and conventions" were assumed between the participants. This attitude seems to extend to harm suffered by spectators as well as fellow participants, perhaps on a parallel application of concepts encapsulated in the defences of volenti non fit injuria and contributory negligence.[55] Thus,

> "in cases involving injury to spectators caused by competitors acting in the ordinary course of play, the test to be applied in determining the issue of negligence is 'whether or not the competitor in question has committed an error of judgment that a reasonable competitor being a reasonable man of the sporting world would not have made.'"[56]

Sometimes this approach is justified because the defender has been presented with a dilemma and has acted in the heat of the moment. Thus, where on rounding a bend, the driver (B) of a car was confronted with another car being

---

[49] See, e.g. *Hunter v Hanley*, 1955 S.C. 200 at 206 per Lord President Clyde: see paras 12–12 to 12–14 below.

[50] *Brown v Rolls Royce Ltd*, 1960 S.C. (HL) 22.

[51] See, e.g. *Henderson v Chief Constable of Fife*, 1988 S.L.T. 361 at 367 per Lord Jauncey; *Lindley v Rutter* [1981] Q.B. 128.

[52] See, e.g. *Horsley v MacLaren (The Ogopogo)* [1971] 2 Lloyd's Rep. 410 (Sup. Ct (Can.)); *Condon v Basi* [1985] 1 W.L.R. 866; *Wooldridge v Sumner* [1963] 2 Q.B. 43; *Marshall v Osmond* [1983] Q.B. 1034. Cf. *Rigby v Chief Constable of Northamptonshire* [1985] 1 W.L.R. 1242.

[53] *Sharp v Highland and Islands Fire Board*, 2005 S.L.T. 855. See also *Andrew v Stevenson* (1905) 13 S.L.T. 581; *Whitefield v Barton*, 1987 S.C.L.R. 259.

[54] *Blake v Galloway* [2004] 1 W.L.R. 2844.

[55] "A person attending a game or competition takes the risk of any damage caused to him by any act of a participant done in the course of and for the purposes of the game or competition notwithstanding that such act may involve an error of judgment or lapse of skill, unless the participant's conduct is such as to evince a reckless disregard of the spectator's safety": *Wooldridge v Sumner* [1963] 2 Q.B. 43 at 68 per Diplock L.J.

[56] *McMahon v Dear* [2014] CSOH 100 at [209] per Lord Jones, quoting *Sharpe v Highland and Islands Fire Board*, 2008 S.C.L.R. 526 at [10] per Lord Johnston.

driven (by W) in the opposite direction on B's (i.e. the wrong) side of the road, B presumed that W would steer across to his own side of the road. When W did not, so that a head on collision seemed inevitable to B unless he took evasive action himself, B swerved onto what for him was the wrong side of the road. Precisely at the same moment, W steered back into his own lane and the inevitable collision occurred. B was held not to have been negligent, even although the accident occurred when he was the one on the wrong side of the road.[57]

However, it should be noted that the courts have tended to take a stricter approach where a driver's "error of judgment" has resulted in harm to an unconnected innocent party. A combination of factors, including the catastrophic damage that may result from a momentary lapse of concentration and the statutory requirement of insurance, leads to this stricter approach. Indeed, "[i]f it were not for insurance, the common law would operate with intolerable harshness in its application to driving."[58]

Inexperience

Although the amateur will not be judged against the standard of care **12–10** reasonably to be expected from a professional,[59] the trainee or newly qualified professional will not enjoy any discount in terms of what is expected by the law because of their inexperience. As the reasonable person does not engage in activities which require special skills without undertaking appropriate instruction or training, it is no excuse for the defender engaging in such activities to argue that he should be judged against an "unskilled" benchmark. Thus, anyone who voluntarily engages in activity which demands a particular level of competence, such as driving a car, will be deemed by the law to have undertaken to deliver the minimum level of competence expected of a responsible person participating in such activity.

This approach might also be justified by applying the principle of "holding out"—a form of personal bar. Thus, a person holding himself out as competent in providing dental services cannot later pick and choose between those aspects of dentistry in which he should be judged against the standard of the expert and those against which he should be judged against the standard of the amateur.[60] Similarly, a newly qualified doctor will be benchmarked against the competent general or specialist (as appropriate to the facts of the case) practitioner.[61]

An often cited case is *Nettleship v Weston*,[62] where the Court of Appeal held a learner driver to owe the skill and care of the ordinary driver to the passenger who sat in with her, but by a majority allowed a deduction of 50 per cent contribution because of his awareness of the risks.

The standard of care to be expected of a child will depend upon the child's age and circumstances.[63]

---

[57] *Wallace v Bergius*, 1915 S.C. 205. For the distinction between errors of judgment and negligence on the part of a police officer driving a car in response to an emergency and with its siren and blue lights operating see *Gilfillan v Barbour*, 2003 S.L.T. 1127 at 1135 per Lord Reed.

[58] *Imbree v McNeilly* [2008] H.C.A. 40 at [23] per Gleeson C.J.

[59] See, e.g. *Wells v Cooper* [1958] 2 Q.B. 265.

[60] *Dickson v Hygenic Institute*, 1910 1 S.L.T. 111.

[61] *Wilsher v Essex AHA* [1987] Q.B. 730 at 750 per Mustill L.J.

[62] *Nettleship v Weston* [1971] 2 Q.B. 691.

[63] Compare, e.g. *Blake v Galloway* [2004] 1 W.L.R. 2844 with *Orchard v Lee* [2009] E.L.R. 178. See also para.3–25 above.

PROFESSIONAL NEGLIGENCE

12–11 Liability of professional persons for negligence presents a range of special issues. First, it may be difficult to demonstrate that a duty of care is owed outside of a contractual relationship, especially where the loss claimed for is purely economic, as is usually the case in claims against accountants, surveyors, solicitors and advocates.[64] Secondly, the standard of care demanded by the law will (in principle) be that of the reasonable member of the relevant profession, which will be a higher standard than that expected of the lay-person. Thirdly, there may be difficulties with regard to causation, particularly in medical negligence cases and especially where the claim is for the loss of a chance.[65] Professionals may also be susceptible to complaints of intentional wrongdoing such as fraud and, in respect of medical treatment in particular, assault. This section will focus on the standard of care demanded of a professional person by the law of negligence.

It should be noted at the outset that the legal considerations do not depend upon the defender being a member of a professional body as opposed to, say, a trade association:

> "If I engage a man to exercise his expertise on my behalf . . . it matters not whether he is to prepare a conveyance of land or to drive a straight furrow across it."[66]

In fact, if an untrained or inexperienced person holds him or herself out as competent in an activity which requires special skills, that person will be judged against the standard to be expected of the competent and experienced person.[67] In general, the law does not distinguish between negligent acts and negligent advice,[68] although the latter is often associated with pure economic loss.

Professional standard of care: medical negligence

12–12 A professional will be judged by the standard expected of the ordinarily competent professional, rather than that of the reasonable person. This was confirmed in the case of *Hunter v Hanley*, where it was claimed that a doctor used an inappropriate needle in treating a patient. However, Lord President Clyde explained that, given the scope for differences in professional opinions, to determine whether a professional has, or has not, discharged the standard of care expected requires a fairly sophisticated analysis:

---

[64] See above at paras 11–25 to 11–39.

[65] See paras 13–08 to 13–09 below. See also J.G. Logie, "Proof of Causation in Medical Negligence Cases", 1988 S.L.T. (News) 25; A.F. Phillips, "Further Reflections on Medical Causation", 1988 S.L.T. (News) 325; A.F. Phillips, "Medical Negligence and No-Fault Compensation", 1989 J.L.S. 239; E. Russell, "Establishing Medical Negligence—A Herculean Task", 1998 S.L.T. (News) 17. Matters are not helped by the problems faced by poor pursuers, see generally D. Sandison, "Medical Negligence Claims: The Paucity of Funding", 1995 J.L.S. 309. The new private legal insurers charge higher premiums for medical negligence cases.

[66] *Arenson v Casson Beckman* [1977] A.C. 405 at 430 per Lord Kilbrandon.

[67] *Dickson v Hygienic Institute*, 1910 S.C. 352. See also *Wilsher v Essex AHA* [1987] Q.B. 730 (trainee); Companies Act 2006 s.174 (two-tier standard of care expected of a director enshrined in statute).

[68] See, e.g. *Clayton v Woodman & Son (Builders) Ltd* [1962] 2 Q.B. 533. An architect gave instructions direct to a bricklayer. The architect knew the instructions would be promptly obeyed and should have realised that they could result in serious injury. In fact, the wall on which the plaintiff was working collapsed, injuring him.

"To succeed in an action based on negligence, whether against a doctor or against anyone else, it is of course necessarily to establish a breach of that duty to take care which the law requires, and the degree of want of care which constitutes negligence must vary with the circumstances ... But where the conduct of a doctor, or indeed of any professional man, is concerned, the circumstances are not so precise and clear cut as in the normal case. In the realm of diagnosis and treatment there is ample scope for genuine difference of opinion and one man clearly is not negligent merely because his conclusion differs from that of other professional men, nor because he has displayed less skill or knowledge than others would have shown. *The true test for establishing negligence in diagnosis or treatment on the part of a doctor is whether he has been proved to be guilty of such failure as no doctor of ordinary skill would be guilty of if acting with ordinary care.*"[69]

The Lord President went on to explain some of the justification for taking such a cautious approach to establishing professional negligence and, in so doing, astutely raised what is even today a formidable hurdle for pursuers in contested medical negligence cases:

"It follows from what I have said that in regard to allegations of deviation from ordinary professional practice ... such a deviation is not necessarily evidence of negligence. Indeed it would be disastrous if this were so, for all inducement to progress in medical science would then be destroyed. Even a substantial deviation from normal practice may be warranted by the particular circumstances. To establish liability by a doctor where deviation from normal practice is alleged, three facts require to be established. First of all it must be proved that there is a usual and normal practice; secondly it must be proved that the defender has not adopted that practice; and thirdly (and this is of crucial importance) it must be established that the course the doctor adopted is one which no professional man of ordinary skill would have taken if he had been acting with ordinary care. There is clearly a heavy onus on a pursuer to establish these three facts, and without all three his case will fail."[70]

Thus, policy factors need to be considered. If the law required rigid adherence to a conservative approach to medicine, defensive practice would be promoted and applied research discouraged: inhibiting the development of medical science.

---

[69] *Hunter v Hanley*, 1955 SC 200 at 204–205 (emphasis added); echoed in the English case of *Bolam v Friern Hospital Management Committee* [1957] 1 W.L.R. 582. See also *Moyes v Lothian Health Board*, 1990 S.L.T. 444; Anon, "Medical Negligence: Hunter v Hanley 35 Years On", 1990 S.L.T. (News) 325. A midwife will be measured against the standard to be expected of the ordinarily competent midwife exercising ordinary skill and care: *Campbell v Borders Health Board* [2012] CSIH 49; 2012 G.W.D. 23–468.

[70] *Hunter v Hanley*, 1955 SC 200 at 206. The "true test" was echoed in England in *Bolam v Friern Hospital Management Committee* [1957] 1 W.L.R. 582 at 586 per McNair J.: "(W)here you get a situation which involves the use of some special skill or competence, then the test as to whether there has been negligence or not is not the test of the man on the top of a Clapham omnibus, because he has not got this special skill. The test is the standard of the ordinary skilled man exercising and professing to have that special skill. A man need not possess the highest expert skill; it is well-established law that it is sufficient if he exercises the ordinary skill of an ordinary competent man exercising that particular art."

That would not be in the interests of society as a whole. But on the other hand, deferring to the autonomy of the medical profession places significant and frequently insurmountable hurdles in the path of the individual pursuer. This is a dilemma that has bedeviled medical negligence cases[71] since *Hunter v Hanley* and its English equivalent, *Bolam v Friern Hospital Management Committee*.[72]

12–13 The test to be applied where a doctor is accused of negligence in treatment has also been accepted as appropriate with regard to diagnosis and to medical advice.[73] It has also been applied where the complaint has been that a doctor has failed to inform the patient of the risks inherent in a medical procedure before obtaining consent from the patient to go ahead with the procedure.[74] In these cases the courts have consistently deferred to a paternalistic approach adopted by the medical profession. Thus, "informed consent" has been defined with reference to the practice of the reasonable doctor rather than the needs of the reasonable patient.[75]

A strict reading of the "true test" as defined by Lord President Clyde effectively provides that the medical profession may regulate itself—if the medical practitioner accused of negligence can lead evidence from even a small group of other medical professionals to condone the practice or procedure that has been adopted, then that appears to be a complete answer to an action in negligence.[76] In reality it may be more subtle, but not by much. There must be a responsible body of medical opinion to support the position taken by the doctor but, generally, whether or not the body of medical opinion is or is not "responsible" is determined by the medical profession rather than by the court. Thus, where there are conflicting opinions propounded by opposing bodies of medical opinion, the court cannot conclude that negligence has occurred just because it prefers one body of opinion over another.[77] It might even be said that for a pursuer to succeed, medical negligence requires to be admitted or proved beyond reasonable doubt!

However, in *Bolitho v City and Hackney Health Authority*,[78] the House of Lords asserted what might, with some generosity, be described as a semi-objective attitude in testing medical opinion. A child who was a patient in the hospital suffered catastrophic brain damage after failure in the child's respiratory system triggered a cardiac arrest. A senior nurse had repeatedly called for a doctor, but the doctor did not attend. Although it was accepted that the doctor was

---

[71] For discussion see, e.g. Anon, "Medical Negligence: Hunter v Hanley, 35 Years On", 1990 S.L.T. 325; D.K. Feenan, "Medical Negligence (Hunter *v* Hanley 35 Years On: A Reply)", 1991 S.L.T. 321; L. Sutherland, "A Single Standard of Care" (1995) Rep. B. 6–11; K. Norrie, "Common Practice and the Standard of Care in Medical Negligence" (1985) J.R. 145.

[72] *Bolam v Friern Hospital Management Committee* [1957] 1 W.L.R. 582. See also *Whitehouse v Jordan* [1981] 1 W.L.R. 246 at 263 per Lord Fraser of Tullybelton.

[73] *Gold v Haringey Health Authority* [1988] Q.B. 481.

[74] *Sidaway v Governors of the Bethlem Royal Hospital and the Maudsley Hospital* [1985] A.C. 871; *Moyes v Lothian Health Board*, 1990 S.L.T. 444; *M's Guardian v Lanarkshire Health Board*, 2013 S.C. 245. See also *Chester v Afshar* [2005] 1 A.C. 134; K. Mason and D. Brodie, "Bolam, Bolam—Wherefore art thou, Bolam?" (2005) Edin. L.R. 398.

[75] Criticised in the dissenting speech of Lord Scarman in *Sidaway v Governors of the Bethlem Royal Hospital and the Maudsley Hospital* [1985] A.C. 871 at 889–890.

[76] *De Freitas v O'Brien* [1995] P.I.Q.R. P281.

[77] *Maynard v West Midlands AHA* [1984] 1 W.L.R. 634; *Gerrard v Royal Infirmary of Edinburgh NHS Trust*, 2005 1 S.C. 192.

[78] *Bolitho v City and Hackney Health Authority* [1998] A.C. 232. See also *Hucks v Cole (1968)* [1993] 4 Med. L.R. 393, decided in 1968 but not reported until 1993.

negligent in failing to respond to the repeated calls to attend the child, the doctor denied liability. The basis for the denial was that the only intervention that would have saved the child would have been to intubate, and the doctor said that she would not have carried out that treatment. The judge had evidence from eight medical experts, all of them distinguished. Five for the plaintiff said that failure to intubate would be negligent and three for the defendants said it would not. The defendants won on the *Bolam* test even although the judge had a feeling that the defendants' evidence did not make sense. The House of Lords retained a very limited place for the courts:

> "The court is not bound to hold that a defendant doctor escapes liability for negligent treatment or diagnosis just because he leads evidence from a number of medical experts who are genuinely of opinion that the defendant's treatment or diagnosis accorded with sound medical practice ...
> The use of 'responsible, reasonable and respectable' all show that the court has to be satisfied that the exponents of the body of opinion relied upon can demonstrate that such opinion has a logical basis. In particular in cases involving, as they so often do, the weighing of risks against benefits, the judge before accepting a body of opinion as being responsible, reasonable or respectable, will need to be satisfied that, in forming their views, the experts have directed their minds to the question of comparative risks and benefits and have reached a defensible conclusion on the matter."[79]

There is some, but not much, evidence that *Bolitho* has emboldened the courts to **12–14** take a more robust approach to testing expert medical opinion. In *Marriott v West Midlands Regional Health Authority*,[80] the English Court of Appeal approved a judge's scrutiny of expert medical opinion to ascertain whether it was based on logic and that the judge, not being convinced that the medical experts properly had considered the relevant risks, was entitled to carry out her own risk assessment. However, such occasions remain rare.

In *Honisz v Lothian Health Board*,[81] Lord Hodge summarised the jurisprudence on how judges should deal with expert evidence in medical negligence cases:

> "First, as a general rule, where there are two opposing schools of thought among the relevant group of responsible medical practitioners as to the appropriateness of a particular practice, it is not the function of the court to prefer one school over the other ... Secondly, however, the court does not defer to the opinion of the relevant professionals to the extent that, if a defender lead evidence that other responsible professionals among the relevant group of medical practitioners would have done what the impugned medical practitioner did, the judge must in all cases conclude that there has been no negligence. This is because, thirdly, in exceptional cases the court may conclude that a practice which responsible medical practitioners have perpetuated does not stand up to rational analysis ... Where the judge is satisfied that the body of professional opinion, on which a defender relies,

---

[79] *Bolitho v City and Hackney Health Authority* [1998] A.C. 232 at 241–242 per Lord Browne-Wilkinson. Cf. *Penney v East Kent Health Authority* [2000] Lloyd's Rep. Med. 41.
[80] *Marriott v West Midlands Regional Health Authority* [1999] Lloyd's Rep. Med. 23.
[81] *Honisz v Lothian Health Board*, 2008 S.C. 235.

is not reasonable or responsible he may find the medical practitioner guilty of negligence, despite that body of opinion sanctioning his conduct. This will rarely occur as the assessment and balancing of risks and benefits are matters of clinical judgment."[82]

In conclusion on the court's approach to medical opinion, it is worth noting the now historic deference of the courts to company directors.[83] It took several high profile corporate scandals to change judicial attitudes, but since the 1980s judges have taken a far more robust approach to the standard of care expected of directors, preferring an objective, rather than a subjective, test.[84] The two-tier test that was adopted is now enshrined in statute.[85] Thus there is precedent for a sea-change in judicial attitudes: there may be scope for the judiciary to develop confidence in testing the logical basis of contested medical opinion. Should this happen, the courts may in future take a more pro-active role in challenging medical practices that are supported by questionable medical opinion.

Professional negligence: the legal profession

12–15   Although in principle Lord President Clyde's "true test" for medical negligence[86] is also applied to professional negligence cases involving practitioners in other skilled areas,[87] in practice it is much easier successfully to sue a solicitor than a doctor. This may be explained by pointing out that judges will undoubtedly feel more comfortable adjudicating on performance in familiar territory than in a field in which the judge is a lay-person. Another factor may be that the client, or the third party affected by the solicitor's acts, may be drawn more quickly to litigation against a negligent solicitor given the relationship between the professional activity and the law. Whatever the reason, solicitors are more frequently found liable in negligence than any other professionals.

However, solicitors and advocates enjoy immunity from liability for negligence with regard to their conduct of criminal cases in court.[88] The justification is that legal representatives may be

"less willing to assist the court by responding fully, frankly and promptly to an invitation to do so made by it in a criminal appeal when defective representation is alleged."[89]

---

[82] *Honisz v Lothian Health Board*, 2008 S.C. 235 at 247–248 per Lord Hodge. See also *Coyle v Lanarkshire Health Board* [2013] CSOH 167; 2013 G.W.D. 37–722.

[83] See, e.g. *Re City Equitable Fire Insurance Co Ltd* [1925] Ch. 407 at 428–429 per Romer J.

[84] *Dorchester Finance Co v Stebbing* [1989] B.C.L.C. 498; *Norman v Theodore Goddard* [1992] B.C.C. 14; *Re D'Jan of London Ltd* [1993] B.C.C. 646.

[85] Companies Act 2006 s.174.

[86] *Hunter v Hanley*, 1955 SC 200 at 205.

[87] So professional negligence must be averred and proved with evidence from suitably qualified witnesses: *Tods Murray WS v Arakin Ltd*, 2011 S.C.L.R. 37 at [92] per Lord Woolman.

[88] *Wright v Paton Farrell*, 2006 S.C. 404. Lord Osborne found that, given the differences in the rules of court procedure in the respective jurisdictions, the rationale for the decision of the House of Lords in *Arthur J S Hall & Co v Simons* [2002] 1 A.C. 615 with regard to immunity in the conduct of criminal proceedings did not transpose into Scots law. For further background in England and Wales, see *Rondel v Worsley* [1969] 1 A.C. 191; *Saif Ali v Sydney Mitchell & Co* [1980] A.C. 198.

[89] *Wright v Paton Farrell*, 2006 S.C. 404 at 414 per Lord President Hamilton.

However, the immunity does not extend to the conduct of civil proceedings.[90]

Solicitors may also incur liability for pure economic loss caused to a third party by the solicitor's negligence. It has always been the case that a solicitor could be sued by a client for breach of contract, or by a third party for an intentional delict, such as fraud, but for a long time it was understood that the decision of the House of Lords in *Robertson v Fleming*[91] precluded a third party claim for pure economic loss outside of contract. However, the House of Lords held that a firm of solicitors were liable in damages for negligence to disappointed legatees in *White v Jones*.[92] Following the reconciliation of two sisters with their father, he instructed solicitors to alter his will in their favour. The solicitors delayed carrying out his instructions and their client died before the alteration was effected. The House of Lords found that a *Hedley Byrne*[93] "special" relationship existed between the solicitors and their client's daughters, and held that the solicitors had breached a duty of care owed to the sisters and that the solicitors were liable for their pure economic loss.

The Scottish courts were initially hesitant in accepting that *White v Jones* represented the law in Scotland,[94] but the decision was followed in *Robertson v Watt & Co*[95] and then in *Holmes v Bank of Scotland*.[96] *White* has since been relied upon in a number of Scottish cases to the extent that it has been said: "There can be little doubt . . . that the principle enunciated in *White v Jones* is applicable in Scotland."[97]

Professional negligence: miscellaneous

A professional standard of care is also expected from a variety of other **12–16** professions including accountants and auditors,[98] insolvency practitioners,[99] architects,[100] surveyors[101] and engineers.[102]

Finally, by way of caution, an attempt to use the *Hunter* test to exculpate builders failed in *Morrisons Associated Companies Ltd v James Rome & Son Ltd*.[103] Lord Cameron said:

> "Counsel argued for the defenders that the position of a builder was the same as a doctor, and that it would, therefore be necessary to show that the defenders had acted in a way which no builder of reasonable skill exercising

---

[90] *Wright v Paton Farrell*, 2006 S.C. 404 at 451 per Lord Osborne.

[91] *Robertson v Fleming* (1861) 4 Macq. 167. The pursuer was held unable to recover in delict but was allowed to recover on the basis of an implied contract, or a *jus quaesitum tertio*.

[92] *White v Jones* [1995] 2 A.C. 207.

[93] *Hedley Byrne & Co Ltd v Heller & Partners Ltd* [1964] A.C. 465.

[94] *See, e.g. Weir v J M Hodge*, 1990 S.L.T. 266.

[95] *Robertson v Watt & Co* Unreported July 4, 1995 IH (2 Div).

[96] *Holmes v Bank of Scotland*, 2002 S.L.T. 544. See also *Hines v King Sturge LLP*, 2011 S.L.T. 2.

[97] *Steven v Hewats*, 2013 S.L.T. 763 at 766 per Lord Tyre. For discussion on the *function* of the *White v Jones* principle see *Milligan's Executors v Hewats*, 2013 S.L.T. 758. Cf. *McLeod v Crawford*, 2010 S.L.T. 1035.

[98] See, e.g. *ADT Ltd v BDO Binder Hamlyn* [1996] B.C.C. 808.

[99] See, e.g. *Macrae v Henderson*, 1989 S.L.T. 523 (although the *Hunter v Hanley* test was held not to apply).

[100] See, e.g. *Atwal Enterprises Ltd v Toner*, 2006 S.L.T. 537.

[101] See, e.g. *Smith v Eric S Bush* and *Harris v Wyre Forest DC* [1990] 1 A.C. 831.

[102] See, e.g. *G. Percy Trentham Ltd v Beattie Watkinson and Partners*, 1987 S.L.T. 449.

[103] *Morrisons Associated Companies Ltd v James Rome & Son Ltd*, 1962 S.L.T. (Notes) 75.

reasonable care would have acted in the circumstances. I do not think this is so. The practice of medicine is only permitted to those who have attained a fixed standard of professional qualifications. Further, the practice of medicine is not an exact science and methods of practice and treatment vary with the movement of professional opinion and the expansion of the horizon of scientific knowledge. The standard of qualification of a builder is not recognised and defined in the same way. An old established craft of the builder is not subjected to the same divisions and movements in professional opinion or fluctuations in diagnosis and prescription ... A builder or any other skilled tradesman is only required to possess a reasonable degree of competence and to display it in his work ... What is the measure of the standard in each case must be judged against the practice ruling in the particular trade at the particular time. I think also that where different opinions as to method may reasonably be held by persons equally skilled in the particular trade or craft, selection of one which has in fact led to certain injurious consequences in preference to another which might have led to a different result is not necessarily proof of negligence ... unless these consequences were within the realm of the reasonably foreseeable as certain or likely to ensue. On the other hand error of judgement however honestly arrived at, does not necessarily exculpate from liability."

He went on to examine the issue of practice and found that it had not been criticised by any practical builder. If it had that would make a difference for a builder but not for a doctor.[104]

Multi-layered standards

12–17   The days of the guild are nearly gone. Professions share each others' functions. Nurses do what doctors did. Estate agents do what lawyers did. Professions are encouraged to be multi-disciplinary and persons to be multi-skilled. Demarcation in the workplace has gone. The one-stop shop is everywhere. Banks sell insurance. Insurers sell financial services. Against that background, an early contract case based on negligence against a company for dentistry work is helpful. The defenders argued that they were only expert in supplying and fitting false teeth, not in removing the teeth in relation to which they only had to do their poor untrained non-qualified best as their operatives were not qualified dentists.[105] It was held that the practitioner holding himself out to do dentistry had to meet the standard of a dentist. Done well, the one-stop shop can be very beneficial. There is the potential for confusion of responsibilities or a gap in responsibility.[106] Obviously, the practical answer to avoid these difficulties is either contractual provisions or statements defining obligations, but they will continue to arise so long as multi-disciplinary operations continue. Within a profession the same principle applies. The less experienced member of the profession, who holds himself out as a specialist or the trainee who does the qualified person's work, is judged by the higher standard, not his own level of competence.[107]

---

[104] The defenders were held liable in contract but not in delict.
[105] *Dickson v Hygienic Institute*, 1910 S.C. 352.
[106] *G. Percy Trentham Ltd v Beattie Watkinson and Partners*, 1987 S.L.T. 449.
[107] *Wilsher v Essex Area Health Authority* [1988] A.C. 174.

PROOF OF NEGLIGENCE AND RES IPSA LOQUITUR

In a negligence action, normally "(n)egligence must be both averred and **12–18** proved."[108] It is the task of the pursuer to prove, on the balance of probabilities, that the defender failed to achieve the standard of care required.[109] To achieve this requires evidence.[110] However, where evidence is not available, the pursuer may attempt to rely upon the doctrine of "res ipsa loquitur" to create an inference of negligence on the part of the defender. This is a rule of evidence[111] as opposed to a rule of substantive law, and asserts that the "facts speak for themselves".[112] The inference of liability created by the application of the maxim may nevertheless be rebutted by the defender if, supported by some evidence, an alternative explanation plausibly can be asserted. In such a case the usual rule is restored—the onus of proof reverts to the pursuer.

In *Scott v London & St Katherine Docks Co* the plaintiff was struck by six bags of sugar which had fallen from a crane operated by the defendants. The plaintiff was unable to adduce evidence of how or why the bags had fallen and so could not prove fault on the part of the defendants. Erle C.J. explained how the doctrine would operate:

> "There must be reasonable evidence of negligence. But where the thing is shown to be under the management of the defendant or his servants, and the accident is such as in the ordinary course of things does not happen if those who have the management use proper care, it affords reasonable evidence, in the absence of explanation by the defendants, that the accident arose from want of care."[113]

Accordingly, there are three elements that must be present for a plea of res ipsa loquitur to succeed:

- sole control of the offending thing by the defender;
- the incident would not normally occur if due care was taken;
- no explanation is given by the defender for the incident.[114]

Logically, the onus of proof falls upon the pursuer with regard to the first two elements, but upon the defender with regard to the third. However, in practice these issues must be raised in the pleadings and the matter will be considered in the round at a proof before answer.[115]

---

[108] *Donoghue v Stevenson*, 1932 S.C. (HL) 31 at 73 per Lord MacMillan.

[109] See, e.g. *Evans v Triplex Safety Glass Co Ltd* [1936] 1 All E.R. 283.

[110] See, e.g. *Glennie v University of Aberdeen* [2013] CSOH 71; 2013 G.W.D. 17–362.

[111] *Ballard v North British Railway Co*, 1923 S.C. (HL) 43.

[112] *David T. Morrison & Co Ltd v ICL Plastics Ltd*, 2013 S.L.T. 413 at 419 per Lady Paton, delivering the opinion of the court.

[113] *Scott v London & St Katherine Docks Co* (1865) 3 Hurl. & C. 596 at 601 per Erle C.J., approved in *Ballard v North British Railway Co*, 1923 S.C. (HL) 43 and *Milliken v Glasgow Corp*, 1918 S.C. 857.

[114] See also *David T. Morrison & Co Ltd v ICL Plastics Ltd*, 2013 S.L.T. 413 at 419 per Lady Paton, delivering the opinion of the court.

[115] *Ballard v North British Railway Co*, 1923 SC (HL) 43 at 53 per Lord Dunedin; *McQueen v Glasgow Garden Festival (1988) Ltd*, 1995 S.L.T. 211; *David T. Morrison & Co Ltd v ICL Plastics Ltd*, 2013 S.L.T. 413 at 419 per Lady Paton, delivering the opinion of the court.

It must be noted that res ipsa loquitur may only be applied if the facts are unknown:

> "Where the circumstances giving rise to the cause of the accident are unknown that doctrine may be of great assistance, but where, as in the present case, all the facts are known, it cannot have any application. It is known exactly how the accident happened and it is unnecessary to ask whether this accident would have happened had there been no negligence; the only question is, do the facts or omissions which are known and which led up to the injury amount to negligence."[116]

Defender in exclusive control

12–19 The defender must be in exclusive control of the offending thing, or of the environment within which the incident occurs.[117] Control may be exercised either personally, or through agents for whom the defender is responsible[118] or would be vicariously liable. Thus, in *Inglis v London Midland & Scottish Railway Co*[119] it was held that res ipsa loquitur would apply where a train carriage door flew open immediately upon leaving a railway station (i.e. immediately after it had been closed by an employee of the defender), but would not apply further into the journey, by which time it could have been tampered with by another person. Res ipsa loquitur has also been invoked to hold the owners of a supermarket liable for spilled yoghurt[120] and the owners of a factory for an explosion in pipes supplying oxygen to a factory.[121]

Incident would not normally occur if due care taken

12–20 This element probably should speak for itself. However, product liability cases have not been consistent: although Lord Wright reckoned that the presence of sulphites in underpants did create an inference of negligence,[122] Lord MacMillan must have imagined that snails might ordinarily enter ginger bottles without negligence![123] Nevertheless, judges have concluded that bags of flour or sugar do not fall on person's heads without negligence.[124] Similarly, railway wagons do

---

[116] *Bolton v Stone* [1951] A.C. 850 at 859–860 per Lord Porter. See also *David T. Morrison & Co Ltd v ICL Plastics Ltd*, 2013 S.L.T. 413 at 419 per Lady Paton, delivering the opinion of the court.

[117] See, e.g. *McDyer v Celtic Football & Athletic Co Ltd (No.1)*, 2000 S.C. 379.

[118] *McQueen v Glasgow Garden Festival (1988) Ltd*, 1995 S.L.T. 211. If control is shared, res ipsa loquitur may be invoked if the pursuer can show that the incident was *not* the defender's fault: *Milliken v Glasgow Corp*, 1918 S.C. 857.

[119] *Inglis v London Midland & Scottish Railway Co*, 1941 S.C. 551. An eight-year-old boy fell out and was killed when a carriage door flew open twenty-six miles into the train's journey.

[120] *Ward v Tesco Stores Ltd* [1976] 1 W.L.R. 810.

[121] *Devine v Colvilles Ltd*, 1969 S.C. (HL) 67. See also *David T. Morrison & Co Ltd v ICL Plastics Ltd*, 2013 S.L.T. 413.

[122] *Grant v Australian Knitting Mills Ltd* [1936] A.C. 85 at 101 per Lord Wright. Cf. *Evans v Triplex Safety Glass Co Ltd* [1936] 1 All E.R. 283.

[123] "There is no presumption of negligence in such a case as the present, nor is there any justification for applying the maxim *res ipsa loquitur*": *Donoghue v Stevenson*, 1932 S.C. (HL) 31 at 73 per Lord MacMillan. Cf. *Lockhart v Barr*, 1943 S.C. (HL) 1. See also *Daniels v White & Sons* [1938] 4 All E.R. 258 where the defendants rebutted an inference of negligence by demonstrating a rigorous manufacturing and inspection process.

[124] *Byrne v Boadle* (1863) 2 Hurl. & C. 722; *Scott v London & St Katherine Docks Co* (1865) 3 Hurl. & C. 596.

not run away of their own accord; nor do motor vehicles.[125] Motor vehicles do not ordinarily skid,[126] or mount the pavement,[127] or veer into oncoming traffic.[128] Properly maintained pipes, whether in factories[129] or on vehicles,[130] do not ordinarily corrode or explode. Medical procedures do not ordinarily result in the patient suffering further injury.[131] Thus:

> "I went into hospital to be cured of two stiff fingers. I have come out with four stiff fingers and my hand is useless. That should not happen if due care had been used. Explain it if you can."[132]

Absence of an explanation

If the defender can provide a plausible alternative explanation for the incident **12–21** that would not involve negligence on the part of the defender, the onus of proof will revert to the pursuer. However, the defender must adduce some evidence to support the alternative innocent explanation.[133] Thus, in a case where a passenger was injured when a tram car suddenly stopped, the defenders could not, without adducing supporting evidence, displace the inference of fault merely by asserting that the driver had to take sudden evasive action to avoid a collision with a motor car driven into the path of the tram.[134] On the other hand, in a case where a passenger was injured when the bus on which he was travelling veered violently, the bus company provided evidence that a man had ran out onto the road in front of the bus. The bus driver's explanation that he had been forced to take sudden evasive action was held sufficient to rebut the presumption of negligence.[135]

---

[125] *Ballard v North British Railway Co*, 1923 S.C. (HL) 43; *Parker v Miller* (1926) 42 T.L.R. 408.

[126] *Richley (Henderson) v Faull (Richley, Third Party)* [1965] 1 W.L.R. 1454.

[127] *Ellor v Selfridge & Co Ltd* (1930) 46 T.L.R. 236.

[128] *Ng Chun Pui v Lee Chuen Tat* [1988] R.T.R. 298 (PC (HK)). Cf. *O'Hara v Central SMT Co Ltd*, 1941 S.C. 363.

[129] *Devine v Colvilles Ltd*, 1969 S.C. (HL) 67; *David T. Morrison & Co Ltd v ICL Plastics Ltd*, 2013 S.L.T. 413.

[130] *Henderson v Henry E Jenkins & Sons* [1970] A.C. 282.

[131] *Cassidy v Ministry of Health* [1951] 2 K.B. 343; *Mahon v Osborne* [1939] 2 K.B. 14. Cf. *Fish v Kapur* [1948] 2 All E.R. 176.

[132] *Cassidy v Ministry of Health* [1951] 2 K.B. 343 at 365 per Denning L.J.

[133] *Mars v Glasgow Corp*, 1940 S.C. 202 at 209 per Lord Moncrieff.

[134] *Mars v Glasgow Corp*, 1940 S.C. 202 at 209 per Lord Moncrieff.

[135] *O'Hara v Central SMT Co Ltd*, 1941 S.C. 363. Cf. *Doonan v SMT Co Ltd*, 1950 S.C. 136.

SECTION IV: LIMITATIONS ON DELICTUAL LIABILITY

CHAPTER 13

CAUSATION AND REMOTENESS OF DAMAGE

INTRODUCTION

Liability in the Scots law of delict generally is based on *culpa* and may be **13–01** summed up in the maxim *damnum injuria datum*, i.e. loss wrongfully caused. The third word (*datum*) recognises a requirement for proof of a connection between cause (*injuria*) and effect (*damnum*).[1] The onus of proof with regard to each of these elements is on the pursuer. Thus, for delictual liability to arise it is not enough that a breach of duty is admitted or proved: the breach of duty must be a *necessary* antecedent with regard to the harm, i.e. the harm would have been avoided "but for" the breach of duty; and the breach of duty must also be *sufficient* to justify liability imposed *ex lege*. From this it may be seen that the causation aspect of the enquiry into delictual liability involves two stages, or questions, which operate cumulatively (i.e. both require affirmative answers) in determining causation:

1. Was the breach of duty an essential pre-requisite "but for" which the harm would not have been suffered? The maxim *causa sine qua non* (cause without which) is often used to denote a "necessary" cause and lawyers talk of the "but-for" test. Recognising that whether a delictual wrong is a *causa sine qua non* the harm is in theory a question of fact determined by evidence,[2] another phrase used to describe this stage is "factual causation".

2. Was the breach of duty the predominant, or effective, cause of the harm? The maxim *causa causans* (cause among causes) is often used to denote a "sufficient" cause, i.e. sufficient to confirm delictual liability. This stage also involves questions of fact, but given the objective of determining whether the delictual wrong is sufficiently causative to justify liability *ex lege*, this stage may be seen in principle as a question

---

[1] "Causation is a mental concept, generally based on inference or deduction from uniformity of sequence as between two events that there is a causal connection between them": *A/B Karlshamns Oljefabriker v Monarch Steamship Co*, 1949 S.C. (HL) 1 at 24 per Lord Wright.

[2] Although the facts exist, they may not be made clear by the evidence available: "Everything has a determinate cause, even if we do not know what it is": *Gregg v Scott* [2005] 2 A.C. 176 at 196 per Lord Hoffmann. Thus, what legal tests are to be applied to the evidence involves a question of law: see, e.g. *Mallett v McMonagle* [1970] A.C. 166 at 176 per Lord Diplock; *Fairchild v Glenhaven Funeral Services Ltd* [2003] 1 A.C. 32 at 110 per Lord Rodger of Earlsferry; *Gregg v Scott* [2005] 2 A.C. 176 at 181–182 per Lord Nicholls of Birkenhead.

of law. Thus the term "legal causation" is often used to distinguish this second stage of the causation enquiry.[3]

It has frequently been said that these questions should be applied in a "common-sense" manner rather than applying scientific or other technical formulae.[4] In most cases this is likely to be relatively straightforward, but as will be seen below "common-sense" decisions in difficult or complex cases can be very controversial,[5] and with hindsight (e.g. when the precedent created comes to be applied in future cases) may not appear to have been based on "common sense" after all.[6] Misguided presumptions masquerading as "common sense" may be displaced by expert evidence.[7]

It is also worth remembering that proof of causation in delict cases is a loaded issue. It is not a dispassionate analysis of cause and effect, rather it is part of an adversarial enquiry into whether the law, reflecting the values of society, should impose delictual liability in a given set of circumstances. It may also be said that the law's approach to causation is so primitive it often operates artificially upon a false premise,[8] i.e. the law insists on recognising a linear process where in reality a much more complex set of circumstances is at large.[9] Thus, notions of culpability may influence judicial decision making, and "policy considerations" often "loom large".[10]

FACTUAL CAUSATION

13–02 The onus of proof is on the pursuer.[11] It is sufficient for the pursuer to lead evidence to show that defender's negligence triggered a chain of events that led

---

[3] Some commentators have begun to conflate causation with remoteness of damage under the heading "scope of liability". This is intended to reflect that policy-based decision making has become more frequent in cases dealing with causation and remoteness issues, although the term (used in a similar context) may be traced back at least as far as Lord MacMillan's speech in *Bourhill v Young*, 1942 S.C. (HL) 78 at 88. Does this confirm that duty, breach, causation and remoteness are just different ways of looking at the same thing? See, e.g. *Roe v Minister of Health* [1954] 2 Q.B. 66 at 85 per Denning L.J.

[4] *Yorkshire Dale Steamship Co Ltd v Minister of War Transport* [1942] A.C. 691 at 706 per Lord Wright. See also *P's Curator Bonis v Criminal Injuries Compensation Board*, 1997 S.L.T. 1180 at 1200 per Lord Osborne.

[5] "One person's commonsense may be another's nonsense": *Equitable Life Assurance Society v Ernst & Young* [2003] P.N.L.R. 23 at 479 per Langley J.

[6] See, e.g. *Sienkiewicz v Greif (UK) Ltd* [2011] 2 A.C. 229 at 291–294 per Lord Brown.

[7] See, e.g. *Clements v Shell UK Ltd*, 1991 G.W.D. 35–2153.

[8] This is especially vivid in medical negligence loss of chance cases: see, e.g. *Gregg v Scott* [2005] 2 A.C. 176.

[9] "Causation is not a chain, but a net. At each point influences, forces, events, precedent and simultaneous, meet and the radiation from each point extends indefinitely. At the point where these various influences meet it is for the judgment as upon a matter of fact to declare which of the causes thus joined at the point of effect was the proximate and which was the remote cause": *Leyland Shipping Co v Norwich Union Fire Insurance Society* [1918] A.C. 350 at 369 per Lord Shaw.

[10] *Wright v Cambridge Medical Group* [2013] Q.B. 312 at 341 per Elias L.J. *Chester v Afshar* [2005] 1 A.C. 134 perhaps provides a paradigm example, where the decision of the House of Lords (albeit by a bare majority) seemed to be driven by a concern that without liability the duty of care owed by a doctor to a patient would be drained of all content.

[11] See, e.g. *McGlinchey v General Motors UK Ltd* [2012] CSIH; 2013 G.W.D. 1–47—extensive testing did not demonstrate that on the balance of probabilities a defect in a handbrake mechanism had caused the injuries sustained by the pursuer.

to the harm claimed for.[12] If the pursuer cannot lead evidence to prove that but for the defender's wrong the pursuer's loss would have been avoided, the pursuer's case is normally doomed. The "but-for" test thus performs an exclusionary function, filtering out irrelevant cases. A famous example occurred in *Barnett v Chelsea and Kensington Hospital Management Committee*[13] where, having taken unwell after drinking a cup of tea, a night watchman attended hospital and was seen by a doctor. The doctor refused treatment and sent the man home, suggesting that if his symptoms persisted he should visit his GP. The man died before he made it home. It transpired that the cup of tea was so contaminated by arsenic that no treatment could have saved the man. So, although the doctor had breached the duty of care he owed the man in refusing treatment, the doctor's delictual wrong was not a *causa sine qua non* the man's death. There was no liability.

The standard of proof is on the balance of probabilities. This is illustrated in *McWilliams v Sir William Arrol & Co.*[14] An experienced steel erector died after falling from a platform some 100 feet above the ground. In an action against the deceased's employer for breach of statutory duty in failing to provide a safety harness, the employer led evidence which the court accepted as proving it was more likely than not that the deceased would not have worn a safety harness even if the employer had complied with the statutory duty. The court held the "but-for" test not to have been satisfied and there was no liability.

A court may be prepared to draw a reasonable inference from established facts.[15] However, courts are reticent to bend the rules on causation, so the facts must be established and the inference must be reasonable. In *Kay's Tutor v Ayrshire and Arran Health Board* an infant child was admitted to hospital suffering from meningitis. Negligence on the part of hospital staff resulted in the infant being given an adult dose of penicillin. The infant's reaction alerted staff to the mistake and immediate remedial action was taken. Fortunately, the child recovered. However, the child had become deaf. The hospital admitted liability for the immediate reaction suffered by the child, but denied liability for the deafness, pointing to a paucity of evidence of a causal connection between an overdose of penicillin and deafness and a substantial body of evidence of a connection between meningitis and deafness. Although expressing sympathy with the child's plight, the House of Lords acknowledged that the evidential gap prevented the pursuers from proving a causal link between the overdose and the deafness.[16]

---

[12] See, e.g. *McGee v RJK Building Services Ltd*, 2013 S.L.T. 428. The defender may attempt to argue that the chain of events was broken by a *novus actus interveniens*: see paras 13–14 to 13–16 below.

[13] *Barnett v Chelsea and Kensington Hospital Management Committee* [1969] 1 Q.B. 428.

[14] *McWilliams v Sir William Arrol & Co and Lithgows Ltd*, 1962 S.C. (HL) 70.

[15] "In my opinion, when a man who has not previously suffered from a disease contracts that disease after being subjected to conditions likely to cause it, and when he shows that it starts in a way typical of disease caused by such conditions, he establishes a *prima facie* presumption that his disease was caused by those conditions . . . That presumption could be displaced in many ways": *Gardiner v Motherwell Machinery and Scrap Co Ltd*, 1961 S.C. (HL) 1 at 17 per Lord Reid.

[16] *Kay's Tutor v Ayrshire and Arran Health Board*, 1987 S.C. (HL) 145 at 167 per Lord Keith of Kinkell. The language used by Lord Keith arguably hints that had there been any medical evidence to indicate the possibility of a connection between the overdose and the deafness the pursuer would have been given the benefit of the doubt.

A defender will escape liability if he can show that a similar outcome would have been probable even if the defender had not acted wrongfully. In *Bolitho v City and Hackney Health Authority*[17] a hospital doctor failed to respond to an emergency pager call and the child patient died. Medical evidence showed that intubation was the only intervention which would have saved the child, but the doctor gave evidence that she would not have intubated the child even had she attended immediately. The House of Lords accepted that a failure to intubate would not in itself be negligent, evidence having been adduced to confirm that her view was condoned by a responsible body of medical opinion.[18] Thus there was no liability. However, had a failure to intubate been itself negligent, the defender would have been liable.[19]

More than one delinquent

13–03   What if two or more distinct delictual wrongs committed by independent persons coincide so as cumulatively to cause the pursuer's harm? Here is an example: lorry driver A while driving on the motorway negligently loses control of his lorry, causing a "pile-up". Other drivers stop to offer help. Another lorry driver (S), who is also driving along the motorway, fails to notice the accident until he cannot avoid ploughing into the stationary vehicles. The impact pushes the stationary vehicles forward and R, one of the drivers who had stopped to help, is knocked down and killed.[20] In this scenario there are two independent negligent acts (by respectively A and S) which combine to result in a single harmful outcome (death of R). If any one of those negligent acts had not occurred, the outcome would not have been realised.[21] In such cases liability will be determined on a joint and several basis;[22] the court apportioning contributions from each party.[23] The pursuer will be entitled to recover all of the damages to which he is entitled from either wrongdoer, and if one wrongdoer pays more than the contribution determined by the court he may seek to recover the difference from the other wrongdoer(s).[24]

It is important to note that joint and several liability will arise only where

---

[17] *Bolitho (Deceased) v City and Hackney Health Authority* [1998] A.C. 232.
[18] See paras 12–12 to 12–14 above.
[19] See also *Coyle v Lanarkshire Health Board* [2013] CSOH 167; 2013 G.W.D. 37–722; *Wright v Cambridge Medical Group* [2013] Q.B. 312. In *Wright*, Lord Neuberger of Abbotsbury M.R. at 329 suggested that the *Bolitho* rule would also apply in cases where a third party was negligent, there being an irrebuttable presumption that where, for example, the delay was in referring a patient to a specialist, the specialist would not act negligently.
[20] These facts occurred in the English case of *Rouse v Squires* [1973] Q.B. 889. See also *Andrews v St Andrew's Ambulance Association*, 1943 S.C. 248.
[21] If the latter wrongful act is unforeseeable from the perspective of the person committing the former wrongful act, the latter may amount to a novus actus interveniens, absolving the former wrongdoer from liability for harm that would not have occurred but for the latter wrongful act. See, e.g. *Wright v Lodge* [1993] 4 All ER 299; *Knightley v Johns* [1982] 1 W.L.R. 349, and paras 13–14 to 13–16 below.
[22] Law Reform (Miscellaneous Provisions) (Scotland) Act 1940 s.3.
[23] Contributions should be determined by causative effect and not by culpability: *Drew v Western S.M.T. Co*, 1947 S.C. 222 at 240 per L.J.C. Cooper. See also, e.g. *Gilfillan v Barbour*, 2003 S.L.T. 1127; *Morris v Fife Council*, 2005 1 S.C. 72.
[24] See *Associated Newspapers Ltd v Dingle* [1961] 2 Q.B. 162 at 188–189 per Devlin L.J. See also *Cairns v Northern Lighthouse Board*, 2013 S.L.T. 645.

distinct delictual wrongs committed independently by more than one wrongdoer combine, effectively so as to become a single wrong,[ ] and cause a single injury, or indivisible harm.[26] If the harm is divisible,[27] or the hazards distinct,[28] each wrongdoer will be liable for only the harm that his wrong caused. Thus, if a person crossing the road at a pedestrian crossing is struck by two vehicles being raced by their respective drivers, if the pedestrian's broken leg is caused by his collision with the car driven by A, and his broken arm is caused by his collision with the car driven by B, A and B will be liable only for the distinct injury each has respectively caused.[29] Resolving the conundrum becomes much more difficult when it is impossible to determine which injury was caused by which driver's negligence.[30]

Where the pursuer has been contributorily negligent, the court will first of all calculate the reduction in overall entitlement to damages[31] before allocating respective contributions to the defenders. An example is *Drew v Western S.M.T. Co*[32] where a van boy was killed when a bus collided with the back of the van he was unloading. The van driver was negligent in failing to ensure the van's lights were visible; the bus driver was negligent in failing to spot the stationary van; and the boy was negligent in the way in which he was carrying out his task.

Indeterminate wrongs

What if there are several potential reasons why a pursuer has suffered harm but **13–04** it is impossible to ascertain which of these would satisfy the "but-for" test? The question arose in *Wardlaw v Bonnington Castings Ltd*,[33] where an employee developed an industrial disease through exposure to silica dust on the atmosphere in his workplace. It was accepted that there were two sources of silica dust: the pneumatic hammer which was operated by the pursuer; and swing grinders operated by other workers. The employer had satisfied the legal requirements with regard to the hammer, but not the grinders. Thus, the silica dust given off by the hammer was lawful dust, whereas the dust from the grinders was unlawful. To satisfy standard causation rules, the pursuer would have to prove on the balance of probabilities that but for the unlawful dust from the grinders, he would have avoided the disease. "Common sense" might suggest that the source most

---

[25] See, e.g. *Ruddy v Chief Constable of Strathclyde*, 2013 S.C. (U.K.S.C.) 126; *Ellerman Lines Ltd v Clyde Navigation Trs*, 1909 S.C. 690; *Grunwald v Hughes*, 1965 S.L.T. 209.

[26] See, e.g. *McGillivray v Davidson*, 1993 S.L.T. 693.

[27] The definition of "divisible" harm is unclear: compare *Holtby v Brigham and Cowan (Hull) Ltd* [2000] 3 All E. R. 421; *Barker v Corus (UK) Plc* [2006] 2 A.C. 572; *Wright v Stoddard International*, 2008 Rep. L.R. 2.

[28] See, e.g. *Fleming v McGillivray*, 1946 S.C. 1; *Reid v Sir Robert McAlpine & Son*, 1986 S.L.T. 108.

[29] See, e.g. *Davis v Catto*, 2012 Rep. L.R. 40.

[30] See, e.g. *Fitzgerald v Lane* [1987] Q.B. 781. Here, liability was apportioned on a joint and several basis. However, given the decision was based on an application of the *McGhee/Fairchild* exception (albeit pre-*Fairchild*), does the decision of the House of Lords in *Barker v Corus (UK) Ltd* [2006] 2 A.C. 572 call into question the approach taken by the English Court of Appeal in *Fitzgerald*?

[31] Law Reform (Contributory Negligence) Act 1945.

[32] *Drew v Western S.M.T. Co*, 1947 S.C. 222.

[33] *Wardlaw v Bonnington Castings Ltd*, 1956 S.C. (HL) 26.

local to the pursuer (i.e. the hammer) would be the most significant. Nevertheless, the House of Lords allowed the claim to proceed, holding that it was sufficient to demonstrate that the unlawful dust made a material contribution to the injury. Lord Reid also ruled that a material contribution would be any contribution that was not de minimis,[34] suggesting that the onus of proof with regard to excluding a contribution as not material would be upon the defender.

A more challenging set of facts presented in *McGhee v National Coal Board*. The pursuer contracted dermatitis having been required by his employer to work in the hot and dusty atmosphere of a brick firing kiln. His skin came into contact with abrasive brick dust while in the kiln (which was not unlawful as the employer had satisfied its legal duties in terms of a safe system of work). His employer, in acknowledged breach of duty, failed to provide washing facilities so that the pursuer had to travel home before having an opportunity to wash the dust off his skin. Medical evidence could not confirm whether the disease was triggered by exposure to dust during, or after, the pursuer's shift at work, nor could it confirm whether prolonged exposure would have a cumulative effect in triggering the disease. Thus, a key distinction between *Wardlaw* and *McGhee* was that in the former case the separate contributions (hammer and grinders) did have a cumulative effect, whereas in the latter it was understood that the skin condition would likely be triggered at the point in time where the dust penetrated his skin which could have happened at any time when he was exposed to the dust. Accordingly, *Wardlaw* could not be applied in the sense that the employer's breach of duty had made a material (i.e. not de minimis) contribution to the injury as such. Nevertheless the House of Lords permitted the claim to proceed, apparently equiparating a material contribution to the injury itself with a material contribution to the *risk* of injury.[35] Thus,

> "the 'but-for' or *sine qua non* test of causation gives way to this considerably more generous test based on the defendant's contribution to the victim's injury."[36]

The decision in *McGhee* was controversial, and seemed to have been discarded as a result of the decision of the House of Lords in *Wilsher v Essex Area Health Authority*, where Lord Bridge declared that *McGhee* "laid down no new principle of law whatever".[37] However, hindsight confirms Lord Bridge's comments were clearly obiter, *Wilsher* being distinguishable on its facts from *McGhee*.[38] An infant born prematurely became blind after contracting retrolental fibroplasia. Although the negligence of the hospital doctor could have caused the condition, there were four other alternative potential causes associated with the premature birth, none of which were connected to the doctor's negligence. The House of Lords insisted on applying the "but-for" test in the traditional manner, and since the plaintiff could not lead evidence to show that on the balance of probabilities the doctor's negligence was the most likely cause the claim failed. Thus, where

---

[34] i.e. insignificant: *Wardlaw v Bonnington Castings Ltd*, 1956 S.C. (HL) 26 at 32 per Lord Reid.

[35] *McGhee v National Coal Board*, 1973 S.C. (HL) 37 at 53 per Lord Reid.

[36] *Barker v Corus (UK) Ltd* [2006] 2 A.C. 572 at 602 per Lord Rodger of Earlsferry.

[37] *Wilsher v Essex Area Health Authority* [1988] A.C. 1074 at 1090 per Lord Bridge of Harwich.

[38] *Fairchild v Glenhaven Funeral Services Ltd* [2003] 1 A.C. 32. See also *Barker v Corus (UK) Ltd* [2006] 2 A.C. 572 at 585–587 per Lord Hoffman.

only one hazard could have led to the harm *McGhee* may be applied,[39] but not where two or more distinct hazards could potentially have led to the harm.[40]

Indeterminate wrongdoers

What if two or more persons independently commit the same delictually **13–05** wrongful act and an individual is harmed, but although the harm could have been caused by only one of the delictual acts it is impossible to tell which was responsible? The "two hunters" conundrum has occurred literally in the United States[41] and in Canada,[42] where two hunters negligently shoot at the same time, a victim is struck by a bullet, but it is impossible to confirm from which gun. The problem was resolved in each of these cases by a reversal of the burden of proof, leaving both hunters liable on a joint and several basis.[43] A similar approach was taken by the English Court of Appeal in *Fitzgerald v Lane*,[44] where a pedestrian using a pelican crossing, having been struck by one negligently driven vehicle, was thrown onto the opposite carriageway where he was struck by another. But is a reversal of the burden of proof the correct approach?

A series of cases dealing with diseases associated with exposure to asbestos fibres have presented the courts with a range of challenges and have resulted in the relaxation of strict rules of causation. As each relaxation then stores up complications that become apparent in subsequent cases, the courts have increasingly been careful to confine the relaxation of rules to cases involving similar facts. Given that it is probably reasonable to expect the occurrence of asbestos related diseases to tail off in the future (the risks of asbestos now being well known and the use of asbestos being more tightly controlled) it may be that we are witnessing a temporary fillip in the law in this area and a return to orthodoxy may be anticipated. Nevertheless, as demonstrated by *Fitzgerald v Lane*, relatively mundane events can throw up complex conundrums in causation, so when asbestos related diseases become a thing of the past, the challenges in causation will remain and may come into focus in different scenarios.

Asbestos is a naturally occurring mineral which enjoys substantial heat insulation properties. Thus, it was used extensively in many industrial and domestic applications, particularly in shipbuilding. However, asbestos is deadly, and inhalation of asbestos fibres can result in hideous diseases. There are three distinct asbestos-related conditions which have been the subject of litigation in negligence: asbestosis, where fibres collect in the lungs inhibiting one's ability to breathe; mesothelioma, a lung cancer which is inevitably fatal and of which little is understood in the medical profession; and pleural plaques, a scarring of the

---

[39] It has been suggested that the *McGhee/Fairchild* principle may be confined to industrial disease cases: see *Porter v Strathclyde RC*, 1991 S.L.T. 446. Cf. *Fairchild v Glenhaven Funeral Services Ltd* [2003] 1 A.C. 32 at 118–119 per Lord Rodger of Earlsferry (commenting on the decision of the English Court of Appeal in *Fitzgerald v Lane* [1987] Q.B. 781). The *McGhee/Fairchild* principle has been applied in a sheriff court decision concerning liability under the Occupiers' Liability (Scotland) Act 1960 where the extra height of a playground swing had materially increased the risk of injury to a 12-year-old child: *Bye v Fife Council*, 2007 Rep. L.R. 40.

[40] In *Wilsher* there were five.

[41] *Summers v Tice*, 119 P. 2d 1 (1948).

[42] *Cook v Lewis* [1951] S.C.R. 830.

[43] In *Arneil v Paterson*, 1931 S.C. (HL) 117, the House of Lords held that where two dogs had together worried some sheep, and it was impossible to tell which dog had killed which sheep, each of the two owners was liable for the whole of the damage. The court did not consider it necessary to reverse the onus of proof.

[44] *Fitzgerald v Lane* [1987] Q.B. 781.

lung tissue which at the time of writing has not been shown to be directly connected with either of the former conditions.[45] Litigation involving asbestos-related diseases has most often been instigated by employees each claiming that their respective employers were in breach of a duty of care by failing to provide a safe system of work, i.e. exposing them to asbestos without taking appropriate precautions to protect the employees from the harmful effects. A common feature has been that pursuers have worked for a series of employers over their working lives, several of whom have negligently exposed the pursuers to asbestos fibres. The difficult question posed by such litigation is how should the law deal with cases where it is impossible to prove which employer's negligence caused the harm.

Because asbestosis operates in a cumulative way (the lungs gradually fill up with asbestos fibres as they are inhaled and breathing capacity is proportionally reduced), each employer's negligence will contribute to the harm suffered by the employee. English decisions[46] have treated liability as several, with each employer who is sued being held liable to pay damages on an aliquot basis, i.e. limited in the case of each defender by the extent to which that defender's wrong contributed to the harm. So if a pursuer was employed by four employers each for five years, and was exposed to similar amounts of asbestos in each employment, each employer should be liable only for one quarter of the damages award appropriate to asbestosis. However, whether this approach is correct has been doubted in Scotland, it being asserted that it is up to the defender to call third parties if it seeks liability to be apportioned.[47]

13–06   Much less is medically understood about mesothelioma and pleural plaques. Mesothelioma in particular is enigmatic in its aetiology. It is not known how many asbestos fibres must be present in one's lungs nor for how long fibres can inhabit the lungs before the disease is triggered. Nor is it known whether an accumulation of fibres in the lungs has any effect on the likelihood of mesothelioma. Indeed, for all medical science has been able to establish, it may be the case that a single fibre is sufficient and that it could have lain dormant in the individual's lungs for decades before the mutation occurs and cancer develops. What is known is that mesothelioma is inevitably fatal and that, upon discovery, life expectancy may be measured at most in months.

In *Fairchild v Glenhaven Funeral Services Ltd*[48] the House of Lords was confronted with a series of claims brought by former employees of the respective defendants, all of whom had contracted mesothelioma attributed to inhaling asbestos fibres at work. Although the respective employers admitted breach of duty, they denied liability, pointing out that the claimants could not satisfy the "but-for" test in causation. In addition to the exposure caused by the respective defendant's negligence, each claimant had also been exposed to asbestos fibres by the negligence of other employers who had employed the respective claimants at different times in their working lives. The claimants had selected the particular defendants because their other previous employers no longer existed. The House of Lords accepted that the claimants could not satisfy the "but-for" test—given

---

[45] *Grieves v FT Everard & Sons Ltd* [2008] 1 A.C. 281.

[46] *Holtby v Brigham and Cowan (Hull) Ltd* [2000] 3 All E.R. 421. Similar treatment is given to "industrial deafness or any of the other dose-related cumulative diseases": *Barker v Corus (UK) Plc* [2006] 2 A.C. 572 at 615 per Baroness Hale of Richmond. If these decisions are correct they are unaffected by s.3 of the Compensation Act 2006 as it is confined to mesothelioma cases.

[47] *Wright v Stoddard International*, 2008 Rep. L.R. 2 at 27–35 per Lord Uist.

[48] *Fairchild v Glenhaven Funeral Services Ltd* [2003] 1 A.C. 32.

the lack of understanding of mesothelioma it was impossible to say that but for the defendants' negligence the claimants would have avoided developing mesothelioma. However, their Lordships considered that to apply the normal rules of causation would lead to an intolerable injustice, and so the requirement to satisfy the "but-for" test should be relaxed.

Their Lordships did not identify a clear and distinct reason for reaching this conclusion. The decision was explained as an extension of the principle postulated by Lord Reid in *McGhee v National Coal Board*.[49] However, it has since been emphasised that although to satisfy the *Fairchild* substitute to the "but-for" test it is sufficient to show that the wrong materially increased the risk of harm, the wrongdoer's liability is not for contributing to the risk of disease as such, but recognises responsibility for the disease itself.[50] There was some concern that refusing a remedy would "empty the duty of content"[51] and a general consensus that there were policy reasons for relaxing the rules here. This lack of clarity raises concerns about the scope of the exception. However, these concerns may transpire to be rather academic given the impetus to return to orthodoxy that has been apparent in subsequent cases.[52] Nevertheless the *Fairchild* exception continues to throw up fresh conundrums.[53]

A question not judicially considered in *Fairchild* was whether in such cases **13–07** the defender should be liable for the whole of the damage, or for only a proportion based on the extent to which the defender had exposed the employee to asbestos, as against the cumulative exposure to which the employee had been subjected by successive employers.[54] The question was considered by the House of Lords in *Barker v Corus (UK) Ltd*.[55] In a majority judgment[56] it was held that liability should be apportioned, thus for defenders smoothing the rough justice

---

[49] *McGhee v National Coal Board*, 1973 S.C. (HL) 37. "Indeed, on one view the principle is easier to apply in the present cases than in *McGhee* since it is not disputed that the men developed mesothelioma as a result of a tort by one of their employers": *Fairchild v Glenhaven Funeral Services Ltd* [2003] 1 A.C. 32 at 112 per Lord Rodger of Earlsferry. Ironically, "*McGhee* must therefore be accepted as an approved application of the *Fairchild* exception": *Barker v Corus (UK) Plc* [2006] 2 A.C. 572 at 584 per Lord Hoffman.

[50] *Grieves v FT Everard & Sons Ltd* [2008] 1 A.C. 281. See also *Durham v BAI (Run Off) Ltd* [2012] 1 W.L.R. 867 at 895–896 per Lord Mance. Is this consistent with the reasoning of the majority in *Barker v Corus (UK) Ltd* [2006] 2 A.C. 572—see especially Lord Hoffmann at 589–590?

[51] *Fairchild v Glenhaven Funeral Services Ltd* [2003] 1 A.C. 32 at 74 per Lord Hoffman; at 112 per Lord Rodger of Earlsferry.

[52] See, e.g. *Gregg v Scott* [2005] 2 A.C. 176; *Barker v Corus (UK) Ltd* [2006] 2 A.C. 572; *Sienkiewicz v Greif (UK) Ltd* [2011] 2 A.C. 229.The *Fairchild* "material contribution" exception has since been applied in other circumstances: see, e.g. *Bailey v Ministry of Defence* [2009] 1 W.L.R. 1052; *Popple v Birmingham Women's NHS Foundation Trust* [2011] EWHC 2320; *Leigh v London Ambulance Service NHS Trust* [2014] Med. L.R. 134.

[53] See, e.g. *Barker v Corus (UK) Ltd* [2006] 2 A.C. 572 (where some of the claimant's exposure to asbestos occurred when he was self-employed); *Sienkiewicz v Greif (UK) Ltd* [2011] 2 A.C. 229 (where only one employer negligently exposed the claimant to asbestos fibres); *Durham v BAI (Run Off) Ltd* [2012] 1 W.L.R. 867 (did the language of an insurance policy effectively exclude *Fairchild* type liability—answer was no).

[54] Neither was the question considered in *Wardlaw v Bonnington Castings Ltd*, 1956 S.C. (HL) 26, nor in *McGhee v National Coal Board*, 1973 S.C. (HL) 37. Both of these cases, along with *Fairchild* have been treated as confirming liability *in solidum* (i.e. joint and several) rather than aliquot: *Wright v Stoddard International Plc*, 2008 Rep. L.R. 2.

[55] *Barker v Corus (UK) Ltd* [2006] 2 A.C. 572.

[56] Lord Rodger of Earlsferry dissented, asserting that proportionate damages would effectively create liability for loss of a chance, contradicting the stance taken by the majority in *Gregg v Scott* [2005] 2 A.C. 176.

created by the decision in *Fairchild*.[57] This outcome looks like a sop to the insurance lobby, and was almost immediately nullified by s.3 of the Compensation Act 2006. It must be noted though that s.3 is restricted to liability for mesothelioma, leaving open whether, if the *Fairchild* exception is applied in any non-mesothelioma case, liability will have to be apportioned on an aliquot basis following *Barker*. That question was addressed obiter by Lord Uist in *Wright v Stoddard International*[58] who, after reviewing the authorities, concluded that the decision in *Barker* was itself confined to mesothelioma cases and, in any event that being an English appeal, *Barker* was not binding in Scotland and the dissenting speech of Lord Rodger was to be preferred.[59]

That mesothelioma cases are in a category of their own was confirmed by the Supreme Court in *Sienkiewicz v Greif (UK) Ltd*. The defendant argued that where there were only two possible triggers for the mesothelioma suffered by the claimant: the defendant's negligence being one and the presence of asbestos in the atmosphere being the other, *Fairchild* would not apply and the usual rules of causation should be applied. This argument was rejected and the court confirmed that the exception would be applied where the negligence materially increased the risk of contraction of the disease: a material risk being a risk that could not be discounted as de minimis. It was also noted that advances in medical science may reveal that at least some of the justification for placing mesothelioma cases on a special footing may transpire to be based on a false premise, and Lord Brown noted that "the law tampers with the but-for test of causation at its peril."[60]

What of pleural plaques? In *Grieves v FT Everard & Sons Ltd*[61] the House of Lords held that as there was no evidence confirming any direct connection between pleural plaques and any diseases as such, the scarring of the lungs was in itself harmless and so there would be no liability. Thus, although pleural plaques confirmed that the individual had been exposed to asbestos, it did not signal an increased risk of developing asbestosis or mesothelioma. Since there was no physical harm as such, and no immediate threat of such,[62] neither could there be liability for mental harm in the form of distress or fear for the future upon discovering such scar tissue on one's lungs. The decision in *Grieves* was also nullified by legislation, although this time only in Scotland.[63]

Loss of chance

13–08   If it is sufficient to bypass the traditional "but-for" test that the defender's wrong has materially increased the risk of the harm, does consistency demand

---

[57] *Barker v Corus (UK) Ltd* [2006] 2 A.C. 572 at 592 per Lord Hoffmann.

[58] *Wright v Stoddard International*, 2008 Rep. L.R. 2. See also *Balfour v William Beardmore & Co Ltd*, 1956 S.L.T. 205.

[59] Lord Uist, at 34, also questioned the correctness of the decision of the English Court of Appeal in *Holtby v Brigham & Cowan (Hull) Ltd* [2000] 3 All E.R. 431 in the context of the law in England and Wales; *Wright v Stoddard International Plc*, 2008 Rep. L.R. 2 at 34.

[60] *Sienkiewicz v Greif (UK) Ltd* [2011] 2 A.C. 229 at 294 per Lord Brown J.S.C.

[61] *Grieves v FT Everard & Sons Ltd* [2008] 1 A.C. 281.

[62] *Page v Smith* [1996] 1 A.C. 155.

[63] Damages (Asbestos-Related Conditions) (Scotland) Act 2009. The legislation was the subject of an ultimately unsuccessful challenge by the insurance industry: *AXA General Insurance Ltd, Petitioners*, 2012 S.C. (U.K.S.C.) 122.

that an exception is also applied where the defender's wrong costs the pursuer the chance of achieving a positive outcome?[64] Consider the following scenario:

A man attends his GP complaining of a swelling under his arm. Following a cursory examination his GP advises that there is a benign growth and that there is nothing to worry about. Over a period of months the swelling gets worse. Nine months after his visit to his GP, the man attends another GP, who sends the man for specialist tests which confirm non-Hodgkins lymphoma—an aggressive cancer. The first GP was negligent in failing properly to diagnose the cancer. If there was a 42 per cent chance of recovery[65] following treatment at the time of the first visit, but only a 25 per cent chance following the second visit, can the man recover damages from the first GP for the reduction of 17 per cent in the chance of recovery?

These were the facts in *Gregg v Scott*.[66] A majority of the House of Lords held that the law did not provide for liability for loss of chance in such circumstances.[67] What was the justification for the decision? It has been said that,

> "in determining what did happen in the past a court decides on the balance of probabilities. Anything that is more probable than not it treats as certain."[68]

Applying this principle, it follows that if the evidence points to the likelihood of an outcome at less than evens, the law presumes that the outcome would not be achieved. So if statistical evidence suggests that out of 100 persons who have cancer at a given stage, 42 of those will recover if they are treated immediately, 42 being less than evens, it was probably the case that the pursuer would not have recovered anyway. Thus, on application of the balance of probability test the pursuer is no worse off as a result of the first GP's negligence. Thus, loss of chance in this context does not qualify as *damnum*. If, however, the chances of survival were 51 per cent at the time of attendance at the first GP, but had reduced by 2 per cent to 49 per cent by the time of attendance at the second GP, the pursuer would recover full compensation![69] Is this fair?

---

[64] A considerable body of academic commentary has been produced on loss of chance. Highlights include: H. Reece, "Losses of Chances in the Law" (1996) M.L.R. 188; J.G. Fleming, "Probabalistic Causation in Tort Law" (1989) 68 Can. Bar Rev. 661; J.G. Fleming, "Probabilistic Causation in Tort Law: A Postscript" (1991) 70 Can. Bar Rev. 136; M. Lunney, "What Price Chance?" (1995) L.S. 2; H.H.A. Stewart, "Medical Lost Chances: challenging the new orthodoxy", 2000 2(5) S.L.P.Q. 147; M. Hogg, "Paul v Ogilvy: A Lost Opportunity for Lost Chance Recovery" (2003) 7 Edin. L.R. 86; J. Stapleton, "Loss of Chance of Cure from Cancer" (2005) M.L.R. 996; M. Hogg, "Re-establishing orthodoxy in the realm of causation" (2007) 11 Edin. L.R. 8; Lord Neuberger of Abbotsbury, "Loss of a chance and causation" (2008) P.N. 206; A. Burrows, "Uncertainty about uncertainty: damages for loss of a chance" (2008) J.P.I. Law 31; H. McGregor, "Loss of chance: where has it come from and where is it going?" (2008) P.N. 2.

[65] Recovery being defined as surviving in a disease free state for 10 years.

[66] *Gregg v Scott* [2005] 2 A.C. 176. See also *Kenyon v Bell*, 1953 S.C. 125; *Hotson v East Berkshire Area Health Authority* [1987] A. C. 750; *McGlone v Greater Glasgow Health Board* [2011] CSOH 63; 2011 G.W.D. 19–459.

[67] Although there may be liability for additional pain and suffering and/or for psychiatric injury: *Oliver v Williams* [2013] Med. L.R. 344.

[68] *Mallett v McMonagle* [1970] A.C. 166 at 176 per Lord Diplock. See also *Simpson v The London Midland and Scottish Railway Company*, 1931 S.C. (HL) 15 at 20 per Lord Dunedin.

[69] An alternative analysis may be carried out on a reduction of "median life expectancy": *Gregg v Scott* [2005] 2 A.C. 176 at 207 per Baroness Hale of Richmond. See also *JD v Mather* [2013] Med. L.R. 291.

It has been suggested that the spirit of the decision in *Gregg v Scott* confirms that there is no place for liability based on a loss of chance in personal injury, and especially medical negligence, cases.[70] Thus, the *Fairchild* exception is further confirmed as narrow in its application[71]—Mr Gregg was denied a remedy where the first GP's negligence had increased the risk of suffering harm in the future.

13–09   Nevertheless, liability for loss of chance has been held competent in claims for economic loss, both north[72] and south[73] of the border. A typical example is where a solicitor has failed to lodge papers with a court before the client's action becomes time-barred. The solicitor may be held liable to pay a proportion of the damages sought in the time-barred action based on an assessment of the chance of success accepted by the judge in the action brought by the client against the negligent solicitor.[74] Another example may be where, having a relative's claim in respect of a deceased whose life was shortened by a delictual wrong,[75] the relative's claim is reduced because his own life expectancy is shortened due to a delictual wrong, the delinquent responsible for the harm to the relative may be liable for the loss of chance of recovering in full the relative's claim in respect of the wrong done to the first deceased.[76] Another example may be where due to an unjustifiably poor reference drafted by a negligent former employer, a job applicant loses the chance of gaining employment.[77]

How then is the distinction between personal injury and economic loss claims justified in terms of liability for loss of chance? Although considerable attention was given to justifying their respective positions by their Lordships in *Gregg v Scott*, with a range of arguments being set out both pro[78] and con[79] the decision, little attention was paid to accounting for the distinction between personal injury and economic loss cases. It may simply be down to the fact that judges are professionals in law but not in medicine, and so are more comfortable in assessing chances in lost opportunities for litigation than in lost opportunities for medical treatment. Nevertheless, the fact that the decision was ultimately based on policy factors rather than principle was acknowledged:

> "It is always likely to be much easier to resolve issues of causation on a
> balance of probabilities than to identify in terms of percentage the effect that

---

[70] *Wright v Cambridge Medical Group* [2013] Q.B. 312 at 334 per Neuberger M.R.; at 337 per Elias L.J.

[71] *Gregg v Scott* [2005] 2 A.C. 176 at 196 per Lord Hoffmann.

[72] *Kyle v P & J Stormonth Darling WS*, 1993 S.C. 57; *Paul v Ogilvy*, 2001 S.L.T. 171; *McCrindle Group Ltd v Willis Corroon Scotland Ltd*, 2002 S.L.T. 209; *McCrindle Group Ltd v Maclay Murray & Spens* [2013] CSOH 72; 2013 G.W.D. 19–389.

[73] *Chaplin v Hicks* [1911] 2 K.B. 786; *Kitchen v Royal Air Force Association* [1958] 1 W.L.R. 563; *Allied Maples Group v Simmons and Simmons* [1995] 1 W. L. R. 1602. See also *Fox v British Airways Plc* [2013] I.C.R. 1257.

[74] See, e.g. *Kyle v P & J Stormonth Darling WS*, 1993 S.C. 57.

[75] See paras 5–19 to 5–22 above.

[76] According to the English Court of Appeal in *Haxton v Philips Electronics UK Ltd* [2014] 2 All E.R. 225, if makes no difference whether the original deceased's, and the relative's, lives are respectively shortened by the same wrong (as was the case on the facts), or by separate wrongs.

[77] See, e.g. *Spring v Guardian Assurance Plc*, 1995 2 A.C. 296 at 327 per Lord Lowry.

[78] *Gregg v Scott* [2005] 2 A.C. 176 at 197–199 per Lord Hoffmann; at 220–221 per Lord Phillips of Worth Matravers; at 233–234 per Baroness Hale of Richmond.

[79] *Gregg v Scott* [2005] 2 A.C. 176 at 189–190 per Lord Nicholls of Birkenhead; at 206 per Lord Hope of Craighead.

clinical negligence had on the chances of a favourable outcome. The reality is a policy factor that weighs against the introduction into this area of a right to compensation for the loss of a chance. A robust test which produces rough justice may be preferable to a test that on occasion will be difficult, if not impossible, to apply with confidence in practice."[80]

A *causa sine qua non* flowchart

It is suggested that it is possible to distill the complex case law on factual **13–10** causation into a flowchart involving four specific questions. The questions are complicated by having to consider the perspective from which the question is posed, i.e. is the question looking at the matter from the perspective of the wrong or from the perspective of the harm? They are further complicated by having to consider whether they are intended to filter out claims, or to permit them to proceed to the next stage, and by having to consider whether they should be answered on the basis of probabilities or possibilities.

Question 1: Does the evidence prove it more likely than not that that the harm was caused by the wrong?[81]

This question is posed from the perspective of the harm[82]—it traces backwards from the harm its cause (or causes). It is determined on the balance of probabilities. It is also permissive—if the answer to the question is "yes", causation is established. A "no" answer leads to the second question.

Question 2: Could the wrong possibly have caused the harm?[83]

This question is posed from the perspective of the wrong and so operates forwards from the wrong. It is determined by possibilities[84] rather than probabilities. It is a filtering question—if the answer is "no", causation will not be established and the claim must fail. A "yes" answer leads to the third question.

Question 3: Is it possible that the harm could have been caused by any other type of injurious agent?[85]

This question is asked from the perspective of the harm and so operates backwards. It is determined by possibilities rather than probabilities. It is a filtering question—if the answer is "yes", causation will not be established and the claim must fail. A "no" answer leads to the fourth question.

---

[80] *Gregg v Scott* [2005] 2 A.C. 176 at 220–221 per Lord Phillips of Worth Matravers.

[81] This question applies the test described in *Mallett v McMonagle* [1970] A.C. 166 at 176 per Lord Diplock.

[82] In one sense this question also performs a filtering function with regard to loss of chance in personal injury (at least those involving medical negligence) cases, since loss of the chance to avoid physical harm is not considered harm (i.e. *damnum*) per se: *Gregg v Scott* [2005] 2 A.C. 176.

[83] This question applies a pre-requisite element of the decisions in *Wardlaw v Bonnington Castings Ltd*, 1956 S.C. (HL) 26; *McGhee v National Coal Board*, 1973 S.C. (HL) 37; and *Fairchild v Glenhaven Funeral Services Ltd* [2003] 1 A.C. 32.

[84] See, e.g. *Kay's Tutor v Ayrshire and Arran Health Board*, 1987 S.C. (HL) 145; *McTear v Imperial Tobacco Ltd*, 2005 2 S.C. 1.

[85] This question applies the decision in *Wilsher v Essex Area Health Authority* [1988] A.C. 1074 as corrected by *Fairchild v Glenhaven Funeral Services Ltd* [2003] 1 A.C. 32.

Question 4: Has the wrong materially contributed to the risk of the harm, where that risk has eventuated?[86]

This question is posed from the perspective of the wrong and so operates forwards. It is determined by application of the de minimis rule—any wrong that is not de minimis is deemed a material contribution. The question is thus permissive—if the answer is "yes", causation is established. However, the question also provides a filter: if the answer is "no", causation is not established.

13–11

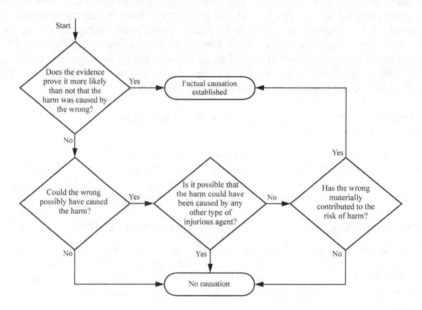

13–12   This flowchart should function effectively provided that the harm is clearly defined. It is suggested that a flawed definition of harm is the reason why the case of *Chester v Afshar*[87] does not appear to fit. The facts were as follows. A patient suffering from back problems was referred to a consultant surgeon, who advised the patient that the appropriate treatment required an operation. The operation carried a low risk of paralysis. The surgeon was negligent in failing to advise the patient of that risk. The patient agreed to the operation, which was carried out competently by the surgeon. The patient suffered paralysis, and sued. The patient admitted that had she been informed of the risk she would probably have gone ahead with the operation anyway, although she would have delayed its timing until she had received a second opinion.[88] Thus, given that the paralysis was an inherent risk in the procedure and could not be attributed to negligence in carrying out the operation, it was impossible to conclude that paralysis would, or could, have been avoided if the surgeon had advised the patient of the risk. It is suggested that had the *damnum* been viewed as the loss of autonomy the patient

---

[86] This question applies the exception from *Fairchild v Glenhaven Funeral Services Ltd* [2003] 1 A.C. 32.
[87] *Chester v Afshar* [2005] 1 A.C. 134.
[88] Cf. *Moyes v Lothian Health Board*, 1990 S.L.T. 444 at 447 per Lord Caplan.

suffered from effectively being denied the opportunity to consider the implications of the risk,[89] then causation could be established on the application of the
principles set out above. However, the majority in the House of Lords held that
the patient was entitled to damages for the paralysis itself, as to find otherwise
would mean that the surgeon's duty to warn was "a hollow one, stripped of all
its practical force and devoid of all content."[90] Thus, issues of culpability may
inevitably creep into what should in theory be an entirely pragmatic analysis into
causation.[91] Indeed, Lord Hope, in his leading speech in *Chester v Afshar*,
acknowledged the role of "policy" in determining factual causation:

> "But the issue of causation cannot be separated from issues of policy ...
> I would prefer to approach the issue which has arisen here as raising an issue
> of legal policy which a judge must decide. It is whether, in the unusual
> circumstances of this case, justice requires the normal approach to causation
> to be modified."[92]

LEGAL CAUSATION

Not only must the delictual wrong be a necessary pre-requisite for the harm to **13–13**
have occurred, it must also be sufficient to attract liability. Put another way, it
may not be enough for the pursuer to show that the wrong was a *causa sine qua
non* the loss; the wrong must also be *causa causans* the loss. Thus we must
consider what status the law demands of a wrong for it to qualify as *causa
causans* the harm. A wide range of terms have been used in this context:
including the real, dominant, efficient, effective, decisive, proximate, direct and
substantial cause of the harm. Many of these terms have been criticised for
a number of reasons. However, in answer to the logical and linguistic
difficulties associated with the exercise of separating out the legal cause of a loss,
judges have emphasised the "common sense" approach to be taken.[93] Thus,

---

[89] This was proposed in his dissenting opinion by Lord Hoffmann: *Chester v Afshar* [2005] 1 A.C.
134 at 147. See also *Goorkani v Tayside Health Board*, 1991 S.L.T. 94 at 95–96 per Lord
Cameron of Lochbroom: " ... the loss, injury and damage sustained as a consequence of the
failure to warn the pursuer of the risk ... is restricted to the degree of distress and anxiety which
arose from the discovery of the risk." It is also submitted that the decision in *Stevens v Yorkhill
NHS Trust*, 2006 S.L.T. 889 confirms that Scots law would have the capacity, based on the *actio
injuriarum*, to determine *damnum* as loss of autonomy (alternatively as affront to dignity) in such
a case.

[90] *Chester v Afshar* [2005] 1 A.C. 134 at 162–163 per Lord Hope of Craighead.

[91] Could the decision be viewed as creating liability for loss of chance in a medical negligence case,
i.e. loss of the chance to take the operation at a different time when, given the relatively low risk
of paralysis, it would be more likely than not that paralysis would not have occurred? If so, is this
decision affected by the decision of the House of Lords in *Gregg v Scott* [2005] 2 A.C. 176?

[92] *Chester v Afshar* [2005] 1 A.C. 134 at 162 per Lord Hope of Craighead. See also *Lamb v Camden
LBC* [1981] Q.B. 625 at 636 per Lord Denning. Cf. J. Stapleton, "Occam's Razor Reveals an
Orthodox Basis for *Chester v Afshar*" (2006) 122 L.Q.R. 426.

[93] "No formula can be devised which will provide a universal touchstone for the infinite variety of
circumstances which may arise. Each case must be judged in the light of its own facts and by
resorting, not to the refinements of the philosophical doctrine of causation, but to the
commonplace tests which the ordinary business man conversant with such matters would adopt":
Yorkshire Dale Steamship Co v Minister of War Transport [1942] A.C. 691 at 702 per Lord
MacMillan. See also, e.g. *Stapley v Gypsum Mines Ltd* [1953] A.C. 663 at 681 per Lord Reid.

"(t)he second inquiry ... involves a value judgment (' ... *ought* to be held liable ... ')."[94]

Whereas the onus of proof is on the pursuer to establish that the delictual wrong is a *causa sine qua non* the loss (i.e. factual causation), the onus is on the defender to challenge its status as *causa causans*. In other words, if the pursuer satisfies the court that the wrong was a necessary pre-requisite for the harm, the status of the wrong is presumed to be sufficient to attract liability. Thus it may be said that the onus of proof shifts at this point to the defender. As well as the range of substantive defences recognised in the Scots law of delict, the defender potentially can deploy at least two arguments within the field of causation to avoid liability: first that the "chain of causation" was "broken" by a novus actus interveniens; and secondly that the wrong did no more than create the opportunity for the harm to be suffered by the pursuer. Closely related to causation proper is the concept of remoteness of damage. Thus:

> "The law has to set a limit to the causally connected losses for which a defendant is to be held responsible. In the ordinary language of lawyers, losses outside the limit may bear one of several labels. They may be described as too remote because the wrongful conduct was not a substantial or proximate cause, or because the loss was the product of an intervening cause. The defendant's responsibility may be excluded because the plaintiff failed to mitigate his loss. Familiar principles, such as foreseeability, assist in promoting some consistency of general approach. These are guidelines, some more helpful than others, but they are never more than this."[95]

Novus actus interveniens

13–14　　Literally, a new act intervening, a novus actus interveniens will break the chain of causation, usually replacing the defender's wrong as the predominant cause of the harm suffered by the pursuer. A novus actus interveniens may typically be the act of a third party, which may or may not be a delictual wrong in itself, but it may be the actions of the pursuer himself[96] (but not of the defender)[97] or it may be a natural event.[98] An example may be where a negligent driver has collided with a pedestrian who suffers non-life threatening injuries that nevertheless require hospital treatment. If on the way to the hospital the pedestrian is killed when the ambulance is involved in a crash, whatever caused that crash becomes the predominant cause of the death. Although but for the driver's negligence the pedestrian would never have been in the ambulance and so would have avoided the crash, the second incident will be treated as a novus actus interveniens, breaking the chain of causation. The negligent driver who ran over the pedestrian will remain liable for the pedestrian's pain and suffering, which would of course terminate at the point of death, but would avoid liability for the death itself.

---

[94] *Kuwait Airways Corpn v Iraqi Airways Co (Nos 4 and 5)* [2002] 2 A.C. 883 at 1091 per Lord Nicholls of Birkenhead.

[95] *Kuwait Airways Corpn v Iraqi Airways Co (Nos 4 and 5)* [2002] 2 A.C. 883 at 1091 per Lord Nicholls of Birkenhead.

[96] *McKew v Holland & Hannen & Cubitts (Scotland) Ltd*, 1970 S.C. (HL) 20.

[97] *Bolitho (Deceased) v City and Hackney Health Authority* [1998] A.C. 232. See also *McLaughlin v Morrison*, 2014 S.L.T. 111 where no causal link was accepted in connecting the criminal act of the pursuer with a criminal act of the defender carried out apparently in retaliation to the first.

[98] See, e.g. *Carslogie Steamship Co Ltd v Royal Norwegian Government (The Carslogie)* [1952] A.C. 292.

Modifying the facts of the scenario may bring into focus questions about the definition of novus actus interveniens: if the original collision left the pedestrian with injuries that could be fatal if not treated quickly, and the ambulance was delayed by a traffic jam on the way to the incident, would the delay amount to a novus actus interveniens so absolving the negligent driver from liability for the death of the pedestrian? What if the negligent driver was caught up in the traffic jam at the time? What if a helicopter was known to be deployed in the area as an air ambulance because traffic jams were common? In Lord Wright's view:

> "To break the chain of causation it must be shown that there is something which I will call ultroneous, something unwarrantable, a new cause which disturbs the sequence of events, something which can be described as either unreasonable or extraneous or extrinsic."[99]

Thus not every event or action following a wrong will amount to a novus actus interveniens. The defender will remain legally responsible for those that do not break the chain of causation,[100] and the law has developed mechanisms to apportion liability among joint wrongdoers[101] or to place some responsibility upon the pursuer[102] where appropriate. What then are the factors that the court will consider in deciding whether an act or event following a wrong amounts to a novus actus interveniens?

Foreseeability[103]

If the act or event is a foreseeable consequence of the defender's wrong, it will **13–15** not break the chain of causation.[104] Whether the act or event is foreseeable may be assessed by considering its probability:

> "Unless the judge can be satisfied that the result of the human action is highly probable or very likely he may have to conclude that all that the reasonable man could say was that it was a mere possibility. Unless the needle that measures the probability of a particular result flowing from the conduct of a human agent is near the top of the scale it may be hard to conclude that it has risen sufficiently from the bottom to create the duty reasonably to foresee it."[105]

---

[99] *The Oropesa* [1943] P. 32 at 39 per Lord Wright.

[100] See also paras 4–02 to 4–03 and 11–20 to 11–24 above.

[101] See, e.g. *Owners of the Boy Andrew v Owners of the St Rognvald*, 1947 S.C. (HL) 70. Liability will be apportioned on a joint and several basis under Law Reform (Miscellaneous Provisions) (Scotland) Act 1940 s.3: see para.13–03 above.

[102] Law Reform (Contributory Negligence) Act 1945. This development justified the abandoning of the "last opportunity rule" attributed to the decision in *Davies v Mann* (1842) 10 M. & W. 546: see, e.g. *Davies v Swan Motor Co (Swansea) Ltd* [1949] 2 K.B. 291.

[103] There is an acknowledged overlap with duty of care issues in negligence here: "In all these cases you will find that the three questions, duty, causation, and remoteness, run continually into one another. It seems to me that they are simply three different ways of looking at one and the same problem": *Roe v Minister of Health* [1954] 2 Q.B. 66 at 85 per Denning L.J. Is this why Lord Hoffmann used the term "scope of liability" in the context of causation and remoteness of damage in *South Australia Asset Management Corp v York Montague Ltd* sub nom. *Banque Bruxelles Lambert SA v Eagle Star Insurance Co Ltd* [1997] A.C. 191 at 212?

[104] See, e.g. *Dorset Yacht Co Ltd v Home Office* [1970] AC 1004 at 1030 per Lord Reid.

[105] *Maloco v Littlewoods Organisation Ltd*, 1987 S.C. (HL) 37 at 68 per Lord MacKay of Clashfern.

It should be remembered that it has also been held that the duty reasonably to foresee extends to events that occur in an abnormal way or to an unexpected extent provided that these consequences are of a type of damage that is foreseeable.[106] Somewhat anomalously, it has been held in England that medical negligence is a foreseeable consequence of an accident, although gross medical negligence constitutes a novus actus interveniens.[107]

Thus, foreseeability may again be seen as a slippery concept which is difficult precisely to define. A range of factors will have an impact, both on the foreseeability test to be adopted, and upon its significance in dealing with the issue. These factors include

> "the nature of the event or act, the time it occurred, the place where it occurred, the identity of the perpetrator and his intentions, and responsibility, if any, for taking measures to avoid the occurrence and matters of public policy."[108]

Reasonableness

13–16   The wrongdoer will not generally be liable for the consequences of unreasonable acts or omissions by the pursuer or by third parties which impact on the consequences of the wrong. Thus, in *Knightley v Johns*,[109] where, after the defendant had overturned his car inside a one-way road tunnel, a police officer instructed a police motor-cyclist to ride through the tunnel against the flow of traffic, the defendant was not liable for the injuries sustained by the motor-cyclist in a collision with another car. The instructions of the police officer in charge were so unreasonable as to amount to a novus actus interveniens.

A mere error of judgment will not amount to a novus actus interveniens. However, in *McKew v Holland, Hannen and Cubitts*[110] because the error of judgment was a consequence of the unreasonable actions of the pursuer, the defenders avoided liability. Mr McKew had sustained a leg injury due to his employer's breach of duty. Because of this sometimes his leg would give way without warning. In spite of this, Mr McKew chose unaided (even although his wife and brother-in-law were on hand to provide support) to descend a steep staircase with no handrail. As luck would have it, his leg gave way some steps from the foot of the staircase, whereupon the pursuer "performed a not inconsiderable acrobatic feat in jumping down ten steps clear,"[111] breaking his ankle in the process! Although the leap itself was considered a mere error of judgment in the House of Lords, Mr McKew's decision to "descend in such a way that when his leg gave way he could not stop himself" was unreasonable. It should have been obvious to him that more care was required "if he had given the matter a moment's thought."[112]

---

[106] *Hughes v Lord Advocate*, 1963 S.C. (HL) 31; *Jolley v Sutton LBC* [2000] 1 W.L.R. 1082. See also *Overseas Tankship (UK) Ltd v Morts Dock & Engineering Co (The Wagon Mound (No. 1))* [1961] A.C. 388; *Simmons v British Steel Plc*, 2004 S.C. (HL) 94.

[107] *Webb v Barclays Bank Plc* [2002] P.I.Q.R. P8.

[108] *Lamb v Camden LBC* [1981] Q. B. 625 at 647 per Watkins L.J.

[109] *Knightley v Johns* [1982] 1 W.L.R. 349.

[110] *McKew v Holland, Hannen and Cubitts*, 1970 S.C. (HL) 20.

[111] *McKew v Holland, Hannen and Cubitts*, 1970 S.C. (HL) 20 at 27 per Lord Guest.

[112] *McKew v Holland & Hannen & Cubitts (Scotland) Ltd*, 1970 S.C. (HL) 20 at 25 per Lord Reid.

The decision in *McKew* may suggest considerable overlap between unreasonable behaviour constituting a novus actun intervenieno and the defence of volenti non fit injuria. Similarly, where a pursuer's acts are not so unreasonable as to break the chain of causation, the defender may be able to rely upon the defence of contributory negligence. Thus, where a woman sustained injury when unsuccessfully trying to escape by climbing through the narrow gap above the door of a public toilet cubicle within which she had become trapped (due to a poorly maintained lock), pleas of novus actus interveniens and volenti were rejected, although damages were reduced by 25 per cent due to the woman's contributory negligence in choosing an obviously hazardous means of escape.[113]

However, if the pursuer's actions albeit unreasonable are actions that the defender is under a duty to prevent, the defender will remain fully liable. For example, if the police detain a known suicide risk but negligently allow the detainee access to the means to take his own life, the police will be prevented from arguing novus actus interveniens, volenti or contributory negligence.[114] Similarly, the suicide of an employee who suffers depression on account of a failure by the employer to provide a safe system of work may not amount to unreasonable conduct which breaks the chain of causation.[115] However, the ex turpi causa non oritur actio rule will preclude liability for the consequences to the pursuer of his own criminal act, even where but for the defender's delictual wrong the pursuer would not have committed the crime.[116]

Policy

Policy considerations tend to be more openly acknowledged and discussed by **13–17** judges when considering a disputed claim that a defender owes a pursuer a duty of care, especially in "novel" cases. However, as is noted above, there is significant overlap between "duty" issues and "causation" issues, especially with regard to the defender's liability for the acts or omissions of third parties, or indeed the pursuer, preceding or following the defender's delictual wrong. The relative economic positions of the parties may be a factor in the decision-making process, i.e. who is best placed to bear the loss or to obtain insurance? Indeed, if liability is based on a "general public sentiment of moral wrongdoing for which the offender must pay"[117] judges may be influenced by a predicted public sentiment of moral outrage if legal logic runs its course.

Thus, the person who behaves instinctively rather than rationally in times of peril should not be measured against a test that is detached from the heat of the moment.[118] Likewise, where the defender's wrong has removed from the victim the personal autonomy required to make rational decisions, the victim should not be prevented from obtaining a remedy from the original wrongdoer just because the victim has acted in a way that would normally be seen as unreasonable,

---

[113] *Sayers v Harlow Urban DC* [1958] 1 W.L.R. 623.

[114] *Kirkham v Chief Constable of Greater Manchester* [1990] 2 Q.B. 283. Cf. *Reeves v Commissioner of Police of the Metropolis* [2000] 1 A.C. 360.

[115] *Corr v IBC Vehicles Ltd* [2008] 1 A.C. 884.

[116] *Gray v Thames Trains Ltd* [2009] 1 A.C. 1339. The turpis causa defence is discussed below at para.14–09.

[117] *Donoghue v Stevenson*, 1932 S.C. (HL) 31 at 44 per Lord Atkin.

[118] See, e.g. *Wallace v Bergius*, 1915 S.C. 205; *Baker v T.E. Hopkins & Son Ltd* and *Ward v T.E. Hopkins & Son Ltd* [1959] 1 W.L.R. 966.

irrational or purely voluntary.[119] After all, the general public sentiment may be anticipated that overall the ultimate harm was still the wrongdoer's fault. But what might the general public sentiment be to fixing the suicidal prisoner, or the suicidal employee driven to depression by their employer, with contributory negligence?[120] And what if the psychiatric injury inflicted by an employer on an employee changes the employee's character so that he commits a serious crime?[121]

Creation of the opportunity to suffer a loss

13–18   A wrongdoer will not be liable where the wrong merely creates the opportunity for the pursuer to suffer a loss. This was asserted by the Court of Appeal in England in *Galoo Ltd v Bright Grahame and Murray*.[122] This was an action brought against the auditors of a company who had, over a period of years, certified the company's accounts as representing a true and fair view of the company's financial position; when in fact they did not. The accounts portrayed a profitable and valuable company, failing to reveal that it was in fact incurring substantial losses and actually worthless. The question was whether, assuming that the auditors had in fact breached a duty of care owed to the company, they were liable for the trading losses suffered as a result of the company's continuing to trade in the belief that it was profitable, when, had the true picture been revealed, the company would have ceased trading immediately. The auditors were held not to be liable: their negligence had merely created the opportunity or set the stage[123] for the company to suffer loss, it was not the catalyst.[124] Thus, the "but-for" test was insufficient in itself to establish liability.

The rationale for the decision in *Galoo* appears to be that the wrong committed by the defender does not disturb the autonomy of the pursuer: although the defender's wrong is an essential pre-requisite of the loss, the autonomous actions of the pursuer amount to the predominant cause of the loss. This rationale has not so far been applied as such outside of pure economic loss cases—and rarely within that field—but it is suggested it could play a significant role in providing a coherent analysis for some difficult cases where the decisions have been criticised as unprincipled. This may be especially apposite in Scots law, given the opportunity to recognise affront, here in the indignity of being deprived of one's autonomy, as *damnum*.[125]

For example, in what have been described as "wrongful conception" cases[126] where conception of an unwanted child has occurred following a failed sterilisation operation, the House of Lords controversially decided that "legal policy" prohibited an award of damages for anything other than the pain and

---

[119] *Kirkham v Chief Constable of Greater Manchester* [1990] 2 Q.B. 283.

[120] *Reeves v Commissioner of Police of the Metropolis* [2000] 1 A.C. 360; *Corr v IBC Vehicles Ltd* [2008] 1 A.C. 184.

[121] *Meah v McCreamer (No.2)* [1986] 1 All E.R. 943; *Gray v Thames Trains Ltd* [2009] 1 A.C. 1339.

[122] *Galoo Ltd v Bright Grahame and Murray* [1994] 1 W.L.R. 1360. See also *JEB Fasteners Ltd v Marks Bloom & Co* [1983] 1 All E.R. 583.

[123] *R v Hughes* [2013] 1 W.L.R. 2461.

[124] *Sasea Finance Ltd (In Liquidation) v KPMG (formerly KPMG Peat Marwick McLintock) (No.2)* [2000] 1 All E.R. 676.

[125] *Stevens v Yorkhill NHS Trust*, 2006 S.L.T. 889.

[126] *McFarlane v Tayside Health Board*, 2000 S.C. (HL) 1; *Rees v Darlington Memorial Hospital NHS Trust* [2004] 1 A.C. 309. These cases are discussed in more detail at paras 11–67 to 11–70 above.

suffering associated with giving birth to a child, but carved out of thin air a "conventional award" of £15,000 for the loss of autonomy in determining the size of one's family. It is suggested that *damnum* in such cases may include: first, loss of autonomy in determining the size of one's family; secondly, the pain and suffering associated with pregnancy and childbirth; thirdly, the costs of the upbringing of a healthy child; and fourthly, the additional costs in providing for a disabled child. The first of these flows directly from the wrong but, since other factors also have a role to play in creating the condition, the wrong may be seen as merely providing the opportunity rather than the legal cause for the second and third. As for the fourth category, it would depend on whether any disability arose independently of the wrong, or as its direct consequence, whether the wrong could be said to merely create the opportunity for the loss or whether it should be treated as the catalyst.

It is suggested that identifying the patient's loss of autonomy as a distinct form of *damnum* would also provide a more coherent resolution in *Chester v Afshar*,[127] and would distinguish liability for the loss of autonomy from liability for the physical incapacity. Even should the surgeon's failure to warn the patient of the risk properly have satisfied the "but-for" test with regard to the paralysis (in that the patient would probably have had the operation at a different time and, given the low level of risk involved, it was more likely than not that paralysis would not have occurred at a different time), the failure to warn merely created the opportunity for the risk to eventuate rather than acting as its catalyst.

It is also suggested that the concept may be open to manufacturers of products which, when used for the purpose for which they were manufactured, are known to carry a likelihood of harm or damage. The most obvious are tobacco and alcohol products. Thus, the tobacco manufacturer, assuming that they have been found to be in breach of duty, may point out that the placing of the product on the market does no more than create the opportunity for the consumer to suffer smoking related diseases, since the smoker chooses to continue smoking. This argument would appear to carry more weight since the dangers of smoking are well known and therefore should be obvious to the smoker.[128] However, what may complicate this example is the addictive quality of the product. As suggested above, the argument that the creation of the opportunity is in itself not enough to establish a causal link sufficient to attract liability is based on the recognition that the pursuer enjoys at least a significant level of autonomy in the making of the decision to engage in or to continue the damaging activity. However, where the addictive quality of the product is thrown into the equation, this undermines the autonomy of the pursuer and so it becomes more difficult to argue that the manufacturer does no more than to create the opportunity for the pursuer to suffer the loss.

Thus it is suggested that the decision in *Galoo* has potential for development so as to provide the defender from whom a remedy for the consequences of his wrong is sought with another string to his bow in challenging the action. This has been described as a "developing area of the law" and it is suggested that the potential scope of its application has yet to be realised.

---

[127] *Chester v Afshar* [2005] 1 A.C. 134. See para.13–12 above.

[128] See, e.g. *McTear v Imperial Tobacco Ltd*, 2005 2 S.C. 1 ("addiction" to tobacco); *Calvert v William Hill Credit Ltd* [2009] Ch. 330 ("addiction" to gambling); *St George v Home Office* [2009] 1 W.L.R. 1670 ("addiction" to drugs and alcohol).

REMOTENESS OF DAMAGE

13–19 Consider the following scenario. A woman is travelling in a taxi on the slip road leaving a motorway on the exit to an airport when it is involved in an accident, caused by another driver's negligence. The woman is injured and has to be taken to hospital by ambulance. She had been intending to board a flight from the airport so as to attend a business meeting where she was due to complete a contract on behalf of her employer. Because she misses the flight, she misses the meeting, and does not complete the contract. Not only does the woman lose the bonus she was anticipating on completing the deal, she is also made redundant because the lost profit puts her employer out of business! Because she no longer has a salary, she is refused the mortgage she had applied for to allow her to buy the house she wanted. Both the woman's and the employer's losses (and those of other employees also made redundant) have been caused by the driver's negligence. Should the driver be liable for all of the consequences of his delictual wrong, or is there a legal boundary line beyond which losses are too remote?

In his classic dictum in *Donoghue v Stevenson*, Lord Atkin said "rules of law arise which limit the range of complaints *and* the extent of their remedy."[129] The "range of complaints" element no doubt was intended to refer to the duty of care concept that was central to the significance of the decision. The duty of care concept as a limiting device therefore draws a legal boundary line based on remoteness of *relationship*. The "extent of their remedy" element would appear to distinguish a separate legal limiting device creating a boundary line.[130] This is the concept of remoteness of *damage*.[131]

It may thus be seen that Lord Atkin refers to legal boundary lines in two separate dimensions. Reverting to the analogy of throwing a stone in a pool of water, ripples will span out horizontally across the surface of the water, striking any objects which protrude the surface. The duty of care device creates a legal boundary line in that horizontal first dimension: objects within that boundary are sufficiently proximate to the splash whereas those beyond the line have too remote a relationship with the splash.[132] The second dimension may be viewed as the *height* of the ripples that strike an object. The second legal boundary line operates in that vertical second dimension: where an object is swamped by a wave that is higher than the boundary line, that "damage" suffered by the object is too remote to attract liability, even although the object itself was within the first dimension boundary line.

As will be seen below, there is perhaps a third dimension to delictual liability which, in the ripples across the pond analogy, may be equated with the *force* by

---

[129] *Donoghue v Stevenson*, 1932 S.C. (HL) 31 at 44 (emphasis added).

[130] Cardozo C.J. also distinguished "amount" from "class" in *Ultramares Corporation v Touche* (1931) 255 N.Y. 170 at 179: "liability in an indeterminate amount for an indeterminate time to an indeterminate class".

[131] Making that distinction at that time is part of what made *Donoghue v Stevenson* such a watershed decision. Before Donoghue, perhaps more so in Scotland than in England, keeping liability within boundaries that society could cope with was achieved by the "remoteness of damage" concept. Distinguishing "duty of care" from "remoteness of damage" was of vital significance in creating the legal landscape in which the modern law of negligence has grown and developed.

[132] It may be better to think of the relationship as being with the person who has caused the splash—the wrongdoer.

which a ripple impacts upon the object in the water. It appears that there is no legal boundary line in this dimension[133]; so no matter the impact of the ripple upon the object, so long as the object itself is within the first legal boundary line, and the height of the wave within the second, delictual liability will arise. Similarly, as will also be seen, if the object is vulnerable to greater harm due to an inherent weakness, liability for the harm actually sustained will not be subject to any additional legal boundaries.[134]

Remoteness of damage may be an issue not only in negligence cases, but indeed in any case involving delictual liability. The assault may cause the victim to suffer more severe injuries than may be predicted; the fraud more serious economic consequences for the victim than were intended[135]; the nuisance more physical, emotional or economic consequences than were reasonably foreseeable; the defamatory statement may "go viral".[136] In principle the intentional wrongdoer is liable for all of the consequences to his intended victim, whether foreseeable or not. However, the rules may differ in detail according to the specific delict at issue and specialist works should be consulted as appropriate.[137]

Subject to special rules applying to specific intentional delicts, in general the **13–20** onus of proof with regard to remoteness of damage issues is on the defender. Although there is some overlap between remoteness of damage and causation, remoteness of damage should be treated as a separate issue. Indeed, the enquiry into causation is in principle carried out from the perspective of the harm (what caused the harm), whereas the enquiry into remoteness of damage is carried out from the perspective of the wrong (how far from the wrong were the consequences). Logically, remoteness of damage becomes an issue only after liability has been established, and so falls for consideration after not only duty, breach and causation have been established, but also after consideration of any defences.

The starting point[138] in any discussion on remoteness of damage is found in the case of *Allan v Barclay*.[139] An employee of the pursuer was injured in a road collision caused by the defender's negligence. The pursuer claimed damages for the costs involved in obtaining replacement cover for the employee while he recuperated. Lord Kinloch had this to say:

> "The grand rule on the subject of damages is, that none can be claimed except such as naturally and directly arise out of the wrong done; and such, therefore, as may reasonably be supposed to have been in the view of the

---

[133] See, e.g. *Hughes v Lord Advocate*, 1963 S.C. (HL) 31; *Simmons v British Steel Plc*, 2004 S.C. (HL) 94. Cf. *Overseas Tankship (UK) Ltd v Morts Dock & Engineering Co (The Wagon Mound (No.1))* [1961] A.C. 388.

[134] The wrongdoer takes his victim as he finds him: *McKillen v Barclay Curle & Co Ltd*, 1967 S.L.T. 41; *Simmons v British Steel Plc*, 2004 S.C. (HL) 94.

[135] See, e.g. *Smith New Court Securities Ltd v Scrimgeour Vickers (Asset Management) Ltd* [1997] A.C. 254.

[136] See, e.g. *Cairns v Modi* [2013] E.M.L.R. 8. See also *Slipper v BBC* [1991] 1 Q.B. 283. Cf. *McManus v Beckham* [2002] 1 W.L.R. 2982.

[137] See, e.g. J.M. Thomson, *Delict* (Edinburgh: W. Green/SULI, 2010); *Stair Memorial Encyclopaedia*.

[138] *Simmons v British Steel Plc*, 2004 S.C. (HL) 94 at 115 per Lord Rodger of Earlsferry.

[139] *Allan v Barclay* (1864) 2 M. 873.

wrongdoer.[140] Tried by this test, the present claim appears to fail. The personal injuries of the individual himself will be properly held to have been in the contemplation of the wrongdoer. But he cannot be held bound to have surmised the secondary injuries done to all holding relations with the individual, whether that of a master, or any other."[141]

As discussed in Ch.3,[142] a modern view of the facts in *Allan v Barclay* would see the pursuer as a secondary victim of the wrong suing for pure economic loss and subject to the exclusionary rule that operates in such cases.[143] Nevertheless, Lord Kinloch's dictum remains important (at least as a starting point if not a grand rule) in the context of the modern understanding of remoteness of damage. However, there is an inherent tension in Lord Kinloch's explanation: harm can be a natural and direct consequence of a wrong without it being reasonably forseeable. This begs the question: if there are two limbs to Lord Kinloch's "grand rule" are they alternatives, or is one intended to be subject to the other?

This tension led to what might be described as the *Polemis/Wagon Mound* dichotomy. In *Re Polemis*[144] due to stevedores' negligence, a wooden plank fell into a ship's hold. When the plank struck the inside of the hold, it apparently generated a spark which ignited fumes in the hold resulting in a fire which consumed the ship. It was accepted that the fire was unforeseeable. However, the court held that a negligent wrongdoer becomes liable for all of the consequences of the negligence, provided these are "natural and direct". Thus, the firm of stevedores was liable.

13–21   In *The Wagon Mound (No.1)*,[145] as a result of stevedores' negligence, furnace oil being loaded onto a ship (The Wagon Mound) moored in Sydney Harbour spilled into the sea. The tide and wind caused the oil to collect around a neighbouring timber wharf owned by the plaintiffs where two ships were berthed. Upon seeing the floating oil, the manager of the plaintiff's wharf took advice on the likelihood of the oil catching fire before allowing workers to commence welding work since the work would likely involve molten pieces of metal falling into the contaminated water. The advice received apparently confirmed the manager's belief that the oil could not be ignited and he gave the order for welding work to continue. Shortly thereafter, a fire started which spread across the oil, destroying the plaintiff's wharf and the two ships. It was accepted that the fire was likely caused by a piece of molten metal created by the welding work

---

[140] Note the obvious influence from the dictum of Alderson B. in *Hadley v Baxendale* (1854) 9 Exch. 341 at 355: "Where two parties have made a contract which one of them has broken, the damages which the other party ought to receive in respect of such breach of contract should be such as may fairly and reasonably be considered either arising naturally, i.e. according to the usual course of things, from such breach of contract itself, or such as may reasonably be supposed to have been in the contemplation of both parties, at the time they made the contract, as the probable result of the breach of it." The rules on remoteness of damage were then accepted as generally similar in both contract and negligence cases.

[141] *Allan v Barclay* (1864) 2 M. 873 at 874 per Lord Kinloch.

[142] At paras 3–04 to 3–06. See also paras 11–14 and 11–40 to 11–43 above.

[143] In the ripples in the pond analogy, the employer would be an object that protruded outside the horizontal dimension boundary line and that was struck only by ricochet ripples emanating from the protruding object representing the employee (which Lord Kinloch indicates falls within the horizontal boundary line).

[144] *Re Polemis* [1921] 3 K.B. 560.

[145] *The Wagon Mound (No.1)* [1961] A.C. 388.

falling onto a rag floating on the oil, which smouldered for long enough to cause the rag to ignite. The court held that as damage by fire (distinguished from damage by pollution) was unforeseeable, the damage was too remote. In so holding, the court expressly questioned the correctness of the approach in *Polemis*.

The dilemma created by this dichotomy seems at first sight to have been resolved by the decision of the House of Lords in the Scottish case of *Simmons v British Steel Plc*.[146] The pursuer suffered a head injury following an accident caused by his employer's negligence. Although he recovered from the head injury, the psychiatric impact of the incident was such that he suffered an exacerbation of a pre-existing skin condition (psoriasis) and never returned to work. The employer admitted liability for the head injury, but argued that the psychiatric harm and psoriasis were too remote. Following *Page v Smith*,[147] the House of Lords held that the thin skull rule applied, and so being required to take his victim as he finds him, the employer was liable for all of the consequences, whether foreseeable or not.

In *Simmons*, the House of Lords took the opportunity to set out the law on remoteness of damage. Lord Rodger summarised the position in Scotland as follows (authorities in footnotes):

"(1) The starting point is that a defender is not liable for a consequence of a kind which is not reasonably foreseeable[148];

(2) While a defender is not liable for damage that was not reasonably foreseeable, it does not follow that he is liable for all damage that was reasonably foreseeable: depending on the circumstances, the defender may not be liable for damage caused by a novus actus interveniens or unreasonable conduct on the part of the pursuer, even if it was reasonably foreseeable[149];

(3) Subject to the qualification in (2), if the pursuer's injury is of a kind that was foreseeable, the defender is liable, even if the damage is greater in extent than was foreseeable or it was caused in a way that could not have been foreseen[150];

(4) The defender must take his victim as he finds him[151];

(5) Subject again to the qualification in (2), where personal injury to the pursuer was reasonably foreseeable, the defender is liable for any personal injury, whether physical or psychiatric, which the pursuer suffers as a result of his wrongdoing.[152]"[153]

---

[146] *Simmons v British Steel Plc*, 2004 S.C. (HL) 94.

[147] *Page v Smith* [1996] 1 A.C. 155.

[148] *McKew v Holland & Hannen & Cubitts (Scotland) Ltd*, 1970 S.C. (HL) 20 at 25 per Lord Reid; *Bourhill v Young*, 1942 S.C. (HL) 78 at 85 per Lord Russell of Killowen; *Allan v Barclay* (1864) 2 M. 873 at 874 per Lord Kinloch.

[149] *McKew v Holland & Hannen & Cubitts (Scotland) Ltd*, 1970 S.C. (HL) 20 at 25 per Lord Reid; *Lamb v Camden LBC* [1981] Q.B. 625; but see *Ward v Cannock Chase DC* [1986] Ch. 546. It is submitted that these should be viewed as causation issues, in other words, relevant to determining culpability/liability rather than to compensation/remoteness of damage.

[150] *Hughes v Lord Advocate*, 1963 S.C. (HL) 31 at 38, 40 per Lord Reid.

[151] *Bourhill v Young*, 1942 S.C. (HL) 78 at 92 per Lord Wright; *McKillen v Barclay Curle & Co Ltd*, 1967 S.L.T. 41 at 42 per Lord President Clyde.

[152] *Page v Smith* [1996] 1 A.C. 155 at 197F–H per Lord Lloyd of Berwick.

[153] *Simmons v British Steel Plc*, 2004 S.C. (HL) 94 at 115 per Lord Rodger of Earlsferry.

Reasonable foreseeability

13–22   Lord Rodger accepted that the correct interpretation of Lord Kinloch's grand rule is that it imposed a filter based on reasonable foreseeability. Lord Hope concurred,[154] taking the view that Lord Kinloch's use of the word "therefore" in connecting the two limbs confirms that although the losses must be "natural and direct", the ultimate test is reasonable foreseeability. Thus, subject to the rules set out below, losses which may be natural and direct, but are not reasonably foreseeable, will be too remote.

A question that has arisen is whether the test of reasonable forseeability differs depending on whether it is being used to assess culpability (duty, breach and causation) or compensation (remoteness of damage). In principle the answer is no.[155] In practice, as will be seen immediately below, the answer is not so clear.

Damage greater in extent than was foreseeable

13–23   This point has often been treated by commentators as a culpability/liability issue, rather than one of compensation/remoteness of damage. However, taking the analogy of the ripples in the pool as set out above, if the "dimension" in question is the force of the impact of the waves rather than the horizontal range of the waves, it is suggested that it is more logical and coherent to treat this issue as one of remoteness of damage.

Lord Rodger qualified this section by reference to "kind of injury". This potentially opens a hornet's nest. How is injury classified by kind? In the *Wagon Mound (No.1)*, which was treated as dealing with compensation rather than culpability, a distinction was made between damage to property caused by pollution (which was foreseeable) and damage to property caused by fire (which was unforeseeable). Thus, the court justified denial of liability for foreseeable consequences (damage to property) caused by unforeseeable means (fire, as distinguished from pollution). On the other hand, in *Page v Smith*,[156] which was treated as dealing with culpability rather than compensation, it was held that the law should not distinguish between physical injury and psychiatric harm suffered by a primary victim who feared for his own personal safety in a minor road accident, but that both should be treated as forms of "personal injury". Thus, the court justified liability for unforeseeable consequences (psychiatric injury) caused by foreseeable means (the mental trauma associated with involvement in a car crash). The two cases appear inconsistent and, if the concept of reasonable foreseeability indeed should operate in the same way irrespective of whether the question is as to culpability or compensation, it follows that one must have been wrongly decided. The treatment of the *Wagon Mound (No.1)* by Lord Lloyd in *Page v Smith*[157] may be viewed as splitting hairs, but it does call into question whether hair-splitting was what was really going on in the *Wagon Mound (No.1)*.[158] Lord Rodger's analysis in *Simmons* seems more consistent with *Page*

---

[154] *Simmons v British Steel Plc*, 2004 S.C. (HL) 94 at 100.

[155] See, e.g. *Bourhill v Young*, 1942 S.C. (HL) 78 at 85 per Lord Russell of Killowen; *Overseas Tankship (UK) Ltd v Morts Dock & Engineering Co (The Wagon Mound (No. 1))* [1961] A.C. 388 per Viscount Simonds (delivering the Opinion of the Court).

[156] *Page v Smith* [1996] 1 A.C. 155.

[157] *Page v Smith* [1996] 1 A.C. 155 at 195–196.

[158] Had the plaintiffs argued that oil floating on water created a foreseeable risk of fire they would have been met with the defence of contributory negligence, which at the time was a complete defence in New South Wales.

v Smith, but he did not assert that *Wagon Mound (No.1)* was wrongly decided on this point,[159] On the other hand, the conflation of psychiatric with physical injury in *Page v Smith* has also been questioned.[160]

Nevertheless, the three-dimensional model of the ripples in the pool analogy may confirm that *Hughes v Lord Advocate*[161] is relevant to compensation rather than to culpability and so properly classified as a remoteness of damage case. In *Hughes*, a boy was severely burned when he tripped over a paraffin lamp. The paraffin vapourised and the mixture ignited in a violent explosion, the effects of which were exacerbated by the confined space in which the accident occurred. Although it was accepted that it was reasonably foreseeable that paraffin would leak out of the lamp if it was dropped, and that the resulting pool of paraffin would catch fire - creating the risk of burning, it was not reasonably foreseeable that the paraffin would vapourise and explode. So the means by which the personal injury was caused (by burning) was foreseeable as was the kind of harm (personal injury), although the extent of the harm was not. The House of Lords held that there was liability.[162] Put in the context of the ripples in the pool analogy: the wave struck an object within the horizontal legal boundary line[163]; the height of the wave was no higher than the vertical boundary line[164]; and that the wave struck with greater force than was foreseeable was irrelevant, there being no boundary line with regard to that dimension.[165]

The defender takes his victim as he finds him

This rule operates in various ways, depending upon the circumstances of the **13–24** case. The limiting effect of the rule was vividly illustrated in the US case of *Dillon v Twin State Gas & Electric Co.*[166] The facts confirm that life is often stranger than fiction. A young boy fell from a bridge to almost certain death but was electrocuted by electricity cables moments before he hit the ground. The cause of death was electrocution but the electricity company's liability for their negligence in failing properly to position the cables was limited to the boy's life expectancy, which was no more than moments.[167]

The rule has been applied to provide that where the thing harmed by the wrong was already imperfect, liability will be limited to reflect the restoration of the thing to its pre-existing imperfect condition. Thus, if a negligent driver crashed

---

[159] Decisions such as *Hughes v Lord Advocate*, 1963 S.C. (HL) 31 and *Jolley v Sutton LBC* [2000] 1 W.L.R. 1082 also call into question the distinction in type of damage made in the *Wagon Mound (No.1)*.

[160] See, e.g. *Grieves v FT Everard & Sons Ltd* [2008] 1 A.C. 281. Cf. *Corr v IBC Vehicles Ltd* [2008] 1 A.C. 184.

[161] *Hughes v Lord Advocate*, 1963 S.C. (HL) 31.

[162] Is this, like *Page v Smith* [1996] 1 A.C. 155, a case of unforeseeable harm by foreseeable means?

[163] The *relationship* between the boy (victim) and the post office workers (wrongdoer) being sufficient for the duty of care to be owed by the latter to the former.

[164] The means by which that kind of damage could be caused being reasonably foreseeable.

[165] "The precise concatenation of circumstances need not be envisaged": *Harvey v Singer Manufacturing Co Ltd*, 1960 S.C. 155 at 172 per Lord MacIntosh; "The foreseeability is not as to the particulars but the genus": *Jolley v Sutton LBC* [2000] 1 W.L.R. 1082 at 1091 per Lord Hoffman. See also *Corr v IBC Vehicles Ltd* [2008] 1 A.C. 184.

[166] *Dillon v Twin State Gas & Electric Co*, 163 A 2d 111 (1932).

[167] In the hypothetical example of the woman missing her flight due to the road accident cited at the beginning of this section, if the plane she was due to catch crashed, killing all passengers, should the court take that into consideration in assessing damages?

into an already damaged car, the negligent driver will be liable for only the extra damage caused.[168]

The set of facts that presented in *Baker v Willoughby*[169] raised a tricky question in light of the rule. The plaintiff suffered a permanent disability in his leg following a road accident caused by the defendant's negligence. The injury restricted his ability to work and he took a job in a scrapyard, where he was shot in his injured leg by robbers. His leg had to be amputated. The lower courts held that the facts that had transpired between the incident and the trial could not be ignored, and held that the driver's liability was restricted to compensate for the harm and suffering associated with the leg injury prior to the amputation, there being no injured leg beyond that point. However, the House of Lords, recognising that the plaintiff would be undercompensated as his damages award against the robbers (assuming he could find and sue them) would be restricted to the *extra* harm they had caused, held that the further injury should not be taken into consideration in assessing damages against the negligent driver.[170]

As a corollary to its limiting effect, the rule that the wrongdoer takes his victim as he finds him may also increase the damages to be paid by the defender. If the wrong triggers or exacerbates a pre-existing condition suffered by the pursuer, even where that condition is latent, the defender will be presumed reasonably to have foreseen that the victim may be affected by such a condition, and will be liable for the additional harm. This is known in personal injury cases as the "thin skull rule" or "eggshell skull rule".[171] Thus, in the *Simmons*[172] case, the defender was liable for the exacerbation of the pursuer's skin complaint.

The thin skull rule was applied by the Inner House in *McKillen v Barclay Curle & Co Ltd*.[173] The pursuer fractured a rib when he fell due to his employer's negligence. Medical evidence confirmed that the injury caused tuberculosis, which the pursuer had suffered previously but from which he had recovered, to flare up again. The employer was held to be liable for the recurrence of the disease.

It was thought that the thin skull rule was confined to cases of physical injury. It has been confirmed that it does not apply in secondary victim psychiatric injury cases.[174] However, in *Page v Smith*,[175] the House of Lords held that the thin skull

---

[168] *Performance Cars v Abraham* [1962] 1 Q.B. 33. See also *Thompson v Smiths Shiprepairers (North Shields) Ltd* [1984] Q.B. 405, where it was held employers were only liable for deafness caused from exposure to noise in the workplace from the point in time where the cause and effect became common knowledge.

[169] *Baker v Willoughby* [1970] A.C. 467.

[170] This decision was questioned, though not overturned, in *Jobling v Associated Dairies* [1982] A.C. 794, where a spinal disease unconnected with the accident overtook the injuries before the trial.

[171] The thin skull rule will not apply to the losses that the pursuer would have suffered anyway (e.g. pain and suffering associated with an operation and convalescence) where the wrong *accelerates* a condition which would have inevitably overtaken the pursuer without the occurrence of the wrong: see, e.g. *Sutherland v North British Steel Group Ltd*, 1986 S.L.T. (Sh. Ct) 29. Cf. *Cutler v Vauxhall Motors Ltd* [1971] 1 Q.B. 418. Likewise, the thin skull rule will not apply if the condition overtakes the harm without being triggered by the wrong: see, e.g. *Jobling v Associated Dairies* [1982] A.C. 794.

[172] *Simmons v British Steel Plc*, 2004 S.C. (HL) 94.

[173] *McKillen v Barclay Curle & Co Ltd*, 1967 S.L.T. 41.

[174] A "control mechanism" being that shock must be foreseeable in a person of normal fortitude—the customary "phlegm": see, e.g. *McLoughlin v O'Brian* [1983] 1 A.C. 410; *Alcock v Chief Constable of South Yorkshire* [1992] 1 A.C. 310; *McFarlane v E.E. Caledonia Ltd* [1994] 2 All E.R. 1; *Robertson v Forth Bridge Joint Board*, 1995 S.C. 364.

[175] *Page v Smith* [1996] 1 A.C. 155.

rule applied to a case of psychiatric injury. The plaintiff suffered a recrudescence of the chronic fatigue syndrome[176] from which he had previously suffered following his involvement in a minor road traffic collision. By a majority, it was held that in primary victim cases psychiatric injury should not be separated from physical injury as a distinct "kind of injury" and that both should be treated as sub-species of "personal injury". Since the plaintiff was a primary victim, the thin skull rule should therefore apply. Thus in the *Simmons*[177] case, the defender was liable for the psychiatric injury arising from the accident experienced by the pursuer.[178]

The thin skull rule may also apply with regard to economic losses deriving **13–25** from property damage, where a victim's impecuniosity exacerbates the costs flowing from an accident. For example, if a pursuer's car is damaged in an accident caused by the defender's negligence, and because the pursuer has a basic car insurance policy which does not provide a replacement car while his is being repaired the pursuer has to hire a car himself, if the pursuer pays more to hire the car than it would have cost the insurance company to hire an equivalent model, the pursuer can nevertheless recover all of the costs from the defender.[179]

Lagden v O'Connor[180] was followed in *Haxton v Philips Electronics UK Ltd*,[181] where the English Court of Appeal held that where a relative of a deceased suffers a diminution in the value of their own dependency claim[182] because the relative's own life expectancy is shortened by the defender's negligence, the relative will be entitled to recover the difference between the reduced value of the dependency claim and its full value, the defender being required to take the victim as he finds him.

It is suggested that the thin skull rule has no place in "pure economic loss" claims. There is indeed no judicial authority to support its application in such cases. In the *SAAMCO* case, where the plaintiff sought from a negligent valuer damages to reflect financial losses exacerbated by a fall in the relevant market, Lord Hoffman appeared to confirm the exclusion of the operation of the thin skull in pure economic loss cases:

> "Rules which make the wrongdoer liable for all the consequences of his wrongful conduct are exceptional and need to be justified by some special policy. Normally the law limits liability to those consequences which are attributable to that which made the act wrongful. In the case of liability in negligence for providing inaccurate information, this would mean liability for the consequences of the information being inaccurate."[183]

---

[176] Myalgic encephalomyelitis (ME).

[177] *Simmons v British Steel Plc*, 2004 S.C. (HL) 94.

[178] *Page v Smith* was followed and the thin skull rule applied by the House of Lords in *Corr v IBC Vehicles Ltd* [2008] 1 A.C. 884.

[179] See, e.g. *Lagden v O'Connor* [2004] 1 A.C. 1067. The pursuer must still act reasonably, which requires taking reasonable steps to mitigate losses: see, e.g. *Whitehead v Johnston*, 2006 Rep. L.R. 25.

[180] *Lagden v O'Connor* [2004] 1 A.C. 1067.

[181] *Haxton v Philips Electronics UK Ltd* [2014] 2 All E.R. 225.

[182] Equivalent to a relatives' claim for loss of support under the Damages (Scotland) Act 2011: see paras 5–19 to 5–21 above.

[183] In *South Australia Asset Management Corp v York Montague Ltd* sub nom. *Banque Bruxelles Lambert SA v Eagle Star Insurance Co Ltd* [1997] A.C. 191 at 213 per Lord Hoffman.

On a final point related to terminology, in his speech in *SAAMCO* Lord Hoffmann made the point that determining the harm for which the wrongdoer is liable is inextricably linked with determining the "scope of the duty".[184] Some commentators have begun to adopt that phrase in distinguishing issues related to compensation (legal causation and remoteness of damage) from those related to culpability, and it has begun to creep into the terminology used in the courts in Scotland.[185] Whether it will transpire to be helpful in adding to the understanding or coherence of this area of law remains to be seen.

---

[184] "The real question in this case is the kind of loss in respect of which the duty was owed. How is the scope of the duty determined?": *South Australia Asset Management Corp v York Montague Ltd* [1997] A.C. 191 at 212 per Lord Hoffmann.

[185] See, e.g. *Newcastle Building Society v Paterson Robertson & Graham*, 2001 S.C. 734; *Royal Bank of Scotland Plc v Bannerman Johnstone Maclay*, 2005 1 S.C. 437; *Preferred Mortgages Ltd v Shanks* [2008] P.N.L.R. 20; *Kirkton Investments Ltd v VMH LLP* [2012] P.N.L.R. 11; *Henderson v Wotherspoon* [2013] P.N.L.R. 28.

CHAPTER 14

DEFENCES

INTRODUCTION

The term "defence" may be encountered in a variety of contexts in the **14–01** investigation into delictual liability.[1] The term may be used generally to describe any challenge put forward by a defender to the pursuer's claim that the defender is liable in delict. In that sense, there are a wide range of grounds on which a pursuer's claim might be challenged, including:

- the pursuer's title and/or interest to sue[2];
- the defender's immunity from suit[3];
- a denial of the facts averred by the pursuer;
- an assertion that the law does not recognise the loss or harm as reparable.[4]

Some challenges will be specific to certain claims in delict. For example, in negligence claims there may be challenges to the various elements of the pursuer's case:

- a denial that the defender owes the pursuer a duty of care[5];
- an assertion that the defender achieved the standard of care demanded by the law.[6]

Likewise, in defamation actions the defender may challenge the pursuer's assertion that the statement complained of is defamatory, or that the pursuer is identified.[7] Indeed, for every delict that is comprised of a group of elements where the onus of proof is upon the pursuer, the defender may escape liability by successfully challenging the existence of any one of the elements cumulatively required for a prima facie valid claim to be established.

---

[1] Alternative terms may be used, e.g. "limiting principles": *Attorney-General v Guardian Newspapers Ltd (No.2)* [1990] 1 A.C. 109 at 280 per Lord Goff of Chieveley. See para.9–09 above.

[2] See Ch.3.

[3] See paras 3–28 to 3–35 and below at 17–02 to 17–09.

[4] See, e.g. *McFarlane v Tayside Health Board*, 2000 S.C. (HL) 1; *Dynamco v Holland, Hannen & Cubitts (Scotland) Ltd*, 1971 S.C. 257; *Rothwell v Chemical and Insulating Co Ltd* sub nom. *Grieves v FT Everard & Sons Ltd* [2008] 1 A.C. 281. Note the effective reversal of the latter decision with regard to delictual liability in Scots law by the Damages (Asbestos-related Conditions) (Scotland) Act 2009.

[5] See Ch.11.

[6] See Ch.12.

[7] See Ch.7.

Further grounds for challenge that are more generic to delictual liability include:

- a challenge to causation—either that the defender's admitted wrong was not a *causa sine qua non* the loss or that it was not *causa causans*[8];
- a contention that the losses claimed are too remote;
- an assertion that the claim is time-barred.[9]

If the claim is for damages for breach of statutory duty a specific ground for challenging the claim will be that the statute does not create a private law right of action.[10] If the defender is being sued as vicariously liable for the delictual conduct of a worker, the defender may assert that the worker is not an employee, or may admit an employee's status but deny that the employee was acting within the scope of employment.[11]

Perhaps with the exception of a challenge based on remoteness of damage (where there may remain liability albeit not for all of the harm for which the pursuer seeks reparation), these are all examples of challenges to the case brought by the pursuer. Thus, these challenges may be distinguished from true defences as such, which may operate to (at least partially) defeat a prima facie valid claim, i.e. a case where the pursuer is successful in proving all of the elements necessary to establish liability for the delictual conduct averred.

Some of these true defences are specific to certain delicts and are dealt with in this work as part of the treatment of these specific examples of delictual wrongs. These include: in assault—self-defence or provocation[12]; in the economic delicts (with the exception of fraud)—lawful justification; in breach of confidence- —public interest; in defamation—*veritas*, fair comment, *in rixa*.[13]

The rest of this chapter will deal with examples of true defences that tend to operate across liability for a range of delictual wrongs, if not universally across delictual liability generally. It will also deal with some miscellaneous challenges to liability which may not fit within the definition proposed above for true defences as such, but nevertheless may limit or extinguish liability for a prima facie valid claim.

CONSENT AND VOLENTI NON FIT INJURIA

14–02 Consent and volenti non fit injuria are variations on a theme: the theme being the concept that no wrong may be done to one who is willing to accept the risk of harm. Thus, both are examples of complete defences, i.e. if either is pled successfully, the defender is absolved from any liability to the pursuer in relation

---

[8] See Ch.13.
[9] See Ch.15.
[10] See Ch.16.
[11] See Ch.4.
[12] Provocation may *mitigate* rather than exclude liability: *Ross v Bryce*, 1972 S.L.T. (Sh. Ct) 76. See also *Ashmore v Rock Steady Security Ltd*, 2006 S.L.T. 207.
[13] Is absolute or qualified privilege a defence as such or a challenge to the pursuer's case? See para.7–19 above.

to that ground of action.[14] The distinction is that "consent" generally requires *active communication of willingness by the pursuer, whereas "volenti"* may be evidenced where the pursuer's conduct indicates *passive* acceptance of a risk. Thus, consent is evidenced by *communication*, whereas volenti is evidenced by *conduct*. Furthermore, consent relates to conduct which carries a risk, whereas volenti relates purely to risk.[15] The distinction may be subtle, but it is important and necessary. Speaking generally, because delictual actions are usually between two parties, if one has in some way agreed or accepted that he should be injured, corrective justice is not engaged. However, applying that general philosophical approach is more difficult: different wrongs involve different aims and to that extent the efficacy of the law could be compromised by applying the same "willingness" rule across all wrongs.

Consent is most relevant to wrongs that involve deliberate conduct, such as assault, where the pursuer's active acceptance of, or agreement to, such conduct provides a defence. The consent is specific to certain conduct and must be communicated prior to the conduct. When we turn to harm through negligence, there is an immediate difference. The defender does not set out to harm. The pursuer cannot therefore, consent in particular and in advance. Yet justice still requires that in some cases the defender be absolved due to the "consent" of the pursuer. It is here that we encounter the phrase volenti non fit injuria (loosely: "a volunteer cannot be wronged").

Conceptually, volenti is more apposite to negligence cases[16]: it is difficult to imagine a state of mind that passively accepts a risk of harm caused by *intentional* conduct; but it is more straightforward to envisage a state of mind that subconsciously "hopes for the best" or "keeps one's fingers crossed" where there is a possibility of harm from another's negligence. Put another way, it is much more difficult to accept the notion of one *passively* running the risk of being punched in the face than it is to accept the notion of one passively running the risk that beyond the gap in the fence one is about to squeeze through there may be an active railway line, a golf driving range, a steep drop or any other dangerous phenomenon that one would expect to be fenced off.

Another conceptual issue to consider is whether the theme underpinning these defences—that no wrong is done to one who is willing—suggests that they are not pure defences as such, but rather are challenges to the suggestion that the defender owed a duty to the pursuer, which in negligence is the first element that

---

[14] It may be pointed out that if no wrong is done then there can be no action to defend. Thus, lack of consent may therefore be seen as a pre-requisite to liability for assault (see paras 6–13 to 6–19 above). However, it is submitted that it would be inimical to fix the onus of proof with regard to consent upon the pursuer, since the logical corollary would be that the law's default position would presume harm to be consensual unless the pursuer proved otherwise.

[15] Alternatively, it might be said that consent relates to the risk associated with the *defender's* conduct, whereas volenti relates to the risk associated with the *pursuer's* conduct. Compare, e.g. *R v Brown* [1994] 1 A.C. 212 with *Titchener v British Railways Board*, 1984 S.C. (HL) 34. The former case was a criminal case—the conviction was the subject of an unsuccessful application to the European Court of Human Rights as an alleged breach of art.8 of the European Convention on Human Rights: *Laskey v United Kingdom* [1997] 24 E.H.R.R. 39.

[16] There are many cases and articles that can be and ought to be read in attempting to understand the position of "consent" in negligence: J.B. Stewart, "Football: Civil Aspects", 1981 S.L.T. (News) 157; W.J. Stewart, "Skiing and the Law: the First Case" (1990) 3 5 J.L.S.S. 27; A. Duff, "Civil Actions and Sporting Injuries Sustained by Professional Footballers", 1994 S.L.T. (News) 175; R. Kidner, "The Variable Standard of Care, Contributory Negligence and Volenti", 1991 L.S. 1; C.G.S. Tan, "Volenti Non Fit Injuria: An Alternative Framework", 1995 Tort L. Rev. 208.

the pursuer must prove in establishing a prima facie case against the defender.[17] If, because the pursuer is willing, the defender can do no wrong to the pursuer, does that mean that the defender does not owe the pursuer any duty to avoid harmful conduct? It is suggested that this analysis does not fit comfortably with the concept of consent, especially in relation to medical procedures: just because I have signed a consent form does not mean that the surgeon no longer owes me a duty of care in carrying out the operation. However, there has been judicial discussion of the volenti defence which is consistent with the analysis that because the pursuer accepted the risk of harm, the defender did not owe a duty of care to the pursuer.[18] Analogising this analysis with the *Caparo*[19] criteria, in negligence cases it might coherently be argued that where there is evidence of the pursuer's passive acceptance of the risk of harm—in other words a voluntary assumption of risk, this would militate against it being fair, just and reasonable to recognise the imposition of an *ex lege* duty of care.

Consent

14–03   Where there is a deliberate conduct wrong, such as assault, then acceptance or agreement to that conduct is a complete defence. This explains why one boxer cannot sue another for a punch. The consent is particular (to conduct within the rules and customs, i.e. a punch and not a bite) and prior. The same applies to medical treatment—where the interference with the patient's body through carrying out, e.g. an operation is intentional.

Because the defence requires evidence of some form of active (as opposed to passive) communication of willingness from the pursuer, it is important to consider how much information the pursuer must be in possession of before the pursuer's consent may be considered sufficient to absolve the defender from liability. Issues may thus arise as to the quality of the consent. If the consent is extorted, then it does not provide a bar to recovery.[20] However, in the medical sphere Scots law has not taken the route of seeking, for example, informed consent.[21] In Scots criminal law it is not possible to consent to inflict serious injury on another, as by a "square go".[22] Similar policy considerations might apply to a civil case.

Volenti non fit injuria

14–04   Volenti non fit injuria loosely translates to "a volunteer cannot be wronged" and is often described as confirming that a wrong is not done to one who is willing. As discussed above, volenti may alternatively be seen as an attack on the pursuer's case or as a self-standing defence. Either way, if pled successfully,

---

[17] See, e.g. *McTear v Imperial Tobacco*, 2005 2 S.C. 1 at 558–559 per Lord Nimmo Smith.

[18] *Titchener v British Railways Board*, 1984 S.C. (HL) 34 at 55 per Lord Fraser of Tullybelton, applying s.2(3) of the Occupiers' Liability (Scotland) Act 1960, which uses language suggesting that a pursuer's assumption of risk negates "obligations" to the pursuer being imposed upon the occupier.

[19] *Caparo Industries Plcv Dickman* [1990] 2 A.C. 605.

[20] *Adamson v Martin*, 1916 S.C. 319.

[21] *Hunter v Hanley*, 1955 S.C. 200; *Moyes v Lothian Health Board*, 1990 S.L.T. 444; *M's Guardian v Lanarkshire Health Board*, 2013 S.C. 245. *Moyes* and *M's Guardian* follow the approach adopted by the majority in *Sidaway v Board of Governors of the Bethlem Royal Hospital* [1985] A.C. 871. See also paras 12–12 to 12–14 above.

[22] *Smart v HM Advocate*, 1975 S.L.T. 65. See also *Laskey v UK* (1997) 24 E.H.R.R. 39. Cf. *Mosley v News Group Newspapers Ltd* [2008] E.M.L.R. 20.

volenti provides a complete barrier to liability: the pursuer will be deemed to have waived his right to a remedy and the defender will be assoilzied.

It is suggested that, unlike consent, volenti requires only passive conduct on the part of the defender which objectively may be seen as demonstrating a willingness to accept the relevant risk.[23] In this way the risk ultimately derives from the pursuer's own conduct, by engaging in or continuing with the activity which carries a foreseeable risk of harm, the pursuer is confirming an assumption of that risk.[24] The pursuer thus assumes responsibility for the risk; which is inconsistent with the defender incurring liability if the risk eventuates. This analysis is consistent with the "no duty" terminology sometimes adopted by judges.[25]

Thus, because in a football match any player (including myself) knows that a bona fide tackle can break my leg, if my opponent does break my leg (which is entirely foreseeable), he is not liable because I have assumed the risk of that harm. I did not really consent to having my leg broken, but I was willing to run the risk. I took a chance and it came out against me. Thus, on ordinary principles of fact-finding, the pursuer can lose if he knew or if he ought to have known of the risk: even the visiting martian cannot say that he was unaware of the risks inherent in a game of football.

However, an awareness of the risk does not necessarily amount to a willingness to accept the risk. It is not sufficient for the pursuer to be merely *sciens* (i.e. aware of the risk); the pursuer must also be *volens* (i.e. have assumed the risk). In other words, *sciens* is necessary but not sufficient. *Sciens* may be nevertheless constructive where the risk is obvious, such as where the risks inherent in a game of football should be obvious even to the passing martian.

Thus, turning to actual cases, the courts have turned against volenti generally, although when presented as "no duty" the anti-volenti cases might be avoided. So in employment cases there must be the clearest possible evidence that the pursuer accepted the risk of the actual harm[26]: it is not sufficient to show that the pursuer continued working knowing of the risk.[27] A tenant had been held volenti prior to the Occupiers' Liability (Scotland) Act 1960 by remaining in a house that was in ill repair,[28] but that has not been followed in a thoughtful sheriff court decision.[29] It is often mentioned in sports cases, especially in regard to spectators, but it is seldom that a spectator can actually be said to have assumed a risk of

---

[23] Although volenti was, in origin, of the nature of a consent defence to particular conduct in advance, a freeman who was allowed to be sold as a slave was denied his right to be declared free: T. Ingman, "A History of the Defence of Volenti Non Fit Injuria", 1981 J.R. 1; A.E. Jaffey, "Volenti Non Fit Injuria", 1985 C.L.J. 87.

[24] The pursuer's assumption of risk must occur prior to, or contemporaneous with, the defender's delictual act. If the pursuer's actions come later, they will not be relevant to a plea of volenti: see, e.g. *Sabri-Tabrizi v Lothian Health Board*, 1998 S.C. 373.

[25] See, e.g. *Titchener v British Railways Board*, 1984 S.C. (HL) 34 at 55 per Lord Fraser of Tullybelton; *Tomlinson v Congleton BC* [2004] 1 A.C. 46.

[26] See generally *ICI v Shatwell* [1965] A.C. 656, where two qualified shot-firers (who were brothers) agreed, contrary to their employer's orders and contrary to statute, to test-fire detonators without taking shelter. One was killed and the other badly injured.

[27] *Smith v Baker & Sons* [1891] A.C. 325; *Stewart's Executrix v Clyde Navigation Trustees*, 1946 S.C. 317. Nevertheless, the damages award may be reduced due to contributory negligence: see, e.g. *Robb v Salamis (M&I) Ltd*, 2007 S.C. (HL) 71.

[28] *Webster v Brown* (1892) 19 R. 765; *Shields v Dalziel* (1894) 24 R. 849.

[29] *Hughes' Tutsix v G.D.C.*, 1982 S.L.T. (Sh. Ct) 70. See also *Neilson v Scottish Homes*, 1999 S.L.T. (Sh. Ct) 2; *Murray v Harringay Arena* [1951] 2 K.B. 529; see especially *Wooldridge v Sumner* [1962] 2 All E.R. 978.

injury.[30] In Scotland's first skiing decision,[31] the sheriff correctly, it is submitted, would not have applied volenti non fit injuria, but would rather have found the pursuer's damages to be reduced by contributory negligence. This would have been the case even although the sheriff considered participants generally accepted some degree of danger.[32]

14–05   As well as a willingness to accept the risk, the law also demands that the pursuer *appreciate* the risk involved for a plea of volenti to succeed. Thus, if the pursuer's perception of the risk is undermined by his mental state, a plea of volenti will fail, especially where the damage to his mental state was itself caused by the defender's delictual wrong—such as where an employee commits suicide after developing clinical depression following sustaining a serious head injury caused by his employer's negligence.[33] This outcome is reinforced where the plea is used to defend a breach of a duty that existed only because of the pursuer's mental state. Thus, where a prisoner who is known by the police to be a suicide risk is arrested, if the prisoner is placed in a cell which provides the means for the prisoner to commit suicide, the police cannot escape liability for negligence by relying on volenti.[34] Likewise, volenti cannot be pled against a rescuer who places himself in danger in order to assist the victim of an accident caused by the negligence of the defender,[35] or against a child who is too young to appreciate the risk.[36]

However, self-imposed inebriation may not be accepted as impacting on a pursuer's perception of the risks inherent in an adventure. In *Morris v Murray*,[37] the plaintiff had spent a substantial part of the day drinking in several pubs with the deceased. After a substantial quantity of alcoholic beverage had been consumed by both, the plaintiff agreed to accept a spin as a passenger in the deceased's light aircraft. The deceased lost control of the plane and it crashed. Although the court left open the possibility that a plea of volenti could be defeated upon the victim being so drunk as to be incapable of appreciating the risk, nevertheless the plea of volenti was upheld.

It should be noted that there is a statutory prohibition on volenti as a defence in relation to a road traffic accident where the motor vehicle is used in circumstances where a motor insurance policy is required to be in force.[38]

---

[30] See *Lamond v Glasgow Corp*, 1968 S.L.T. 291 for a full statement in the context of sport. See also *Lewis v Buckpool Golf Club*, 1993 S.L.T. (Sh. Ct) 43. Cf. *McMahon v Dear* [2014] CSOH 100.

[31] *Garven v White Corries* Unreported June 21, 1989 Fort William sheriff court.

[32] *Pitts v Hunt* [1991] 1 Q.B. 24. *Ashton v Turner* [1981] Q.B. 137 takes a firm line.

[33] *Corr v IBC Vehicles Ltd* [2008] 1 A.C. 884.

[34] *Reeves v Commissioner of Police for the Metropolis* [2000] 1 A.C. 360. The House of Lords also rejected a plea of novus actus interveniens, but did permit a reduction of damages for contributory negligence on the part of the prisoner. Cf. *Calvert v William Hill Credit Ltd* [2009] Ch. 330.

[35] "If . . . A by negligence places B in peril in such circumstances that it is a foreseeable result that someone will try to rescue B and if C does so try—ought C in any appropriate sense to be described as a 'volunteer'? In my judgment the answer is No": *Baker v T.E. Hopkins & Son Ltd.* [1959] 1 W.L.R. 966 at 976 per Morris L.J.

[36] *McGlone v British Railways Board*, 1966 S.C. (HL) 1 at 18 per Lord Pearce. Cf. *Titchener v British Railways Board*, 1984 S.C. (HL) 34; *Devlin v Strathclyde RC*, 1993 S.L.T. 699.

[37] *Morris v Murray* [1991] 2 Q.B. 6.

[38] Road Traffic Act 1988 s.149. See, e.g. *Winnik v Dick*, 1984 S.C. 48. The statutory prohibition is restricted to volenti and does not prohibit other defences including ex turpi causa non oritur actio or contributory negligence: see, e.g. *Ashton v Turner* [1981] Q.B. 137; *Pitts v Hunt* [1991] 1 Q.B. 24.

Where volenti may fail, the defence of contributory negligence should be considered a full back position.[39]

Waiver

A notice of waiver may preclude liability. However, any such notice **14–06** purporting to exclude liability in the course of a business will now be subject to the Unfair Contract Terms Act 1977,[40] which renders void any attempt to exclude liability for death or personal injury caused by a breach of duty. Other non-contractual disclaimers of liability will generally be required to be fair and reasonable in the circumstances.

CONTRIBUTORY NEGLIGENCE

Contributory negligence is a plea to the effect that the defender failed to take **14–07** reasonable care for his own safety. Prior to the implementation of the Law Reform (Contributory Negligence) Act 1945 this was a complete defence, so older cases should be read with caution. However, the 1945 Act now provides that the court may attribute fault between the parties in proportion to their share of the responsibility. The onus is on the defender to establish the defence. All that need be shown is that the pursuer's carelessness was a co-operating cause of his injuries or loss, i.e. the pursuer's own fault contributed to the accident or exacerbated the harm. The pursuer's conduct may be careless or intentional, including suicide.[41] Although contributory negligence does depend upon foreseeability of harm to oneself, there is no need to show a breach by the pursuer of a duty of care as such, owed to himself or to anyone else.[42]

The defence is commonly encountered in workers' cases, slipping and tripping cases and in road traffic accident cases, a common instance being where injuries are exacerbated by a failure to wear a seatbelt.[43] Motor vehicles are frequently described as tantamount to dangerous weapons,[44] and so it has been held to be unlikely for a pedestrian to be held to be more liable than a car driver,[45] unless the pedestrian is considerably under the influence of alcohol.[46]

Although each case will be determined by its own facts, it is accepted that there are two general factors to consider in assessing the apportionment of

---

[39] See, e.g. *Sayers v Harlow Urban DC* [1958] 1 W.L.R. 623.

[40] Unfair Contract Terms Act 1977 s.16, as amended by s.68 of the Law Reform (Miscellaneous Provisions) Scotland Act 1990.

[41] *Reeves v Commissioner of Police for the Metropolis* [2000] 1 A.C. 360; *Corr v IBC Vehicles Ltd* [2008] 1 A.C. 884.

[42] *Jones v Livox Quarries* [1952] 2 Q.B. 608.

[43] *Froom v Butcher* [1976] Q.B. 286. Cf. *Mackay v Borthwick*, 1982 S.L.T. 265 (accepted that, exceptionally, it was not careless where the pursuer was not wearing a seatbelt because she was suffering from a hiatus hernia); *Pace v Cully*, 1992 S.L.T. 1073 (taxi driver advised by the police that is was safer not to wear a seatbelt in case he was attacked by passengers—failure to wear a seatbelt merely an error of judgment). A similar approach has been taken where a motorcyclist was not wearing a crash helmet: *Capps v Miller* [1989] 1 W.L.R. 839.

[44] See, e.g. *Jackson v Murray*, 2013 S.L.T. 153; *Eagle v Chambers* [2004] R.T.R. 9.

[45] *Eagle v Chambers* [2004] R.T.R. 9. Cf. *Jackson v Murray*, 2013 S.L.T. 153.

[46] See, e.g. *Malcolm v Fair*, 1993 S.L.T. 342; *Little v Glen* [2013] CSOH 153; 2013 G.W.D. 31–630. Cf. *McNab v Bluebird Buses Ltd*, 2007 Rep. L.R. 36. See also *Kemp v Secretary of State for Scotland*, 2000 S.L.T. 471.

liability: viz blameworthiness and causative potency.[47] Nevertheless, the influence of these factors is difficult to determine with any degree of precision and
appeal judges tend to be slow to interfere with the assessment of a judge of first
instance.[48]

Even if the pursuer's conduct that is called into question might be described as
blameworthy, it will not justify a reduction in the award of damages unless it has
more than de minimis causative potency. Thus, where the pursuer is complaining
about negligence in the treatment of compulsive behaviour such as addictions to
gambling,[49] smoking, or consuming alcohol or drugs,[50] the lifestyle choices
themselves will not trigger the defence as they will generally be "too remote in
time, place and circumstance" from the defender's negligence and so "no more
than part of the history".[51] However, the defence may be engaged if the pursuer
continues to smoke in circumstances where he made aware that smoking will
exacerbate harm caused by a defender's negligence.[52]

14–08   While it is a contradiction in terms, it is thought that findings of 100 per cent
may be made.[53] It is, however, more logical that the defender be absolved if the
defender's contribution was de minimis or less.[54] Where two or more defenders'
delictual wrongs combine to cause indivisible harm to a pursuer, if the harm is
exacerbated by the pursuer's own negligence, a proportionate reduction in
damages under the Law Reform (Contributory Negligence) Act 1945 should be
determined prior to the allocation of contribution between joint wrongdoers.[55]

The defence has been extended to liability in negligence for pure economic
loss,[56] but has been held not to apply to fraud.[57]

The defence has been held available against children. In *Banner's Tutor v
Kennedy's Trustees*,[58] a five-year-old girl got out of the back of a minibus and ran
into a lorry. She had been expressly warned by the minibus driver not to go out

---

[47] *Davies v Swan Motor Co (Swansea) Ltd* [1949] 2 K.B. 291 at 326 per Lord Denning. See also
Stapley v Gypsum Mines Ltd [1953] A.C. 663.
[48] *Grant v Sun Shipping Co Ltd*, 1948 S.C. (HL) 73. See also *Robb v Salamis (M&I) Ltd*, 2007 S.C.
(HL) 71, where an oil platform worker was injured when he fell while descending a ladder from
a top bunk. The ladder was removable and its hooks had not properly been engaged in the rail of
the top bunk. The pursuer was aware that this was a common problem. The House of Lords
refused to interfere with the assessment of the lower courts of a reduction of 50% for contributory
negligence.
[49] *Calvert v William Hill Credit Ltd* [2009] Ch. 330.
[50] *St George v Home Office* [2009] 1 W.L.R. 1670.
[51] *St George v Home Office* [2009] 1 W.L.R. 1670 at 1684 per Dyson L.J.; *Jones v Livox Quarries*
[1952] 2 Q.B. 608 at 616 per Denning L.J.
[52] *Badger v Ministry of Defence* [2006] 3 All E.R. 173. See also *Barrett v Ministry of Defence*
[1995] 1 W.L.R. 1217.
[53] See, e.g. (obiter) in *McEwan v Lothian Buses Plc*, 2006 Rep. L.R. 134 at 137 per Lord Emslie
(contributory negligence assessed at 75%); (obiter) in *Robb v Salamis (M&I) Ltd*, 2003 G.W.D.
33–949 (contributory negligence confirmed at 50% by the House of Lords at 2007 S.C. (HL) 71).
Cf. (also obiter) *Robb v Salamis (M&I) Ltd*, 2005 S.L.T. 523 at 541 per Lord Penrose (delivering
the opinion of the court). See also *Skipton Building Society v Lea Hough & Co* [2000] P.N.L.R.
545.
[54] See, e.g. *Murphy v East Ayrshire Council*, 2012 S.L.T. 1125; *Little v Glen* [2013] CSOH 153;
2013 G.W.D. 31–630.
[55] *Fitzgerald v Lane* [1989] A.C. 328 at 338–339 per Lord Ackner. See also *Drew v Western S.M.T.
Co*, 1947 S.C. 222.
[56] *Platform Home Loans Ltd v Oyson Shipways Ltd* [2000] 2 A.C. 190; *Skipton Building Society v
Lea Hough & Co* [2000] P.N.L.R. 545. See also *Billig v Council of the Law Society of Scotland*,
2007 S.C. 32.
[57] *Standard Chartered Bank v Pakistan National Shipping Corp (No.2)* [2003] 1 A.C. 959.
[58] *Banner's Tutor v Kennedy's Trustees*, 1978 S.L.T. (Notes) 83.

until he opened the door but he did not take any actual steps to prevent her getting out. The court held that she was a girl of usual intelligence and had parental guidance about roads and had seen heavy traffic. She was held to be 20 per cent liable for the accident and her damages were reduced accordingly. The age of the pursuer impacts on the determination of blameworthiness.[59] Thus, in *Jackson v Murray*,[60] the Inner House marginally reduced a finding of 90 per cent contributory negligence to 70 per cent. A 13-year-old girl ran across a rural road from behind a school minibus and was struck by a driver who had not taken into account the potential danger created by the presence of the school minibus.

Conduct that consists of a response to an emergency created by the defender does not constitute contributory negligence, in terms of the so-called "agony rule".[61] Thus, it is not contributory negligence to swerve onto the wrong side of the road when, having driven around a blind bend, the pursuer is confronted with another vehicle being driven directly towards the his vehicle.[62] However, acting in the agony of the moment will not always exculpate the pursuer—it depends upon the circumstances. Thus, where due to a defective lock a woman became trapped in the cubicle of a public toilet, she was held to be 25 per cent contributorily negligent when she was injured in a futile attempt to escape through the gap between the top of the door and the ceiling.[63] Similarly, the "dilemma rule" provides an exemption from the defence where the defender's delictual wrong presents the pursuer with a dilemma and the pursuer picks what transpires to be the wrong course of action.[64]

Illegality: ex turpi causa

The maxim ex turpi causa non oritur actio,[65] which applies in contract, has been applied as a defence to delict claims too. Its appearance in delict arises from the reluctance of courts to award damages to one wrongdoer caused by another wrongdoer.[66] However, instances of such situations range from the safe-blower who blows up his confederate who is keeping watch, to a case where a person injures a passenger when infringing some traffic regulation.[67] The question has been regularly debated in England and has been considered in some detail by the House of Lords.[68]

14–09

---

[59] Compare, e.g. *Galbraith's Curator ad Litem v Stewart (No.2)*, 1998 S.L.T. 1305 (eight-year-old boy injured on building site: no contributory negligence) with *McCluskey v Wallace*, 1998 S.C. 711 (four-year-old run over in street: 20% contributory negligence). See also *McKinnell v White*, 1971 S.L.T. (Notes) 61.

[60] *Jackson v Murray*, 2013 S.L.T. 153.

[61] *Laird Line v U.S. Shipping Board*, 1924 S.C. (HL) 37.

[62] *Wallace v Bergius*, 1915 S.C. 205.

[63] *Sayers v Harlow Urban DC* [1958] 1 W.L.R. 623. Foreseeability of panic in a trapped occupant of the lavatory prevented the plaintiff's actions amounting to a novus actus interveniens. Her panic confirmed that her actions were not truly volenti.

[64] *Clayards v Dethick* (1848) 12 Q.B. 439.

[65] No action arises out of an immoral transaction.

[66] See generally, A.H. Hudson, "Crime, Tort and Reparation—What Solution?", 1984 S.L.T. (News) 321; A.H. Hudson, "Crime, Tort and Reparation: A Common Solution", 1992 S.L.T. (News) 203.

[67] See, e.g. *Currie v Clamp's Executor*, 2002 S.L.T. 196.

[68] *Gray v Thames Trains Ltd* [2009] 1 A.C. 1339. The English Court of Appeal has also given the matter a degree of analysis: *Pitts v Hunt* [1991] 1 Q.B. 24; *Ashton v Turner* [1981] Q.B. 137.

Australian cases have shown something of a lead in moving away from a rigorous application of the maxim.[69] Similarly in England, the circumstances of each case will be taken into account[70]—so, for example, suicide will not necessarily be viewed as triggering the rule where suicide is the very thing that the defendant owes a duty to prevent.[71] Nevertheless, where a victim of a railway accident caused by the negligence of the defending railway company suffered post traumatic stress disorder, which so altered his personality that he stabbed to death a pedestrian who stepped into the path of his car, the turpis causa rule applied, it being based on a public policy that prevented a person recovering damages for the consequences of his own criminal act.[72]

The general approach for Scots law has been set out in *Weir v Wyper*,[73] which reconsidered much previous authority. A 16-year-old girl went on a trip with two men and another girl. One of the men and the other girl left the car, leaving the girl with the defender at night, in the dark, in a place she did not know. Knowing that he held only a provisional licence, she asked the defender for a lift home. The defender began showing off by driving very fast and braking violently when it was necessary to stop. The car left the road and overturned. Lord Coulsfield, it is submitted, quite properly concluded that the maxim was not to be rigorously applied nor, if the defence was restated or explained as an aspect of public policy, was it to be a complete bar to claims. The proper course was to take each case on its merits and it is probably only in cases of significant criminal activity that the defence would have a chance of success.

The defence was treated as applicable to a case of an injured passenger who was knowingly in a stolen car, which on the balance of probabilities it was accepted he had helped steal.[74] It should be mentioned that such cases are sometimes argued on the basis of a public policy against recovery[75] and yet others are argued on the basis that, in negligence cases, it is impossible to fix a standard of duty of care—for example, as between the safe-blower and his lookout, the court will not trouble to inquire as to the standards of the reasonable man out doing a burglary.[76] This latter argument seems unnecessary and may

---

[69] See *Jackson v Harrison* (1978) 138 C.L.R. 438; *Progress and Properties v Craft* (1976) 135 C.L.R. 651 moving away from *Smith v Jenkins* (1970) 119 C.L.R. 397. The Australian position was analysed in *Weir*, below. See also R.W. Kostal, "Currents in the Counter-reformation: illegality and the duty of care in Canada and Australia" (1995) Tort L. Rev. 100.

[70] Thus trivial wrongs, or immoral but not illegal conduct, are unlikely to trigger the defence: see, e.g. *Mosley v News Group Newspapers* [2008] E.M.L.R. 20.

[71] *Kirkham v Chief Constable of Greater Manchester* [1990] 2 Q.B. 283. Cf. *Stone & Rolls Ltd (In Liquidation) v Moore Stephens (A Firm)* [2009] 1 A.C. 1391, where a "one-man" company had engaged in a serious fraud, the turpis causa principle prevented the company from claiming its auditors were in breach of a duty of care to detect that fraud.

[72] *Gray v Thames Trains Ltd* [2009] 1 A.C. 1339.

[73] *Weir v Wyper*, 1992 S.L.T. 579, considering the earlier Scottish authority *Sloan v Triplett*, 1985 S.L.T. 294; *Ashcroft's C.B. v Stewart*, 1988 S.L.T. 163; *Duncan v Ross Harper & Murphy*, 1993 S.L.T. 105; *Wilson v Price*, 1989 S.L.T. 484 and *Winnik v Dick*, 1984 S.L.T. 185.

[74] *Duncan v Ross Harper & Murphy*, 1993 S.L.T. 105. See also *Andersen v Hameed*, 2010 Rep. L.R. 132.

[75] Thus it has been held in England that the public policy that underpins the ex turpi causa rule also precludes recovery of compensation for the consequences of the claimant's own criminal act even where that has been perpetrated because of a personality change brought on by the defendant's negligence: *Gray v Thames Trains Ltd* [2009] 1 A.C. 1339.

[76] For a case along these lines see the case of the escaping prisoner *Vellino v Chief Constable of Manchester* [2002] 1 W.L.R. 218. The Scottish Law Commission, *Report on Civil Liability* (HMSO, 1988), Scot. Law Com. No.115 proposes a classification of the defence in cl.9 of its draft Contribution in Damages (Scotland) Bill.

well have been a way out of the otherwise draconian effect of subscribing fully to the turpis causa rule

For the turpis causa defence to apply, there must be a sufficient causal link between the unlawful act and the harm. Thus, the defence was held not to apply where a motor-car was used as a weapon to carry out a serious assault on an individual who had immediately previously been involved in a criminal attack on premises which were owned by relatives of the defender. The pursuer had, along with others and as part of a campaign between rival criminal enterprises, gathered outside a bar where they had thrown objects at the building, apparently intending to goad the occupants into the street so as to carry out an attack. One of the attackers was shot in the leg and the group retreated in two vehicles, stopping on the street a short distance from the bar. The victim alighted from one vehicle and, while standing beside the other, was struck when the defender, whose uncle owned the bar that had been attacked, deliberately drove her car at the pursuer, who was severely injured. The defender had been in a nearby shop at the time of the attack on the bar and had not been in any danger. Lord Jones in the Outer House held that the defence was bound to fail.[77]

Again, contributory negligence may be pled as a fall-back position.[78]

NECESSITY

Necessity may protect a defender against action in certain circumstances, **14–10** particularly where there has been an emergency. So it is permissible to trespass in order to save life or property.[79] So too, force-feeding of a prisoner has been held not to be actionable on this basis.[80] Necessity may also be used, albeit in limited circumstances, to justify the imposition of unwanted medical treatment.[81] If there are general principles of law crossing pedagogic and doctrinal boundaries, then cases from the criminal law, used carefully, should assist. The High Court has recently reviewed and clearly acknowledged the defence, which for a long time has been regarded with suspicion. In *Moss v Howdle*,[82] it was decided that a defence of necessity (albeit it is a form of a wider defence of coercion) is available where the accused had no choice but to do what he did, as where he is in immediate danger of death or serious bodily harm. However, the defence of necessity cannot be used to justify malicious damage in pursuit of the "enforcement" of customary international criminal law.[83]

STATUTORY AUTHORITY

In many examples this may take the form of a statutory immunity, such as that **14–11** enjoyed with regard to otherwise delictual acts done by trade unions and others

---

[77] *McLaughlin v Morrison*, 2014 S.L.T. 111.

[78] See, e.g. *Taylor v Leslie*, 1998 S.L.T. 1248.

[79] *Cope v Sharpe* [1912] 1 K. B. 496. See also *Rigby v Chief Constable of Northamptonshire* [1985] 1 W.L.R. 1242. Cf. *Monsanto Plc v Tilly* [2000] Env. L.R. 313.

[80] *Leigh v Gladstone* (1949) 26 T.L.R. 139.

[81] *Re B (A Minor) (Wardship: Sterilisation)* [1988] A.C. 199; *Re F (Mental Patient)* [1990] 2 A.C. 1. The English authorities were followed in *L v L's Curator ad Litem*, 1997 S.L.T. 167. See also *Re T (Adult: Refusal of Treatment)* [1993] Fam. 95.

[82] *Moss v Howdle*, 1997 S.C.C.R. 215.

[83] *Lord Advocate's Reference (No. 1 of 2000)*, 2001 J.C. 143.

"in contemplation or furtherance of a trade dispute".[84] If Parliament has authorised some conduct, then it will not be actionable unless it could as easily be done without causing harm. In *Lord Advocate v North British Railways*,[85] waste that was being disposed of under statutory authority was left near an army barracks. The purpose of the statute could as easily have been served by not leaving it, so the defence was not available.

DAMNUM FATALE

14–12 *Damnum fatale* is one of the few defences available to a defender who is subject to strict liability. Sometimes referred to as "Act of God", or force majeur, it refers to a happening that no human foresight could provide against such as an earthquake in Edinburgh or a volcanic eruption in Thurso, but not heavy rain in Greenock.[86]

MISCELLANEOUS RELATED MATTERS

Assignation and subrogation

14–13   It is quite clear that a claim may be assigned at any time to someone else. Any defences available against the original party will be valid against the assignee.[87] A claim may be transferred by way of subrogation, that is, where the insurer has indemnified his insured for a loss for which another person is legally liable, he is entitled to proceed against that party without the need of an assignation. By the Third Parties (Rights Against Insurers) Act 1930, if an insured person becomes bankrupt or unable to pay, then anyone who has incurred a loss covered by the insurance may proceed directly against the insurer. The Road Traffic Act 1972 makes insurance compulsory in respect of the risk of death or personal injury to third parties (including passengers). The insurer[88] must satisfy any judgment against any insured, notwithstanding that they may be entitled to avoid the policy.[89] There is a similar arrangement in respect of employers in terms of the Employers' Liability (Compulsory Insurance) Act 1969.

Contribution and relief

14–14   The Law Reform (Miscellaneous Provisions) (Scotland) Act 1940 s.3(1) (as amended) provides:

> "Where in any action of damages in respect of loss or damage arising from any wrongful acts or negligent acts or omissions two or more defenders are in pursuance of the verdict of a jury or the judgment of a court found jointly

---

[84] Trade Union and Labour Relations (Consolidation) Act 1992 s.219: see para.3–41 above. For a discussion on statutory discretion see paras 17–02 to 17–03 and see para.16–03 below.

[85] *Lord Advocate v North British Railways* (1894) 2 S.L.T. 71. See also *Bell v McGlennan*, 1992 S.C. 41.

[86] *Greenock Corp v Caledonian Railway Co*, 1917 S.C. (HL) 56.

[87] See A. Young, "Rights of Relief on Assignation in Settlements", 1992 S.L.T. (News) 225.

[88] Or the Motor Insurers Bureau under the Uninsured Drivers Scheme. Note also the Financial Services Compensation Scheme under the Financial Services and Markets Act 2000.

[89] But there is some safeguard where the policy is obtained, e.g. by a misrepresentation.

and severally liable in damages or expenses, they shall be liable inter se to contribute to such damages or expenses in such proportions as the jury or the court, as the case may be, may deem just."

This allows the court to apportion liability between defenders sued jointly and severally according to their responsibility for the loss.[90] As liability is generally joint and several, the pursuer will be entitled to enforce his decree in full against any party. The party paying then has to recover the proportions for which he is not responsible from the other wrongdoers and to do that he may have to exercise his right of relief. If all the wrongdoers are not parties to the one action, the position is more complicated. While there may remain a common-law right of relief, in practice the position is now regulated by statute. Section 3(2) of the 1940 Act provides that:

"Where any person has paid any damages or expenses in which he has been found liable in any such action as aforesaid [a section 3(1) action] he shall be entitled to recover from any other person who, if sued, might also have been held liable in respect of the loss or damage on which the action was founded, such contribution, if any, as the court may deem just."

At common law, there is a right of relief against a wrongdoer by a person who is vicariously liable for him. So, for example, where an employee injured another employee, the employer's liability insurers were held entitled to proceed against him.[91] In this particular area, there are a number of extra-legal considerations, the most significant of which is that certain insurers have agreed not to exercise this legal right against employees unless there has been collusion or wilful misconduct.

The facts, read short, of *Caledonia North Sea Ltd v London Bridge Engineering Ltd*,[92] were that an oil platform, the Piper Alpha, exploded with enormous loss of property and loss of life. The owner-occupiers settled damages actions with the various claimants on the owner-occupiers. The owner-occupiers then sought indemnity from the 146 sub-contractors for the payments made by their insurers and underwriters. At first instance, six of seven test cases were dismissed. Because the contractors by their indemnity and the insurers by their contracts covered the same loss, they were co-debtors and the insurers would be able to sue for a proportion of their losses by way of contribution. It was also found at first instance that the insurers could have proceeded by subrogation and the owners would have had to have transferred their rights against the contractors to the insurers. On reclaiming it was held that as between the contract of insurance and the contract containing the indemnity, the latter was the primary obligation, being part of a mutual arrangement in a wider contractual relationship whereas the pursuers' insurance arrangements were intended for their own benefit and were *res inter alios acta* as respects the defenders and that the actions were properly brought by the insurers in name of the pursuers. Although decree had been pronounced in respect of the claims by the relatives and the claims had thereby been extinguished, the sums paid in terms of those decrees remained

---

[90] For discussion on the circumstances where liability may be joint and several see paras 4–04 and 13–03 above.

[91] *Lister v Romford Ice & Cold Storage Co Ltd* [1957] 1 All E.R. 125.

[92] *Caledonia North Sea Ltd v London Bridge Engineering Ltd*, 2002 S.C. (HL) 117.

sums paid in respect of liabilities arising from the injuries or deaths, and could be recovered by the pursuers if the settlement was reasonable in the circumstances. After a hearing before the House of Lords, all but one appeal was settled (*Norton No.2 Ltd*) which was dismissed. It was also held that a settlement taking into account the possibility of an award of damages in a foreign court which is later relied upon as a claim of indemnity, is not a matter of asking a Scottish court to award foreign damages and is permitted.[93]

The use of third party procedure, available in the sheriff court as well as the Court of Session, allows a defender to call any party who might be liable to contribute or indemnify as a third party to the action. This frequently prevents the need for a separate action of contribution or relief. Actions of contribution and relief are subject to a two-year limitation period, commencing on the date when the right to contribution or relief accrued.[94] It is essential for a claim of relief that there should be a Scottish decree against the claimant, but it does not have to have been obtained in a contested action.[95]

Extinction: decree and res judicata

14–15   It has been held to be a

> "sound principle that where a natural or legal person suffers damage as a result of a single negligent act, that gives rise to a single right to obtain reparation which must be pursued in one action."[96]

Thus, a delictual claim is discharged by decree and satisfaction of the decree. The cause—providing, of course, that the decree was not taken in absence—is res judicata and cannot be raised again. The onus of proof is however upon the defender to demonstrate that his liability has already been wholly discharged.[97]

Decree of *absolvitor* (the defender is *assoilzied*, i.e. absolved) prevents the action being raised on a different basis, as where an action is raised for personal injuries instead of for damage to property, or for a negligent misstatement instead of fraud.[98] An acquittal in a criminal matter is not res judicata and a victim of crime, or their family if the victim is deceased, may raise a civil action to vindicate the wrong.[99] Common law negligence and breach of statutory duty are in most circumstances not different *media concludendi*[100] but it depends on the nature of the negligence and the terms of the statutory duty. A finding of an employment tribunal may constitute res judicata in a later civil action.[101]

---

[93] *Caledonia North Sea Ltd v London Bridge Engineering Ltd*, 2002 S.C. (HL) 117.

[94] Prescription and Limitation (Scotland) Act 1973 s.8A.

[95] *Comex Houlder Diving Ltd v Colne Fishing Co Ltd*, 1987 S.C. (HL) 85. The Scottish Law Commission have reported on the questions of contribution and relief, annexing a draft Contribution in Damages (Scotland) Bill (Scottish Law Commission, *Report on Civil Liability*). See the analysis of relief in A. Young, "Rights of Relief", 1992 S.L.T. (News) 225 and *Comex Houlder Diving Ltd v Colne Fishing Co Ltd (No.2)*, 1992 S.L.T. 89.

[96] *Smith v Sabre Insurance Co Ltd*, 2013 S.C. 569 at 594 per Lord Brodie delivering the opinion of the court.

[97] *Irving v Hiddleston*, 1998 S.C. 759.

[98] On this point see, generally, *Gibson & Simpson v Pearson*, 1992 S.L.T. 894.

[99] *Mullan v Anderson*, 1996 Rep. L.R. 47.

[100] i.e. the ground of action. See *Matuszczyk v NCB*, 1955 S.C. 418.

[101] *British Airways Plc v Boyce*, 2001 S.L.T. 275.

There was a divergence of authority on the common practical point that arises where accidents cause both personal injuries and property damages. In *McPhee v Heatherwick*,[102] a motorcyclist sued the driver of a motorcar in the small debt court, on the ground of his negligent driving, for damages consisting of the excess on his insurance policy and the value of his crash helmet. The driver admitted liability and consented to decree. The motorcyclist's insurers, who were unaware of the small debt action, raised a summary action against the driver in the name of the motorcyclist, on the same ground, for the cost of replacing the motorcycle. The defender pleaded res judicata. This was upheld by Sheriff McPhail.

The point in *McSheehy v MacMillan*[103] was different. The pursuer raised a small claim against the defender for damages consisting of the excess on his insurance policy, loss of a vehicle and non-reclaimable insurance. The defender admitted the claim and decree was granted of consent. The pursuer's insurers subsequently raised a summary cause against the defender in the name of the pursuer in respect of the same collision for the cost of repairing the vehicle. The defender pleaded res judicata. The sum sued for in the action of £798 represented the sum paid by the pursuer's insurance company to the pursuer in settlement of his claim under his policy. In terms of the policy, there was a right of subrogation to the insurance company to use the pursuer's name in an action to recover their outlay. It should be noted that for the purposes of this case it was accepted that the *media concludendi* were the same—liability for harm caused by the negligent driving. That may not always be the case where different claims are put forward but whatever the case this was not argued out in *McSheehy*. Instead, Sheriff Lockhart considered that the subject-matter was different and on that basis he came to a different result.

The tension between these two decisions appears now to have been resolved in favour of Sheriff MacPhail's analysis in *McPhee* by the decision of the Inner House in *Smith v Sabre Insurance Co Ltd*.[104] The pursuer had been involved in a road accident caused by the negligence of another driver who was insured with the defenders. The pursuer had obtained decree in proceedings brought in Stirling Sheriff Court for personal injury and for the cost of repairs to his car. He subsequently raised a separate action in the Outer House for the costs associated with hiring a replacement car while his own was being repaired. The defenders pled *res judicata*. The Inner House upheld the decision of Lord Bannatyne that the *media concludendi* of the two actions was the same and that *McPhee* was correctly decided whereas the reasoning of Sheriff Lockhart in *McSheehy* ran counter to the authorities.

Decree of dismissal (in favour of the defender) only prevents an action being raised on the same point of law and so an action may be raised again on the same facts but on a different ground of law.

Discharge, compromise and settlement

A delictual action can be discharged on any terms and the discharge can be in any form. Acceptance of social security benefits does not imply a discharge. Only **14–16**

---

[102] *McPhee v Heatherwick*, 1977 S.L.T. (Sh. Ct) 46. The analysis of Sheriff MacPhail was approved by Lord Macfadyen in *Irving v Hiddleston*, 1998 S.C. 759 at 770, and by the Inner House in *Smith v Sabre Insurance Co Ltd*, 2013 S.C. 569 at 592.
[103] *McSheehy v MacMillan*, 1993 S.L.T. (Sh. Ct) 10.
[104] *Smith v Sabre Insurance Co Ltd*, 2013 S.L.T. 665.

the party in whose favour the discharge is granted can found upon it. If an action is raised against a number of persons jointly and severally, a discharge may be a discharge of one and not the others, but may be read as a discharge of the whole ground of action. The discharge of one joint wrongdoer does not prevent others subsequently claiming a right of relief against that party. A case can be compromised or settled with or without the court's permission on any terms. It is important that the settlement is clearly expressed. The onus of establishing a discharge by settlement is on the defender.[105] An advocate, but not a solicitor, can compromise a case without authority from his client. In practice, discharge may be effected by a separate minute which is a formal offer of settlement and if it includes an offer of the expenses of the action it will have the effect of imperilling the offeree for expenses if he is not subsequently awarded more than the offer by the court. It is one of the skills of the experienced agent to pitch such offers at the right level. In defamation cases, the offer must include a withdrawal of the alleged defamatory statement.

In *Irving v Hiddleston*,[106] the facts and legal background were different from the res judicata cases discussed above, although all the same authorities were canvassed. The pursuer's first solicitors settled her claim for damages. A sum was accepted in respect of solatium. Payments were also made in respect of her excess and loss of use. The pursuer's condition got worse and she sued in the Outer House. It was accepted that the claim for solatium was ruled out. However, no claims had previously been put forward for loss of wages or employability or for services. The actual ruling in this case was that the compromise did not encompass the new claims—put another way that the compromise amounted to no more than a partial settlement confined to its terms. Thus it is essentially a contract case deciding the meaning of certain terms agreed between the parties.

---

[105] *Irving v Hiddleston*, 1998 S.C. 759.
[106] *Irving v Hiddleston*, 1998 S.C. 759.

CHAPTER 15

PRESCRIPTION AND LIMITATION

INTRODUCTION

The concepts of prescription of obligations and limitation of actions are of **15–01** significant practical importance both for the litigant and for the professional legal adviser. Actions become "time-barred" after a period of time has elapsed. Thus, the victim of a delictual act then loses the opportunity to pursue a remedy and, if there has been a failure to lodge a claim timeously with the correct court, the professional adviser may be liable to the frustrated litigant in damages for negligence.

> "In this area of law, certainty is of central importance. So far as possible, everyone must know precisely when a claim exists and when it has pre-scribed." [1]

The rules, set out in the Prescription and Limitation (Scotland) Act 1973,[2] are complex, and although there is unfettered judicial discretion to extend some time limits the occasions when judges exercise this discretion remain rare.

There are several justifications for providing that actions become time-barred after a certain period. Policy reasons include the need for legal certainty and the avoidance of the threat of litigation in perpetuity.[3] Practical reasons include the deterioration in physical evidence and in human recollection over time,[4] as well as problems associated with maintaining insurance to protect against liabilities arising years after an activity has ceased.

The difference between limitation and prescription is simple but important. *Limitation* recognises that the obligation to make reparation continues but renders the obligation unenforceable. In practice the defender must tender a plea which in effect operates as a defence.[5] *Prescription* completely extinguishes the obligation, effectively preventing the court from entertaining the action and requiring the sheriff or Lord Ordinary to note that the action is no longer

---

[1] *David T Morrison & Co Ltd v ICL Plastics Ltd*, 2012 S.L.T. 813 at 814 per Lord Woolman.

[2] As amended by the Law Reform (Miscellaneous Provisions) (Scotland) Act 1980, the Prescription and Limitation (Scotland) Act 1984, the Law Reform (Miscellaneous Provisions) (Scotland) Act 1985, the Consumer Protection Act 1987 and the Protection from Harassment Act 1997.

[3] "The purpose of prescription is to cut off stale claims": *David T Morrison & Co Ltd v ICL Plastics Ltd*, 2012 S.L.T. 813 at 814 per Lord Woolman. The law should not permit "liability . . . for an indeterminate time": *Ultramares Corporation v Touche* (1931) N.Y. 170 at 179 per Cardozo C.J.

[4] See, e.g. *B v Murray (No.2)*, 2008 S.C. (HL) 146.

[5] The pursuer may choose not to take the plea: *A v Glasgow City Council* sub nom. *F v Quarriers*, 2010 S.C. 411 at 417 per Lord President (Hamilton); *J v Fife Council*, 2007 S.L.T. 85.

competent.[6] With this in mind it is suggested that the appropriate terminology to adopt is respectively limitation of *actions* and prescription of *obligations*. It is important to note that in many cases, an obligation may prescribe before the limitation period would otherwise have expired.

A table providing an overview of the basic time periods is provided at the end of this chapter.

LIMITATION

15–02 A limitation period of three years[7]—often called the "triennium"—applies respectively to actions with regard to personal injuries,[8] reputational harm,[9] harassment[10] or product liability under the Consumer Protection Act 1987.[11] Any other claims in delict, such as for economic loss or damage to property other than under the Consumer Protection Act 1987, are not subject to limitation, although the relevant obligations will be subject to prescription. The three year computation will exclude any period where the person suffering harm was under a legal disability such as nonage or unsoundness of mind,[12] and the court has discretion to permit the commencement of an action outside of the triennium where the court considers it to be equitable in the circumstances.[13]

The commencement of the limitation period varies depending on the nature of the wrong and on the nature of the harm.

In *personal injury* cases normally the period begins on the date when the injuries were sustained. However, if the wrong was in the form of a continuing delictual act such as failure to maintain a safe system of work, the triennium runs from the date when the wrongful act ceased.[14] Furthermore, the commencement of the triennium will be delayed if the court considers that it would not have been reasonably practicable[15] in the circumstances for the victim to have previously become aware of all of the following three facts[16]:

---

[6] Although the onus of proof of prescription is on the defender: see, e.g. *Strathclyde RC v W.A. Fairhurst*, 1997 S.L.T. 658; *Glasper v Rodger*, 1996 S.L.T. 44.

[7] In December 2013 the Scottish Government announced a proposal to increase the time period to five years: *Civil Law of Damages: Issues in Personal Injury—Scottish Government Response to the Consultation* (December 19, 2013) found at *http://www.scotland.gov.uk/Publications/2013/12/7197* [Accessed June 12, 2014].

[8] Prescription and Limitation (Scotland) Act 1973 ss.17 and 18.

[9] Prescription and Limitation (Scotland) Act 1973 s.18A.

[10] Within the meaning of s.8 of the Protection from Harassment Act 1997: Prescription and Limitation (Scotland) Act 1973 s.18B.

[11] Prescription and Limitation (Scotland) Act 1973 ss.22B and 22C.

[12] For a discussion on unsoundness of mind see *Bogan's Curator Bonis v Graham*, 1992 S.C.L.R. 920. In December 2013 the Scottish Government announced a proposal to replace the term "unsoundness of mind" with a reference to the pursuer's being "incapable" for the purposes of the Adults with Incapacity (Scotland) Act 2000: *Civil Law of Damages: Issues in Personal Injury—Scottish Government Response to the Consultation.*

[13] Prescription and Limitation (Scotland) Act 1973 s.19A.

[14] Prescription and Limitation (Scotland) Act 1973 s.17(2)(a). See *Mather v British Telecommunications Plc*, 2001 S.L.T. 325.

[15] In December 2013 the Scottish Government announced a proposal to replace the term "reasonably practicable" with a term that increases the subjectivity of the test. The term "excusably unaware" was put forward so as to enable the circumstances of the pursuer, such as education, intelligence or occupation, to be taken into account: *Civil Law of Damages: Issues in Personal Injury—Scottish Government Response to the Consultation.*

[16] See generally with regard to "historic abuse" cases: *M v O'Neill*, 2006 S.L.T. 823; *M v Hendron*, 2007 S.C. 556; *B v Murray*, 2008 S.C. (HL) 146; *A v N*, 2009 S.C. 449; *G v Glasgow City Council*, 2011 S.C. 1; *W v Glasgow City Council*, 2011 S.C. 15.

- the injuries in question were sufficiently serious to justify his bringing an action—on the assumption that the defender did not dispute liability and was able to satisfy a decree[17];
- the injuries were attributable in whole or in part to an act or omission;
- the defender was a person, or vicariously liable with regards to a person, to whose act or omission the injuries were attributable in whole or in part.[18]

If, before the expiry of the triennium as outlined above, the victim dies as a result of the personal injury, a claim with regard to the death is subject to a three year limitation period running from the date of the death.[19] Here, the triennium may be extended where the *pursuer*[20] was under a legal disability such as nonage or unsoundness of mind. Again, the court may acknowledge a delay in the commencement of the triennium where it would not have been reasonably practicable in the circumstances for the pursuer to have become aware of both of the following facts:

- the injuries were attributable in whole or in part to an act or omission;
- the defender was a person, or vicariously liable with regards to a person, to whose act or omission the injuries were attributable in whole or in part.[21]

Note that the *terminus a quo*, i.e. the point from which time will run, thus occurs **15–03** on the concurrence of *injuria* and *damnum*. Death, in being dealt with separately in s.18, is clearly treated as a form of *damnum* distinct from personal injuries. However, personal injuries incorporate physical and derivative psychiatric injuries[22] and the two will be treated as indivisible where they are consequent on a single wrongful act or course of wrongful conduct. Thus, should a wrongful act cause immediate physical injuries, the triennium will run from the point when the pursuer becomes aware of the three statutory facts set out in s.17(2)(b), and should psychiatric injuries caused by the same legal wrong manifest following

---

[17] In *Blake v Lothian Health Board*, 1993 S.L.T. 1248 the Lord Ordinary pointed out that just because injuries could not be described as "trivial" did not mean that they were sufficiently serious to justify an action, especially considering the disproportionate cost and trouble in bringing an action for a claim apparently worth no more than £200. See *Ferla v Secretary of State for Scotland*, 1995 S.L.T. 662 for the impact of having already lodged a claim with the Criminal Injuries Compensation Scheme. See also *W v Glasgow City Council*, 2011 S.C. 15.

[18] Prescription and Limitation (Scotland) Act 1973 s.17(2)(b). The onus of proof rests on the pursuer to show that he did not have constructive knowledge before he acquired actual knowledge of these facts: *Elliott v J. & C. Finney*, 1989 S.L.T. 208; *Agnew v Scott Lithgow Ltd. (No.1)*, 2001 S.C. 516. Cf. *Clark v Scott Lithgow Ltd*, 2006 Rep. L.R. 16.

[19] Note that death that is not attributable to the legal wrong has no impact on the running of the triennium.

[20] Including a relative pursuing an action under s.4 of the Damages (Scotland) Act 2011.

[21] Prescription and Limitation (Scotland) Act 1973 s.18.

[22] See *Page v Smith* [1996] A.C. 155; *Simmons v British Steel Plc*, 2004 S.C. (HL) 94. Cf. *Grieves v FT Everard & Sons Ltd* [2008] 1 A.C. 281.

the expiry of the triennium, any action in respect of the psychiatric injury will be subject to limitation.[23]

In *reputational harm* cases, including defamation, *convicium* and malicious falsehood, the three year limitation period runs from the point where the communication that is the subject of the complaint first came to the attention of the pursuer.[24]

In *harassment* cases, the three year limitation period runs from the date when the harassment ceased, subject to a delay where the court considers it would not have been reasonably practicable in the circumstances for the victim to have become aware that the defender was a person responsible for the alleged harassment or vicariously liable with regard to such a person.[25]

In *product liability* cases brought under s.2 of the Consumer Protection Act 1987 the limitation rules are broadly similar to those applying to personal injury. Thus, subject to the exceptions regarding nonage and unsoundness of mind,[26] and to the discretion of the court to extend the period where equitable,[27] an action must be commenced within three years of the date the court considers it would have been reasonably practicable in the circumstances for the victim to have become aware of all of the following four facts:

- there was a defect in a product;
- the damage was caused or partly caused by the defect;
- the damage was sufficiently serious to justify the pursuer in bringing an action on the assumption that the defender did not dispute liability and was able to satisfy a decree;
- the defender was a person liable for the damage under the s.2 of the 1987 Act.[28]

Similar to the position with regards to personal injury: if, before the expiry of the triennium as outlined above, the victim dies as a result of personal injury caused by the defective product, an action with regard to the death is subject to a three year limitation period running from the date of the death. Again, the triennium may be extended where the *pursuer*[29] was under a legal disability such as nonage or unsoundness of mind. Again, the court may recognise a delay in the commencement of the triennium where it would not have been reasonably practicable in the circumstances for the pursuer (or the original victim) to have become aware at an earlier stage of the following three facts:

- there was a defect in a product;
- the damage was caused or partly caused by the defect;

---

[23] *A v Glasgow City Council* sub nom. *F v Quarriers*, 2010 S.C. 411, departing from the approach taken in *Carnegie v Lord Advocate*, 2001 S.C. 802 and *Shuttleton v Duncan Stewart & Co Ltd*, 1996 S.L.T. 517.
[24] Prescription and Limitation (Scotland) Act 1973 s.18A.
[25] Prescription and Limitation (Scotland) Act 1973 s.18B.
[26] Prescription and Limitation (Scotland) Act 1973 ss.22B(5) and 22C(3).
[27] Prescription and Limitation (Scotland) Act 1973 ss.22B(6) and 22C(5).
[28] Prescription and Limitation (Scotland) Act 1973 s.22B(3).
[29] Including a relative pursuing an action under s.4 of the Damages (Scotland) Act 2011.

- the defender was a person liable for the damage under the section 2 of the 1987 Act.[30]

As noted above, commencement of an action outside of the triennium may be **15–04** permitted where the court considers it equitable in all the circumstances.[31] The court has an unfettered discretion to make a decision by examining the broad question "where do the equities lie?"[32] Without prejudice to the important principle that each case turns on its own facts,[33] it has been suggested[34] that factors to consider may include:

- the conduct of the pursuer in the period between the incident and the commencement of proceedings including an explanation for failure to bring proceedings timeously[35];
- likely prejudice to the pursuer if permission to bring proceedings out of time is not granted[36];
- Likely prejudice to the defender if permission to bring proceedings out of time is granted.[37]

However, it must be emphasised that these factors will not necessarily all be relevant in a particular case and certainly do not provide an exhaustive list.[38] Other factors to have been considered include:

- the pursuer's lack of knowledge of a legal right[39];
- the conduct of the parties' legal representatives[40];
- the availability of an alternative action against a third party—such as a legal representative responsible for a delay in bringing an action timeously.[41]

---

[30] Prescription and Limitation (Scotland) Act 1973 s.22C(2).

[31] Prescription and Limitation (Scotland) Act 1973 s.19A. In December 2013 the Scottish Government announced a proposal to add a detailed non-exhaustive list of factors for the court to consider when asked to exercise its discretion to allow a case to proceed outwith the limitation period: *Civil Law of Damages: Issues in Personal Injury—Scottish Government Response to the Consultation.*

[32] *Forsyth v A.F. Stoddard & Co. Ltd*, 1985 S.L.T. 51 at 55 per Lord Justice-Clerk Wheatley.

[33] Which means that the relevant facts may have to be investigated in order to permit the court to exercise discretion: see, e.g. *A v N*, 2009 S.C. 449; *G v Glasgow City Council*, 2011 S.C. 1; *W v Glasgow City Council*, 2011 S.C. 15.

[34] *Carson v Howard Doris Ltd*, 1981 S.C. 278 at 282 per Lord Ross.

[35] See, e.g. *M v Hendron*, 2007 S.C. 556.

[36] See, e.g. *Ferla v Secretary of State for Scotland*, 1995 S.L.T. 662.

[37] See, e.g. *Bogan's Curator Bonis v Graham*, 1992 S.C.L.R. 920; *M v O'Neill*, 2006 S.L.T. 823; *B v Murray*, 2008 S.C. (HL) 146, where the House of Lords approved the decision of the Lord Ordinary that the evidential prejudice that the defenders would suffer because of the delay was itself sufficient to confirm the equities pointed to a refusal to exercise discretion under s.19A.

[38] See, e.g. *Donald v Rutherford*, 1984 S.L.T. 70 at 75 per Lord Cameron, and at 78 per Lord Dunpark; *Forsyth v A.F. Stoddard & Co Ltd*, 1985 S.L.T. 51 at 53 per Lord Justice-Clerk Wheatley, and at 55 per Lord Hunter.

[39] See, e.g. *Comber v Greater Glasgow Health Board*, 1989 S.L.T. 639; *B v Murray*, 2008 S.C. (HL) 146.

[40] See, e.g. *Forsyth v A.F. Stoddard & Co Ltd*, 1985 S.L.T. 51; *Bogan's Curator Bonis v Graham*, 1992 S.C.L.R. 920; *McCluskey v Sir Robert McAlpine & Sons Ltd*, 1994 S.C.L.R. 650.

[41] See, e.g. *Donald v Rutherford*, 1984 S.L.T. 70; *Forsyth v A.F. Stoddard & Co Ltd*, 1985 S.L.T. 51; *Clark v McLean*, 1994 S.C. 410. Cf. *Elliott v J.C. Finney (No.1)*, 1989 S.L.T. 605; *Ferguson v McFadyen*, 1992 S.L.T. 44.

Prescription

15–05 It should be noted at the outset that obligations to make reparation with regard to death or personal injuries do not prescribe if the harm occurred on or after September 26, 1964[42]—although actions with regard to such obligations are subject to limitation.[43]

Other obligations to make reparation will prescribe, i.e. the obligations will be extinguished, upon the expiry of the relevant prescriptive period. With the exception of obligations under s.2 of the Consumer Protection Act 1987 which are subject to a 10 year prescriptive period,[44] and obligations to make contributions between wrongdoers[45] which are subject to a two year prescriptive period,[46] there are two periods to bear in mind:

- a "short" prescriptive period of five years ("the quinqennium");
- a "long-stop" prescriptive period of 20 years.

With the exception of reparation for reputational harm[47] and for death or personal injury,[48] obligations to make reparation normally prescribe after five years.[49] Such obligations clearly include those to make reparation for damage to property and economic loss (with the aforesaid exception of those arising under the Consumer Protection Act 1987). However, if such an obligation does not prescribe after five years, e.g. because the damage remains latent, the obligation to make reparation will inevitably prescribe after 20 years upon the expiry of the long-stop prescriptive period. Apart from the two exceptions noted above,[50] obligations to make reparation which are subject to limitation prescribe after 20 years.

As a general rule, the prescriptive periods run from the date, often referred to as the *terminus a quo*, when the delict is complete, i.e. when the *injuria* manifests in *damnum*:

> "The right to raise such an action accrues when *injuria* concurs with *damnum*. Some interval of time may elapse between the two ... and ... in such circumstances time is to run from the date when *damnum* results, not from the date of the earlier *injuria*."[51]

---

[42] Such obligations as had not already prescribed were made imprescriptible by the Prescription and Limitation (Scotland) Act 1984 (amending s.7(2) of the 1973 Act) made from the date of its coming into force—September 26, 1964.

[43] Obligations in respect of death or personal injuries occurring before September 26, 1964 remain subject to the long-stop 20 year prescriptive period.

[44] Prescription and Limitation (Scotland) Act 1973 s.22A. Note that there is nothing to prevent the victim of damage caused by a defective product attempting to fall back on a claim for reparation at common law, which will then be subject to the 20 year long-stop prescriptive period.

[45] Under s.3(2) of the Law Reform (Miscellaneous Provisions) (Scotland) Act 1940.

[46] Prescription and Limitation (Scotland) Act 1973 s.8A.

[47] Including defamation, *convicium* and malicious falsehood: Prescription & Limitation (Scotland) Act 1973 s.18A.

[48] Prescription and Limitation (Scotland) Act 1973 Sch.1.

[49] Prescription and Limitation (Scotland) Act 1973 s.6(1).

[50] i.e. obligations to make reparation for damage under Pt 1 of the Consumer Protection Act 1987 (which prescribe after 10 years) and obligations to make reparation for death or personal injury that arose on or after September 26, 1964 (which do not prescribe).

[51] *Dunlop v McGowans*, 1980 S.C. (HL) 73 at 81 per Lord Keith of Kinkell. See also *Renfrew Golf Club v Ravenstone Securities Ltd. (No.3)*, 1984 S.C. 22; *Osborne & Hunter Ltd v Hardie Caldwell*, 1999 S.L.T. 153.

It has been settled law since at least the case of *K v Gilmartin's Executrix*[52] that for the purposes of the long-stop prescriptive period, physical and psychiatric injuries attributed to a single wrongful act or course of wrongful conduct will be treated as indivisible. Thus, where the obligation to make reparation has prescribed due to physical injury being apparent to the pursuer prior to September 26, 1964, any obligation to make reparation with regard to psychiatric injury manifesting on or after September 26, 1984 will have already prescribed.

However, where the obligation to make reparation arises from damage caused by a continuing delictual act, such as a nuisance,[53] prescriptive periods run from the time the wrongful conduct ceased.[54] Also, the running of the five year prescriptive period will be suspended (but not restarted) during any period where the original victim was under a legal disability by reason of nonage or unsoundness of mind,[55] and will likewise be suspended for any period during which the pursuer refrains from making a relevant claim with respect to the obligation by reason of the defender's fraud, or because of words or conduct inducing error on the part of the pursuer.[56]

Where the damage is latent,[57] the five year prescriptive period will run from **15–06** the point where the victim became aware, or with reasonable diligence would be expected to have become aware of the harm caused by the delictual act.[58] This is known as the "discoverability formula" and will require the pursuer to know not only that harm has occurred but also that the harm is attributable to the legal wrong before time will begin to run.[59] The court may consider whether in the circumstances of the particular case the law requires the exercise of reasonable diligence. For example, where professional negligence was alleged of a solicitor in failing to take a proper title, the Inner House held that time ran from the point where the error was noticed by the clients rather than from the point where the error was made, and that the clients would not necessarily have failed to exercise reasonable diligence where they had not taken steps to check that their solicitors had completed the conveyancing transaction according to their instructions.[60]

---

[52] *K v Gilmartin's Executrix*, 2004 S.C. 784.

[53] Note that the obligation to abate a nuisance is subject only to the long-stop prescriptive period so, whereas an action for *damages* with regard to a nuisance normally prescribes within five years, an application for an *interdict* prescribes only after 20 years. It is unclear whether an application for an interdict is subject to s.7 (which allows for interruption by a relevant claim or relevant acknowledgement) or s.8 (which does not allow for interruption).

[54] Prescription and Limitation (Scotland) Act 1973 s.11(2).

[55] Prescription and Limitation (Scotland) Act 1973 s.6(4)(b).

[56] Prescription and Limitation (Scotland) Act 1973 s.6(4). See *BP Exploration Operating Co Ltd v Chevron Transport (Scotland)*, 2002 S.C. (HL) 19.

[57] It has been held in the context of the quinquennial prescriptive period that time will not run until a latent defect is revealed by actual damage: *Renfrew Golf Club v Ravenstone Securities Ltd (No.3)*, 1984 S.C. 22.

[58] Prescription and Limitation (Scotland) Act 1973 s.11(3). Note that this exception does not apply in respect of the long-stop 20 year prescriptive period: Prescription and Limitation (Scotland) Act 1973 s.11(4).

[59] *Dunfermline DC v Blyth & Blyth Associates*, 1985 S.L.T. 345; *Kirk Care Housing Association Ltd v Crerar and Partners*, 1996 S.L.T. 150. Knowledge of a concurrence of *injuria* and *damnum* will trigger the quinqennium even if the identity of the wrongdoer is not known to the victim: *Greater Glasgow Health Board v Baxter Clark & Paul*, 1990 S.C. 237.

[60] *Glasper v Rodger*, 1996 S.L.T. 44.

Reliance on the doctrine of res ipsa loquitur has been described as the "antithesis"[61] of "awareness not only of the fact of loss having occurred, but of the fact that it is a loss caused by negligence."[62] Thus, prescription may be deferred with reference to s.11(3).

All prescriptive periods are subject to interruption where a relevant claim is made,[63] or, with the exception of product liability claims under Pt 1 of the Consumer Protection Act 1987, by a relevant acknowledgement by the defender.[64] Such interruptions serve to restart applicable prescriptive periods.

TIME LIMITS IN OTHER RELATED CASES

15–07 Legal proceedings brought under the Human Rights Act[65] or under the Scotland Act[66] for acting incompatibly with Convention rights must be brought within one year of the taking place of the act complained of.[67] A court or tribunal may extend this period if it considers this to be equitable with regard to all of the circumstances.[68]

	Limitation period	Short prescriptive period	Long prescriptive period
Death/personal injury before 26 September 1964	3 years		20 years
Death/personal injury on or after 26 September 1964 (excluding damage under Consumer Protection Act 1987 Part 1)	3 years		Do not prescribe
Reputational harm	3 years		20 years
Harassment under the Protection from Harassment Act 1997	3 years	5 years	20 years
Economic loss		5 years	20 years

---

[61] *David T Morrison & Co Ltd v ICL Plastics Ltd*, 2013 S.L.T. 413 at 419 per Lady Paton delivering the opinion of the court.

[62] *Glasper v Rodger*, 1996 S.L.T. 44 at 47 per Lord Hope of Craighead.

[63] i.e. the formal service on the defender of relevant papers with regard to a claim brought via relevant court or arbitration proceedings, or a claim lodged with regard to the defender's bankruptcy or insolvency, or diligence: Prescription and Limitation (Scotland) Act 1973 s.9(1). See also *Boyle v Glasgow Corp*, 1975 S.C. 238 at 250 per Lord Justice-Clerk Wheatley.

[64] i.e. such performance towards implement of the obligation as is sufficient to confirm its continued existence, or an unequivocal written admission by or on behalf of the defender: Prescription and Limitation (Scotland) Act 1973 s.10(1).

[65] Human Rights Act s.7(5)(a)

[66] Scotland Act 1998 s.100(3B)(a).

[67] Or within one year of the ceasing of a continuing act: *Somerville v Scottish Ministers*, 2008 S.C. (HL) 45 at 65 per Lord Hope of Craighead.

[68] Human Rights Act 1998 s.7(5)(b); Scotland Act 1998 s.100(3B)(b).

	Limitation period	Short prescriptive period	Long prescriptive period
Damage to property		5 years	20 years
Damage under Consumer Protection Act 1987 Part 1	3 years		10 years
Contributions between wrongdoers under s.3(2) Law Reform (Misc. Prov.) (Scotland) Act 1940			2 years

SECTION V: SPECIFIC LIABILITY REGIMES

CHAPTER 16

BREACH OF STATUTORY DUTY

INTRODUCTION

Although the influence of civilian traditions historically shaped the development **16–01** of Scots law, the recent influence of English law has prevented Scots law from following civilian systems to their codifying conclusions. Thus, common law, in the sense of non-statutory law, might be said to be the equivalent of the natural environment of Scots law, whereas legislation forms the built environment so adding to the legal landscape. It follows that, subject to the exception of desuetude for pre-1707 Scots Acts, statute may supplement or supplant common law, but not vice versa.[1] Thus, statute takes priority over the common law.

A growing number of statutes and other legislative instruments[2] impose "duties" on individuals and/or public bodies.[3] These regulate an ever-widening range of activities, including various social responsibilities of public bodies in areas such as education, housing, building control, transport infrastructure and welfare etc; employment relationships and safety in the workplace and in other premises; the manufacture and supply of consumer goods and services; road traffic—and the list goes on. Several of these statutes are explicit in providing for liability by means of a private law civil action to victims of a breach of the statutory duty. These statutes usually also stipulate whether liability requires proof of intention,[4] or is fault-based,[5] strict,[6] or absolute.[7] Conversely, some statutes specifically *exclude* civil liability for breach.[8] However, difficulties arise where, as is very often the case, statutes (including delegated legislation) create "duties" but are silent on whether breach of those duties can lead to civil liability. Then, it is for the courts to

---

[1] See, e.g. *X (Minors) v Bedfordshire CC* [1995] 2 A.C. 633 at 765 per Lord Browne-Wilkinson; *Downsview Nominees v First City Corp* [1993] A.C. 295 at 316 per Lord Templeman.

[2] e.g. the "six pack" of regulations created under the Health and Safety at Work Act 1974: see paras 21–09 to 21–24.

[3] A detailed treatment is found in K. Stanton et al., *Statutory Torts* (London: Sweet & Maxwell, 2003).

[4] e.g. Protection from Harassment Act 1997.

[5] e.g. Occupiers' Liability (Scotland) Act 1960.

[6] e.g. Animals (Scotland) Act 1987; Consumer Protection Act 1987 Pt I.

[7] e.g. Factories Act 1961 (relevant provisions now repealed). For discussion of the terminology see *Allison v London Underground* [2008] I.C.R. 719 at 729–730 per Smith L.J.

[8] e.g. Health and Safety at Work Act 1974. Note that until October 2013 s.47(2) of the Act provided that the "six pack" of regulations *did* provide for civil liability unless otherwise stated. The presumption was reversed upon the implementation of s.69 of the Enterprise and Regulatory Reform Act 2013.

work out, or second-guess,[9] whether it was the intention of Parliament to create civil liability:

> "It has long ago been decided that the mere fact that a duty has been created by a statute will not entitle a person injured by the breach of that statutory duty to claim damages from the person upon whom the duty is imposed[10] and the Courts have frequently had to determine whether a particular statutory obligation does or does not confer a right upon a person injured by its breach to damages for that injury. The solution in each case must depend upon what the intention of Parliament was in enacting the obligation in question, and what persons consequently have a right to enforce it or to found upon it as a basis for a claim of damages."[11]

It should be noted that an action for breach of statutory duty is distinct from a common law negligence action.[12] In some cases there have been attempts to circumvent statutory interpretation by arguing that a parallel duty of care is imposed by the common law.[13] The courts tend to be reticent in accepting this argument, holding that the policy aspect of the *Caparo*[14] test militates against supplementing or supplanting statutory duties, especially when these are imposed on public bodies with respect to their public functions.[15] However, it should also be noted that where they claim to have suffered harm due to a breach of a statutory duty by a public authority, pursuers may have an alternative string to their bow in the form of s.8 of the Human Rights Act 1998,[16] which provides the court with the power to make an award of damages in just satisfaction if the pursuer can show that the breach of duty amounts to a breach of a relevant provision of the European Convention on Human Rights.[17]

ACTION FOR BREACH OF STATUTORY DUTY: FACTORS

16–02 Where a statute creating a duty is silent on the matter, there are several elements that a court will consider in determining whether a civil remedy may be pursued by an individual who claims to have suffered harm attributable to a breach of that

---

[9] See, e.g. *Island Records Ltd v Corkindale* [1978] Ch. 122 at 135 per Lord Denning M.R.

[10] *Atkinson v Newcastle Waterworks Co* (1877) 2 Ex. D. 441 at 448 per Lord Cairns L.C.

[11] *Pullar v Window Clean*, 1956 S.C. 13 at 20 per Lord President Clyde.

[12] See, e.g. *London Passenger Transport Board v Upson* [1949] A.C. 155 at 168 per Lord Upjohn. A pursuer may aver breach both of statutory duty and of a common law duty of care as alternatives: see, e.g. *Millar v Galashiels Gas Co Ltd*, 1949 S.C. (HL) 3; *Bux v Slough Metals Ltd* [1973] 1 W.L.R. 1358.

[13] See, e.g. *X (Minors) v Bedfordshire CC* [1995] 2 A.C. 633.

[14] Whether it is fair, just and reasonable to recognise an *ex lege* duty of care: *Caparo Industries Plc v Dickman* [1990] 2 A.C. 605. See paras 11–61 to 11–63 above.

[15] See, e.g. *X (Minors) v Bedfordshire CC* [1995] 2 A.C. 633. See Ch.17.

[16] See also Scotland Act 1998 s.100(1) and (3).

[17] See, e.g. *Jain v Trent Strategic Health Authority* [2009] 1 A.C. 853; *Mitchell v Glasgow City Council*, 2009 S.C. (HL) 21. Note that such a claim for just satisfaction is distinguishable from an action for breach of statutory duty *per se*: *Somerville v The Scottish Ministers*, 2008 S.C. (HL) 45 at 57 per Lord Hope of Craighead. The distinctive features extend to time-bar and also to title to sue: see *Axa General Insurance Ltd, Petitioners*, 2012 S.C. (U.K.S.C.) 122. For further discussion see Ch.17.

duty. This is, therefore, a specialised area of statutory interpretation.[18] A good example is *Cutler v Wandsworth Stadium Ltd (in liquidation)*.[19] This was an action raised by a bookmaker for damages against a licensed dog track for their refusal to allow him space on their premises to carry on bookmaking. The bookmaker founded on the Betting, Gaming and Lotteries Act 1934 s.11(2), which provided that so long as a totalisator (state bookmaking system) was being lawfully operated from a licensed dog track, the occupier could not exclude any person from the track by reason only that he proposes to carry on bookmaking on the track; and had to take such steps as are necessary to secure that there is available for bookmakers space on the track where they can conveniently carry on bookmaking. Every person who contravened or failed to comply with, any of the provisions was made guilty of an offence. Now, while it is clear that Parliament was imposing a duty on the stadium proprietor it is not clear from reading the Act when, if at all, and if so in what circumstances, a person might be able to sue in the civil courts for a failure to carry out the duty. In the House of Lords, Lord Reid identified certain issues that can help to determine the question. He asked: for whose benefit was this sub-section intended? And, as Law Lords usually do, he provided an answer to his own question: I think that it was primarily intended for the protection of those members of the public who might wish to bet on these tracks. Not for bookmakers then—the idea was to provide competition for the state-run totalisator. Another factor for Lord Reid was that, "if the legislature had intended to create such [civil] rights, [one] would expect to find them capable of reasonably precise definition."[20] This the bookmaker was unable to do since, for example, there were many answers to the question "How many bookmakers must be allowed in?"—all that ask, or just enough to leave enough space for the dogs? Lord Reid concluded by pointing out that the statute imposed a criminal penalty that was "appropriate and sufficient for the general obligation imposed."[21]

That, then, is the sort of issue with which this head of liability deals. Other issues arise in other cases and it is possible to set out a list of requirements the presence of which might lead to success, and the absence of which are likely to bring defeat for the pursuer.[22] It should already be clear that matters of policy such as social and economic issues will bear significantly on the courts' decisions, undermining the predictability of a particular outcome.[23] Nevertheless, as Lord McCluskey put it, "[i]t is essential to look at the statute founded upon."[24]

---

[18] D.M. Walker, *The Scottish Legal System: An Introduction to the Study of Scots Law*, 8th edn (Edinburgh: W. Green, 2001), pp.413–432. A good example of the legal method to be applied is provided in *Morrison Sports Ltd v Scottish Power Plc*, 2011 S.C. (U.K.S.C.) 1.

[19] *Cutler v Wandsworth Stadium Ltd (in liquidation)* [1949] 1 All E. R. 544. This case was influential and approved in *Pullar v Window Clean*, 1956 S.C. 13.

[20] *Cutler v Wandsworth Stadium Ltd* [1949] A.C. 398 at 417.

[21] *Cutler v Wandsworth Stadium Ltd* [1949] A.C. 398 at 418.

[22] See also *X (Minors) v Bedfordshire CC* [1995] 2 A.C. 633 at 731–732 per Lord Browne-Wilkinson.

[23] Compare, e.g. *Richardson v Pitt-Stanley* [1995] Q.B. 123 with *Quinn v McGinty*, 1999 S.L.T. (Sh. Ct) 27. Is it satisfactory that whether a breach of a statutory duty is actionable at private law is determined by the priorities individual judges put on the various factors at play—put another way, what safeguards exist to prevent the question being determined by judicial whim?

[24] *Weir v East of Scotland Water Authority*, 2001 S.L.T. 1205 at 1210.

Statutory duty on defender

16–03   The statute must tell the defender to do, or not to do, something. It is not
enough that the statute permits the defender to do or to refrain from doing
something.[25] Thus, a private law civil action will be incompetent if the act
complained of falls within any discretion conferred by the statute. The courts
have generally refused to adjudicate where a complaint is made about a public
body in respect of "matters of policy", such as the prioritisation and allocation
of finite resources.[26] However, limits have been suggested. A distinction has been
made between policy decisions and operational decisions,[27] and the latter have
been held to be justiciable in a civil action. Even in matters of discretion,
although the court is likely to be wary of imposing liability for bona fide
mistakes, it has been suggested that Parliament could not intend that discretion
be exercised in an irrational way.[28]

The court's own view on whether there should be liability is irrelevant:

> "All that it is necessary to show is duty to take care to avoid injuring; and
> if, the particular care to be taken is prescribed by statute, and the duty to the
> injured person to take the care is likewise imposed by statute, and the breach
> is proved, all the essentials of negligence are present. I cannot think that the
> true position is, as appears to be suggested, that in such cases negligence
> only exists where the tribunal of fact agrees with the legislature that the
> precaution is one that ought to be taken. The very object of the legislation
> is to put that particular precaution beyond controversy."[29]

Duty to protect the pursuer as an individual

16–04   This point is illustrated by *Cutler* above, where although there may have been
some intention by Parliament to help bookmakers generally, it was essentially
members of the public who were being protected. Many statutory duties have
been interpreted as intended to provide general protection for the community at
large, rather than specific civil remedies for individuals. Indicators may be
deemed to include:

- the size of class of persons Parliament intends to protect: Parliament
  may have intended to provide a private law remedy for a limited class
  of persons as defined in the statute[30];
- whether the duty is imposed with regard to individual relationships
  (such as the relationship between employer and employee)[31] or community relationships (such as between a local authority and the community)[32];

---

[25] Thus it is necessary to distinguish statutory "duties" from statutory "powers" which are clearly
discretionary: *East Suffolk Rivers Catchment Board v Kent* [1941] A.C. 74; *Stovin v Wise* [1996]
A.C. 923; *Gorringe v Calderdale Metropolitan BC* [2004] 1 W.L.R. 1057; *Mitchell v Glasgow
City Council*, 2009 S.C. (HL) 21; *MacDonald v Aberdeenshire Council*, 2014 S.L.T. 2.

[26] See, e.g. *O'Rourke v Camden LBC* [1998] A.C. 188 at 193 per Lord Hoffmann.

[27] See *Anns v Merton LBC* [1978] A.C. 728 at 754 per Lord Wilberforce.

[28] See *Dorset Yacht Co Ltd v Home Office* [1970] A.C. 1004 at 1031 per Lord Reid; *X (Minors) v
Bedfordshire CC* [1995] 2 A.C. 633 at 736–737 per Lord Browne-Wilkinson.

[29] *McMullan v Lochgelly Iron and Coal Co*, 1933 S.C. (HL) 64 at 67 per Lord Atkin.

[30] Employees have been held to constitute a limited class: see, e.g. *Groves v Lord Wimborne* [1898]
2 Q.B. 402; *Black v Fife Coal Co Ltd*, 1912 S.C. (HL) 33.

[31] See, e.g. *McMullan v Lochgelly Iron and Coal Co*, 1933 S.C. (HL) 64.

[32] *X (Minors) v Bedfordshire CC* [1995] 2 A.C. 633.

- what is being protected: health and safety interests tend to be prioritised over economic interests.[33]

In the leading case of *Pullar v Window Clean*, the idea of a class of persons protected of which the pursuer must be a member was explained by Lord President Clyde:

> "If the class of persons for whose protection it is alleged that the duty was imposed is indefinite and difficult to define, this would tend to exclude the construction of the section which would give a right to civil damages for breach ... and would favour the view that the legislature intended the sanction of prosecution for a penalty as appropriate and sufficient for the obligation imposed by the section ... But where the predominant purpose of the statute is manifestly the protection of a particular class of workmen by imposing on their employers for instance the duty of taking special measures to secure their safety then the inference is readily drawn that the legislature intended to confer on these workmen a right to sue for damages where the duty is not fulfilled ... Accordingly, before a right to civil damages can arise out of the statutory duty imposed there must be a manifest or clear intention to confer such a right and a definite class of persons upon whom the right is so conferred."[34]

In *Pullar*, the pursuer was a window cleaner who fell when he stepped onto the outside window ledge to clean the outside of a sash window. No provision had been made to facilitate the cleaning of the outside of the window from inside the premises, even although the relevant building regulations, which were administered and enforced by the Dean of Guild Court, appeared to require that.[35] The legislative purpose was related to planning and building control; it was not "designed to constitute a charter for window-cleaners."[36]

In *Weir v East of Scotland Water Authority*,[37] the duty on the defenders to provide a supply of wholesome water was held to be owed to every domestic consumer within the defender's area and thus not a sufficiently defined limited class of the public. Is this not a question of a big defined class—they are defined by having pipes into their houses and perhaps paying water rates?[38]

Enforceable by civil action

As indicated above, some statutes expressly provide for private law civil **16–05** action, whereas some others specifically exclude this. Here we are dealing with those statutes that, having imposed duties on identifiable persons, are silent on

---

[33] *Cutler v Wandsworth Stadium Ltd (in liquidation)* [1949] 1 All E. R. 544. See also *Morrison Sports Ltd v Scottish Power Plc*, 2011 S.C. (U.K.S.C.) 1 at 11 per Lord Rodger of Earlsferry (delivering the opinion of the court).

[34] *Pullar v Window Clean*, 1956 S.C. 13 at 22.

[35] On closer inspection, Lord President Clyde found that the legislation conferred a discretion on the Dean of Guild Court: *Pullar v Window Clean*, 1956 S.C. 13 at 23.

[36] *Pullar v Window Clean*, 1956 S.C. 13 at 17.

[37] *Weir v East of Scotland Water Authority*, 2001 S.L.T. 1205.

[38] Can "road users" be a defined and limited class? See, e.g. *Roe v Sheffield City Council* [2004] Q.B. 653 at 672–673 per Pill L.J. Cf. *Phillips v Britannia Hygienic Laundry Co Ltd* [1923] 2 K.B. 832 at 840 per Bankes L.J.: "In my view the public using the highway is not a class; it is itself the public and not a class of the public."

the matter. It is submitted that if the function of such a statute is to codify an aspect of the law where it had previously been accepted by the courts that breach of a common law duty sounded in a civil action pursuable by the victim, in the absence of express provisions it should be presumed that Parliament intended that the ability of the victim to sue for breach of a now statutory duty be continued.[39]

The express provision of criminal sanctions or some other specific enforcement mechanism, such as by a statutory regulator, will be presumed to exclude a private law civil action.[40] The presumption is that inclusion of specific criminal sanctions or a dedicated enforcement mechanism excludes an implied right to a civil remedy, subject to an exception where the protection is clearly intended to be enjoyed and enforceable by a defined and limited class.[41] Similarly, if the statute provides for a statutory complaints procedure the courts will presume that Parliament did not intend for there to be a parallel remedy pursuable by civil action through the courts.

If within a statute certain duties are expressly justiciable by civil action but the statute is silent on others, the "natural inference"[42] is that Parliament did not intend breach of those other duties to sound in a private law civil action.

Even where a statutory scheme makes provision for regulations to be implemented with the express purpose of protecting persons and property, in itself that will be insufficient to discover an implied intention by Parliament to confer upon individuals a right to a private law remedy. In *Morrison Sports Ltd v Scottish Power Plc*, the pursuers were tenants in a property destroyed by a fire that was traced to an electricity meter which had been subject to a makeshift repair. The Supreme Court reversed the decision of the Inner House:

"Looked at as a whole, therefore, the scheme of the legislation, with its carefully worked-out provisions for various forms of enforcement on behalf of the public, points against individuals having a private right of action for damages for contraventions of regulations made under it."[43]

A court may be prepared to grant an interdict, at least on an interim basis where the test is on the balance of convenience, to prevent a breach of a statutory duty even where an action for damages for harm following such breach would not be competent.[44]

---

[39] Codifying statutes, e.g. Occupiers' Liability (Scotland) Act 1960; Animals (Scotland) Act 1987 tend not to be silent on the matter.

[40] The opposite, i.e. that absence of penal sanction creates a presumption that a private law civil action is competent, does not necessarily follow: *R v Deputy Governor of Parkhurst Prison, ex p. Hague* [1992] 1 A.C. 58. Cf. *X v Bedfordshire CC* [1995] 2 A.C. 633 at 731 per Lord Browne Wilkinson; *Doe d. Murray, Lord Bishop of Rochester v Bridges* (1831) 1 B. & Ad. 847 at 859 per Lord Tenterden.

[41] *Lonhro Ltd v Shell Petroleum Co Ltd* [1982] A.C. 173 at 185 per Lord Diplock. See also *Nicol v Caledonian Newspapers Ltd*, 2002 S.C. 493 at 509–510 per Lady Paton.

[42] *Morrison Sports Ltd v Scottish Power Plc*, 2011 S.C. (U.K.S.C.) 1 at 5 per Lord Rodger of Earlsferry (delivering the opinion of the court).

[43] *Morrison Sports Ltd v Scottish Power Plc*, 2011 S.C. (U.K.S.C.) 1 at 11 per Lord Rodger.

[44] See *Duchess of Argyll v Duke of Argyll* [1967] Ch. 302. Cf. *Nicol v Caledonian Newspapers Ltd*, 2002 S.C. 493 at 510 per Lady Paton.

Although not conclusive, where the activity of a public body that is the subject of the complaint is amenable to judicial review, courts may be reticent in recognising the competence of a parallel civil action.[45]

Harm within scope of statutory duty

Where a statutory provision does provide for a private law remedy, the **16–06** pursuer's claim will nevertheless fail if the harm falls outside the scope of the statutory duty. If the statute imposes the duty for a particular purpose, the claim must be related to that purpose. The principle is illustrated in the well-known case of *Gorris v Scott*.[46] The Contagious Diseases (Animals) Act 1869 required sheep and cattle that were being transported by ship to be housed in pens of a certain specification. The purpose of the legislation was to prevent overcrowding so as to avoid the spread of disease. The action was brought when a number of the plaintiff's sheep were swept overboard the defendant's ship, the plaintiff arguing that the sheep would not have been lost if the shipowner had complied with the statutory duty. The Court of Exchequer dismissed the claim, holding that the harm was outside the scope of the statutory duty.

Gorris v Scott was distinguished in *Grant v National Coal Board*.[47] The Coal Mines Act 1911 s.49 required that the "roof and sides of every travelling road ... shall be made secure." A roof collapsed and a worker was injured when the bogie on which he was travelling collided with the debris which had fallen onto the road. The defender argued that the scope of the provision extended only to harm caused by *falling* debris, as opposed to *fallen* debris. The House of Lords held that the section was intended to protect workmen and so a worker would be entitled to a remedy if he was injured as a consequence of a breach of the statutory duty, i.e. that the roof had not been made secure.

LIABILITY FOR BREACH OF STATUTORY DUTY

Breach of duty

The pursuer must still show a breach of the duty imposed. The content of the **16–07** duty is a matter of interpretation of the legislation. This is a specialised matter of pleading. Sometimes the standard required will be reasonable care as in common-law liability, but other standards exist, mainly because statutes have usually been passed to impose a higher degree of care. Thus, sometimes there is absolute liability or cases where something must be achieved so far as it is reasonably practicable; or an Act may allow a defence of impracticality only, regardless of how unreasonable it would be to take certain steps. Examples of these can be seen in the treatment of the Factories Acts. In *Edwards v National*

---

[45] *R v Deputy Governor of Parkhurst Prison, ex p. Hague* [1992] 1 A.C. 58 at 173 per Lord Jauncey of Tullichettle. See also, e.g. *Phelps v Hillingdon LBC* [2001] 2 A.C. 619.

[46] *Gorris v Scott* (1873–74) L.R. 9 Ex. 125. See also *Carroll v Andrew Barclay & Sons Ltd*, 1948 S.C. (HL) 100 (duty to fence machinery was to prevent worker falling into machine, not to prevent parts of the machine flying out and striking a worker).

[47] *Grant v National Coal Board*, 1956 S.C. (HL) 48. The approach taken by the House of Lords may be compared to *Hughes v Lord Advocate*, 1963 S.C. (HL) 31. See also *Donaghey v Boulton & Paul Ltd* [1968] A.C. 1.

Coal Board[48] the following formulation of reasonable practicability was offered:

> "Reasonably practicable is a narrower term than physically possible and seems to me to imply that a computation must be made by the owner in which the quantum of risk is placed in one scale and the sacrifice involved in the measures necessary for averting the risk (whether in money, time or trouble) is placed in the other, and that, if it be shown that there is a gross disproportion-the risk being insignificant in relation to the sacrifice—the defendants discharge the onus on them. .... The questions he has to answer are: (a) what measures are necessary and sufficient to prevent any breach ... (b) are these measures reasonably practicable?"[49]

If the duty is an absolute one then only the happening of the prohibited thing need be proved.[50] There is no need to prove fault.

Causation

16–08   Normally it is essential to show that the harm was caused by the breach of the statutory duty.[51] A statute can make proof of causation unnecessary.[52]

Remoteness of damage

16–09   There seems to be no clear direct authority on remoteness of damage in statutory liability cases. Probably the same approach would be taken as in liability at common law. Some suggestions that the same rule does apply can be found in *Drew v Western SMT*. A boy was killed as a result of a breach of a statutory regulation as to the lighting of vehicles. Lord McKay in the Second Division said:

> "So much explained, then, it is enough to say by preliminary that I cannot find any grounds whatever in fact or in law for giving the benefit of 'remoteness' whether that be treated as remoteness in time, or remoteness in logic, to the maintenance, contrary to a safety statute, of an unlit obstacle in the full and public path likely to be taken by approaching traffic from behind."[53]

In the Outer House, in the well-known *McKew v Holland & Hannen & Cubitts (Scotland) Ltd*,[54] Lord Robertson applied traditional remoteness of damage doctrine to what was both a common law and statutory claim. The leading English text book suggests the possibility that an "old" remoteness rule such as that in *Polemis* might apply in these cases, even although that rule was departed from some time ago in England for ordinary negligence cases.[55] In view of the

---

[48] *Edwards v National Coal Board* [1949] 1 K.B. 704.
[49] *Edwards v National Coal Board* [1949] 1 K.B. 704 at 712 per Asquith L.J.
[50] See, e.g. *John Summers & Co Ltd v Frost* [1955] A.C. 740.
[51] *Wardlaw v Bonnington Castings*, 1956 S.C. (HL) 26.
[52] e.g. Compensation Act 2006 s.3.
[53] *Drew v Western SMT*, 1947 S.L.T. 92 at 95.
[54] *McKew v Holland & Hannen & Cubitts (Scotland) Ltd*, 1968 S.L.T. 12.
[55] See the discussion in Stanton et al., *Statutory Torts* (2003), para.9.025.

decision in *Simmons v British Steel*,[56] it unlikely that there would be enthusiasm for that, but it is true to say that different considerations might apply.

Defences

There remains one more speciality of liability for breach of statutory duty and **16–10** that is that the defence of volenti non fit injuria is normally presumed not to apply, on the basis that if Parliament had intended a duty to be so restricted, it would have said so. This is well illustrated by the case of *Wheeler v New Merton Board Mills Ltd*.[57] A boy was employed to clean the blades of a machine. There was a lever that he was to use to stop the machine to let him do this. Either through pressure of work or over eager application to his task, his practice was to try to clean the blades while the machine was still in operation. Scrutton L.J. takes up the story:

> "He went on for three months taking shaving out of the knives while the machine was still working, and by good luck he did so for three months without having his fingers cut off, but at last the evil day came when he lost his hand and fingers."

The court held that he was not defeated by the plea of volenti. It should be noted that Parliament can include such a defence should it so wish, as it has in the Occupiers' Liability (Scotland) Act 1960 and the Animals (Scotland) Act 1987. That Parliament does this indicates that the inapplicability of the volenti defence is not restricted to cases under the Factories Acts. Nevertheless, unless excluded by statute, it is possible for conduct to amount to contributory negligence reducing or completely excluding liability.[58]

---

[56] *Simmons v British Steel*, 2004 S.C. (HL) 94.
[57] *Wheeler v New Merton Board Mills Ltd* [1933] 2 K.B. 669. Cf. *ICI Ltd v Shatwell* [1965] A.C. 656.
[58] See, e.g. *Robb v Salamis (M & I) Ltd*, 2007 S.C. (HL) 71; *John Summers & Co Ltd v Frost* [1955] A.C. 740.

CHAPTER 17

LIABILITY OF PUBLIC BODIES

INTRODUCTION

17–01 As has been seen above,[1] there are difficulties enough with the concept of the duty of care in the context of private law, i.e. the law between persons. However, the matter becomes even more complicated when public authorities are involved. Delict is part of private law, concerned with relationships among individuals. However, public law concerns the relationship between the individual and the State.[2] Sometimes—indeed perhaps quite often—public authorities cause loss to individuals through their acts or omissions. Where the acts or omissions are associated with a function that is not "public" in character, the public body will be susceptible to delictual liability in the same circumstances as private persons or organisations.[3] It is where the acts or omissions called into question relate to functions which are "public" in character that the difficulties arise. The matter is not made difficult if the relevant statute specifies a "private law" liability upon a public authority for breach of a statutory duty to act or to refrain from acting.[4] However, statutes rarely do. Often a difficulty in dealing with a case where the authority has failed to act is because often there may be very good political reasons for not acting, such as a lack of resources. Thus, there is a basic question as to whether a case arising from the performance or otherwise of a public function should be *justiciable* in a private law action by the courts at all. Furthermore, public law remedies are available in judicial review proceedings against public authorities and, unlike the position in England and Wales,[5] the

---

[1] See Ch.11.

[2] See generally J. Sopinka, "The Liability of Public Authorities: Drawing the Line" (1993) 1 Tort L. Rev. 123; D. Brodie, "Public Authorities and the Duty of Care", 1996 J.R. 127; J.J. Doyle, "The Liability of Public Authorities" (1994) 1 Tort L. Rev. 189; D. Brodie, "Public Authority Liability: The Scottish Approach" (2007) Edin. L.R. 254.

[3] See, e.g. *X (Minors) v Bedfordshire CC* [1995] 2 A.C. 633 at 729 per Lord Jauncey of Tullichettle. Thus a local authority will equally be vicariously liable for the negligent driving of a van driver as any private employer. Equally, complications related to liability for pure economic loss, or to secondary victims, or for professional negligence etc. will all apply in the same way as in any other delictual actions.

[4] See Ch.16. An obvious suggestion might be the Occupiers' Liability (Scotland) Act 1960, but closer examination reveals that liability is for "private" rather than "public" activity: taking care to ensure the safety of premises as an occupier is a function shared with any other occupier of premises, taking care to ensure the safety of *public* roads is not: see paras 18–16 to 18–17 below.

[5] See, e.g. *Stovin v Wise* [1996] A.C. 923 at 953 per Lord Hoffmann: "I think that the minimum preconditions for basing a duty of care upon the existence of a statutory power, if it can be done at all, are, first, that it would in the circumstances have been irrational not to have exercised the power, so that there was in effect a public law duty to act, and secondly, that there are exceptional grounds for holding that the policy of the statute requires compensation to be paid to persons who

range of remedies that may be awarded by the Scottish courts includes damages. Complicating matters even more, the Human Rights Act 1998 requires public bodies to act consistently with the European Convention on Human Rights and the remedy of damages for "just satisfaction"[6] may be sought in parallel to, or as an alternative to, a private law remedy. Accordingly, the basic policy question must be addressed: is it fair, just and reasonable that a public authority may even in principle incur liability at common law in delict? Unravelling that question reveals that issues may involve both *public* policy and *legal* policy matters.[7]

Such policy questions were first dealt with head-on by the House of Lords in *Home Office v Dorset Yacht Co Ltd*.[8] Their Lordships rejected an argument that liability of public bodies should be confined to circumstances defined specifically in statute:

> "The reason for this is, I think, that Parliament deems it to be in the public interest that things otherwise unjustifiable should be done, and that those who do such things with due care should be immune from liability to persons who may suffer thereby. But Parliament cannot reasonably be supposed to have licensed those who do such things to act negligently in disregard of the interests of others so as to cause them needless damage."[9]

So negligent performance, or otherwise, of a statutory function may in principle be justiciable in a private law action in delict. However, that is far from the end of the matter:

> "The problem which this type of action creates is to define the circumstances in which the law should impose, over and above, or perhaps alongside, these public law powers and duties, a duty in private law towards individuals such that they may sue for damages in a civil court."[10]

CO-EXISTENCE OF A STATUTORY DUTY AND A COMMON LAW DUTY OF CARE

Justiciability: discretion and the policy/operational dichotomy

An action against a public body for breach of statutory duty will be subject to **17–02** the usual analysis of whether Parliament intended to confer a common law remedy.[11] This is a *legal* policy question. A further distinction has been made in actions against public bodies between the exercise of a statutory discretion and

---

suffer loss because the power was not exercised." If Lord Hoffmann is hinting that a private law remedy might be required to fill a gap in English public law, if that gap does not exist in Scots law, should the Scottish courts go their own way and say that coherence demands that no private law action is competent against a public authority with regard to the performance of its "public" functions?

[6] Human Rights Act 1998 s.8. See Ch.2.

[7] See above at paras 11–62 to 11–63 for discussion of a distinction between public policy and legal policy.

[8] *Home Office v Dorset Yacht Co Ltd* [1970] A.C. 1004. The facts are explained at para.11–20 above.

[9] *Home Office v Dorset Yacht Co Ltd* [1970] A.C. 1004 at 1031 per Lord Reid. See also Lord Pearson at 1056.

[10] *Anns v Merton LBC* [1978] A.C. 728 at 754 per Lord Wilberforce.

[11] See Ch.16.

the practical implementation of a statutory power. Thus, whether or not to close a school, or to build a new school, or to change the boundaries between school catchment areas falls within the discretion of a local authority. Likewise, determining whether to provide tuition in subjects in addition to those prescribed by statute is a policy matter within the discretion of the local authority. These are matters of *public* policy and it follows that if such decision making can be challenged in the courts at all, it must be via a public law mechanism.[12] However, overcrowding the school, or employing too few teachers to deliver the curriculum may be an operational matter:

> "The fact that the school is being run pursuant to a statutory duty is not necessarily incompatible with a common law duty of care arising from the proximate relationship between a school and the pupils it has agreed to accept. The distinction is between (a) taking care in exercising a statutory discretion whether or not to do an act and (b) having decided to do that act, taking care in the manner in which you do it."[13]

This distinction has been described as "convenient, and illuminating"[14] yet it does not provide a touchstone of liability.[15] Many so-called operational powers involve the exercise of discretion, such as the staffing of the school in the example given above. Nevertheless,

> "(i)t can safely be said that the more 'operational' a power or duty may be, the easier it is to superimpose on it a common law duty of care."[16]

Equally, although Parliament may confer a wide discretion on public bodies, the discretion is unlikely to be completely unfettered. The public law concept of "Wednesbury unreasonableness"[17] arguably has a broad equivalent in private law delict actions against public bodies. Thus,

> "(T)here must come a stage when the discretion is exercised so carelessly or unreasonably that there has been no real exercise of the discretion which Parliament has conferred. The person purporting to exercise his discretion has acted in abuse or excess of his power. Parliament cannot be supposed to have granted immunity to persons who do that."[18]

---

[12] It might be asserted that challenge normally should be confined to the political process, i.e. through the ballot box.

[13] *X (Minors) v Bedfordshire CC* [1995] 2 A.C. 633 at 735 per Lord Browne-Wilkinson. Thus, having decided to demolish a wall (a matter of discretion), a duty of care was owed by a local authority to the proprietors of neighbouring buildings in planning how operationally the demolition was carried out: *K2 Restaurants Ltd v Glasgow City Council* [2013] CSIH 49; 2013 G.W.D. 21–420.

[14] *Anns v Merton LBC* [1978] A.C. 728 at 754 per Lord Wilberforce.

[15] *Rowling v Takaro Properties Ltd* [1988] A.C. 473 at 501 per Lord Keith of Kinkell.

[16] *Anns v Merton LBC* [1978] A.C. 728 at 754 per Lord Wilberforce.

[17] *Associated Provincial Picture Houses Ltd v Wednesbury Corp* [1948] 1 K.B. 223.

[18] *Home Office v Dorset Yacht Co Ltd* [1970] A.C. 1004 at 1031 per Lord Reid. "If the decision complained of falls outside the statutory discretion, it can (but not necessarily will) give rise to common law liability": *X (Minors) v Bedfordshire CC* [1995] 2 A.C. 633 at 738 per Lord Browne-Wilkinson.

Thus, it is suggested that a public body's discretion to consider public policy matters in making decisions operates in two dimensions. There is a wide, but not unfettered, discretion within the policy dimension, although where the body acts outside of its discretion it is reiterated that a "public law" remedy (the Scottish courts can award damages) is more logical since the challenge to the body will be that it is acting ultra vires. In terms of the operational dimension, there is a degree of "headroom" within which the body may exercise discretion, and if the body is acting within that range it cannot be said to have been acting wrongfully. The boundaries to discretion inevitably will be difficult to define, although reference may be made to the ambit of statutory powers and to the exercise of powers bona fide in the interests of the public.[19] Nevertheless, mere errors of judgment in the exercise of discretion will not breach the standard required by the law.[20] However, if the public body strays substantially beyond the extent of its headroom in its operational activity so that it is clearly acting unlawfully, it may be susceptible to liability in delict. In theory, delictual liability might arise through "intentionally" wrongful acts, such as defamation or assault. In practice, pursuers are more likely to aver negligence—unintentional acts or omissions which have as their reasonable and probable consequence injury to others. Although the foreseeability element may be satisfied, that is not enough for the necessary pre-requisite duty of care to be owed by the public body to the pursuer. Not only must there be a relationship of sufficient proximity between them[21] but further public policy questions may arise, examples of which are explored below.[22]

The following diagram is intended to illustrate the two-dimensional model **17–03** explained above:

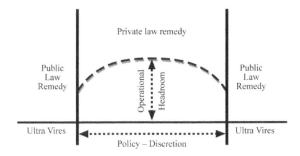

As the diagram is intended to illustrate, it is suggested that the "headroom" for discretion in operational activity reduces as the exercise of discretion in policy approaches the boundaries of what is intra vires.

---

[19] See, e.g. *Hallett v Nicholson*, 1979 S.C. 1 at 9 per Lord Dunpark; *Bonthrone v Secretary of State for Scotland*, 1987 S.L.T. 34 at 41 per Lord Grieve.

[20] It should be clear then that there is substantial overlap between the issue of justiciability and breach of a private law duty, prompting the question which is the chicken and which the egg? See, e.g. *Barrett v London Borough of Enfield* [2001] 2 A.C. 550 at 591 per Lord Hutton; *Duff v Highland and Islands Fire Board*, 1995 S.L.T. 1362 at 1363 per Lord McFadyen.

[21] See, e.g. *Thomson v Scottish Ministers*, 2013 S.C. 628.

[22] Thus, the second and third criteria from the tri-partite test in *Caparo Industries Plc v Dickman* [1990] 2 A.C. 605 loom large: see, e.g. *Mitchell v Glasgow City Council*, 2009 S.C. (HL) 21.

A brief history of liability of public bodies in negligence

England and Wales

17–04   It might be said that in the *Dorset Yacht* case the House of Lords confirmed that the gate was not absolutely closed to private law claims in negligence against public bodies. The gate might then be said to have been opened wide by the House of Lords in *Anns v Merton BC*,[23] although what complicated that decision was an erroneous classification of the harm as physical, when it should have been classified as pure economic loss. Efforts were made to close the gate again across a range of cases,[24] and ultimately *Anns* was overruled by *Murphy v Brentwood DC*,[25] when the House of Lords took the opportunity to confirm that both cases involved liability of a public body for pure economic loss. What is often forgotten in this discussion is that a major part of the decision in *Murphy* was also that the building legislation was not intended to create such liability in negligence.[26]

While the debate around classifying these cases as involving pure economic loss caused a focus on proximity issues, another case actually decided on proximity enjoys an enduring fame because of the public policy issues which were highlighted. Ironically, what recently has been referred to as the "core principle"[27] deriving from the House of Lords decision in *Hill v Chief Constable of West Yorkshire*[28] was discussed in an obiter statement by Lord Keith, with whom three of his fellow Lordships agreed, and expanded upon only by Lord Templeman. Treating this discussion as a core principle effectively creates an immunity enjoyed by the police from liability in negligence with regard to their function in the investigation and suppression of crime, justified as to hold otherwise would result in the police carrying out their functions in a "detrimentally defensive frame of mind"[29] and would cause "more harm than good".[30] *Hill* immunity was rapidly applied by the English courts to protect the police from liability for negligence in the performance of other policing activities, such as investigating why a burglar alarm was activated,[31] and dealing with reports of malfunctioning traffic lights[32] and of hazards on a roadway.[33] *Hill* was also applied to provide immunity to the Crown Prosecution Service[34] and to the

---

[23] *Anns v Merton BC* [1978] A.C. 728. For the facts, see para.11–27 above.

[24] See, e.g. *Yuen Kun Yeu v Attorney-General of Hong Kong* [1988] A.C. 175; *Rowling v Takaro Properties Ltd* [1988] A.C. 473.

[25] *Murphy v Brentwood DC* [1991] 1 A.C. 398.

[26] It might be said here that the judiciary, as an organ of the State, was closing ranks with public authorities, as an executive organ of the State.

[27] See, e.g. *Brooks v Commissioner of Police of the Metropolis* [2005] 1 W.L.R. 1495 at 1509 per Lord Steyn; *Smith v Chief Constable of Sussex Police*, sub nom. *Van Colle v Chief Constable of Hertfordshire Police* [2009] 1 A.C. 225; *Smith v Ministry of Defence* [2014] A.C. 52.

[28] *Hill v Chief Constable of West Yorkshire* [1989] A.C. 53. For the facts, see para.11–61 above. The facts in *Hill* were distinguished from *Rigby v Chief Constable of Northamptonshire* [1985] 1 W.L.R. 1242 where the police were held liable for fire damage to a building into which they fired a CS gas canister without checking first that fire extinguishing equipment was on hand.

[29] *Hill v Chief Constable of West Yorkshire* [1989] A.C. 53 at 63 per Lord Keith of Kinkell.

[30] *Hill v Chief Constable of West Yorkshire* [1989] A.C. 53 at 64 per Lord Templeman.

[31] *Alexandrou v Oxford* [1993] 4 All E.R. 328.

[32] *Clough v Bussan* [1990] 1 All E.R. 431.

[33] *Ancell & Ancell v McDermott* [1993] 4 All E.R. 355.

[34] *Elguzouli-Daf v Commissioner of Police of the Metropolis* [1995] Q.B. 335.

Coastguard Service,[35] although perhaps curiously not to the fire brigade[36] or ambulance service.[37]

In *Osman v Ferguson*,[38] *Hill* immunity was applied to "strike out" a claim brought against the police for failing to prevent a teacher killing a pupil's father and injuring the pupil. However, upon application to the European Court of Human Rights, the court held that the rule in *Hill*, creating effectively a blanket immunity from liability enjoyed by the police, was a disproportionate interference with the applicant's rights under art.6 of the European Convention on Human Rights.[39] The impact of the European Court of Human Rights' decision in *Osman* resulted in the courts taking a more cautious approach to applying any blanket immunity to the police, or to other emergency services or public bodies.[40]

During the period between the *Hill* decision in the House of Lords and the **17–05** *Osman* ruling by the European Court of Human Rights, the House of Lords also dealt with *X (Minors) v Bedfordshire CC*,[41] which might be described as one of a trend in English cases which evinced an enthusiasm for protection of public bodies.[42] This was a series of cases brought against local authorities which fell broadly into two groups. The first were complaints that local authorities had acted negligently in failing to protect children from abuse carried out by their parents or others looking after the children. The second group of cases were complaints that local authorities had been negligent in failing to deal properly with children who had special educational needs. Drawing heavily on the policy arguments considered in the *Hill* case, the House of Lords held that decisions falling within a public body's statutory discretion were not justiciable in a private law action. Thus, the court rejected the claims that the children were owed a duty of care by the local authorities with regard to those functions which were purely "public" in nature. Where, however, the local authority operated a service which was also provided by private bodies, such as the provision of psychological advice by persons employed by its education service, a duty of care could be owed to the children.

Following the decision of the European Court of Human Rights in *Osman*, the courts in England and Wales appeared to be less bold in protecting public bodies from liability in negligence. In another child abuse case, *Barrett v Enfield LBC*,[43] the House of Lords were careful to distinguish the facts from those in *X* so as to take into consideration the criticism of the European Court of Human Rights. The House of Lords held that once a child was actually taken into care by a local

---

[35] *OLL Ltd v Secretary of State for Transport* [1997] 3 All E.R. 897. Lord Bingham of Cornhill, in his dissenting speech in *Smith v Chief Constable of Sussex* sub nom. *Van Colle v Chief Constable of Hertfordshire* [2009] 1 A.C. 225 at 266, felt bound to say that "a law of delict which denies a remedy on facts such as these, in the absence of any statutory inhibition, fails to perform the basic function for which such a law exists."

[36] See, e.g. *Capital & Counties Plc v Hampshire CC* [1997] QB 1004.

[37] See, e.g. *Kent v Griffiths* [2001] Q.B. 36.

[38] *Osman v Ferguson* [1993] 4 All E.R. 344.

[39] *Osman v United Kingdom* (2000) 29 E.H.R.R. 245.

[40] See, e.g. *Barrett v Enfield LBC* [2001] 2 A.C. 550; *Phelps v Hillingdon LBC* [2001] 2 A.C. 619.

[41] *X (Minors) v Bedfordshire CC* [1995] 2 A.C. 633.

[42] See also, e.g. *Elguzouli-Daf v Commissioner of Police of the Metropolis* [1995] Q.B. 335; *Stovin v Wise* [1996] A.C. 923; *Mulcahy v Ministry of Defence* [1996] Q.B. 732; *OLL v Secretary of State for the Home Department* [1997] 3 All E.R. 897; *Harris v Evans* [1998] 1 W.L.R. 1285.

[43] *Barrett v Enfield LBC* [2001] 2 A.C. 550.

authority, the authority would be deemed to have assumed responsibility to the child and would owe a duty of care to the child on that basis. In *Phelps v Hillingdon LBC*[44] the House of Lords went further, and expressed doubts concerning the decision in *X*. It was held that there was no justification for a blanket immunity with regard to education officers carrying out assessments of children to determine special educational needs. The House of Lords held that the local authority could be vicariously liable for a breach of a duty of care owed by its employees to children in diagnosing specific learning difficulties such as dyslexia.

Meanwhile, some of the plaintiffs in *X* had applied to the European Court of Human Rights, arguing that the local authority's failure to prevent them continuing to suffer from neglect and abuse amounted to a breach of art.3 of the Convention (freedom from torture or degrading treatment) and that the denial by the UK courts of the opportunity to seek a remedy amounted to a violation of arts 6 and 13.[45] Although the court held unanimously that there had been a breach of art.3 and by a majority that there had been a violation of art.13, by a majority the court held that there had been no violation of art.6.[46] The significance here is that the European Court of Human Rights carried out a review of its previous decision in the *Osman* case, and concluded that in reaching its decision in that case it had failed to appreciate the operation of the "strike-out" procedure in the English civil courts or that the fair, just and reasonable criterion as applied by the domestic courts in *Osman v Ferguson* and deriving from the decision in *Hill* was an intrinsic element of the duty of care rather than disclosing the operation of an immunity.[47]

17–06   In its statement to the European Court of Human Rights, the UK government had asserted that

> "the exclusion was not a blanket exclusion of liability but a carefully and narrowly focused limitation which applied only in respect of the investigation and suppression of crime, and even then not in every case."

In this light it is ironic that the court's review of *Osman* in *Z* may be seen to have emboldened the House of Lords in re-asserting the "core principle" in *Hill* and in returning to an approach which tended to protect public bodies from liability in negligence.

In *D v East Berkshire Community Health NHS Trust*,[48] the Court of Appeal asserted that the wider effects of the decision of the House of Lords in *X* could not survive the coming into force of the Human Rights Act 1998, as the effect of the Act was that public authorities, including health and education authorities, had an obligation to respect a child's human rights.[49] Thus, it was no longer legitimate to conclude that no common law duty of care could be owed to children who were suspected to be the victims of child abuse; the rule in *X* being restricted to the core proposition that a duty of care would not be owed to a child

---

[44] *Phelps v Hillingdon LBC* [2001] 2 A.C. 619.

[45] For more detailed discussion of these and other Articles of the European Convention on Human Rights see Ch.2.

[46] *Z v United Kingdom* (2002) 34 E.H.R.R. 3.

[47] *Z v United Kingdom* (2002) 34 E.H.R.R. 3 at 138.

[48] *D v East Berkshire Community Health NHS Trust* [2004] Q.B. 558.

[49] This case is an example of the rare phenomenon of the Court of Appeal refusing to follow a precedent set in the House of Lords!

with regard to a decision as to whether or not the child should be taken into care. Nevertheless, as later confirmed by a majority decision of the House of Lords,[50] the Court of Appeal considered that it was not fair, just or reasonable to extend the law so as to impose on the health authorities a duty of care owed to such a child's parents. The facts in question were that a child was wrongly suspected of being subjected to sexual abuse (it transpired that the child was actually suffering from a rare skin disease) and the medical professionals openly accused the child's father of being responsible, denying him access to the child. In proceedings brought by the father in negligence, it was held that to impose a duty of care owed to the parents would create a conflict of interest for the health professionals, given that the interests of the child were paramount in such a case.[51]

The return to the "core principle" in *Hill* was completed by the unanimous decision of the House of Lords in *Brooks v Commissioner of Police of the Metropolis*.[52] The claimant was with his friend, Stephen Lawrence, when the two of them were set upon in a racist attack as a result of which Stephen died. Aggravating the impact of the experience on the claimant, he was initially treated by the police as a suspect, and he claimed damages from the police for false imprisonment and for negligence resulting in his psychiatric injury. The House of Lords held that it would not be fair, just and reasonable to impose a duty of care upon the police owed to a potential suspect or witness:

"But the core principle of Hill's case has remained unchallenged in our domestic jurisprudence and in European jurisprudence for many years. If a case such as the Yorkshire Ripper case, which was before the House in Hill's case, arose for decision today I have no doubt that it would be decided in the same way. It is, of course, desirable that police officers should treat victims and witnesses properly and with respect . . . (b)ut to convert that ethical value into general legal duties of care on the police towards victims and witnesses would be going too far. The prime function of the police is the preservation of the Queen's peace. The police must concentrate on preventing the commission of crime; protecting life and property; and apprehending criminals and preserving evidence. . . . A retreat from the principle in Hill's case would have detrimental effects for law enforcement. Whilst focusing on investigating crime, and the arrest of suspects, police officers would in practice be required to ensure that in every contact with a potential witness or a potential victim time and resources were deployed to avoid the risk of causing harm or offence. Such legal duties would tend to inhibit a robust approach in assessing a person as a possible suspect, witness or victim. By placing general duties of care on the police to victims and witnesses the police's ability to perform their public functions in the interests of the community, fearlessly and with despatch, would be impeded.

---

[50] *D v East Berkshire Community Health NHS Trust* [2005] 2 A.C. 373.

[51] Once again, on a complaint to the European Court of Human Rights, the court found that the decision of the domestic courts was incompatible with the Convention—this time insofar as denying that a duty of care could be owed to the parents breached their rights under art.13 (the right to an effective remedy) given that the accusations and denial of access was itself a breach of art.8 (the right to respect for private and family life): *MAK v United Kingdom* (2010) 51 E.H.R.R. 14.

[52] *Brooks v Commissioner of Police of the Metropolis* [2005] 1 W.L.R. 1495.

It would, as was recognised in Hill's case, be bound to lead to an unduly defensive approach in combating crime."[53]

17–07 In his speech in *Brooks*, Lord Nicholls had suggested that there may be exceptional cases where the core principle in *Hill* should not be applied.[54] Lord Steyn imagined that the "core principle" may not apply in cases of "outrageous negligence".[55] The House of Lords soon had the opportunity to consider this suggestion in *Smith v Chief Constable of Sussex*.[56] Following an assault, the claimant concluded his relationship with his partner and reported the assault to the police. Later, over a period of two months, the claimant received a series of threats of violence and death from his former partner, which were reported to the police. However, the police did not apprehend the former partner, leaving him free to attack the claimant with a claw hammer, causing serious injury. Lord Bingham, in a dissenting judgment, proposed a "liability principle" that

> "that if a member of the public (A) furnishes a police officer (B) with apparently credible evidence that a third party whose identity and whereabouts are known presents a specific and imminent threat to his life or physical safety, B owes A a duty to take reasonable steps to assess such threat and, if appropriate, take reasonable steps to prevent it being executed."[57]

However, this liability principle was not accepted by the remaining Law Lords, who did not consider the facts to fall into an exceptional category of case so as to justify deviating from the core principle in *Hill*.

What can be seen in these cases is a tendency of the English courts, and the House of Lords in particular, to default to a position which protects public authorities from liability in negligence. The European Court of Human Rights' ruling in *Osman v United Kingdom*[58] may be said to have caused a temporary "hiccup" in this approach, but following the European Court's review of its *Osman* decision in *Z v United Kingdom*,[59] the default position of the English courts was reinforced and in particular the House of Lords was emboldened in asserting and applying the "core principle" in *Hill*.

---

[53] *Brooks v Commissioner of Police of the Metropolis* [2005] 1 W.L.R. 1495 at 1509–1510 per Lord Steyn.

[54] *Brooks v Commissioner of Police of the Metropolis* [2005] 1 W.L.R. 1495 at 1498 per Lord Nicholls of Birkenhead. See also *Robinson v Chief Constable of West Yorkshire Police* [2014] P.I.Q.R. P14 at P250 per Hallett L.J. and P253 per Arnold J.

[55] *Brooks v Commissioner of Police of the Metropolis* [2005] 1 W.L.R. 1495 at 1511 per Lord Steyn. Could "outrageous negligence" be an example of *culpa lata*? (See paras 1–22 to 1–23 above.)

[56] *Smith v Chief Constable of Sussex* sub nom. *Van Colle v Chief Constable of Hertfordshire Police* [2009] 1 A.C. 225. *Van Colle* was dealt with together with Smith. In *Van Colle* it was alleged that the police had violated art.2 of the ECHR (right to life—*Van Colle* was killed). However, the House of Lords concluded that the evidence did not evince a "real and immediate risk" to the claimant's life. It is suggested that the facts in *Smith* did evince a real and imminent risk to the claimant's life, which should have been apparent to the police. Although *Smith* survived the attack, might he better have been advised to pursue a case for breach of art.3 (the right not to be subject to inhuman and degrading treatment)?

[57] *Smith v Chief Constable of Sussex* sub nom. *Van Colle v Chief Constable of Hertfordshire Police* [2009] 1 A.C. 225 at 261.

[58] *Osman v United Kingdom* [1993] 4 All E.R. 344.

[59] *Z v United Kingdom* (2002) 34 E.H.R.R. 3.

Scotland

What was the situation In Scotland and what was the view of the Scottish **17-08** courts? Like their English counterparts, the Scottish courts had long recognised that there could be no liability for acts that fell within a statutory discretion.[60] However, a duty of care could be owed where "the discretionary stage of its exercise has ceased and the executive stage has begun,"[61] but there would be no liability for errors of judgment. An exercise of a power would only be improper where it either was "not authorised by statute or . . . not made bona fide in the interests of the public within the limits of any statutory discretion."[62] *Hill* was not embraced with the same vigour that seemed to have been applied in the English courts.[63]

In *Duff v Highlands and Islands Fire Board*,[64] the fire brigade left after they thought they had put out a fire. It broke out again and burnt down the property and one beside it. Lord Macfadyen rejected arguments of public immunity based on *Hill*. While on the evidence the brigade were assoilzied, the fact that the brigade had gone into action, and thus moved from the discretion stage to the executive/operational stage, meant that ordinary principles of liability applied.[65] *Forbes v Dundee Council*[66] represented the arrival into Scotland of the contemporaneous English approach, where Lord Nimmo-Smith applied the reasoning of the House of Lords in *X (Minors) v Bedfordshire CC*.[67] A woman lost her footing when leaving a large shop. She did not trip on a dangerous step but her rhythm of walking was broken by the irregular spacing of the steps, not conforming in this regard (it was alleged) to the building regulations which the defenders were charged by statute to apply. Although Lord Nimmo-Smith accepted that the issue of reasonable foreseeability of harm of the kind that happened was sufficiently stated to entitle the pursuer to a proof before answer, he dismissed the action, considering that the trend was away from imposing civil liabilities on local authorities. He did not think that there was enough in *Duff* to support the dicta in favour of liability in that case.

However, Lord Hamilton's judgment in *Gibson v Orr* appeared to halt the encroachment of the English approach upon Scottish jurisprudence. A bridge carrying a public road across the River Kelvin collapsed following heavy rainfall. Police officers attended the north side of the bridge, which they coned off. They remained at the scene for over an hour with the blue light on their police vehicle flashing, so as to warn drivers approaching from the south side of the bridge of the hazard. However, when they left the scene, they were aware that no barrier or warning had been erected on the south side. A few minutes later, a car was driven onto the bridge from the south side and fell into the river. Two of the occupants of the car died, although the pursuer escaped. The defender disputed that a duty of care was owed by the police officers to the occupants of the car, relying inter alia on *Hill* immunity. Following an extensive review of the

---

[60] See, e.g. *Hallett v Nicholson*, 1979 S.C. 1.

[61] *Bonthrone v Secretary of State for Scotland*, 1987 S.L.T. 34 at 41 per Lord Grieve.

[62] *Hallett v Nicholson*, 1979 S.C. 1 at 9 per Lord Dunpark.

[63] See, e.g. *Johnstone v Traffic Commissioner*, 1990 S.L.T. 409

[64] *Duff v Highlands and Islands Fire Board*, 1995 S.L.T. 1362.

[65] Although scepticism may be detected in Lord MacFadyen's judgment with regard to an argument that there was no duty to respond to the emergency call. See also *Burnett v Grampian Fire and Rescue Service*, 2007 S.L.T. 61; *Aitken v Scottish Ambulance Service*, 2011 S.L.T. 822.

[66] *Forbes v Dundee Council*, 1997 S.L.T. 1330.

[67] *X (Minors) v Bedfordshire CC* [1995] 2 A.C. 633.

authorities, Lord Hamilton rejected the application of *Hill* immunity to the facts, stating that

> "(a)lthough in Scotland the police function in relation to the investigation and suppression of crime and that in relation to the protection of life and property stem from the same statutory provision, it does not follow, in my view, that the same considerations apply to both functions in relation to immunity from suit."[68]

Lord Hamilton refused to accept the reasoning on public policy applied in several English cases[69] which he deprecated as illustrating "a tide in the English courts towards a wide interpretation of Lord Keith's and Lord Templeman's observations in *Hill*."[70] He did suggest that the tide may be running less strongly following the *Osman*[71] ruling in the European Court of Human Rights, but this was before the follow-up decision in *Z*.[72] Although Lord Hamilton also rejected the application of the "assumption of responsibility" concept as artificial in the context of police officers voluntarily assuming responsibility for persons in their charge, he nevertheless held that because the police had "taken control" of the situation, the tests of foreseeability and proximity were made out, and there were no compelling reasons why it would not be fair, just and reasonable to recognise the imposition of a duty of care.

17–09 However, if *Gibson v Orr* heralded a distinctive Scottish approach to liability of public authorities, that might be described as a false dawn following the reasoning of the House of Lords in *Mitchell v Glasgow City Council*. The Scottish judge Lord Hope had this to say:

> "Public policy was at the root of the decision in *Hill v Chief Constable, West Yorkshire* about the scope of the duty owed by the police which the House followed in *Brooks v Commissioner of Police of the Metropolis* and again in *Smith v Chief Constable, Sussex Police* ... I would take the same approach to this case."[73]

The extent to which Lord Hope's dictum has undermined the position taken by Lord Hamilton in *Gibson v Orr*[74] has yet fully to be addressed in the Scottish courts. In *Thomson v Scottish Ministers*[75] it was claimed that the Scottish Prison Service owed a duty of care to a woman who was murdered by a prisoner who at the time had been permitted a temporary release allowing him to visit his own home. The Inner House confirmed that there was insufficient proximity for a duty of care to be recognised, there being no "special relationship" between the Scottish Prison Service and the victim. In that sense, the decision of the Inner House followed the ratio in *Hill*. However, although the court did not consider

---

[68] *Gibson v Orr*, 1999 S.C. 420 at 437.
[69] *Clough v Bussan* [1990] 1 All E.R. 431; *Alexandrou v Oxford* [1993] 4 All E.R. 328; *Ancell & Ancell v McDermott* [1993] 4 All E.R. 355. Lord Hamilton also "respectfully disagreed" with the approach taken by Lord Nimmo Smith in *Forbes v City of Dundee DC*, 1997 S.L.T. 1330.
[70] *Gibson v Orr*, 1999 S.C. 420 at 437.
[71] *Osman v United Kingdom* (2000) 29 E.H.R.R. 245.
[72] *Z v United Kingdom* (2002) 34 E.H.R.R. 3.
[73] *Mitchell v Glasgow City Council*, 2009 S.C. (HL) 21 at 32 per Lord Hope of Craighead. The facts are explained at para.11–65 above.
[74] *Gibson v Orr*, 1999 S.C. 420.
[75] *Thomson v Scottish Ministers*, 2013 S.C. 628.

the matter in detail, it was said that the application of the fair, just and reasonable test would have produced the same outcome, given the implications for the proper functioning of the Scottish Prison Service and the Parole Board, carrying at least a hint of the "core principle" from *Hill*. On the other hand, Lord Hamilton's judgment in *Gibson v Orr* has been referred to with approval since the decision of the House of Lords in *Mitchell*. In particular, although it was held on the facts that the council did not owe a duty of care to the pursuer, in *MacDonald v Aberdeenshire Council*[76] the conclusion that duties of care were owed by the police in *Gibson v Orr*, by the fire service in *Burnett v Grampian Fire and Rescue Services*,[77] and by the ambulance service in *Aitken v Scottish Ambulance Service*[78] were all referred to with approval. Thus, there may still be scope for the Scottish courts in continuing a distinctive approach to liability of public authorities, especially, as pointed out at the beginning of this chapter, taking into consideration the fact that damages are a competent remedy in judicial review proceedings in the Scottish courts.

FAIR, JUST AND REASONABLE TEST: FACTORS

Statutory powers or statutory duties?

It has consistently been held that statutory powers do not automatically **17–10** translate into statutory duties.[79] In other words, where a public authority enjoys a statutory power to do something, it does not follow that the authority owes a duty to anyone who may be affected to implement that power. Thus, no duty of care was owed where severe flooding was not curtailed because a public authority permitted unnecessary delays in repairing a sea wall.[80] Likewise, there is no duty to remove a mound of earth obstructing the view at a road junction,[81] or to paint road markings.[82]

Raising standards

One factor that was swiftly dispatched by Lord Keith in *Hill v Chief Constable* **17–11** *of West Yorkshire Police*,[83] was that to impose a duty of care might raise standards. However, trusting that a public body invariably applies its best endeavours to the performance of a function was doubted by Lord Steyn in

---

[76] *MacDonald v Aberdeenshire Council*, 2014 S.L.T. 2.
[77] *Burnett v Grampian Fire and Rescue Services*, 2007 S.L.T. 61.
[78] *Aitken v Scottish Ambulance Service*, 2011 S.L.T. 822.
[79] See Ch.16.
[80] *East Suffolk Rivers Catchment Board v Kent* [1941] A.C. 74. The House of Lords' assertion that if a duty of care was owed, there could only be liability for making the situation worse rather than not making it better was criticised by Lord MacFadyen in *Duff v Highlands and Islands Fire Board*, 1995 S.L.T. 1362 and was described by Lord MacPhail as appearing "not to have been accepted in the law of Scotland" in *Burnett v Grampian Fire and Rescue Services*, 2007 S.L.T. 61 at 72.
[81] *Stovin v Wise* [1996] A.C. 923. However, if the mound featured in Scotland, and constituted a "hazard" which was not obvious to the road-user, a duty may be owed: see, e.g. *MacDonald v Aberdeenshire Council*, 2014 S.L.T. 2 at 15 per Lord Drummond Young.
[82] *MacDonald v Aberdeenshire Council*, 2014 S.L.T. 2; *Gorringe v Calderdale Metropolitan BC* [2004] 1 W.L.R. 1057. Cf. *McKnight v Clydeside Buses Ltd*, 1999 S.L.T. 1167.
[83] *Hill v Chief Constable of West Yorkshire Police* [1989] A.C. 53 at 63.

Brooks,[84] and in *Smith v Chief Constable of Sussex,*[85] Lord Bingham declared that it could no longer be supported. Thus, raising standards may be a factor in *favour* of recognising a duty of care.

Deflection from principal purpose

17–12 In *Hill*, Lord Keith thought that recognising the imposition of a duty of care upon the police would lead to increased litigation. He commented that

> "[a] great deal of police time, trouble and expense might be expected to have to be put into the preparation of the defence to the action and the attendance of witnesses at the trial. The result would be a significant diversion of police manpower and attention from their most important function, that of the suppression of crime."[86]

The point was echoed in *Smith v Chief Constable of Sussex,*[87] and expanded by Lord Hope in *Mitchell v Glasgow City Council*:

> "(T)he defenders would have had to determine, step by step at each stage, whether or not the actions that they proposed to take in fulfilment of their responsibilities as landlords required a warning to be given, and to whom. And they would have had to defer taking that step until the warning had been received by everyone and an opportunity given for it to be acted on. The more attentive they were to their ordinary duties as landlords the more onerous the duty to warn would become ... As in the case of the police, it is desirable too that social landlords, social workers and others who seek to address the many behavioural problems that arise in local authority housing estates and elsewhere, often in very difficult circumstances, should be safeguarded from legal proceedings arising from an alleged failure to warn those who might be at risk of a criminal attack in response to their activities. Such proceedings, whether meritorious or otherwise, would involve them in a great deal of time, trouble and expense which would be more usefully devoted to their primary functions in their respective capacities."[88]

On the other hand, it may not be unfair, unjust or unreasonable to recognise a duty of care if its imposition would not impede or deter the public body from carrying out its principal or statutory functions.[89]

Detrimentally defensive practice

17–13 A concern expressed emphatically in *Hill* was that to impose a duty of care upon the police with regard to the functions of investigation and suppression of

---

[84] *Brooks v Chief Constable of the Metropolis* [2005] 1 W.L.R. 1495 at 1509.
[85] *Smith v Chief Constable of Sussex* sub nom. *Van Colle v Chief Constable of Hertfordshire Police* [2009] 1 A.C. 225 at 262. Lord Bingham had previously opined to similar effect: *D v East Berkshire Community Health NHS Trust* [2005] 2 A.C. 373 at 392.
[86] *Hill v Chief Constable of West Yorkshire Police* [1989] A.C. 53 at 63. See also *X (Minors) v Bedfordshire CC* [1995] 2 A.C. 633 at 750 per Lord Browne-Wilkinson.
[87] *Smith v Chief Constable of Sussex* sub nom. *Van Colle v Chief Constable of Hertfordshire Police* [2009] 1 A.C. 225 at 2684 per Lord Brown of Eaton-under-Heywood.
[88] *Mitchell v Glasgow City Council*, 2009 S.C. (HL) 21 at 32.
[89] See, e.g. *Braes v Keeper of the Registers of Scotland*, 2010 S.L.T. 689 at 714 per Temporary Judge M.G. Thomson QC. Cf. *Santander v Keeper of the Registers of Scotland*, 2013 S.L.T. 362.

crime would necessarily result in the police adopting a "detrimentally defensive frame of mind"[90] and would cause "more harm than good"[91] Again, this concern has been doubted, at least in other contexts.[92] Nevertheless, it has been re-stated in recent cases, and was cited as a further justification for the decision in *Mitchell*.[93]

In *Jain v Trent Strategic Health Authority*, the claimants sought damages for the economic loss they suffered when their nursing home was forcibly closed. The health authority had, on the basis of a slipshod investigation and inaccurate information, sought cancellation of the registration of the nursing home in ex parte[94] court proceedings. The claimants had received no notice, and so were unable to intervene to contest the application. The order was granted, but four months later successfully appealed. However, by the time the appeal was heard, the business was ruined. The House of Lords held that no duty of care was owed by the health authority to the claimants. Lord Scott of Foscote reviewed the authorities and concluded:

> "that where action is taken by a state authority under statutory powers designed for the benefit or protection of a particular class of persons, a tortious duty of care will not be held to be owed by the state authority to others whose interests may be adversely affected by an exercise of the statutory power. The reason is that the imposition of such a duty would or might inhibit the exercise of the statutory powers and be potentially adverse to the interests of the class of persons the powers were designed to benefit or protect, thereby putting at risk the achievement of their statutory purpose."[95]

Conflicts of interest

In *Hill*, Lord Templeman made it clear that he thought to impose a duty of care **17–14** to individual victims or witnesses of crime would create a conflict—their duty to the individual distracting the police from their role in serving the public.[96] This conflict between the duty to the community and the duty to the individual has been recognised in many subsequent cases,[97] even beyond those brought against strictly public bodies.[98] Conflicts between the interests of various interested parties have also been highlighted as rendering it unfair, unjust or unreasonable to recognise a duty of care owed to one group or individual, where that may

---

[90] *Hill v Chief Constable of West Yorkshire Police* [1989] A.C. 53 at 63 per Lord Keith of Kinkell.

[91] *Hill v Chief Constable of West Yorkshire Police* [1989] A.C. 53 at 64 per Lord Templeman.

[92] See, e.g. *Barrett v Enfield LBC* [2001] 2 A.C. 550 at 568 per Lord Slynn of Hadley; *Phelps v Hillingdon LBC* [2001] 2 A.C. 619 at 672 per Lord Clyde.

[93] *Mitchell v Glasgow City Council*, 2009 S.C. (HL) 21 at 32 per Lord Hope of Craighead.

[94] Court proceedings brought by one person without any other being required to respond.

[95] *Jain v Trent Strategic Health Authority* [2009] 1 A.C. 853 at 867–868.

[96] *Hill v Chief Constable of West Yorkshire Police* [1989] A.C. 53 at 65.

[97] See, e.g. *Elguzouli-Daf v Commissioner of Police of the Metropolis* [1995] Q.B. 335 at 349–350 per Steyn L.J. (Crown Prosecution Service owes no duty to the person it prosecutes); *Brooks v Commissioner of Police of the Metropolis* [2005] 1 W.L.R. 1495 at 1509–1510 per Lord Steyn (police owe no duty of care to a witness to a crime); *Mitchell v Glasgow City Council*, 2009 S.C. (HL) 21 at 32 per Lord Hope of Craighead (public housing provider owes no duty to tenant not to house beside dangerous neighbour).

[98] See, e.g. *Marc Rich & Co AG v Bishop Rock Marine Co Ltd* [1996] A.C. 211 at 240 per Lord Steyn.

operate at the expense of the interests that are paramount. Examples include the potential conflict between the interests of children and their parents in cases of suspected child abuse,[99] and between the interests of residents and proprietors in cases of suspected mismanagement of nursing care homes.[100]

Conflicts will not arise in every case, and in some circumstances the situation may be more finely balanced. Thus, in *Swinney v Chief Constable of Northumbria*, the Court of Appeal refused to strike out a claim on the application of *Hill*. The plaintiff was a police informant who had provided the police with information pertinent to the identification of the driver of a vehicle which had struck and killed a police officer who was trying to flag it down. The informant's details had been within a brief-case which was stolen from a police car, and the informant thereafter received anonymous death threats. Ward L.J. considered that there was "no overwhelming dictate of public policy to exclude the prosecution of this claim."[101] He went on to confirm that in general the police should be free to carry out their activities unfettered by the threat of litigation, and that the greater public good "quite rightly" outweighs individual hardship.[102] However, the facts of this case disclosed a countervailing public interest that citizens should be able to trust the police to keep sensitive information confidential as otherwise would discourage informants from coming forward. The Court of Appeal unanimously allowed the case to go to trial, although at trial it was held that the police had achieved the standard of care demanded in the circumstances.[103]

Assumption of responsibility

17–15   In *Elguzouli-DAF v Commissioner of Police of the Metropolis* Lord Justice Steyn suggested[104] that *Hill*[105] immunity might not apply where there is some form of assumption of responsibility by the police. The concept, ultimately deriving from the decision of the House of Lords in *Hedley Byrne*,[106] was applied by the Court of Appeal in *Swinney*[107] to find that a special relationship existed between the police and the informant arising from an assumption of responsibility to the informant by the police. Likewise, in *Barrett*,[108] it was accepted that a duty of care was owed by a local authority to a child once it had taken that child into care and so had assumed a responsibility for the child. Similar approaches have been taken to suicidal prisoners[109] and hospital patients.[110] However, it is

---

[99] *X (Minors) v Bedfordshire CC* [1995] 2 A.C. 633 at 750–751 per Lord Browne-Wilkinson; *A v Essex CC* [2004] 1 W.L.R. 1881 at 1899–1901 per Hale L.J. (delivering judgment of the court); *D v East Berkshire Community Health NHS Trust* [2005] 2 A.C. 373 at 405–408 per Lord Nicholls of Birkenhead at 415–416 per Lord Rodger of Earlsferry and at 418–420 per Lord Brown of Eaton-Under-Heywood.

[100] See, e.g. *Jain v Trent Strategic Health Authority* [2009] 1 A.C. 853 at 868 per Lord Scott of Foscote.

[101] *Swinney v Chief Constable of Northumbria* [1997] Q.B. 464 at 486.

[102] *Swinney v Chief Constable of Northumbria* [1997] Q.B. 464 at 487.

[103] *Swinney v Chief Constable of Northumbria (No.2)* (1999) 11 Admin. L.R. 811.

[104] *Elguzouli-DAF v Commissioner of Police of the Metropolis* [1995] Q.B. 335 at 348.

[105] *Hill v Chief Constable of West Yorkshire* [1989] A.C. 53.

[106] *Hedley Byrne & Co Ltd v Heller & Partners Ltd* [1964] A.C. 465.

[107] *Swinney v Chief Constable of Northumbria (No.1)* [1997] Q.B. 464.

[108] *Barrett v London Borough of Enfield* [2001] 2 A.C. 550.

[109] See, e.g. *Kirkham v Chief Constable of Greater Manchester* [1990] 2 Q.B. 283; *Reeves v Commissioner of Police of the Metropolis* [2000] 1 A.C. 360.

[110] See, e.g. *Savage v South Essex Partnership NHS Foundation Trust* [2009] 1 A.C. 681; *Rabone v Pennine Care NHS Foundation Trust* [2012] 2 A.C. 72.

important to note that an assumption of responsibility must be *voluntary* before it might override other policy reasons for denying a duty of care owed by a public body. Thus, in *Gibson v Orr*[111] it was held that merely "taking control" of a hazard was insufficient in itself, and in *Mitchell*,[112] it was held that merely providing housing for social tenants did not amount to a voluntary assumption of responsibility so as to create a duty of care. Likewise, in *X and Y v London Borough of Hounslow*,[113] it was held that mere engagement with a statutory function did not of itself amount to a voluntary assumption of responsibility, and in *Desmond v Chief Constable of Nottinghamshire*,[114] the English Court of Appeal held that a police officer will not voluntarily have assumed responsibility to a victim or witness of crime in the performance of normal operational duties.

EUROPEAN CONVENTION ON HUMAN RIGHTS

As stated in the introduction to this chapter, delictual liability of public **17–16** authorities is now made even more complex by the possibility of liability under s.6 of the Human Rights Act 1998. Where the acts or omissions that are the subject of the complaint occurred on or after October 2, 2000,[115] an alternative remedy of damages for just satisfaction for breach of s.6 may be pursued as a self-standing claim.[116] The impact of the Human Rights Act 1998 on delictual liability is discussed in more detail in Ch.2 above.

MISFEASANCE IN OFFICE—WRONGFUL ADMINISTRATION

Public officers may be a category of person who can be held liable for dishonest **17–17** abuse of power, notwithstanding the law of negligence.[117] The difficulty in establishing negligence liability against public authorities as discussed above makes this approach of interest to pursuers.

As referred to above, Scotland now has a very well developed system of judicial review. Within that system damages or reparation may be claimed. It remains of course that judicial review is only a procedure and it is still possible to ask what is the substantive right. Often it may well be abuse of power or

---

[111] *Gibson v Orr*, 1999 S.C. 420.

[112] *Mitchell v Glasgow City Council*, 2009 S.C. (HL) 21.

[113] *X and Y v London Borough of Hounslow* [2009] P.T.S.R. 1158. The facts are explained at para.11–66 above.

[114] *Desmond v Chief Constable of Nottinghamshire* [2011] P.T.S.R. 1369. The plaintiff had been arrested on suspicion of carrying out a sexual assault, but released when the investigating officer concluded that he was not responsible. This information was included in an enhanced criminal record certificate sought by the claimant in relation to his application for a job as a teacher.

[115] For example, in *Jain v Trent Strategic Health Authority* [2009] 1 A.C. 853, the House of Lords recognised that had the facts occurred on or after this date the claimants would have been able to a claim under s.6.

[116] Examples already include *Savage v South Essex Partnership NHS Foundation Trust* [2009] 1 A.C. 681; *Mitchell v Glasgow City Council*, 2009 S.C. (HL) 21; *Thomson v Scottish Ministers*, 2013 S.C. 628; *Rabone v Pennine Care NHS Foundation Trust* [2012] 2 A.C. 72; *Smith v Ministry of Defence* [2014] A.C. 52.

[117] C.T. Reid, "Damages for Deliberate Abuse of Power", 1988 S.L.T. (News) 121.

misfeasance in public office and these are the wrongs for which reparation may be ordered.[118]

There was an early discussion, based on Professor Walker's work, in a case argued before Lord Ross:

> "The expression 'a tort which is called misfeasance in public office' sounds strange to Scottish ears. However, the question which arises is whether some equivalent would be recognised by the law of Scotland . . . The validity of a claim such as that made by the present pursuers does not depend upon there being any precise Scottish authority. There is no such thing as an exhaustive list of named delicts in the law of Scotland. If the conduct complained of appears to be wrongful, the law of Scotland will afford a remedy even if there has not been any previous instance of a remedy being given in similar circumstances. As Professor Walker puts it at p.9: 'The decision to recognise a particular interest, and consequently to grant a remedy for its infringement, is a question of social policy, and the list recognised has grown over the years. In considering whether or not to recognise particular interests the courts have had regard to such factors as the moral obliquity of the defenders' conduct, the capacity of the parties to bear the loss, and the consistency of recognition with what is conceived to be public policy.' In my opinion, deliberate misuse of statutory powers by a public body would be actionable under the law of Scotland at the instance of a third party who has suffered loss and damage in consequence of the misuse of statutory powers, provided that there was proof of malice or proof that the action had been taken by the public authority in the full knowledge that it did not possess the power which it purported to exercise. I have reached this conclusion on a consideration of the English authorities referred to above and having regard to the general principles applicable under the law of Scotland to abuse of legal process which are referred to by Professor Walker in Ch.24 of his work on Delict."[119]

In *Watkins v Secretary of State for the Home Department*, Lord Hope said that it is normal practice for rules regulating the conduct of public officers to be the same, or substantially the same, in Scotland as in England.[120] This point was accepted by Lord Bonomy in *Phipps v Royal College of Surgeons of Edinburgh*.[121] Recent developments have been in the Commonwealth and in England. The ingredients of the tort were set out in *Three Rivers DC v Bank of England (No.3)*[122]:

- the defendant must be a public officer;
- the act complained of must be exercised as a public officer;
- the public officer must act in bad faith;
- the claimant must prove that the public officer knew that the act was outwith his powers;

---

[118] See the discussions in *Micosta S.A. v Shetland Islands Council*, 1986 S.L.T. 193 and *Shetland Line (1984) Ltd v Secretary of State for Scotland*, 1996 S.L.T. 653.
[119] *Micosta S.A. v Shetland Islands Council*, 1986 S.L.T. 193 at 198.
[120] *Watkins v Secretary of State for the Home Department* [2006] 2 A.C. 395 at 410.
[121] *Phipps v Royal College of Surgeons of Edinburgh* [2010] CSOH 58; 2010 G.W.D. 27–544.
[122] *Three Rivers DC v Bank of England (No.3)* [2003] 2 A.C. 1 at 191–195 per Lord Steyn.

- the claimant must prove that the public officer knew that his act would probably harm the claimant, or a class of persons to which the claimant belonged.

A public officer may thus be liable for loss, injury and damage resulting from action known to be unlawful and likely to cause harm.[123] The claim can succeed on targeted malice or on recklessness—conduct in the face of a serious risk of loss due to an act or omission that was known to be unlawful but which was deliberately disregarded—it not being essential to prove spite, ill-will or specific intent to injure.[124] It may be raised against a public authority or a public officer. In England, the class of public officers is wide and can in some circumstances include police officers. Again in England, there is the suggestion that a "police" case could circumvent the probable cause requirement there.[125] It might also assist in circumventing some judicial protection of social work departments and the like.[126] Bad faith is of the essence.

FAILED OR INADEQUATE IMPLEMENTATION OF EUROPEAN UNION LAW

Known as "Eurotort" or "Eurorep", this head of liability has been described as **17–18** a new and emerging tort. It is included here because it inevitably involves vertical claims, i.e. against the State. It is similar to statutory liability in that (a) there may be no express provision for damages, indeed no UK provision at all, and (b) it is the national system of law, particularly that dealing with compensation in the civil courts, that gives effect to the right of damages on breach. The first manifestation was in relation to the competition policy of the European Community.[127] It was suggested in one case that a breach of these provisions might be actionable in the UK courts for damages.[128]

Francovich

The next development is in relation to the enforcement of Community law **17–19** generally. The methods provided by the Treaty have not always been adequate. The decision in the landmark case *Van Gend en Loos v Nederlandse Tarief Commissie*[129] declared that certain Treaty Articles could have direct effect[130] in the Member States and later decisions declared that regulations and directives[131] can have this effect too. That is not the end of the matter, for the problem with directives is that, as they are frequently addressed to a Member State with instructions to achieve an objective, there is the possibility, that the Government

---

[123] *Dunlop v Woollahra Municipal Council* [1982] A.C. 158; *Racz v Home Office* [1994] 2 A.C. 45.
[124] *Three Rivers DC v Bank of England (No.3)* [2003] 2 A.C. 1; *Akenzua v Secretary of State for the Home Department* [2003] 1 W.L.R. 741. Cf. *Phipps v Royal College of Surgeons of Edinburgh* [2010] CSOH 58; 2010 G.W.D. 27–544.
[125] *Clerk & Lindsell on Torts*, edited by A. Dugdale and M. Jones, 20th edn (London: Sweet & Maxwell, 2013), para.17–138.
[126] *Clerk & Lindsell on Torts*, edited by Dugdale and Jones (2013), para.17–141.
[127] For Community law generally, see "European Community Law and Institutions", *Stair Memorial Encyclopaedia*, Vol.10.
[128] *Garden Cottage Foods v Milk Marketing Board* [1984] A.C. 130.
[129] *Van Gend en Loos v Nederlandse Tarief Commissie* [1963] 1 C.M.L.R. 105.
[130] See *Stair Memorial Encyclopaedia*, Vol.10, para.81.
[131] See *Stair Memorial Encyclopaedia*, Vol.10, paras 89–93.

will not implement or will improperly implement the directive. This failure heretofore had been thought only challengeable at the supranational level of the Commission suing the Member State before the European Court of Justice. Some directives, indeed many directives, allow the Member State some considerable discretion. If it is not exercised then there is a gap in the Community enforcement mechanism.[132] This was plugged in *Francovich*. The case arose out of Directive 80/987, which was intended to provide workers with a minimum level of protection in the event of the insolvency of their employers. The deadline for implementation was October 23, 1983. The Italian Government failed to implement the directive and was sued by the Commission, who obtained a ruling against Italy. Nonetheless, nothing had been done by May 1991. *Francovich* is in fact two cases, raised separately and later joined, whereby workers who were uncompensated sought damages against the State for payment of wages as provided by the directive or alternatively for compensation for the loss as a result of the failure of the State to implement the directive.[133] On a preliminary ruling,[134] it was held that the directive just failed to meet the twin criteria for direct effect as the State had a considerable discretion. The court did allow the compensation claim. The full effectiveness of rules of Community law would be undermined and the protection of the rights which they create weakened if individuals were unable to obtain reparation when their rights were infringed as a result of Member State's violation of Community law.[135] There are three conditions for such a case:

1. the result prescribed by the directive must involve the attribution of rights to individuals;
2. the content of those rights must be identifiable from the provisions of the directive;
3. a causal link must exist between the violation of the Member State's obligation and the damage suffered by the injured person.[136]

It is for the national courts to decide the form of the reparation process. However, the national systems must designate the competent courts and forms of proceedings which may be used to pursue such Eurorep cases.

Factortame

17–20   The European Court of Justice took the law a stage further in two joined cases.[137] In *R. v Secretary of State for Transport, ex p. Factortame Ltd*,[138] companies owned and operated by Spanish citizens sought judicial review complaining of the illegality of a UK statute and related regulations. A first ECJ

---

[132] What follows is indebted to G.H. Downie, "New Right to Damages in Community Law" (1992) 37 J.L.S.S. 424; see also C. Boch and R. Lane, "A New Remedy in Scots Law: Damages from the Crown for Breach of Community Law", 1992 S.L.T. 145.
[133] *Francovich v Italy* (C-6/90) [1992] I.R.L.R. 84.
[134] See *Stair Memorial Encyclopaedia*, Vol.10, paras 239–244.
[135] *Francovich v Italy* (C–6/90) [1992] I.R.L.R. 84 at [34].
[136] *Francovich v Italy* (C–6/90) [1992] I.R.L.R. 84 at [40].
[137] For a detailed analysis see M.G.J. Upton, "Crown Liability in Damages under Community Law [Parts 1 & 2]", 1996 S.L.T. (News) 175 and 211.
[138] *R. v Secretary of State for Transport, ex p. Factortame Ltd* (C-48/93) [1990] 2 A.C. 85; [1991] 1 A.C. 603.

reference declared that any national rules precluding remedies enforcing Community law were inapplicable and so injunctions could be brought against the Crown and national courts could declare UK legislation inapplicable. In the second reference, the UK legislation was ruled to have been contrary to EU law. It was changed by the UK Parliament as a result. The plaintiffs then sought the damages they had claimed in the original judicial review—they had, after all, been precluded (they said) from fishing by what had been declared to be illegal legislation. It was held that such a right to damages did arise.

Brasserie

In *Brasserie du Pecheur S.A. v Germany*,[139] French brewers complained that **17–21** the German law on beer duty was contrary to EU law and that they had sustained a loss as a result. They, too, were entitled to recover damages. The ECJ based its rules for establishing liability on its existing rules on non-contractual liability of the Community. Community law confers a right to reparation where three conditions are met:

1. the rule of law infringed must be intended to confer rights on individuals;
2. the breach must be sufficiently serious;
3. there must be a direct causal link between the breach of the obligation resting on the state and the damage sustained by the injured parties.

In deciding whether the matter was sufficiently serious the decisive test is whether the Member State had manifestly and gravely disregarded the limits on its discretion. Certain factors can be taken into account (so can others not listed by the court) in approaching that question:

a. the clarity and precision of the rule breached;
b. the measure of discretion left to the Member State;
c. whether the infringement and any damage caused were intentional or voluntary;
d. whether any error of law was excusable;
e. the contribution, if any, a Community institution might have made;
f. the adoption or retention of national measures.

Where there has been (a) a judgment finding an infringement established; (b) a preliminary ruling; or (c) an established body of ECJ jurisprudence, then the breach is sufficiently serious.

A number of practical points were also laid down in the joint cases. The obligation to make reparation did not depend on a condition based on any concept of fault (intentional or negligent) beyond that of a serious breach of community law. The extent of reparation must be commensurate. The local system may set the criteria but they must not be less favourable than those applying to similar claims based on domestic law and must not be such as in practice make it impossible or excessively difficult to obtain reparation. Damages for loss of profit could not be ruled out as many cases involve commerce. Exemplary damages, where they apply nationally, could not be ruled out

---

[139] *Brasserie du Pecheur S.A. v Germany* (C-46/93) [1996] 2 W.L.R. 506.

either.[140] The date from which damages would be payable was not cut off at the date of a decision—there was no temporal limitation.

Beyond

17–22   An example based on the foregoing jurisprudence is *Dillenkofer v Germany*.[141] The plaintiffs lost money when their holiday companies went bust. They sued the State for failure to have implemented the directive on package travel swiftly enough to have covered their cases. The court referred to the *Brasserie* criteria and the *Francovich* criteria. The court explained that although *Francovich,* another non-transposition case, did not expressly mention the need for serious breach, it was implied within it. Thus failure to transpose within the set time-limit is per se a serious breach. In this case, the rights conferred and the persons on whom they were conferred was clear.[142]

Another example, this time showing the wide reach of the liability, is *Kobler v Republik Osterrich*,[143] in which the ECJ held that the *Brasserie* criteria could apply to the decision of a court at last instance as being part of the state apparatus. To be actionable, the *Brasserie* criteria still have to be met and in *Kobler*—an interpretation of a length of service increment—the breach was not sufficiently manifest. This head of liability will increase as the years go by.[144]

In the context of a case for *Francovich* damages for personal injury, the Court of Appeal in England has held that limitation periods run from the date on which the personal injury was suffered.[145] The practical difficulty here is that the pursuer will be required to exhaust all domestic remedies before pursuing a *Francovich* claim, which may inevitably mean that limitation periods will already have expired.

---

[140] Although a claim for exemplary damages was rejected by the Divisional Court as part of the *Factortame* litigation: *R v Secretary of State for Transport ex p. Factortame Ltd (No.5)* [1998] 1 C.M.L.R. 1353.

[141] *Dillenkofer v Germany* [1997] 2 W.L.R. 253.

[142] The United Kingdom joined the case to argue that late transposition should not be a matter of liability per se and that it would have to be shown that it was a manifest and grave breach. The directive was implemented by the United Kingdom in the Package Travel, Package Holiday and Package Tours Regulations 1992 (SI 1992/3288).

[143] *Kobler v Republik Osterrich* [2004] 2 W.L.R. 976.

[144] See also *R. v Ministry of Agriculture and Fisheries, ex p. Hedley Lomas (Ireland) Ltd* [1996] 3 W.L.R. 787; *R. v HM Treasury, ex p. British Telecommunications Plc* [1996] 3 W.L.R. 203. The increased size of the Community will naturally generate more litigation.

[145] *Spencer v Secretary of State for Work and Pensions* [2009] Q.B. 358. See also *R v Secretary of State for Transport ex p. Factortame Ltd (No.6)* [2001] W.L.R. 942.

CHAPTER 18

OCCUPIERS' LIABILITY

A person who occupies, or otherwise is in control of premises, may incur **18–01** delictual liability to others affected by what is done with or on those premises by the occupier on a variety of legal bases, including nuisance, *aemulatio vicini*[1] or perhaps the Roman *quasi-delicts*,[2] or common law negligence.[3] However, where due to the state of the premises themselves—or, with regard to the state of the premises, due to anything done or not done on those premises— injury or damage is suffered by persons *who have entered onto premises* controlled by the occupier, delictual liability of the occupier for that harm is now dealt with by the Occupiers' Liability (Scotland) Act 1960. The broad purpose of the Act is to provide that occupiers must take reasonable care for persons entering onto their premises. It is not a duty of insurance, although the more dangerous the activity the more care must be taken. The Act also extends to damage to property situated on the relevant premises, even where the person to whom the property belongs is not physically present on the premises.[4] However, it must be noted that the Act does not create a general liability on an occupier of premises to take any care for persons who have not entered onto the premises, such as adjoining proprietors or passers-by. Such persons must look to general principles of liability for unintentional harm, nuisance and other related delicts for protection of their interests. There is also a related cluster of cases discussing whether employers' liability regulations also give protection to non-workers entering the workplace.[5]

Historical background

Although the 1960 Act supersedes the common law, it is important to **18–02** understand the context in which the Act was passed. The Act was passed to amend the Scots common law, which had been strongly influenced by English principles imposed in 1929 by the House of Lords in *Dumbreck v Addie & Sons*.[6]

---

[1] See paras 8–08 to 8–18 above.

[2] See paras 18–18 to 18–25 below.

[3] See, e.g. *Maloco v Littlewoods Organisation Ltd*, 1987 S.C. (HL) 37; *Bolton v Stone* [1951] A.C. 850.

[4] Occupiers' Liability (Scotland) Act 1960 s.1(3)(b).

[5] *Banna v Delicato*, 1999 S.L.T. (Sh. Ct) 84; *O'Brien v Duke of Argyll's Trs*, 1999 S.L.T. (Sh. Ct) 88; *Layden v Aldi GmbH & Co KG*, 2002 S.L.T. (Sh. Ct) 71; *Mathieson v Aberdeenshire Council*, 2003 S.L.T. (Sh. Ct) 91; *Donaldson v Hays Distribution Services Ltd*, 2005 1 S.C. 523; *Brown v East Lothian Council*, 2013 S.L.T. 721.

[6] *Dumbreck v Addie & Sons*, 1929 S.C. (HL) 51.

Prior to 1929 Scots law made no distinction between categories of person entering onto premises in the context of delictual liability of occupiers. However, English law, with its traditional emphasis on property, classified persons entering onto premises into three rigid categories: invitee; licensee and trespasser. A duty to take reasonable care was owed by the occupier to invitees, but with regard to licensees (persons entitled but not invited to enter onto the premises) the duty was merely not to create a trap or allow hidden dangers to exist on the property. Trespassers were afforded the lowest duty: effectively they entered property at their own risk.

The 1960 Act was passed in response to the *First Report of the Law Reform Committee for Scotland*,[7] which had recommended the restoration of the pre-1929 position in Scotland, based on general principles of *culpa*.[8] Accordingly, although the 1960 Act purports to supersede the common law, it may be seen as ejecting an interloper in the common law and restoring consistency with modern traditions in the Scots law of delict. Given that statutory occupiers' liability in Scotland thus incorporates common law concepts, it is perhaps not surprising that the courts are willing to entertain cases pled under the 1960 Act and under the common law in the alternative.

Thus, although a similar duty is now owed by the occupier to persons (and their property) entering onto the premises no matter whether they are invited or unwanted, the status of the pursuer will be relevant to determining what care a reasonable occupier actually would be expected to take.[9]

THE SCOPE OF THE OCCUPIERS' LIABILITY (SCOTLAND) ACT 1960

18–03 Section 1(1) of the Act appears to provide that the Act supersedes the common law where the Act applies.[10] This would suggest that it is vitally important to understand where the boundary lies between delictual liability at common law and that under the 1960 Act, as a strict interpretation of this provision would imply that an action at common law would be incompetent where the 1960 Act applies. However, in practice, cases have proceeded on alternative common law and statutory pleas.[11] Nevertheless, care should be taken in ensuring that pleadings are based on the 1960 Act in circumstances where it applies. It is

---

[7] Law Reform Committee for Scotland, *First Report of the Law Reform Committee for Scotland* (HMSO, 1957), Cmnd.88.

[8] A parallel reform occurred in England and Wales, resulting in the Occupiers' Liability Act 1957, now supplemented by the Occupiers' Liability Act 1984.

[9] See *McGlone v BRB*, 1966 S.C. (HL) 1.

[10] Cf. s.2(2) which recognises "enactment *or rule of law*" (emphasis added) as alternative sources of a stricter duty, arguably condoning alternative liability at common law. It is clear that the 1960 Act does not preclude parallel statutory liability. Thus, there may be parallel liability under the Animals (Scotland) Act 1987 or with regard to statutory duties owed by employers to employees: see, e.g. *Beggs v Motherwell Bridge Fabricators Ltd*, 1998 S.L.T. 1215. In *Simmons v British Steel Plc*, 2002 S.L.T. 711 the Lord Ordinary (Kingarth) found the defenders liable under various statutory duties imposed upon them as employers, and at common law, even although the harm to the pursuer was caused by what was done by the defenders on their premises, which was where the pursuer suffered the accident causing the harm. This aspect of the Lord Ordinary's decision was condoned by the House of Lords: *Simmons v British Steel Plc*, 2004 S.C. (HL) 94.

[11] See, e.g. *Bell v Scottish Special Housing Association*, 1987 S.L.T. 320; *Hill v Lovett*, 1992 S.L.T. 994; *Dawson v Scottish Power*, 1999 S.L.T. 672; *Fegan v Highland Council*, 2007 S.C. 723; *Porter v Scottish Borders Council*, 2009 Rep. L.R. 46; *Kelly v Riverside Inverclyde (Property Holdings) Ltd* [2014] CSOH 86; 2014 G.W.D. 18–355.

suggested that a convenient rule of thumb is to assess the locus of concurrence of *damnum* and *injuria*. If the alleged delict is completed upon relevant premises, then pleadings should aver a case under the Occupiers' Liability (Scotland) Act 1960. However, should the alleged delict be completed elsewhere, then the 1960 Act will not apply and an alternative ground for liability must be averred.

The long title to the 1960 Act refers to "the liability of occupiers ... by reason of the state of the premises or of anything done or omitted to be done thereon." Although this language is repeated in s.1(1), the Act itself goes no further in defining what is meant by the "state" of the premises or the range of activity carried out upon the premises that is within the scope of the Act. If the purpose of the Act is to amend the law of Scotland as to the *liability* of occupiers, then it is submitted that the range of activity that relates to occupation of premises and so falls within the scope of the Act remains as it was treated at common law.

In *Muir v Glasgow Corp*[12] Lord Wright appeared to make a distinction between dangers in the structural condition of premises, which would be subject to the then common law on occupiers' liability, and dangers in the use of the premises, where the ordinary principles of the law of negligence would apply. This distinction has been described in England and Wales as being between "occupancy" duties and "activity" duties.[13] It follows from the above that the words "anything done or omitted to be done thereon" should be interpreted as being confined in their application to activity related to the state of the premises, rather than extending to activity coincidentally carried on within the premises that is not directly connected to the structural condition of the premises.

Thus, mesothelioma contracted from inhaling asbestos fibres that fall from insulation already fitted to premises properly may be the subject of a claim under the 1960 Act,[14] whereas mesothelioma contracted from inhaling asbestos fibres from insulation being manufactured within premises, or while being fitted to premises, may not.[15] The pleadings in the latter case should therefore be based on a breach of a common law, as opposed to statutory, duty of care.

Courts in England and Wales have recognised that the duty of occupiers under the Occupiers' Liability Act 1957 extends to taking reasonable steps to ensure the safety of persons on the occupiers' premises where the occupier has permitted a contractor to use the premises for, e.g. a firework display[16] and a fund-raising fair.[17] However, these decisions subsequently have been questioned in the

---

[12] *Muir v Glasgow Corp*, 1942 S.C. (HL) 3 at 14–15.

[13] *Fairchild v Glenhaven Funeral Services Ltd* [2002] 1 W.L.R. 1052 at 1084 per Brooke L.J. delivering the opinion of the court. This distinction does not appear to have been considered judicially in Scotland since the 1960 Act came into force. Although the Occupiers' Liability Act 1957, which applies in England and Wales, is significantly different from the 1960 Act—and indeed much of the judicial consideration of these issues in the English courts has been concerned with the interpretation of statutory provisions on liability for contractors with no direct equivalent in the 1960 Act—the language in s.1(1) of the 1957 Act concerning liability for activity carried out on premises is broadly similar: " ... the duty which an occupier of premises owes ... in respect of dangers due to the state of the premises or to things done or omitted to be done on them."

[14] See in England under the Occupiers' Liability Act 1957: *Smith v Ministry of Defence* [2005] EWHC 682.

[15] *Fairchild v Glenhaven Funeral Services Ltd*, [2002] 1 W.L.R. 1052. This decision of the Court of Appeal was not disturbed by the House of Lords: *Fairchild v Glenhaven Funeral Services Ltd* [2002] 3 W.L.R. 89.

[16] *Bottomley v Todmorden Cricket Club* [2004] P.I.Q.R. 18.

[17] *Gwilliam v West Hertfordshire Hospitals NHS Trust* [2003] Q.B. 443.

English courts,[18] and it has been pointed out in *Honeybourne v Burgess*[19] that the purported statutory basis[20] has no equivalent in the Occupiers' Liability (Scotland) Act 1960. Nevertheless, in *Mallon v Spook Erections Ltd*[21] the operators of an open-air market were held liable under the 1960 Act to an 11-year-old girl who was scalded when a cup of soup she purchased from a stall-holder spilled over onto her hands. She was not tall enough to see over the counter and so could not see that the soup was delivered without a lid on the cup.[22]

An inherently dangerous use of premises may fall within the scope of the 1960 Act. Examples may include the keeping of dangerous animals, including dogs,[23] or the handling of hazardous substances.[24] However, in *Honeybourne v Burgess*[25] it was held that an assault by a nightclub bouncer had nothing to do with the state of the premises or with anything done or not done on those premises. This continuing subtlety of the distinction between "occupancy" duties and "activity" duties arguably may justify the pragmatic approach taken by the courts in Scotland in permitting cases to proceed on alternative statutory and common law pleas.

Premises

18-04   An essential question to ask is what is meant by "premises" ("land" being apparently self-explanatory). This term is not defined in the Act and so is a matter to be determined in each case. Buildings clearly qualify as premises. The Act also imposes liability for certain areas that (as they have been separately described) are not premises as such and may be described as notional premises.[26] So the following are covered by the Act: fixed or moveable structures,[27] including any vessel,[28] vehicle or aircraft. This provision in its terms covers most modes of transport and it will be a question of statutory interpretation whether, for example, a hoist or a ski-tow fall within the statutory definitions. It follows that to qualify as notional premises, the property in question must be capable of occupation. The act applies to *exits* from premises, presumably where the pursuer has already entered on the premises.[29]

Land may be in public or private ownership and includes open land, public parks, car parks, open-air markets and sports grounds. An open area of land attracted liability when Mrs Cairns, a grandmother, tripped in a concealed hole at a Butlins holiday camp. The defenders denied the existence of a hole on the basis

[18] See, e.g. *Glaister v Appleby-in-Westmorland Town Council* [2010] P.I.Q.R. P6.
[19] *Honeybourne v Burgess*, 2006 S.L.T. 585. See also *West v Castlehill LLP*, 2009 G.W.D. 1–4.
[20] Occupiers' Liability Act 1957 s.2(4).
[21] *Mallon v Spook Erections Ltd*, 1993 S.C.L.R. 845. See also *Hazard v Glasgow Pavilion*, 1994 G.W.D. 13–850. Cf. *Falconer v Edinburgh City Transport Longstone Social Club*, 2003 Rep. L.R. 39.
[22] The stallholders themselves were liable only at common law as the girl had not entered their van.
[23] See, e.g. *Hill v Lovett*, 1992 S.L.T. 994.
[24] *Dunn v Carlin*, 2003 G.W.D. 5–130. See also *Honeybourne v Burgess*, 2006 S.L.T. 585 at 588 per Lady Smith.
[25] *Honeybourne v Burgess*, 2006 S.L.T. 585.
[26] Occupiers' Liability (Scotland) Act 1960 s.1(3).
[27] Scaffolding qualifies: *Poliskie v Lane*, 1981 S.L.T. 282; *Morton v Glasgow City Council*, 2007 S.L.T. (Sh. Ct) 81.
[28] Including an oil rig: *Clark v Maersk Co Ltd*, 2000 S.L.T. (Sh. Ct) 9.
[29] See *Duff v East Dunbartonshire Council*, 2002 Rep. L.R. 98.

of regular inspections. The court held there was a hole and because they had regular inspections they must have been negligent and missed it[30]

However, it has long been settled that the duty of an occupier of land does not extend to taking active measures to protect others from dangers arising from obvious features of the landscape, whether these features are natural or man-made.[31]

Part 1 of the Land Reform (Scotland) Act 2003 provides everyone with the right of access to land, and to cross land, for recreational activity and for educational purposes, including where these activities are being pursued for profit,[32] subject to the exercising of these rights responsibly.[33] The 2003 Act imposes reciprocal obligations on landowners to use and manage the land responsibly with regard to access rights,[34] but makes no changes to the duty of care owed by an occupier to persons exercising their rights of access under the Act.[35]

The special case of the liability of landlords of premises is discussed at para.18–15 below.

Although private roads and footpaths fall within the scope of the Act,[36] roads and pavements under public control are generally thought to be treated outside the scope of the Act. These are discussed at paras 18–16 to 18–17 below.

Who can sue?

The Act specifies to whom an occupier's duty is owed. There is therefore no **18–05** need to revert to the common law in order to determine whether or not a contested duty of care is owed. Thus, neither the neighbourhood test,[37] nor the *Caparo* tri-partite test,[38] nor concepts such as assumption of responsibility[39] are relevant to statutory occupiers' liability. The duty unequivocally is owed to "persons entering on the premises".[40] It follows that in order to have title to sue, it is sufficient that the pursuer was physically present on the premises in question at the time the injury or damage was inflicted. This is the case where the pursuer suffers personal injury, whether that be physical or psychiatric, and there is no

---

[30] *Cairns v Butlins*, 1989 G.W.D. 40–1879.

[31] *Hastie v Magistrates of Edinburgh*, 1907 S.C. 1102; *Stevenson v Glasgow Corporation*, 1908 S.C. 1034; *Taylor v Glasgow Corp*, 1922 S.C. (HL) 1; *Fegan v Highland Council*, 2007 S.C. 723. The approach taken in England and Wales is similar: *Donoghue v Folkstone Properties Ltd* [2003] Q.B. 1008; *Tomlinson v Congleton BC* [2004] 1 A.C. 46.

[32] Land Reform (Scotland) Act 2003 s.1.

[33] Land Reform (Scotland) Act 2003 s.2.

[34] Land Reform (Scotland) Act 2003 s.3.

[35] Land Reform (Scotland) Act 2003 s.5(2). A local authority may be deemed occupier for the purposes of the Occupiers' Liability (Scotland) Act 1960 if it has made a "path order" delineating an existing or new path under s.22 of the 2003 Act. See also *Johnstone v Sweeney*, 1985 S.L.T. (Sh. Ct) 2, which includes discussion of the unreported Inner House decision in *McQueen v Vale of Leven District Council* Unreported January 24, 1973 CSIH. See also the tangential discussion in *McDougall v Tawse*, 2002 S.L.T. (Sh. Ct) 10, and see D.J. Cusine and R. Paisley, *Servitudes* (Edinburgh: W, Green/SULI, 1998), para.21.28.

[36] See, e.g. *Beggs v Motherwell Bridge Fabricators Ltd*, 1998 S.L.T. 1215.

[37] *Donoghue v Stevenson*, 1932 S.C. (HL) 31 at 44 per Lord Atkin.

[38] *Caparo Industries Plc v Dickman* [1990] 2 A.C. 605.

[39] *Henderson v Merrett Syndicates* [1995] 2 A.C. 145 at 180–181 per Lord Goff of Chieveley.

[40] Occupiers' Liability (Scotland) Act 1960 s.1(1). Note that to enjoy title to sue, the pursuer must not also be the occupier, i.e. the person in control: *Harrison v West of Scotland Kart Club*, 2004 S.C. 615.

reason in principle why liability under the Act could not extend to pure economic loss.[41]

The 1960 Act may have a surprising impact on liability for secondary victims, which the common law generally precludes.[42] For example, where a pursuer suffers psychiatric injury in witnessing the harm inflicted upon a primary victim in breach of the occupiers' statutory duty, it follows that the pursuer (as a secondary victim) may bring a claim for damages for psychiatric injury against the occupier under the 1960 Act if the pursuer was physically present on the premises in question when witnessing the harm.[43] It is submitted that in such cases[44] a secondary victim would be able to circumvent the common law control mechanisms given that the only prerequisite for the imposition of the duty of care under the 1960 Act is the physical presence of the pursuer on the premises in question.[45] However, even where the harm to the primary victim is itself covered by the 1960 Act, if the pursuer witnesses the immediate aftermath of the accident elsewhere, such as in a hospital, the pursuer would have to bring a claim under the common law, where the "control mechanisms" applying to secondary victims suing for psychiatric would thus apply.

However, the pursuer's physical presence on the premises in question is not required where the damage is to property. The 1960 Act extends a duty upon the occupier with regard to "the property of persons who have not themselves entered onto the premises."[46] Thus, the owner of property that is hired to a contractor engaged to work on premises has title to sue the occupier under the Act if the property is damaged by the failure of the occupier to take reasonable

---

[41] The Act does not qualify the "injury or damage" (s.2(1)) that it covers. It is presumed, therefore, that the Act extends liability to all forms of injury or damage reparable at common law. Lord Osborne perhaps hints at the potential for liability for economic loss under the 1960 Act in his judgment in *Hines v King Sturge LLP*, 2011 S.L.T. 2 at 13–14. Ultimately each case must turn on its own facts and it may be difficult in practice to establish a duty of care with regard to pure economic loss. Nevertheless, the categories of negligence are never closed: see, e.g. *Glaister v Appleby-in-Westmorland Town Council* [2010] P.I.Q.R. P6. *Glaister* also indirectly involved a claim for psychiatric injury. In *Barker v Anders Stokka* [1969] 1 Lloyd's Rep. 319, the plaintiff's case for damages for psychiatric injury as a primary victim of a breach of the Occupiers' Liability Act 1957 (which applies in England and Wales) failed on causation.

[42] See, e.g. *Perrett v Collins* [1998] 2 Lloyd's Rep. 255 (physical injury); *Coleridge v Miller Construction Ltd*, 1997 S.L.T. 485 (damage to property and pure economic loss); *Alcock v Chief Constable of South Yorkshire* [1992] 1 A.C. 310 (psychiatric injury).

[43] An example would be the bystanders present within the premises in circumstances similar to those of the Hillsborough tragedy.

[44] And possibly also in secondary victim physical injury cases. An example may be if, due to the state of premises, machinery being used on the premises was damaged and so made unsafe. If subsequently a person operating the machinery (still situated on the premises) was physically injured due to the state of the machinery, the chain of causation could be traced back through the damage suffered by the primary victim (the owner of the damaged machinery) to the occupier's breach of statutory duty. If the occupier's statutory duty to the physically injured person is automatic by virtue of his being upon the premises at the time of the injury, then does it matter if the pursuer is a primary or secondary victim? Would the same be true of property on the premises damaged by machinery on the premises which itself had been damaged by the state of the premises themselves? Arguably, liability would circumvent the impediments set out in *Marc Rich v Bishop Rock Marine Co Ltd (The Nicholas H)* [1996] A.C. 211 (for discussion see paras 11–16 to 11–19 above).

[45] In *Robertson v Forth Road Bridge Joint Board (No.2)*, 1995 S.C. 364 the Inner House rejected a submission that an employer's duty of care to employees would circumvent the secondary victim control mechanisms. However, no plea was taken by the pursuers on the Occupiers' Liability (Scotland) Act 1960. Could it have been argued that the 1960 Act applied?

[46] Occupiers' Liability (Scotland) Act 1960 s.1(3)(b).

care with regard to the state of the premises or anything done or not done on the premises.[47] If it is accepted that human gametes which are harvested and stored (e.g. where intended to be used for future conception) remain the "property" of the person from whom the material was harvested, it is suggested that whoever is responsible for the storage owes a duty of care with regard to the state of the premises (including the conditions in which the gametes are stored) to the "owner" of the gametes as occupier under the 1960 Act.[48]

Who should be sued?

When suing under the 1960 Act we need to determine who is the occupier. **18–06** Here we gain some assistance from the Act.[49] It defines "occupier of premises" as "a person occupying or having control of land or other premises." However, we still require to know what is meant by occupying or having control. To resolve this question regard is had to the law as it applied before the Act. This is still effectively determined by the common law which is expressly saved in the statute.[50] The test is one of possession and control and will be a matter of fact in each case: "an occupier's liability is based on his capacity to act so as to make the premises safe."[51] An example is *Telfer v Glasgow DC*.[52] The Co-operative Society was in the course of selling property to Glasgow District Council. Both the Council and the Society were sued in respect of an injury sustained on the property. It was held, inter alia, that the Society was the occupier. It had the keys and the de facto power to exclude others.

Ownership is not necessary nor indeed is any form of title, however limited. Where property is leased, the tenant, subject to the landlord's repairing duty, will normally become the person in control of the premises, and thus the occupier under the 1960 Act. Utilities exercising statutory powers of access may usurp the owner's occupation of premises and so take control. Similarly, an independent contractor may have control while in occupation of property, as was seen in *Poliskie v Lane*.[53] However, the involvement of an independent contractor does not of itself mean that the "primary" employer or owner escapes liability,[54] especially where the normal occupier retains some control over the premises.[55] Even where substantial control is relinquished by the normal occupier, there may be liability with regard to the selection of the contractor or, depending upon the facts of the case, a more general residual liability,[56] especially where the purpose

---

[47] It is submitted that in similar circumstances to *North Scottish Helicopters Ltd v United Technologies Corp Inc*, 1988 S.L.T. 77, where the pursuer enjoys a right tantamount to ownership in the property concerned, a claim under the 1960 Act for pure economic loss may be feasible.

[48] The point was not considered in *Holdich v Lothian Health Board*, 2014 S.L.T. 495. Nor was the point raised in the earlier English equivalent: *Yearworth v Bristol NHS Trust* [2010] Q.B. 1

[49] Occupiers' Liability (Scotland) Act 1960 s.1(1).

[50] Occupiers' Liability (Scotland) Act 1960 s.1(2).

[51] *Gallagher v Kleinwort Benson (Trs) Ltd*, 2003 S.C.L.R. 384 at 393 per Lord Reed.

[52] *Telfer v Glasgow DC*, 1974 S.L.T. (Notes) 51. See also *Feely v Co-operative Wholesale Society*, 1990 S.L.T. 547 at 549 per Lord Dervaird. And see also for an independent contractor pursuer himself being in control: *Poliskie v Lane*, 1981 S.L.T. 282.

[53] *Poliskie v Lane*, 1981 S.L.T. 28.

[54] Reflected in statutory safety regulations such as the Lifting Operations and Lifting Equipment Regulations 1998.

[55] See, e.g. *Dawson v Page*, 2012 Rep. L.R. 56. The Lord Ordinary's conclusion that the defender was occupier was not challenged upon appeal: 2013 S.C. 432.

[56] *McDyer v The Celtic Football and Athletic Co Ltd*, 2000 S.L.T. 736. See also *Mallon v Spook Erections Ltd*, 1993 S.C.L.R. 845.

of relinquishing control involves a use of the premises which is intrinsically dangerous.[57]

Nor is ownership sufficient, as was made clear in *Pollock v Stead & Simpson Ltd*[58] in which a case against one of the defenders based solely on infeftment was dismissed.[59] In *Murray v Edinburgh DC*,[60] the pursuer was a home help and was injured when a wooden panel containing a ventilator fell onto her wrist when she was working in a council house tenanted by an individual. The case under s.2(1) failed as it was not averred that the defenders were in occupation and control.

In *Todd v British Railways Board*,[61] the pursuer alleged that he slipped on a pavement in Waverley station while employed as a conductor. The issue arose because it was not clear whether British Railways Board or Railtrack were responsible partly due to the allocation of functions set up under the Railways Act 1993. While that Act transferred ownership, Lord Penrose correctly thought that irrelevant. It was held that the case was relevant under the Act on the basis that it was said that the premises were a train station. The pursuer is not always so fortunate in these multiple-defender cases. *Gallagher v Kleinwort Benson (Trs) Ltd*[62] demonstrates vividly the importance of drafting pleadings in such cases. Lord Reed identified three requirements that had to be averred and proved where the pursuer had fallen from the roof of a building in multiple occupation: first that the defender had control; secondly that that control gave rise to a duty of care; and thirdly that the duty of care was owed to the pursuer as opposed to some other person. There were nine defenders but the pleadings did not disclose a full set of requirements against any one. Similarly, in *Meek v SRC*,[63] where the pursuer fell on to a concrete "beach" when the promenade gave way, the Regional Council, District Council and Scotrail were all released at legal debate. It is open to a court to find all or some defenders liable and apportion liability.[64]

Standard of care

18–07   The duty and the standard of care are laid down by the Act. To succeed the pursuer must bring himself within the terms of the Act[65]:

> "The care which an occupier of premises is required, by reason of his occupation or control of the premises, to show towards a person entering thereon in respect of dangers which are due to the state of the premises or to anything done or omitted to be done on them and for which the occupier is in law responsible shall, except in so far as he is entitled to and does extend, restrict, modify or exclude by agreement his obligations towards that person, be such care as in all the circumstances of the case is reasonable to see that that person will not suffer injury or damage by reason of any such danger."

---

[57] *Muir v Glasgow Corp*, 1943 S.C. (HL) 3; *Bottomley v Todmorden Cricket Club* [2004] P.I.Q.R. 18.

[58] *Pollock v Stead & Simpson Ltd*, 1980 S.L.T. (Notes) 76.

[59] See also comments in *Clark v Maersk Co Ltd*, 2000 S.L.T. (Sh. Ct) 9.

[60] *Murray v Edinburgh DC*, 1981 S.L.T. 253.

[61] *Todd v British Railways Board* Unreported February 24, 1998 CSOH.

[62] *Gallagher v Kleinwort Benson (Trs) Ltd*, 2003 S.C.L.R. 384.

[63] *Meek v SRC* [2001] Scot. H.C. 92.

[64] *Nicol v Advocate General for Scotland* [2003] Scot. C.S. 65.

[65] Occupiers' Liability (Scotland) Act 1960 s.2(1).

This provision can be summarised to the effect that the occupier must take such care as is reasonable in all the circumstances. Thus it is "appropriate to adopt a similar approach to the calculus of risk as with common law negligence."[66] The test used in determining foreseeability of harm is accordingly an objective one, asked from the perspective of the reasonable person rather than the specific occupier.[67] It is nevertheless a statutory duty and it is important to try to fit specific cases into the statutory definition of the duty. Despite the positive formulation of the duty, it seems now to be settled that it imposes no evidentiary burden upon the occupier. The pursuer will still have to show the circumstances which give rise to liability, i.e. by the leading of credible evidence to confirm that the harm was reasonably foreseeable[68] and to show how and why the duty was breached,[69] with reference to what was required to fulfil the duty.[70] A pursuer cannot merely aver that he has suffered an accident on premises and put the onus on the defender to prove that he took reasonable care.[71] Thus, a woman who fell when the signpost she was leaning on gave way did not succeed as it was not established that the defenders should have known of the defect.[72] Likewise, a woman who was injured when she fell down a flight of steps outside her workplace while trying to escape from a swooping seagull did not succeed as she adduced no evidence to confirm that the gull had been nesting on the defender's building or that her employer as occupier had been aware of any previous attacks from nesting birds.[73] However, in *McDyer v The Celtic Football and Athletic Co Ltd*[74] the Inner House allowed the doctrine of res ipsa loquitur to apply to the extent of allowing that the doctrine meant that the pleadings that narrated control and an accident were sufficient where an item fell on the pursuer from above.[75]

Previously decided cases can illustrate what the rule set out in the statute means. It certainly would cover many a derelict building,[76] poor lighting,[77] leaving things lying about over which people can trip,[78] the failure to find a hole

---

[66] *Phee v Gordon*, 2013 S.C. 379 at 388 per Lord Hodge delivering the opinion of the court—for detailed consideration of the calculus of risk at common law see above at paras 12–04 to 12–10.

[67] *McGlone v British Railways Board*, 1966 S.C. (HL) 1. See also *Wardle v Scottish Borders Council*, 2011 S.L.T. (Sh. Ct) 199.

[68] *Dawson v Page*, 2013 S.C. 432; *Kelly v Riverside Inverclyde (Property Holdings) Ltd* [2014] CSOH 86; 2014 G.W.D. 18–355.

[69] See, e.g. *Atkinson v Aberdeen City Council*, 2002 G.W.D. 22–737; *Glennie v University Court of the University of Aberdeen* [2013] CSOH 71; 2013 G.W.D. 17–362.

[70] See, e.g. *McGuffie v Forth Valley Health Board*, 1991 S.L.T. 231; *Bonham v Pentland Housing Association Ltd*, 2013 G.W.D. 7–165.

[71] See *Wallace v City of Glasgow DC*, 1985 S.L.T. 23; *Walker v Eastern Scottish Omnibuses Ltd*, 1990 G.W.D. 3–140; *Miller v City of Glasgow DC*, 1989 G.W.D. 29–1347. For notes on the law in practice see D. Kinloch, "Slippery Substances", 1995 Rep. B. 4–7.

[72] *Walker v Eastern Scottish Omnibuses Ltd*, 1990 G.W.D. 3–140.

[73] *Kelly v Riverside Inverclyde (Property Holdings) Ltd* [2014] CSOH 86; 2014 G.W.D. 18–355.

[74] *McDyer v The Celtic Football and Athletic Co Ltd*, 2000 S.L.T. 736. See also *Black v CB Richard Ellis Management Services Ltd*, 2006 Rep. L.R. 36.

[75] Applying *Devine v Colvilles*, 1969 S.C. (HL) 67.

[76] *Telfer v Glasgow DC*, 1974 S.L.T. (Notes) 51.

[77] *Millar v Fife Regional Council*, 1990 S.L.T. 651; although it is perfectly possible to descend a stair in the dark and it may only be where the absence of light is unexpected that there may be liability: *Teacher's Trs v Calder* (1900) 2 F. 372.

[78] *McMillan v Lord Advocate*, 1991 S.L.T. 150.

during regular inspections of land,[79] leaving a surface slippery because wet.[80] In *Kirk v Fife Council*,[81] the pursuer was injured when he slipped playing five-a-side football. It was established there had been water on the floor such that under their policy the defenders ought to have called-off the game. In the case of a landlord, an example is leaving a toilet bowl damaged.[82] Allowing a house to become damp such that it affected a child's asthma has fallen within the Act.[83]

18-08   Whether or not to be safe common stairs should be lit is a matter of fact and degree.[84] A man succeeded when he fell down stairs leaving premises he had visited as a salesman. It was held that the steps were dangerous because of the lack of a warning, either by notice or by a coloured warning strip.[85] However, a woman who fell down a set of steps when leaving a shop did not succeed in showing a breach of the 1960 Act where the shop had not fitted a handrail—the shop had another signposted alternative disabled access, it had satisfied all of the statutory requirements and there was no evidence that a handrail would have prevented the accident. Hindsight is irrelevant—it also made no difference that an additional notice had been installed at the steps since the accident.[86] Nevertheless, where the reasonable person would be expected to foresee that warning notices would alleviate the possibility of accident, such as in warning novice golfers of the dangers of badly hit golf balls,[87] the occupier will have a duty to put up notices unless the cost would be disproportionate.

However, it has long been settled that the duty of an occupier of land does not extend to taking active measures to protect others from dangers arising from obvious features of the landscape, whether these features are natural or man-made.[88] Thus, the Forestry Commission did not owe a duty to a woman who strayed from their land onto an unmaintained footpath from which she slipped and fell onto a rock. The poor condition of the footpath was obvious.[89] Likewise, there was no liability where a woman fell from a cliff when she bent down from

---

[79] *Cairns v Butlins*, 1989 G.W.D. 40–1879.

[80] *Todd v British Railways Board*, 1998 G.W.D. 11–568; *Black v CB Richard Ellis Management Services Ltd*, 2006 Rep. L.R. 36. Cf. *Dawson v Page*, 2013 S.C. 432; *Porter v Scottish Borders Council*, 2009 Rep. L.R. 46.

[81] *Kirk v Fife Council*, 2001 G.W.D. 36–1398. Cf. *Glennie v University of Aberdeen* [2013] CSOH 71; 2013 G.W.D. 17–362.

[82] *Hughes' Tutrix v Glasgow DC*, 1982 S.L.T. (Sh. Ct) 70.

[83] *Guy v Strathkelvin DC*, 1997 S.C.L.R. 405.

[84] *Davie v Edinburgh Corp*, 1977 S.L.T. (Notes) 5.

[85] *Cole v Weir Pumps Ltd*, 1995 S.L.T. 12.

[86] *Brown v Lakeland Ltd*, 2012 Rep. L.R. 140.See also *Connelly v Whitbread Plc* [2012] CSIH 51; 2012 G.W.D. 23–466.

[87] *Phee v Gordon*, 2013 S.C. 379.

[88] *Hastie v Magistrates of Edinburgh*, 1907 S.C. 1102; *Stevenson v Glasgow Corp*, 1908 S.C. 1034; *Taylor v Glasgow Corp*, 1922 (S.C.) (HL) 1. The approach taken in England and Wales is similar: *Donoghue v Folkstone Properties Ltd* [2003] Q.B. 1008; *Tomlinson v Congleton BC* [2004] 1 A.C. 46.

[89] *McCluskey v Lord Advocate*, 1994 S.L.T. 452. See also *Leonard v The Loch Lomond National Park Authority*, 2014 Rep. L.R. 46. Cf. *Anderson v Scottish Ministers*, 2009 Rep. L.R. 122, where, surprisingly, the defenders admitted that the facts as proved rendered them liable under the 1960 Act. The editor's note at the end of the report is duly sceptical. There is a full discussion of this general topic and some very interesting comparative material in D. Mckenzie et al., "Civil Liability for Injury and Damage Arising from Access to the Scottish Countryside" (1997) 2 S.L.P.Q. 214.

a bench on which she had been sitting to pick up her personal stereo, which she had dropped:[90]

> "There is no doubt that the general law remains as stated in the somewhat historic cases of *Stevenson*[91] and *Taylor*[92] to the effect that in general terms an occupier of land containing natural phenomena such as rivers or cliffs, which present obvious dangers, is not required to take precautions against persons becoming injured by reason of those dangers unless there are special risks such as unusual or unseen sources of danger."[93]

However, where hidden dangers, or traps, are concealed upon the land in question, the occupier will incur a duty to take reasonable precautions to minimise the associated risks. This exception may be traced back to the case of *Black v Caddell*,[94] where the occupiers of a disused coal pit were liable when a man travelling on an adjacent road was killed when he fell from his horse directly into the hidden shaft. Thus, in *Cowan v Hopetoun House Preservation Trust*,[95] the defenders were liable (subject to a 75 per cent reduction for the pursuer's contributory negligence) to a visitor taking part in a guided night bat-walk in the grounds of Hopetoun House. At the end of the tour the pursuer took a short-cut across a lawn towards the car park, where in the darkness he fell into a "ha-ha" (a trench dug as a feature in the grounds in the eighteenth century) and broke his ankle.

Allurements to children

An occupier will be expected to take into account the propensity for children **18–09** to be attracted to unusual features or installations and the additional risks that such allurements might pose given the lack of experience or judgement to be anticipated in children. Thus, a local authority was held liable for failing to keep bright berries out of the reach of young children who were visitors to a public park and were of such an age that it would be reasonable to foresee that they would be attracted to the berries and not understand that the berries were poisonous.[96]

Nevertheless, an occupier will not be liable where a child's actions are so reckless as to be beyond the scope of reasonable foresight, such as where a 14-year-old jumps from a height of five feet onto a flimsy skylight cover on the

---

[90] *Fegan v Highland Council*, 2007 S.C. 723. See also *Graham v East of Scotland Water Authority*, 2002 S.C.L.R. 340.

[91] *Stevenson v Glasgow Corp*, 1908 S.C. 1034.

[92] *Taylor v Glasgow Corp*, 1922 (S.C.) (HL) 1.

[93] *Fegan v Highland Regional Council*, 2007 S.C. 723 at 729 per Lord Johnston.

[94] *Black v Caddell* (1804) M. 13905, affirmed by the House of Lords at (1812) 5 Pat. App. 567. It has apparently been suggested that the defenders in this case unsuccessfully argued that the death of the victim was a benefit, rather than a loss to his family, given his "dissipated habits"! See *Rankin v Waddell*, 1949 S.C. 555 at 562 per Lord Jamieson.

[95] *Cowan v Hopetoun House Preservation Trust*, 2013 Rep. L.R. 62. See also *Cruikshank v Fife Council*, 2002 G.W.D. 2–87; *Duff v East Dunbartonshire Council*, 2002 Rep. L.R. 98.

[96] *Taylor v Glasgow Corp*, 1922 S.C. (HL) 1. A seven-year-old boy died after eating berries from a belladonna shrub growing in Glasgow's Botanical Gardens. See also, e.g. *Telfer v Glasgow Corp*, 1974 S.L.T. (Notes) 51 (the attraction of derelict buildings as a "glorified adventure playground" at 51 per Lord Stott); *Wardle v Scottish Borders Council*, 2011 S.L.T. (Sh. Ct) 199. For an English example that was ultimately dealt with by the House of Lords see *Jolley v Sutton LBC* [2000] 1 W.L.R. 1082.

roof of a school.[97] Volenti non fit injuria,[98] or as a fall-back contributory negligence,[99] may also exclude or limit occupiers' statutory liability to children.

Actings of others

18–10   Liability extends to a failure to take into account the actings of other parties, such as visitors to land or premises. Thus, in *Phee v Gordon*,[100] a golf club was liable for failure to take reasonable precautions to alert novice golfers to the dangers of poorly hit balls. In *Mallon v Spook Erections Ltd*[101] the operators of an open-air market were held liable under the 1960 Act to an 11-year-old customer of one of the market stall-holders who was injured because the stall's counter from which she was served hot soup was too tall for her to see over. In *Hosie v Arbroath Football Club Ltd*, the club was held liable when fans forced down a door by their sustained pressure injuring the pursuer. There were safety devices available and in use that would have prevented the door being lifted off.[102] The facts of *Hazard v Glasgow Pavilion*[103] are unusual. A person fell from a stage after being hypnotised by a performer and a proof before answer was allowed. In *Dunn v Carlin*,[104] the Inner House upheld a finding of liability on an occupier in respect of his having petrol exposed that did ignite and injure the pursuer, who later died. The pursuer had not proven that one of the employees of the defender had been smoking while decanting petrol. However, the Inner House made very clear that the act relates to the state of the premises, which *with the exposed petrol* was dangerous.

However, the occupier cannot take care of things about which he does not know or ought not to know. In *Falconer v Edinburgh City Transport Longstone Social Club*,[105] the pursuer slipped on residual body oil from a male strip show. Her case failed because there was neither averment nor proof that the occupiers knew or ought to have known that there would be oil on the floor at the interval. In such a situation, a case against the showmen might have been indicated but, of course, they may be difficult to find or convene.

While cases involving dog bites or other injuries by animals are now likely to be dealt with under the Animals (Scotland) Act 1987, in principle, the Occupiers' Liability (Scotland) Act 1960 applies to an occupier's conduct in keeping animals on premises and it was so held in the Outer House in *Hill v Lovett*.[106]

---

[97] *Devlin v Strathclyde Regional Council*, 1993 S.L.T. 699. See also *Pierce v West Sussex CC* [2014] E.L.R. 62, where, in holding that there was no liability where a child had damaged his hand when swinging a punch which accidentally hit a metal drinking fountain, the English Court of Appeal emphasised that the test to be applied was whether, as an objective fact, visitors to a school were reasonably safe in using the premises.

[98] For discussion see, e.g. *Titchener v British Railways Board*, 1984 S.L.T. 192; *Devlin v Strathclyde Regional Council*, 1993 S.L.T. 699.

[99] See, e.g. *Telfer v Glasgow Corp*, 1974 S.L.T. (Notes) 51; *Wardle v Scottish Borders Council*, 2011 S.L.T. (Sh. Ct) 199; *Morton v Glasgow City Council*, 2007 S.L.T. (Sh. Ct) 81.

[100] *Phee v Gordon*, 2013 S.C. 379.

[101] *Mallon v Spook Erections Ltd*, 1993 S.C.L.R. 845.

[102] *Hosie v Arbroath Football Club Ltd*, 1978 S.L.T. 122 at 124–125. Another case based on the act, that the club should have had more turnstiles and all of them manned was, on the facts alleged, unsuccessful.

[103] *Hazard v Glasgow Pavilion*, 1994 G.W.D. 13–850.

[104] *Dunn v Carlin*, 2003 G.W.D. 5–130.

[105] *Falconer v Edinburgh City Transport Longstone Social Club*, 2003 Rep. L.R. 39.

[106] *Hill v Lovett*, 1992 S.L.T. 994. It was also opined that there may well have been employer's liability upon one defender for failing to provide a safe place of work, per Lord Weir at 997.

The status of the pursuer

As a result of there being no express categories of victim, it does not matter, **18–11** in principle, whether someone is on the premises by invitation or as a trespasser: the standard of care, in both cases, is still reasonable care. However, as a matter of fact and circumstance, the pursuer's mode of entry is still relevant. These points were considered in *McGlone v British Railways Board*.[107] A boy aged 12 climbed up a transformer belonging to the board. It was surrounded on three sides by a large fence and on the other by the railway. A gap between the fence and a wall was restricted by barbed wire in a fan shape. There were signs saying, "Danger—overhead live wires". The boy was badly burned as a result of an electric shock sustained when he came into contact with one of the wires high up the transformer. The court held that although the barrier was not impenetrable, it indicated to the victim that he would be in danger and that was enough to implement the duty of care. Lord Reid expressed the view that the degree of care to be shown could vary depending on whether the person was trespassing or not. Lord Reid's opinion has not, in any way, resulted in an under-the-table categorisation of victims: instead it usefully serves to make courts and advisers remember that the Act refers every case back to its own circumstances.

McGlone was considered again by the House of Lords in *Titchener v British Railways Board*.[108] A 15-year-old girl and her 18-year-old boyfriend were struck by a train as they crossed a busy railway line. The girl was injured and the boy killed. The girl alleged the board should have inspected for gaps in the fence and repaired them. However, she admitted that she was aware of the dangers of trains and said she usually looked both ways. It was held that the existence and extent of a duty to fence will depend upon the circumstances of the case, including the age and intelligence of the particular person entering on the premises. Thus the board owed no duty to that particular pursuer in these particular circumstances to repair the fence.[109] Indeed, Lord Fraser said that if it had been necessary to do so, he would have held that the board owed her no duty to provide a fence at all. This applies generally so that an obvious danger does not require to be fenced or signposted.[110]

Titchener was followed in *Devlin v Strathclyde Regional Council*.[111] A 14-year-old boy was killed when, after he and some friends had "bounced" on a skylight cover on the roof of a local school, the deceased jumped from a height of five feet onto the cover, which gave way. The Lord Ordinary (Coulsfield) held that even making allowances for youth and excitement, the boy's actions could not be described other than as reckless, and so were beyond the scope of reasonable foresight. Furthermore, as was the position of the House of Lords in

---

[107] *McGlone v British Railways Board*, 1966 S.C. (HL) 1.

[108] *Titchener v British Railways Board*, 1984 S.C. (HL) 34. Cf. *Wardle v Scottish Borders Council*, 2011 S.L.T. (Sh. Ct) 199. See also *Morton v Glasgow City Council*, 2007 S.L.T. (Sh. Ct) 81.

[109] The "no duty" conclusion reflects the language of s.2(3) of the 1960 Act. However: "On this analysis of the facts it is possible to formulate the result either by saying that, at the critical moment, that is when the appellant crossed the line, the respondent Board owed no duty to the appellant, or that the duty they owed to the appellant had been discharged by the time she crossed the boundary fence, or that the accident was not caused by any breach of duty on the part of the respondent Board, or alternatively that, having assumed the risk involved, the respondent Board was covered by the doctrine *volenti non fit injuria*": *Titchener v British Railways Board*, 1984 S.C. (HL) 34 at 52 per Lord Hailsham.

[110] *Stevenson v Glasgow Corp*, 1908 S.C. 1034; *Taylor v Glasgow Corp*, 1922 (S.C.) (HL) 1; *Fegan v Highland Regional Council*, 2007 S.C. 723.

[111] *Devlin v Strathclyde Regional Council*, 1993 S.L.T. 699.

Titchener, his Lordship would have been prepared to hold that the claim would be subject to the defence of volenti non fit injuria had the occupier been held to have been in breach of duty.

A more routine example is *Dawson v Scottish Power*,[112] in which the pursuer's 11-year-old son was injured when he went to retrieve his football which had landed in the defenders' substation. He tried to climb over a fence and impaled his finger on a spike at the top. The fence was six-feet high but its height had reduced effectively to four feet as a result of the build up of rubble. It was, as a matter of common sense and the evidence of a health and safety expert, reasonably foreseeable that a boy would try to climb over a fence for his ball and six feet or two metres was the safe height.

Higher duties

18–12   The 1960 Act does not relieve an occupier of any higher duty of care incumbent upon him[113] such as the employer's duty to provide for his employees under employers' liability legislation.

Causation

18–13   Consistent with liability at common law, the onus is on the pursuer to lead evidence to establish causation—or at least that the breach of the occupier's statutory duty is causa sine qua non the injury or damage complained of.[114] Thus, where the pursuer cannot adduce evidence to suggest that, on the balance of probabilities, the precautions contended to be missing would have prevented the harm, the pursuer's claim will fail. So if a court is not persuaded that had a handrail been fitted to a staircase the pursuer would have avoided injury, there will be no liability upon the occupier.[115]

The *McGhee/Fairchild*[116] exception has been applied to a case brought under the 1960 Act. In *Bye v Fife Council*,[117] a 12-year-old child fell 2.3 metres from a swing which had been installed in the playground of a public park. It was found that the swing was 0.5 metres taller than the British Standard, and, had the swing been installed compatibly with the British Standard, the maximum height from which the child could have fallen would have been 1.8 metres. Although the sheriff held that non-compatibility with the British Standard was not of itself negligence, the local authority had breached its duty as an occupier by installing a swing that was 0.5 metres taller than the standard. Furthermore, although the medical evidence was that the child may have suffered the same injury (a ruptured spleen) had she fallen only 1.8 metres, the sheriff accepted that the greater height from which the child had fallen materially increased the risk of injury, and on application of the *McGhee/Fairchild* exception, confirmed that the local authority were liable. It would be difficult to predict what might have been decided had this decision been appealed, given the caution which has been

---

[112] *Dawson v Scottish Power*, 1999 S.L.T. 672.
[113] Occupiers' Liability (Scotland) Act 1960 s.2(2).
[114] See Ch.13 above.
[115] See, e.g. *Brown v Lakeland Ltd*, 2012 Rep. L.R. 140.
[116] *McGhee v National Coal Board*, 1973 S.C. (HL) 37; *Fairchild v Glenhaven Funeral Services Ltd* [2003] 1 A.C. 32.
[117] *Bye v Fife Council*, 2007 Rep. L.R. 40.

expressed in the application of the exception in other cases: "the law tampers with the but-for test of causation at its peril."[118]

A plea of novus actus interveniens is competent.[119]

Notices, assumption of risk and consent

It is possible to exclude the duty by agreement but not by a simple notice or **18-14** warning. However, such notice or warning will be a circumstance to be accorded whatever weight is appropriate.[120] Further, there is statutory control of agreements where premises are used as business premises. Section 16 of the Unfair Contract Terms Act 1977 provides:

> "Where a term of a contract purports to exclude or restrict liability for breach of duty arising in the course of any business or from the occupation of any premises used for business purposes of the occupier, that term—(a) shall be void in any case where such exclusion or restriction is in respect of death or personal injury; (b) shall in any other case, have no effect if it was not fair and reasonable to incorporate the term in the contract."

There is no obligation to a person entering on the premises in respect of a risk which that person has willingly accepted as his.[121] There was an extensive evaluation of the law in *Hughes' Tutrix v Glasgow DC*,[122] a landlord's case in which a child injured her hand on a broken toilet bowl:

> "Since the 1960 Act, the old law no longer exists, and this case is not raised in contract. The defence of *volenti* is specifically retained in the 1960 Act, by virtue of s. 2(3) ... The landlord's obligation under s. 3 is the same as is required of an occupier in terms of s. 2, and so s. 2(3) would apply in this case. Professor Walker says of that section: 'The application of the maxim [*volenti non fit injuria*] to landlord and tenant cases is probably further limited by the effect of the Occupiers' Liability (Scotland) Act, 1960, s. 3, which imposes on a landlord towards his tenants and sub-tenants the duties of care owed by an occupier towards his visitors, so that only clear evidence of voluntary acceptance of specific known risks (s. 2 (3)) could be sufficient to make the maxim applicable' (Delict, p.352). I accept that in this case there was a specific known risk, but I think that it is open to me to hold that the defenders have not shown that, in all the circumstances, the pursuer 'willingly' accepted the danger, far less that it can be inferred that she agreed to what would be tantamount to a variation of her contract (*c.f.* Rankine on Personal Bar, pp.76–87) to the effect of relieving the defenders of their obligation to repair the bowl."[123]

---

[118] *Sienkiewicz v Greif (UK) Ltd* [2011] 2 A.C. 229 at 294 per Lord Brown J.S.C.

[119] Although it was ultimately dismissed in *Murdoch v Moray Council*, 2005 Rep. L.R. 83.

[120] *McGlone v British Railways Board*, 1966 S.C. (HL) 1.

[121] Occupiers' Liability (Scotland) Act 1960 s.2(3).

[122] *Hughes' Tutrix v Glasgow DC*, 1982 S.L.T. (Sh. Ct) 70. See also *Dawson v Scottish Power*, 1999 S.L.T. 672 in which the boy had been warned of the danger by his father and understood the risk. However, Lord MacLean commented s.2(3) was not pled. There was a finding of contributory negligence.

[123] *Hughes' Tutrix v Glasgow DC*, 1982 S.L.T. (Sh. Ct) 70 at 73 per Sheriff Gordon.

In *Titchener*, it was reiterated that the part of the Act which deals with acceptance of risk merely put into words the principle expressed by the maxim volenti non fit injuria. In *Titchener*, it was stated that if there had been a duty of care this "volenti" subsection would have applied to exclude liability. In evidence, the pursuer had said that she had known she was "taking a chance". In the case of the male strippers discussed above, had the occupiers been liable for allowing body oil on to the floor upon which the pursuer slipped, the pursuer would not have been held to have assumed that risk.[124]

Consistently with cases pursued under the common law, contributory negligence may be pled to reduce the award of damages.[125] There have been several cases where damages awards in favour of injured children have been reduced due to a finding of contributory negligence. For example, in *Wardle v Scottish Borders Council*,[126] a nine-year-old was injured when falling from exposed rafters (described as an allurement to children) while playing in a shelter in her school playground. The occupier was liable subject to a 50 per cent reduction of damages for contributory negligence. In *Morton v Glasgow City Council*,[127] a 14-year-old was injured in a 15-foot fall from scaffolding easily accessible to children. The occupier was liable for failing to install a suitable fence but subject to a 25 per cent reduction for contributory negligence.

Landlord and tenant

18–15   The Act makes special provision for cases involving landlord and tenant. This is important, for the tenant is the person in actual occupation and would normally seem to be the occupier for the purposes of the Act. The landlord under a lease may, however, be the one who has the responsibility for certain aspects of the state of the premises. While the tenant is entitled to pursue a claim against the landlord for a breach of an obligation under the lease, this is a contractual right[128] which would not be available to his guests or members of his family. Accordingly, the Act makes the landlord liable instead of the tenant, if under the lease the landlord is responsible for the maintenance or repair of the premises.[129] The most important question is, of course, whether the landlord is responsible in the first place: this will be determined by the contract of lease. Apart from any special terms in the lease there are two major implied conditions.

1. There is an implied warrandice that the subjects let are fit for the purpose for which they are let. In an urban lease the landlord is impliedly obliged to maintain the subjects in a tenantable and habitable condition, having put them in such a state at entry.
2. There is a statutorily implied condition that subjects are and will be maintained reasonably fit for human habitation.[130]

---

[124] *Falconer v Edinburgh City Transport Longstone Social Club*, 2003 Rep. L.R. 39.
[125] See, e.g. *Cowan v Hopetoun House Preservation Trust*, 2013 Rep. L.R. 62; *Heary v Phinn*, 2013 S.L.T. (Sh. Ct) 145; *Sayers v Harlow UDC* [1958] 1 W.L.R. 623.
[126] *Wardle v Scottish Borders Council*, 2011 S.L.T. (Sh. Ct) 199.
[127] *Morton v Glasgow City Council*, 2007 S.L.T. (Sh. Ct) 81.
[128] Subject to contract law precedents unhelpful to the tenant: in particular *Webster v Brown* (1892) 19 R. 765. Cf. in delict: *Hughes' Tutrix v Glasgow DC*, 1982 S.L.T. (Sh. Ct) 70.
[129] Occupiers' Liability (Scotland) Act 1960 s.3(1).
[130] Housing (Scotland) Act 2001 (social landlords) and Housing (Scotland) Act 2006 (private landlords). See also *Haggarty v Glasgow Corp*, 1963 S.L.T. (Notes) 73; 1964 S.L.T. (Notes) 95.

Accordingly, in most cases where someone is injured in a council house they will have a possible delictual remedy against the landlord even if they do not have a contractual right under the lease. Lord Johnston decided in the Outer House that s.3 of the 1960 Act effectively overruled the effect of the existing common-law rule which relied upon privity to deny the tenant's claim.[131]

However, claims brought under s.3 of the Occupiers' Liability (Scotland) Act 1960 will only succeed if negligence can be proved against the landlord. Thus, where the lease makes the landlord responsible for repairs, if the landlord has not been made aware of the need for a repair the landlord cannot be held liable.[132] Awareness may be actual—where the tenant has communicated the repair requirement to the landlord, or constructive—where, e.g. the issue is related to general wear and tear which has been permitted to create a danger due to a failure on the part of the landlord to carry out routine maintenance.[133]

Landlords may also incur liability under s.3 where they are obliged to maintain common parts of premises which are divided into separate leases. However, if the offending part of the premises is used exclusively by one tenant it may not fall within the common parts, and so require intimation of the issue to the landlord to trigger a duty incumbent upon he landlord under s.3.[134]

ROADS AND FOOTPATHS

Historically, liability in respect of roads developed separately from occupiers' **18–16** liability,[135] while liability for premises was subject to the older "English" tripartite system. Accordingly it is still thought that a different regime applies to public roads and footpaths. This may be on the basis of history or because authorities do not have sufficient possession and control to fall within the plain words of the Act.

In practice, despite a brave attempt by the then Sheriff Principal at Glasgow to state the law in an open ended way in *King v Strathclyde Regional Council*,[136] the Inner House balkanised pavement cases in the daily cited case of *Gibson v Strathclyde Regional Council*. The following, sometimes obvious, practical propositions can be extracted from that case:

1. liability is for fault;
2. the general rule applies that a pursuer's personal injury case should not be dismissed on relevancy unless it is bound to fail if proved, the onus of establishing that being on the defender[137];
3. a daily inspection case cannot normally be supported merely by a bald averment that it would be reasonable and practicable to do that[138];

---

[131] *Guy v Strathkelvin DC*, 1997 S.C.L.R. 405: the common-law rule was in *Cameron v Young*, 1908 S.C. (HL) 7.

[132] See, e.g. *Bell v North Ayrshire Council*, 2007 Rep. L.R. 108.

[133] Or perhaps a combination: see, e.g. *Muir v North Ayrshire Council*, 2005 S.L.T. 963.

[134] See, e.g. *Kirkham v Link Housing Group Ltd*, 2012 Hous. L.R. 87.

[135] See *MacDonald v Aberdeenshire Council*, 2014 S.L.T. 2 at 11–15 per Lord Drummond Young for a brief history.

[136] *King v Strathclyde Regional Council* Unreported January 8, 1991 Glasgow sheriff court.

[137] *Gibson v Strathclyde Regional Council*, 1993 S.L.T. 1243 per Lord Justice-Clerk Ross at 1245H–K.

[138] *Gibson v Strathclyde Regional Council*, 1993 S.L.T. 1243 per Lord Justice-Clerk Ross at 1246A; Lord Weir at 1248B.

4. it is possible, without averments of proper practice, to establish a daily inspection case giving rise to an inference of negligence, although the circumstances should be, on one view, special, exceptional and obvious,[139] or perhaps better the subject of averment.[140]

The arguments often made by pursuers were made in this case and largely rejected, particularly the point that the pursuer seldom has the knowledge of what is reasonable or practicable, the daily burden of roads administration being beyond their knowledge and in the absence of private or public funding, that of their professional advisers. Older cases, quite naturally, suggesting that defects in roads infer fault were not adopted, although depending on the circumstances. That said, it is possible to establish a case based on prior reports of danger.[141] The Sheriff Principal at Glasgow has emphasised, it is submitted correctly, that an averment of *a dangerous state* does not require *Gibson* averments anent inspection (save in the alternative).[142] However, most cases have to rely on the arguing that the defenders have failed to meet the standard they themselves have currently agreed.[143] Proving the case requires information held by the defenders.[144]

18–17   As public authorities are involved in roads and pavement cases, it should not be forgotten that general principles of liability apply.[145] These general principles derive from a distinct tradition in Scots law, traceable to the *lex aquilia*, and so the position in Scotland is not the same as the position in England and Wales.[146] A roads authority will be liable in negligence for failure to take reasonable steps to deal with a "hazard" under its control. Hazards may include low bridges,[147] sink holes, collapsed bridges[148] and other dangers that would create a significant risk to the road user. The hazard must fall under the control of the roads authority. There will be no liability for obvious dangers, such as:

"bends, blind summits, visible road junctions, and the fact that the driver's view is restricted, whether by buildings, vegetation or features of the land and the configuration of the road. In all such cases, a careful driver should slow down and look carefully ahead. If he does not do so, the accident is his own fault."[149]

---

[139] *Gibson v Strathclyde Regional Council*, 1993 S.L.T. 1243 per Lord Weir at 1248A.
[140] *Gibson v Strathclyde Regional Council*, 1993 S.L.T. 1243 per Lord Justice-Clerk Ross at 1246H.
[141] *McGeouch v SRC*, 1985 S.L.T. 321; *Syme v Scottish Borders Council*, 2003 S.L.T. 601.
[142] *Letford v Glasgow City Council*, 2002 Rep. L.R. 107.
[143] "Delivering the Best Value in Highway Maintenance: Code of Practice for Maintenance Management" (July 2001) reported and discussed in R. Conway, *Personal Injury Practice in the Sheriff Court*, 2nd edn (Edinburgh: W. Green, 2003), Ch.18. See, e.g. *Campbell v Highland Council*, 2005 S.L.T. (Sh. Ct) 141; *Nugent v Glasgow City Council*, 2009 G.W.D. 24–392.
[144] The issues are discussed for England in D. Turner, "Pre-action protocol: tripping up over disclosure", 2003 P.I.L.J. 18 (Aug), 2–4 and there is a style specification in Conway, *Personal Injury Practice in the Sheriff Court* (2003), p.303.
[145] *MacDonald v Aberdeenshire Council*, 2014 S.L.T. 2.
[146] *MacDonald v Aberdeenshire Council*, 2014 S.L.T. 2 at 17 per Lord Drummond Young. For the position in England and Wales see *Stovin v Wise* [1996] A.C. 923; *Gorringe v Calderdale Metropolitan BC* [2004] 1 W.L.R. 1057.
[147] *McKnight v Clydeside Buses Ltd*, 1999 S.L.T. 1167.
[148] *Gibson v Orr*, 1999 S.C. 420.
[149] *MacDonald v Aberdeenshire Council*, 2014 S.L.T. 2 at 15 per Lord Drummond Young.

According to Lord Drummond Young,

> "(T)his state of the law strikes a fair and reasonable balance between the interests of drivers and their passengers on one hand and the interests of the roads authority on the other hand. Roads authorities are under a public law duty to maintain the roads under their care, and it seems fair that they should be held to minimum standards not just in public law but as a matter of delictual liability in civil law. Eliminating hazards, in the sense discussed above, is the minimum that can be expected of them. The fundamental fairness of such a duty is supported by consideration of the insurance implications of an accident. Third party motor insurance is of course compulsory, and if an accident is caused by a driver's fault those who are injured, including his passengers, may expect to obtain recovery from his insurer. If the driver is not at fault, however, there can be no recovery, from the insurer or the driver. If an accident occurs because of a hazard, in the sense discussed above, the critical point is that there is no fault on the part of the driver; it is the road that is dangerous rather than the driver. In such a case, therefore, passengers will only recover anything if the roads authority is liable. ... Furthermore, for a roads authority that deals conscientiously with its responsibilities, the cost of eliminating hazards will be part of its normal running expenses."[150]

Although the wording of the Roads (Scotland) Act 1984 s.34 (which provides that a roads authority must take such steps as they consider reasonable to prevent snow and ice endangering the safe passage of pedestrians and vehicles over public roads) seems to impose a specific positive obligation on an authority to take steps, it has been held to reflect the common law and there is no fault where a reasonable system is in place.[151] The power to mark roads and the like and the existence of foreseeability of injury is not itself sufficient to create a duty to mark roads,[152] although it might be possible to make a case if there is evidence of special risks known to the authority.[153] In *Kemp v Secretary of State for Scotland*,[154] it was held that the roads authority was liable for having a raised kerb at the edge of a footpath that caused the pursuer to fall into the path of traffic. There was evidence from a police office and a consulting engineer that the design was a hazard.[155] It was held in *McKnight v Clydeside Buses Ltd*[156] that the roads authority was under an obligation to mark low bridges where it knew or ought to have known it constituted a danger, such as in this case where there had been many accidents before. Roadworks need to be properly marked and regard may be had to the "traffic signs manual".[157]

---

[150] *MacDonald v Aberdeenshire Council*, 2014 S.L.T. 2 at 15.

[151] *Grant v Lothian Regional Council*, 1988 S.L.T. 533; *Syme v Scottish Borders Council*, 2003 S.L.T. 601; *MacDonald v Scottish Ministers*, 2004 Rep. L.R. 16; *Ryder v Highland Council*, 2013 S.L.T. 847. See for the English position at common law: *Sandhar v Dept of Transport* [2005] 1 W.L.R. 1632.

[152] *MacDonald v Aberdeenshire Council*, 2014 S.L.T. 2; *Gorringe v Calderdale Metropolitan BC* [2004] 1 W.L.R. 1057.

[153] *Murray v Nicholls*, 1983 S.L.T. 194.

[154] *Kemp v Secretary of State for Scotland*, 2000 S.L.T. 471.

[155] There was one-third contributory negligence as the pursuer was drunk.

[156] *McKnight v Clydeside Buses Ltd*, 1999 S.L.T. 1167.

[157] *MacKenzie v Perth and Kinross Council*, 2003 G.W.D. 4–101.

THE ROMAN QUASI-DELICTS

18-18 The Roman quasi-delicts is a special category of obligations involving strict liability including for the wrongs of third parties. The extent to which the Roman quasi-delicts are part of Scots law is uncertain. However, that they arise *ex lege* is certain and they are, therefore, appropriately considered in the law of delict. Unfortunately they have little in common in either Roman or Scots law. However, when it is remembered that the term "delict" originally had a morally blameworthy connotation, this may help explain why they were put together, in that in these cases the defender has not been especially bad (as opposed to the actual person who poured, threw, placed or suspended the offending item). With perhaps the difficult exception of the *judex qui litem suam fecerit* (the judge who makes a cause his own), they involve liability being established without proof of fault on the part of the defender and have suggestions of vicarious liability. Their reception into Scots law is not, as shall be seen, without difficulty. The interests protected are sometimes the integrity of the person, but extend also to property. As there are no Scots cases directly in point on the strict liability of the *judex,* that head of liability is not dealt with in this book.[158]

The *actio de effusis vel dejectis* and the *actio de positis vel suspensis*

18-19   Roman law imposed a penalty on the occupier of premises:

>   i. from which something was poured or thrown out, striking the victim (the *actio de effusis vel dejectis*), and
>   ii. where something was placed on or suspended from a building which fell causing loss, injury or damage (the *actio de positis vel suspensis*).

Poured and thrown

18-20   The remedy has been recognised as part of Scots law, but not clearly so.[159] In *Gray v Dunlop*,[160] the pursuer's pupil son was walking along a street about 5pm when some, understandably unidentified, person emptied a pot of urine upon him. An action was raised against the occupier of the premises, which were a model lodging house (a sort of hostel for down-and-outs). No fault could be proved against the occupier and so it was important for the pursuer that strict liability should be established. The sheriff refused to accept that there could be liability without fault and refused the claim. Notwithstanding that decision, Professor Walker and Professor Stein incline to the view that the *actio de effusis vel dejectis* is part of the law of Scotland.[161] This case must now be read subject to the dicta in the opinion of the court in *McDyer v Celtic Football and Athletic*

---

[158] See D.M. Walker, *The Law of Delict in Scotland*, 2nd edn (Edinburgh: W. Green/SULI, 1981), pp.285–286.
[159] Bankton, I, iv, 32; Kames, I, i, 1; Hume, iii, 186; and see P. Stein, "*The actio de effusis vel dejectis* and the Concept of Quasi-Delict in Scots Law" (1955) 4 I.C.L.Q. 356. W.M. Gordon, "Householders' Liabilities" (1982) 27 J.L.S.S. 253.
[160] *Gray v Dunlop*, 1954 S.L.T. (Sh. Ct) 75.
[161] See Walker, *The Law of Delict in Scotland* (1981), pp.285–286 and Stein, "*The actio de effusis vel dejectis* and the Concept of Quasi-Delict in Scots Law" (1955) 4 I.C.L.Q. 356.

Company Ltd,[162] discussed below. While that case dealt with the *actio de posito et suspenso*, it is clear that the preferred view was that these two quite different heads of liability have come into Scots law in some kind of related way.

Placed and suspended

The *actio de positis vel suspensis* was considered in *MacColl v Hoo*.[163] Miss **18–21** MacColl discovered that her motor car had been dented by a slate that had fallen from premises occupied by Mr Hoo. She sued relying on the *actio*. The sheriff at first instance allowed the claim, accepting that it was part of the law of Scotland, and did not require proof of fault. On appeal, the sheriff principal rejected the claim, taking the view that there can be no liability without fault. In *McArthur v Matthew Cleland Public House Proprietors*, another lady was unsuccessful in claiming for damages for injury caused by a slate falling from the roof of the defenders' public house. The sheriff had allowed the case to proceed on the basis of the possibility of res ipsa loquitur being established. The sheriff correctly rejected res ipsa loquitur because the fall of a slate could be explained other than by the defenders' negligence. However, it may well be that if there had been more facts alleged in the pleadings sufficient to infer fault, the case would have proceeded—averments that the roof was generally in a poor state of repair prior to the accident, or (in the sheriff principal's view) that the building was newly built.[164]

The *actio de posito* came up for consideration before the Inner House in *McDyer v Celtic Football and Athletic Company Ltd*.[165] The pursuer was injured in the defenders stadium when attending the European Summer Special Olympic Games. A piece of wood fell on him from a temporary construction attached to the roof. One of the grounds pled by the pursuer was that there was strict liability to the pursuer in terms of the *actio de positis vel suspensis* for causing or allowing a piece of timber to be placed or suspended from the said stadium canopy where it could fall upon the pursuer who was in a part of the stadium where the public were likely to pass or congregate. The *actio* was the subject of learned debate and consideration. It seems the Inner House was convinced that the *actio* had been received. In this case, however, it would not be applicable because the incident took place *inside* the stadium.[166] The Occupiers' Liability Act would apply and thus averments of strict liability were irrelevant.

These special factual situations have come into Scots law as instances of liability providing there is *culpa*. We then reach the difficult question since *R.H.M. Bakeries v Strathclyde Regional Council*,[167] albeit with the assistance of

---

[162] *McDyer v Celtic Football and Athletic Company Ltd*, 2000 S.L.T. 736. The subsequent proof is noted at 2001 S.L.T. 1387.

[163] *MacColl v Hoo*, 1983 S.L.T. (Sh. Ct) 23.

[164] *McArthur v Matthew Cleland Public House Proprietors*, 1981 S.L.T. (Sh. Ct) 76 at 77. In *MacColl* the home was completed in July 1979 and the slate fell in December of that year.

[165] *McDyer v Celtic Football and Athletic Company Ltd*, 2000 S.L.T. 736. The subsequent proof is noted at 2001 S.L.T. 1387.

[166] This conclusion is disputed on analysis of the Roman law: Tammo Wallinga, *"Effusa vel deiecta* in Rome and Glasgow"* (2002) 6 Edin. L.R. 123. He goes so far as to say the Praetor would have found strict liability. In *Burns v Boots UK Ltd*, 2011 Rep. L.R. 124, the matter was not raised, but it is suggested that the facts may provide an example of an opportunity to test whether the *actio de positis vel suspensis* has been received into Scots law so as to create strict liability.

[167] *R.H.M. Bakeries v Strathclyde Regional Council*, 1985 S.C. (HL) 17. See paras 8–16 to 8–17 above.

Kennedy v Glenbelle,[168] namely to determine "what is *culpa*?" If there is distinct "nuisance *culpa*", is there a distinct "roman quasi-delict *culpa*"? There seems little point in admitting that the law has infused special cases but in no way treats them specially. It is thus possible that the practical result is that the defender in such cases has more explaining to do and that the burden of averment on the pursuer is lifted at least to some extent.[169] It may be that they are treated as simple cases of "negligence or inadvertency" and only of merit in identifying some situations where it might be easier to establish liability, at least to the extent of establishing prima facie liability against which the defender must offer averment and, if after the pursuer's proof there is a case to answer, proof. As a matter of convenience, on that analysis, a court could ordain a defender to learn at proof.

The praetorian edict *nautae caupones stabularii*

18-22   The praetor was a Roman magistrate elected annually. When he demitted office, his edicts were handed down to the next praetor and eventually this grew into a body of law equivalent to legislation—most praetors being content to leave the previous edicts alone. This particular edict related to the liability of sailors (*nautae*), innkeepers (*caupones*) and stable keepers (*stabularii*).[170] These particular trades are said to have been singled out because of the propensity of people involved in them to be in league with pirates or highwaymen. The hotel-keeper or carrier could arrange to have the guest's baggage or the consigned goods stolen for a share in the booty. The carrier or innkeeper would then be able to plead that it was not his fault. To remedy this, the edict imposed strict liability for the simple happening unless there had been a *damnum fatale*.[171] In its modern form in Scots law, it applies to carriers of goods (not carriers of passengers), hotel-keepers and stable-keepers.

While the law of contract will often be applicable in many such cases, since we are concerned with liability in delict it is not essential that a contract exists: for example, in a case where a purported contract for accommodation is void, if goods are stolen from the hotel there is still liability under the edict. The liability of both the carrier and hotel proprietor has been adjusted by statute.

Carriers

18-23   *Nautae,* or carriers by sea, are strictly liable unless they can show the damage to goods was caused by *damnum fatale* or act of the Queen's enemies.[172] It is, therefore, to no avail to show that all reasonable precautions were taken.[173] The particular law is, however, substantially modified and stated in international conventions and legislation and is not dealt with in this book.[174] The common carrier of goods (but not of people) by land is, by analogy, held strictly liable for

---

[168] *Kennedy v Glenbelle*, 1996 S.C. 95.

[169] This is largely the same problem encountered not only with nuisance but with the discussion of the diversion of the natural course of a stream discussed above.

[170] J. MacKintosh, "The Edict *nautae caupones stabularii*" (1891) 3 J.R. 306.

[171] See para.14–12 above.

[172] Mackenzie Stuart, "Liability of Common Carriers" (1926) 3 8 J.R. 205.

[173] *Rae v Hay* (1832) 10 S. 303.

[174] See *Gloag and Henderson: The Law of Scotland*, edited by Lord Eassie and H.L. MacQueen, 13th edn (Edinburgh: W. Green, 2012), Chs 21, 22 and 23.

the goods carried. It is no defence to show that the goods were stolen.[175] Only the defences of *damnum fatale* and act of the Queen's enemies are available. The Carriers Act 1830 affects the edictal liability. It prevents the carrier excluding liability by advertisement or notice. It does allow special contracts to be made so long as reasonable care is taken to bring the terms to the attention of the consignor. It also excludes the carrier's liability for certain specified goods,[176] unless their nature and value, if over £10, was declared when deposited.

Hotel proprietors

The Hotel Proprietors Act 1956 now regulates the inn-keeper's liability: "[a]n **18–24** hotel within the meaning of this Act shall, and any other establishment shall not, be deemed to be an inn." Hotel

> "means an establishment held out by the proprietor as offering food, drink and, if so required, sleeping accommodation, without special contract, to any traveller presenting himself who appears able and willing to pay a reasonable sum for the services and facilities provided and who is in a fit state to be received."[177]

On such a proprietor there falls strict liability subject to the defences of *damnum fatale* and act of the Queen's enemies. But the Act offers additional protections to the hotel proprietor: sleeping accommodation has to have been booked at the time of the loss and the loss must have occurred between the midnight before arrival and the midnight after departure. There is no special strict liability in respect of motor vehicles in hotel car parks. The proprietor can limit his liability to £50 for any one article and £100 in aggregate if he has conspicuously displayed a notice in terms of the Schedule to the Act.[178] But the restriction does not apply where fault or vicarious liability is actually established, where the property was deposited for safe custody or if the goods were offered for deposit and not accepted.

Stable-keepers

Stable keepers have not received the benefit of any special legislation and are **18–25** strictly liable for any damage to the beast subject to the defences of *damnum fatale* and act of the Queen's enemies.[179]

---

[175] *MacAusland v Dick* (1787) Mor. 9246.
[176] For example, jewellery, watches and lace.
[177] Hotel Proprietors Act 1956 s.1.
[178] Hotel Proprietors Act 1956 s.2.
[179] See *Mustard v Paterson*, 1923 S.C. 142.

CHAPTER 19

PRODUCT LIABILITY

INTRODUCTION

19–01 Product liability like many other areas now involves the application of both the common law and statute. It is another area which usually involves unintentional harm. The general common law duty to take reasonable care has been supplemented by a special statutory form of strict liability by the Consumer Protection Act 1987.[1] Not all cases are covered by the Act, so the common law is still relevant.

THE COMMON LAW

19–02 Scots law did recognise delictual liability outwith contract in respect of injuries caused by products in some circumstances. In one case, the liability was upon the person who left a dangerous machine in a public place.[2] In another case, the owner was liable even although the pursuer's injuries were the result of the acts of another: two children played with the door of a shed on waste ground and it fell on another as a result of its insufficiency.[3] It would not have fallen if the boys had not climbed up the door and lifted a drop bar. On the other hand, where the goods were intrinsically safe, there was no liability.[4] Mention has already been made of the case of *Donoghue v Stevenson* in the context of liability for unintentional harm generally.[5] However, while that case has a wide *ratio* establishing proximity as a basis of liability, it also has a narrow *ratio* which is a suitable beginning from which to look at product liability. That narrow *ratio* is apparent from a dictum of Lord Atkin:

> "A manufacturer of products, which he sells in such a form as to show that he intends them to reach the ultimate consumer in the form in which they left him, with no reasonable possibility of intermediate examination, and with the knowledge that the absence of reasonable care in the preparation or

---

[1] This only applies to damage attributable to defective products arising after March 1, 1988, where the product has been supplied after that date.
[2] *Campbell v Ord* (1873) 1 R. 149.
[3] *Findlay v Angus* (1887) 14 R. 312.
[4] *Duff v National Telephone Co* (1889) 16 R. 675.
[5] See paras 11–02 to 11–03 above.

putting up of the products will result in an injury to the consumer's life or property, owon a duty to the consumer to take that reasonable care."[6]

It has been accepted that the principle could apply to services as much as goods.[7] However, where there is a general public awareness that particular products are dangerous, such as alcohol or tobacco, if a person then chooses to consume such products there will be no breach of the duty of care owed by the manufacturer to the consumer.[8]

The intermediate examination point requires some clarification. In *Donoghue*, the seller of the ginger beer could not be expected to open the bottles to check for decomposed snails. However, if the bottle had been translucent, the retailer might have been expected to check for obvious impurities. In the case of *Grant v Australian Knitting Mills Ltd*,[9] the issue was whether it was possible to recover in respect of dermatitis contracted as a result of injurious chemicals being present in the plaintiff's underwear. The difference between this case and *Donoghue* was that the retailer took the underpants from their pack and placed them on his shelves, whereas the alleged snail in *Donoghue* remained in its bottle until the contents were consumed by Mrs Donoghue. The Privy Council refused to accept the significance of that distinction. There was no need for the product to remain exactly as it had been put out by the manufacturer. On the other hand, it was stated that the defect in the product has to remain "hidden and unknown to the consumer". The *Grant* case is also of interest because it was held that the plaintiff did not have to prove the mechanism of the harm—it was possible to establish the cause by an inference from the proven facts.

The issue of intermediate examination and the general question of causation are interrelated. The issue of intermediate examination can be analysed as whether the cause of the accident was the fault of the manufacturer or due to another cause.[10] The case of *Evans v Triplex Safety Glass Co Ltd*[11] illustrates this. It is also a convenient example of how the common law fails to offer what many consider to be adequate protection for the consumer. Mr Evans bought a car. The manufacturers of the car had fitted a windscreen manufactured by the defenders. When Mr Evans was driving his car the windscreen disintegrated and injured people in the car. The accident could have been due to faulty fitting of the windscreen or could have been due to other causes such as faulty manufacture of the windscreen. Because *Evans* failed to prove fault on the part of the

---

[6] *Donoghue v Stevenson*,1932 S.C. (HL) 31 at 57. Lord Rodger has traced the legal ancestry of the *Donoghue* snail back to a cigar stub in a Coca-Cola bottle in Tennessee: "Lord Macmillan's Speech" (1992) 108 L.Q.R. 236 at 244. In a vehement dissent, Lord Buckmaster quoted from Lord Anderson's judgment in *Mullen v Barr & Co*, 1929 S.C. 461: "In a case like the present, where the goods of the defenders are widely distributed throughout Scotland, it would seem little short of outrageous to make them responsible to members of the public for the condition of the contents of every bottle which issues from their works": *Donoghue v Stevenson*, 1932 S.C. (HL) 31 at 43. Lords Anderson and Buckmaster were respectively clearly criticising the potential for liability of the manufacturer to an indeterminate class (of consumers). Do the facts of *Sutradhar v Natural Environment Research Council* [2007] Env. L.R. 10 prove them right? What if, rather than a decomposed snail, or mouse, in a bottle of juice, the defective product was a spice which was then used by a wide range of manufacturers of ready meals?

[7] *Haseldine v C.A. Daw & Son Ltd* [1941] 3 All E.R. 156.

[8] *McTear v Imperial Tobacco*, 2005 2 S.C. 1.

[9] *Grant v Australian Knitting Mills Ltd* [1935] All E.R. 209.

[10] For a discussion of the modern relevance of intermediate examination, see *Murphy v Brentwood DC* [1990] 3 W.L.R. 414.

[11] *Evans v Triplex Safety Glass Co Ltd* [1936] 1 All E.R. 283.

manufacturer either of the car or of the windscreen, he lost his case. It was such difficulties that led to calls for liability independent of fault, to which we now turn.

THE CONSUMER PROTECTION ACT 1987 PT I

19–03 This statute implements an EEC Directive[12] and it is expressly stated in the Act that it has to be construed to comply with the Directive.[13] For some time there had been moves to introduce some form of strict liability, but no domestic solution had come to fruition.[14] There are many matters of policy reflected in such a system. In the main, liability is placed on the person most able to prevent an accident in the first place—the producer. Secondly, the cost of an accident is removed from the consumer, who generally would find it expensive to insure, and passed to someone else more likely to be able to obtain insurance cover on reasonable terms. The Act provides a limited form of strict liability for defective products, which does not, however, replace any existing liability in delict.[15] Broadly speaking, there is strict liability on a producer for damages caused by a defective product. Each of the key elements in this liability is defined by the statute. The following treatment is intended to give a broad view of the Act, but does not deal with every aspect of it.

Product

19–04 "Product" means any goods or electricity and includes any goods comprised in another product whether by virtue of being a component part or raw material

---

[12] Council Directive 85/374/EEC of 25 July 1985 on the approximation of the laws, regulations and administrative provisions of the Member States concerning liability for defective products.

[13] Consumer Protection Act 1987 s.1(1). This is no platitude. It had been anticipated that the Commission might challenge the UK's implementation of the directive as being too restrictive to liability in places. Such a case did emerge: *Commission v UK* [1997] All E.R. (E.C.) 481, and this very provision convinced the court that the United Kingdom had complied, for if this provision were given effect to, the UK law would comply with EC law. That is an optimistic view of the approach of UK courts to legislation! See generally A.M. Clark, *Product Liability* (London: Sweet & Maxwell, 1989); J. Blaikie, "Product Liability" (1987) 32 J.L.S. 325; A. Clark, "Liability for Defective Products" (1981) 26 J.L.S. 398; A. Clark, "Product Liability: The New Rules", 1987 S.L.T. (News) 257; A. Clark, "Conceptual Basis of the Product Liability" (1985) 48 M.L.R. 325; A. Clark, "US Product Liability" (1982) 27 J.L.S. 514; W.C.H. Ervine, "Product Liability and Part 1 of the Consumer Protection Act 1987" (1988) SCOLAG 21; P.R. Ferguson, "Pharmaceutical Products Liability", 1992 J.R. 226; P.R. Ferguson, "Compensation for Alleged Vaccine Injury" (1994) 39 J.L.S. 80; C. Newdick, "The Future of Negligence in Product Liability" (1987) 103 L.Q.R. 288; C. Newdick, "The Development Risk Defence", 1988 C.L.J. 455; J. Stapleton, "Products Liability Reform—Real or Illusory", 1986 6 O.J.L.S. 392; D. Powles, "Product Liability—A Novel Dimension in Scots Law", in A.J. Gamble (ed.), *Obligations in Context* (Edinburgh: W. Green, 1990), p.33; R. Freeman, "Product Liability, defective goods" [2001] J.P.I.L. 26; G. Junor, "Beyond the Common Law—The (potential) reach of product liability", 2001 Rep. B. 41–5; P. Balen, "An introduction to product liability claims" [2002] J.P.I.L. 3.

[14] European Convention on Products Liability in regard to Personal Injury and Death (Strasbourg: January 27, 1977) ("the Strasbourg Convention"); the Law Commission and the Scottish Law Commission, *Liability for defective products* (HMSO, 1977), Law Com. No.82 and Scot. Law Com. No.45, Cmnd.6831; *The Pearson Report on Civil Liability* (1978), Cmnd.7054.

[15] Consumer Protection Act 1987 s.2(6). Cf. *Tesco Stores Ltd v Pollard* (2006) 103(17) L.S.G. 23.

or otherwise.[16] Thus both the car and the windscreen in a case like *Evans* would be products. "Goods" is further defined as including "substances, growing crops and things comprised in land by virtue of being attached to it and any ship, aircraft or vehicle."[17] For Scotland the reference to "attached" means becoming heritable by accession to heritable property.[18] There is no liability in respect of any defect in any game or agricultural produce, which is defined as being any produce of the soil or stock farming or fisheries so long as the supply was at a time when it had not undergone an industrial process.[19] A new European Union directive included agricultural produce too.[20]

It has been held to apply to vaccine,[21] to an elasticated strap,[22] and, in principle, to a condom.[23]

Defect

The Act provides a definition of "defect", which exists "if the safety of the **19–05** product is not such as persons generally are entitled to expect."[24] Realising that this would not answer every problem or might lead to diverging judicial opinions, the Act provides that while all the circumstances of the case should be taken into account, the following must be considered:

1. "the manner in which and purposes for which, the product has been marketed, its get-up, the use of any mark in relation to the product and any instructions for, or warnings with respect to, doing or refraining from doing anything with or in relation to the product;
2. what might reasonably be expected to be done with or in relation to the product; and
3. the time when the product was supplied by its producer to another."[25]

This is sometimes referred to for convenience as a consumer expectation test. In *A v National Blood Authority*,[26] the plaintiffs had been infected with Hepititis C as a result of transfusions. The defendants' argument was based simply on the

---

[16] Consumer Protection Act 1987 s.1(2). See also J. Stapleton, "Software, Information and the Concept of Product" (1989) 9 Tel Aviv Stud. in Law 47; R. Colbey, "Personal Injury Claims Arising out of Food Poisoning" [1994] J.P.I.L. 294.

[17] Consumer Protection Act 1987 s.45 (1).

[18] Consumer Protection Act 1987 s.45(5).

[19] Consumer Protection Act 1987 ss.2(4) and 1(2).

[20] "Extension of Product Liability Directive" (1998) 43 J.L.S. 45; Directive 1999/34/EC: "Article 1 Directive 85/374/EEC is hereby amended as follows: 1. Article 2 shall be replaced by the following: 'Article 2 For the purpose of this Directive, "product" means all movables even if incorporated into another movable or into an immovable. "Product" includes electricity.' 2. In Article 15, paragraph 1(a) shall be deleted." Given effect in England and Wales by the Consumer Protection Act 1987 (Product Liability) (Modification) Order 2000 and in Scotland (late) by the Consumer Protection Act 1987 (Product Liability) (Modification) (Scotland) Order 2001.

[21] *A v National Blood Authority* [2001] 3 All E.R. 289.

[22] *Abouzaid v Mothercare (UK) Ltd* [2001] T.L.R. 136.

[23] *Richardson v LRC Products Ltd* [2000] P.I.Q.R. P164.

[24] Consumer Protection Act 1987 s.3(1).

[25] Consumer Protection Act 1987 s.3(2). See A. Stoppa, "The Concept of Defectiveness in the Consumer Protection Act 1987: a critical analysis", 1992 L.S. 210.

[26] *A v National Blood Authority* [2001] 3 All E.R. 289. See generally, J.M. Williams, "Product Liability—Hepatitis C litigation" [2001] J.P.I.L. 238.

focus of the legislation—the consumer expectation test. They said that consumers would not expect anything other than reasonably available precautions. Burton J. made his decision based on the distinction between standard and non-standard products and then asked whether the non-standard risk was accepted. He held it was not. In *Abouzaid v Mothercare (UK) Ltd*,[27] the plaintiff injured his eye as the result of the recoil of an elasticated strap on the defenders product. In the Court of Appeal, the judge's decision that this was a breach of the consumer expectation test was upheld and it was emphatically pointed out that this was so even though there was no negligence. In *Richardson v LRC Products Ltd*,[28] it was held that a consumer would not expect a condom to be 100 per cent safe from bursting. In *Tesco Stores Ltd v Pollard*,[29] the Court of Appeal held that a product satisfied the consumer expectation test if it performed as persons generally were entitled to expect, even where the product did not perform to a British Standard certificate.

The pursuer must lead evidence to prove that the product was defective and that the defect caused the harm.[30] In *McGlinchey v General Motors (UK) Ltd*,[31] the pursuer parked a car on a gradient and claimed to have applied the handbrake, leaving the car out of gear. She said that as she stood at the rear of the car, it rolled back and trapped her leg against a metal bollard. Testing the handbrake on the car revealed no defect, although the handbrake did fail to engage on two or three occasions upon more rigorous testing following its removal from the car. The Lord Ordinary's conclusion that the pursuer had failed to prove on the balance of probabilities that a defect caused her injuries was upheld by the Inner House.

Producers and suppliers

19–06   In the first place, liability is on the producer. This includes the manufacturer, but may also include the person who wins or abstracts raw materials. Someone who processes agricultural products is a producer. Someone who simply packages goods is not a producer.[32] As well as the producer, other persons may be liable in respect of the same product,[33] namely any person who holds himself out as the producer by putting his brand on the goods (sometimes known as an "own brander") and a person who imports goods from outside the European Community in the course of his business to supply them to another (an "importer").[34] Further, in addition to those liable above as producers, there is liability too on the supplier of goods, for example, a retailer, but only if:

1. the victim requests that the supplier reveal one or more of the producers;
2. that request is made within a reasonable time after damage occurs, and at a time when it is not reasonably practicable for the victim to identify all of the producers himself; and

---

[27] *Abouzaid v Mothercare (UK) Ltd* [2001] T.L.R. 136.
[28] *Richardson v LRC Products Ltd* [2000] P.I.Q.R. P164.
[29] *Tesco Stores Ltd v Pollard* (2006) 103 (17) L.S.G. 23.
[30] *B (A Child) v McDonald's Restaurants Ltd* [2002] EWHC 490 (QB).
[31] *McGlinchey v General Motors (UK) Ltd* [2012] CSIH 91; 2013 G.W.D. 1–47.
[32] Consumer Protection Act 1987 s.2(2)(a), although he may be liable under another head.
[33] Consumer Protection Act 1987 s.2(2)(b); s.2(2)(c).
[34] It goes without saying that students must be familiar with the ever increasing membership of the European Community.

3. the supplier fails to identify the producer or the person who supplied to him.[35]

The value of this provision is to encourage the supplier to reveal the person who produced the article. Once the provision is appreciated in the business community, it is likely that steps will be taken to record the source of products and components so that liability can be avoided by a supplier by complying with the request and naming the person who supplied to him. Any persons who are liable are liable jointly and severally.[36] These provisions make it likely that a person in the position of the plaintiff in *Evans*[37] would succeed. He could sue either the car manufacturer or the windscreen manufacturer, both of whom are prima facie liable.[38]

Damages

The damages recoverable are limited by the Act. Damages are recoverable for **19–07** personal injuries, death or damage to the pursuer's property. Damage to the product itself or damage to a product caused by one of its defective component parts, is not recoverable.[39] Damages can only be recovered in respect of property, which is

"of a description of property ordinarily intended for private use, occupation or consumption; and intended by the person suffering the loss or damage mainly for his own private use, occupation or consumption."

In any event, even if not a business asset, the value of the property damaged must exceed £275. However, it should be noted that this limit does not apply to personal injuries or death.

Defences

It is crucial to know the defences for they affect the scope of liability **19–08** significantly. They are:

Compliance with any requirement imposed by or under any enactment or with any Community obligation

This is self explanatory.

The defender did not supply

This covers a situation where someone takes the product away from the **19–09** defender, as by theft or mistake. The point was litigated in *Veedfeld v Arhus Amtskommune*,[40] an ECJ case on a preliminary ruling from Denmark. The product in question was kidney flushing fluid used in kidney transplants. It was

---

[35] Consumer Protection Act 1987 s.2(3).

[36] Consumer Protection Act 1987 s.2(5).

[37] *Evans v Triplex Safety Glass Co Ltd* [1936] 1 All E.R. 283.

[38] Although the windscreen manufacturer plausibly could rely upon the defence in s.4(1)(d) if he could lead evidence to confirm that the defect did not exist at the time of supply to the car manufacturer.

[39] Consumer Protection Act 1987 s.5(1) and (2).

[40] *Veedfeld v Arhus Amtskommune* [2001] T.L.R. 358.

argued, inter alia, by the defendants that they were not liable as the product had not been "put into circulation" in terms of the directive. That argument failed.

The supply is not in the course of a business by someone who is not one of the producer class or, if he is, he is so by virtue of things not done with a view to a profit

19–10 Blaikie has well explained this provision by saying,

> "the commercial producer who gives his product away for nothing ... cannot rely on this defence. However the lady who makes confectionery for the cake and candy stall at the church sale of work would not be liable."[41]

In the same way, it is perfectly permissible to make a present for a person's birthday, without attracting strict liability. In the case of *Veedfeld v Arhus Amtskommune*,[42] noted above, an ECJ case on a preliminary ruling from Denmark, the product in question was kidney flushing fluid used in kidney transplants, It was argued, inter alia, by the defendants that they were not liable as the product had not been manufactured for an "economic purpose" in terms of the directive. That argument failed. This was not a charitable supply as envisaged by art.7(c).

The defect did not exist at the relevant time

19–11 Generally, the relevant time is the time of supply. This will allow a defence where it can be shown that someone else has tampered with the product.

The state of scientific and technical knowledge at the relevant time was not such that a producer of products of the same description as the product in question might be expected to have discovered the defect if it had existed in his products while they were under his control

19–12 This is often known as the "development risks defence".[43] The directive provided that the Commission would review in 1995 whether Member States should be allowed to continue to permit this and other provisions. There are arguments for and against it. Not to have it inhibits entrepreneurs and inventors or at least puts their costs up.[44]

There was concern during the passage of the legislation that the United Kingdom's form of the defence narrated above did not properly implement the Directive.[45] Article 7(e) of the Directive provides a defence that

---

[41] Blaikie, "Product Liability" (1987) 32 J.L.S.S. 325 at 328.

[42] *Veedfeld v Arhus Amtskommune* [2001] T.L.R. 358.

[43] P. Spink, "The Consumer Protection Act the State of the Art Defence" (1997) 42 J.L.S.S. 416.

[44] See R. Goldberg, "The Development Risk Defence and Medicinal Products" (1991) 36 J.L.S.S. 376.

[45] See, e.g. Clark, *Product Liability* (1989), Ch.8; Blaikie, "Product Liability" (1987) 32 J.L.S. 325; Ervine, "Product Liability and Part 1 of the Consumer Protection Act 1987" (1988) SCOLAG 21; Newdick, "The Future of Negligence in Product Liability" (1987) 103 L.Q.R. 288; Stapleton, "Products Liability Reform—Real or Illusory" (1986) 6 O.J.L.S. 392.

"the state of scientific and technical knowledge at the time when he put the product into circulation was not such as to enable the existence of the defect to be discovered."[46]

Eventually this divergence led to a challenge by the Commission before the ECJ in *Commission v United Kingdom*.[47] The ECJ treated the Commission's argument as being that the United Kingdom had converted the intended strict liability regime into a negligence liability. The United Kingdom did not challenge the submission that the Directive set out an objective test but argued instead that read together the United Kingdom's version interpreted in the light of s.1(1) of the Act did not infringe the obligation to deliver the directive. The ECJ agreed. In so doing, the court accepted that the directive defence (and thus the UK's defence) required it to be shown that the producer had complied with the most advanced knowledge available on an objective analysis, but the producer would be able to argue that the knowledge was not accessible. This is nowhere near saying that the court agreed with a negligence standard. Most people familiar with the way in which UK's courts construe UK legislation will be surprised that the ECJ thought that the UK's courts would ignore the generous words of the UK's defence to impose a liability based on s.1(1). Semantically, the UK defence seems to allow more room for danger than the EC Directive even as more liberally explained by the court, especially in cases where information was reasonably accessible, but a reasonable producer did not find it. UK courts in all fairness ought, of course, now to interpret the UK statute, not according to the semantics of UK statutory interpretation, but by the hermeneutics of the United Kingdom in Europe. In *A v National Blood Authority*,[48] a defence was taken under direct reference to art.7(e). The pursuers had contracted hepititis C from the defender's vaccine. This was a case where the risk was known, but it was not possible to identify which particular item among many would be dangerous, in that the defenders knew that some blood would be dangerous but not that any particular blood was dangerous. The defence failed. In *Abouzaid v Mothercare (UK) Ltd*,[49] doubt was expressed as to whether a database showing an absence of previous incidents came within the category of scientific or technical knowledge.

It was said (obiter) in *Richardson v LRC Products Ltd* that this defence would not have availed condom manufacturers:

"unless the case had shown that there was a defect of which the leading evidence of available scientific knowledge was ignorant. The test provided by the statute is not what the defendants knew, but what they could have known if they had consulted those who might be expected to know the state of research and all available literature sources. This provisions is ... not apt to protect a defendant in the case of a defect of a known character,

---

[46] Note the comments in W.A. Wilson, "The Product Liability Directive", 1980 S.L.T. 1 which suggests that the final UK version was one which had been rejected even before the directive came into being.

[47] *Commission v United Kingdom* (C-300/95) [1997] All E.R. (E.C.) 481.

[48] *A v National Blood Authority* [2001] 3 All E.R. 289. See Williams, "Product Liability—Hepatitis C litigation" [2001] J.P.I.L. 238.

[49] *Abouzaid v Mothercare (UK) Ltd* [2001] T.L.R. 136.

merely because there is no test which is apt to reveal its existence in every case."[50]

Defect in a product in which the defender's product is comprised

19–13   This is a defence only if the defect is wholly attributable to the design of the subsequent product or to compliance by the defender with instructions given by the final producer. Again this would cover cases like *Evans*. It is a valuable protection for component makers who do not know what their product is to be used for, where bolts are subjected to inordinate stress and strains by the "assembling" manufacturer.

Contributory negligence is recognised[51]

19–14   It can be seen then that it is impossible to understand fully the scheme of strict liability without comprehending the defences, a position which obtains equally in the other statutory strict liability scheme under the Animals (Scotland) Act 1987.

Time bar

19–15   There are complicated time-bar provisions providing broadly that there shall be a limitation period of three years from the time the victim was aware, or it was reasonably practicable for him to be aware, of the essential facts to ground an action. There is a long-stop prescriptive period of 10 years.[52]

---

[50] *Richardson v LRC Products Ltd* [2000] P.I.Q.R. P164 at 172 per Ian Kennedy J. at 172.
[51] Consumer Protection Act 1987 s.6(4); and see *McGlinchey v General Motors (UK) Ltd* [2012] CSIH 91; 2013 G.W.D. 1–47.
[52] See Ch.15. For the effect of time-bar on the issue of substitution of one defender for another see *O'Byrne v Aventis Pasteur MSD Ltd* [2010] 1 W.L.R. 1412.

CHAPTER 20

LIABILITY FOR ANIMALS

INTRODUCTION

Historically, the law has treated animals specially.[1] This is unsurprising when **20–01** most legal systems have their historical roots in essentially agricultural communities: animals constitute stock, machinery and wealth in such communities. Some animals clearly and notoriously can be so harmful to person or property that taking reasonable care that they do not cause harm is not perceived as being sufficient for the welfare of the community. Thus there is a tradition of the imposition of stricter forms of liability—a tradition that continues to the present day. Animals in law are things, but things capable of considerable independent action.[2] Scots law was systematically and extensively reformed by the Animals (Scotland) Act 1987.

STRICT LIABILITY BEFORE THE 1987 ACT

Prior to the Animals (Scotland) Act 1987 coming into force, at common law a **20–02** person in charge of a wild animal or an animal that could be shown to have vicious propensities was strictly liable for the harm that it caused. The fact that reasonable care was taken was not a sufficient defence—effective precautions had to have been taken. So when a dog with vicious propensities managed to break its chain and then bit a passer-by, it was not sufficient to show that the chain looked strong and usually held the dog.[3] Certain animals were deemed to have the vicious propensities required to attract strict liability and were described as ferae naturae (i.e. feral by nature, such as lions, tigers, elephants,[4] bears and boars). This was in distinction to domesticated animals—*domitae naturae* (such as dogs, cats, and cattle, including bulls!),[5] whose damage did not attract strict liability unless they could be shown to have previously exhibited dangerous

---

[1] See, e.g. B.S. Jackson, "Liability for Animals in Scottish Legal Literature" (1977) J.R. 139; D.L. Carey Miller, "A Statutory Substitute for Scienter" (1973) J.R. 61; D.L. Carey Miller, "The Scottish Institutional Writers on Animal Liability" (1974) J.R. 1; J. Blackie, "The Provoking Dogs Problem 2", 1993 J.L.S. 148. See also Scottish Law Commission, *Report on Civil Liability in Relation to Animals* (HMSO, 1985) Scot. Law Com. No.97.

[2] The Germans have gone so far as to recast the BGB to provide a separate section for animals: See Blackie, "The Provoking Dogs Problem 2", 1993 J.L.S. 148; See also P. Handford, "The Dog Act in the New South Wales Court of Appeal", 1995 Tort Law Rev. (Note), p.5.

[3] *Burton v Moorhead* (1881) 8 R 892.

[4] Tame elephants were deemed naturally dangerous because of their size: *Behrens v Bertram Mills Circus Ltd* [1957] 1 All E.R. 583.

[5] *Clark v Armstrong* (1862) 24 D. 1315.

propensities.[6] These categories were categories of law and it was not competent to show that a particular animal ferae naturae was, as a matter of fact, domesticated.

Defences were available to a defender who could show:

1. that the beast was provoked by the complainer;
2. that the beast was actually still under control;
3. that the animal was improperly loosed by a third party, or
4. *damnum fatale.*

Strict liability was also imposed by two statutes. The Winter Herding Act 1686 extended strict liability for damage to crops caused by straying livestock beyond the growing season to include the winter period. The Dogs Act 1906 rendered the owner of a dog strictly liable in damages for injury done to cattle including horses, sheep, oats and swine without proof of negligence or vicious propensities.[7] Both were repealed by the Animals (Scotland) Act 1987. However, the Guard Dogs Act 1975 was expressly stated not to create any civil liability but is now to an extent incorporated in the 1987 Act.

The common law: negligence

20–03 Whether or not we are concerned with statutory liability under the Animals (Scotland) Act 1987, the general principles of negligence are still relevant. This was also the case historically where at common law liability based on *culpa* operated in parallel with strict liability.[8] Thus, in *Henderson v John Stuart (Farms) Ltd*[9] a farmworker, who was an experienced stockman, was attacked and fatally injured by a Friesian dairy bull. He had been cleaning out its box, which was not fitted with baffles or escape gaps. It was not averred that the bull (which is, of course, *domitae naturae*) had dangerous propensities. It was held that there was no need to aver dangerous propensities to state a relevant case in negligence. The action was founded on breach of the employer's duty to his employee to provide a safe system of work by failing to follow normal practice in relation to looking after bulls.

Where fault is required, the pursuer must lead evidence to prove fault, unless fault may be inferred by application of the doctrine of res ipsa loquitur.[10] However, the mere fact that an animal is in a different place than where its owner intended it to be is insufficient to create such an inference—the pursuer must aver and prove that the animal's escape is attributable to the defender's fault.[11]

The standard of care required at common law is that of reasonable care. Thus, where a playful black labrador dog had shown no tendency to behave aggressively or unpredictably, her owner was not at fault in allowing her to run off the

---

[6] Liability for *domitae naturae* that had not previously exhibited dangerous propensities was based on *culpa*: see below.

[7] Liability under the 1906 Act would be joint and several where two or more dogs acted together in worrying livestock: *Arneil v Paterson*, 1931 S.C. (HL) 117.

[8] There may be liability for intentional delictual wrongs where an animal effectively is used as a weapon: see, e.g. *Ewing v Earl of Mar* (1851) 14 D. 314.

[9] *Henderson v John Stuart (Farms) Ltd*, 1963 S.C. 245; and see also *Hill v Lovett*, 1992 S.L.T. 994.

[10] See paras 12–18 to 12–21 above.

[11] *Dobbie v Henderson*, 1970 S.L.T. (Sh. Ct) 27. Cf. *Daniel Logan & Son v Rodger*, 1952 S.L.T. (Sh. Ct) 99.

lead with other dogs in a field which was also occupied by several dog owners. When the dog collided with one of the other owners, causing a severe knee injury, it was thus held to be "an unfortunate and unforeseeable collision ... a pure accident."[12]

A court may hold that damage caused by an animal is too remote a consequence of the defender's negligence to attract liability. In *Cameron v Hamilton's Auction Marts Ltd* a cow, already in an excited state, escaped from an auction house through an unsecured gate. It got into a shop, climbed a staircase and then fell through the floor, turning on a tap in the process. The court held that the damage and flooding to the shop was too remote to attract liability, either from the auction house or from the farmer who owned the cow. Sheriff Hector McKechnie QC said:

> "One cannot help sympathising with the pursuer in her loss, but I feel forced to the conclusion that a gate-crashing, stair-climbing, floor-bursting, tap-turning cow is something *sui generis,* for whose depredations the law affords no remedy unless there was foreknowledge of some such propensities."[13]

Liability is not confined to property damage or physical injury to the person, and has been held to extend to psychiatric injury in the form of nervous shock.[14] In principle at least, there is no reason why liability may not extend to pure economic loss suffered by a primary victim.

There may also be liability connected to the keeping, or use, of animals, but on different grounds. Thus it was held in *Hill v Lovett*[15] that under the Occupiers' Liability (Scotland) Act 1960 (as well as at common law) there was liability for the lack of care in allowing a person to enter a garden in which there were two territorially defensive dogs. Liability may also arise under the law of nuisance.[16] A proof before answer was allowed in one case where it was alleged that requiring a police officer to walk a police dog on a slippery surface breached reg.12 of the Workplace (Health, Safety and Welfare) Regulations 1992.[17] It is not impossible that a worker who has to lift animals could raise a case based on the manual handling regulations, if not the common law.[18]

Common law: Animals on the roads

It has often been accepted that, as in the law of England, the mere presence of **20–04** an animal on the road does not infer liability.[19] But reasonable care must still be

---

[12] *Welsh v Brady*, 2008 S.L.T. 363 at 366 per Lord Malcolm.
[13] *Cameron v Hamilton's Auction Marts Ltd*, 1955 S.L.T. (Sh. Ct) 74 at 79. Contrary to popular myth cows can and do climb downstairs too, although the design of their knees and hips prevent them from descending such steep stairs as are likely to be found within a shop.
[14] See, e.g. *Gilligan v Robb*, 1910 S.C. 856.
[15] *Hill v Lovett*, 1992 S.L.T. 994.
[16] See, e.g. *Ireland v Smith* (1895) 3 S.L.T. 180; *Shanlin v Collins*, 1973 S.L.T. (Sh. Ct) 21; *Wheeler v J J Saunders Ltd* [1996] Ch. 19.
[17] *Flynn v Lothian and Borders Police*, 2010 G.W.D. 30–626.
[18] See the facts of the unsuccessful common law case of *McCormick v City of Aberdeen DC*, 1993 S.L.T. 1123. Success may now be more difficult on account of the reversal of the burden of proof by s.69 of the Enterprise and Regulatory Reform Act 2013.
[19] *Clark v Armstrong* (1862) 24 D. 1315; *Milligan v Henderson*, 1915 2 S.L.T. 156; *Fraser v Pate*, 1923 S.L.T. 457 and *Anderson v Wilson's Trs*, 1965 S.L.T. (Sh. Ct) 35 in which it was held that darkness did not constitute a special circumstance attracting liability.

taken by persons grazing livestock, albeit in the context of the existence of open countryside.[20] In *Fraser v Pate*,[21] a motorcyclist sued a farmer said to have allowed his sheep to stray on to the highway. Considerable reliance was placed on an English case, *Heath's Garage Ltd v Hodges*.[22] The court accepted the Lord Ordinary's analysis that there was no liability because there was no duty owed by the farmer to the road-user.[23] It may, however, be observed that there was a curious examination of the domestic/wild animal dichotomy, which in the circumstances is of doubtful relevance. While the distinction is a valid one so far as the conduct of animals according to their nature by way of biting, goring or otherwise injuring people is concerned it can hardly be said that a man-eating tiger equally infers liability to its keeper should it decide instead to throw itself upon someone's motor cycle. On the actual point, the case may well have been properly decided on the law of negligence on the facts of the use of roads at the time. It is an open question how far animals may be allowed to stray without inferring negligence in today's conditions where many people expect to be able to drive without even seeing a horse. Lord Anderson, it should be noted, concurred on the basis that

> "nothing we are deciding in this case is to be taken as encouraging carelessness on the part of farmers in the discharge of their duty of taking all proper precautions to ensure their gates and fences are sufficient to confine bestial to their grazings."[24]

The trend now is to permit proof before answer to evaluate factors such as the locality and the conditions. In *Sinclair v Muir*,[25] the Second Division allowed a proof before answer on appeal in the case of a motorcyclist knocked over by a charging bull on the road. In *Gardiner v Miller*,[26] the pursuer collided with a horse that had escaped, the basis of the case, however, being the failure to have a gate that could not easily be left open by strangers. A proof before answer was allowed. In *Wark v Steel*,[27] the pursuer was a pedal cyclist who collided with a horse, the sheriff substitute followed *Fraser* and dismissed the action. On appeal, the sheriff allowed a proof before answer and the pursuer succeeded at the proof. Note the distinction in that case between the "great unfenced areas in the highlands" and the "populous country" where there is regularly fencing to be found. The authorities were reviewed in *Swan v Andrew Minto & Sons*,[28] where the pursuer collided with one of two black cows belonging to the defenders, which had strayed on to an A-road from adjacent land. The cows were grazing on opposing grass verges and so blocked the whole road. It was alleged, inter alia, that the defenders ought to have erected a stockproof fence and inspected it

---

[20] *Sinclair v Muir*, 1933 S.N. 42, 62; *Colquhoun v Hannah* Unreported October 31, 1942 CSOH; *Glasgow Herald*, July 31, 1943; *Gardiner v Miller*, 1967 S.L.T. 29.

[21] *Fraser v Pate*, 1923 S.L.T. 457.

[22] *Heath's Garage Ltd v Hodges* [1916] 2 K.B. 370.

[23] It is submitted that a modern approach to this case would be that there was a duty, but that on the facts it was not breached.

[24] *Fraser v Pate*, 1923 S.L.T. 457 at 460.

[25] *Sinclair v Muir*, 1933 S.N. 42 at 62. See also *Davidson v McIrvine*, 2007 S.L.T. (Sh. Ct) 71 where it was held not to be reasonably foreseeable that a bull kept in a barn would escape through fields and cause damage on a road.

[26] *Gardiner v Miller*, 1967 S.L.T. 29.

[27] *Wark v Steel*, 1946 S.L.T. (Sh. Ct) 17.

[28] *Swan v Andrew Minto & Sons*, 1998 Rep. L.R. 42.

and to have taken care that it should have remained so. The defenders averred, inter alia, that the cows jumped over the fence and the pursuer while denying that, said that the fence should then have been higher.[29] The sheriff founding on the cases after *Fraser*, correctly it is submitted, allowed a proof before answer.[30]

It is also worth noting a different approach to liability argued in *Bennett v J Lamont & Sons*,[31] in which livestock got onto the road through a wall that had allegedly fallen into disrepair. The pursuer averred that under common law a roads authority had a duty to take reasonable care to keep the road safe for road users as a result of their statutory duty under s.1(1) of the Roads (Scotland) Act 1984. This included a duty to take reasonable care to avoid dangers to road users from reasonably foreseeable hazards that could arise on the road from adjacent land and its use and to carry out inspections annually to this end. The roads authority, therefore, knew or ought to have known about the wall and the potential danger arising, and should have taken reasonable care to see to it that the wall was maintained in a way that obviated danger to road users and was sufficient to contain livestock. It was held that to impose a duty of care on a roads authority would be a considerable and onerous extension of the duties imposed on roads authorities given the many miles of unfenced road in Scotland adjacent to which animals might roam, and would not be fair, just or reasonable.[32] This case of course raises bigger issues. By not suing the keeper of the animals, the pursuer perilled his case on the difficult cases discussed elsewhere in the text relating to the liability of public authorities.[33]

ANIMALS (SCOTLAND) ACT 1987

The Act covers many matters relating to animals and only the parts dealing with liability for animals are dealt with in this book. It creates a new form of strict liability, specifically replacing that set out above[34] while preserving any liability under the general law relating to negligence.[35] **20–05**

Upon whom does liability fall?

The Act imposes liability on a "keeper of an animal" as defined by the Act.[36] **20–06**
A person is a keeper if he owns the animal or has possession of it, or he has actual

---

[29] Inter alia, the defenders relied on D.M. Walker, *The Law of Delict in Scotland*, 2nd edn (Edinburgh: W. Green, 1981), pp.632-634; on *Clark v Armstrong* (1862) 24 D. 1315 and, of course, *Fraser v Pate*, 1923 S.L.T. 457. They also relied on *Milne v Macintosh*, 1952 S.L.T. 84 which was a droving case and *Fraser v Lyle* Unreported February 3, 1998 Paisley sheriff court.

[30] In the most recent case, proof before answer was allowed in a case where a motorist sued for injuries sustained when he collided with one of the defenders cows. It was necessary to know the facts: *Wormald v H J Walker & Co*, 2004 S.C.L.R. 733.

[31] *Bennett v J Lamont & Sons*, 2000 S.L.T. 17.

[32] The third limb of the tri-partite test in *Caparo Industries Plc v Dickman* [1990] 2 A.C. 605 specifically was applied.

[33] See Ch.17.

[34] Animals (Scotland) Act 1987 s.1(8)(a). The argument that essentially fault was required and that the Act had been intended to simplify the previous law rather than radically alter it was (it is submitted, rightly) rejected in *Foskett v McClymont* (1998) Rep. L.R. 13.

[35] A negligence case was run in parallel to a statutory case in *Fairlie v Carruthers*, 1995 S.L.T. (Sh. Ct) 56.

[36] Animals (Scotland) Act 1987 s.5.

care and control of a child under the age of 16 who owns the animal or has possession of it. If the animal has been abandoned or has escaped, liability is not avoided until another person acquires ownership or comes into possession of it.[37] The Crown does not acquire ownership of an animal if it is abandoned. A person is not liable as a keeper if he is detaining a stray animal under section 3 of the Act, nor if he is otherwise temporarily detaining it with a view to restoring it as soon as is reasonably practicable to its owner or a possessor of it. Beware the Queen's corgis for, although the Act expressly binds the Crown, proceedings cannot be brought against Her Majesty.[38]

Types of animals

20–07 Reading the Act as a whole it is possible to put animals into three categories.

1. Animals belonging to a species whose members generally are by virtue of their physical attributes or habits likely (unless controlled or restrained) to injure severely or kill persons or animals, or damage property to a material extent.
2. Dogs and dangerous wild animals (as defined by the Dangerous Wild Animals Act 1976).[39]
3. Cattle, horses, asses, mules, hinnies, sheep, pigs, goats and deer.[40]

These are not distinct categories. The first category is the general category and the other two are specific statutory examples of animals which will fall within the Act. Thus animals in the second category are

> "deemed to be likely (unless controlled or restrained) to injure severely or kill persons or animals by biting or otherwise savaging, attacking or harrying."

That is not to say that other animals not listed in the Dangerous Wild Animals Act 1976 might not yet fall within the first category. This view is now confirmed by the decision in *Foskett v McClymont*,[41] a case in the best tradition of the *Dandy*. The pursuer, a research student, siting a radar installation with permission, was returning from his work. He said he met an animal that would not let him past. He said the defender had told him how to deal with such an eventuality—he waved his arms at it, shouted at it and tapped it on the nose twice. The bull (as it turned out to be) charged him and tossed him over a wall on to stinging nettles. There was no argument about a common-law case. The argument that because cattle are deemed to damage land meant that a bull could not cause personal injury was rightly rejected. More difficult was the decision that an averment that a bull is a species of animal whose members are by virtue

---

[37] Contrast this with the common law position where a strict liability case was not allowed where a bullock had escaped from the custody of its owner: *Stillie v Wilson*, 1988 S.C.L.R. 108. However, the Inner House held that the facts should be established first: 1990 S.L.T. 145.
[38] Animals (Scotland) Act 1987 s.6.
[39] Animals (Scotland) Act 1987 s.1(3)(a). The Act was applied to a dog without difficulty in *O'Neil v Coyle*, 1995 G.W.D. 21–1185.
[40] Animals (Scotland) Act 1987 s.1(3)(b).
[41] *Foskett v McClymont* (1998) Rep. L.R. 13.

of their physical attributes or habits likely severely to injure persons, etc was held sufficiently specific. While it was appreciated that some bulls are docile and some not, it is not clear whether this was thought to be as a result of genetics (which is the foundation of the language of "species"). The defenders were probably entitled to more specification. The Act incorporates the Dangerous Wild Animals Act 1976. That Act, in its Schedule (and see Dangerous Wild Animal Act 1976 (Modifications) Order 1984 art.1 (SI 1984/1111), makes zoological Linnaen descriptions of species authoritative and so it might reasonably be assumed that the proper course was to plead a zoological species. The defender's experts would really need to know what animal was being discussed. Similarly, animals in the third category are

> "deemed to be likely (unless controlled or restrained) to damage to a material extent land or the produce of land, whether harvested or not."

The phrase "attack or harry" was considered in *Fairlie v Carruthers*,[42] and was held not to include a case where a frisky dog knocked a person over while it was being exercised. It was considered that "harrying" implied continual harassing or worrying behaviour such as "chasing" and so was not constituted by one single incident where all that occurred was that the pursuer was knocked over. Attack was more difficult because it seemed to require some form of intent and it would not be appropriate to look into the mind of a dog! With respect, the decision is correct but there is no question of looking for intent—if objectively the act is an attack, that is the end of the matter. Nevertheless, the sheriff did consider that the dog's behaviour was more consistent with an accident than an "attack". Thus, what the sheriff really did was to look objectively at the evidence and see whether he was satisfied that it was an attack or an accident.

Causation

Once a keeper of an appropriate animal has been found it need only be shown **20–08** that the injury or damage complained of is "directly referable" to (as opposed to "caused by") the physical attributes or habits of the animal. Thus, a human victim may rely upon strict liability under the Act if she is injured even when a dog harries or attacks another animal rather than the pursuer herself.[43]

Defences

The Act provides its own defences and exclusions.[44] **20–09**

1. There is no liability for injury in the form of a disease transmitted by means unlikely to cause severe injury. Thus, if your panther licks my hand and I acquire some hideous disease I do not have the benefit of the strict liability.
2. The mere presence of an animal on a road or other place does not incur strict liability. Thus, there is no strict liability where, e.g. I ski into a reindeer in the Cairngorms, or again, where I trip over the proverbial sleeping dog lying on the pavement or drive into it.[45]

---

[42] *Fairlie v Carruthers*, 1995 S.L.T. (Sh. Ct) 56.

[43] *Flynn v Lothian and Borders Police*, 2010 G.W.D. 30–626.

[44] Set out in s.1(4), s.1(5) and s.2 of the Animals (Scotland) Act 1987.

[45] Although such may be actionable in negligence: see para.20–04 above.

3. There can be apportionment of liability between owner and possessor.

4. The fault of the pursuer is a defence, in effect allowing the defence of contributory negligence.[46]

5. There is statutory provision to allow for the voluntary assumption of risk. If you stick your head in the lion's mouth and you lose your head you have probably taken a chance that will leave the keeper free of liability. (If he said, as owners of animals tend to say, "It's all right, he'll not hurt you", that might affect the nature of the risk which was accepted and might in any event be a negligent misstatement.)

6. There is a defence if the person (or other animal) injured had been on the land where the beast was without authority, *unless* the animal was kept wholly or partly for the purpose of protecting persons or property, in which case there is no defence *unless* the keeping of the animal and the use made of it was reasonable, and, if the animal is a guard dog within the terms of the Guard Dogs Act 1975, there has been compliance with s.1 of the Act. The Guard Dogs Act 1975 penalises the use of a guard dog unless its handler (being a person who is capable of controlling the dog) is present and the dog is under his control, if not actually tied up. Notice of the dog's presence must be displayed at every entrance to the property. The Dangerous Wild Animals Act 1976 forbids the keeping of any dangerous wild animal as defined in the Act without a licence. The keeper must insure against third party liabilities, which seemed to imply a right of action (now confirmed by the 1987 Act). The list of dangerous animals includes: wolf, jackal, foxes and dogs (except the domestic dog and the common red fox), cassowary, old world monkey, mangabey, baboon or mandrill, alligator, emu, cobra or mamba, lions, tigers, cheetahs, gibbons and gila monsters, orangutans and chimpanzees, ostriches and grizzly bears, vipers and rattlesnakes.[47]

When all of the above is taken into account, the Animals (Scotland) Act 1987 places liability without proof of fault on the keeper of the appropriate type of animal for injury or damage (providing it is referable to the category of beast) unless the claimant is at fault, has assumed the risk or failed to take care for his own safety. It is not a defence to show *damnum fatale*, nor the intervention of a third party.

---

[46] Such a plea was taken but not argued and would not have found favour in *Fairlie v Carruthers*, 1995 S.L.T. (Sh. Ct) 56.

[47] Note that the common names, such as those listed, are not definitive: that is only the case with the zoological terms listed in the Schedule.

CHAPTER 21

EMPLOYERS' LIABILITY

COMMON LAW

For some time, an employer has been held to have a personal duty to take **21–01** reasonable care for his employees' safety.[1] At an early stage in the industrial revolution, it was appreciated that the common law did not adequately provide for the victims of industrialisation and so there has been a long series of statutory interventions creating various forms of absolute liability.[2] Nonetheless, the common law developed to a stage where it was held that an employer personally owed a duty of reasonable care to his workmen—a non-delegable duty which was not fulfilled by entrusting it to a competent foreman. The classic statement of the duty is in *English v Wilsons & Clyde Coal Co*[3]:

> "To take reasonable care, and to use reasonable skill, first, to provide and maintain proper machinery, plant, appliances, and works; secondly, to select properly skilled persons to manage and superintend the business; and thirdly, to provide a proper system of working."

Thus, the employer's duty is described under three heads. Nevertheless, the employer's common law duty of care is an aspect of the general law of negligence,[4] and so it should be noted at the outset that these categories are neither rigid nor conclusive, e.g. it is clear that the employer's duty extends to providing a safe place of work.[5] Thus, the case law makes it clear that not only does the employer's duty apply with regard to employees' physical injury; it also applies with regard to employees' economic loss[6] and psychiatric injury.[7] However, the courts have tended to take a conservative approach in those areas, applying general rules restricting the circumstances in which the law recognises a duty of care, rather than recognising that the contractual nature of the

---

[1] See *Hislop v Durham* (1842) 4 D. 1168.
[2] See the Employers' Liability Act 1880 and the Workmen's Compensation Act 1897.
[3] *English v Wilsons & Clyde Coal Co*, 1937 S.C. (HL) 46. The Supreme Court dealt more generally with the concept of non-delegable duty of care in *Woodland v Essex CC* [2014] A.C. 537.
[4] *White v Chief Constable of South Yorkshire Police* [1999] 2 A.C. 455 at 506 per Lord Hoffmann.
[5] See, e.g. *Latimer v AEC Ltd* [1953] A.C. 643 (albeit this case failed on its facts). A parallel statutory duty may be owed under the Occupiers' Liability (Scotland) Act 1960.
[6] See, e.g. *Spring v Guardian Assurance* [1995] 2 A.C. 296.
[7] See, e.g. *Barber v Somerset CC* [2004] 1 W.L.R. 1089.

relationship between employer and employee transcends the concerns of liability to an indeterminate class that most of these rules appear to be cautious of.[8]

Provide and maintain proper machinery, plant, appliances, and works

21–02   This covers a wide variety of equipment including equipment directly associated with the type of work carried out, e.g. ladders for a window cleaner, vehicles for a driver etc: equipment ancillary to the work, e.g. soap in a washroom[9]; and equipment on which an employee may be working, e.g. a ship.[10] Equipment or plant may be in the form of animals.[11] The common law duty is to take reasonable care.

So, where a plaintiff was injured when a piece of a drift (a kind of chisel) broke and entered his eye, a claim was made under the first head. However, as the drift had been purchased from a reputable supplier, this was held sufficient to discharge the employer's duty of reasonable care—the employer is not, at common law, an insurer of his workman's safety.[12] However, the result of that particular decision was changed by the Employers' Liability (Defective Equipment) Act 1969, which imposes a system of strict liability, deeming the negligence of the supplier to be the negligence of the employer, while allowing the employer to maintain a claim against the supplier.[13]

Select properly skilled persons

21–03   The second head comprises the duty to provide the employee with competent fellow workers, a duty breached in the case of *Hudson v Ridge Manufacturing*,[14] where an employee, well known to the employer as a practical joker, tripped up a fellow employee, who was a cripple, causing him injury. That the duty is, however, still one of reasonable care is illustrated by a contrasting Scottish case of *McLean v Remploy Ltd*,[15] in which the pursuer tripped over a length of yarn tied across her path by fellow employees. There was no liability as such conduct could not be expected.[16] Where an employee acting outwith the scope of employment causes intentional harm to a fellow worker, the employer may be personally liable because of the "special" nature of the relationship.[17] In addition, there may be liability where a complaint made to an employer about a

---

[8] See, e.g. *Robertson v Forth Road Bridge Joint Board (No.2)*, 1995 S.C. 364; *White v Chief Constable of South Yorkshire Police* [1999] 2 A.C. 455; *Keen v Tayside Contracts*, 2003 S.L.T. 500. Cf. *Harrhy v Thames Trains Ltd* [2003] EWHC 2286.

[9] See, e.g. *Ralston v Greater Glasgow Health Board*, 1987 S.L.T. 386.

[10] See, e.g. *Coltman v Bibby Tankers Ltd (The Derbyshire)* [1988] A.C. 276.

[11] Thus there may be parallel statutory liability under the Animals (Scotland) Act 1987, which may be strict. See Ch.20.

[12] *Davie v New Merton Board Mills* [1959] A.C. 604.

[13] See para.21–25 below.

[14] *Hudson v Ridge Manufacturing* [1957] 2 Q.B. 348.

[15] *McLean v Remploy Ltd*, 1994 S.L.T. 687.

[16] And see the similar but more gruesome English case, *Smith v Crossley Bros Ltd* (1951) 95 Sol. Jo. 655.

[17] See, e.g. *Ward v Scotrail Railways Ltd*, 1999 S.C. 255—proof before answer allowed where employer had failed to intervene in case of alleged sexual harassment by a colleague. The employer may also be vicariously liable if the wrongful conduct is closely connected with the employment: see *Majrowski v Guy's and St Thomas's NHS Trust* [2007] 1 A.C. 224. Cf. *Vackuviene v J Sainsbury Plc*, 2013 S.L.T. 1032.

colleague is ignored where it would be reasonable to carry out an investigation, especially where the employee is then victimised by other colleagues.[18]

System of working

The third head demands that the working system should be reasonably safe. **21–04** For example, an employer was held liable where he failed to provide a window cleaner with blocks that would prevent the window he was cleaning falling on his fingers.[19] On the other hand, an employer was absolved when a workman used a ladder, which had wheels at the top, upside down so that the wheels were on the ground. Worse, the pursuer ordered the apprentice (who was holding the foot of the ladder) to move away. The pursuer fell.[20] Another ladder case further illustrates the wide scope of "system". In *McGregor v AAH Pharmaceuticals*,[21] the employee did not use the stepladders provided but clambered up shelves, despite a booklet instructing that this ought not to be done. The employee won. The ladders were not close enough and, although there had been reprimands for a failure to use ladders, there had been no disciplinary proceedings.

Stress at work

The duty on an employer to provide a safe system of work extends to the **21–05** psychiatric health of employees. Thus, in *Walker v Northumberland CC*,[22] a local authority was held liable for failing to relieve the pressure of work on an employee who then had a nervous breakdown. However, he had already had one. So far as the first breakdown was concerned, it had not been reasonably foreseeable. After that it was foreseeable.[23] It has accordingly been accepted that stress is potentially actionable in Scotland and cases have been settled on that assumption. The requirement of foreseeability was confirmed in *Rorrison v West Lothian College*,[24] where it was held that a case of psychiatric injury could not succeed because the foundation in earlier complaints was not made out[25] and, in any event, the resulting psychiatric injury was difficult to pin down. In *Fraser v State Hospitals Board for Scotland*,[26] it was accepted that the conditions at the employees' workplace — disciplinary proceedings and the like — were in law a cause of his later breakdown. However, while there was no reason why the general duty on an employer to avoid exposing employees to unnecessary risk of injury should be restricted to physical injury, in this case, that there was nothing that the employers did which was, or ought to have been perceived by them as,

---

[18] See, e.g. *W v Commissioner of Police for the Metropolis* [2000] 1 W.L.R. 1607.

[19] *General Cleaning Contractors v Christmas* [1953] A.C. 180.

[20] *Russell v Motherwell Bridge Fabricators Ltd*, 1992 G.W.D. 14–827; see also reg.16 of the Workplace (Health, Safety and Welfare) Regulations 1992 (SI 1992/3004) (see para.21–13 below).

[21] *McGregor v AAH Pharmaceuticals*, 1996 S.L.T. 1161.

[22] *Walker v Northumberland CC* [1995] 1 All E.R. 737.

[23] See also *Petch v Customs and Excise Commissioners* [1993] I.C.R 789.

[24] *Rorrison v West Lothian College*, 1999 Rep. L.R. 102.

[25] A case will often be doomed to fail if there is not even an averment why the defender knew or ought to have known that the pursuer was at risk: *Smith v Advocate General for Scotland*, 2001 G.W.D. 3–139. See also *Chapman v Lord Advocate*, 2006 S.L.T. 186. Cf. *Catleugh v Caradon Everest Ltd*, 1999 G.W.D. 32–1554: although foreseeability could be established by two breakdowns in tears this case failed because of the inadequate specification of the contractual or other relationship between the parties.

[26] *Fraser v State Hospitals Board for Scotland*, 2001 S.L.T. 1051.

a potential cause of psychiatric illness. The present position is that the *Hatton*[27] guidelines are considered valuable in Scotland. They are accordingly worthy of repetition.

(1) There are no special control mechanisms applying to claims for psychiatric (or physical) illness or injury arising from the stress of doing the work the employee is required to do. The ordinary principles of employer's liability apply.

(2) The threshold question is whether this kind of harm to this particular employee was reasonably foreseeable: this has two components (a) an injury to health (as distinct from occupational stress) which (b) is attributable to stress at work (as distinct from other factors).

(3) Foreseeability depends upon what the employer knows (or ought reasonably to know) about the individual employee. Because of the nature of mental disorder, it is harder to foresee than physical injury, but may be easier to foresee in a known individual than in the population at large. An employer is usually entitled to assume that the employee can withstand the normal pressures of the job unless he knows of some particular problem or vulnerability.

(4) The test is the same whatever the employment: there are no occupations which should be regarded as intrinsically dangerous to mental health.

(5) Factors likely to be relevant in answering the threshold question include:

(6) The nature and extent of the work done by the employee. Is the workload much more than is normal for the particular job? Is the work particularly intellectually or emotionally demanding for this employee? Are demands being made of this employee unreasonable when compared with the demands made of others in the same or comparable jobs? Or are there signs that others doing this job are suffering harmful levels of stress? Is there an abnormal level of sickness or absenteeism in the same job or the same department?

(7) Signs from the employee of impending harm to health. Has he a particular problem or vulnerability? Has he already suffered from illness attributable to stress at work? Have there recently been frequent or prolonged absences which are uncharacteristic of him? Is there reason to think that these are attributable to stress at work, for example because of complaints or warnings from him or others?

(8) The employer is generally entitled to take what he is told by his employee at face value, unless he has good reason to think to the contrary. He does not generally have to make searching enquiries of the employee or seek permission to make further enquiries of his medical advisers.

(9) To trigger a duty to take steps, the indications of impending harm to health arising from stress at work must be plain enough for any reasonable employer to realise that he should do something about it.

(10) The employer is only in breach of duty if he has failed to take the steps which are reasonable in the circumstances, bearing in mind the

---

[27] *Sutherland v Hatton* [2002] 2 All E.R. 1, approved by the House of Lords sub nom. *Barber v Somerset CC* [2004] 1 W.L.R. 1089.

magnitude of the risk of harm occurring, the gravity of the harm which may occur, the costs and practicability of preventing it, and the justifications for running the risk.

(11) The size and scope of the employer's operation, its resources and the demands it faces are relevant in deciding what is reasonable; these include the interests of other employees and the need to treat them fairly, for example, in any redistribution of duties.

(12) An employer can only reasonably be expected to take steps which are likely to do some good: the court is likely to need expert evidence on this.

(13) An employer who offers a confidential advice service, with referral to appropriate counselling or treatment services, is unlikely to be found in breach of duty.

(14) If the only reasonable and effective step would have been to dismiss or demote the employee, the employer will not be in breach of duty in allowing a willing employee to continue in the job.

(15) In all cases, therefore, it is necessary to identify the steps which the employer both could and should have taken before finding him in breach of his duty of care.

(16) The claimant must show that that breach of duty has caused or materially contributed to the harm suffered. It is not enough to show that occupational stress has caused the harm.

(17) Where the harm suffered has more than one cause, the employer should only pay for that proportion of the harm suffered which is attributable to his wrongdoing, unless the harm is truly indivisible. It is for the defendant to raise the question of apportionment.

(18) The assessment of damages will take account of any pre-existing disorder or vulnerability and of the chance that the claimant would have succumbed to a stress related disorder in any event.[28]

Hatton has been influential in many subsequent Scottish cases. In *Stevenson v* **21–06** *East Dunbartonshire Council*,[29] Lord Bonomy allowed proof before answer, albeit with considerable hesitation, in a stress at work case where there had been two letters from a GP one mentioning severe mental and physical stress. In *Taplin v Fife Council*,[30] Lord Philip dismissed a case alleging psychiatric injury from stress. The pursuer had been moved in 1995 as a result of a diagnosis of hypothyroidism and on account of stress due to working conditions. She broke down again in 1998 having complained about a lack of resources. His Lordship applied dicta in *Hatton*: there had to be foreseeability of actual psychiatric injury in the pursuer as an individual. The complaints in this case were about resources rather than any effect on the pursuer.[31] In *Donaldson v Scottish Ministers*,[32] Lord Woolman dismissed a claim brought by a prison officer who was known by his employer previously to have suffered psychological problems, but who had been

[28] *Sutherland v Hatton*, [2002] P.I.Q.R. P21 at 42.
[29] *Stevenson v East Dunbartonshire Council*, 2003 S.L.T. 97. See discussion in A.J. Bowen, "*Stevenson v East Dunbartonshire Council*, 2003 S.L.T. 97", 2003 S.L.T. (News) 29.
[30] *Taplin v Fife Council*, 2003 G.W.D. 1–27.
[31] See also the English case *Bonser v UK Coal Mining Ltd*, 2003 T.L.R. 388 which failed absent sufficient prior indicators which would have alerted the employer.
[32] *Donaldson v Scottish Ministers*, 2009 S.L.T. 240. Cf. *Fletcher v Argyll and Bute Council*, 2007 S.L.T. 1047.

certified by his medical practitioner that she was fit to return to work. The employer was entitled to assume that the pursuer was able to perform his duties, and although it was known that a prisoner had made threats against the pursuer, could not reasonably have foreseen that the mere presence of that prisoner in the area where the pursuer worked would put him at risk of psychiatric injury.

In *Pratt v Scottish Ministers*,[33] the Inner House upheld the findings of the Lord Ordinary (Lord Brodie), who had held that the prison service owed a duty of care to provide a prison guard with a system of early counselling and support, following the prison guard's ingestion of blood from a prisoner who was known to be an intravenous drug user. However, the claim failed: it being held that the employer was not in breach of its duty as the employer was aware that the prison guard was attending a hospital as the best qualified source of advice. That being the case, it had not been demonstrated that the employer should have known that workplace support remained a necessary part of the therapeutic process. In any event, the employee had failed to establish causation in proving that but for the lack of workplace support he would have avoided the psychiatric injury.

21–07   That *Hatton* provides guidance in the form of general principles rather than a rigid set of criteria was confirmed in *Flood v University of Glasgow*[34] where the Inner House permitted the case to proceed to a proof before answer. Flood, who was employed as a lecturer, had found her workload progressively increased and eventually complained to her employer that she was doing the work of three and a half employees and working 100 hours per week when she was contracted to work 32.5. Her employer persuaded her not to resign, promising that she would receive relief and assistance. However, no relief or assistance was provided, and the pursuer eventually resigned due to developing a long-term stress related illness. The Inner House confirmed that the requirement of foreseeability was discharged given that the employer had acknowledged the extent of the issue in persuading the employee to remain in post and in promising relief and assistance. The Inner House also held that, in those circumstances, the pursuer would not be required to spell out specifically what steps the employer should have taken to address the excessive workload.

However, psychiatric injury to employees caused by work-related stress has been distinguished from psychiatric injury caused by shock. Where the employee suffers psychiatric injury triggered by shock from the sudden appreciation of harm to others, unless the pursuer may be classified as a primary victim as an involuntary participant in the cause of the other's injury or death,[35] the employee will generally be treated as a secondary victim. Thus, the employee will be subject to the control mechanisms applied to secondary victims in psychiatric injury negligence cases, even where the averred negligence is on the part of the employer.[36]

---

[33] *Pratt v Scottish Ministers*, 2013 S.L.T. 590.
[34] *Flood v University of Glasgow*, 2010 S.L.T. 167. See also *Hartman v South Essex Mental Health and Community Care NHS Trust* [2005] I.C.R. 782 at 794 per Scott Baker L.J.
[35] *Alcock v Chief Constable of South Yorkshire Police* [1992] 1 A.C. 310; *Dooley v Cammell Laird & Co Ltd and Mersey Insulation Co Ltd* [1951] 1 Lloyd's Rep. 271; *Campbell v North Lanarkshire Council*, 2000 S.C.L.R. 373; *Salter v UB Frozen & Chilled Foods Ltd*, 2004 S.C. 233. See also *Anderson v Christian Salvesen Plc*, 2006 S.L.T. 815.
[36] See *White v Chief Constable of South Yorkshire* [1999] 2 A.C. 455; *MacFarlane v E. E. Caledonia* [1994] 2 All E.R. 1; *Robertson v Forth Road Bridge Joint Board (No.2)*, 1995 S.C. 364; *Keen v Tayside Contracts*, 2003 S.L.T. 500. See paras 11–54 to 11–59 above for discussion of duty of care to secondary victims in psychiatric injury cases.

A generalised common law duty

Nonetheless, merely because a case does not fall within one of these three **21 08**
heads does not signify that it is of no merit. It might still fall within the general
obligation to take reasonable care for the workman's safety.[37] An example of a
novel situation is *Collins v First Quench Retailing Ltd*.[38] The employers of a
shop assistant who was working on her own at the time were liable when the shop
was robbed. She had expressed concerns about her vulnerability in the past.
Double-manning would have prevented a robbery like this even although there
were two robbers and a look-out. From the evidence, one of the things important
about double-manning was not so much to balance up the numbers but because
of the criminal fraternities' knowledge of the requirement for corroboration in
criminal cases. Robbery was likely in the area and in particular at this off-sales
shop. General warnings had been issued by the police. So the case does not mean
that every shop needs to have two members of staff. There may be other
precautions, such as physical screens, or in other areas there may be no need to
do anything at all. On one view the case can be seen as an ordinary third-party
intervention case and not requiring any special treatment.[39] It is possible to
restrict it to potential robbery in vulnerable situations, issues of staffing levels
being relatively familiar in other areas of employers' liability for example, where
a helper may be required to foot a ladder or to back out a lorry. Finally, it is
notable for the rejection of any economic argument relating to the cost of double-
manning where double-manning was actually in use in other shops and on
occasions when weighed against the danger arising to a person—especially
where there had been an earlier incident.

The usual rules on causation and remoteness of damage apply, and the
employer may invoke the usual defences to negligence in order to escape or
reduce liability.

STATUTORY LIABILITY

Prior to October 2013, s.47 of the Health and Safety at Work Act 1974 contained **21–09**
a presumption that breach of regulations made under the 1974 Act carried civil
liability unless this was specifically excluded. This presumption was reversed
from October 2013 by s.69 of the Enterprise and Regulatory Reform Act 2013.
Accordingly, s.47 of the 1974 Act now states that, unless specifically provided
for within regulations, there will be no civil liability for breach of the regulations
as such.[40] At the time of writing none of the relevant regulations provide
explicitly for civil liability for breach. Thus, in future liability will be based on
common law negligence.[41] The impact of the change is at the time of writing

---

[37] *Longworth v Coppas International (UK) Ltd*, 1985 S.L.T. 111, although see *Forsyth v Lothian Regional Council*, 1995 G.W.D. 4–204.

[38] *Collins v First Quench Retailing Ltd*, 2003 S.L.T. 1220. For a case note see E. Russell, "Lone Workers — The Employer's Duty in Respect of Double Manning and Security Screens", 2003 S.L.T. (News) 241.

[39] See paras 11–20 to 11–24 above.

[40] Criminal liability for breach of the regulations remains.

[41] It has been acknowledged that a claim for negligence at common law is almost inevitably more difficult to establish than a claim for breach of statutory duty: *Cairns v Northern Lighthouse Board*, 2013 S.L.T. 645 at 656 per Lord Drummond Young.

unclear.[42] If the courts accept that the employer's common law duty of care encapsulates the duties set out in the various regulations, the significance of the change will be that where employers breach the statutory duties, employees will no longer be able to sue their employers for breach of statutory duty as such: employees will have to sue in negligence and so will have to aver, and subsequently lead evidence to prove, that the employer's acts or omissions with regard to the duties set out across the regulations fall below the common law standard, i.e. of reasonable care.[43] On the other hand, if the courts refuse to accept that employers' common law duty of care to their employees encapsulates the duties set out across the regulations, where an employee is injured due to an employer's breach of such a statutory duty, before reaching the proof of negligence stage the employee will need to persuade the court that there is a parallel common law duty owed by the employer to the employee. Given the general reticence of the courts to recognise parallel common law duties,[44] this could mean that much of what follows here will no longer be accepted by the courts as creating liability. The following text should be read in the light of this uncertainty.

The "six-pack" batch of European-inspired regulations made under the Health and Safety at Work Act 1974 provides a partial code for employers' duties, it is reasonably internally coherent and it had frequently been litigated prior to the October 2013 change to s.47 of the Health and Safety at Work Act 1974. It is ironic that an articulate judicial explanation setting out justifications for the strict liability approach shortly preceded this change:

> "There are important economic reasons for taking such an approach, and indeed for making the protection afforded by such legislation applicable to all employees, whether or not they are employees of the person in breach of the legislation. The underlying economic theory is that the cost of workplace accidents is part of the cost of production of a good or service, and the most efficient way of absorbing that cost is by passing it to the ultimate consumer as part of the price of the product. In this way the cost can be insured against efficiently by the employer, with the premiums being reflected in the price. This is much more efficient than expecting employees to insure against the possible cost of injury through an accident at work; such a course would require a multiplicity of policies, and would not cater well for employees on short term contracts, or who simply chose to spend their income on other things. Moreover, strict liability has a further advantage over fault based liability in that it acts as an incentive to reduce the incidence of hazardous activities; the employer knows that if the risk of injury eventuates he will be liable, and thus he is encouraged to take steps to reduce the frequency with which the risk is incurred. Strict liability also

---

[42] For example, given that the directives themselves will continue to have "vertical effect" it is likely that public sector employees will still be able to pursue strict liability claims against employers in breach of the "six pack" regulations. Private sector employees will not.

[43] *Davidson v Lothian and Borders Fire Board*, 2003 S.L.T. 939 illuminates the practical difference in pursuing a fault-based claim at common law as against pursuing a strict liability claim under relevant regulations.

[44] See Ch.16. See also, e.g. *White v Chief Constable of South Yorkshire* [1999] 2 A.C. 455; *Robertson v Forth Road Bridge Joint Board (No.2)*, 1995 S.C. 364; *Keen v Tayside Contracts*, 2003 S.L.T. 500 on conservative approaches to applying the common law to employment relationships.

encourages employers to do their utmost to ensure the least possible risk to employees' health and safety. These economic reasons can perhaps be supplemented by the moral argument that those who consume a good or service should pay a proper price for it, including the cost of compensating those injured in the production of the good or service in question. For all these reasons, strict liability has become the norm in European Union inspired legislation governing health and safety at work."[45]

Some cases will turn on existing UK statutes and regulations, but by far the bulk **21–10** of cases have been taken under the "six pack" of regulations derived from EU legislation. There was an interpretative background built up over years of considering UK statutory cases, which could yield to an EU interpretation where appropriate. A "eurorep" action is generally possible for defective transposition of EU directives and such was certainly possible in relation to these regulations.[46] The fact that the United Kingdom chose to retain many of its linguistic formulations opens the possibility of such challenge, and unless provisions are added to EU derived regulations to permit claims for breach of statutory duty, there may even be the possibility of such challenge with regard to the change made by s.69 of the Enterprise and Regulatory Reform Act 2013 to s.47 of the Health and Safety at Work Act 1974!

Where statutory duties are expressed as "absolute" (i.e. equipment *must* be safe by statute), it is not a defence to say that the required precautions would make the machine unusable.[47] Down the scale from absolute, some duties are expressed as if absolute, but the defender is given the proviso that he is only liable insofar as it was not reasonably practicable to provide some effective precaution. The phrase "practicable" was defined and its practical effect as effecting a reversal of the onus of proof was established in *Nimmo v Alexander Cowan & Sons Ltd*,[48] a Scottish House of Lords decision dealing with the Factories Act 1961:

> "In construing a statute and determining the incidence of the burden of proof the parties' respective means of knowledge and spheres of responsibility are important factors to be taken into account together with the form and content of the relevant statutory provisions. On a true construction of section 29(1) it is for the defenders to aver and prove by way of excuse for the unsafety of the working place that they had made it safe so far as reasonably practicable or that it was not reasonably practicable to make it any safer".[49]

---

[45] *Cairns v Northern Lighthouse Board*, 2013 S.L.T. 645 at 654–655 per Lord Drummond Young.

[46] *McTighe v East & Midlothian NHS Trust*, 1998 S.L.T. 969. The pursuer argued without objection (and without success) that reg.5 of the Provision and Use of Work Equipment Regulations 1992 in allowing suitability to be judged by reference to reasonable foresight did not comply with the foundation European Directive allowing the pursuer to make a claim under the euro-rep head, the defenders being an emanation of the state. See also *Cross v Highland and Islands Enterprise*, 2001 S.L.T. 1060 and *Taylor v Glasgow City Council*, 2002 S.L.T. 689.

[47] *Summers v Frost* [1955] A.C. 740. There are no examples of such absolute liability applicable in Scotland at the time of writing.

[48] *Nimmo v Alexander Cowan & Sons Ltd*, 1967 S.C. (HL) 79.

[49] See *Rae v Strathclyde Joint Police Board*, 1999 S.C.L.R. 793 for s.7 of the Offices Shops and Railway Premises Act 1963.

There was a major revision of the approach to United Kingdom statutory language in the mid-1990s. In *Mains v Uniroyal Englebert Tyres Ltd*,[50] it was held that it was proper to construe s.29(1) in a way more favourable to the pursuer than heretofore — that is by not glossing the statute by making "safe" depend upon reasonable foreseeability.[51] However, *Mains* was doubted by the Supreme Court in *Baker v Quantum Clothing Group*,[52] and in any event reasonable foreseeability must inevitably be a requirement for liability at common law following the effective exclusion of civil liability for breach of statutory duty resulting from the implementation of s.69 of the Enterprise and Regulatory Reform Act 2013 from October 2013.[53]

The "European" rules

21-11   The European Council Directive 89/391 of June 1989 on the Introduction of Measures to Encourage Improvements in the Safety and Health of Workers at Work,[54] often known as the "Framework Directive", provided for the introduction of measures to encourage improvements in the safety and health of workers at work.[55] It was not intended to reduce levels of protection already achieved in individual Member States. It declared a general duty on employers "to ensure the safety and health of workers in every aspect related to the work."[56] The measures necessary for the safety and health of the employees were to be implemented and reviewed by avoiding risks, evaluating the risks which cannot be avoided and combating the risks at source.[57] The Framework Directive is applicable subject only to any more stringent requirements imposed by a particular directive. The following domestic legislation should be interpreted "purposively" so as to give effect to the objectives of the European legislation.[58]

Management of Health and Safety at Work Regulations 1992

21-12   These regulations are the principal mode of implementation by the United Kingdom of the aforementioned Framework Directive. When originally promulgated, by virtue of reg.15, breach of a duty imposed by these regulations did not confer a right of action in any civil proceedings,[59] subject to some exceptions later introduced.

---

[50] *Mains v Uniroyal Englebert Tyres Ltd*, 1995 S.C. 518. In England, a similar approach was taken by the Court of Appeal in *Larner v British Steel Plc* [1993] I.C.R. 551.

[51] Followed in *Beggs v Motherwell Bridge Fabricators*, 1998 S.L.T. 1215. See the discussion of the case in a different context in *McGhee v Strathclyde Fire Brigade*, 2002 S.L.T. 680. *Mains* was, it is submitted correctly, influential in *Taylor v Glasgow City Council*, 2002 S.L.T. 689.

[52] *Baker v Quantum Clothing Group* [2011] 1 W.L.R. 1003.

[53] Changing s.47 of the Health and Safety at Work Act 1974 so as to create a presumption against civil liability for breach of statutory duty.

[54] European Council Directive 89/391 of June 1989 on the Introduction of Measures to Encourage Improvements in the Safety and Health of Workers at Work [1989] OJ L183 (the "Framework Directive").

[55] Framework Directive art.1.1.

[56] Framework Directive art.5.

[57] Framework Directive art.6.2.

[58] *Taylor v Glasgow City Council*, 2002 S.L.T. 689 at 697 per Lord Carloway.

[59] See *Mitchell v Campbeltown Shipyard Ltd*, 1998 G.W.D. 12–616; *Cross v Highland and Islands Enterprise*, 2001 S.L.T. 1060.

Workplace (Health, Safety and Welfare) Regulations 1992

A "workplace" is defined in a complicated way and some applications of it **21–13**
require reference to the principal Act, but the basic definition is

> "any premises or part of premises which are not domestic premises and are
> made available to any person as a place of work, and included (a) any place
> within the premises to which such person has access while at work; and (b)
> any room, lobby, corridor, staircase, road or other place used as a means of
> access to or egress from the workplace or where facilities are provided for
> use in connection with the workplace other than a public road."[60]

The workplace equipment, devices and systems must be maintained in an
efficient state (from a health and safety point of view), in an efficient working
order and in good repair. Cleaning must take place as appropriate.[61] The
regulation can comprehend failures of maintenance or provision.[62] Regulation 6
provides for ventilation. Regulation 7 provides for the temperature being
reasonable, but not by means of any injurious or offensive fumes. Sufficient
thermometers must be produced.

Regulation 8 provides for suitable and sufficient light which, so far as is
reasonably practicable, shall be by natural light. Emergency lighting is required
if there would otherwise be exposure to danger. In *Miller v Perth and Kinross
Council*,[63] the defenders were held liable for a failure to provide suitable and
sufficient lighting in part of their school, which resulted in the pursuer, a cleaner,
falling. Cleanliness and freedom from waste is required by reg.9 and extends to
the floor wall and ceiling. So far as is reasonably practicable, waste material must
not be allowed to accumulate.[64] This is in addition to the provisions set out below
in relation to slipping, tripping and falling. Regulation 10 on room dimensions
and space requires free space to work and move about in.

Regulation 11 provides for the worker to have a suitable work station with a
suitable seat, suitable referring as much to the person actually using it as the task
in hand.[65] In *Simmons v British Steel Plc*,[66] a worker was injured when the tubes
that supplied his cutting tool became snagged, causing him to fall. It was possible
for the tubes to be safely contained in drums. The employers were held liable
under regs 11(2) and 12(3) and under common law as the workstation was not
suitable. In *Butler v Grampian University Hospital NHS Trust*,[67] it was held that
a toilet was not a workstation albeit the outpatient assistant alleged injury at that
place while working at taking a patient to the toilet — work*station* suggested a
set up for work. (It was, however, a work*place*.)

Regulation 12 states inter alia:

---

[60] As defined in the Roads (Scotland) Act 1984 s.151 (Workplace (Health, Safety and Welfare)
Regulations 1992 (SI 1992/3004) reg.2(1)).

[61] Workplace (Health, Safety and Welfare) Regulations 1992 (SI 1992/3004) reg.5.

[62] *Butler v Grampian University Hospital NHS Trust*, 2002 S.L.T. 985.

[63] *Miller v Perth and Kinross Council*, 2001 G.W.D. 40–1530.

[64] Workplace (Health, Safety and Welfare) Regulations 1992 (SI 1992/3004) reg.9(3).

[65] In addition to the Code of Practice there is an HSE guidance publication called *Seating at Work*,
HSG 57 ((HMSO, 1997).

[66] *Simmons v British Steel Plc*, 2002 S.L.T. 711.

[67] *Butler v Grampian University Hospital NHS Trust*, 2002 G.W.D. 18–610.

"(1) Every floor in a workplace and the surface of every traffic route in a workplace shall be of a construction such that the floor or surface of the traffic routes is suitable for the purpose for which it is used. (2) Without prejudice to the generality of paragraph (1), the requirements in that paragraph shall include requirements that (a) the floor, or surface of the traffic route, shall have no hole or slope, or be uneven or slippery so as, in each case, to expose any person to a risk to his health or safety; (b) every such floor shall have effective means of drainage where necessary. (3) So far as is reasonably practicable, every floor in a workplace and the surface of every traffic route in a workplace shall be kept free from obstructions and from any article or substance which may cause a person to slip, trip or fall."[68]

21–14 In *Gilmour v East Renfrewshire Council*,[69] a teacher slipped on a chip on a ramp leading from the school canteen. There was no system of checking for chips on the ramp and she did not offer to allege an inspection regime. Cases on regs 5(1), 12(2) and (3) were held relevant as was a common law case. The chip was inefficient, the ramp was physically in a state of unevenness and it was not kept free from any article which might cause a person to slip trip or fall.[70]

Regulation 13 provides against falls or falling objects, which should normally be prevented other than by providing personal protective equipment such as hard hats and the like. So far as is practicable, every tank, pit or structure where there is a risk of a person in the workplace falling into a dangerous substance (as defined) in the tank, pit or structure, must be securely covered or fenced.[71] Where necessary, for reasons of health and safety, windows or other translucent surfaces in a wall must be of safety material or protected against breakage of the material and be[72] marked to make it apparent. Windows, skylights and ventilators must be capable of being opened and closed[73] and cleaned safely.[74] Regulation 17 provides that workplace must be organised in such a way that pedestrians and vehicles can circulate in a safe manner and the traffic routes[75] must be suitable, but the duty is only to the standard of reasonable practicability for a workplace which is not a new workplace, modification, extension or conversion. Sensibly, motor vehicles and pedestrians are to be kept apart.

Doors and gates must be suitably constructed, including being fitted with any necessary safety devices.[76] In *Beck v United Closures & Plastics Plc*,[77] Lord McEwan held that doors that had to be used to make machinery work were

---

[68] Employers cannot ignore articles which are part of the manufacturing process as opposed to usual fixtures: *Simmons v British Steel Plc*, 2002 S.L.T. 711.

[69] *Gilmour v East Renfrewshire Council*, 2004 Rep. L.R. 40.

[70] There is an interesting series of cases considering whether this provision allows a person who is not a worker to claim to be owed the same duty. See Ch.18.

[71] Workplace (Health, Safety and Welfare) Regulations 1992 (SI 1992/3004) reg.13(5).

[72] Workplace (Health, Safety and Welfare) Regulations 1992 (SI 1992/3004) reg.14.

[73] Workplace (Health, Safety and Welfare) Regulations 1992 (SI 1992/3004) reg.15. See also British Standard BS 8213 Part 1: 2004.

[74] Workplace (Health, Safety and Welfare) Regulations 1992 (SI 1992/3004) reg.16. Account may be taken of devices fitted to the building.

[75] By Workplace (Health, Safety and Welfare) Regulations 1992 reg.2, a "traffic route" is a route for pedestrian traffic, vehicles or both and includes any stairs, staircase, fixed ladder, doorway, gateway, loading bay or ramp.

[76] Workplace (Health, Safety and Welfare) Regulations 1992 (SI 1992/3004) reg.18.

[77] *Beck v United Closures & Plastics Plc*, 2001 S.L.T. 129.

encompassed by the protection of reg.18 and rejected the argument that they were excluded on not being part of the workplace.[78] The House of Lords has confirmed the regulation extends to a door closer.[79]

Escalators and moving walkways must function safely and have an emergency stop button which is easily identifiable and readily accessible.[80] Suitable and safe sanitary conveniences must be provided at readily accessible places and they must be ventilated and lit, clean and orderly. Men and women must not share facilities.[81] Suitable and sufficient washing facilities must be available at readily accessible places. There must be showers if required by the nature of the work.[82] An adequate supply of wholesome drinking water must be provided which must be readily accessible at suitable places and provided with cups unless supplied in a convenient jet.[83] This explains the many "water-coolers" that have sprung up in offices all over the country.[84] Suitable and sufficient "accommodation" must be provided for clothing[85] and facilities for changing.[86] Suitable and sufficient rest facilities must be provided and facilities to eat meals.[87] Exemptions may be made from all the regulations in respect of the home forces or visiting forces.[88]

Provision and Use of Work Equipment Regulations 1998

"Use" in relation to work equipment means any activity involving work **21–15** equipment and includes starting, stopping, programming, setting, transporting, repairing, modifying, maintaining, servicing and cleaning, and related expressions must be construed accordingly. Driving a forklift truck could be use,[89] as can repairing a door closer.[90]

---

[78] He did, however, hold that reg.5(1) of the Workplace (Health, Safety and Welfare) Regulations 1992 (SI 1992/3004) did not apply, the doors neither constituting a "workplace" nor a "device".

[79] *Spencer-Franks v Kellogg Brown & Root Ltd*, 2008 S.C. (HL) 159.

[80] Workplace (Health, Safety and Welfare) Regulations 1992 (SI 1992/3004) reg.19. See also HSE, *Ergonomic Aspects of Escalators used in Retail Organisations*, CRR12/1989 (HMSO, 1989); *Safety rules for the construction and installation of escalators and passenger conveyors*, British Standard BS 5656–1: 2013.

[81] Workplace (Health, Safety and Welfare) Regulations 1992 (SI 1992/3004) reg.20.

[82] Workplace (Health, Safety and Welfare) Regulations 1992 (SI 1992/3004) reg.21. Perhaps had this been in place *McGhee v National Coal Board*, 1973 S.C. (HL) 37 might never have happened. Detailed guidance is given in the Code of Practice right down to the number of "wash stations" per person which ought to be there.

[83] Workplace (Health, Safety and Welfare) Regulations 1992 (SI 1992/3004) reg.22.

[84] But only to the extent that it has given the vendors a reason to sell the product. It seems clear from the Code of Practice that a sink with cups which can be washed is fine.

[85] Workplace (Health, Safety and Welfare) Regulations 1992 (SI 1992/3004) reg.23.

[86] Workplace (Health, Safety and Welfare) Regulations 1992 (SI 1992/3004) reg.24.

[87] Workplace (Health, Safety and Welfare) Regulations 1992 (SI 1992/3004) reg.25. Regulation 25(3) requires that rest areas must include suitable arrangements to protect non-smokers from discomfort caused by tobacco smoke. There is now a prohibition on smoking in wholly or substantially enclosed premises used wholly or mainly as a place of work: Smoking, Health and Social Care (Scotland) Act 2005 and the Prohibition on Smoking in Certain Premises (Scotland) Regulations 2006 (SSI 2006/90).

[88] Workplace (Health, Safety and Welfare) Regulations 1992 (SI 1992/3004) reg.26. See also *Mulcahy v Ministry of Defence* [1996] Q.B. 732 and *Smith v Ministry of Defence* [2014] 1 A.C. 52 for a general consideration of the army as employer.

[89] *Hunter v Murray*, 2002 G.W.D. 13–445.

[90] *Spencer-Franks v Kellogg Brown & Root Ltd*, 2008 S.C. (HL) 159.

"Work equipment" means any machinery, appliance, apparatus, tool or installation for use at work.[91] It was held and had been a matter of dispute, in *Beck v United Closures & Plastics Plc*,[92] that heavy doors required to be used to start machinery were in fact "work equipment".[93] A forklift truck can be work equipment.[94] A bolt joining together two pieces of railway track[95] was work equipment, as was a door-closer.[96] A ladder provided for the use of entry to and exit from a bunk on an oil rig was held to be work equipment.[97] However, a table which was not being used for working was not work equipment.[98]

"Suitable" means suitable in any respect which it is reasonably foreseeable will affect the health and safety of any person.[99] Every employer must ensure that work equipment is so constructed or adapted as to be suitable for its purpose.[100] The doors in *Beck v United Closures & Plastics Plc*[101] were not suitable. They had a faulty locking mechanism, which combined with the force needed to close them and the positioning of the handles made them unsuitable. The ladder in *Robb v Salamis (M & I) Ltd*[102] was unsuitable. It was not fixed to the bunk and was portable. It should have been anticipated that the ladder may not properly be lodged on the brackets of the bunk before a worker placed his weight on it. Another reg.4 case failed where although it was accepted that an L-Bar was work equipment, the use to which it had been put was the problem — it had been jumped upon: it was perfectly *suitable* if used as intended.[103] In *Horton v Taplin Contracts Ltd*,[104] it was held in relation to scaffolding that where the accident had been caused by the deliberate act of a fellow servant during an altercation, this was not to say the *equipment* was unsuitable.

In selecting work equipment, the employer must have regard to the working conditions and to the risks that exist including the risks posed by use of the equipment.[105] The employer must ensure that work equipment is used only for operations for which, and under conditions for which, it is suitable.[106] The risk of a forklift truck being dragged back when trying to move a heavy lorry is the kind of risk which might be encompassed.[107]

---

[91] Provision and Use of Work Equipment Regulations 1998 (SI 1998/2306) reg.2. For comment generally see C. Goddard, "Work Equipment" [2000] J.P.I.L. 220.

[92] *Beck v United Closures & Plastics Plc*, 2001 S.L.T. 1299.

[93] Obviously the cases discussed below provide other examples of what is or may be work equipment.

[94] *Hunter v Murray*, 2002 G.W.D. 13–445.

[95] *Kelly v First Engineering Ltd*, 1999 Rep. L.R. 106. Lord Abernethy approved reference to previous legislation with regard to the definition of work equipment.

[96] *Spencer-Franks v Kellogg Brown & Root Ltd*, 2008 S.C. (HL) 159.

[97] *Robb v Salamis (M & I) Ltd*, 2007 S.C. (HL) 71.

[98] *Mackie v Dundee City Council*, 2001 G.W.D. 11–398.

[99] Provision and Use of Work Equipment Regulations 1998 (SI 1998/2306) reg.4.

[100] Provision and Use of Work Equipment Regulations 1998 (SI 1998/2306) reg.4(1).

[101] *Beck v United Closures & Plastics Plc*, 2001 S.L.T. 1299. See also *Simmons v British Steel Plc*, 2002 S.L.T. 711.

[102] *Robb v Salamis (M & I) Ltd*, 2007 S.C. (HL) 71.

[103] *Paton v Tube Developments Ltd*, 2001 Rep. L.R. 132 (Note).

[104] *Horton v Taplin Contracts Ltd* [2003] I.C.R. 179.

[105] Provision and Use of Work Equipment Regulations 1998 (SI 1998/2306) reg.4(2).

[106] Provision and Use of Work Equipment Regulations 1998 (SI 1998/2306) reg.4(3). See the facts of *Smith v Crossley Bros* (1951) 95 S.J. 655.

[107] *Hunter v Murray*, 2002 G.W.D. 13–445.

Maintenance

There is a general duty to ensure work equipment is maintained in an efficient   **21-16**
state, in efficient working order and in good repair.[108] In *McMullan v Glasgow
Council*,[109] the pursuer was a 21-stone electrician, who fell from a swing-back
stepladder. He said one of the treads broke off. A common law case failed, but
a statutory case based on the absolute duty in the regulation succeeded.[110] In
McTighe v East & Midlothian NHS Trust,[111] a nurse failed in a lifting case based
on regs 4 and 5. The equipment in question was the bed in which the patient was
positioned, a part of which gave way. In *McLaughlin v East and Midlothian NHS
Trust*,[112] a hospital employee was injured when a curtain rail surrounding a bed
fell on her and she succeeded in her case based on regs 4 and 5.

Information, instruction and training must be given. In *Barrie v Glasgow City
Council*,[113] the pursuer was injured by his slab-cutting Stihl saw. The petrol-
driven saw jammed in use and the pursuer said that he could not switch it off and
put it down because of the location of the switch. He alleged breaches of regs 7
and 8. He had had training. However, the case failed because jamming was not
seen as a possible source of danger as opposed to a nuisance. In any event, the
pursuer failed to establish that the alleged breach caused his injuries. So far as
reasonably practicable, maintenance must be possible when the machine is
stopped.[114]

Effective measures have to be taken to keep dangerous machinery safe.[115]
Regulation 12 provides that special hazards must be prevented especially by
using appropriate measures to minimise the effect of the hazards as well as to
reduce the likelihood of it occurring, those hazards being parts falling or being
ejected from the work equipment; rupture or disintegration of its parts; its
catching fire or overheating; or its discharging gas or liquids which are used or
stored in the equipment; the explosion of the equipment or article or substance
produced, used or stored in it.[116] Employers must ensure protection from things
at a very high or low temperature against burns scalding or searing.[117] Where
appropriate, equipment must have controls to start and vary equipment. It must
only be possible to operate said control by deliberate action of the control unless
part of the normal operating cycle of an automatic device.[118] A safe stop control
must be provided where appropriate and one which operates in priority to other
controls.[119] In some circumstances, an emergency stop device needs to be

---

[108] Provision and Use of Work Equipment Regulations 1998 (SI 1998/2306) reg.5.
[109] *McMullan v Glasgow Council*, 1998 G.W.D. 17–874.
[110] It was conceded in *Beck v United Closures & Plastics Plc*, 2001 S.L.T. 1299 that the duty under
reg.6 was absolute. This has been superseded by the change to s.47 of the Health and Safety at
Work Act implemented in October 2013 by s.69 of the Enterprise and Regulatory Reform Act
2013.
[111] *McTighe v East & Midlothian NHS Trust*, 1998 S.L.T. 969.
[112] *McLaughlin v East and Midlothian NHS Trust*, 2000 Rep. L.R. 87.
[113] *Barrie v Glasgow City Council*, 2000 Rep. L.R. 46.
[114] Provision and Use of Work Equipment Regulations 1998 (SI 1998/2306) reg.22.
[115] Provision and Use of Work Equipment Regulations 1998 (SI 1998/2306) reg.11.
[116] Provision and Use of Work Equipment Regulations 1998 (SI 1998/2306) reg.12(3) specifies the
risks.
[117] Provision and Use of Work Equipment Regulations 1998 (SI 1998/2306) reg.13.
[118] Provision and Use of Work Equipment Regulations 1998 (SI 1998/2306) reg.14.
[119] Provision and Use of Work Equipment Regulations 1998 (SI 1998/2306) reg.15.

fitted.[120] Suitable and sufficient lighting must be provided.[121] Every employer must ensure that work equipment is marked in a clearly visible manner with any appropriate marking for reasons of health and safety.[122] Warnings unambiguous, easily perceived and easily understood must be displayed where appropriate.[123]

Personal Protective Equipment at Work Regulations 1992

21–17   Personal protective equipment (PPE) means all equipment (including clothing affording protection against the weather) which is intended to be worn or held by a person at work and which protects him against one or more risks to his health or safety, and any accessory designed to meet that objective.[124] It has been held in the circumstances of one case that a bolt was not PPE.[125] The regulations do not apply to ordinary working clothes which do not specifically protect health and safety; offensive weapons; portable devices for detecting and signalling risks and nuisances; PPE used for travelling on the road; where used during the playing of competitive sports or where there is other statutory provision as defined.[126] Every employer must ensure that suitable PPE is provided to his employees who may be exposed to risk to their health or safety while at work, except where and to the extent that such risk has been adequately controlled by other means which are equally or more effective. PPE is not suitable unless it is appropriate for the risk involved, it takes account of ergonomic requirements and the state of health of the person who wears it, it fits, so far as reasonably practicable it is effective without itself increasing the overall risk, it complies with the law.[127] The PPE is to be compatible where more than one item is in use.[128] Before choosing the PPE the employer has to carry out an assessment which, in all but the most routine cases, ought to be recorded.[129] An employer was found liable where a workman having to mow grass with a lawnmower on wet grass did not have suitable non-slippy shoes.[130] The PPE must be maintained in an efficient state, in efficient working order and in good repair which includes replacement and cleaning.[131] Accommodation has to be provided for the PPE when not in use.[132] The employee is to be provided with such information, instructions and training as is adequate and appropriate to enable the employee to know the risks, the manner in which it is to be used and any action the employee is to take to make it work properly.[133] The information must be

---

[120] Provision and Use of Work Equipment Regulations 1998 (SI 1998/2306) reg.16.

[121] Provision and Use of Work Equipment Regulations 1998 (SI 1998/2306) reg.21.

[122] Provision and Use of Work Equipment Regulations 1998 (SI 1998/2306) reg.23.

[123] Provision and Use of Work Equipment Regulations 1998 (SI 1998/2306) reg.24.

[124] Personal Protective Equipment at Work Regulations 1992 (SI 1992/2966) reg.2. For a case under the common law considering the benefits and problems of PPE in the form of padded protective trousers for a chain saw operator see *Douglas v Lord Advocate*, 1996 Rep. L.R. 143.

[125] *Kelly v First Engineering Ltd*, 1999 Rep. L.R. 106.

[126] Personal Protective Equipment at Work Regulations 1992 (SI 1992/2966) reg.3.

[127] Personal Protective Equipment at Work Regulations 1992 (SI 1992/2966) reg.4.

[128] Personal Protective Equipment at Work Regulations 1992 (SI 1992/2966) reg.5.

[129] Personal Protective Equipment at Work Regulations 1992 (SI 1992/2966) reg.6.

[130] *Mitchell v Inverclyde DC*, 1998 S.L.T. 1157.

[131] Personal Protective Equipment at Work Regulations 1992 (SI 1992/2966) reg.7.

[132] Personal Protective Equipment at Work Regulations 1992 (SI 1992/2966) reg.8.

[133] For a case which failed on the regulations see *Cameron v Kvaerner Govan*, 2000 G.W.D. 40–1508 but it may be noted that a common law case of vicarious liability in respect of the failure by fellow workmen to appreciate the danger in the operation succeeded.

"comprehensible to the persons to whom it is provided".[134] The code indicates that the help is extensive including theoretical and practical training. Reasonable steps must be taken to ensure that the kit is properly used.[135] The employee is himself under a duty to use the kit and report its loss or defective condition.[136]

Health and Safety (Display Screen Equipment) Regulations 1992

Prior to these regulations there was barely any regulation at all in this field.[137] **21–18** After the legislation, a case at common law was successful before the Court of Appeal for a form of work-related upper limb disorder (not repetitive strain injury but PDA4) in connection with work like that covered by these regulations, but it failed before the House of Lords.[138] The key definitions are as follows: "display screen equipment" means any alphanumeric or graphic display screen, regardless of the display process involved (in what follows, such are called screen); "use" means use in or in connection with work; "user" means an employee who habitually uses display screen equipment as a significant part of his normal work; "workstation" means an assembly comprising:

(i) display screen equipment (whether provided with software determining the interface between the equipment and its operator or user, a keyboard or any other input device);
(ii) any optional accessories to the display screen equipment;
(iii) any disk drive, telephone, modem, printer, document holder, work chair, work desk, work surface or other item peripheral to the display screen equipment; and
(iv) the immediate work environment around the display screen equipment.[139]

The guidance indicates that an ordinary television screen is outside the rules, but microfiche readers are within the rules. The guidance also shows that there may be some difficulty in ascertaining who is a user. The guidance offers seven criteria that can be weighed up in making a decision. They are dependency, discretion, training, prolonged spells of over one hour, daily use, fast information transfer and criticality of errors. Drivers' cabs, screens on board a means of transport, portables (not in prolonged use), calculators and window typewriters are excluded from the regulations.[140] Portables, which undoubtedly include laptop computers and probably cover tablets and smart-phones, in prolonged use are covered. A suitable assessment must be carried out.[141]

Daily work on screens is to be planned to provide interruptions to reduce the workload.[142] In the guidance, it is pointed out that short, frequent breaks are

---

[134] Personal Protective Equipment at Work Regulations 1992 (SI 1992/2966) reg.9.
[135] Personal Protective Equipment at Work Regulations 1992 (SI 1992/2966) reg.10.
[136] Personal Protective Equipment at Work Regulations 1992 (SI 1992/2966) reg.11.
[137] These implement Directive 90/270/EEC - display screen equipment. See I.J. Lloyd and M.J. Simpson, "The Computer at Work", 1992 S.L.T. (News) 177.
[138] *Pickford v Imperial Chemical Industries Plc* [1998] 1 W.L.R. 1189. See generally, B. Langstaff, "Upper Limb Disorders: Work Related or Unrelated?" [1994] J.P.I.L. 14.
[139] Health and Safety (Display Screen Equipment) Regulations 1992 (SI 1992/2792) reg.1.
[140] Health and Safety (Display Screen Equipment) Regulations 1992 (SI 1992/2792) reg.1(4).
[141] Health and Safety (Display Screen Equipment) Regulations 1992 (SI 1992/2792) reg.2.
[142] Health and Safety (Display Screen Equipment) Regulations 1992 (SI 1992/2792) reg.4.

better than occasional, long breaks.[143] The employer must provide eye tests.[144] Adequate health and safety training in relation to the equipment used is to be given.[145] The users must be told about all aspects of health and safety relating to their workstations and the measures taken by the employer to comply.[146]

Manual Handling Operations Regulations 1992

21–19 This regulation has been the most commonly litigated, probably because such injuries are so frequent.[147] Fatalities are rare but as at 1992 HSE information suggested that more than a quarter of all reported accidents were due to manual handling and about a third of three-day injuries. The regulations should be interpreted purposively in accord with the European background.[148]

Manual handling operation

21–20 "Manual handling operations" means any transporting or supporting of a load (including the lifting, putting down, pushing, pulling, carrying or moving thereof) by hand or by bodily force. "Load" includes any person and any animal.[149] Many of the cases considered in the other paragraphs of this section directly, or indirectly apply this definition.

In *Cullen v North Lanarkshire Council*,[150] an employee had to unload debris consisting of old wooden fencing from the back of a pickup truck. He stood on the materials to be unloaded and threw them into a skip, which stood beside the truck. While he was holding a section of fencing above his head, he caught his heel on some of the remaining material and fell backwards off the platform of the truck, sustaining injuries when his left shoulder struck the ground. After proof, the defenders were absolved—their argument that this was not so much handling as the imposition of a load. However, the Inner House, it is submitted correctly, held that neither the terms in which the regulations were expressed, nor the terms of the directive which they were intended to implement, restricted the applicability of the regulations to a risk of injury arising from the *imposition* of a load, as opposed to activities *with* a load.[151]

In the earlier case of *Fraser v Greater Glasgow Health Board*,[152] a nursing auxiliary, who hurt her back lifting a patient, sued. She was assisting a staff nurse who had already trained her in lifting. The staff nurse instructed a certain mode

---

[143] This was thought to be common sense for secretaries with tasks other than typing in the House of Lords decision in *Pickford v Imperial Chemical Industries Plc* [1998] 1 W.L.R. 1189.

[144] Health and Safety (Display Screen Equipment) Regulations 1992 (SI 1992/2792) reg.5.

[145] Health and Safety (Display Screen Equipment) Regulations 1992 (SI 1992/2792) reg.6.

[146] Health and Safety (Display Screen Equipment) Regulations 1992 (SI 1992/2792) reg.7.

[147] For comment generally, see J. Levy, "Manual handling" [2001] J.P.I.L. 130; J.H. Zindani, "Manual Handling Law: The End of Laissez-faire", 2000 J.P.I.L. 2; A.J. Bowen, "Manual handling: A Foreseeable Possibility or a Duty of Insurance," 2002 S.L.T. (News) 189.

[148] *Taylor v Glasgow City Council*, 2002 S.L.T. 689.

[149] Lord Carloway has pointed out that this formulation differs from the European directives in that it speaks only of manual handling operations and does not include in the definition any reference to risk of injury: *Taylor v Glasgow City Council*, 2002 S.L.T. 689.

[150] *Cullen v North Lanarkshire Council*, 1998 S.L.T. 847.

[151] Subsequent and similar is *Purdie v City of Glasgow Council*, 2002 Rep. L.R. 26. where the pursuer was injured while shovelling magazines into a JCB. A magazine blew under the pursuers foot causing him to lose his footing. While the movement of the load was a less prominent feature, it was still the case that the facts could give rise to the inference that the risk had not been properly addressed and a proof before answer was allowed.

[152] *Fraser v Greater Glasgow Health Board*, 1996 Rep. L.R. 58.

of lifting. The defenders were held liable primarily because the lift had not been properly co-ordinated, the pursuer having one of her hands in the wrong place. While she was successful at common law, obiter, the Manual Handling Regulations were held not to be applicable as they were said to apply to regular operations and not to an emergency. In *Nicolls v City of Glasgow*,[153] the pursuer had to shift bales of hay with a wheelbarrow. The bales restricted the worker's view. The injury was due to a jolt on the uneven surface rather than straining and was within the regulations. In *McBeath v Halliday*[154] it was accepted that fitting electrical wiring to a floodlighting column was a manual handling operation. Cases not encompassed within the regulation include a complaint of tennis elbow from using a spanner to tighten bolts.[155] Where it is clear the operation in question is to be carried out mechanically, and not manually, the regulations are not engaged.[156]

Regulation 4

This regulation has been extensively considered. Each employer must, so far **21–21** as reasonably practicable, avoid the need for his employees to do any manual handling which involves a risk of their being injured.[157] If manual handling is necessary then the employer must assess the risk of their being injured according to the details in the schedule to the regulations.[158] Where it is not reasonably practicable to avoid the need for his employees to undertake any manual handling operations at work which involve a risk of their being injured the employer must take appropriate steps to reduce the risk of injury to the lowest level reasonably practicable[159] and must give general indications and, where possible, precise indications on the weight of each load and the heaviest side of any whose centre of gravity is not positioned centrally.[160] Employees have a duty to make use of any system laid down to comply with reg.4(1)(b)(ii).[161] Not unreasonably, standing the language, cases have split consideration of circumstances according to whether they fall within reg.4(1)(a) or 4(1)(b).

Risk of injury

It has not entirely been settled as to how risk of injury is to be treated. It is **21–22** possible to look to the general kind of operation which could have been foreseen as likely to bring about the kind of injury which happened.[162] Such a view is not that different to the common law. It is possible to desiderate that the particular task be within the foreseeable risk.[163] It is possible to say that the word should

---

[153] *Nicolls v City of Glasgow* Unreported December 23, 1996 Glasgow sheriff court.
[154] *McBeath v Halliday*, 2000 G.W.D. 2–75.
[155] *King v Carron Phoenix Ltd*, 1999 Rep. L.R. 51 (obiter).
[156] *Delaney v McGregor Construction (Highlands) Ltd*, 2003 G.W.D. 10–290.
[157] Manual Handling Operations Regulations 1992 (SI 1992/2793) reg.4(1)(a).
[158] Manual Handling Operations Regulations 1992 (SI 1992/2793) reg.4(1)(b)(i).
[159] Manual Handling Operations Regulations 1992 (SI 1992/2793) reg.4(1)(b)(ii).
[160] Manual Handling Operations Regulations 1992 (SI 1992/2793) reg.4(1)(b)(iii). Assessments of risk must be reviewed: Manual Handling Operations Regulations 1992 (SI 1992/2793) reg.4(2).
[161] Manual Handling Operations Regulations 1992 (SI 1992/2793) reg.5.
[162] *Taylor v Glasgow City Council*, 2002 S.L.T. 689 per Lord Marnoch at 690–691. See generally the helpful note: A.J. Bowen, "Manual Handling: A foreseeable Possibility or a duty of insurance?", 2002 S.L.T. (News) 189.
[163] *Taylor v Glasgow City Council*, 2002 S.L.T. 689 per Lord Reed at 692–693.

be read unencumbered by foreseeability—that the actual facts complained of are examined to see if there is a manual handling operation and whether these facts involve a risk of injury—if so, there is an almost irresistible inference of liability absent the reasonably practicable defence which precludes this regulation establishing a duty of insurance.[164] It is respectfully submitted the third is the best view. In analysing the facts of a case, it can be easy to say that there was a risk of injury—not necessarily based on foreseeability, but upon history, whether personal or communal. This is a jury question, perhaps instructed in the context. So while a danger foreseen is a risk, so is a danger well-known without having to foresee it. When we wonder whether we expose our children or our workers to a risk, we utilise the foreseeability of our reason—we also consult our written, folk and craft experience. The language of the law is here both logic and experience. A category of danger foreseen does not necessarily mean that a particular operation was risky.

The relationship of regulation 4(1)(a) and 4(1)(b)

21-23   The first analysis is whether or not it is reasonably practicable to avoid the need for manual handling at all. The employer should ask himself whether he can simply say to his staff: "do not lift those bales". He can and should say this if he has a bale-lifting machine to hand. If it is not reasonably practicable for him to do this—perhaps there is no such thing as a bale-lifting machine—then he must follow reg.4(1)(b). The defender carries the onus of raising the reasonably practicable proviso.[165]

The elements of regulation 4(1)(b)

21-24   There are elements: (i) the making of a risk assessment; (ii) the taking of appropriate preventative measures and (iii) provision of information. There is no need for the assessment to take any particular form.[166] A training course attended by a worker can constitute a suitable and sufficient assessment of the manual handling operations to be undertaken.[167] A particular assessment, in order to be suitable and sufficient, must be related to the manual handling operations which may require to be performed in each discrete task.[168] The present state of the cases is that the failure to prepare an assessment is not itself sufficient for liability.[169] Where the employer has complied with reg.4(1)(b)(ii) and (iii), he ought to be able to argue that any breach of reg.4(1)(a) is not causative. Most certainly, a failure to carry out the desiderated assessment ought to be admitted as relevant to show the care which was or was not being lavished on the pursuer.[170] A failure to provide written instructions in relation to he fitting of electrical wiring can be a breach of reg.4(1)(b)(ii).[171] An employer has been found in breach in relation to the lifting of a slab with a crowbar.[172] Where the

---

[164] *Taylor v Glasgow City Council*, 2002 S.L.T. 689 per Lord Carloway at 697–698; specifically critiqued by Lord Reed in detail at 691–692.
[165] *Aiken v Board of Management Aberdeen College*, 2000 G.W.D. 2–74.
[166] *Brown v East and Midlothian NHS Trust*, 2000 S.L.T. 342.
[167] *Brown v East and Midlothian NHS Trust*, 2000 S.L.T. 342.
[168] *Brown v East and Midlothian NHS Trust*, 2000 S.L.T. 342.
[169] *Logan v Strathclyde Fire Board* Unreported January 12, 1999 CSOH; *Birse v ALPS Electric (Scotland) Ltd*, 2002 G.W.D. 15–513.
[170] *Birse v ALPS Electric (Scotland) Ltd*, 2002 G.W.D. 15–513.
[171] *McBeath v Halliday*, 2000 G.W.D. 2–75.
[172] *Skinner v Aberdeen City Council*, 2001 G.W.D. 16–657

employer has provided and instructed the use of proper equipment but this is ignored by the worker will still result in the employee failing.[173]

In *McIntosh v City of Edinburgh Council*,[174] decided after the leading case *Taylor*,[175] a worker hurt himself while trying to return a three piece ladder weighing 50kg to his van. It got stuck in grass causing him to lose his balance. It was held that the ladder was a load in terms of reg.2(1). A man lifting a ladder of this weight involved a foreseeable possibility of injury engaging the regulations. Some helpful judicial guidance on the interpretation of *Taylor* can be found in the decision of Lord McEwan in *McIntosh*. He read *Taylor* as a majority decision, which he would have had to have followed despite his own sympathies being with the opinion of Lord Carloway. The Inner House in *McDougall v Spiers*,[176] agreed that risk includes "foreseeable possibility" and it is even better if that possibility is that which allegedly occurs.

In one English case, the regulations supported a case where there had been no accident during an actual manual handling operation but an eventual collapse due to extended heavy lifting.[177]

Employer's Liability (Defective Equipment) Act 1969

This Act sets out to help the workman who is injured by his work equipment. **21–25** It is not affected by s.69 of the Enterprise and Regulatory Reform Act 2013. The basic law is that reasonable care is required and so a workman injured by equipment purchased from a responsible supplier would be forced to sue the supplier and not his employer.[178] The Act provides that the fault is that of the employer if an employee suffers personal injury in the course of his employment in consequence of a defect in equipment provided by his employer for the purposes of the employer's business and the defect is attributable wholly or partly to the fault of a third party (whether identifiable or not).[179] Contributory negligence is a defence and the employer has a right of indemnity against the supplier. "Equipment" includes any plant and machinery, vehicle, aircraft and clothing. "Equipment" has been held to include a ship,[180] soap,[181] and a ventilation system,[182] but not actuators which were a part of the product being assembled as opposed to a tool.[183]

A weakness in the Act is that it has been interpreted as there still being a necessity to show something wrong with the article. Thus a man failed to recover damages when he was injured when a knife he was using broke. It was held that the most probable cause of the breakage was a previous fall and thus the provisions of the Employer's Liability (Defective Equipment) Act 1969 did not apply.[184]

---

[173] *Urquhart v Biwater Industries Ltd*, 1998 S.L.T. 576: the pursuer did not use the crane provided but tried to lift concrete blocks himself.

[174] *McIntosh v City of Edinburgh Council*, 2003 S.L.T. 827.

[175] *Taylor v Glasgow City Council*, 2000 S.L.T. 670.

[176] *McDougall v Spiers*, 2003 S.C. 491.

[177] *Knott v Newham Healthcare NHS Trust* [2002] All E.R. (D) 216: See the note H. Immanuel, "Causation — justice for nurses?" 2002 P.I.L.J. Nov/Dec 1.

[178] *Davie v New Merton Board Mills Ltd* [1959] A.C. 604.

[179] Employer's Liability (Defective Equipment) Act 1969 s.1(1).

[180] *Coltman v Bibby Tankers Ltd* [1988] A.C. 276.

[181] *Ralston v Greater Glasgow Health Board*, 1987 S.L.T. 386.

[182] *Yuille v Daks Simpson Ltd*, 1984 S.L.T. 115.

[183] *Loch v British Leyland UK Ltd*, 1975 (Notes) S.L.T. 67.

[184] *Marshall v D.B. Marshall (Newbridge) Ltd*, 1991 G.W.D. 30–1807.

A "defect" includes everything which renders the plant, etc. unfit for the use for which it is intended when used in reasonable way and with reasonable care.[185] Thus soap, which was in itself not said to be in any way defective, was defective within the Act where it could be used safely with gloves but was not safe without. A ventilation system was defective where clips which provided the suspension link from roof trusses for the support of ducting and trunking were insufficient for their purpose.[186] In *Edwards v Butlins*,[187] the Inner House reversed the decision to decide that where the defenders pleadings can be read as accepting that the equipment was defective, then the pursuer does not have to bring home liability to one of the two possible actual wrongdoers.

---

[185] *Yarmouth v France* (1887) 19 Q.B.D. 647 at 658 per Lindley L.J., quoted with approval by Lord Kincraig in *Ralston v Greater Glasgow Health Board*, 1987 S.L.T. (Notes) 386 at 387.
[186] *Yuill v Daks Simpson Ltd*, 1984 S.L.T. 116.
[187] *Edwards v Butlins*, 1998 S.L.T. 500.

INDEX